Paris

The Complete **Residents'** Guide

Passionately Publishing...

EXPLORER

Paris Explorer 1st Edition ISBN 13 - 978-9948-03-383-7 ISBN 10 - 9948-03-383-3

Front Cover Photograph: La Grande Arche de la Défense – Victor Romero

Printed and bound by Emirates Printing Press, Dubai, United Arab Emirates.

Explorer Publishing & Distribution
PO Box 34275, Dubai
United Arab Emirates
Phone   +971 (0)4 340 8805
Fax   +971 (0)4 340 8806
Email   info@explorerpublishing.com
Web   www.explorerpublishing.com

Welcome...

You've just made living in Paris a whole lot easier by buying this book. In the following pages you'll find out everything you need to know to get settled into – and then get the most out of – your new life in one of the world's most exciting cities. From finding schools and apartment-hunting to drinking cocktails and cabaret, we can tell you how and where to do it.

The **General Information** chapter (p.2) fills you in on Paris' economy, history, geography and culture, and provides details of how to get around and where to stay when you first arrive. There's also essential insider info to be found, covering everything from who to call in an emergency to tipping etiquette.

The **Residents** chapter (p.46) takes away all the headaches involved in setting up your new home. With information on visas, residential areas, healthcare, schools and red tape, this section will tell you how to deal with all the formalities of living in a new city.

After settling in, take a look at **Exploring** (p.132). This section guides you through the different neighbourhoods in Paris, telling you all about its museums, architecture and parks, and detailing annual festivals and where to go to see more of France. There's also a checklist of must-dos to work your way through so you won't miss a thing.

If you've still got time on your hands, move on to **Activities** (p.210). Here you'll find out where to play football, how to join a choir, and where to learn French. If you'd prefer to indulge, there's also a wealth of well-being options to digest, with some of Europe's finest spas to be found in the city.

Now that you're living in Paris, you'll also have full access to all the retail that one of the world's best **Shopping** cities has to offer (p.242). We've got a whole chapter dedicated to helping you discover the top markets, department stores and high streets in which to splash the cash.

Don't spend it all in the shops though – save some for the evening. Our **Going Out** chapter (p.304) gives you a detailed run-down on Paris' premier places for eating, drinking, partying and where to find the best live music, theatre and comedy.

Nearly all of the places of interest have colour-coded references that correspond to the detailed **Maps** (p.372) in the back of the book – use these for everything from taking the metro to exploring the cobbled back streets and you'll be looking like a local in no time.

And if you think we have missed something, please let us know. Go to www.explorerpublishing.com, fill in the Reader Response form, and share the knowledge with your fellow explorers. On the website you'll find community forums, articles, product updates and more, so log on and start exploring.

The Explorer Team

Alexander Maksik is an expert resident of Paris after negotiating the tricky city streets and seemingly endless paperwork for five years. He has previously worked as a dishwasher, prep-cook, lifeguard, construction worker, sous-chef, actor, bartender, pizza delivery boy, producer and teacher. He recently finished his first novel and is working on a collection of essays. **Ultimate Paris must-do:** Ride your bike from Montmartre to St-Germain des Prés at dawn stopping on the Seine to watch the sunrise. **Best city memory:** Drinking cold rosé from the bottle on the Pont-des-Arts with his girlfriend in the summer.

Explorer's Paris
There are so many things the Paris Explorers love about this buzzing city: opera at the Palais Garnier (p.167), a picnic at the Bois de Vincennes (p.184), the 360° views from the top of Montparnasse Tower (p.191), the annual Chasse aux Trésors treasure hunt (p.42), daytrips to Champagne (p.203) or the Loire valley (p.202), spending wintry weekends seeking shelter in snug cafes (p.336), eating pastries (p.340), listening to jazz at the Parc Floral (p.190), discovering tiny neighbourhood bars (p.344), staying up until dawn on Nuit Blanche to explore the city's attractions (p.42), standing at one end of Pont Alexander III looking at Les Invalides during sunset (p.166), and just enjoying the energy of living in one of the most thrilling cities in the world.

Alicia Sheber has a background in wine and a mother who taught French, so it was only a matter of time before she made her way to Paris. Today she shares her time between Paris and London creating luxury hospitality interiors. **Favourite daytrip:** Wine lovers will adore the vineyards of Beaune which craft the Bourgogne region's amazing pinot noirs and chardonnays. **Best place to drink with the locals:** Every year the wine tasting magazine *La Revue du Vin du France* hosts a Salon des Grands Crus which offers a chance to try the best wines for a reasonable price.

Amanda MacKenzie first came under Paris' spell while studying for her French degree, and she still hasn't found a good excuse for leaving. When she's not reporting on the city's cultural and hotel scene, Amanda likes prowling around medieval castles and playing jazz. **Best place to drink with the locals:** Your local, of course! Where better to sit it out when you've locked yourself out of your apartment and have hours to wait for spare keys? **Best thing about living in Paris:** The people. They're generous, polite and very opinionated. Until you can dazzle them with a more persuasive argument, of course.

Night owl **Mira Lotfallah** hails from LA but has been in Paris for three years. She prefers sunrises to sunsets, but as a freelance fashion and beauty writer Mira always looks like she's had her eight hours sleep. **Best view:** From the top of the stairs at the Sacré-Coeur (p.160) in Montmartre. **Best city memory:** Walking along the Seine with friends and being invited aboard a boat to enjoy the sun and a few bottles of rosé. The afternoon was spent sharing conversation and laughs with strangers – one of whom turned out to be a French pop star. Only in Paris!

*Having trouble navigating your way around fast-paced Paris? Look no further than the **Paris Mini Map**, an indispensable pocket-sized aid to getting to grips with the roads, areas and attractions of this exciting city.*

*Now that you've moved to Paris, it won't be long before you're playing host to wave upon wave of visiting family and friends – and we've got the perfect guide to help them get the most out of their sightseeing. Packed with info on Paris' shops, restaurants and tourist spots, you can't go wrong with the **Paris Mini Explorer**.*

Novelist **Sarah Gilbert Fox** didn't choose to come to Paris; en route to Prague, sickness struck and she was ordered to stay for three weeks – which quickly turned into three months. After a chance meeting she became directeur général of the *Bonjour Paris* website, and then Paris became her life and passion. **Favourite Paris cultural experience:** Coming across an incredible musician in the metro. They have to audition to play there! **Best city memory:** Sitting at a cafe, having a grand crème, watching the world go by… it's a seat in the best theatre.

Although freelance writer **Sarina Lewis** has spent three years in Paris, it has barely allowed enough time to explore the city's countless fashion boutiques and eateries – but not for want of trying! Brought up between Australia and India with a stint in southern California, the journalist (who has written for a variety of food guides and magazines across the globe) now calls Paris home. **Ultimate Paris must-do:** A three-hour, wine-fuelled Sunday lunch with friends at place du Marche St Catherine on a chilly autumn afternoon. **Favourite Paris cultural experience:** An early evening aperitif at a terrace cafe with a view.

Stephen Leonard has travelled the globe extensively, but Paris captured his heart. Enchanted by the rich history and culture, but befuddled by French politics and bureaucracy, Stephen writes a weekly column on Parisian life for online publication *The Nervous Breakdown*. **Best thing about living in Paris:** Wide, shady sidewalks and architectural wonders make it the greatest city in the world to visit on foot. **Favourite Paris cultural experience:** La Fête de la Musique (p.41), when Parisians celebrate the first day of summer with concerts and jam sessions on practically every street corner, playing late into the night.

Thanks…

In addition to our team of outstanding authors, whose expert advice and remarkable research have ensured the Paris Explorer is the most up-to-date and comprehensive guide to expat life in the city, there are a number of other people who have made great contributions towards making this book what it is. Massive thanks go to: Helen Spearman and Shawn Zuzarte for services beyond the call of duty, Katie Drynan for her tireless translation tasks, and Jodie Quinn for providing moral support and food parcels.

Where are we exploring next?

- Abu Dhabi
- Amsterdam
- Bahrain
- Barcelona
- Beijing*
- Berlin*
- Boston*
- Brussels*
- Cape Town*
- Dubai
- Dublin
- Geneva
- Hong Kong
- Kuala Lumpur*
- Kuwait
- London
- Los Angeles*
- Moscow*
- New York
- New Zealand
- Oman
- Paris
- Qatar
- San Francisco*
- Shanghai
- Singapore
- Sydney
- Tokyo*
- Vancouver*
- Washington DC*

* Available 2008

Where do you live?
Is your home city missing from our list? If you'd love to see a residents' guide for a location not currently on Explorer's horizon please email editorial@explorerpublishing.com.

Advertise with Explorer…
If you're interested in advertising with us, please contact sales@explorerpublishing.com.

Make Explorer your very own…
We offer a number of customization options for bulk sales. For more information and discount rates please contact corporatesales@explorerpublishing.com.

Contract Publishing
Have an idea for a publication or need to revamp your company's marketing material? Contact designlab@explorerpublishing to see how our expert contract publishing team can help.

www.explorerpublishing.com

Life can move pretty fast, so to make sure you can stay up to date with all the latest goings on in your city, we've revamped our website to further enhance your time in the city, whether long or short.

Keep in the know...

Our Complete Residents' Guides and Mini Visitors' series continue to expand, covering destinations from Amsterdam to New Zealand and beyond. Keep up to date with our latest travels and hot tips by signing up to our monthly newsletter, or browse our products section for info on our current and forthcoming titles.

Make friends and influence people...

...by joining our Communities section. Meet fellow residents in your city, make your own recommendations for your favourite restaurants, bars, childcare agencies or dentists, plus find answers to your questions on daily life from long-term residents.

Discover new experiences...

Ever thought about living in a different city, or wondered where the locals really go to eat, drink and be merry? Check out our regular features section, or submit your own feature for publication!

Want to find a badminton club, the number for your bank, or maybe just a restaurant for a hot first date?

Check out city info on various destinations around the world in our residents' section – from finding a Pilates class to contact details for international schools in your area, or the best place to buy everything from a spanner set to a Spandau Ballet album, we've got it all covered.

Let us know what you think!

All our information comes from residents which means you! If we missed out your favourite bar or market stall, or you know of any changes in the law, infrastructure, cost of living or entertainment scene, let us know by using our Feedback form.

AMOUAGE

Gold

EAU DE TOILETTE

The most valuable perfume in the world

Contents

Contents

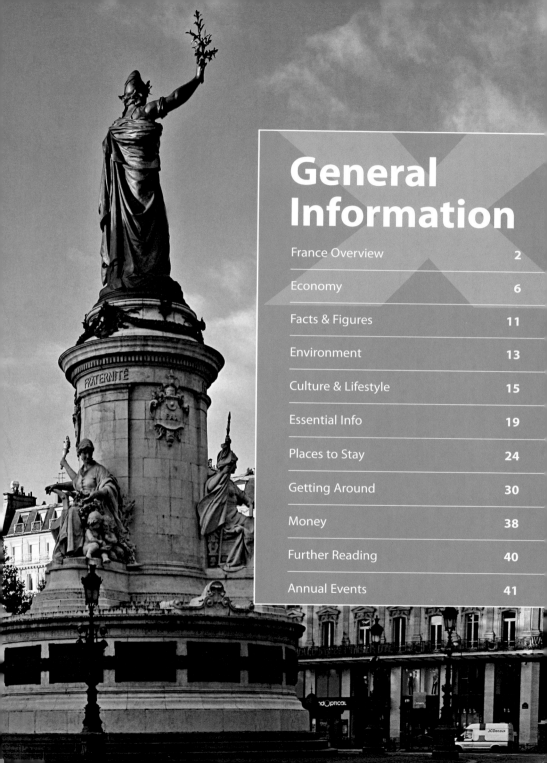

General Information

General Information

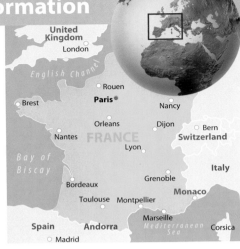

Geography

Due to its roughly six-sided shape, France has been dubbed *L'Hexagone* by its inhabitants. Paris sits in the north of the hexagon along the River Seine, which runs north-west out of the city to the English Channel. While bordered by six other western European nations, mainland France also enjoys over 3,400 kilometres of coastline: the North Sea and English Channel to the north; the Mediterranean Sea on its southern border; and the Atlantic Ocean to the west.

Mainland France is notable for its geographical diversity. It shares two mountain ranges with several neighbours: the Alps, along its eastern borders with Italy and Switzerland; and the Pyrenees, which separate it from Spain to the southwest. The Massif Central mountain region rests within France's borders in the centre of the country.

As popular as its peaks are with skiers, France's Loire Valley is world famous for its wine and castles. The Loire River runs from the mountains of the Massif Central, north to Orléans, then veers westward to the Atlantic. The Rhone River snakes between the Alps to its east and the Massif Central to the west, reaching the Mediterranean at the port city of Marseilles. East of Marseilles, France's famed Côte d'Azur stretches along the Mediterranean.

Rich in fertile farmland, France ranks second internationally behind the United States as an exporter of agricultural products. In addition, France is rich in forestland. The forest of Fontainebleau, for example, covers 280 sq km to the south of Paris.

Regions & Departments

France is divided into 26 regions, established by the Fifth Republic. Paris is located in the Île de France region. Of the 26 regions, 21 sit within mainland France, with a 22nd, the Mediterranean island of Corsica, off its south-eastern coast.

The other four are French overseas territories comprising the Departments d'Outre Mer (DOM). They are: Réunion, in the Indian Ocean, Martinique and Guadeloupe (also known as the French Antilles), and French Guiana, in South America. France also holds several overseas protectorates, called Collectivités d'Outre Mer, which exercise more self-governance. Most notable among these are French Polynesia and New Caledonia, the latter of which will hold a 2011 referendum on the question of independence.

The regions are divided further into 100 departments. Each DOM constitutes a department within itself. Each department, in turn, is made up of *arrondissements* or *communes*, each with its own town hall and local mayor.

Fact Box

Paris Coordinates: 48°52'0"N, 2°19'59"E

France Mainland Borders: Andorra, Belgium, Germany, Italy, Luxembourg, Monaco, Spain, Switzerland

Total Mainland Area: 551,000km sq

Total Area - France (including Corsica and DOM): 675,000km sq

Total Area - Paris: 86.9km sq

Total Coastline: Mainland and Corsica: 3,427km; French Guiana: 378km; Guadeloupe: 306km

Highest Point: Mont Blanc, 4,808m

The city of Paris consists of 20 *arrondissements*, which spiral out clockwise from the centre of the city. Because of this spiraling pattern, the map of Paris is often said to resemble a snail's shell.

Major Cities

As the most popular tourist city in the world and with a metropolitan population of nearly ten million, Paris dwarfs all other French cities by comparison. However, other major cities do exist. Marseilles is the largest port city on the French Mediterranean; Toulouse is the European centre of aerospace industry and home to Airbus; Lyon is the east-central city known as the French capital of gastronomy; Strasbourg, located on the German border, is home to the European Parliament and European Court of Human Rights; Bordeaux is considered the world's wine capital and holds the annual Vinexpo, the biggest worldwide event for the wine industry; and Le Havre, on the English Channel, is the largest export port city in France.

What's in a Name?
Paris takes its name from the Parisii, the Celtic tribe that originally established fishing outposts along the Seine around 250 BC.

History

Lutèce

Originally named Lutèce, Paris was a thriving city in Roman Gaul. As the Roman Empire declined, Atilla the Hun's marauding forces encroached upon France from the east. The prayers of Saint Geneviève were answered when Atilla's army surprisingly turned south before entering the city. Saint Geneviève remains the patron saint of Paris, her statue standing guard over the Pont de la Tournelle.

Paris, Capital of Kings

In 508 AD, Clovis I, the first king of the Franks, established his capital in Paris. Though Charlemagne moved the French capital to Aachen, Paris reassumed its status as capital city thanks to Hugues Capet.

The Île de la Cité, the larger of the two islands that form Paris' heart, saw construction begin on the Cathedral of Notre Dame during the 12th century, while the Left Bank developed as a centre of learning. As Latin was the language of scholars, the area became known as the Latin Quarter. Meanwhile on the Right Bank, building began on the original Louvre Palace.

From the roof of Notre Dame

Know Your Left From Your Right

Paris is famously divided into the Rive Gauche, or Left Bank, and the Rive Droite, the Right Bank. This may seem confusing, since the Seine clearly divides the city into upper and lower portions. The left and right notations refer to the banks' placement in relation to the direction in which the river flows, which is east to west. To face the same direction as the river flow, stand with your back to the front entrance of Notre Dame Cathedral.

A History of Violence

While kings, scholars and clergy lived well in the capital, the poor and merchant classes began to crumble under intolerable living conditions. Charles V quashed a 1358 rebellion and built the infamous Bastille fortress to defend against insurrections. Great political instability and religious intolerance culminated in the St Bartholomew's Day Massacre in 1572, when nearly 3,000 Protestants were killed by Catholic mobs. A Protestant king, Henri IV ascended to the throne only after he converted to Catholicism in 1594, uttering his famous line, 'Paris is well worth a mass'. Henri IV proved worthy of Paris as well, creating the Place des Vosges and the Louvre's Cour Carrée.

Paris continued to bloom in the 17th century, which saw construction of the magnificent Palais du Luxembourg, the Palais Royal, and the rebuilt Sorbonne. Political unrest persisted in the city, however, and Louis XIV moved the court to Versailles, twenty kilometres west of the city.

Revolution & Terror

French nobility lived lavishly at Versailles while people starved in the capital's streets. On July 14, 1789, an angry Paris mob ransacked the arsenal and freed a handful of political prisoners at the Bastille, sparking the French Revolution.

The following years saw the city descend into a bloody 'Reign of Terror', where a guillotine was erected at the current-day Place de la Concorde. There, in 1793, Louis XVI and his queen, Marie Antoinette, were both beheaded.

19th Century Paris

Order was finally restored to the city by the young army officer, Napoleon Bonaparte. Later crowning himself Emperor, Napoleon I expanded the French Empire through military conquests. He transported Egyptian obelisks to the city and built the Roman-style church of La Madeleine.

Paris received a mid-century makeover, thanks to Emperor Napoleon III's prefect Baron Haussmann. Demolishing many neighbourhoods, Haussmann made way for the wide boulevards for which Paris is known today. Napoleon III also commissioned a monument to his uncle's military victories, the Arc de Triomphe, at the head of the Champs-Élysée.

In 1889, the Eiffel Tower was constructed as a temporary structure during the World Exhibition held in Paris. The tower, an iron and steel symbol of modern architecture, proved useful as a radio antenna and endures as the symbol of Paris.

War

Though Paris never became a battleground during the first world war, French casualties were painfully high, and the city suffered through periods of rationing and flu epidemic. Between wars, Paris was the alluring, exotic city that drew literary giants and jazz luminaries to its cafes and clubs, but when the Depression hit, a city and a nation were plunged into disarray and became easy pickings for vengeful German forces, who occupied Paris in June 1940. The government evacuated Paris and took up residency in Vichy, where it became a puppet of the Nazi regime.

Nazi rule lasted four years, marked by the forced deportation of Paris' Jewish residents from their homes along the rue des Rosiers in the Marais district. Their destination was Auschwitz. However, it was also a period of heroism, as the French Resistance movement fought clandestinely against their oppressors.

As Allied forces advanced towards Paris in the summer of 1944, Resistance movements within the city stepped up, skirmishing with German commandant Von Choltitz's troops. General Leclerc's French army division arrived to find Von Choltitz in retreat, thus sparing the city any major damage.

End of the Empire

As post-war France's empire crumbled, immigrant influxes from former colonies saw a need for inexpensive housing, and unattractive *banlieues* were created outside of Paris, where great poverty and strong racial divisions exist to this day. Charles De Gaulle, second world war hero, came out of retirement to assume the reigns in 1958 as first president of the Fifth Republic. De Gaulle quit the presidency 10 years later, his popularity waning partly due to the Algerian War and the series of student riots in May 1968.

Modern Marks

Fifth Republic presidents have followed in the footsteps of kings before them, putting their own stamps on the city, to varying degrees of success. While the bizarre tube and glass facade of the Centre Pompidou and the Pyramid at the Louvre have become interesting novelties, other modern constructions such as the Opéra Bastille and the universally detested Tour Montparnasse are often met with revulsion.

Jacques Chirac left office in May 2007 after 12 years as president, a period marked by scandal, *banlieue* rioting, economic stagnation and political promises left unfulfilled. New President Nicolas Sarkozy, son of immigrants and champion of a smaller government, hopes to reinvigorate the economy by relaxing taxes on businesses.

Paris Timeline

250BC	Celtic Parisii tribe establishes fishing village on banks of the Seine
52BC	Julius Caesar seizes control of Gaul, quashing revolt led by Vercingetorix
250AD	St. Denis, Paris' first bishop, martyred at Montmartre
506	Clovis I makes Paris capital of his Merovingian dynasty
987	Hugues Capet establishes Capetian Dynasty, which will last in France until the Revolution
1100	Famous monk Abelard begins teaching in Paris
1150	Population: 50,000
1163	Construction begins on Cathedral of Notre Dame de Paris
1257	Sorbonne (University of Paris) opens
1320	Population: 250,000
1328	England's Edward III claims throne of France; French nobles disagree, Hundred Years' War begins, lasts 109 years
1572	St Bartholomew's Day Massacre
Mid-17th century	population: 500,000
1789	On July 14 the French storm the Bastille. Revolution ensues
1792	September 22 – 'Day 1 of Year 1 of the French Republic' proclaimed
1804	Napoleon crowns himself emperor
Early 19th century	Population: 900,000
1870-1871	Prussian army sieges Paris for four months; citizens eat zoo animals
1889	Moulin Rouge cabaret opens
1900	Paris metro makes first trip
1914	'Miracle of the Marne': 600 Parisian taxis help transport reserve infantry to early WWI battle
1924	Paris hosts Summer Olympic Games
1927	Charles Lindbergh feted in Paris for intercontinental flight
1928	Roland-Garros tennis stadium opens
1968	Massive student protests in Latin Quarter
1995	Bomb explodes in St. Michel RER train station, killing eight
1998	Host country France wins football World Cup
2001	Socialist Bertrand Delanoë elected mayor
2005	Lance Armstrong makes 7th Tour de France victory lap on Champs-Élysée
2007	Nicolas Sarkozy elected President

Leading Industrial Sectors

Telecommunications (including
    communication satellites)
Aerospace and Defence
Shipbuilding (naval and specialist ships)
Pharmaceuticals
Nuclear and Electrical Power
Electronics
Construction and Civil Engineering
Chemicals
Automobile production (3.5m units in 2005)
Transport equipment
Research and development (2.3% of GDP)

France Overview

While France's GDP growth remains stagnant and unemployment rates are relatively high, the Republic is still the sixth largest economy in the world and boasts a low poverty rate thanks to high taxes (almost 50% of GDP in 2005) that pay for a solid system of social services. GDP is around $2 trillion, or about $30,100 per capita.

Privatisation

The days of François Mitterand's Socialist Party-controlled government are long gone. Jacques Chirac, who became president in 1995 after Mitterand's fourteen years in office, ushered in an era of economic privatisation, which newly elected President Nicolas Sarkozy looks to continue. Many formerly public sectors such as banks and insurance companies have been privatised, while other large companies such as Air France and France Telecom have seen moves in that direction and are already publicly traded on the stock exchange. Sarkozy hopes to rejuvenate businesses by easing tax burdens.

Average Yearly Salaries

Accountant	€ 39,000
Communications Director	€ 52,000
Database Administrator	€ 51,000
Electronics Engineer	€ 53,000
HR Manager	€ 92,000
IT Consultant	€ 65,000
Lawyer (in-house)	€ 63,000
Marketing Director	€ 96,000
Sales Director	€ 55,000

Job Market

In 2006, Prime Minister Dominique de Villepin spearheaded the controversial Contract de Première Embauche (CPE) law, designed to help people entering the job market find jobs more quickly. Hoping to encourage businesses by extending the new worker employment trial period to two years, he saw his plans backfire, as young people staged a series of demonstrations throughout Paris and the provinces, accusing the government of treating them as disposable labour. While the law was passed, and ratified, by Chirac, the president made a special decree aimed at diffusing the unrest, saying that he did not want the law to be put into practice.

The economy is driven by the services sector, comprising 77% of the GDP, while industry makes up 20%. Agriculture accounts for a little over 2%. France's largest export partners are its neighbors within the EU, chiefly Germany (15%), Spain (10%), and UK (9%), as well as the US (7%).

Paris Overview

Paris is easily the most populous and economically important city in France, accounting for about 29% of the national GDP, but the city does not have one go-to industry that drives its economy, such as the aerospace industry in Toulouse. Rather, the over five million-strong workforce is spread out over many fields. Business services make up around 17%, while commerce and manufacturing account for 13% and 12%, respectively. Though Paris is the most popular tourist destination in the world, the tourism industry accounts for less than 4% of the metropolitan GDP; further evidence of a diverse economy.

Gross Domestic Product

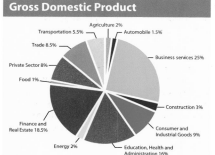

Agriculture 2%
Transportation 5.5%
Automobile 1.5%
Trade 8.5%
Business services 25%
Private Sector 8%
Food 1%
Construction 3%
Finance and Real Estate 18.5%
Consumer and Industrial Goods 9%
Energy 2%
Education, Health and Administration 16%

Strategic Location

When enticing businesses to move to Paris, location is often overlooked. The fact is, that while the European Union has shifted eastward due to new members in recent years, Paris is still excellently located within western Europe, a short TGV ride away from London and Brussels, and easily reachable by plane from many other western European destinations.

Economy

Arc de Triomphe

Need a Job?
For more information on working in Paris, including contact details for recruitment agencies, see Work in the Residents chapter, p.54.

Where Parisians Work

Though major business districts do exist within Paris, most notably on the Right Bank in the western portion of the city, the last half-century has seen incredible development in the western suburbs of Paris. The La Défense business district is a complex of fantastic skyscrapers a few kilometres west of the city that serves as home to many company headquarters. Suburbs to the north and south of Paris have also become work hubs, contributing to the heavy traffic and packed Paris metro and RER trains during peak hours, as commuters make their way in and around the city.

Tourism

Describing Paris as a popular tourist destination is like saying French wine tastes good. Paris is the most popular tourist destination in the entire world; year in, year out. In 2006, the city welcomed 27 million visitors, over ten times its population. It should therefore come as no surprise that 12% of the Paris workforce is involved in some aspect of the tourism industry.

Be they scruffy students backpacking through Europe, retirees who come for the ambience, or families on holiday, tourists of all ages and background know Paris cannot be beaten for its variety, its culture, and its joie de vivre.

Hotels

Over 1,500 hotels, 'aparthotels', campsites, and youth hostels offer over 80,000 rooms to accommodate the tourist influx. Though hotels are reasonably spread throughout the city, the highest concentration is found in the 8th, 9th, 10th and 17th *arrondissements*, all on the Right Bank. The 9th has the most hotels (179), while the 19th and 20th have the least (17 each). Some 60% of visitors are foreign, a third of which is North American or British.

Top Spots

In a city featuring 455 parks and gardens, 210 theatres, 171 churches and 157 museums, the number one tourist attraction is Notre Dame Cathedral (estimated to have received 13 million visitors in 2005), followed by Sacré Coeur Basilica at Montmartre. Their figures are helped by the fact that entry to both is free. The Louvre Museum is in third place, followed by the Eiffel Tower and the Centre Pompidou.

Key Paris Projects

Ever since Baron Haussmann carved out wide boulevards and spurred citywide rebuilding efforts in the latter half of the 19th century, Paris has undergone frequent facelifts. Currently, the eastern and north-eastern parts of the city are seeing the majority of new construction. While real estate is always at a premium, aesthetics and ecology remain of utmost importance, as architects and city planners strive to create functioning, environmentally sound works of art within which Parisians can live, work, and play.

7

Ateliers de Paris

30 rue du Fg Saint-Antoine
12th

The 12th *arrondissement* has recently seen completion on the Ateliers de Paris building, a complex of workshops dedicated to new development in the areas of fashion and design. Located on rue de Faubourg St Antoine, the space brings together artists and designers in a new way, connecting them with major industry drivers.

Bibliothèque Médiathèque Bagnolet

109/115 rue de Bagnolet
20th

Spring 2009 brings with it the public opening of this modern, five storey library. With over 4,000 square metres of space, the library will be largely dedicated to a DVD and CD collection and will also house a meeting room large enough to accommodate 100 people.

Carreau des Halles

Les Halles
1st

The Forum des Halles will be demolished to make way for an innovative combination of green space and shopping in central Paris, due for completion in 2012. La Canopée, a futuristic glass ceiling will cover much of the grounds. Along with retail space, a 3,000 square metre conservatory and a '21st century cafe' will overlook 4.3 hectares of park space. Eco-friendly, the park's glass canopy will contain solar cells, and its unique structure will allow for rain-gathering to form a reservoir with which the gardens can be watered.

Grand Projet de Renouvellement Urbain

Various Locations

The Grand Projet de Renouvellement Urbain (GPRU) was started in 2001 with the long term objective of improving the quality of life in 11 chief neighbourhoods throughout the city. Many projects are planned or are underway in the northern 18th and 19th *arrondissements*, including the improvement of public squares as well as the construction or renovation of low-cost housing. The 12th and 20th *arrondissements* are currently undergoing improvement to traffic flow problems on avenue de la Porte de Vincennes, rue Noël Ballay and rue Fernand Fourreau.

'Le 104'

104 rue d'Aubervilliers
19th

01 40 05 51 71 | www.104.fr

The 19th century building and former municipal funeral services headquarters was set to open its doors again in early 2008, welcoming contemporary artists and their fans. The 35,000 square metre property will house all sorts of artists and will be able to hold up to 5,000 people - artists and visitors - within its walls. As part of a larger urban renewal project for north-east Paris, 'Le 104' will feature a large main hallway, from which visitors will find artwork in all its stages, from conceptualisation to exhibition.

Paris Biopark

13th

Located in the 13th *arrondissement*, Paris Biopark is developing into a centre for public health companies and biotechnology firms, as well as a small financial district. With 700,000 square metres of office space and another 450,000 square metres of activity space, the facility has enough space for 60,000 workers. Along with numerous small biotech firms, various companies in other sectors already taking up residence there include the Accor Group, Les Caisses d'Epargne and La Caisse des Dépôts.

Paris Philharmonic

185-193 blvd Serrurier
19th

September 2009 will see ground-breaking on the future Philharmonie de Paris, in Parc de la Villette. A joint venture between the City of Paris and the national government, the symphony hall will hold 2,400 spectators for orchestra performances. The Paris Orchestra will make its home there, while jazz concerts will be scheduled, as well as musical groups from around the world. The 20,000 square metre space will be a place of learning too, with many private rehearsal rooms. The Philharmonic is due to open in November 2012.

International Relations

France is a charter member of the European Union, which grew out of the ashes of the second world war. France and Germany, bitter enemies that fought three wars against each other in the 75 year period ending in 1945, forged an economic pact in 1950. A year later, six Western European nations signed a treaty allying each's coal and steel industries, and in 1958 the European Economic Community was born, renamed the European Union in 1992.

A founding member of the United Nations as well as NATO, France plays a central role within the 27 member strong European Union.

Most nations' embassies and consular offices are located within Paris' 7th, 8th and 16th *arrondissements*, on the Right Bank.

Challenging the US

Nicolas Sarkozy did not wait long after being elected to challenge the United States. Though perceived as much more pro-America than his predecessor Jacques Chirac, Sarkozy mentioned in his first post-election speech that he planned to seek President George Bush's signature on the Kyoto Protocol. France, a leader in the cause to reduce CO_2 emissions, is an important international player on the environmental scene.

Political Parties

Numerous political parties span the political spectrum, from the Revolutionary Communist League Party (who received 4% of the 2007 first round presidential vote) to the extreme right National Front Party (10%). Third-place finisher François Bayrou ran on the centrist Union for French Democracy (UDF) ticket, garnering 18% of the vote. After the elections, Bayrou created the Democratic Movement Party, which won three seats in the June 2007 legislative elections.

Government & Politics

France's Fifth Republic was established by the constitution of 1958. The president is the head of the Republic, governing in accord with a bicameral legislature. While regional and local governments exist, the constitution guarantees all French live under the same law, citing the ideals of Liberté, Egalité and Fraternité, which trace back to the Revolution.

Elections

Presidential elections usually consist of two rounds. Several candidates run in the first round, and if no one receives a majority of the popular vote, the top two candidates from the first round advance to a run-off held two weeks later. Legislative elections occur a month after.

Hôtel de Ville

Executive Branch

The presidential candidate receiving the majority of the popular vote in the second round becomes president, officially taking office ten days after the election. He is elected to a five-year term of office, and currently there are no term limits. Upon election, he names his prime minister and ministers, tasked with proposing the bulk of all new laws.

Legislative Branch

Le Parlement votes a new law into existence and is responsible for voting on the state budget. It comprises two houses: the popularly elected

Pont Royal and the Louvre

Assemblée Nationale and the Sénat. There are 577 members of the Assemblée Nationale, known as *députés*. They are elected to five-year terms coinciding with the president's tenure. *Sénateurs*, 321 in total, are named by locally elected officials and serve for six years.

Judiciary Branch

The judiciary is divided into civil and administrative branches. Respectively, the Cour de Cassation and the Conseil d'Etat are the highest courts in France. The Conseil Constitutionel, if invoked, is responsible for ensuring the constitutionality of new laws. Concerning trials, an appellate court system exists to check lower court rulings. Popular juries are only used in serious criminal cases. For all other cases the *magistrats*, or judges, are responsible for court decisions.

The Current Government

Nicolas Sarkozy was elected the sixth President of the Fifth Republic in May 2007, replacing Jacques Chirac. Sarkozy appointed François Fillon as his Prime Minister and named fifteen other ministers – seven of which are women. President Sarkozy is a member of the Union for a Popular Movement Party (UMP). The UMP garnered a strong majority of votes in the Assemblée Nationale, considered a necessity if the president hopes to implement change. The party holding the second largest number of seats in the Assemblée Nationale is the Socialist Party (PS). PS Party presidential candidate Ségolène Royal was the first woman to appear on a second round presidential ballot, garnering 47% of the vote.

Local Government

Each of the 26 regions of France has its own Regional Council, which is charged with some state functions. Likewise, each department consists of a General Council, and each *commune* is governed by a Municipal Council, at the head of which is a mayor.

Population

An estimated 2.2 million people live within Paris' twenty *arrondissements*, an additional four million living in the near suburbs. 11.4 million inhabitants call the Île de France department home. Though Paris is over 2,000 years old, a young populace courses through its city streets. Well over half the city's residents are under 40, and 49% of residents over age 15 are unmarried. Paris is a city that moves. 20% of all inhabitants have lived in the city for less than five years, and only about one in three residents can actually claim Parisian birth. Constantly in flux, the city has seen slightly declining numbers in recent years, due to the growth of its suburbs.

National Flag

The national flag consists of three equal vertical bands of blue, white and red. The blue and red denote the colours of Paris, while the white represents the king. The flag dates from the Revolution and was officially recognised as the national flag in 1794. The flag waves from all state buildings and is most prominent on Bastille Day, July 14.

Local Time

Paris is located in the Central European Time Zone (UCT +1). Like all European countries within its time zone, it recognizes Central European Daylight Time (UCT+2), beginning the last Sunday in March and lasting until the last Sunday in October.

Social & Business Hours

The famous 35 hour French working week is complicated. First of all, it is not applied to all sectors of the labour force. For instance, executives and members of liberal professions (doctors and lawyers, for example) are exempt, meaning they work much longer hours on average.

In order to circumvent its limitations, companies often just insist their employees produce more within the time span allotted. Most employees who do adhere to the 35 hour week choose to work overtime during the first of a two-week period, then take a day off during the second. Others, especially parents, choose to take

Time Zones

Athens	+1
Beijing	+6
Chicago	-7
Denver	-8
Dubai	+2
Dublin	-1
Hong Kong	+6
Jakarta	+5
Johannesburg	0
Kuala Lumpur	+6
London	-1
Los Angeles	-9
Mexico City	-7
Montreal	-6
Moscow	+2
Mumbai	+3.5
Munich	0
New York	-6
Perth	+9
Prague	0
Rio de Janeiro	-5
Rome	0
Seoul	+7
Singapore	+6
Sydney	+8
Tokyo	+7
Toronto	-6
Wellington	+10

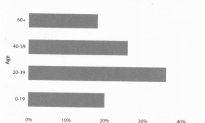

Paris Population Age Breakdown

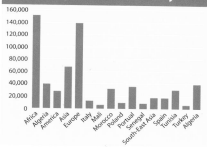

Foreign Population – Nationality

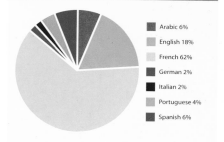

Population by Principal Language

- Arabic 6%
- English 18%
- French 62%
- German 2%
- Italian 2%
- Portuguese 4%
- Spanish 6%

Wednesday afternoons off, as children only have half-days of school on Wednesdays. Children also have morning sessions on Saturday, although this will soon be scrapped. However long one chooses to spend at work, the average working week begins Monday morning at 09:00 and ends Friday afternoon at 18:00.
The French usually take an hour for lunch between noon and 14:00, and dinner is usually no earlier than 20:00. French children usually have a snack at 17:00, when they return home from school. Government offices open at 09:00 or 10:00 and close between 17:00 and 18:00. Most shops close at 19:00. Large grocery shops stay open until 21:00 or 22:00, while smaller convenience stores remain open later. On Sunday, most shops are closed.

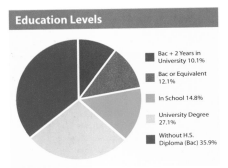

Education Levels

- Bac + 2 Years in University 10.1%
- Bac or Equivalent 12.1%
- In School 14.8%
- University Degree 27.1%
- Without H.S. Diploma (Bac) 35.9%

◀ *Pentecost Monday*

A stir over Pentecost Monday has occurred over a 2004 government decision to revoke the holiday. This decision stemmed from the excessively hot summer of 2003, when approximately 15,000 senior citizens died due to inadequate or non-existent home cooling systems. The government decided to provide cooling systems free of charge for poverty-stricken senior citizens, hoping to pay for the programme by asking citizens to donate their day's wages to the government. Pandemonium ensued at the idea of losing a vacation day, and many companies still give their employees the day off, paying the government out of their own pockets.

Public Holidays

Five civil and six Catholic holidays dot the French calendar. Though France holds firm to the idea of separation of church and state, somehow when it comes to vacation days the French prove to be quite devout.
Le pont, or 'the bridge', is a time-honored tradition where most French workers cash in accrued overtime to create four day weekends whenever holidays fall on Tuesdays or Thursdays. For instance, as the Ascension always falls on a Thursday, the following Friday is a de facto holiday as well, which the French refer to as 'taking the bridge'.

Public Holidays

Public Holidays	
New Year's Day	January 1
Labour Day	May 1
1945 Armistice Day	May 8
'La Fête Nationale', or Bastille Day	July 14
Assumption	August 15
All Saints' Day	November 1
1918 Armistice Day	November 11
Christmas	December 25
Easter Monday	One day after Easter
Ascension Thursday	39 days after Easter
Pentecost Monday	50 days after Easter

Photography

Paris has to be one of the most photogenic, and photographed, cities in the world, and Parisians are used to tourists toting all manner of camera and video equipment, but that doesn't mean they like it. When taking a photo of a stranger, either be discreet, or ask for permission. Street performers will gladly pose for photos, as long as they receive a few coins for their trouble.
Tripods are officially not allowed in front of major sites, and police will usually ask that they be put away. In addition, photography of restricted areas within Charles de Gaulle Airport is not allowed.

Population Statistics

Life Expectancy:

Females born in 2004: 83.8 yrs.
Males born in 2004: 76.7 yrs.
Source: INED (Institut National d'Etudes Démographiques), 2005

Gender Breakdown:

Females: 31,631,156
Males: 29,907,166
Source: INED, 2007

Weather on the Web
*The website
www.meteofrance.com
has detailed forecasts
and clickable weather
maps. For up-to-date
information on the air
quality in the Île de
France region, visit
www.airparif.asso.fr
which is available in
French and English.*

Climate

Paris is generally temperate, ranging from average lows in January of 4.7°C to average highs in July and August of 20°C. Extreme cases of cold and heat have been recorded, most recently in August 2003, when the mercury soared above 35°C for a record nine consecutive days, leading to thousands of deaths throughout the country. In the last 30 years, the coldest day on record in Paris was January 17, 1985, with a low of -13.9°C. On average, Paris can expect to see 25 sub-zero days per year (but it rarely snows), and 43 days where the temperature surpasses 25 degrees.

There is no rainy season, though thunderstorms are most frequent between May and August. Precipitation is spread relatively evenly throughout the year. On especially windy and stormy days, Paris' parks and gardens will close, to protect people from falling branches.

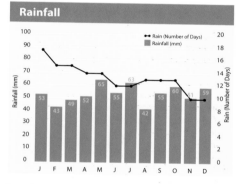

Flora & Fauna

With large green spaces within the city and acres of woodland to the west, east and south, Paris and its environs present a diverse ecological makeup for a big city. Technically part of the 16th *arrondissement*, the Bois de Boulogne in western Paris covers a space of nearly 8.5 square kilometres. On the other side of the city, the Bois de Vincennes is even larger at nearly 10 square kilometres. Both feature several lakes and wooded areas, and are favourites of all species, human and otherwise. New York's Central Park and Hyde Park in London are dwarfed in comparison.

The rest of Paris' Île de France region is even more diverse. While 20% of the region's land may be urban, the other 80% is rural landscape. Nearly a quarter of the region is wooded, the forests predominantly composed of oak trees, most notably in the Forest of Fontainebleau, to the south of Paris. Île de France counts fifty rivers in its territory, all branches of the Seine, lending sustenance to its arable land.

Flora

Perhaps the flower most commonly associated with Paris, the fleur de lys, literally 'lily flower', is not actually a lily, and didn't originally have any roots in Paris. Legend has it that Clovis I, the fifth century king of the Franks, won a decisive battle at Vouillé, about 200 kilometres south-west of Paris. Yellow irises were abundant in the area, and to commemorate the important victory, Clovis incorporated a stylized version of the flower into his coat of arms. Though eventually misinterpreted as a lily instead of an iris, the fleur de lys has become a lasting symbol of French royalty and French culture in general.

13

Fauna

A half-hour journey south of Paris leads to the Forest of Fontainebleau, where two species of deer – the large red deer and the smaller roe deer – can be found in their natural habitat. Wild boar, foxes, and species of wildcats also call Île de France home.

Birds

In Paris itself, 213 species have been spotted, 73 of which nest in the city. The common kestrel, a bird of prey from the falcon family, may seem a bit elitist, preferring to make its home in such prized spots as Notre Dame Cathedral and the Eiffel Tower.

Take Action ◀
If you're passionate about the environment and want to do more to protect it, visit www.greenpeace.org/france for details of how to get involved with Greenpeace in France.

Environmental Issues

It is hard to live in Paris and not notice how the city and its people care about ecology. From city greening efforts to its recycling programme, the City of Paris is engaged in many projects to improve the environment.

Green Spaces

A movement to create more green spaces within the city has seen the creation of many new parks and gardens, with several more under construction. The 17th *arrondissement*'s Parc Clichy-Batignolle became the largest green area in north-western Paris in June 2007. Likewise, the Jardin des Grands Moulins along the Seine in Paris' 13th *arrondissement* opened in June 2007 and contains a 2,000 sq m play area for children. Major renovation on the 43,000 sq m green space in the heart of Paris, at Les Halles was scheduled to begin in 2008.

Water Quality

Parisian tap water is drinkable, and the city is taking measures to improve the quality of water by replacing or renovating 54,000 pipes and water conduits throughout the city over the next six years. The cleaning of the River Seine is also a popular issue as, like other city rivers, it has been misused and polluted through the years. From the early 1990s, city planners have been working on reducing pollution levels in the Seine. Swimming in the portion of the Seine within Paris' city limits is not advisable today, though it is a goal for the future.

Air Quality

A study of the first six years of the millennium revealed that Paris and its suburbs saw its air quality attain a rating of 'very good' or 'good' for 82% of days, while air quality for slightly over 7% of days was graded as 'poor' or 'very poor'. In order to improve air quality, the city is continuing efforts to reduce the number of vehicles on the streets. In December 2006, the new T3 tramway line opened along the southern ring of the city (see p.36). July 2007 saw the debut of the mayor's Vélib' network of bicycle stations (p.35) consisting of 15,000 bikes around Paris aimed at encouraging people to cycle instead of use cars within the city. The scheme was a success from the off, with thousands of commuters turning to pedal power.

Recycling

All Parisian homes are expected to recycle, putting plastics, aluminium and paper products in yellow-topped bins, while non-recyclable objects go in green-topped bins. In addition, 1,000 large, green receptacles are installed about the city, accepting all glass recyclables. In city parks, the yellow receptacles serve the same purpose as the yellow cans in homes, further aiding city recycling efforts.

Culture

Paris is a giant canvas of museums, theatres, concert halls and monuments dedicated to its artists, past and present, and Parisians take great interest in these offerings, lining up for exhibitions and packing opera houses. Many theatres and halls begin posting metro station advertisements for plays or concerts six months in advance, knowing the culture-hungry community will quickly snap up the tickets.

Exit sign

Rich Cultural Heritage

Paris' history is intertwined with its love of art and its ties to the Catholic church. In the Middle Ages, Paris grew in prominence as a result of its status as a place of religious worship, welcoming Catholics to its magnificent Notre Dame Cathedral and the Sainte Chapelle. It became a magnet for students at the same time, growing rapidly into the European seat of higher education. Continuing through the centuries, Paris has been an inspiration to its residents and its visitors. Museums like the Louvre and the Musée d'Orsay house priceless works of art, and lesser known galleries throughout the city nurture burgeoning talents. The Panthéon serves as the final resting place for French greats, while the Académie Française ensures the language of those greats is protected. Classic Haussmann-style apartment buildings stand across the street from new wave glass-facade structures, denoting a city at once rich in history yet moving forward.

Recent Racial Tensions

This dichotomy between tradition and modernity is as evident in its varying architecture as it is in the clash of social classes that has rocked the city and the nation in recent years. Immigrant waves began arriving from former colonies in the 1950s, adding a new spice to Parisian life. France was not ready for such changes, and integration has been difficult for many.

The *banlieue* riots in October and November 2005 stemmed from the accidental deaths of two boys from the eastern suburb of Clichy-sous-Bois who thought the police were chasing them. After weeks of unrest throughout the country, order was restored, but tension remains high. The 2007 election of right-wing 'law and order' President Nicolas Sarkozy only served to remind many non-European French citizens and immigrants that their culture remains at odds with some of the traditions of France.

L'Académie Française
Created by Cardinal Richelieu in 1635 to codify spelling and grammar, the main aim of the Académie today is to protect the French language against anglicisms such as 'le parking' and 'les people'.

Language

French is the only official language of France, and therefore Paris. French is a Romance language, descending from Latin, with influences from the original Celtic and Germanic tribes who inhabited parts of Gaul before and during the Roman era. French is spoken by 300 million people worldwide.

Verlan

Adolescents of every country speak a language all their own, and France is no exception. In the 1970s and 80s, suburban teenagers began speaking Verlan, a kind of reverse-syllable language. L'envers means backwards. When the word is pronounced, it sounds like 'lanver' which, when the syllables are reversed, becomes verlan. Many of these reverse words are spelled phonetically making it even more difficult for a foreigner to identify. Examples include zarbi (bizarre), meuf (femme) and kébri (briquet - a cigarette lighter).

Basic French

Accidents		Numbers	
Accident	Un accident	Zero	Zéro
Ambulance	Ambulance	One	Un
Doctor	Médecin	Two	Deux
Driver's licence	Permis de conduire	Three	Trois
Help!	Au secours!	Four	Quatre
Hospital	Hôpital	Five	Cinq
Insurance	l'assurance	Six	Six
Papers	Des papiers, des documents	Seven	Sept
Police	La police	Eight	Huit
Sorry	Je suis désolé	Nine	Neuf
Introduction		Ten	Dix
I am from	Je viens de	Hundred	Cent
My name is	Je m'appelle	Thousand	Mille
What is your name?	Comment vous appelez-vous?	**Basic**	
Taxi / Car Related		Excuse me	Excusez-moi
Airport	Aéroport	No	Non
East	Est	Pardon	Pardon
Far	Loin de	Please	S'il vous plaît
Hotel	Hôtel	Thank You	Merci
Is this the road to...?	C'est la rue qui va à...?	Yes	Oui
Left	Gauche	You're Welcome	De rien
Near	Près de	**Greetings**	
North	Nord	Good morning, hello	Bonjour
Petrol Station	la station service	How are you?	Ca va?
Restaurant	Restaurant	Fine, thank you	Bien, merci
Right	Droite	Goodbye	Au revoir
Road, street	Rue	**Questions**	
Roundabout	Rondpoint	How much does that cost?	Combien ça coute?
Slow down	Ralentissez	How much?	Combien?
South	Sud	How?	Comment?
Stop	Arrêtez	What?	Quoi?
Straight ahead	Tout droit	When?	Quand?
Traffic light	Le feu	Where?	Où?
West	Ouest	Why?	Pourquoi?

English Spoken

While anglophone expats can survive in Paris without speaking more than cursory French, it is a limiting way to live in a city that can offer so much. It is also very difficult to get practical things done, like speaking with a building superintendent, without a good grasp of the language. Though nearly every Parisian speaks at least a few words of English, the average Parisian would only be capable of carrying on a limited conversation. English is the language of business and tourism, and as such one can expect those working in such areas to speak on a higher level.

While street signs are not in English, many restaurants do have English language menus. Additionally, Paris cinemas often show films in VOST (Version Originale, Sous-Titres Français) which is usually abbreviated to VO, and means the film will be the original with French subtitles.

Religion

The once dominant Roman Catholic faith has seen its numbers diminished considerably in France over the last thirty years. Though the government does not compile statistics on religion, most independent polls reveal that the majority of French do not actively practise

Église de la Sainte-Trinité

The Veil Affair
The government's strict interpretation of separation between church and state clashed with its stance on freedom of religion in the 1990s in what is now known as 'The Veil Affair'. Muslim girls were restricted from wearing their veils in public school, as it represented an 'ostentatious' public display of religion. This remains a hot issue among some religious communities.

any faith, and an increasing percentage indicates they are atheist or agnostic. While the number of 'culturally Catholic' French people is somewhere around 85%, actual regular churchgoers make up a tiny constituency.

Catholic churches still dominate the landscape of Paris. Protestant churches are represented in smaller numbers. A community of several hundred thousand Jews resides in Paris, predominantly in the Marais quarter. The 5th *arrondissement* is home to La Mosquée de Paris (p.163). Built after the first world war, it is the central place of worship for an increasing Muslim population.

The French government is secular, meaning it adheres to no religion, while at the same time guaranteeing freedom of worship. In 1995, Parliament created a Commission on Cult Activities, reporting a list of cults that it considers potentially dangerous, including the Church of Scientology and Jehovah's Witnesses.

Despite its secular claims, half of France's national holidays are Catholic feast days. No other faith's holy days are officially recognized by the state.

Places of Worship

Name	Area	Phone	Denomination
American Cathedral	8th	01 47 20 17 92	Episcopalian/Anglican
American Church In Paris	7th	01 40 62 05 00	Interdenominational
Church of Jesus Christ of Latter-Day Saints	4th	01 44 61 90 50	LDS
Grande Mosquée de Paris	5th	01 45 35 97 33	Muslim
Kehilat Gesher	17th	01 39 21 97 19	Reformed Jewish
Paroisse Luthérienne de la Trinité	13th	01 45 82 47 11	Lutheran
St Joseph's Catholic Church	8th	01 42 27 28 56	Roman Catholic
St Michael's Church	8th	01 47 42 70 88	Anglican
Synagogue de la Victoire	9th	01 45 26 95 36	Jewish

National Dress

No, Parisian men do not all wear berets, and the women aren't all wearing fishnet stockings and stiletto heels. In fact, the only people wearing berets are the tourists. There really isn't a national dress in France, especially not in cosmopolitan Paris. While clichéd visions of stripe-shirted mimes stick in the heads of many people who have never visited Paris, new arrivals may be disappointed to discover that Parisians dress more or less like people in London or New York. In the summertime men prefer three-quarter Capri pants to shorts. Suits are de rigueur for men in a business setting, though an increasing number of men currently choose to go tie-less. A la mode for businesswomen are jacket-skirt combinations. In general, Parisians prefer sober, dignified shades to garish colours.

Food & Drink

Other options **Eating Out** p.305

The word 'cuisine' is French in origin, which indicates how important French cooking is to the rest of the world, specifically the western world. While the French did not invent food, the advances that French chefs have made in its preparation and presentation over the last 500 years are known and respected by culinary artists and fans everywhere.

A Rich History

The French tradition of *haute cuisine*, literally 'high cuisine', dates back to the mid 16th century, when Catherine de Medici arrived from Italy to marry the future French King Henri II. Importing her own team of chefs, she combined their skill and the French crown's wealth to nurture cuisine as an art form. Later, Louis XIV's Versailles feasts were known for their many courses, the first instance where food was not served all at once. Down through the years, famous French chefs such as La Varenne, Carême, Escoffier and Bocuse have codified, refined, and developed French cuisine into what it is today. While traditional French cuisine is rather elaborate, featuring heavy sauces, it underwent a makeover in the 1960s. Nouvelle cuisine ('new cuisine') developed from the kitchens of Paul Bocuse and others, and featured lighter cooking techniques. Many of today's tables feature a fusion of the old and the new.

Varied Menus

The French menu is rich and varied, representative of France's different regions. Parisian chefs take the best the nation has to offer – foie gras from the south-west, creamy sauces from Normandy, south-east spices, and sausages from the north-east, to name a few – and refine each dish for their customers. Wine remains an essential part of any fine meal, as does a plate of assorted cheeses, also representing all regions of France.

But Paris not only features great indigenous cuisine. Immigrants from North Africa have brought with them their own specialties. Paris' Chinatown community in the 13th *arrondissement* offers a variety of good Chinese restaurants, and of course several English pubs and American burger joints dot the capital.

Habits

Despite a plethora of great restaurants throughout the city, Parisians do not eat out very often, as dinners can be expensive. Children usually eat lunch in school cafeterias (*cantines*). Most French companies subsidise their employees' lunches in *cantines* or provide restaurant coupons, which can be redeemed in most restaurants, grocery stores and *boulangeries* throughout the city. Breakfast is usually a light meal consisting of bread and jam or cereal, with juice and a hot beverage.

While all neighbourhoods have their own market areas, some of which are open six days a week, more and more Parisians choose to buy their food in larger, American-style supermarkets. Monoprix and Champion are two of the larger city supermarket chains, used for convenience and variety. Smaller grocery stores, known as *épiceries*, cater to late-night shoppers, staying open past midnight. Outside the city, huge supermarkets called *hypermarchés* such as Carrefour and Leclerc welcome suburban shoppers.

Eating Establishments

Paris has many different kinds of eating establishments, some of whose names denote the type of fare you can expect to find:

Café: traditionally a place to go for drinks, from coffee to a few different wines and other alcoholic drinks. Cafés may serve sandwiches and other quick, lighter meals.

Bistro: serves most of what can be found on a café menu, plus a few more meal choices, such as the ubiquitous steak frites - steak and fries. The name bistro actually comes from the Russian word bystro, meaning 'quickly'. Russian troops occupying Paris after the Napoleonic Wars shouted this at restaurateurs, demanding their food be served quickly.

Brasserie: Originally from the Alsace region, these were traditionally breweries (hence the name). Today there is not a noticeable difference between a brasserie and a bistro.

18

In Emergency

French emergency teams are efficient, friendly and quick to respond. Only one problem: operators won't necessarily speak English. Therefore, it is advisable that when calling to have a list of important phrases on standby to get the help you need. If you have a recurring or permanent health problem and do not speak French, ask someone who does to write out your particular health conditions in French, and carry the information in your wallet or purse. In addition, the number 112 can be called from any cell phone. This is a European emergency number, and English-speaking operators are available.

There are three main emergency response branches within France:

SAMU – The Service d'Aide Médicale d'Urgence deals with serious medical emergencies, providing ambulances and trained emergency response teams.

Sapeurs-Pompiers – The sapeurs-pompiers are firefighters by trade, but also have life-saving medical training. Often the sapeurs-pompiers are the first response team at accident scenes.

Police – If you are a victim of a crime or domestic dispute, call the police. In non-emergencies, do not call the police emergency line.

Common Emergency Phrases

Help!	Au secours!
This is an emergency	C'est un cas d'urgence
My name is…	Je m'apelle…
My phone number is…	Mon numéro de telephone est…
My address…	Mon adresse…
I need an ambulance	J'ai besoin d'une ambulance
Heart attack	une crise cardiaque
Stroke	une attaque cérébrale
To be choking	s'étouffer
To be poisoned	s'empoisonner
To bleed	saigner
Diabetic	diabétique
Labour	accouchement/accoucher

Emergency Numbers

English-Speaking European Emergency Number	112
National Emergency Numbers	
Police (emergency)	17
SAMU	15
Sapeurs-pompiers	18
Lost\Stolen Items	
Lost Property	08 21 00 25 25
Lost/Stolen Credit Cards	08 92 70 57 05
Paris Emergency Numbers/Hotlines	
24 Hour Pharmacy	01 45 62 02 41
Anti-poison Centre	01 40 05 48 48
Dental Emergency	01 43 37 51 00
Domestic Violence Hotline	01 40 33 80 60
Pediatric Emergency	01 44 09 84 85
Rape Victim Hotline	08 00 05 95 95
SOS Help (English-language helpline)	01 46 21 46 46
Veterinary Emergency	01 43 96 23 23

Women

In general, women should not feel especially unsafe in Paris. A woman walking alone is not at all uncommon. If taking the metro late at night, it is advisable to sit in the first train car; the driver is just on the other side of the window in the front and can intervene or call for further assistance in a case of harassment. Long metro transfer corridors such as Châtelet – Les Halles and Montparnasse should not be traversed alone at night. Les Halles, in the 1st *arrondissement*, is notoriously unsafe at night and should be avoided by men and women alike. If bothered by someone, the best strategy is to ignore the person and walk away.

Women's Organisations

Several organisations and women's groups exist in Paris. The Women of the American Church group (01 40 620 500) holds an annual workshop aimed at helping women transitioning to Paris. Other organisations include:

Sisters: an association of African American women and other Anglophone women of colour, founded in 1993, providing support and networking services for its members. Phone 01 53 01 08 96.

19

Embassies & Consulates

Australia	01 40 59 33 00
Austria	01 45 55 95 66
Belgium	01 43 80 61 00
Canada	01 44 43 29 00
Denmark	01 44 31 21 21
Finland	01 44 18 19 20
Germany	01 42 99 78 00
Greece	01 47 23 72 28
Ireland	01 45 00 20 87
Italy	01 45 44 38 90
The Netherlands	01 43 06 61 88
New Zealand	01 45 00 24 11
Norway	01 47 23 72 78
Portugal	01 47 27 35 29
South Africa	01 45 55 92 37
Spain	01 44 43 18 18
Sweden	01 44 18 88 00
Switzerland	01 49 55 67 00
United Kingdom	01 42 66 91 42
United States	01 43 12 22 22

American Catholic Women's Organization: part of the St Joseph's Church located in the 8th, the group holds many activites around the year, including lectures, luncheons and classes. Phone 01 42 27 28 56.
WICE: originally the Women's Institute for Continuing Education, an organisation providing cultural and educational programmess to the Anglophone community. Email wice@wice-paris.org.

Children

Large parks like Parc Monceau in the 8th (p.186) or the Jardin du Luxembourg in the 6th (p.184) provide green lawns, fountains, rides and play areas, but on sunny weekends they are packed. Restaurants are not always kid-friendly, though some larger chains like Hippopotamus (www.hippopotamus.fr) or Hard Rock Café in the 9th (01 53 24 60 00) are welcoming and provide children's menus.
Museums like Cité des Sciences (p.169) provide fun learning experiences for children aged 3 and up. The always popular *guignols*, French marionettes, put on shows in many parks around town. There is also a little place called Disneyland Paris (p.188) which has been known to entertain a child or two. Childcare and babysitting services are abundant, the majority regulated by the city government. Visit the City of Paris website (www.paris.fr) for more information.

La Maison des Personnes Handicappés
La Maison des Personnes Handicappés de Paris opened its doors in 2006. With a staff of 120 and an annual budget of €1.2 million, the centre provides counselling and services for people with disabilities in Paris.

People With Disabilities

Paris is making strides to accommodate people with disabilities, though many buildings, pavements and metro stations remain a challenge for the wheelchair-bound. For instance, many restaurant bathrooms are found in the basement, down staircases that even the able-bodied might find difficult to navigate, and metro stations that date from the first half of the 20th century shouldn't be counted on to have lifts. For this reason, whenever visiting a new place in Paris, check beforehand to learn what services are provided.
On the plus side, metro platform edges are marked with raised strips to warn the sight-impaired, and the city is installing audio indicators at traffic lights to ensure safe crossing.

Dress

Paris is a centre of fashion, and Parisians reflect that in the way they choose to dress. While styles differ, count on dressing 'business casual' for a night out on the town. Nicer restaurants will turn away customers dressed in ripped jeans, flip-flops or tracksuits. Baseball caps are increasingly worn around the city, but never in polite society; better to arrive cap-less to a restaurant or to someone's home.
Weather-wise, Paris weather is unpredictable. While mornings may dawn grey and rainy, the afternoon might present blue skies and warmer weather so plan appropriately. Parisians take advantage of any chance to sunbathe in parks and along the Seine and it is not uncommon to see men and women wearing revealing swimsuits. Indoors, air conditioning is rarely too cold. On the contrary, many buildings and homes do not have air-conditioning units, so keep this in mind.

Paris performance artist

Dos & Don'ts

No Smoking

Although around one quarter of French adults are smokers, as of February 2007 they have been banned from smoking in most public places. While it is still possible to smoke in restaurants, cafes and bars, the glory days for nicotine lovers are numbered. By 2008, in theory at least, even Paris' eating and drinking establishments were due to become tobacco-free.

Tu or Vous?

Tu is the familiar form of the word 'you', usually used with friends and family. *Vous* is the polite form, used with people you don't know well, or people who are in a position of seniority. General rule: use *vous* with the neighbouhood baker and your boss. But the under 40 crowd tends to be more informal. Don't be outraged if *tu* is commonplace in your office. When in doubt, let the native decide.

La Bise

Likewise for the famous French double-cheek kiss, known as *la bise*. General rule: men will give *la bise* to women they are familiar with in a social setting. Men shake hands with most other men, but do give *la bise* to close friends and family. Women give *la bise* to female and male friends and family. Office setting? Again, let the French lead.

Right of Way

Road signs can be confusing in France, as can road rules. Most importantly, remember the right of way. If you see a red and white triangular sign marked in the center with a symbol that resembles a rocket, you have the right of way. If the triangle is marked with an 'X' instead, beware of vehicles entering on the right. They have the priority!

Crime & Safety

Other options **In Emergency** p.19

Victims of Crime

Victims of a crime must file a formal complaint report at a local police station. Depending on the immediacy and severity of the crime, one should either call the police emergency number (17) or a local station number. See the table on p.19 for more numbers.

Paris is a relatively safe city, with typical big city issues. Overall, 2006 saw a mild reduction in the crime rate (-1.2%), with a strong 9.9% reduction in crimes committed in metro, RER and train stations, an area of concern for the 19,000 police officers of Paris. Crime has declined steadily over the last several years. Most crimes are non-violent in nature, such as pickpocketing, especially in touristy areas or on the metro.

Pickpockets tend to work in pairs. A common technique involves one person distracting you, perhaps with a confusing question or a request for change, while a second person goes for your goods. Pickpockets like to work the metro because they will know its corridors better than you, and there's always a train arriving to quickly put distance between you and them. When in tight confines, such as metro cars and elevators, pay extra attention to those around you. Most importantly, use common sense. Don't let a stranger carry your bag, don't excessively display valuables such as cameras or mobile phones, and be vigilant.

As a general rule, do not walk alone at night in the large metro transfer stations such as République, Châtelet-Les Halles or Montparnasse. The area around République is known for its drug trade, while Les Halles is populated by petty criminals and prostitutes. When taking the metro after dark sit in the first car. If an incident occurs, knock on the front window to alert the driver of the train.

Traffic Violations

It was a custom in recent election cycles for the president, after taking office, to annul all outstanding traffic fines. When 'law and order' President Nicolas Sarkozy took office in May 2007, he declared there would be no more amnesty.

French traffic law involves a point system. Depending on the severity of an infraction, points are deducted from one's licence. Using a mobile phone while driving will cost you two points and €22. Speeding fines start at €135 and rise to €1,500, with points ranging from one to six. Driving with an alcohol level between 0.5g/L and 0.8g/L results in a €135 fine, six points off the licence and three years' suspended licence. Over a 0.8: €4,500 fine, six points deducted, three years' suspended licence and two years in prison.

9,000 Parisians were injured in traffic accidents in 2006, with 64 deaths. The most common causes of accidents were speeding violations and changing lanes without warning.

Getting Arrested

In the unfortunate instance that you are arrested in Paris, you can rest assured that no matter what you did, you won't get the death penalty as it does not exist in France. You have the right to a state-provided lawyer. For most crimes you cannot be held under guard for more than 48 hours without being charged. If, however, you are involved in organised crime, human trafficking, or terrorism, the 48 hour rule does not apply. There are no juries for lesser infractions. Nine-member citizen juries are only called in for heavy crimes.

Prison Time

In 2000, Véronique Vasseur, a doctor (now a politician) at Prison de la Santé, caused a national stir with her book denouncing the deplorable condition of the prison. Parliamentary investigations were undertaken to review the French prison system and ensuing reports described the state of French prisons as a 'humiliation to the Republic'. Problems remain, chiefly overcrowding and the need to modernise, but the Justice Ministry website does state that prisoners do have the chance to engage in sports, work and educational programs, and can rent TVs. There is a parole system, and only in some cases are basic rights like voting taken away.

Police

Paris' Préfecture de Police falls under direct jurisdiction of the Interior Ministry. With a ratio of nearly a thousand officers per *arrondissement*, armed police presence is evident. Recognisable in their dark blue uniforms with Police emblazoned across the back, police take the streets in motorised vehicles, on horseback, by foot, bike and rollerblade. Traffic officers wear white or blue shirts and are mainly identifiable by their whistling and white-gloved waving at drivers. Police vehicles are white with red and blue stripes, with the word Police written on each side. Officers are usually approachable and ready to help someone in need.

Préfecture de Police, Île de la Cité

Lost/Stolen Property

Stolen items should be reported to the nearest police station immediately. See the table on p.19 for numbers to call when you have lost something within Paris. French mobile phones come equipped with an IMEI number, a unique phone ID number. This IMEI can be found by pushing *#06# on the keypad. Keep this number in a safe place, and if your phone is lost, call your service provider and give this number. Service can be suspended, and in some cases the phone can be traced.

Tourist Information

There are ten official Paris welcome centres dotting the city and the flagship office, the Pyramides centre, is just off l'Avenue de l'Opéra in the 1st. There, you can find Paris tourist information (museums, things to do, special events); make hotel reservations; book excursions and shows; and purchase 'Paris Visite' (transport) and museum passes. The Pyramides centre is open every day from 09:00 to 19:00, June to October; and from 10:00-19:00 Monday to Saturday, and 11:00-19:00 Sundays November to May. Most other centres offer similar services. The Carrousel du Louvre centre, located in the inverted Louvre pyramid, offers information on the Île de France region. Visit http://en.parisinfo.com/our-welcome-centres for the locations of all the offices throughout Paris.

Tourist Information

Name	Area	Phone
Anvers	8th	08 92 68 30 00
Carrousel du Louvre (Île de France)	1st	08 92 68 30 00
Clemenceau	8th	08 92 68 30 00
Gare de Lyon	12th	08 92 68 30 00
Gare de Nord	10th	08 92 68 30 00
Montmartre	18th	08 92 68 30 00
Paris Expo / Porte de Versailles	15th	08 92 68 30 00
Pyramides	1st	08 92 68 30 00

Place Vendôme

Eiffel Tower

23

Places to Stay

Visitors to Paris can choose from a variety of lodging options, depending on budget, duration of stay, and location. Hotels are plentiful and reasonably dispersed throughout the city. In addition, aparthotels, hostels and a campsite welcome travellers. Another increasingly popular option made easy by the internet is direct-from-owner apartment rental, which can usually be booked for a stay as short as one week and will probably cost less than a hotel.

Hotels

Other options **Weekend Break Hotels** p.204

Nearly 1,500 hotels accommodated the droves of tourists arriving to the French capital in 2006. Over 75,000 rooms may seem like a lot, but in peak months lodging is tight and visitors should book early when planning trips in the months of June, September and October, when city hotel occupancy rates run over 80%. (September was the busiest month in 2006, with a rate of 87.5%.) On the flip side, bookings are a lot easier and less expensive in January and February with occupancy at a low of 64.4%. Predictably, the 8th and 9th *arrondissements* have the most hotels (317), catering especially to business travellers while on the other side of the Seine, the smaller 5th and 6th *arrondissements* flex their tourist muscles, with 181 hotels.

The hotel rating system runs from zero to four stars. An overwhelming majority of hotels - 78% - received ratings of two or three stars. Six top-range hotels have earned a rating above four stars and are known as '4 Luxe' hotels. In addition, some hotels fall outside the rating systems and call themselves 'Palace' hotels.

Compared to other major cities, Paris' budget and mid-range rack rates are reasonable. A two star hotel runs €86 on average, while three star hotels cost €158 per night. When climbing into the luxury hotel level, costs shoot up to €361. All taxes are included within the price.

Main Hotels

Palace	Phone	Website	Map
Four Seasons Hôtel George V	01 49 52 70 00	www.fourseasons.com/paris	p.387 D4
Hôtel de Crillon-Concorde	01 44 71 15 00	www.crillon.com	p.388 A4
Hôtel Meurice	01 44 58 10 10	www.meuricehotel.com	p.398 B1
Le Bristol Paris	01 53 43 43 00	www.hotel-bristol.com	p.387 F3
Four Luxe			
Hôtel de Vendôme	01 55 04 55 00	www.hoteldevendome.com	p.398 B1
Hôtel Fouquet's Barrière	01 40 69 60 00	www.fouquets-barriere.com	p.387 D4
Hôtel Plaza Athénée	01 53 67 66 65	www.plaza-athenee-paris.com	p.397 E1
Hôtel Scribe Paris	01 44 71 24 24	www.sofitel.com	p.388 C4
L'Hôtel	01 44 41 99 00	www.l-hotel.com	p.398 C3
Four Star			
Hôtel Lutetia	08 00 05 00 11	www.lutetia-paris.com	p.398 B3
Pavillon de la Reine	01 40 29 19 19	www.pavillon-de-la-reine.com	p.400 C3
Terrass Hôtel	01 46 06 72 85	www.terrass-hotel.com	p.382 C4
Villa d'Estrées	01 55 42 71 11	www.hotelvilladestreesparis.com	p.399 E4
Three Star			
Abbatial Saint Germain	01 46 34 02 12	www.abbatial.com	p.409 F1
Hôtel Arc De Triomphe Étoile	01 56 68 90 00	www.atehotel.com	p.386 C2
Hôtel Duo	01 42 72 72 22	www.duoparis.com	p.399 F3
Hôtel Kleber	01 47 23 80 22	www.kleberhotel.com	p.386 B4
Hôtel Sully Saint Germain	01 43 26 56 02	www.sully-saint-germain-hotel.com	p.409 F1
Hôtel Victor Hugo	01 45 53 76 01	www.bestwestern.com	p.386 B4

Main Hotels

31 ave George V
8th
Ⓜ *Alma – Marceau*
Map p.387 D4 **1**

Four Seasons Hôtel George V

01 49 52 70 00 | *www.fourseasons.com/paris*
Located steps away from the Champs-Élysée, the George V has 245 rooms, many of which have private terraces overlooking the sights of Paris. Elegant restaurant Le Cinq offers views of the courtyard and garden, and has earned two Michelin stars. One of the finest spas in all of Paris (p.238) offers a thorough menu of therapies as well as VIP treatment rooms. In-room massages are also available.

10 place Concorde
8th
Ⓜ *Gare du Nord*
Map p.388 A4 **2**

Hôtel de Crillon-Concorde

01 44 71 15 00 | *www.crillon.com*
One of the most prestigious hotels in Paris, it is hard to beat the Crillon for its location, looking out on Place de la Concorde, minutes away from the Champs-Élysée to the west and the Tuileries Gardens to the east. It offers 103 rooms, 39 suites, and five luxury apartments. Les Ambassadeurs restaurant serves classic French cuisine, and hosts the gourmet Sunday 'Brunch du Monde.'

1 place Vendôme
1st
Ⓜ *Concorde*
Map p.398 B1 **3**

Hôtel de Vendôme

01 55 04 55 00 | *www.hoteldevendome.com*
Lending its name to the famous Place Vendôme in which it is located, the hotel is prized for its proximity to Paris' best high-end jewellery shops. With only 18 rooms and 11 suites, the hotel provides itself on its ability to provide individual service to its clients. There's a cosy restaurant and British-style bar with plush leather armchairs and a grand piano.

11 rue du Temple
4th
Ⓜ *Hôtel de Ville*
Map p.399 F3 **4**

Hôtel Duo

01 42 72 72 22 | *www.duoparis.com*
Formerly known as the Axial Beaubourg, this funky and modern hotel mirrors the lively spirit and colour of its neighbourhood, the Marais quarter. Friendly and helpful staff add to the positive atmosphere and the 39 rooms, including suites, are surprisingly large for the price and location. Some rooms have free Wi-Fi, and there's a small gym for guests to use.

46 ave George V
8th
Ⓜ *Alma – Marceau*
Map p.387 D4 **5**

Hôtel Fouquet's Barrière

01 40 69 60 00 | *www.fouquets-barriere.com*
When sheer opulence just isn't enough, this hotel takes things to a whole new level, offering a 24 hour personal butler service to its guests. Located on the Champs-Élysée, the 107 room modern palace prides itself on its luxurious suites, interior garden and panoramic view of the city. There's a choice of bars and restaurants, and a luxury spa with a large indoor pool.

45 blvd Raspail
6th
Ⓜ **Sèvres Babylone**
Map p.398 B3 **7**

Hôtel Lutetia

08 00 05 00 11 | *www.lutetia-paris.com*
The 230 room art deco-style Lutetia is minutes away from the Jardin du Luxembourg and St-Germain des Prés, and many other Left Bank sights. The popular hotel bar is a favourite among local celebrities and features piano music and jazz sessions each night from Wednesday to Saturday. Other facilities include a business centre and gym.

228 rue de Rivoli
1st
Ⓜ **Concorde**
Map p.398 B1 **8**

Hôtel Meurice

01 44 58 10 10 | *www.meuricehotel.com*
Family-friendly packages and proximity to the Tuileries Gardens make this luxury hotel popular with kids. Its 160 rooms are furnished in Louis XVI style while the penthouse Belle Etoile Suite features a 300 square metre terrace providing a 360° panorama of the Parisian skyline. Dining options include the showpiece Restaurant le Meurice.

25 ave Montaigne
8th
Ⓜ **Alma – Marceau**
Map p.397 E1 **9**

Hôtel Plaza Athénée

01 53 67 66 65 | *www.plaza-athenee-paris.com*
Located on one of the most chic streets in Paris, this hotel won the 2006 'Prix Villégiature' for Best Hotel Service in Europe. World famous chef Alain Ducasse oversees the cuisine in its five restaurants. The hotel's 188 rooms include 43 suites. There's a well-equipped fitness centre and spa treatments are available.

15 place Vendôme
1st
Ⓜ **Opéra**
Map p.398 B2 **10**

Hôtel Ritz Paris

01 43 16 45 33 | *www.ritzparis.com*
Carrying on the tradition of its first head chef Auguste Escoffier, the hotel houses its own Ritz Escoffier School, where amateurs and professionals alike can enroll in cooking courses. The classic Roman and Greek marbled health club features one of the best swimming pools in the city.

1 rue Scribe
9th
Ⓜ **Opéra**
Map p.388 C4 **11**

Hôtel Scribe Paris

01 44 71 24 24 | *www.sofitel.com*
Falling between the Opéra and Place Vendôme, this Sofitel group member is conveniently situated near the Grands Magasins (department stores such as Galleries Lafayette and Printemps) as well as the central city business district. Redecorated in 2006, the hotel offers 213 rooms and 11 suites.

L'Hôtel

13 rue des Beaux-Arts
6th
Ⓜ **Saint-Germain-des-Prés**
Map p.398 C3 **13**

01 44 41 99 00 | www.l-hotel.com
The name says it all, as if it was the only hotel in Paris and for a long list of former lodgers, it was. Originally part of Queen Margot's palace, Oscar Wilde called it home, and names like Dali and Sinatra grace its guest list. There's a small indoor pool which can even be reserved for private swimming.

Le Bristol Paris

112 rue du Faubourg Saint Honoré
8th
Ⓜ **Miromesnil**
Map p.387 F3 **14**

01 53 43 43 00 | www.hotel-bristol.com
Children are VIPs at this luxury hotel located on the ultra-fashionable rue du Faubourg Saint Honoré. Hippolyte the Bunny brings special treats to kids' rooms, and a special kids' gourmet menu can be enjoyed at the restaurant or in the room. With top-class dining, drinking and leisure facilities, adults will be equally well catered-to.

Pavillon de la Reine

28 place des Vosges
3rd
Ⓜ **Bastille**
Map p.400 C3 **15**

01 40 29 19 19 | www.pavillon-de-la-reine.com
This elegant 56 room hotel overlooks one of the most beautiful squares in all of Europe, the dazzling Place des Vosges, built by Henri IV in 1605. The hotel has an attractive bar and lounge area. After breakfasting on freshly baked breads from the boulangerie next door, explore the hip Marais quarter.

Terrass Hôtel

12-14 rue Joseph-de-Maistre
18th
Ⓜ **Place de Clichy**
Map p.382 C4 **16**

01 46 06 72 85 | www.terrass-hotel.com
The only four-star hotel in artsy Montmartre, this building dating from 1900 offers 98 rooms, a cozy piano bar, and terrace dining with panoramic views over Paris. The Terrass is just minutes away from the Sacré Coeur Basilica and the Moulin Rouge, as well as art galleries, boutiques and restaurants.

Villa d'Estrées

17 rue Gît le Coeur
6th
Ⓜ **Cité**
Map p.399 E4 **17**

01 55 42 71 11 | www.hotelvilladestreesparis.com
This ten-room boutique hotel is excellently located in the heart of Paris' Left Bank, a stone's throw from the Seine and five minutes from Notre Dame Cathedral. Each room and the lobby are decorated in the rich Napoleon III style. Free Wi-Fi is available.

27

Hotel Site ◀

*For a guide to the
capital's many hotels,
plus information on
furnished rentals and
campsites, visit
www.parisinfo.com
and click the Hotels &
Accommodation link.*

Hotel Apartments

For longer stays, 'aparthotels' (hotel apartments) provide visitors with hotel service and apartment living conditions. Advantages to staying in an aparthotel include fully-furnished apartments, private kitchens, business centres, wireless internet access, and 24 hour reception service. However, most lack character and some are in shady areas. The Citadines chain is the best known, with fifteen aparthotels spread throughout the city. Chains like Citadines conform to the same rating system hotels with which hotels are categorised. Citadines' flagship property, the Citadines Paris Opéra Vendôme, is comparable to a four-star hotel.

Numerous websites, such as www.paris.craigslist.org contain ads offering direct-from-owner apartment rentals as well. While amenities may be fewer and regulation non-existent, the experience of staying in an actual Parisian apartment for a week or a month is often worth it.

Hotel Apartments			
Four Star	Area	Phone	Web
Citadines Paris Opéra Vendôme	9th	08 25 33 33 32	www.citadines.com
Three Star			
Appart'hôtel Paris	19th	01 40 03 67 52	www.appartcity.com
Citéa Paris La Villette	19th	01 44 72 42 00	www.citea.com

Bed & Breakfasts

Bed and breakfasts, known as *chambres d'hôtes*, are often inexpensive and pleasant alternatives to hotels. Frequently situated in older buildings, B&Bs vary in quality and amenities. If you don't mind tight quarters or sharing a bathroom, the quaint charm and more personal touch may prove the perfect home base while in Paris.

With countless websites touting hundreds of B&Bs, a safe bet is to stick with those places adhering to the 'Hôtes Qualité Paris' charter. A joint effort by the Paris City Council and the Paris Convention and Visitors Bureau, the 2005 charter provides an outline of standards for B&Bs. The B&B providers listed below have signed the charter and adhere to the charter rules.

Bed & Breakfasts			
France Lodge Locations	2 rue Meissonier	01 56 33 85 80	www.francelodge.fr
Good Morning Paris	43 rue Lacépède	01 47 07 28 29	www.goodmorningparis.fr
Une Chambre en Ville	10 rue Fagon	01 44 06 96 71	www.chambre-ville.fr

Motels

Paris does not have a motel culture. While there aren't any small rest houses where you can pull up your car and bunk cheaply for the night, there are options for those just passing through. With 51 properties throughout Paris, the no-frills Ibis Hotel chain is short on character, but moderately priced and clean. Outside of the city, try the even cheaper Formule 1 chain.

Motels			
Formule 1 Roissy Aéroport	Roissy	08 91 70 54 36	www.hotelformule1.com
Hôtel Ibis Paris Bastille Faubourg Saint Antoine	11th	01 48 05 55 55	www.ibishotel.com
Hôtel Ibis Paris Sacré Cœur	18th	01 46 06 99 17	www.ibishotel.com
Hôtel Ibis Paris Tour Montparnasse	15th	01 45 48 95 52	www.ibishotel.com

Hostels

Four youth hostels around Paris belong to the French branch of the International Youth Hostelling Network. Most rooms contain four to six beds, while collective living areas allow guests to mingle. All ages are welcome in French hostels, as long as you have purchased a membership card in your home country. Otherwise, purchase a 'Guest Card' at the hostel of your destination. After paying a €2.90 supplement for each of the first six nights, you gain a full one-year membership. Due to hostel popularity, there is a maximum stay limit of four nights. Visit www.fuaj.org for more information on locations and prices.

Hostels		
Cite des sciences	Le Pres Saint Gervais	01 48 43 24 11
Clichy	Clichy	01 41 27 26 90
D'Artagnan	20th	01 40 32 34 56
Jules Ferry	11th	01 43 57 55 60

Campsites

Other options **Camping** p.214

Yes, you can camp in the Bois de Boulogne. There are 75 bungalows and 435 spaces for mobile homes or tents available on a year-round basis for those who want to rough it while visiting Paris. Prices vary depending on the season, but two people can expect to pay between €11 and €16.50 per night to pitch a tent. Shuttles run regularly from the campground to a city access point (Porte de Maillot metro station). Campground services include a restaurant, small store, snack shop, laundry room and game room, as well as a new children's play area. Opportunities to camp to the east of Paris along the Marne also exist.

Campsites			
Camping du Bois de Boulogne	16th	01 45 24 30 00	www.campingparis.fr
Paris Est Camping	Champigny sur Marne	01 43 97 43 97	www.campingparis.fr

L'Hôtel

Hôtel Meurice

Getting Around

Other options **Exploring** p.132

Mayor Bertrand Delanoë has made it a mission to improve circulation within the city. The southern rim T3 tram line that opened in December 2006 allows some commuters to avoid heading into the heart of the city to transfer metro lines while some existing metro lines such as the 4 are expanding to reach deeper into the suburbs. Recent years have also seen an increase in bus and taxi only lanes, which allows those modes of transportation smoother movement within Paris. Most recently Delanoë's Velib' bicycle rental scheme went into effect in July 2007 and some 15,000 bicycles are available at hundreds of mini-stations around the city. All these efforts are to reduce one of the greatest aggravations of Parisian life: traffic. No matter how wide the boulevards are, no matter how many other transport options Parisians have, the fact remains that there are too many vehicles clogging the streets. Anyone who has experienced the massive rush-hour backups on the *périphérique*, the highway that forms a ring around Paris, or sat in an endless traffic jam on one of the autoroutes entering the city at the end of a long weekend, realises the need to continue to work towards improving this situation.

Air

Two airports service metropolitan Paris, easily reachable by RER train or bus. All major carriers fly direct to Paris, and most major cities can be reached direct. With a fleet of 380 aircrafts, Air France, a subsidiary of the Air France KLM Group, flies to 185 destinations (98 within Europe) in 83 countries.

Airport Numbers	
Paris - Orly	
Information	01 49 75 15 15 (06:00 to 23:45)
Medical centre	01 49 75 45 12 (24 hour)
Lost and found	
Terminal Sud	01 49 75 34 10
Terminal Ouest	01 49 75 42 34
Police	01 49 75 43 04 (24 hour)
Customs	01 49 75 09 10 (24 hour)
Paris - Roissy CDG	
Information	01 48 62 22 80 (24 hour)
Medical centre	01 48 62 28 00 (24 hour)
Lost and found	
Terminal 1	01 48 62 13 34
Terminal 2	01 48 16 63 83
Police	01 48 62 31 22 (24 hour)
Customs	01 48 62 62 85 (24 hour)

Airports

Counterfeiting
Any baggage may be inspected by Customs. In France, any person who buys or holds a counterfeited product is liable to pay a fine of €300,000 and faces up to three years of imprisonment.

Though officially known as Aéroport Roissy-Charles de Gaulle, the French just call the main Paris airport Roissy, referring to the nearby town of the same name, 25km north-east of Paris. Made cool by U2's usage of it for their *Beautiful Day* video, the airport lost a little lustre four years later when part of the brand-new Terminal 2E collapsed, killing four. While 2E is still being rebuilt, the airport remains the busiest in continental Europe. 200,000 passengers pass through its three terminals every day, and with room to expand, those numbers should increase in the decade to come. The just completed Satellite 3 (S3), connected to 2E by the new CDGVAL tram system, was specially designed to handle the largest commercial jets.

Terminal 1, an ugly, grey doughnut full of criss-crossing tubes taking disoriented passengers up and down its insides, is the oldest of the three. It services several non-Air France international carriers and sits far from Terminals 2 and 3. The CDGVAL now connects the old terminal with the others in just a few minutes, whereas until April 2007 a painfully slow shuttle was the only means between terminals. If arriving by RER, make sure to note that Terminal 1 is a different RER stop from Terminals 2 and 3.

Terminal 2 is divided into six halls, labeled A-F. The terminal, which opened in 1996, is the polar opposite of its predecessor. Its bright corridors, moving walkways and open design make for a first-class airport. As with any modern international airport, Terminal 2 features plenty of duty-free shops, restaurants, and amenities such as a beauty salon and massage station. Internet terminals are found in 2D and 2F. Wi-Fi access is available

Airlines

Aeroflot Russian Airlines	01 42 25 43 81	www.aeroflot.fr/eng
Air Canada	08 25 88 08 81	www.aircanada.com
Air China	01 42 66 16 58	www.us.fly-airchina.com
Air France	08 20 32 08 20	www.airfrance.fr
Air Tahiti Nui	08 25 02 42 02	www.airtahitinui.com
British Airways	08 25 82 54 00	www.britishairways.com
Cathay Pacific	01 41 43 75 75	www.cathaypacific.com
Continental Airlines	01 71 23 03 35	www.continental.com
Delta Airlines	08 11 64 00 05	www.delta.com
El Al Israel Airlines	01 40 20 90 90	www.elal.co.il
Emirates Airlines	01 53 05 35 35	www.emirates.com
Finnair	08 21 02 51 11	www.finnair.com
Iberia Airlines	08 25 80 09 65	www.iberia.com
Icelandair	01 44 51 60 51	www.icelandair.net
Japan Airlines	01 44 35 55 50	www.fr.jal.com
KLM	08 90 71 07 10	www.klm.com
Korean Air	01 42 97 30 80	www.koreanair.com
Lot Airlines	01 47 42 05 60	www.lot.com
Lufthansa	08 26 10 33 34	www.lufthansa.com
Northwest Airlines	08 90 71 07 10	www.nwa.com
Pakistan International Airlines	01 56 59 22 60	www.piac.com.pk
Qantas	08 11 98 00 02	www.qantas.com.au
Singapore Airlines	08 21 23 03 80	www.singaporeair.com
Tap Airlines	08 20 31 93 20	www.flytap.fr
Thai Arlines	01 44 20 70 80	www.thaiair.com
United Airlines	08 10 72 72 72	www.united.com
US Airways	08 10 63 22 22	www.usairways.com

Electronic Check-In

Electronic check-in kiosks do exist in Terminal 2 and occasionally even work, though often it's just as fast to wait in the queue.

everywhere. When flying into or out of Terminal 2, pay special attention to which hall (A-F) is indicated on your ticket, as each hall acts as its own mini-terminal.
The smaller Terminal 3 handles charter flights and budget air carriers such as easyJet. Orly Airport, located south of the city, is Paris' second airport. Much calmer and smaller, it services European destinations as well as some destinations in the Middle East, Africa and the Caribbean.

Airport Transfers

Costing €8.50 one way, Roissybus runs daily between the Paris Opéra (stop at the corner of rue Scribe and rue Auber) and Roissy CDG. The average commute time is between 45 and 60 minutes. Buses run at 15 minute intervals from 06:00 to 19:00, and 20 minute intervals from 19:00 to 23:00, stopping at all three terminals.
Costing €6 one way, Orlybus runs daily between south Paris' Denfert-Rochereau metro-RER station and Orly. Average commute time is 30 minutes. Buses run at 15-20 minute intervals from 06:00 to 23:30.

Boat

Several years ago, the City of Paris formed a committee to discuss a mass transit system on the Seine. Nothing ever came of it. The closest thing Paris has is the Batobus, which is really only used by tourists.
The Batobus (01 44 11 33 99, www.batobus.com) has eight stops between the Eiffel Tower and the Jardin des Plantes. Times differ throughout the year, with maximum hours from 10:00 to 21:00 May to September. No service in February. Day tickets cost €11, with two-day, monthly, and season passes available. See also p.195.

31

Bus

Paris' RATP bus network is as extensive and efficient as its metro system, most lines running from 07:00 to 20:30, with no Sunday service. Steer clear of the bus at peak travel times, as trip durations can increase greatly. Most bus lines continuously circulate, and waits at covered stops are not unbearable. From after midnight until 05:30, forty-two 'Noctilien' lines run throughout the city.

A bus ticket costs the same as a metro ticket, €1.50, but tickets are not transferable between metro and bus. Tickets can be purchased individually on the bus (no exact change required), but the better and slightly cheaper option is to buy a *carnet*, a pack of ten tickets which can be used on the metro, tram, RER or bus. Pass Navigo cards are the way to go if you'll be making multiple daily trips over a calendar week or month. Remember, in order to exit a bus, you must signal the driver by pressing the buttons on the grip poles. While waiting at bus stops serving multiple lines, make sure to stand up and make yourself visible to a bus driver as he approaches.

For bus routes and times, the little red book L'Indispensable proves… indispensable. In addition, the RATP website (www.ratp.fr) contains an English-language tool which allows you to enter in start and finish points and reports the best method of transport (metro, bus, tram) to get you to where you need to go, as well as an estimation of time.

Car

Other options **Transportation** p.124

As with the rest of continental Europe, driving is done on the right side of the road. Compared to other major cities, Paris' streets are wide and its main conduits well-maintained. However, driving within Paris city limits should be avoided as streets are often congested, parking spaces are hard to find and expensive, and traffic police are constantly setting up random checkpoints and speed traps.

Even if you don't mind those inconveniences, navigation itself can be difficult and frustrating. Bus and taxi-only lanes are common throughout the city, and you must remain vigilant of road signs indicating where private autos are allowed to go. In addition, good luck negotiating the wild, wild, west roundabout at Arc de Triomphe, with 12 streets radiating from it. Several other interesting roundabouts around town will also leave the novice Paris driver spinning in circles, literally.

On city streets and multi-lane highways alike, passing another vehicle from the right is illegal. All passing must be done from the left.

The iconic Citroën 2CV

Speed limits within the city are marked by red and white circular signs reading either

30 or 50kph. (Some special cases may see 15kph.) On the *périphérique*, the maximum speed limit is 80kph. Maximum speed limit on French autoroutes is 130kph. Permanent radar cameras are set up along the *périphérique* and autoroutes to nab speeders, though signs indicate when you're nearing a radar camera, and websites offering directions, such as www.mappy.fr, always

Paris Explorer 1st Edition

Are you always taking the wrong turn?

Whether you're a map person or not, these pocket-sized marvels will help you get to know the city – and its limits.

Explorer Mini Maps
Fit the city in your pocket

mark camera locations to help you out. Heading into the city, the only road where a toll must be paid is the A14 tunnel in the west of the city, but using the rest of France's highway system can get pricey, with frequent tolls along the way.

Right of Way

An important law to grasp right away is the right of way. Generally at intersections, vehicles at the right have priority. This may seem logical, but keep in mind that Parisian streets do not have familiar red stop signs. Even if the street you're on is much busier and larger than a side street to the right, the vehicle on the right has priority. On the *périphérique*, this holds true as well. Vehicles entering the Paris ringroad have priority over those already on it. There are some exceptions to the right of way rule. French autoroutes do not follow the rule, and some city streets are marked with a yellow, diamond-shaped sign which marks them as *prioritaire*.

Parking

Parking is a special nightmare. Expect to pay a lot in an underground garage, or try jamming your car into whatever small spot might present itself. For kerb-side pay spots, first park, then look for the green parking ticket distributor box. These automatic distributors no longer accept change or notes. A special parking card, *une carte de stationnement*, can be bought at any *tabac* throughout the city, and works in the same way that a pre-paid calling card does. Insert the card into the meter, punch in how much time you'll need, and place the ticket on the front dash. Maximum time limit permitted in a parking space outside one's *arrondissement* is two hours. Within your *arrondissement*, with a resident card (*carte de resident*) obtained at your local town hall (*mairie*) you can stay put for one week.

Baby & Child Safety Seats

France has strict laws governing children's safety seat requirements. Five separate categories of seats (0, 0+, 1, 2, and 3) are used for children from infancy until they reach 36 kg.

Hiring a Car

Renting cars in Paris, while not advised, is not excessively expensive. Three-day packages start as low as €33/day with unlimited mileage. Weekly packages start at around €235 for a compact, €295 for a mid-size. Expect to pay around €50/day for a compact, €60/day for a mid-size on average. Book in advance from July to September, when car-less Parisians rent cars for vacations. Chauffeured luxury cars and limousines can be rented in a variety of ways: airport or city transfer, hourly, partial day or full day. CDG airport transfers start at around €180 for a Mercedes S Class, which is also about the hourly starting rate. The best car-hire deals and the widest selection are usually found online. See table for contact information.

Car Rental Agencies

Ada	08 25 16 91 69	www.ada.fr
Avis	08 20 05 05 05	www.avis.fr
Budget - Paripark	01 45 87 04 04	www.paripark.fr
Car'Go	08 25 16 17 16	www.cargo.fr
Europcar	08 25 35 83 58	www.europcar.fr
Hertz	08 00 25 10 00	www.hertz.fr
National / Citer	01 45 72 02 01	www.nationalciter.fr
Prestige Limousines	01 40 43 92 92	www.prestige-limousines.fr
Renault Rent	01 44 37 20 20	www.renaultparis.fr
Rent A Car	08 91 70 02 00	www.rentacar.fr
Royal Ways Limousine	01 40 55 92 92	www.location-voiture-chauffeur.eu
Sixt SAS	08 20 00 74 98	www.sixt.fr

Cycling

Other options **Cycling** p.218

Traditionally not a popular form of transportation, bicycles recently made a huge entry onto the Parisian street scene, thanks to the new Velib' scheme. Around 20,000 bicycles are available to the public for short-term rental at bike stations which can be found roughly every 300 metres. It costs €29 to use the system for a year. Short duration subscriptions – daily and weekly – can also be purchased at any station for €1 and €5, respectively. Regardless of which subscription you have, the first 30 minutes of each ride are free. You pay €1 for the first extra half-hour, then €2 for each half-hour after. With the short-term subscriptions these fees are deducted from your bank account, while annual pass holders have a prepaid account.

With the advent of Velib', the City of Paris has stressed for all cyclists the need to follow traffic laws. Cyclists are not permitted to ride on pavements and must respect the right of way. Cyclists are encouraged to wear helmets, though it is not currently the law.

Free Ride

Inevitably this will happen: you put your ticket into the slot, take it back, and proceed through the turnstile, and someone slides through right after you on your ticket. Depending on how you feel about letting others travel for free, you can attempt to avoid this by being vigilant upon entry (and RER exits).

Metro

With nearly 300 stations, the metro's 14 lines along with its five express (RER) lines, serve 4.5 million people per day and 62 stations connect to at least one other line. The largest underground station in the world is Paris' Châtelet–Les Halles.

The familiar, violet 't' tickets were phased out in July 2007, replaced by white 't+' tickets, which sell for €1.50 and are also valid on buses and trams. A better deal is a carnet, ten tickets for €11.10. In addition, monthly passes, known as Pass Navigo cards, afford unlimited trips within Paris for €53.50. Stations open at 05:30 and close at 01:00, except Saturday nights, when they stay open an extra hour. During peak times, there is never a wait of more than a couple of minutes. Digital clocks in most stations indicate waiting times.

RER times are posted on video screens and on poster boards in the station. Make sure to look at the electronic boards on RER platforms indicating which stops the train will make. Additionally, whereas upon exiting the metro system you need not re-enter your ticket in the automated slots, RER lines require ticket verification upon entry *and* exit. Keep your ticket on you until you have exited the station. Metro guards usually stand by exit points to verify you paid. If you're caught without a ticket, the fine is €25, payable on the spot.

Motorbike & Scooter

Easier to park and scoot through traffic jams than cars, *les deux roues*, or two-wheelers, have a certain following in Paris. Whereas the number of motorbikes and scooters has seen steady increase in recent years, they still only account for around 7% of motorised vehicle traffic within the city limits. However, motorbike riders make up nearly half of all traffic accident victims; a good reason why helmets are mandatory.

The City of Paris has made efforts to increase two-wheeler parking spaces over the last few years, more than doubling the number since 2000 to 29,000. Parking spaces must be used; it is illegal to lock a bike up to a signpost or other such pole.

Taxi

All taxis carry white lights on their roofs. In principle when the light is on, the taxi is free. Off, and it's engaged.

Taxi service is regulated by the Préfecture de Police, which outlines exactly what a taxi driver can and cannot do. Paris taxi drivers are a finicky lot; while they are not allowed to, they will try and refuse less profitable trips, and they hate taking four passengers, even if they technically can by charging a small supplement.

All taxis are metered and start once you have given your destination. The meter should display €2 at the start of a trip and the minimum trip charge is €5.50. Count on paying a small supplementary fee after midnight. From CDG airport, expect to pay around €40 to the city centre and from Orly, it's a little over half that. Supplementary charges for baggage are minimal.

Hailing a taxi can prove a challenge. Better to seek out a taxi stand, recognisable all over the city by their white-domed call-boxes. There are 28 *grandes stations* around Paris that are supposed to have taxis present at all times. For a map of all taxi stands, visit www.paris.fr, type 'taxi' in the search box then look for the link to the PDF document.

Taxi Companies	
Les Taxis Bleus	08 91 70 10 10
Taxis G7	01 47 39 47 39

Taxi Numbers

Recently, the City of Paris made available a new phone number for those seeking taxis: 01 45 30 30 30. Call the number and give your coordinates. You'll be connected with the nearest taxi stand, and a taxi will come and pick you up. However, be aware: when you call a taxi, the meter starts the moment they are engaged. Alternatively, try either of the companies listed in the table above.

Train

France prides itself on its fast and efficient trains. Its Train à Grande Vitesse (TGV), or high-speed train, goes from Gare du Nord to Brussels in less than an hour and a half, and to London in under three hours. The newest in the TGV family, TGV Est, goes from Paris Gare de l'Est to Strasbourg in two hours 20 minutes. All tickets can be purchased at any of Paris' six train stations, SNCF shops around town, or online at www.voyages-sncf.com, run by Société Nationale des Chemins de Fer (SNCF), France's national railway company.

Tram

Paris' tram lines provide clean and quiet accompaniment to their big brothers, the metro, bus and RER. The newest to join the family, the T3 line along the city's southern rim, is the only tramway fully within the city limits. In its first six months of its existence (it opened mid-December 2006), the T3 welcomed five million passengers, and its popularity has spurred discussion on extending it eastward.

Tickets work the same for the tram as they do for the other public transit systems – make sure you validate your ticket upon entry.

Walking

Take a Tour

For some insider info and a glimpse of the Paris you may have missed, book yourself onto a walking tour. See p.199 for details of the companies offering tours in and around the city.

When in Paris, you should never forget the best mode of transportation: legs. Paris was made to be enjoyed on foot and nearly all main roads feature wide, shaded pavements as well as clearly marked crossings.

Paris' famous bridges traversing the Seine are equally safe for pedestrians. Several, in fact, are pedestrian-only, including the Pont des Arts and the newest bridge in Paris, the Passerelle Simone de Beauvoir.

You should pay attention to two things when on a stroll in Paris: drivers who don't obey traffic lights, and presents left behind by dogs. Paris' 200,000 dogs leave 16 tonnes of waste on the streets every day, and while laws exist forcing owners to clean up after their pets, you won't walk long in residential districts before having to tiptoe around some mess left behind by a dog and their less than caring owner.

Taxi

SNCF train service

Vélib'

The T3 Tram

Classic metro entrance

Money

Nearly all Parisian restaurants and shops accept electronic payment, though some smaller groceries and bakeries will demand cash. All Parisians carry bank debit cards (known as *cartes bancaires*) with small electronic chips embedded in them, known as *puces*. The chip is a security measure to ensure stolen cards can't be used, as it requires the entry of a PIN, with no signature required. Don't worry if you don't have a card with a chip, cashiers will simply swipe your card the old-fashioned way, then ask you for a signature.

Financial Planning
For details of pensions and financial planning, turn to p.59 in the Residents chapter. There's also a table listing the cost of basic items in Paris.

Local Currency

The euro replaced the French franc in 2002, and is currently used in 13 member states of the European Union (forming the Eurozone). Though originally weak against the dollar, the euro has risen steadily over its existence.

One euro is broken into 100 centimes. Coins are available in 1c, 2c, 5c, 10c, 20c, 50c, €1, and €2 denominations. Notes come in denominations of €5, €10, €20, €50, €100, €200, and €500.

Exchange Rates		
Foreign Currency(FC)	1 Unit FC = €x	€1 = xFC
Australia	0.61	1.63
Bulgaria	0.51	1.95
Canada	0.69	1.44
China	0.09	10.41
Hong Kong	0.09	10.78
India	0.01	56.06
Japan	0.006	158.12
Kuwait	2.57	0.38
Lebanon	0.0004	2.09
Malaysia	0.2	4.86
New Zealand	0.53	1.88
Norway	0.12	8
Oman	1.87	0.53
Qatar	0.19	5.03
Russia	0.028	35.21
Saudi Arabia	0.1	9.32
Singapore	0.47	2.1
South Africa	0.1	9.97
Switzerland	0.61	1.63
Thailand	0.022	44.68
United Kingdom	1.47	0.67
United States	0.74	1.34
Unites Arab Emirates	0.19	5.08
* Rates correct at time of going to print		

Banks

It is impossible to live anywhere in Paris and not be within a couple of blocks of a bank. Popular banks include BNP Paribas, Société Générale, Crédit Lyonnais, Crédit Agricole, and Caisse d'Epargne. All are internationally recognised, and all have numerous branches throughout the city. Most open Monday to Friday from 09:00 to 17:00, and many have Saturday hours. Some branches close for an hour during lunch. While bank employees are usually friendly and helpful, don't count on exchanging money or even getting them to break a large note for you. For more information on banks, see the Bank Accounts section in the Residents chapter (p.58).

Main Banks		
Barclays	08 10 09 09 09	www.barclays.fr
BNP-Paribas	08 20 82 00 01	www.bnpparibas.fr
Caisse d'Epargne	08 21 01 02 22	www.caisse-epargne.fr
Crédit Agricole	01 47 20 17 40	www.credit-agricole.fr
HSBC	01 55 69 74 54	www.hsbc.fr
La Poste	36 39	www.laposte.fr
Société Générale	39 33	www.societegenerale.fr

ATMs

You should have no problem withdrawing cash from ATMs, or *distributeurs*, as they are widely accessible throughout the city. Mostly connected to banks or post offices, you will also find them at supermarkets and hotels. Upon inserting your card, most ATM screens will offer a choice of languages in which you may conduct your business. ATMs support the two global ATM networks, Cirrus and Plus, which will be indicated on the machine.

Money Exchanges

Name	Phone	Web
Le Comptoir des Tuileries	01 42 60 17 16	www.cdt.fr
Multi Change	01 40 15 61 16	www.multi-change.com

Several currency exchange places are found along the Champs-Élysée, as well as other popular tourist areas, such as near Notre Dame Cathedral or L'Opéra. Depending on how much you're looking to exchange, it is worth comparing a few before choosing. Commission rates vary, and some 'No Commission' places take a flat fee. Most bureaux de change are open from around 09:00 to 19:00. Larger hotels will exchange money too, but the rates are not competitive.

Credit Cards

While credit cards are accepted nearly everywhere, even at your larger neighbourhood fruit stands, often there is a minimum purchase requirement of around €10 to €15 in smaller shops. If your credit card is lost or stolen, or if there is fraudulent activity on it, contact the Centre Nationale d'Opposition on 08 92 70 57 05. No matter who issued your credit card, this agency should be able to help you cancel it *tout de suite*. Also, report it to your local Préfecture de Police as soon as possible. Most credit card companies have their own numbers to call as well so make sure you keep these details in a safe place at home.

Traditionally, since the introduction of plastic, the French have used bank debit cards. However, credit cards have become increasingly popular. Though they haven't reached the epidemic proportions they have in the US, a marked spike in rising personal debt has occurred in recent years among the French, and it is a burgeoning cause of national concern.

Tipping

The French have a bad reputation as stingy tippers when travelling but it's not their fault. In France, service industry workers don't expect large tips, and many don't expect anything at all, so no one's accustomed to giving large *pourboires*. In most places, such as restaurants, service charges are included in the price. Leave change – no more than a couple of euros – for waiters, taxi drivers, and hair stylists. In fancy restaurants and hotels where an international clientele is common, tipping is more frequent and larger, but it is not common to add a tip on a credit card payment.

Former Paris HQ of Crédit Lyonnais

Shakespeare & Co bookshop

Newspapers & Magazines

Catering to a large Anglophone expat community, several newspapers provide English-language reporting on local Paris and France news, available around town at ubiquitous news kiosks and shops or by subscription.

The Connexion is a monthly English-language French newspaper, geared toward expats. It's €2.40 at newsstands, while an annual subscription costs €26. Established in 1987, *French News* is the other large expat voice in France. Also a monthly paper, a year's subscription costs €28. Smaller monthly newsletter-style free publications like *The Paris Times* are distributed at popular Anglophone locales around town, such as Indiana restaurants and Starbucks. An excellent free source for classified ads is FUSAC, which you'll find anywhere Anglophones tend to frequent. For a French-published paper with an international flair, check out *Le Monde Diplomatique*, a monthly magazine published in French and English by French daily *Le Monde*. A yearly €41 subscription knocks about 25% off the stiff cover price. The *International Herald Tribune* is edited and published in Paris, costs €2, and is located everywhere. A plethora of the latest copies of other international periodicals are equally available around town. Top French dailies such as *Le Figaro*, *Le Monde*, *Le Parisien*, and *Libération* can be found beside their Anglophone brethren, all selling for less than €2.

Books

Paris attracts writers like Hollywood does actors, resulting in billions of pages about the city. Englishman Stephen Clarke's novel *A Year in the Merde* became a word-of-mouth bestseller in Paris a few years ago, and his latest, *Talk to the Snail*, is a non-fiction work which serves up his humorous observations on the French. American journalist Adam Gopnik's *Paris to the Moon* is a compilation of his *New Yorker* magazine dispatches as well as hitherto unpublished journal entries which reveal an American family's five-year love affair with the city. British novelist Polly Platt's book, *French or Foe* delves into the French culture and tells you how to ask directions without getting a snooty look.

Michelin's *Guide Rouge* is still the bible for French cuisine, to the extent that some restaurants' fortunes have been made and others' downfalls precipitated by the simple addition or subtraction of a star in this book.

Websites

Search the internet for Paris and you'll be bombarded with millions of websites (many of which, admittedly, feature the infamous Ms Hilton rather than the French capital). The selection in the table should help you find the information you're after.

Websites

www.allocine.fr	Film showtimes
www.bonjourparis.com	Info and articles for expats
www.expatica.com	French news and expat guide
www.fusac.fr	Online small ads
www.maps.google.com	Searchable map site
www.meteo-paris.com	Paris weather
www.pagesjaunes.fr	Paris yellow pages
www.pap.fr	Property for sale and rent
www.paris.craigslist.org	Community classifieds
www.paris.fr	City of Paris official site
www.paris.org	Paris news and events
www.parisdailyphoto.com	Daily photo blog
www.parisinfo.com	Official tourist site
www.parisnotes.com	Useful info for expats
www.parisvoice.com	Webzine
www.ratp.fr	Metro and RER info
www.theparisblog.com	Expat blogs

Paris Annual Events

There is always something happening in Paris, and usually you don't have to go far to find it. Be it a modern sculpture exhibit in the Luxembourg, free concerts around town, or a chocolate convention, no one can complain of boredom in Paris.

Arènes de Montmartre

27 rue Chappe
18th
August-September

01 48 40 62 49 | *www.mysterebouffe.com*

The three-week festival revives the popular Italian Commedia dell'Arte form of theatre in the open air of the historical Montmartre neighbourhood. Running from late August to the first week of September, the festival is put on by the Mystère Bouffe troupe.

Armistice Day

place Charles de
Gaulle - Etoile
8th
November 11

www.paris.fr

Recognising the end of the first world war, and all soldiers who died in combat, the holiday is marked by a ceremony where the president lays a wreath at the Tomb of the Unknown Soldier under the Arc de Triomphe.

Bastille Day

ave Champs-Élysée
8th
July 14

www.paris.fr

The national holiday, known in France as 14 Juillet, is celebrated with an impressive military parade down the Champs-Élysée and fireworks around the city at night.

Chinese New Year

place d'Italie
13th
January or February

08 92 68 30 00 | *www.mfa.gov.cn/eng*

Paris' Chinese community puts on an exciting show in welcoming the traditional Chinese New Year, occuring in January or early February. Parades and spectacles attract everyone to Chinatown, located in the 13th *arrondissement*.

Christmas Season

Various Locations
December

www.paris.fr

In December Paris transforms into a unique winter wonderland, with ice skating rinks at Montparnasse train station and in front of the Hôtel de Ville. Shoppers and strollers alike make sure to pass by the special holiday displays in the department store windows of Printemps (p.292) and Galeries Lafayette (p.291).

Festival Paris Cinéma

Various Locations
July

01 55 25 55 25 | *www.pariscinema.org*

In 20 cinemas and venues throughout Paris, this annual event draws cinephiles with its selection of 300 films, its star-studded guest list, and its low prices (€4 per film, or €20 for all you can watch).

Fête de la Musique

Various Locations
June 21

www.fetedelamusique.fr

Summer officially kicks off with a night of music unlike any other. Popular bands play on stages erected around town, while everyone with a guitar and a mic finds somewhere to jam. On the only night of the year where the city suspends its sound restriction laws, all kinds of music can be heard throughout Paris.

Fête du Travail

Various Locations
May 1

Known as May Day in Anglophone countries, May 1 is a popular holiday, marked by the exchanging of small bouquets of lilies of the valley (*muguets*). Unless it falls on a Wednesday, many Parisians take advantage of the long weekend to escape the city.

41

French Open

Stade Roland Garros
16th
May-June

www.rolandgarros.com

Paris welcomes the best tennis players in the world for the second Grand Slam event on the annual ATP tour, contested on the famed terre battue at Stade Roland Garros. Played out just to the west of the 16th *arrondissement*, the tournament is a source of Parisian pride and passion.

Journées du Patrimoine

Various Locations
September

www.journeesdupatrimoine.culture.fr

Held on the third weekend of every September, France's Heritage Days offer Parisians and tourists alike the opportunity to visit buildings and locales usually closed to the public. Annually, around 12 million lovers of art and architecture take advantage of this special weekend.

La Chasse aux Trésors

Various Locations
July

www.tresorsdeparis.fr

The Paris Treasure Hunt was a great success in 2006 when it debuted, sponsored by the City of Paris, and its 2007 sequel proved more popular. Several hunts take place in pre-determined *arrondissements*, affording everyone the opportunity to spend a few adventurous hours discovering or re-discovering a Parisian quarter while solving clues and interacting with local characters who hold the keys to the treasure.

New Year's Eve

Various Locations
December 31

www.paris.fr

New Year's celebrations touch both sides of the calendar, kicking off with year-end parades and cultural events around Paris and the Île de France region.

Nuit Blanche

Various Locations
October

www.paris.fr

The first Saturday night in October never ends with museums staying open extra late during this 'White Night' and admission is often free. The City of Paris' goal is to make art accessible to all and art exhibits of all kinds imaginable are on display into the wee hours.

Paris Fashion Week

Carrousel du Louvre
2nd
July

www.modeaparis.com

Heavy hitters of the fashion world finish a whirlwind tour of international fashion capitals with a breathless haute couture showing at the Carrousel du Louvre. Over a few days in July, industry experts display their wares and divulge the next great trends.

Paris Marathon

Champs-Élysée to
ave Foch
April

www.parismarathon.com

Nearly 30,000 runners took part in the 2007 Paris Marathon, leaving a trail of paper cups and sweat behind them. The race attracts huge crowds, with an estimated 250,000 lining the streets for the April run through Paris.

Paris Plage

Various Locations
July-August

www.paris.fr

For those who can't escape August's heatwave, the City of Paris brings the beach to them. Stretching along both sides of the Seine, sandy swaths welcome sunbathers, with umbrellas and lounge chairs included! Cool off under misting machines and stay at night for free weekend concerts on the river. See p.183 for more details.

Annual Events

Various Locations
Dates tbc

Printemps des Musées
www.paris.fr

Piggybacking on the successes of La Fête de la Musique and Nuit Blanche is this fast-becoming tradition, which sees many museums stay open until 01:00 on one spring night, with free admission to all.

15th
February-March

Salon d'Agriculture
www.salon-agriculture.com

Former President Jacques Chirac rarely missed this popular agricultural convention held at Porte de Versailles every year. 'The largest farm in Europe' exhibits the finest specimens of cattle, swine and more in the great hall, while other halls offer tastings and lessons in green tourism.

15th
October

Salon du Chocolat
www.chocoland.com

Strategically timed right around Halloween, this enormous chocolate convention attracts chocolatiers from around the world and gives adults reason to trick or treat, walking the corridors and sampling the delights. Special shows and cooking exhibitions are staged throughout the event run to add to the fun.

Various Locations
June-July

Summer Sales

Les soldes are a big deal in Paris, with stores opening extra early on the first morning (the last Wednesday in June). Large department stores like Printemps (p.292) and Galeries Lafayette (p.291) are extra busy all through July, as prices are continually marked down and bargains are to be had. Winter sales take place in January and are just as big.

Champs-Élysée
8th
July

Tour de France
www.letour.fr

Cycling's greatest race finishes on one of the most famous streets in the world, the Champs-Élysée, where spectators watch the competitors complete eight laps before finishing at Place de la Concorde at the base. Even post-Lance, this is an exciting and festive finale to an extraordinary three-week endurance event.

Cour Napoléon at the Louvre

Residents

Residents

Euro So Strong ◀
The euro is strong and getting stronger. If you're coming from a nation with a currency that is weak against the euro you might consider sending some money home each month. The euro is expected to continue to maintain its strength, though there are certain analysts who expect the EU to weaken the euro to help European exports.

Overview

Paris. Absolutely without peer, this is the most beautiful city in the world. No other city combines physical beauty, history and quality of life the way that Paris does. The city, and its myths have been drawing foreigners for a very long time and many of them arrive with black and white visions of lovers on the corner, artists in cafes, strolling philosophers and airy apartments with sweeping views of the Seine. How do you ease yourself into that fantasy world without enduring too much disappointment or suffering? This chapter aims to walk you through every conceivable aspect of living in Paris, from visas to taxes, apartments to hospitals, so that you spend less time in a queue sorting through paperwork and more time living the way you've dreamt of doing.

Paris is an expensive city, but depending upon your lifestyle, it is still relatively easy to save money. If you're here working legally you will have excellent healthcare provided by the state, an outstanding public transportation system and, perhaps most importantly, a culture that is not devoted to making money. The French generally do not flash their money around. Wealthy people drive tiny cars. They walk. They take the metro. The culture of consumption is not nearly as prevalent in Paris as it is in other international cities and the discussion of money is considered vulgar.

Aside from basic savings accounts (*comptes d'épargne sur livret*) any investment plan you can find in a modern, financially stable country, you can find in France. It is an excellent idea to talk to a financial planner about any investments you plan to make in France, and if you don't speak French it is crucial. Financial planners who specialise in serving international clients are, obviously, the best bet and there are many working in Paris. See the table on p.60.

If you speak French reasonably well, consider discussing your plans with your banker. French banks offer personalised service and rely on personal relationships to keep customers. It's a good idea to develop a relationship with your bank contact and discuss your financial plans with them so make sure you find someone you feel comfortable with and trust. You can easily change banks and new laws make it the bank's, not your, responsibility to deal with the paperwork.

One of the advantages of working with an international bank is that they often offer services targeted to expats and are better-equipped to handle international investment plans.

Buying property in France is perhaps the most common foreign investment. See p.64 for details.

Considering Paris

Paris has much to offer. Some would say that no other city offers more. Rightfully famous for food, music, art, cafe life, fashion and film, Paris offers its residents (especially those with a bit of money) endless opportunities. There is music on the street, the cafes are full, the Seine is lovely at sunset, people picnic on the Pont des Arts. You can walk nearly everywhere and the city is reasonably safe. Compared to New York or London, Paris is a bargain. However Paris, as with all cities, has its problems. The city can feel impenetrable to the foreigner and Parisians themselves can be cold and unwelcoming. Strikes and bureaucracy are national pastimes. If you're not French, finding real employment here is very difficult. Sadly, if you're not white, it can become even more so. Paris is an old city in an old country and the French, generally speaking, like things the way they are. Change, if it happens at all, happens slowly in France. Ideally you'll be hired before you arrive and your new employer will take care of all aspects of your relocation, including housing and visas.

If you're not an EU citizen you simply won't find (legal) work otherwise. With an EU passport you can legally work in France, but you'll need to either be very talented or speak French well enough to survive inside a French company. If you do manage to be hired to work in Paris, you'll see that the social charges which are taken from your salary are enormous.

Think Ahead
If you have children, contact prospective schools before you arrive; there are a wealth of options and choosing a school can be overwhelming. See p.119.

Before You Arrive

As you prepare to leave home make sure that you have all your paperwork in order. Contact your bank, insurance and credit card companies and make sure that all of them know that you will be living abroad. None of them should be surprised to see that you're making transactions from France; often a credit card company will temporarily freeze your account if there are suddenly charges being made in a foreign country. Notify the post office, telephone and television providers, newspapers, magazines and so on that you will be leaving the country and make certain that you have telephone service up to your last day in your home country. Ensure that you have all important documents in a single file and leave a copy of this file with a trusted friend at home. If in doubt, bring the document. You'll soon find that the French are swayed by three things; love, dogs and documents. Keep in mind that not all medications are available in France and consider filling prescriptions before you leave or speak with your doctor about substitutes. It is possible, depending upon where you've received your driving licence, to exchange it for one in France.

When You Arrive

Even if you've been hired from abroad to be the president of Chanel, if you're not French you will spend much of your first few weeks waiting in queues, waiting to fill out forms and then filling out forms. Just try to remember that soon you'll be strolling along the Seine, amazed that you now live in one of the most wonderful cities in the world.

Residency/Visas – if you don't hold an EU passport you're most likely only authorised to stay in France for three months. If you're planning on staying longer you'll need to be ready. See Documents on p.49.

Assemblée Nationale

Find a place to live – if it's possible (and if you have the money) consider hiring a relocation company (p.98). This can save an enormous amount of time, energy and headaches. Otherwise, make sure you have a place to live for a few weeks (see Places to Stay on p.24) and prepare for more absurdity.

Furnish your home – it's all out there; antiques, IKEA and much more so it helps to have an idea of what you want before you arrive, otherwise you'll be overwhelmed by the choices. See Home Furnishings on p.265.

Cars – unless you're living in the suburbs or somewhere with guaranteed parking it is not a good idea to have one. See Getting Around on p.30.

Get a life – meeting people in Paris isn't difficult; meeting Parisians is more so. See Social Groups on p.230.

Essential Documents

With the exception of your passport, all documents which you plan to use in an official capacity in France, must be translated into French. Do not make the mistake of relying on people's ability to speak your language.

Don't leave home without:

• Passports
• Visas
• Passport photos
• Birth certificates
• Marriage certificates
• Financial certificates
• School records
• Dental and medical records
• Credit cards
• Insurance papers (including copies of your past driving record)
• Vehicle documents (if shipping your car)
• Veterinarian papers (if shipping your pet)
• Driving Licences
• Inventory of safety deposit box
• Relocation material and instructions (if your move is being taken care of by an employer)
• Wills, trusts, powers of attorney
• Moving company documents or contracts
• Prescriptions (and/or letters from your doctor with the French name of whatever medications you may take)

When You Leave

You'd be well-advised to tie things up officially when you leave Paris; all that form-filling at the beginning means that there is plenty to be undone so it's not a simple case of jumping on a plane and waving your friends goodbye.

Shipping – shipping is very expensive. Keep in mind that customs in France can be rigid so make sure that you have the proper paperwork for whatever you're shipping (or carrying) out of the country. Unless you deeply love your furniture, your motorcycle or your refrigerator, just sell it. Websites like www.paris.craigslist.org, www.ebay.fr, and www.fusac.fr are all excellent resources for selling (and buying) household contents.

Landlord – be sure that you leave your apartment precisely as you found it, so fill in holes and touch up the paint, otherwise you may never see your deposit. Fighting landlords is difficult enough in France. You certainly don't want to be in a battle from thousands of miles away.

The Whole World's Your Home

Explorer Residents' Guides are going global with new titles for locations as far flung as Dublin and New Zealand. So if you fancy living abroad check out the complete list of current and upcoming Explorer guides on our website www.explorer˙ publishing.com. Remember, life's a trip... all you need to do is pick a destination.

Join The Queue
September and October are the worst possible months to visit your friendly préfecture*; queues during these months can mean waiting as long as five hours, so bring a good book. The* carte de séjour *office opens at 09:00 and closes at 16:00.*

Documents

You're not the only person who wants to live in Paris. Immigrants come by the thousands every month – both legally and illegally. France's new right-wing president Nicolas Sarkozy, who won the election on a 'tough on immigration' platform, has promised to make it far more difficult for foreigners to live and work here. The easiest, most painless way to move to France is to be hired from abroad. Most employers will provide a full relocation package; however, with or without an employer's support the level of bureaucracy in France will make the process of becoming and staying legal a frustrating one. Find comfort in knowing that the French are as frustrated by it as you are. Know what they know; arrive prepared for any request – passport photos, rent notices, electricity bills, marriage certificates, bank statements, and on and on. Have it all in hand before you get in the queue.

Entry Visa

If you don't have an EU passport or a contract to work in France and are arriving from North America or Japan you may stay, but not work, in France for 90 days without a visa. If you're arriving from any other country a tourist visa is compulsory. For these visas you must be able to convince the embassy that you have the appropriate funds to support your trip and that you are travelling for the purposes of tourism, business or a family visit. If you'd like to stay longer you must first obtain the appropriate visa from the French consulate in your home country. This inevitably requires documentation, some of which may need to be translated into French by a certified translator and then notarised. Visas usually take approximately three weeks to process but may take three months, or in some cases, even longer. Regardless of why you want to come to France, unless you're planning on staying for less than three months, you should begin the process in your home country. Do not make the mistake of arriving in France without proper documentation; legally, you will not be able to stay and you will not be able to work.

If you have the means to stay in France without working you may apply for a long-term visa (*visa de long séjour*) which will allow you to stay in France without working.

Residence Visa

To begin the residency process, you are obliged to go to your local *préfecture de police* office within one week of your arrival in France. If your request is accepted you will be granted a receipt (*récépissé*). It is likely that you will have to return to the *préfecture* several times before finally being given your receipt. When you do receive your *récépissé* you will be legal to either work or study (depending upon your request) for three months. It is possible (even likely) that you will have to return to renew your receipt before your final card is ready.

Under normal circumstances you will be granted a *carte de séjour temporaire* which is valid for one full year. There are seven variations of these cards – *visiteur*, *salarié*, *étudiant*, *vie privée*, *commerçante*, *scientifique* and *artistique*. Each, of course, requires different supporting documentation. When your card expires it will be necessary to return to the *préfecture* and demonstrate that you are continuing to meet the card's initial requirements.

At the time of your third *carte de séjour* renewal you may apply for a 10 year *carte de resident* and after your tenth renewal you have the legal right to that card. Remember that upon arriving in France it is crucial to begin the process immediately.

When you arrive at the *préfecture* make sure that you have the following documentation:
• A valid passport
• A minimum of three passport photos (it is best to have these done in France so that you don't risk the wrong angle or size.)

- A *justificatif de domicile* proving where you live. A utilities bill is preferred.
- A medical certificate issued by a French doctor.
- A full translation of your medical insurance. The translation must be made by a *traducteur assermenté*.
- Your registration documentation if you're a student.
- Proof of resources. For employees this means a copy of your contract (*contrat de travail*) and, if possible, your three most recent payslips (*bulletins de paie*).
- If you are self-employed you must provide evidence such as memberships to trade unions and VAT numbers.
- If you are retired you must provide evidence that you can support yourself financially. You will need notarised account documents and proof of comprehensive health insurance which covers you in France. Remember that all documents must be translated by an official translator.

It is not necessary to be a citizen or a resident of France to purchase property here. This may change as there is increasing anger over sky-rocketing Paris real-estate prices and many blame wealthy foreign investors for making it impossible for Parisians to buy homes here.

Nationality

Children who are born in France by at least one French parent are French at birth. Children who are born in France by two foreign parents may become French only if by their 18th birthday they have lived in France for at least five years since the age of 11.

You may obtain French nationality if:
- Your spouse is French and you've been married for a minimum of one year.
- You were born in France and have lived there for at least five consecutive years.
- Your children are French and you've lived in the country for at least five consecutive years.

Student Visas

If you've entered France on a student visa and have enrolled at a university or in a study-abroad programme eligible for a *carte de séjour*, you will most likely avoid much of the complications described above. However, it is essential that you have the required physical examination and pick up your card when you're asked to. Be certain that before you arrive at the *préfecture* that you have all university or programme registration documents with you. These documents (along with your student visa) serve as evidence that you have entered France legally and for the specific purpose of studying.

If you're a returning student you should submit requests for renewal through your university. Most universities have offices that are responsible for making these processes easier for their students.

Vos Papiers
You should make a habit of carrying some form of ID, whether it's a driving licence, bank card, your carte de sejour, *an official ID card or passport copy.*

ID Card

France does have an official ID card system, but residents are not obliged to get one. These cards can be used as proof of ID in many official procedures, but a current passport will also suffice in such instances. An ID card, or *Carte Nationale d'Identité*, can be obtained from the local *préfecture*, but for non-French nationals the process is very complicated. Unless you decide you absolutely must have one, you're advised not to bother.

The police have the right to stop you at any time and ask to see identification. If you're not carrying any ID and have less than €2 you can be charged for public vagrancy and taken to jail. The police even have the right to hold you for up to 48 hours without charging you. In short, always carry identification.

Driving Licence

Other options **Transportation** p.124

If you're in possession of a valid driver's licence (*permis de conduire*) from an EU or EEA country, you may drive in France with that licence until it expires. If you plan to stay in France for an extended period of time it is a good idea (and your right) to exchange your national licence for a French one. While both French and EU/EEA licences allow you the same rights, you would be well advised to acquire as many official French documents as possible. The more documentation you have the better, and when you've just arrived, one official set of paperwork may allow you to receive another so take advantage of the opportunity.

If you have a valid driver's licence from a non-EU or EEA country and are 18 years old you may drive legally under your national or state licence for one year from the date you received your first *carte de séjour*. Technically (as with all documents) you must have an official French translation of your driver's licence. Students are allowed to use their up-to-date home licences for the duration of their studies.

After having lived in France for one year anyone not driving under an EU/EEA licence must convert to a French driving permit. If you're fortunate enough to have arrived in France from one of the US states with a reciprocity agreement you may simply exchange your licence for a French one. If not, you'll need to pass a highway code exam and a driving test.

The following US States have a reciprocity agreement with France: Colorado, Connecticut, Delaware, Florida, Illinois, Kansas, Kentucky, Michigan, New Hampshire, Ohio, Pennsylvania, South Carolina, Virginia.

The following Canadian provinces have reciprocity agreements with France: Newfoundland, Labrador, Ontario, Quebec.

Additionally, all Australian and South African territories have agreements with France.

If you are a legally licensed driver from any of the aforementioned states, regions or countries you may go directly to your local *préfecture de police* and apply for a French driver's licence. Make sure that you apply three months before the end of your first year. If you wait, you may not be able to benefit from the reciprocal agreement.

It may be worth your time to check with the French consulate in your home country or state to determine whether a reciprocal agreement has been recently negotiated.

To exchange your licence, apply directly to the Préfecture de Police, 1 rue de Lutèce, in the 4th; 01 58 80 80 80 (metro: Cité). The office you're looking for is the *service de permis de conduire*. Their hours are: Monday to Thursday 08:35 to 16:45, Friday 08:35 to 16:15.

Without the benefit of a reciprocal agreement you will have to take a written exam (*code*) and the driving test (*pratique*). If you are already licensed in another country it is not necessary to enroll in driving lessons. Keep in mind, that driving tests in France must be done in a 'dual-command car'. It is therefore necessary to arrange your test through a driving school. It is probably worth your time to take some classes so that you're familiar with French laws. Some driving schools provide lessons in English and will arrange for you to take the test outside of Paris and with a translator. See p.52 for more information.

The process of getting a French driver's licence takes, on average, two months. The *préfecture* demands this waiting period. If you arrive in France without a driver's licence, or you were under 16 when you were granted your licence, you will need to enroll in a drivers' training course and 20 hours of driving with an instructor is required.

Driving Schools

There are several driving school devoted to English speakers but one of the best is the Fehrenbach Driving School near La Défense. They have an excellent reputation and are very well-known in France, but be warned – like other similar schools, they're expensive. If you can speak French well, find a school near you and avoid the extra costs of lessons in English.

Driving Schools				
Name	Address	Area	Phone	Web
C.I.R Plus Avron	18 rue d'Avron	20th	01 43 48 40 06	na
Fehrenbach Driving School	53 blvd Henri-Sellier	Suresnes	01 45 06 31 17	www.frenchlicense.eu
Massena	Centre Commercial Massena, 13 place de Venetie	13th	01 45 70 74 55	na

Birth Certificate & Registration

For a child to be French he or she must be born to at least one French national. If both parents are not French the child is not French but a child born on French soil may be entitled to later apply for French residency.

There are two options under the law:

Someone who has lived in France for five years between the ages of 11 and 18 is entitled to French nationality. They will be given a French passport upon application for a national identity card, assuming that they provide a birth certificate from the town hall (showing that the birth took place in France) and a school certificate demonstrating that the child has the necessary years of residency.

Otherwise, when the child is 13, his or her parents may ask for French nationality if the child has lived in France for the preceding five consecutive years.

The child will have to appear at the Tribunal d'Instance in the *mairie*. If all of the documentation is in order, the national identity card will be provided within a few months. The new 'loi Chevènement' allows for a third option:

The applicant must have been born in France and have lived there continuously for eight years. Additionally, between the age of 10 and 21 they must have spent at least five years in the French school system. Those eight years must be proven on a monthly basis, though a '*certificat de scolarité*' is enough to prove residency for the school year. The school certificate is also used to prove that the five year requirement has been met and, in this case, it does not have to be continuous residency.

When a child is born in France, regardless of nationality, the child will be granted a birth certificate (*extrait de l'acte de naissance integral*). A representative from the city hall or *mairie* will be present in the maternity ward to register the child's birth and will then take care of all the paperwork necessary for declaring the birth of the child to the local *mairie*. You will then have two days following the birth of the child to go to the *mairie* and sign the official birth certificate. You will then be given copies which are necessary for everything from French social security to school registration; ensure that you have these copies and that you make additional copies.

Make sure that you request several *fiches d'etat civil*. This file will be necessary to apply for a passport along with other official administrative requests. Again, the golden rule is to always err on the side of too much paperwork.

Be precise and be careful when you write your child's name. If the parents of the child are not married the child will automatically take the father's last name. There is a law on the books which allows the child to take both names, but many administrators cross their arms and refuse to apply the law so insist if it is important to you. One way to avoid what can become an administrative nightmare is to use an alias. You will have the opportunity to fill in your child's *nom d'usage* as one last name, and the other's last name as the *nom de famille*.

You're advised to consult your own embassy or consulate if you have questions regarding children born abroad. See p.20 for contact details.

Livret de Famille

Once you're married in France you'll receive a livret de famille, a small booklet (much like a passport) that will serve to record the initial marriage and all subsequent family events such as births, deaths and divorces. Each marriage is looked upon as the beginning of a history. You may also obtain a marriage certificate by requesting one in writing. Send your request to the town hall where you were married and ask for an extrait d'acte de mariage. Make certain that you indicate when and where you were married in your request.

Marriage Certificate & Registration

Assuming that you're in Paris legally, getting married in France shouldn't be a problem. Obviously, your home country will have its specific laws regarding marriages abroad and it will be important to check with your consulate to determine the ramifications of getting married abroad.

For a marriage to be legal in France it must, before any religious ceremony takes place, be performed by an *officier de l'état civil*, and this usually means the mayor (or one of his deputies) of the town where you or your spouse is living. French law requires that at least 10 days before the civil ceremony is performed an announcement of the impending marriage be posted at the town hall (*mairie*). These announcements are called banns. Each town hall has different requirements. Once you've decided that you want to get married contact your *mairie*. Keep in mind that some town halls will ask for your complete wedding file 10 days before the banns are to be posted.

Remember that no religious ceremony may take place before the civil ceremony is completed. Any officiating clergy will ask to see a *certificat de celebration civile* before he or she will perform the ceremony.

The majority of French town halls will require foreigners to present the following documents before they will marry you, but confirm particular requirements with your local town hall:

- Valid passport and/or your *carte de séjour*
- Birth certificate translated (officially) into French
- A certificate of celibacy (*attestation tenant lieu de declaration en vue de marriage ou de non-remariage*). This is not a confirmation of your virginity, but a document which confirms that you are not presently married to someone else
- Affidavit of law (*certificat de coutume*). This certificate confirms that you may, as a foreign citizen, be legally married in France. These certificates may only be executed by a lawyer who is licensed to practise law in both your home country and in France
- A medical certificate (*certificat medical prenuptial*) less than three months old which proves that you've been given a prenuptial exam by a doctor
- Proof of residence (*justacatifs de domicile*) in the city where you will be married, such as electricity bills or rent forms
- Prenuptial agreement (*certificat du notaire*). This certificate is only required if you are signing a prenuptial agreement. It must be completed by a certified notary.

Death Certificate & Registration

To obtain a death certificate (*acte de décès*) you must submit a written request to the mayor's office of the town (or *arrondissement*) where the death took place. Your request should include the full name of the deceased person, the date and the location of the death. If you are confronted with a death during your time in France there are, not surprisingly, some formalities you'll need to respect. A doctor must certify the death and you need to register it (in person) within 24 hours at the *mairie*. There you must present the death certificate and the deceased's *carte de sejour* if applicable. The *mairie* must then provide its approval before any service can officially take place.

Each individual country has its own laws regarding the transportation of bodies. It is therefore crucial that you contact the appropriate consulate as soon as possible. Certain countries have strict requirements concerning the way the body has been treated. This process can be complicated, difficult and expensive.

*Office buildings in
La Défense*

Working in Paris

Paris, like most major international cities, has a large population of foreign workers. The city draws people from the provinces as well as people of all walks of life from around the world. There are immigrants here from every continent in the world, with large African and Asian populations. If you are able to work legally and speak French well, there are many opportunities for employment here. As with any other country, depending upon various factors (education, age, and sadly skin colour) your chances will either rise or fall. It is important to remember that, generally speaking, the French often put a high value on background and heritage.

If you're willing to do manual labour for little pay there's no shortage of work, but the higher you move up the ladder the more difficult finding work will be. France has the slowest growing 'large EU' economy. Considering that France is the sixth wealthiest nation in the world, unemployment is high at 8.7% and public debt is at 66% of the GDP. In the poor suburbs where unemployment hovers around 40% there has been a marked increase in tension. The recent riots have sparked a lot of political talk but not a lot of action. One thing is certain, with the conservative Nicolas Sarkozy as France's new president it will become increasingly difficult to relocate to France, let alone find work here.

Because of the stagnating job market many of France's young, skilled job force has been seeking employment in other countries and some estimates have 40,000 French citizens working in the Silicon Valley's technology industry.

If you want to live and work in France it is important to consider that social charges and taxes are high. On the other hand, France has one of the finest healthcare systems in the world and the quality of life in Paris can be exceptional.

Working Hours

Generally and officially the French working week is 35 hours long. In Paris people generally work from 09:00 to 17:00 with a full hour's lunch break, while outside of the capital people tend to begin work earlier, starting around 08:00 and finishing around 16:00. Of course hours vary widely depending upon given professions and positions. People who have completed higher-level studies, such as graduate degrees, tend to be given *cadre* contracts and are often expected to work far longer than 35 hours per week. Depending upon the employer these *cadres* are given upwards of seven extra vacation days as compensation.

Those employees without *cadre* contracts generally work under a worker contract (*agent de matrisse*), which is a set 35 hour work week. How they're paid for overtime depends greatly upon their employer.

All French employees are guaranteed five weeks of annual holiday after they've worked for their employer for one full year. President Sarkozy has pledged to make the French working week longer than 35 hours and to allow employers more freedom, but general strikes are expected in protest.

Business Councils & Groups

American Chamber of Commerce in France	www.amchamfrance.org
Chamber of Commerce & Industry Portal	www.cci.fr
Chambre Régionale de Commerce et d'Industrie	www.paris-iledefrance.cci.fr
Paris Chamber of Commerce & Industry	www.ccip.fr
UCCIFE (Union of Overseas French Chambers of Commerce and Industry)	www.uccife.org

Finding Work

With unemployment rates rising and a stagnant French economy it is important to seriously consider your options before arriving in Paris; unless you can do a job that a French person can't do and are able to prove this, you will have a very difficult time finding work. Without question, the safest bet is to find a job before you leave home. With a few exceptions, unless you're from an EU country, you won't even be considered for an interview as it is an expensive and complicated process for companies operating on French soil to employ someone who is not allowed to work in France. In addition to the recruitment agencies listed in the table below, the websites www.expatica.com and www.monster.fr (in French) are good places to start when job hunting.

Finding Work Before You Arrive

With the exception of labourers, housekeepers, bartenders and language teachers, most people who find work in Paris do so before they arrive. As in any city, there's always a way to get by legally or otherwise, but if you're interested in a career with a full-time, legitimate contract, find a job before you arrive. Nearly every major international company has offices in France and if you can convince one of them that you are more capable than anyone they can hire in France, you may find yourself a job. It is crucial though to remember that Paris is a very popular relocation destination and positions are hard to come by. Depending upon a variety of factors, such as legal status, ability to speak French, expertise and past experience, it is a good idea to attend local job fairs and contact specific companies of interest directly. As is true anywhere in the world, the more experience you have, and the more specialised that experience, the more likely you'll be to find work in Paris.

Keep in mind that while it is becoming more common to search for a job via the internet, French employers expect your cover letters to be hand-written. Handwriting is taken very seriously in France and the analysis of a prospective employee's handwriting is a common practice.

Finding Work While You're In Paris

If you're already in France and are searching for work there are a few things to consider. In France, it is exceptionally rare and very difficult to change careers. For most people, whatever you've studied in school determines your future. A lawyer does not, at 30 years old, become a doctor. A middle-aged doctor does not become an accountant. When searching for work, make sure that whatever job you're applying for is supported by your CV. It is extremely important to use whatever connections you may have. Networking is crucial in Paris and it is a city composed of countless, and seemingly impenetrable, social circles.

Keep in mind that by law anyone offering a job must create a written job description, submit that description to the ASSEDIC (the national unemployment office) and advertise the position in newspapers. Technically an employer may only hire a non-French citizen if, after an exhaustive search, no French person can be found to do the job.

Work To Live

The French claim that they work to live and that 'Anglo-Saxons' live to work. True or not, this is the general attitude. Despite the rising popularity of Starbucks and other American chains selling food and drink in take-away containers, the French love to leave work, sit down and have a real lunch. It is considered profoundly unhealthy – physically, emotionally, perhaps even morally, to eat lunch sitting at your desk. Don't do it. Take advantage of the long lunch hour and prepare for offices to shut down at lunchtime. This is not to say that the French don't work hard, but there is generally less pressure to move constantly forward, to make more money, to grow. This makes life in Paris more comfortable and less stressful, but it also may have put France behind its more ambitious neighbours.

Finding Work

Club TELI	04 50 52 26 58	www.teli.asso.fr
Euro London Appointments Paris	01 53 43 94 52	www.eurolondon.fr
Expatica ▶ p.44	na	www.expatica.com
GR Interim	01 42 61 16 16	www.groupe-gr.com
Monster	na	www.monster.fr

Voluntary & Charity Work

Not surprisingly there are many opportunities for volunteer and charity work in Paris. Depending upon your proficiency in French there are a variety of possibilities. As in your home country, places like hospitals, schools and shelters are always looking for people willing to donate their time. It is perfectly legal to work as a tourist volunteer in France as long as you're not being paid.

The following organisations are good places to start: American Cathedral Junior Guild (www.juniorguild.online.fr), Armée du Salut (Salvation Army; www.armeedusalut.fr), and Health Network International (www.hni-paris.org).

Working as a Freelancer/Contractor

If you're interested in freelance or contract work while living in Paris you need to do so under a *travailleur indépendant* permit. Keep in mind that working under this status requires that you pay a monthly sum to social security, which is paid to different administrations depending upon the type work you do. Unless you're an artist, musician, journalist or author (all of whom have their own administrations), the majority of self-employed workers in France will pay into URSSAF. More information can be found at www.urssaf.fr.

Initially this is an expensive and complicated process requiring a great deal of paperwork, but ultimately it is worth your effort. With *travailleur indépendant* status you will benefit from the same social insurance coverage granted to all legal workers in France. Additionally, you'll become more attractive to prospective employers who are cautious when it comes to offering permanent contracts which are notoriously difficult and expensive to get out of.

Employment Contracts

The French love paperwork and without proper documentation you are powerless. You may have spent 17 years working for Francois Mitterand, but if you don't have the paperwork to prove it, in the eyes of the French government, it never happened.

This is to say that you are not employed unless you have a signed contract in French. Some employers will offer their foreign employees a translated version of the official French contract – if yours does then consider it a gift, but also keep in mind that the only document which carries any legal weight is that contract drafted in French.

There are essentially two different French employment contracts:

CDI (*Contract Duration Indeterminée*): an ongoing contract which is very difficult for an employer to end.

CDD (*Contract Duration Determinée*): a contract with a determined duration. It may not exceed one year and is then only renewable once for a period of no more than six months.

In either case, all of your employment benefits should be included and clearly articulated in your contract.

As a *salarié*, your contract grants you certain rights and your employer will pay your *charges sociales*. You are then entitled to a variety of legal benefits including generous unemployment and health insurance. For the first three months of employment, employers have the right to annul your contract. However, you are entitled to all the benefits that a regular *salarié* would have.

Maternity leave is granted for all female employees, allowing six weeks before giving birth and ten weeks afterwards. With a third child, mothers are granted eight weeks before birth and 18 weeks afterwards. These rights are not negotiated and are the same no matter what your position. Fathers are granted 11 consecutive days paternity leave.

Labour Law

It is famously difficult to fire an employee in France; the French worker is protected on all sides and it is always the employer who is looked upon with suspicion. All dismissals must follow very strict procedures and an employer must request a meeting (in writing) with the employee in question, and the employee has the right to have a co-worker or union rep present during the meeting. The dismissal itself must be executed with a written document which explains precisely the legal reasons for the firing.

If you are fired, you are entitled to severance pay, payment of time worked until your last day worked and any due holiday pay. Depending upon many factors, such as your position at the company, the reason for being fired, and the level of goodwill that exists between the two parties involved, the conditions can change dramatically. French labour law is more codified and complicated than you can imagine so if you suspect you're going to be fired, find a solicitor.

Recommended Labour Law Firms

Ravisy & Associés	www.prudhommes.fr	01 53 10 99 99	Firm specialising exclusively in workers' rights
Stéphanie Pailler	spailler@pons-francois.com	01 45 53 06 55	Reputable lawyer specialising in labour law
Coblence & Associes	www.coblence-avocat.com	01 53 67 24 24	Bilingual lawyers specialising in international clients

Changing Jobs

As long as you have the legal right to work in France you may change jobs as often as you wish. However, if you resign from a position and don't find work before your present *carte de séjour* expires you may find yourself in a bad situation. For many foreign workers, it is their contract which got them into the country and working legally in the first place. The ideal situation is to find a new job before leaving the old position, otherwise you may find yourself without a job and a valid *carte de séjour*. If you do decide to leave your job before finding another position, time it so you leave immediately after you have renewed your *carte de séjour*.

Generally, people don't move from job to job and the notion that there is always something better, more money to be made, or more to achieve is not part of the national attitude, so you may find it quite difficult to change careers or even to change sectors.

Company Closure

If your company shuts their doors and you have been employed under a French contract you are protected by the government. It is under these conditions that you will be thankful for having paid those high social charges.

The first step is to register with the French unemployment agency, ASSEDIC (www.assedic.fr) immediately and you will be granted an interview during which you'll be officially registered. You will then be given an interview with the French employment agency ANPE (www.anpe.fr). Even if you have no intention of using the ANPE services, it is crucial to have your initial interview. ASSEDIC will pay you a monthly unemployment allowance assuming that you satisfy the following criteria:

• You were dismissed and did not resign of your own freewill
• You've contributed to French social security for a minimum of six months within the previous 22 months
• You're less than 60 years old
• You're physically capable of working

Bank Accounts

Depending upon what you're accustomed to, banking in France (as with most other service-based industries) may not be a pleasant experience. If you're used to friendly service and eager-to-help tellers and bank managers it is likely that you'll be frustrated and, at times, enraged in your new Parisian bank. The notion that the customer is always right is, quite literally, a foreign one.

French banks dominate the banking landscape. The only major international player is Barclays. In addition to the major privately owned banks in France, the French post office (La Poste) provides full banking services and is, in fact, the nation's most popular bank. La Poste has the advantage of being able to provide services everywhere there's a post office, which is to say in nearly every village, town and city in France. Their hours are better, but bear in mind that the queues at Parisian post offices are notoriously long and slow.

To open a bank account in France you will need to provide your passport, your *carte de séjour*, and proof of address such as a bill. Make sure that the bill includes your full name and address.

The most common, and useful, account is a standard checking account. You'll be granted a chequebook, a debit card (*carte bleue*) and a book of RIBs (*relevé d'identité bancaire*) forms that provide all the codes associated with your account, bank and branch. When setting up any kind of account, including gas, telephone and television, you will be asked for an RIB. This form allows the service provider to deduct money directly from your account and it also allows an employer to deposit money directly into your account. This is standard practice in France and nearly all regular transactions are executed this way. Depending upon your bank and the specific details of your account, you may have a minimum balance. Certain banks provide overdraft insurance while others will penalise you seriously. If you don't have a residence visa you may still get a bank account but you will not be given a debit card or provided with overdraft insurance. It is common to charge an annual fee for your debit card.

Nearly all banks provide internet and telephone banking, and given the standards of customer service in Paris it is a good idea to find a bank which provides the most thorough internet capabilities.

Banking hours in France are generally 09:00 to 17:00 from Monday to Friday. Some branches will close for an hour or even two for lunch. Some banks are open on Sundays.

Banks

Name	Phone	Web	Online Banking	Tele-Banking
Barclays	08 10 09 09 09	www.barclays.fr	✓	✓
BNP-Paribas	08 20 82 00 01	www.bnpparibas.fr	✓	✓
Caisse d'Epargne	08 21 01 02 22	www.caisse-epargne.fr	✓	✓
Crédit Agricole	01 47 20 17 40	www.credit-agricole.fr	✓	✓
HSBC	01 55 69 74 54	www.hsbc.fr	✓	✓
La Poste	36 39	www.laposte.fr	✓	✓
Le Crédit Lyonnaise	39 38	www.lcl.fr	✓	✓
Société Générale	39 33	www.societegenerale.fr	✓	✓

Offshore Investments

While it is illegal for offshore investment companies to advertise their products in France, it is generally legal for French residents to invest offshore. As with any investment, it is advisable to consult with a qualified and reputable financial advisor before signing any papers. Generally speaking, offshore investing is not particularly common in France except for the very rich.

The most popular offshore tax havens in Europe are Switzerland, Luxembourg and the Republic of Ireland. The very wealthy often escape to Monaco where the interests of the rich are considered above all others.

No matter what you decide to do, it is important to remember that while living in France, profits you make on your offshore investments need to be declared to the French tax authority.

Cost Of Living

Apples (per kg)	€ 2
Aspirin (pack of 24)	€3
Baguette	€0.80
Bananas (per kg)	€2
Beer (six pack)	€6
Bottle of house wine (restaurant)	€12
Bottle of wine (off licence)	€5
Burger	€3
Bus (10km journey)	€1.40
Cappucino	€3
Car rental (per day)	€35
Carrots (per kg)	€0.95
CD album	€15
Chocolate bar	€1
Cigarettes (pack of 20)	€4
Cinema ticket	€7
Eggs (dozen)	€3
Fresh chicken (per kg)	€3
Fresh fish (per kg)	€4
Golf (18 holes)	€45
Haircut (female)	€55
Haircut (male)	€25
House wine (glass)	€4
Milk (litre)	€1.50
Orange juice (1 litre)	€5
Petrol (gallon)	€1.17
Photo printing (per copy)	€0.10
Pint of beer	€3.50
Pizza	€10
Postage stamp	€0.54
Postcard	€1
Potatoes (per kg)	€1.50
Rice (1kg)	€2
SMS message	€0.10
Soft drink	€1.21
Strawberries (per punnet)	€2.50
Sugar (2kg)	€2
Taxi (10km journey)	€10
Toothpaste (tube)	€3
Water 1.5 litres (restaurant)	€5
Water 1.5 litres (supermarket)	€0.75

Financial Planning

Pensions

If you are receiving your pension in a foreign account, the French tax authority considers that this money has already been taxed and will not tax it further. You're better off keeping your money abroad and using it as you need it. However, there are two important considerations:

• The cost of transferring money can be high so make as few transfers as possible.

• Consider the impact of the exchange rate. If you're bringing money from the US into France you are, at the time of print, losing 30% on the exchange without considering any bank charges.

Depending upon what kind of company you're working for you may have investment options in France or abroad. Keep in mind that governments are making it more and more difficult to invest outside of the country you're living in. Only recently have French companies begun offering company sponsored retirement plans. The first, *assurance de vie* is similar to an IRA, and a PEA (*Plan d'Epargne en Action*)is essentially a stock portfolio made up of nearly entirely French stocks. Both offer tax advantages.

Again, with something as important and complex as international retirement, you should talk to an international financial consultant for advice.

Cost of Living

Keep in mind that prices vary dramatically from neighbourhood to neighbourhood; a beer in St-Germain des Prés can be more than twice the cost of a beer in the 19th.

Taxation

From the moment you arrive in France, you will be taxed on any personal income. The following is a list of some of the primary French taxes you may have to pay:

• Impot société – Tax based on corporate profit

- Impot su le revenu – Income tax. You must file a tax return between February and March. The date is announced by the government and if you're a registered employee you can be sure you'll be notified
- TVA – Taxe sur la valeur ajoutée (VAT) which is an automatically included sales tax
- Taxe foncière – Property tax. An annual tax paid by the owner of their property
- Taxe professionelle – Professional tax, paid by business owners for the right to run a business in France
- Taxe d'habitation – Habitation tax. An annual tax paid by the person or persons living in (or on) a property
- Rédevance – Television tax. Perhaps the most surprising to newcomers to France, the *rédevance* is the tax you pay for the right to watch French television. If you have a television which is plugged in, you have to pay the price.

Anyone living and working in France, citizen or otherwise, must pay the same taxes at the same rates. If you choose not to pay your taxes you can be imprisoned, fined or deported. For detailed information on French taxes, visit the website of l'Administration Fiscale on www.impots.gouv.fr.

Financial Advisors		
AXA Investment Managers	01 44 45 70 00	www.axa-im.com
Axis Strategy Consultants	01 39 21 74 61	www.axis-strategy.com

Legal Issues

The French legal system, as with many others, distinguishes between civil and criminal law. Civil actions are judged in public (except in cases of divorce or child custody) by tribunals and appeals courts.

Criminal actions are also judged by one of three types of tribunal:

- Police Tribunals – where fines or prison sentences of up to two months may be imposed
- Correctional Tribunals – where sentences can range from community service up to 10 years in prison
- Assize Trials – where prison terms may be as long as 30 years

France is a democracy, but do remember that France follows the Napoleonic code so the burden of proof is on the accused, not the accuser. All court proceedings are, of course, held in French.

There is a strong police presence in Paris, particularly in the parts of the city that attract tourists, and you should avoid confrontations with the police. As an expat you are always vulnerable to being thrown out of the country, so consider this before you enter into any kind of illegal situation.

Adoption

Adoption has been legal in France since 1923. Over the last 10 years an average of 5,000 children were adopted annually; 1,500 are French with the rest from foreign nations. Of those children adopted from abroad, 27% come from Eastern Europe, 25% from Africa, 20% from South America and 19% from Asia.

To adopt in France, couples must have been married for a minimum of two years and unmarried singles must be at least 28 years old to legally adopt. In either case, adopting parents must obtain an agreement provided by the local administration. France allows for two classifications of adoption: full adoption and simple adoption. A full adoption is irrevocable and will not maintain any official ties to the biological parents. Simple adoption allows the child to keep his or her family name and grants the child inheritance rights to the biological parents' possessions.

France and Luxembourg are the only two European nations which allow women to give birth anonymously.

Divorce

Getting divorced in any country is complicated and often painful. As an expat abroad the process may become more difficult, so if you and your spouse are of the same nationality you might consider returning home to be divorced. Consider where your assets are; if you're dividing assets which are primarily based in France you may find it easier to be divorced there. Consider also where you and your spouse will be living after the divorce. Will one of you stay in France? Will both of you? These are important considerations. Are you married to a French citizen? Where were you married? Do you have children? Where were they born? Are they French nationals? Generally, France considers foreigners legally married abroad to be legally married in France. If you do decide to get divorced in France, a judge will determine custody as well as child support payments.

Making a Will

French law respects wills that have been legally made in foreign countries. However, if you plan to live in France as an official resident it is recommended that you have a will drafted in French and notarised by a French *notaire*. This is particularly important if you own 'immovable property' in the country, such as apartments, houses or land.

To make a will in France you must be at least 18 years old and be of sound mind (*sain d'esprit*). There are three kinds of legally accepted wills available in France:

- Holographic Will: To be legal it must be entirely hand written and state the location, day, month and year it is made. Each page must be numbered and signed.
- Authentic Will: Considered the most legally secure, an authentic will must be signed before two notaries and two witnesses, read publicly and registered by a notary in the national database of wills.
- Mystic Will: Rarely used, the mystic will may be typed or handwritten. It is then notarised and sealed in an envelope not to be opened until the death of the testator.

Visit www.notaires.fr for a list of notaries in France and further information in English. Unless the testator has lived in France for less than six years, a 'death tax' will be charged on all inheritance which derives from both inside and outside of France.

Palais des Congrès

Palais de Justice

Paris apartments

Housing

For many foreigners moving to Paris, the notion of owning an apartment with views over the rooftops is part of the dream. But, if you want to live in the centre of the city, be prepared to pay extortionate prices. Whether to rent or buy is a question difficult to answer. How long will you stay in Paris? What can you afford? Often the apartment you can afford to rent is not the apartment you can afford to buy. If you do buy, are you doing so as an investment? Do you plan to rent the apartment when you're not in Paris? Long term or short term? All of these factors will play a role in helping you decide where and if to buy.

Renting in Paris

Paris is unlike other cities; it is a city thriving with life and to live in its centre is to become part of that life. On the other hand, if you're arriving with three children and a minivan, you might consider living in one of the suburbs where you'll find larger houses with gardens. There will be space, parking, quiet and increased safety, and with high quality public transport it's usually only a short train ride to the Louvre. Of course, this isn't always the case and if enjoying Paris is important for you and your family, consider your new home's proximity to public transport.

Your rent usually includes water and building maintenance. In theory, the landlord is responsible for the upkeep of the apartment itself. This does not, however, extend to appliances that may come with the apartment. For example, if you move into a studio which includes a refrigerator and it breaks down two months into your stay, you're responsible for replacing it.

If you have gas heating the cost is shared between the tenants and is dramatically less expensive than electric heating. All other utilities are paid for separately and individually, but air conditioning is rare in Paris. Occasionally, parking is included in the rent but very infrequently.

Start Looking ◄
The American Church in Paris (www.acparis.org) has a good bulletin board and is a great place to start on your search for an apartment. It's an even better place to find a room for rent in someone else's apartment.

A standard rental contract for an unfurnished apartment is three years. Don't be frightened by the seemingly long duration of the lease. French law always favours the 'little guy' and as a tenant that's you; the long duration of your lease exists to protect you from the landlord. If you want out, simply give three months' notice and you're free. And if you're transferred with your job, you only need one month's notice and a letter from your employer. If, however, the landlord wants you out he needs to wait for the full term of the lease. If, at the end of three years, the landlord wants you out they will need to send you a letter six months before the end of the lease. If there's no letter, the three years is automatically renewed. These laws apply only to unfurnished apartments. If you rent a furnished apartment the lease is one year. To leave early you must give a month's notice. At the end of one year the lease is automatically renewed. Rent is paid monthly and is automatically deducted from your bank account. Negotiating your rent is, in most instances, unheard of. There is such high demand for apartments in Paris that landlords have their pick of tenants and because laws favour the tenant so heavily, landlords are very careful about choosing their prospective tenants. In addition to your rent you'll need to pay a security deposit which is usually two months' rent.

A good place to look for apartments that don't carry an agency fee is the weekly publication *De Particulier a Particulier*, an excellent source for independent owners to sell or rent their property. You can also search the website which is available in English at www.pap.fr. *FUSAC* is a monthly English language collection of advertisements which includes a large selection of apartments for rent or sale. Depending upon your budget you may also find apartments advertised in the *International Herald Tribune* but these tend to be at the upper end of the scale. The website www.paris.craigslist.org has also become an excellent place to find apartments to rent, both short and long term as well as sublets and roommate situations. Another excellent resource is www.seloger.co.uk.

Shop Around
Keep in mind that agencies don't usually have exclusive rights to a property, and you may find the same property in another window so it's worth looking around as one agent may charge less than the other.

Real Estate Agents

Because there's no central real estate database in Paris, individuals often need to do a lot of leg work (or hire someone to do it for them) to find a place to live. Don't be surprised if agents don't return your calls, or generally seem uninterested by your desire to pay them money. Real estate agents in Paris all have window displays, which showcase their best properties. Agencies must be certified by the *préfecture de police* and you should only do business with agencies that have a professional ID number, a guarantor and insurance. All of these things must, by law, be printed on all contracts and official correspondence. All agencies charge a non-refundable fee if you use their services to secure an apartment.

The Lease

Before you move into your apartment you will need to sign a copy of the *état des lieux*, a document evaluating the state of the apartment. Make sure that anything that isn't up to par is marked in detail and take photographs. By law you must have tenant's insurance and provide proof to your landlord that you're covered.

In general, you will be asked to prove that you make at least three times the monthly rent and it is not uncommon for a prospective landlord to ask for personal financial details including extensive financial records, your employment contract, and even your parents' financial records. The lease itself is called the *droit de bail* or *contrat de location* and to be valid it must be drafted by a notary and written in French. You

Real Estate Agents

Agence Dauphine	01 43 54 43 43	www.dauphine-immo.com
Barnes	01 55 61 92 92	www.barnes-paris.com
Capitale Partners	01 42 68 35 60	www.capitale-partners.com
Cattalan-Johnson	01 45 74 87 77	www.cattalanjohnson.com
Century 21	01 69 11 12 21	www.century21france.fr
Chasseur d'Appartement	01 55 02 32 55	www.chasseurdappartement.com
De Circourt Associates	01 43 12 98 00	www.homes-paris.com
First Address	01 56 24 83 02	www.1aparis.com
My Flat in Paris	01 44 53 98 09	www.myflatinparis.com
Paris Housing Services	01 45 55 21 37	www.paris-housing.com
Satimmo	01 40 33 55 55	www.satimmo.fr
Segur	01 56 58 68 68	www.segur.fr
Seine et Cité	01 53 68 64 02	www.seineetcite.com
SFI	01 43 80 10 17	www.groupe-sfi.com
Tradinvest	01 48 74 63 64	www.tradinvest.com
Vivre a Paris	01 44 54 97 97	www.vivre-a-paris.eu

have no legal right to have the lease written in another language and if one is provided to you, make sure that you have the original in French reviewed by your lawyer or relocation agent before signing. The lease will be signed by you and by the landlord or occasionally by an estate agency on the landlord's behalf.

Main Accommodation Options

The majority of people who live in Paris live in apartments. There is an enormous range when it comes to price – you can find a room for a few hundred euros per month and you can spend upwards of €10,000 per month for a loft looking out over the Seine. As is true anywhere else, location is key. What you get for your money in St-Germain des Prés is not what you get in the 19th. Know what you want before you arrive and decide what it is you're willing to give up; if you want to live in a house, odds are you're not going to find one in Paris. There are exceptions, but to buy or rent a house in the city is brutally expensive, and even if you have the money it may be difficult to do. If you're set on living in a house with a garden and a parking space, consider the suburbs where this is infinitely more affordable. Serviced apartments or 'aparthotels' are available as well. If you don't have the time to find a perfect, personal and charming place you can find very comfortable serviced apartments throughout the city, often in very desirable locations. These serviced apartments offer the amenities of a hotel but with fully equipped kitchens included. The Citadine (www.citadines.com) apartments in St-Germain des Prés, for example, directly face the Seine and sit on some of the cities most valuable property.

Furnished apartments provide the comforts of home but without the services provided by aparthotels. By renting a furnished apartment you'll save yourself the trouble of starting from scratch or shipping your belongings to Paris. This is, of course, a matter of taste. If you're happy to live with someone else's things and can afford to pay a bit more per month, consider a furnished apartment. Another advantage to living in a furnished apartment is that there is less hassle when it comes to the lease. As mentioned, a furnished apartment is not subject to the same laws as an unfurnished property. On the downside, this means it is far easier for a landlord to throw you out should they wish.

Housing Abbreviations

agence s'abst	no agencies
asc	elevator
bal	balcony
bns	bathrooms
box	parking
calme	quiet
carac	charming
ch	additional monthly charges
chauf	heating
chb	bedroom
com	commission
coq	cute
cuis	kitchen
cuis eq	equipped kitchen
dche	shower
et. el	high floor
imm	building
imm anc	old building
imm mod	contemporary building
imm nf	new building
imm rec	newly built building
imm. pdt	stone building
interméd	agent
jar	garden
kit	kitchenette
m2	square metre
moq	carpeting
pr cpl	couples requested
rav	lovely
ref nf	recently remodelled
slle	large room
ss	without
stdg	high style, class, etc
tcc	everything included
terr	terrace
wc	toilet separate from bathroom
chauf	heating

Other Rental Costs

Aside from your initial deposit, the agency fee and your monthly rent there are other fees to consider. As mentioned on p.60, you'll need to pay an annual habitation tax and, depending upon your phone, internet and cable services, you may need to pay a deposit for those too. Keep in mind that there is an increasingly competitive home services market developing in France and there are some excellent deals to be had if you shop around. It is uncommon for parking to be provided with an apartment; if you have a car or expect to purchase one, consider your options when deciding where to live. There are many underground parking garages in Paris, which sell monthly passes. The mayor would like to ban cars altogether from the centre of the city and is pushing hard to accomplish this.

Buying Property

Paris has a booming property market. Recently foreigners, particularly North Americans, have been the subject of bad press. Wealthy Americans are blamed for the sky-rocketing property prices. They come to Paris, pay absurd prices for small apartments, and drive hard-working French men and women out of the city. Whoever or whatever is to blame for the escalating prices, one thing is certain – apartments in Paris are expensive. Will they continue to be expensive? Will that one bedroom apartment for €800,000 be worth more than that in ten years? If you think so, and you've got the money, buy. Renting is always easier and safer, but it isn't much of an investment.

The property market in Paris is growing quickly. Everyone has a different opinion. It seems that every other day someone somewhere pronounces the market maxed out and yet property continues to become more and more expensive. This is particularly true in central Paris. If you consider the speed with which formerly run-down Paris neighbourhoods are becoming gentrified you might be inspired to buy something fast. On the other hand, there are those who don't believe that the market can sustain any more million-euro properties. If you're interested in buying property to renovate, or land on which to build, you will need the advice of an expert. Any new buildings or structural changes to old buildings must be cleared by the town hall. Before you can hammer a single nail you'll need the permission of your local *mairie*.

Buying To Let

If you plan on renting your property you'll need to declare the rent as income, and pay the appropriate taxes. Additionally, you'll have to pay the annual property tax (*taxe foncière*) which all property owners in France are required to pay. On the other hand, it will be your renter who pays the annual habitation tax (*taxe d'habitation*). Renting your property can be a good investment and an excellent way to pay back a mortgage. However, remember that French law seriously favours the tenant. Once you become a landlord you put yourself seriously at risk. Screen potential tenants scrupulously. Also, consider renting your apartment as a furnished vacation rental on a weekly or month to month basis. You have a lot more protection this way on the off chance that your tenant decides to build a meth lab in your new marble bathroom.

Property Report

Before you can sell a property you must have an energy evaluation to determine the amount of energy the property consumes. The report will evaluate energy consumption along with determining the presence of asbestos and lead.

Selling Property

The buyer will contact a notary who will then serve as an agent for both the seller and the buyer. Make sure that any particular terms (are you selling all the fixtures or do you plan to take them with you? What about the dishwasher? Refrigerator? Gargoyles?) are stipulated precisely in the contract. Anything that can be detached and taken away should be indicated in the contract. The buyer will then pay a 10% deposit to the notary or agent.

Once you sign the sale agreement, you are committed to the sale. If you withdraw, you must return the deposit to the buyer and pay him a 10% compensatory fee. While the buyer has a cooling off period, you do not. See Real Estate Law over the page.

Mortgages

Getting a mortgage is a fairly simple process in France and very similar to other countries. If you pay taxes in France it's possible to have a mortgage without a down payment, but UK and other EU residents must pay a minimum of a 15% deposit. If you are a resident of a non-EU country and pay taxes there, you're required to pay a minimum of a 20% deposit. Most banks and lenders in France charge a flat 1% fee usually with a maximum of €1,500. To qualify for a mortgage in France you must be able to demonstrate that you have sufficient income to cover the monthly payments. You must have a life insurance policy, which covers the terms of your mortgage. The French government maintains strict laws which limit the amount of money a person may spend each month on a mortgage: one third of your monthly income may be devoted to your monthly expenditures such as credit card payments or a pre-existing mortgage. Whatever remains after those payments are made may then be used to cover your new mortgage and the cost of mandatory life insurance. By law, all French mortgages must be covered by life insurance and usually your lender will insist that you use their policies. Every bank operating in France offers mortgages so, if you have a good relationship with your banker, speak with them about mortgage options. If you don't speak French well or aren't familiar with French property law, it's advisable to consult with a bank that specialises in expat investment.

Mortgage Providers

Barclays	08 10 09 09 09	www.barclays.fr
BNP-Paribas	08 20 82 00 01	www.bnpparibas.fr
Caisse d'Epargne	08 21 01 02 22	www.caisse-epargne.fr
Crédit Agricole	01 47 20 17 40	www.credit-agricole.fr
HSBC	01 55 69 74 54	www.hsbc.fr
Societé Générale	39 33	www.societegenerale.fr

Other Purchasing Costs

In addition to the usual costs of purchasing a property the most significant cost will be the fees you pay to the notary. This is an expense that many are surprised by, but be certain that it's a requirement and there's no way around it. You should expect to pay a minimum of 8% of the total purchase price but additionally you'll also need to pay a 4% property registration fee to the city. An important note, while French tax payers have the right to include notary fees in their mortage, foreigners paying taxes abroad must pay the fees directly and in cash. Agencies charge 4-10% and who pays the fee, buyer or seller, depends entirely on the individual deal.

Real Estate Law

The Deed is Done
Once you sign the deed the notary will sign it as a legal witness and then register the deed with the city. The notary will keep the original document and send you an official copy.

Regardless of whether or not you plan to buy with cash or take out a mortgage, there are certain flat fees you'll have to pay directly. First, on the day you sign the sales agreement (*compromis de vente*) you will be obliged to pay your deposit, approximately 10% of the purchase price. Pay your deposit to the notary or real estate agent who is representing you and do not make the mistake of paying directly to the seller. In this way, the deposit will be kept by the mediating agent or notary until completion, otherwise you risk a dishonest seller vanishing with a large sum of your money.
Once you've made an offer and it has been agreed upon by the seller you'll sign a contract (*compromis de vente* or *promesse de vente*). If you're planning on buying with a mortgage the name on the sales contract must be the same as on the mortgage. You will have to pay your deposit on the day of the signing. Once you've signed, you have seven days to change your mind which is the time to have your structural engineer make an inspection of the property. Remember that even if you do change your mind, you'll need to give a specific reason, otherwise you may lose your deposit.
If you decide to buy the property, you'll need to have the full amount of cash in your French bank account and ensure that it is open to transfer on the day of completion. Also, from the moment the money is transferred it is your insurance which will cover the property and you'll need proof that the property is insured. Before the closing you'll be sent the final deed (*projet de l'acte*). At the final meeting, you'll need to provide both your birth certificate and your passport along with your marriage certificate if appropriate.

Residential Areas

Other options **Exploring** p.197

The city of Paris is made of 20 sections or *arrondissements*, which spin out in a widening spiral from the centre of the city. Paris is often described as a city made up of many different villages and it's an apt description to keep in mind when choosing your future home. Simply because a given *arrondissement* is not famous for its history or cobbled streets, you may find a little corner of the city with a perfect *boulangerie* and florist, a friendly cheese seller, a small park full of kids, unpretentious and welcoming neighbours and discover that living far from avenue Foche isn't so bad. Expats tend to live in one of seven different *arrondissements*: the 1st, 4th, 5th, 6th, 7th, 8th and 16th. Of course there are exceptions, but you will find that the greatest population of expats, particularly Anglo expats, is in these neighbourhoods. Not surprisingly, these happen to be the most expensive neighbourhoods in the city. Each has its clear advantages – charm, safety, familiarity and beauty among others – but don't dismiss other lesser-known *arrondissements* simply because they're unfamiliar; there is a lot to be said for being the only expat on the block. The same is true in the suburbs, and expats tend to end up in Neuilly-sur-Seine, St Cloud, Versailles or St Germain-en-Laye. But again, there are many other charming, beautiful, villages within a short train ride or drive from Paris.

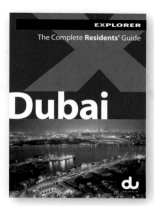

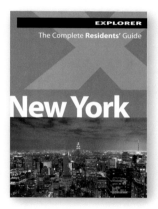

Tired of writing your insider tips…

…in a blog that nobody reads?

The Explorer Complete Residents' Guide series is growing rapidly, and we're always looking for literate, resident writers to help pen our new guides. So whether you live in Tuscany or Timbuktu, if writing's your thing, and you know your city inside out, we'd like to talk to you.

Apply online at www.explorerpublishing.com

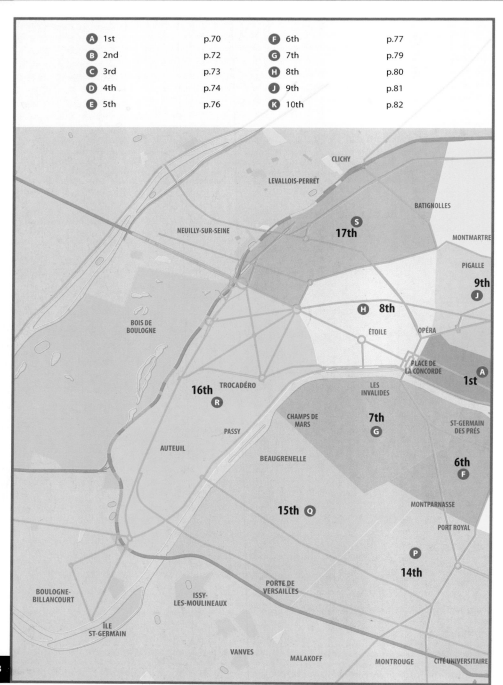

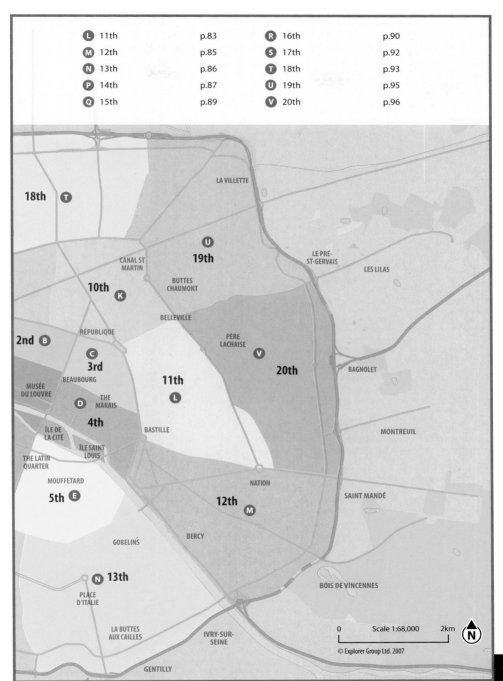

18th **T**

LA VILLETTE

U
19th

CANAL ST
MARTIN

LE PRÉ-
ST-GERVAIS

LES LILAS

10th
K

BUTTES
CHAUMONT

BELLEVILLE

RÉPUBLIQUE

PÈRE
LACHAISE

2nd **B**

C
3rd

V

20th

BAGNOLET

BEAUBOURG

MUSÉE
DU LOUVRE

D THE
MARAIS

11th
L

ÎLE DE
LA CITÉ

4th

BASTILLE

MONTREUIL

ÎLE SAINT
LOUIS

THE LATIN
QUARTER

MOUFFETARD

NATION

SAINT MANDÉ

5th **E**

12th
M

GOBELINS

BERCY

N **13th**

BOIS DE VINCENNES

PLACE
D'ITALIE

LA BUTTES
AUX CAILLES

IVRY-SUR-
SEINE

0   Scale 1:68,000   2km

N

© Explorer Group Ltd. 2007

GENTILLY

Map p.398, p.399
Area **A** p.68

Best Points
A fast-moving, often glamorous, lively neighbourhood; includes some of the city's most beautiful areas.

Worst Points
Has some of central Paris' most dangerous corners; seedy, congested, noisy and dirty; terrible parking and a crush of people.

1st

To the east, in the direction of Chatelet and Les Halles, the 1st can be seedy, congested and a magnet for petty crime, but the north-eastern section is becoming deeply trendy. Rue Etienne Marcel, the dividing line between 1st and 2nd, is the epicentre of fashion victims while hip boutiques blend with the increasingly touristic rue Montorgueil. To the west, the *quartier* becomes increasingly bourgeois, staid and attractive where it includes some of the city's most valuable property – the Palais Royale and place Vendome included. The Jardin des Tuileries and the Louvre to the south and the western tip of the Île de la Cité make up the rest of the *arrondissement*. While one of the smaller *arrondissements,* the level of variety is enormous.

Accommodation

Anything from some of Paris' most expensive and desirable property to unattractive, mildly dangerous, and relatively inexpensive apartments are available. An apartment on place Dauphine is a rare and expensive find while an apartment on the eastern side of Les Halles is to be avoided.

Shopping & Amenities

From the ultra-expensive to flea-market cheap, the 1st offers an entire range of possibilities. To the east you'll find tacky T-shirt shops, tattoo parlours and a vast variety of fastfood. In other directions you'll find some of the most exclusive shopping in Paris and some of the most expensive restaurants in the city, if not the world, including the exquisite, three-starred Grand Vefour (01 42 96 56 27) in the north-eastern corner of the Palais Royale. Le Ritz Health Club (p.232) is one of the most luxurious in France.

Entertainment & Leisure

There's a wide variety of restaurants, cafes, and bars as well as some of the city's most famous jazz clubs. The Jardin des Tuileries, square du Vert Gallant, place Dauphine, place Vendome and Pont Neuf all find their home in the 1st. You can have a classic drink at the Hotel Ritz (p.345), a casual coffee in a cafe on rue Montorgueil, or spend an evening with hipsters in black from all over the world in the bar at the Hotel Costes (p.345). A wonderful place for lunch is the well-known Le Fumoir (p.349).

Healthcare

Médic-Halles (15 rue Louvre, 01 42 33 23 32) is a private clinic offering basic health services. And for free, anonymous AIDS testing go to CIDAG (43 rue Valois, 01 42 97 48 29).

Transport

Chatelet-Les Halles serves as a transportation hub, allowing access to every corner of Paris and beyond. All of the RER trains pass through Les Halles as do most Metro and bus lines. On the other hand, parking is an absolute nightmare and is to be avoided.

Safety & Annoyances

Because the *quartier* draws so many tourists there is a high level of pickpockets and petty criminals roaming the streets. Of course, there are certain areas which are more prone to these dangers than others; Chatelet and Les Halles are notorious. The park between St Eustache and Chatelet Les Halles should be avoided at night (it is a haven for drug dealers) while rue St Denis was once crawling with sex workers. While there are still prostitutes along this street, it is becoming increasingly gentrified with organic food stores taking the place of sex shops. Pay particular attention to your surroundings when you're walking through the labyrinth metro station at Chatelet and avoid it entirely at night.

Residential Areas

Apartments on rue de Rivoli

Cruising past the Conciergerie

The Louvre

Église Saint-Eustache

Place des Victoires

Map p.389
Area **B** p.69

2nd

Markedly less touristic than the 1st, the *quartier* has become increasingly trendy over the last years. The rue Etienne Marcel which demarcates the southern border between the 1st and 2nd is the epicentre of young designers. As you move north to the east you'll find a less pretentious environment, full of Jewish tailors and their workshops. Far less expensive than the area around Etienne Marcel it is a comfortable and safe neighbourhood albeit a bit noisy in the mornings. To the west the neighbourhood becomes more bourgeois (and rather soulless) as you move toward the Grands Boulevards and the Opéra Garnier (p.167). To the south around the Bibliothèque Nationale is a section devoted to Asian, primarily Japanese, restaurants.

Best Points
Wide variety of neighborhoods from the gritty to the painfully hip; good restaurants, bars and excellent shopping; central with quick access to everywhere.

Worst Points
Often congested and noisy in the north-west; to the north east rather soulless and becomes a ghost town in the evening.

Accommodation

As is generally the case in Paris, the further north you go the less expensive the accommodation. In the 2nd, the further you move away from Etienne Marcel the less expensive the apartments. Keep in mind that there is not a single park in this *arrondissement* and that it can become claustrophobic to the north and certain areas lack charm. On the other hand, you're more likely to find a bigger apartment for less and you'll certainly be living among Parisians rather than expats and tourists.

Shopping & Amenities

For the trendy, the shopping along Etienne Marcel is heaven. Paris' famous enclosed shopping galleries are found primarily in the 2nd and in the 9th. Near the French stock market, la Bourse, you'll find a wide variety of stores selling collectible coins. For one of the best food stores in Paris, visit G Detou (58 rue Tiquetonne, 01 42 36 54 67) where you can find everything from spices and almonds to chocolate and cranberries. For the ultimate in designer gyms, l'Usine (8 rue de la Michodière, 01 42 66 30 30) is the place.

Entertainment & Leisure

As with nearly every *quartier* in Paris there is a wide variety of eating and drinking establishments in the 2nd. There are classic bistrots, popular wine bars, and a huge variety of Japanese restaurants in the area. The beautiful Bibliothèque Nationale is a wonderful place to spend an afternoon reading and there are often exhibitions held ranging from photography to rare books. The more you move in the direction of the Opéra Garnier the less funky the area becomes and you'll find the bars less populated by the young and the hip and more by the besuited and the wealthy.

Housing in the 2nd

Healthcare

Centre de Santé Reamur is a health clinic provided at very low cost by the French social security and offers full medical services including dental care. Centre de Planification (2 rue Vivienne, 01 42 60 93 20) offers family planning treatments.

Transport

The area is well-serviced by public transportation and relatively car-friendly.

Saftety & Annoyances

The congestion and lack of green spaces mean you might find yourself escaping elsewhere to relax. The 2nd is fairly safe but with all areas popular for socialising, extra care should be taken at night.

Map p.400
Area **C** p.69

Best Points
A fast-growing, young and exciting neighborhood; the Marais and the north-western corner are full of excellent shopping of all varieties; rapidly gentrifying neighborhoods but there's still time to buy.

Worst Points
Can be excruciatingly noisy and clogged with traffic; the north-eastern corner maintains a scruffy edge and can be unpleasant in the evening.

3rd

The 3rd has experienced a major resurgence to become one of the most desirable neighbourhoods in the city. Full of interesting boutiques and restaurants, the 3rd makes up the northern section of the Marais, the famous Jewish and gay quarter which is now a major tourist hub. While the southern end of the Marais has become overrun with tourists and is extremely expensive, almost on a par with St-Germain des Prés, the 3rd (particularly the northern section) is more liveable and less developed as a tourist destination. Full of art galleries and hip boutiques, the area around rue de Bretagne has great shopping and a charming covered market. Not quite as hip and nowhere near as pretentious as the Etienne Marcel neighbourhood, it's a wonderful, lively, brimming place to live.

Accommodation

It has become increasingly difficult to find inexpensive housing in the more desirable parts of the 3rd, particularly those considered part of the Marais. Still, it's possible to find reasonably priced apartments to the north. Be careful however, the area to the north-west, around rue St Martin has an entirely different feeling than the area around square du Temple and is far less safe. On the other hand, if you're looking to stay in Paris for a long time or are interested in making an investment, this might very well be the neighbourhood to do it in. The further south you go the more expensive the property.

Shopping & Amenities

There is superb shopping of every variety in the 3rd. The marché des Enfants Rouges (p.298) is a small covered market and an excellent place to come for lunch on a weekend. Hip boutiques along rue de Turenne and rue Charlot seem to change hands daily and as you descend into the true Marais the shopping is endless.

Entertainment & Leisure

Take a picnic to square du Temple or go for a stroll through the meandering streets in the Marais. Get a table on the sidewalk at La Perle (p.348) and watch the young and hip wander past. For something with more substance get a table at l'Ami Louis (32 rue Vertbois, 01 48 87 77 48) one of Paris' most reliable classics; no better roast chicken to be found. Have a drink at Andy Wahloo (p.344) or spend an afternoon with the locals in square Emilie Chautemps, you'll feel far from the sometimes oppressive hipness of the southern end of this *arrondissement*.

Healthcare

The nearest major hospital is the Hotel Dieu (p.112) just in front of Notre Dame. The city of Paris also offers a clinic, the Centre de Santé (01 48 87 49 87) at 4 rue Maire.

Transport

The 3rd offers excellent public transportation options which is a good thing given the fact that parking is such a nightmare. At the north-east corner of the 3rd is the République metro from which you can find metros going in all directions. The neighbourhood is also well-served by the public buses.

Saftety & Annoyances

Generally, the 3rd is safe, but as with anywhere in the city, you should avoid parks and dark corners at night. The streets are generally lively at all hours and as gentrification continues the neighbourhood becomes safer. The northern end, particularly towards boulevard St Martin, can be relatively dangerous. The 3rd is particularly congested, with a great deal of commerce taking place on rue St Martin, rue Beaubourg, rue Turenne and rue de Turbigo. Delivery trucks and traffic noise can be intense during business hours.

Map p.400
Area **D** *p.69*

4th

Best Points
Some of the most coveted real estate in Paris (if not in France) is here; wonderful restaurants, shopping and views of the Seine; charming streets, the Île-St Louis, the Marais, and beautiful squares.

One of Paris' most desirable and expensive neighbourhoods, the 4th is full of winding streets, charming buildings and includes the Marais, Paris' gay and Jewish quarter. Brimming with streetlife, expensive boutiques, great bars (most of which are gay), Jewish restaurants and art galleries, tourists have descended in droves, but with so many people the crush can be overwhelming and claustrophobic. This is the city's very first neighbourhood and it is appropriately full of history. The Île St Louis and the Île de la Cité are beautiful islands, smack in the middle of the Seine, dripping with charm (and tourists). If you can afford to live on one of these islands and can find an apartment big enough to be comfortable in, consider it seriously. It doesn't get much more picturesque, but you'll need a lot of money and a lot of luck; apartments on a *quai* with a view are precious and hard to come by no matter how much money you have. Central, lively, beautiful and safe, this is a lovely place to find yourself, but remember that living in the 4th you'll often hear English spoken as often as any other language and that locals have often become intolerant of foreigners.

Worst Points
Throngs of tourists and astronomical property costs make the 4th a difficult and, for some, unappealing place to live; can be utterly charmless and claustrophobic around rue de Rivoli and west of rue du Temple.

Accommodation

From tiny garrets to exquisite apartments with sweeping views in all directions, the 4th is expensive and in high demand. The least expensive corners are in the west and the closer you get to boulevard Sébastapol, the cheaper and less charming the streets. Keep in mind that any apartment marked as Beaubourg is likely not going to be as charming as an apartment at the other end of the *arrondissement*. One of the quieter, more comfortable and less expensive sections of the 4th is around the metro Sully Morland, a perfect neighbourhood for a family. Here you'll find more room to breathe and fast access to the Seine, Bastille and the Latin Quarter.

Shopping & Amenities

BHV (p.290) is a Paris institution; a department store just across the street from the Hôtel de Ville with an extraordinary hardware section in the basement. The recently opened BHV Homme is an enormous, beautifully designed men's store selling everything from haircuts to designer suits. If you'd like something a bit less corporate, explore the myriad boutiques between rue des Archives and place des Vosges. The Marais is one of the best shopping districts in the city and here you can find anything you want from shoes and jewellery to furniture. Stores here favour independent and funky designers to the ultra-expensive established houses like Chanel and Gucci you'll find in the 1st and the 8th.

Entertainment & Leisure

The 4th has some of the best green spaces in central Paris and an afternoon lying on the grass in place des Vosges can be magical. No matter how crowded the city becomes, you can always find a quiet place to sit in the sun along the *quais* ringing the islands. The square de l'Île de France on the eastern point of the Île de la Cité always catches a breeze and is a perfect place on a hot summer's day as is square Barye. For an absolutely true Parisian brasserie experience there is nowhere in the world like Bofinger (5 rue de la Bastille, 01 42 72 87 82), a gorgeous Belle-Epoque brasserie in the western end. For a purely English-speaking bar experience the Lizard Lounge (18 rue Bourg Tibourg, 01 42 72 81 34) offers good, strong cocktails and excellent poetry readings.

Healthcare

Apart from the nearby Hôtel Dieu (p.112), there's the Hôpital Esquirol (4 rue Rivoli).

Transport

There is a vast array of public transportation in this part of town. The area around Sully Morland is slightly isolated but one stop on the metro or a few stops on the bus gets you to Bastille, a major transportation hub. Be warned of the terrible parking.

Safety & Annoyances

The 4th is relatively safe but avoid square de la Tour St Jaques and the area around the Centre Pompidou at night. The only real annoyances are the crowds, the crush of tourists and the overall lack of space.

Approaching place des Vosges

Apartments in the 4th

Rooms with a view

Map p.409, p.410
Area **E** p.69

5th

The 5th is a large, hilly *arrondissement* that spreads east along the Seine and south towards the 13th and 14th. This is the legendary Latin Quarter where, in the middle-ages, university students communicated in Latin (hence the name). It is an *arrondissement* with a liberal intellectual reputation, full of leftist students and professors. The Sorbonne, Pantheon and famous rue Mouffetard are here. Popular with tourists and students, the 5th remains a sort of university village, vibrant and full of good bars and winding streets.

Best Points

Provides a large variety of ambience; this vast arrondissement includes chic and exclusive neighbourhoods, universities, excellent markets and great bars; some of the most Parisian of Parisian streets are here – the 5th offers a bit of everything.

Accommodation

Apartments are expensive towards the river and around the Pantheon, but the further you go away from the 6th and the Seine, the less expensive the area. Apartments along boulevard St Germain and near Jardin du Luxembourg are expensive and hard to come by. It's still possible to find reasonable prices off boulevard St Michel towards Port Royal.

Shopping & Amenities

There are excellent outdoor markets in the 5th, most notably at Maubert Mutualité (p.298) and place Monge (p.298). The famous candle-maker Diptyque maintains a quiet corner on boulevard St Germain. For outdoor goods, visit Au Vieux Campeur (p.273) with stores on and around rue des Écoles. The rue Mouffetard was once a market street full of independent vendors but it is fast becoming a generic tourist trap. La Piscine Club Pontoise (19 rue de Pontoise, 01 55 42 77 88) is a public pool and gym.

Worst Points

Tourist-heavy – many shops cater to busloads of foreigners; can be loud and raucous at night, particularly during the school year.

Entertainment & Leisure

For one of the most beautiful picnic spots in the city wander down to the quai Saint Bernard at sunset and watch the light change looking up at Notre Dame. The Jardin des Plantes (p.190) is a lovely park for a stroll or a run, for true relaxation there are countless student bars and cafes around place de la Contrescarpe and place St Geneviève. Le Piano Vache (8 rue La Place, 01 46 33 75 03) is a classic. Le Pré Verre (8 rue Thénard, 01 46 33 75 03) offers inventive food at reasonable prices. St Michel is a zoo of tourist-trap restaurants, bars and cafes.

Education

The 5th is home to some of France's most famous universities including the Sorbonne, and École Normale Supérieure.

Healthcare

Groupe Médical Gobelins (4 avenue Gobelins, 01 43 31 31 08) provides basic medical care. The military hospital HIA Val de Grâce (01 40 51 40 00) is on boulevard de Port Royal.

Transport

Depending upon where in the 5th you are, transportation can either be excellent or a bit tricky. Near the river and up the hill toward Cardinal Lemoine, Jussieu, Monge and Censier Daubenton there's adequate metro access. However, there's a large area that is simply not served by the metro at all. Keep this in mind when choosing where to live. Parking is horrendous around St Michel but deeper in the 5th it can be tenable.

Safety & Annoyances

The 5th is fairly safe. The streets are usually crowded with people and full of tourists, which means a large police presence and safe walking at night. Avoid the areas around the Jardin des Plantes and Val de Grace after dark. St Michel, as with all tourist-heavy areas, is a magnet for pickpockets – particularly around the St Michel fountain. Be careful along the quais in the evening as square Tino Rossi often attracts drug dealers.

Map p.398
Area ⑤ p.68

6th

In terms of property value, the 6th is the most expensive *arrondissement* in Paris. One of the most popular tourist destinations in the city, the 6th includes the chic neighbourhood of St-Germain des Prés, Jardin Luxembourg, perfect Parisian streets, famous restaurants and cafes, and superb shopping. This is an area very popular with expats and tourists. And to stroll boulevard St Germain, or spend an evening on the Pont des Arts or in the Jardin Luxembourg is to understand why. This is the way newcomers to Paris often want the city to be; charming, pristine, safe and comfortable. With a long history of famous residents from Hemingway to Sartre it is an *arrondissement* that conjures images (often in black and white) of writers in cafes. Many of the cafes remain but most of that bohemian spirit has been lost with the sky-rocketing rents and tour buses.

Best Points
Physically beautiful, safe, well-taken care of and home to some of the city's most famous cafes, boulevards and monuments; the 6th looks like the Paris of the movies.

Accommodation

Expensive. Very expensive. Because of its popularity, location, history, conveniences and beauty, prices are high and getting higher. Your euro will go much further in just about every other part of Paris and you'll be stunned to discover how little you get for a lot of money in this part of town. However, if you can afford to choose where and how you live, you will be living among French politicians, publishers, famous writers, actors and designers. Apartments facing Jardin du Luxembourg or place St Sulpice are rare but worth the search. Equally difficult to find, and more expensive, are those around the Institut de France. Keep in mind that living around Odéon can be very noisy at all hours of the day or night and that living in this part of the 6th means battling waves of tourists from May through to September.

Worst Points
Absolutely packed with tourists from April to October; the 6th can feel a bit like Disneyland and English often seems to be the dominant language; not the place to live if you're looking to blend in with the locals.

Shopping & Amenities

From small, independent boutiques along rue du Four to one of the world's most famous and exclusive department stores, Le Bon Marché (p.292), the 6th offers shoppers endless choices. For simple, inexpensive clothes, furniture, houseware and stationery, Muji (27 rue St Sulpice, 01 46 34 01 10) is a good place to start. Beautiful

Jardin du Luxembourg

The Complete **Residents'** Guide

bespoke shirts at JLR (28 rue St Sulpice, 01 40 46 06 77) are reasonably priced and of excellent quality. One of the world's best food markets is the obscenely expensive La Grande Epicerie (p.261). If you're in the market for a fashionable sex toy, stop by Sonia Rykiel Woman (6 rue Grenelle, 01 49 54 66 21) where the famous designer has created a classy St-Germain des Prés sex shop.

Entertainment & Leisure

One of the most beautiful places to spend any time at all is the Pont des Arts and a summer evening here with a bottle of wine is magical. Jardin du Luxembourg (p.184), is a flawless park and offers some of Paris' best people-watching.

Apartments in the 6th

Famous cafes abound; Café de Flore (p.337), Café des Deux Magots (p.339) are two of many grand cafes. Both offer absurd prices, gorgeous terraces and wonderful people watching. Both are a long way from their heydays but it's possible to spend a winter's afternoon without feeling too much like a tourist. During the summer on the other hand you'll be squeezed in with people struggling with maps, being sneered at by fed-up waiters.

Education

France's most famous art school, l'École Nationale Supérieure des Beaux-Arts is on rue Bonaparte. And one of France's best language schools, the Alliance Francaise (101 boulevard Raspail, 01 42 84 90 00) is also in the 6th. The private university, l'Institut Catholique (21 rue d'Assas, 01 44 39 52 52) offers an excellent French language programme.

Healthcare

There are two major health clinics, the Centre de Santé Saint Michel (p.113) and the Institut Arthur Vernes (36 rue d'Assas, 01 44 39 53 00).

Transport

Most of the 6th is well-served by public transportation. However, the south-west corner is markedly less so. Parking, on the other hand, is far better on the southern end than near the Seine where it is nearly impossible.

Safety & Annoyances

The 6th is very safe. If you're reasonably alert and experienced living in a city, this is one of the safest neighbourhoods in Paris. However, be aware of your surroundings, particularly during the summer when pickpockets cruise the tourist-heavy areas.

78

Map p.397, p.398
Area **G** *p.68*

7th

The 7th spreads out like a clam shell from the southern end of avenue de Breteuil, north-east and west towards the Seine. Bourgeois, quiet and wealthy, it's expensive, safe and conservative. With the exception of the area on the border of the 15th, the streets are dead at night. Most of the government ministries are here which means a constant security presence. The area is attractive, but overall soulless and lacking any kind of real energy – not the place for people who crave an active streetlife or an artistic energy.

Best Points
Quiet, safe, clean residential neighbourhoods with beautiful parks and river views; Paris' most famous landmark is here.

Accommodation

The north-western corner is very expensive, and property prices towards the Seine rival those in the 6th. The same is true around the Champ de Mars. The areas away from the river and the 6th are less expensive. The 7th is good for families; with many parks and good parking the area provides a suburban feel in the heart of Paris.

Worst Points
Dull, bourgeois, often empty streets; not particularly diverse and nearly no streetlife.

Shopping & Amenities

Rue Cler is an excellent market street offering superb food shopping. One of the finest boulangeries in Paris is Stéphane Secco (20 rue Jean Nicot, 01 43 17 35 20) where you will find extraordinary breads and pastries. For the latest in modern furniture, the Conran Shop (117 rue de Bac, 01 42 84 10 01) is a good source. One of the best chocolate stores in the city, Debauve et Gallais (30 rue St Pères, 01 45 48 54 67), looks more like a jewellery store and sells chocolate covered ginger among other delicious things.

Entertainment & Leisure

The Champs de Mars and the Esplanade des Invalides offer great views of the Eiffel Tower, and are good places to run or take kids. Both are excellent places to have a picnic and spend a summer's day. The Musée d'Orsay (p.171) as well as the Musée Rodin (p.178) are both in the 7th offering exquisite art in spectacular environments. One of the city's finest restaurants, Arpege (84 rue Varenne, 01 47 05 09 06) maintains three Michelin stars, or for something more simple, have dinner at Café du Marché (38 rue Cler, 01 47 05 51 27) and stay after for drinks. The restaurant at the new Musée Branly, Les Ombres (27 quai Branly, 01 47 53 68 00) offers some of the finest views in Paris from one of its most beautiful rooms.

Education

Paris' biggest military school, l'École Militaire faces the Eiffel Tower. The American University of Paris (p.122) is here too, providing classes in English and offers BA/BS degrees. The Lennen Bilingual School (p.121) offers bilingual education for grades K-3.

Healthcare

Air France operates a busy international vaccination centre (01 43 17 22 00) at 148 rue de L'université. The Hôpital St Jean de Dieu (15 rue Oudinot) is a small hospital in the southern end.

Transport

Parts of the 7th are not very well-served by public transportation and without a car, you may find yourself doing a lot of walking to your metro stop each morning, or making several changes to get to work. On the other hand, parking is better here than other areas and many of the apartment buildings have good parking nearby or provide it.

Safety & Annoyances

The area is about as safe as you can get, though you should always be alert when walking alone at night. It's often difficult to find a taxi.

Map p.387
Area **H** p.68

8th

Home to the Champs-Élysée and wealthy foreign residents, the 8th is one of the few Paris neighbourhoods where obnoxious displays of wealth are common. Ferraris roar up avenue George V and money seems to be everywhere in the Golden Triangle – the area bordered by avenues Montaigne and Georges V and the Champs-Élysée. The 8th lacks a cohesive sense of community, but it can be very appealing. The Parc Monceau (p.186) is lovely as are the beautiful Haussmann-era apartment buildings lining the wide avenues.

Best Points

Picture-perfect avenues, lovely views, exclusive shopping, superb restaurants and wonderful parks; a very comfortable place to live for the wealthy.

Accommodation

Predictably, apartments within the *Triangle d'Or* are exorbitant, as is any property below the Champs-Élysée. However, as you move west away from rue de Courcelles prices tend to drop quickly and it is still possible to find very attractive housing around boulevard Malsherbes. Of course, the closer you get to Parc Monceau the less likely you are to find reasonably priced apartments. Near Gare St Lazare property value is far lower.

Worst Points

Can be dangerous around the Gare St Lazare; the flashy cars, relentless traffic and throngs of tourists along the Champs-Élysée drive many away.

Shopping & Amenities

The shopping is world famous along avenue Montaigne and, of course, along the Champs-Élysée. Sadly, the Champs has quickly come to resemble a generic (albeit a beautiful) mall, with Adidas, Virgin, McDonalds and the other usual suspects now present. Fast losing its appeal, there's a movement to bring back some of its independence and charm. If you have money to spend, you'll find every luxury brand in the world available between avenues George V and Montaigne. Drugstore Publicis (133 avenue des Champs-Élysée, 01 44 43 79 00) is good for sandwiches, prescriptions and designer handbags.

Entertainment & Leisure

There's no shortage of restaurants, bars and clubs in the 8th. Taillevent (p.323) is a Paris institution and one of the city's most expensive restaurants, serving exquisite food flawlessly prepared. If you can get in, Le Baron (p.360) is one of the city's coolest, most exclusive and pretentious clubs. For high quality Lebanese food, Al Diwan (30 avenue George V, 01 47 23 45 45) is a good bet. The Parc Monceau (p.186) is a beautiful park full of wealthy schoolkids during the week and a good place for a run or a picnic.

Education

The Bilingual Montessori School (p.119) offers year-long programmes to toddlers aged 2-6 at 23 avenue George V.

Healthcare

The full-service medical and dental centre Centre Medical COSEM (15 rue Rome, 01 42 94 14 11) offers a variety of in and out patient services. For specialised testing, Montaigne Santé (53 avenue Montaigne, 01 42 25 60 31) provides bilingual care.

Star Driver

Driving l'Etoile, Paris' famous giant roundabout which circles the Arc de Triomphe, can be terrifying and frustating. Try to stay calm, and keep an eye on your mirrors!

Transport

Public transport is excellent; Charles De Gaulle–Etoile serves as a major transport hub as does Gare St Lazare. Taxis are plentiful and there's no shortage of buses. Parking is expensive and difficult. Traffic can be awful in the southern section; less so in the north.

Safety & Annoyances

Although parts of the 8th are very wealthy, it lacks a sense of neighbourhood and petty crime can be high – particularly along the Champs-Élysée where crowds of young thugs spend their time looking for victims. Walking along the famous avenue can be unsettling on a weekend evening. Be careful too around Gare St Lazare. The traffic congestion during rush hour can be intense around Etoile, along the river and on the bridges.

Map p.388, p.389
Area **J** p.68

9th

Spread out like a butterfly in the centre of the city, the 9th can be scrappy, dull, lively and scruffy, depending on where you're living. Vastly less expensive than any of the first eight *arrondissements*, the 9th offers newcomers wide variety in nearly every realm. The neighbourhood around place St George and rue des Martyrs has experienced a recent resurgence and maintains a cosy feeling. As you move north and north-west the 9th becomes increasingly working-class and, in parts, much less safe.

Best Points

Aside from the famous shopping along boulevard Haussmann, the increasingly hip 9th is relatively untouched by tourists; neighbourhoods retain their charm and much remains to be discovered here.

Accommodation

The 9th is a good place to find a deal. From rue de Chateaudun the streets begin to climb upwards toward Montmartre which means you might find yourself in an apartment with a view of the city. Most desirable are the areas around place St George and west, rue des Martyrs, and the south-west corner which borders the 2nd. There are discoveries to be made to the north of St Trinité but the 9th isn't nearly as refined as other *arrondisements* so you'll be far from the expat ghettos of other areas.

Worst Points

Still very gritty and, in certain corners, dangerous, not a green space to be found.

Shopping & Amenities

One of the best market streets is rue des Martyrs which climbs steeply toward Pigalle, while Galeries Lafayette (p.291) and Printemps (p.292), along with shops like Zara and H&M, cover the area around boulevard Haussmann. If you're looking for something more independent try Wochdom (72 rue Condorcet, 01 53 21 09 72) an excellent vintage clothing store. The internationally famous auction house Drouot has several addresses along rue Drouot; exploring this area you'll find auctions of all shapes and sizes from coins to art. Cinedoc (01 48 24 71 36) sells all things cinema in their lovely shop at 45 passage Jouffroy. After being entirely renovated, the swimming pool Georges Drigny (18 Bochart de Saron, 01 42 76 78 04) reopened in 2007.

Entertainment & Leisure

One of the main problems with the 9th is that it lacks open space; there isn't a single park of note in the entire *arrondissement*. That said, the views can be lovely as you go up the hill. There are endless nightlife options towards Blanche, but remember that those very friendly women around Pigalle only find you charming if you have money to spend. Around the Opéra Garnier you'll find a lot of post-work happy hours. To the north is a far funkier, more interesting scene. For excellent, authentic pizza La Pizzetta (22 avenue Trudaine, 01 48 78 14 08) is the place – some say it has the best pizza in Paris. One of the best of the grand cafes is the Café de la Paix (01 40 07 36 36) on place de l'Opéra.

Healthcare

Centre Médical Europe (44 rue Amsterdam, 01 42 81 93 33) offers complete medical services, as does Centre Médical et Dentaire Opéra (01 44 51 68 28) but with the added benefit of dental services.

Transport

Well-served by public transport, St Lazare serves as a hub for both commuter trains and metro. The north-western corner can be a bit isolated from metro service but the bus service is excellent. Not particularly car friendly, the 9th is hilly and can often be choked with traffic around Opéra and along boulevard de Clichy.

Safety & Annoyances

The 9th is generally less safe than the previous *arrondissements* and to live here means being on guard more often. However, if you're used to big city living you'll be fine. In the northern corners and along boulevard de Clichy you should be particularly aware.

Map p.390
Area **K** p.69

10th

In a very short time parts of the 10th have gone from grubby, to edgy, to cool, to drastically hip. Those who keep track say the 10th is over. All of which is to say that the area around Canal St Martin has undergone a major gentrification. While it isn't the Seine, Canal St Martin provides a lovely backdrop for a burgeoning community of young families and hipsters too lazy to move on to the next edgy quarter. But the 10th is bigger than the Canal St Martin and it still has its share of unattractive, rough and tumble areas. On the other hand, those areas are home to a variety of immigrant communities providing wonderful restaurants and shopping not found in the centre of the city. If you can find a place on the Canal St Martin you'll have the luxury of open space and water, without paying the prices of Seine-side housing.

Best Points
Thriving neighbourhoods full of great streetlife, restaurants, bars and shops; a lively, exciting place to live.

Worst Points
Rapidly gentrifying neighbourhood, which means quickly rising rents and real estate prices; many corners are still dangerous and downright ugly; can be very noisy and congested.

Accomodation

The most desirable neighbourhood runs along the canal from rue de Lancry north towards La Villette. As the area expands and gentrifies, property north along the canal will become more expensive. For those who are looking for an investment, consider buying along the canal around Louis Blanc which is not as polished as its southern neighbours. Rent in the 10th varies widely: inexpensive around the Gare de l'Est and Gare du Nord; more expensive the closer you get to the 2nd and 3rd. The neighbourhood around Chateau d'Eau is unsafe, particularly at night, and not at all recommended.

Shopping & Amenities

Along and around Canal St Martin there is wonderful shopping. Antoine et Lili (95 quai Valmy, 01 40 37 41 55) offers several canal-side storefronts offering quirky clothes for women and kids and assorted housewares. There's also a tea room and bakery. Boutiques become furniture stores and end up as bookstores in the ever-changing Canal St Martin neighbourhood and it's a great place to wander on a weekend.

Entertainment & Leisure

Chez Prune (36 rue Beaurepaire, 01 42 41 30 47) has been around for years and still draws a fun crowd. For something more upscale, have a drink at the Hôtel du Nord (102 quai de Jemmapes, 01 40 40 78 78) made famous by Marcel Carné's film of the same name. Long walks along the canal or a bike ride are recommended ways to spend Sunday afternoons. Further north is the Point Ephemere (200 quai de Valmy, 01 40 34 02 48), a performing arts centre where you can see anything from international DJs and rockers to art expositions.

Healthcare

Hôpital St Louis (see table on p.111), a major city hospital, sits just across the canal from Chez Prune.

Residential street in the 10th

Transport

The 10th is well-served by metro and train; République, Gare de l'Est and Gare du Nord provide access to anywhere in the city. Traffic can be heavy around the stations and on boulevard Magenta, but otherwise isn't as bad as other quarters.

Safety & Annoyances

The 10th has its share of problems and even along the canal you're best to be alert in the evening. Generally you should avoid the area around Chateau d'Eau and be particularly aware behind the Hôpital Saint Louis. The boulevard Magenta to the north can also be iffy at night.

Map p.401
Area ⓛ p.69

Best Points
Exciting neighbourhoods with wonderful streetlife; great nightlife, music and art scene; excellent transportation.

Worst Points
Loud, chaotic and often gritty and choked with traffic; not always safe at night in certain corners.

11th

One of the most exciting and interesting *arrondissements*, the 11th offers a wonderful array of restaurants, bars, cafes, galleries, architecture and open markets. From the Opéra Bastille, the area spreads north and west like a fan and there's something for nearly everyone here. While the Oberkampf area, once the height of cool, has become overrun with chintzy bars, Bastille seems to be succumbing quickly to the fate of St Michel with its crush of fastfood and generic bars and there is still much to discover there. This is an excellent place to live if you want your city life to be noisy, unpredictable and influenced by people from all over the world.

Apartments in the 11th

Accommodation

Not long ago property was very inexpensive but over the last 10 years prices have risen rapidly. Still, compared to more central *arrondissements*, you'll find things reasonable. The most desirable areas are Oberkampf in the north and Faidherbe-Chaligny in the south. The closer you get to Nation the less lively and more residential the neighbourhoods become. Also desirable and quite expensive are the areas around Chemin Vert and Filles du Calvaire which border the 3rd. Real estate agents have begun to call this pocket of the 11th 'the Marais' and indeed if you find a nice apartment reasonably priced between Bastille and Filles du Calvaire its worth some serious consideration. The closer you get to place des Vosges the more expensive.

Shopping & Amenities

One of Paris's best vintage shops, Come on Eileen (16-18 rue Taillandiers, 01 43 38 12 11) near Ledru Rollin sells beautiful clothes in near-perfect condition. For superb organic bread, l'Autre Boulange (43 rue de Montreuill, 01 43 72 86 04) is a cozy and charming bakery selling a wide variety of breads not often found in standard Parisian *boulangeries*. The Wine Loft (100 rue de la Folie Méricourt, 01 44 73 97 80) sells a great selection of French wines. For a well-equipped, reasonably priced gym, Body Gym (157 rue du Faubourg Saint-Antoine, 01 43 42 42 33) is a good bet.

Entertainment & Leisure

With no shortage of eating or drinking establishments the 11th is a great place to live if you like to go out. To the east you'll find Père Lachaise (p.167), not technically in the *arrondissement* but on the border and easy to access. Otherwise, there are few options if you want to spend an afternoon in the park. For a good meal in a cozy, traditional restaurant go directly to Cartet (62 rue de Malte, 01 48 05 17 65) for wonderful roast lamb. For great Moroccan food, Mansouria (11, rue de Faidherbe, 01 43 71 00 16) provides excellent and warm service. For something cool to drink, the Café Charbon (109 rue Oberkampf, 01 43 57 55 13) is a classic. One of the best places to see a live concert is the Café de la Danse (5 passage Louis Phillipe, 01 47 00 57 59).

Education

Rencontres et Echanges (84 rue de la Folie Mericourt, 01 53 36 81 10) provides a kindergarten and a bilingual nursery school for children between 18 and 30 months.

Healthcare

The closest major hospital is the Hôpital Saint-Antoine (p.112).

Transport

The 11th is very well-served by public transportation. Three major public transport hubs at République, Bastille and Nation combined with solid bus coverage allows quick access to anywhere in the city.

Safety & Annoyances

The 11th is a very busy, cramped and rapidly changing area and construction can seem endless along Faubourg Saint-Antoine, as can the traffic. The traffic at Bastille can be harrowing when it isn't at a standstill. The 11th is more or less a safe area but you'll need to be streetwise to live there; the bars and cafes around Bastille attract a variety of drunks, vagrants, junkies, pickpockets and tourists which is often a bad combination. Far calmer and safer are the areas around Faidherbe Chaligny and along boulevard Beaumarchais. Be particularly careful north-west of République.

Place de la Bastille

Rue du Faubourg

Residential street in the 11th

Map p.411, p.412
Area **M** p.69

12th

If you're looking for charming streets and picturesque cafes this isn't the place. The 12th has little to offer in terms of beauty or Parisian charm, but there's a lot of space, good parking and inexpensive housing. There's easy access to the city's largest *bois*, the Bois de Vincennes (p.184). Certain neighbourhoods are up and coming but most tend toward the nondescript and dull. A family might be very happy living in the east end, close to the Bois de Vincennes, in a large, inexpensive apartment with parking included.

Best Points

Relatively unexplored by tourists, the 12th offers a variety of benefits; quiet streets, local bars, good restaurants and excellent parks.

Accommodation

The most interesting, lively and charming part of the 12th is the area around avenue Ledru Rollin between avenue Daumesnil and rue du Faubourg Saint-Antoine. Here you'll have the wonderful Marché Alligre at your doorstep, the Bastille just down the street and the Seine within a quick walk. You'll find good restaurants and cafes and a real village feel. Otherwise, head to the Bois de Vincennes where you'll escape the crush of the city, have good chances with parking and access to more open space than most Parisians do.

Worst Points

Can feel far from central Paris; lacks the streetlife of other neighbourhoods; areas around the train tracks and Gare de Lyon are absent of atmosphere and can feel abandoned.

Shopping & Amenities

One of the best markets in Paris is the Marché Aligre on place d'Aligre. Here you can find tremendous personality and great variety; it's the perfect place to shop and to make friends with local vendors. The avenue Dausmenil provides some lovely shopping for original design in anything from furniture and fashion to flutes. The Cour St Emilion is an outdoor shopping plaza more American in feeling than anything you'll find in the city. Boutiques, restaurants and bars line the cobbled walkway. The Club Med Waou (45 rue des Pirogues de Bercy, 01 44 67 83 50) is one of the best gyms in the city.

Entertainment & Leisure

One of the most interesting, albeit little known, parks in Paris isn't really a park at all but a long garden walkway which runs from the Bastille to the Jardin de Reuilly. The Promenade Plantée (p.138) was created to make use of an abandoned bit of railway track, much of which runs along an elevated viaduct. Le Parc de Bercy is a beautifully maintained and landscaped modernist park, particularly attractive toward the Cour St Emilion. The entire neighbourhood around Bercy is in the throes of a resurgence, a sure sign of which is the recent addition of a Starbucks. For excellent Sardinian food, Sardegna a Tavola (1 rue de Cotte, 01 44 75 03 28) is the place. And for quality grilled meats, Les Broches á l'Ancienne (22 rue St Nicolas, 01 43 43 26 16) is superb. Le square Trousseau (1 rue Antoine-Vollon, 01 43 43 06 00) serves delicious bistro food overlooking a lovely square – a great place to go for lunch before or after shopping at the Marché Aligre.

Healthcare

There are four major hospitals spread across the 12th from the Bastille east: the Hôpitals Quinze Vingts (28 rue de Charenton, 01 40 02 16 04), Saint-Antoine (p.112), Rothschild (p.111) and Armand-Trousseau (p.110). If you need medical care this is the place to live!

Transport

The 12th is well-served in all directions with easy access to RER, metro, bus and train lines via the Gare de Lyon, Bastille, Nation and the nearby Gare d'Austerlitz. Parking tends to be better the further east you go.

Safety & Annoyances

This is a generally safe *arrondissement*, but you should be alert around the Bastille and along the many dark, empty streets at night. Also be cautious around the Gare de Lyon which, as is the case with most train stations, attracts petty thieves.

Map p.409, p.410, p.419 ◄
Area Ⓝ p.69

13th

Perhaps one of Paris' strangest *arrondissements* mixing perfectly cute villages with shockingly ugly high rises, the 13th offers everything from excellent restaurants and a booming modern art scene to rejuvenated riverfront. There's very little that's cohesive about the 13th – you can feel far from Paris wandering among the strange wasteland of the Porte d'Italie while only a few metro stops away you'll be overwhelmed by the charming village of the Butte Aux Cailles. Home to one of Europe's biggest and best Chinatowns, the 13th thrives with authentic and inexpensive restaurants and fantastic markets. The Bibliothèque Nationale de France (p.190) faces the river and has become the centrepiece of a growing riverfront neighbourhood.

Best Points ◄

The wonderful, hidden Buttes Aux Cailles neighbourhood; vast variety of Asian restaurants and markets spread out through the 13th; a thriving modern art scene.

Accommodation

The most expensive part of the 13th is that closest to the 5th. The Butte Aux Cailles neighbourhood, a lovely village made up of tiny houses and apartment buildings perched on a hill, is fast becoming the place to be. Also desirable is the area around Gobelins. If you want to gamble on riverfront property, consider the area around the Pont de Tolbiac. Generally, prices are less expensive as you move east. The south-eastern section of the 13th is gloomy and ugly; unless your love of Chinese culture and food trumps your need for aesthetic beauty, look elsewhere.

Worst Points ◄

Has some of the city's ugliest architecture – entire blocks of truly horrible buildings; far from the rest of Paris with mediocre public transportation.

Shopping & Amenities

For some of the best shopping in the city (and some of the least expensive) try the Tang Frères (several outlets including 48 avenue Ivry) an incredible Chinese supermarket with a huge selection specialising in Chinese products. Prices here are far cheaper than at other supermarkets and the products far more interesting. By no means is the Tang Frères the only place to shop; you will find all sorts of excellent stores, big and small here, and it is well-worth your time to explore. There is also a massive shopping centre at place d'Italie which includes a Club Med Gym, cinemas and the usual shopping mall fare.

Entertainment & Leisure

An evening out in the Butte Aux Cailles makes you feel what Paris might have been many years ago. The pace of life seems to be slower. There are excellent restaurants here; eating in Chinatown is a pleasure and an excellent escape from spiceless French cooking. Lao-Viet (24 boulevard Massena, 01 45 84 05 43) offers excellent, very inexpensive Laotian and Vietnamese food. With the installation by MK2 (one of France's leading cinema chains) of MK2 Bibliothèque (128-162 avenue de France, 01 56 61 44 04) the neighbourhood around the Bibliothèque Nationale François Mitterand is exploding with development. With 14 screens, four restaurants and three film and book boutiques, going to the cinema can be a full evening's experience.

Healthcare

The area is home to one of the city's largest hospitals, la Pitié-Salpetrière (p.112). Also, Hôpital Broca (p.111) provides full medical services.

Transport

A large portion of the 13th is poorly served by public transportation. If you decide to live here pay close attention to the distance you'll need to walk to find a metro. On the other hand, driving in the 13th is relatively painless.

Safety & Annoyances

The 13th is relatively safe, but be careful around the Porte d'Ivry and along the quais at night – no matter how fast the area is developing there are still dark corners to avoid.

Map p.408, p.418
Area **P** p.68

Best Points
Famous cafes, beautiful parks, great history, excellent restaurants and hidden pockets; great little museums.

Worst Points
Not very well-served by public transportation; the hideous Tour Montparnasse has created horrible neighbourhoods in its shadow.

14th

The 14th offers some lovely, charming neighbourhoods many of which feel like quiet villages and, with a long history of artist and writer residents, the *arrondissement* has managed to preserve a great deal of its quiet charm. Sadly, the once legendary boulevard Montparnasse has become overbuilt and increasingly ugly, but to the south there is much to discover. The Parc Montsouris (p.186) and the small streets to the north have changed little and offer a respite from busier, more hectic neighbourhoods. The Montparnasse cemetery is lovely and while some monstrous modern architecture (most notably the Tour Montparnasse) has scarred the landscape, the 14th has maintained a sense of identity. That so many legends lived, played and worked here is often reason enough for newcomers to set-up shop. Josephine Baker, Hemingway, F Scott Fitzgerald, Henry Miller, Sartre, James Joyce and Man Ray to name a few, were all residents for a time.

Accommodation

The prospect of living beneath the shadow of the Tour Montparnasse isn't very appealing to most. However, living here offers about as central and convenient a neighbourhood as is possible in the 14th. For more charm and more substance Pernety is an infinitely more interesting choice. The best place to live is near the Parc Montsouris on one of the little streets like rue Georges Braques and north. The Villa Seurat was fictionalised as the Villa Borghese in Henry Miller's *Tropic of Cancer* and the street still retains a quiet, magical feel. Generally, apartments or houses here are very hard to come by, but worth the search.

Shopping & Amenities

There's a bit of everything here. Around Montparnasse there are seedy sex shops, giant commercial centres, seemingly endless cinema and the grand cafes that have long ago lost their magic. To the south you'll find rue Daguerre with its superb outdoor market. One of the best hairstylists in the city and perhaps offering the best prices is Naoko (19 rue Delambre, 01 43 27 55 33). Just up the street is the exquisite fish shop, Poissonerie du Dome (4 rue Delambre, 01 43 35 23 95) where you'll find some of the best fish in the city.

A quiet street in the 14th

Entertainment & Leisure

Parc Montsouris (p.186) is perfect for spending a summer's day. Also recommended is a stroll through the Cimetiere du Montparnasse. If you're a fan of photography, one of the best small museums in the city is the Fondation Cartier-Bresson (2 impasse Lebouis, 01 56 80 27 00). The extraordinary Fondation Cartier (pour l'Art Contemporain) (p.156) provides exhibitions and performances throughout the year – both are off the beaten path. For a night of jazz, the Petit Journal (13 rue du Commandant René Mouchotte, 01 43 21 56 70) is a relaxed place with a fun, unpretentious crowd. For a superb, reasonably priced meal made by a culinary star, get a table at Le Régalade (49 avenue Jean Moulin, 01 45 45 68 58).

Transport

The 14th is well-served in the north but the south offers little in terms of metro service. Take particular note of the area between Porte d'Orleans and Porte de Vanves. This is a good place to have a car, with easy access to the ring road and southern suburbs.

Healthcare

There are six hospitals in the 14th: Léopold Bellan (19 rue Vercingoetroix, 01 40 48 68 68), Maternité Baudelocque et Port Royal (123 Port Royal), Sainte-Anne (1 rue Cabanis, 01 45 65 87 41), Saint Joseph (185 rue Lausserand, 01 44 12 33 33), Saint Vincent de Paul (82 avenue Denfert-Rochereau, 01 47 34 40 44) and Universitaire (42 boulevard Jourdan, 01 56 61 66 25).

Safety & Annoyances

This area is safe, but be alert in the dark, quiet streets in the south and particularly careful around the Porte de Vanves and the Porte d'Orléans. Around Montparnasse station can also be dangerous and is often full of drunks and beggars. Traffic can be awful in the north but is generally better in the south.

Apartments in the 14th

Map p.406, p.407
Area ⊙ *p.68*

15th

While far from being exciting, the 15th does offer calm, quiet residential neighbourhoods. More people live here than in any other *arrondissement,* but with so many quiet streets it doesn't feel that way. There's not a single major monument or tourist draw within the borders, although there is much within walking distance. As a result the 15th changes slowly and adapts more to local residents' needs than to tourists. With many parks and small squares throughout, this is a good place for families, but if you're craving energy and streetlife, look elsewhere.

Best Points
Great markets and restaurants; maintains a real local residential feeling; good nightlife; two lovely parks; well served by public transportation.

Accommodation

The most expensive, and often the most desirable, corner of the 15th is along avenue de Suffren near the Eiffel Tower and the Champ de Mars, but even here you need to be very careful; there are horrible modern apartments within a stone's throw of the Eiffel Tower. The La Motte-Piquet Grenelle areas can be busy and cramped, and remarkably different in feeling to their posh neighbours in the 7th. Finding an apartment in the 15th can be tricky as each street seems to have its own personality, and along the Seine there's a strange collection of Japanese tourist hotels which has sapped the area of its personality. Better and more lively neighbourhoods include rue du Commerce.

Worst Points
Can feel dull and empty in sections with the area around Gare Montparnasse seriously lacking in charm.

Shopping & Amenities

The Village Suisse (p.265) offers 150 boutiques selling very high-end antiques. There's an excellent outdoor food market at Dupleix beneath the elevated metro and the fantastic bakery Quartier du Pain (74 rue St Charles, 01 45 78 87 23) is worth a trip for the pistachio and cherry *tarte* alone. The very bourgeois rue de Commerce offers standard shopping with Gap and Zara among others lining the street. There's an excellent Club Med Waou Gym on the 22nd floor of the Hôtel Sofitel (8 rue Louis Armand).

Entertainment & Leisure

Parc André Citroen (p.185) is a modern park on the Seine, and Parc George Brassens (p.186) in the south-western corner is beautiful. Allée des Cygnes, the thin island in the Seine, is a nice place to spend an afternoon. For arguably the best Thai food in the city make a reservation at Erawan (76 rue de la Fédération, 01 47 83 55 67). For something more traditionally French, head for Le Petit Plat (49 avenue Emile-Zola, 01 45 78 24 20), and if you're in the mood for clubbing try Amnesia (24 rue de l'Arrivée, 01 56 80 37 37).

Education

The city's best known bilingual school, Ecole Active Bilingue (p.120), has a campus at 15 rue Edgar Faure. The American Kindergarten (3 bis rue Emile Duclaux, 01 42 19 02 14) offers an American-style kindergarten to children aged 3-5.

Healthcare

The 15th is home to four major hospitals, one of which, Necker - Enfants Malades (p.112), is specifically for children. The other three provide full services to adults and children: Hôpital Europeen G. Pompidou (p.111), Saint-Michel (p.113), and Vaugirard (p.111).

Transport

Much of the 15th is poorly served by the metro; there are huge areas that require long walks to a station, but usually the bus service makes up for it.

Safety & Annoyances

With the exception of the area around the above-ground metro, the 15th is quite safe. Traffic is bad between Bir Hakiem and Cambronne, but better towards the south-west.

Map p.395, p.404, p.405
Area **R** p.68

16th

Home to a disproportionate amount of expat families, particularly Americans, in terms of streetlife, diversity and culture, the 16th is about the least interesting *arrondissement* in the city. Very wealthy and scrubbed clean, you'll find enormous apartments and villas, expensive cars, dogs and clothes on display. Deeply conservative – both socially and politically – this is where the old money lives. If you're an artist of any kind or you seek a vibrant, unpredictable, exciting neighbourhood, keep on looking. But if you want something safe, quiet and staid, somewhere with gorgeous architecture and access to one of Paris' most beautiful parks, the 16th is the right place to live.

Best Points
Beautiful residential buildings; spectacular parks and views; great restaurants.

Worst Points
Inundated by Americans; dull, conservative and bland; very little in the way of nightlife and lacking a cafe scene.

Accommodation

If you have money to spend, or a company willing to spend it on you, you can find truly breathtaking apartments and houses here. place Victor Hugo is a magnet for expat families. English is spoken everywhere, and shopkeepers and waiters are usually bilingual. The English-speakers in the cafes are not tourists; they live here and have created a strong community. As a result you won't as often be treated as a tourist if you walk into a shop without speaking French well. Popular areas include avenue Foch, place and avenue Victor Hugo, and Trocadero (with spectacular views of the Eiffel Tower). With the Bois de Boulogne at your doorstep, the 16th can feel a lot like an urban suburb. With the exception of Auteuil, which is a dash less snooty and far more lively, the rest of the lovely streets are empty at night.

Shopping & Amenities

There's no end to the shopping. Anything you want (with the exception of anything 'ethnic') is here – the usual slate of luxury brands in Passy and along avenue Victor Hugo, a superb outdoor market on avenue du President Wilson, and fantastic speciality shops. For exquisite roast chickens you'll need to reserve one at the Boucherie Dufrenoy (11 rue Dufrenoy, 01 45 04 59 76). For excellent bread and pastries, Carton (150 avenue Victor Hugo, 01 47 04 66 55) is one of the best. For flawless croissants Bechu (118 avenue Victor Hugo. 01 47 27 97 79) will sell them to you as they once did to Aristotle Onassis. The best gym in the 16th is the Club Med Waou at 18 rue de Chanez (01 46 51 88 18). If you're a man looking for an excellent haircut, Pierre at Clémentine Coiffure (01 47 27 62 09) is your man.

Entertainment & Leisure

The Bois de Boulogne is a wonderfully beautiful expanse of lawns, lakes and trails and, on sunny days, you can take a rowing boat around the largest of the park's lakes. The amount of open space is a great luxury and it is easy to forget you're in the city. Not surprisingly, the 16th has its share of expensive, starred restaurants and perhaps the most famous of these is Astrance (4 rue Beethoven, 01 4050 8440), consistently ranked among the best restaurants in the world. For something less expensive, Paris Seize (18 rue des Belles Feuilles, 01 47 04 56 33) serves excellent Italian food in a cramped and convivial dining room. For a drink with an incredible view consider suffering some of the most pretentious service in the city and take a table on the terrace of the Café de l'Homme (17 place du Trocadero, 01 44 05 30 15) while an excellent bistro with excellent service is Le Stella (133 avenue Victor Hugo, 01 56 90 56 00).

Education

The International School of Paris (p.120) provides Pre-K to 12th grade education in English. The Bilingual Montessori School (p.119) offers the Montessori method to students in English. Eurecole (5 rue Lubeck, 01 40 70 12 81) offers trilingual (German, English and French) education to students from nursery school up to 7th grade. For a

90

Catholic education, Institut de la Tour (86 rue de la Tour, 01 45 04 73 35) is a private high school with an English speaking section.

Healthcare
The hospitals Henri Dunant (95 rue Michel Ange, 01 40 71 24 24) and Sainte-Périne (p.111) both provide full medical care.

Transport
Fairly well-served, Charles De Gaulle – Etoile serves as a major hub for both metro and RER lines, but there are sections, particularly towards the southern end, which are a long walk from public transportation. On the other hand, with the exception of Etoile and along the quais, traffic is not as bad as it is in other areas. If you have the money to live in the 16th you've probably got the money for parking.

Safety & Annoyances
While the 16th is generally very safe because there is so little streetlife, it is easy to find yourself alone on a dark street. No matter how nice the architecture, you should be aware of your surroundings, particularly around the Bois de Boulogne, which is somewhere to absolutely avoid after dark.

Housing options in the 16th

Map p.381, p.386, p.387
Area **S** p.68

17th

Unlike the 16th, the 17th offers tremendous diversity from the ultra-chic and upscale Parc Monceau to the truly gritty La Fourche. The leafy and very wealthy bourgeois neighbourhoods to the west, lined with lovely 19th century architecture, fade to the north-east and become less and less upscale until becoming entirely working class, dirty and full of character. The difference between the area around Parc Monceau and that around boulevard Bessieres is vast so there's something for every taste here.

Best Points

Tremendous variety – from the very expensive to the downright cheap; excellent restaurants, bars, cafes and markets spread out across the arrondissement; much to discover here.

Accommodation

To the south-west of boulevard Malsherbes property is very expensive, where neighbourhoods are sedate and rents are high. It's a good place to live with a family but the most up and coming neighbourhood is Batignolles, centred around the lovely square des Batignolles. This is a hip area, brimming with life, in the throes of a resurgence. There are interesting stores, good restaurants, and an increasingly lively cafe and bar scene so this is an excellent place to buy; a safe, growing neighbourhood with a strong sense of community. The further you move north, the less safe the area, but there are plenty of charming, if not a bit sketchy, streets around La Fourche and place de Clichy. The best bet if you're looking to invest, or for a good neighbourhood to settle in, is the quadrant formed by rue Boursault, rue Cardinet, avenue de Clichy and boulevard des Batignolles.

Worst Points

Out of the way; far from central Paris; dull in certain areas; dangerous in others.

Shopping & Amenities

Fantastic food shopping abounds. The market on avenue des Ternes is as good as any in the city, the market street of rue de Levis is also superb as is the covered Marché Batignolles. Boulangerie Conan (38 rue Batignolles) serves some of the best baguettes in Paris. There's a Club Med Waou gym at 1 place du General Koenig (01 40 68 00 21).

Entertainment & Leisure

Parc Monceau (p.186) is one of Paris' most beautiful parks; crowded on weekends, there's excellent people watching here. Square de Batignolles is a good place for a quiet weekend stroll. For the best kebab in all of Paris, Doner Kebab (43 rue des Batignolles) is the place. Two of Paris' finest restaurants Michael Rostang, (20 rue Rennequin, 01 47 63 40 77) and Guy Savoy (18 rue Troyon, 01 43 80 40 61) are not to be missed if you can afford not to miss them. For a drink on a sunny afternoon grab a table outside at l'Endroit (67 place Doctor Félix Lobligeois, 01 42 29 50 00), and for solid fare in a great neighbourhood bistro overseen by the friendly Eddy Santini, visit Le Manoir (7 rue Moines, 01 46 27 54 51).

Education

Les Petit Dragons (01 42 28 56 17) is an international kindergarten at 2 rue Jacquemont.

Healthcare

Centre Médicale et Dentaire (12 avenue Grande Armée, 01 43 80 48 07) provides full medical and dental care in a private clinic.

Transport

One of the main drawbacks to living in the 17th is the lack of metro service. There are vast areas that have no service at all with only three lines that run through the *arrondissement*, and even the bus service is thin. Parking can be very difficult as well, though traffic is reasonably mild except around Porte Maillot and place de Clichy.

Safety & Annoyances

The 17th runs the gamut from very safe to quite dangerous. Generally, be careful around place de Clichy and anywhere north of the La Forche Metro.

Map p.382, p.383, p.384 ◀

Area ❶ *p.69*

18th

Though the 18th is best known for Montmartre and its accompanying tourist attractions, the majority of the *arrondissement* is made up of working-class immigrants. There is a large African community, centred around rue de la Goutte d'Or and northwards, where you'll find a vibrant neighbourhood full of restaurants specialising in everything from Senagalese food to Cote d'Ivoire cooking. While Montmartre is a heavy tourist draw there are plenty of Parisians here. As with St-Germain des Prés and Montparnasse, Montmartre has a wonderful history of artist and writer residents – most notably Pablo Picasso, who lived and worked here for many years.

Best Points ◀
Some of Paris' most famous landmarks and views, including Sacré Coeur and Moulin Rouge; charming, beautiful streets; exciting night life; great street scene.

Accommodation

The most desirable neighborhood in the 18th lies between Sacré Coeur and rue Caulaincourt, with boulevard de Clichy as the southern border. The further you get away from Pigalle the more charming and less seedy the streets are. Less than 10 years ago there were deals to be found here but property has become increasingly expensive as the neighbourhood continues to clean up. Depending upon where you live and how close or far you are from a metro stop, living in the 18th can feel very far away from the rest of the city. On the other hand, the views from the hill are some of the best in the city, there is a real village feel and away from the tourist traps around Sacré Coeur, beautiful old cobbled streets host charming little cafes. If you can find a place with a view and a balcony, consider it seriously.

Worst Points ◀
Far from the centre of the city and from open spaces; can be very seedy in certain areas, and seriously dangerous in others; packed with tourists.

Shopping & Amenities

There's an excellent outdoor market on rue de la Goutte d'Or where you'll find a breathtaking variety of, well, everything. Prices are low and the exoticism is high. Tati, a chain of discount stores selling everything from wedding dresses to football boots has its most famous outlet on rue de Rochechouart. It is an experience not to be missed, but don't expect quality. The world's best flea markets are just outside the

Housing in Montmartre

18th, a short walk from the Porte de Clignacourt. The best gym around is the Club Montmartrois (60 rue Ordener, 01 42 52 50 50).

Entertainment & Leisure

Aside from the Cimetière de Montmartre there is little in the way of open green space. Keep this in mind when you're considering a charming apartment on a steep street; the neighbourhood can feel a bit claustrophobic. There's great eating and drinking here, however. A great place for a drink, a simple meal and a pose is Le Sancerre (35 rue des Abbesses, 01 42 58 08 20). La Fourmi (74 rue des Martyrs, 01 42 64 70 35) has been around forever and remains a reliable place for a drink. Next door, Le Divan du Monde (75 rue des Martyrs, 01 42 52 02 46), a former brothel, is one of the best small-venue concert halls in the city.

Education

Le Petit Cours (104 rue Ordener, 01 46 06 80 33) offers bilingual Pre-K up to Primary School for children from 2 years.

Healthcare

The Hôpital Bichat Claude-Bernard (p.110) provides full medical services.

Transport

Parking is practically impossible around Sacré Coeur; further to the north and north-east it's far better.

Safety & Annoyances

Although Pigalle has become trendy and a lot of money is being injected into this former village, crime is still a problem. Along boulevard de Clichy and Rochechouart be particularly aware. Generally you should avoid Chateau Rouge at night and be aware in areas north. This is not to say that these neighbourhoods are to be avoided – there's a vibrant, cultural life here, but remember when you're there that you're not in St-Germain des Prés.

Montmartre

94

Sacré Coeur

Map p.385, p.391
Area U p.69

Best Points

Relatively unexplored by expats, the nineteenth has lovely parks, a canal, and a wide diversity of residents.

Worst Points

Dangerous in places; scruffy and ugly in others; far from the city centre.

19th

The 19th is a little-known *arrondissement* that, depending upon the neighbourhood, can be a great place to live. It's important to choose carefully, however. Still a bit scruffy all over, the 19th is still awaiting the big resurgence that some of its neighbours have enjoyed. On the other hand because it's still on the fringes there are deals to be had and discoveries to be made. Home to everyone from immigrants to old-money families, there's something for everyone here.

Rue de Belleville

Accommodation

The most desirable place to live is around the lovely Buttes-Chaumont. There's little else to recommend with the exception, perhaps, of the area around Parc de la Villette though you'd need to be very sure of living here. The residential neighbourhoods around Buttes-Chaumont can offer calm and quiet living but not much else.

Shopping & Amenities

While not somewhere you'll want to spend much time at night, place des Fêtes has an excellent outdoor market. For one of the best wood-fired bakeries in the city, Véronique Mauclerc (83 rue Crimée, 01 42 40 64 55) makes incredible organic bread and pastries – an absolute artist. Club Rem Gym (72 rue Romainville, 01 42 49 59 59) has basic facilities.

Entertainment & Leisure

MK2 (7 Quai de la Loire) has two giant cinemas complete with shops, restaurants and a boat which gives movie-goers access to either side of the *quai*. La Villette (p.185), a hyper-modern park, hosts a combination of playgrounds, performance spaces, museums and concert halls. Fast becoming one of the city's cultural centres, it's a great place to bring kids or spend a summer evening watching free films on the giant screen. The Buttes-Chaumont (p.185) is a spectacular park and one of the best (and most dog-friendly) in the city. For classic food beside a fireplace, Relais des Buttes (86 rue Compans, 01 42 08 24 70) is a charming, cosy place.

Education

The Conservatoire National Superieur de Musique et de Danse de Paris (209 avenue Jean-Jaurès, 01 40 40 45 45) makes its home in Parc de la Villette.

Healthcare

The Hôpital Robert Debré (48 boulevard Sérurier) provides full medical services.

Transport

With only four metro lines covering a fairly large *arrondissement,* it's possible to feel stranded. Around the Buttes-Chaumont however there's good coverage both by bus and by metro. Parking is easy here (for Paris).

Safety & Annoyances

The 19th has a bad reputation and indeed there are many areas you should avoid. Stalingrad is a hangout for dealers, but around the Buttes-Chaumont it's relatively safe.

Map p.392, p.402
Area **V** p.69

Best Points

Lively, exciting, up and coming neighborhoods; a fresh cultural scene and a fantastic diversity reflected in the streetlife and restaurants; a diverse local population; great nightlife and the world's most famous cemetery – Père Lachaise.

Worst Points

Still scruffy around the edges; some truly depressing (and depressed) corners with a variety of dangerous areas; far from central Paris and not particularly well-served by public transportation.

20th

This is by far the coolest, hippest, most up and coming *arrondissement* in Paris. As with every city in the world, the cool follow the poor, who live where it's cheap, who are expelled by the trendy who drive the property value up. Nowhere in Paris is that more obvious than in the 20th. In the middle of a major resurgence, this *arrondissement* still has its share of scruffy neighbourhoods but if you want to invest, this is the place to do it. Far out of the way but with a wide variety of advantages to recommend it, this is a great place to live. With a thriving art and music scene, safe ethnic areas, the world's most famous cemetery and some lovely residential neighbourhoods the 20th is well worth a look.

Accommodation

The centre of the scene is around Menilmontant, from Gambetta north to rue de Belleville. Everywhere you look you'll see buildings, streets being redone, and property being sold fast. This is the new Canal St Martin some say, and others complain. Whatever your opinion about gentrification two things are true; it's inevitable and it's happening here. The place Gambetta is lovely and would be a great place to live with a family, while north along rue Sorbier and west towards the 11th is the centre of cool where hipsters are arriving in droves. Further north in Belleville, Paris' second largest Chinatown is rapidly getting cleaned up. Here you can get lovely views of the city, particularly from the Parc de Belleville. Though it'll be a few years before it's entirely cleaned up, buying around rue Piat might be an excellent investment. Further east is far less attractive with the exception of the little village of streets between the Hôpital Tenon and boulevard Mortier. While you'd be lucky if you had the opportunity to buy one, there are occasionally beautiful little houses for sale just south-east of Père Lachaise, where the neighbourhood becomes increasingly residential. Particularly nice are the streets around rue dest Vignoles and rue Vitruve.

Shopping & Amenities

The best thing about the 20th is that while there is plenty of cool and hip shop there are also Tunisian bakeries, Chinese markets, Senegalese bookstores, and Vietnamese, Chinese, Thai and Laotian (to name a few) restaurants. It's the various influences here that makes the area so appealing. One of the best and most diverse markets in the city is the Marché Belleville which runs along boulevard de Belleville. The best bakeries in the 20th are Au 140 (140 rue de Belleville, 01 46 36 92 47) and La Flute Gana (226 rue des Pyréneés, 01 43 58 42 62). Club Med Gym has an outlet near Bagnolet (63/65 rue de Bagnolet, 01 43 70 07 07). For truly everything, the Puces de Montreuil (avenue Montreuil) is an incredible flea market with a collection beyond the imagination – from toothbrushes to radios.

Entertainment & Leisure

Père Lachaise is always worth a stroll anytime of year. The Parc de Belleville (p.185) is

Apartments in the 20th

increasingly attractive and more and more people spend their days lying in the sun on its lawns. The lovely village Charonne feels far from everything and is great for a glass of wine. For an excellent, utterly unpretentious bistro try Bistro des Soupirs (49 rue de la Chine, 01 44 62 93 31). La Fleche d'Or (p.347) was *the* club well before the *New York Times* wrote about it, while La Maroquinerie (p.347) is a great place to see live music. Have a Sunday brunch at the Café Fontaine (2 place Gambetta, 01 43 66 32 75).

A neighbourhood park in the 20th

Healthcare
Hôpital Tenon (p.111) provides full medical care.

Transport
Much of the 20th isn't served by metro so be careful when you're looking for an apartment. Bus service is also spotty but traffic isn't bad and parking is easy.

Safety & Annoyances
Be on your guard toward place des Fêtes and east to Porte des Lilas and also around Porte de Bagnolet. Belleville and Menilmontant are in flux and it is important to remember that just because the neighbourhood is hip, doesn't make it always safe. There's a great deal of construction going on here and plans for even more so make sure you know what's next in the neighbourhood before you sign.

Beyond The Périphérique

If you're moving to Paris with your family, or you'd like more space than is usually possible in the city, consider living in one of the suburbs that surround Paris. The most exclusive (and most populated by wealthy expats) of these are Neuilly-sur-Seine (home to the Marymount International School and the American Hospital), Boulogne, St Cloud (home to the American School of Paris), St Mandé and Vincennes. All of these share similar advantages; they're quiet, safe, often very attractive and are in close proximity to parks and countryside.

The suburbs in the west have the added advantage of being close to several of Paris' largest international schools. Here it is possible to find accommodation far closer to what you might be used to at home. If you have the money, you can find houses with gates and yards and driveways. You can join country clubs and stroll quiet suburban streets and generally live a safe suburban life within a quick drive to your children's schools.

There are other suburbs which are less exclusive and more interesting – both Montreuil and Montrouge are good examples of places that attract a more diverse group of residents and offer more in the way of culture and cafe life. Keep in mind that if you're a staunch Republican you might think twice about moving your family to Montreuil: the city government is officially Communist and the headquarters of France's most powerful ultra liberal labour union, the CGT, is based here.

Further from Paris, Versailles and St Germain-en-Laye both draw a large community of North American and British residents. St Germain-en-Laye is particularly convenient given that it is home to an international school with a full American section.

It's also possible to find charming little villages not far from Paris. While these are often not served by direct public transportation, life here can feel genuinely foreign and authentic in a way that living in St Cloud will not.

Keep in mind that many of the suburbs around Paris, while safe, are profoundly unattractive and soulless. Generally speaking, stay away from the northern suburbs which are generally unpleasant and home to increasing tension and violence.

97

Setting up Home

Once you've decided on where you'll live and in what kind of accommodation, you'll be ready for what can be the most enjoyable part of moving to Paris – making your home, furnishing it, and, finally, actually living in this magical city. For your own sanity, remember that things move slowly here and that customer service is a rare privilege, not a right. Expect the worst and occasionally you'll be pleasantly surprised.

Relocation Companies		
A Good Start In France	01 45 50 25 30	www.agoodstart.fr
Cosmopolitan Services Unlimited	01 44 90 10 10	www.cosmopolitanservices.com
Crown Relocations	01 45 73 66 00	www.crownrelo.com
Executive Relocations	01 47 55 60 29	www.executive-france.com
France Global Relocations	01 53 20 01 01	www.fgrelocation.com
Paris Relocation Service	01 53 30 41 19	www.prs.fr

Moving Services

Unless you've hired a relocation service to take care of the move, you'll be on your own and the success will be due to your tenacity and ingenuity as much as anything else. Moving services are readily available and there seems to be an ever-growing list of services available. If you can afford a relocation service, particularly if you don't speak French well, you should seriously consider employing their services. On the other hand, if you already live in Paris or are simply moving a few things to your apartment you might consider either renting a van or finding someone 'off the books' to do it for you. Paris is full of people who would be happy to find work doing anything at all – ask around, someone always knows someone. Of

Removal Companies		
AVS	01 43 66 66 10	www.avsdemenagement.com
Clark & Rose	01 44 30 03 30	www.clarkandrose.co.uk
Crown Relocations	01 45 73 66 00	www.crownrelo.com
ParisDem	01 43 67 70 40	www.parisdem.com
STPS	01 43 67 00 11	www.stps-star.com

course, if you're moving a precious antique desk, get it done professionally; undocumented labourers don't offer insurance. Moving is expensive in general and shipping is very expensive. You have to consider whether you'd rather spend €5,000 moving your own furniture to Paris or spend that money in the Paris flea markets or in one of the many ultra-modern design stores. All of this depends on your taste and your level of sentimentality.

Furnishing Your Home

It is possible to rent (and occasionally buy) a furnished apartment. If you're only planning on staying in Paris for a limited time, consider renting a furnished flat as this is the easiest and most convenient way to move to the city. Of course, your taste may not always match your landlord's and your version of furnished may not quite be the same as that of the French. The same is true with unfurnished flats; it's not uncommon for the previous tenant to take everything they added – from extra locks to entire kitchens. Make sure you're very clear about what you're getting before you sign anything. The cheapest and most convenient way to furnish your apartment is to make a trip to one of the several IKEAs throughout the city (p.265) but people are always leaving Paris so it's not difficult to find 'everything must go fast' moving-out sales. Craigslist (www.paris.craigslist.org) and FUSAC (www.fusac.fr) are both excellent web sources, as is eBay (www.ebay.fr). Rich or poor, Paris is a playground for the home decorator – from Armani Casa to street sales.

Many employers provide general moving-in allowances which you can use at your discretion, and corporate housing is often offered fully-furnished.

Happy Shopper
The Shopping chapter starting on p.241 is chock full of information on what and where to buy, including a section on Home Furnishings & Accessories.

Second-Hand Sales

The second hand market in Paris is booming. Les Puces St-Ouen (p.296), the most famous flea market in the world, is extraordinary and often extraordinarily expensive. Throughout the year there are endless *brocantes* and *vide greniers*, essentially organised neighbourhood sales where vendors sell, well, everything. Prices vary considerably and they are usually advertised with flyers.

Tailors

Other options **Tailoring** p.284

The city is full of exquisite fabric stores. At open air markets and flea markets you'll often find people (generally called *tapissiers*) set up with samples of their upholstery and swatches of possible fabrics. Bring your chairs and expect to get them back the next week, in the same place.

Tailors			
B et S Décoration	97 rue Jouffroy d'Abbans	17th	01 46 36 66 80
Confort et Harmonie	78 rue Pierre Demours	17th	01 46 22 59 41
Coté Maison	15 rue Convention	15th	01 45 78 03 67
CPM Artisans	8 rue Boulets	11th	01 43 73 61 99
Fernand Letivant	79 rue Menilmontant	20th	01 46 36 66 80

Household Insurance

Household insurance is not an option in France; if you live somewhere you must, by law, carry household insurance. Break-ins are not uncommon, particularly in expensive neighbourhoods. If you plan to furnish your apartment expensively you might consider supplemental insurance, but generally speaking insurance isn't expensive at all, with a basic policy costing aroung €100 per year. As a tenant you're responsible for any damage (such as fire and water) which originates from your apartment and this includes not only your apartment, but the entire building. The minimum coverage allowed by law covers any damage caused by the tenant to the property, however, it is advisable to buy multi-risk

Household Insurance		
AGF	01 45 96 36 10	www.agf.fr
AXA	01 42 22 02 29	www.axa.fr
Chubb	01 70 36 65 00	www.chubb.com
GAN	01 48 74 40 20	www.gan.fr
MAAF	08 20 30 08 20	www.maaf.fr

insurance which will cover your own property as well. If you need to file a claim, contact your insurance agent immediately both by telephone and registered letter (*recommandé*). If something has been stolen you'll need to prove that you owned it. As with all official processes in France, documentation is the key so take photographs and keep receipts.

Laundry Services

While it is common to find washing machines in French homes, you'll find that dryers are far less common, but this is changing and more and more you'll find compact combination washer/dryer units. Laundrettes are available throughout the city, as are *pressings* where you can have dry-cleaning done as well as basic laundry. Keep in mind that these tend to be far more expensive than in other cities. Many dry-cleaners will deliver your clothes to your home, but rarely free of charge. Most dry-cleaners have a prominently posted sign warning that they're not responsible for damage done to zippers, buttons and other adorning items. Prices vary widely between neighbourhoods.

Domestic Help

Only the very wealthy employ live-in maids or staff in Paris, but regular maid service is quite common. All services are available, from uniformed live-in maids to once a month cleaning services. As always, in Paris you can have anything you can afford. There are reliable agencies that provide full domestic services. Alternately, a good option (and often less expensive) is to

Domestic Help Agencies		
Adhap	01 40 60 90 04	www.adhap.fr
Adom	08 10 12 21 29	www.adom.fr
Adomo	08 10 26 25 24	www.adomo.fr
Menage	08 00 60 66 06	www.menage.fr
Shiva	08 11 46 46 46	www.shiva.fr

ask for a reference from your building's *concierge*. Depending upon their responsibilities, maids are paid, on average, €20 per hour and are hired nearly exclusively on a part-time basis. Keep in mind that 50% of what you pay for domestic help is tax deductible.

Babysitting & Childcare

Babysitting and childcare services are abundant in Paris. The English-speaking mothers support group, Message (www.messageparis.org) is an excellent resource for parents with small children. There are three possibilities to consider when searching for childcare: agencies based in France, home-based agencies and independent babysitters. Assitantes Maternelles are registered childcare providers who take care of children in their own homes. For information contact your local *mairie*. Créches are available in every town and *arrondissement* in France and offer

Babysitting & Childcare		
La Bambinerie	01 42 80 64 88	www.labambinerie.fr
La Compagnie des Familles	01 40 21 22 24	www.lacompagniedesfamilles.fr
Reves d'Enfants	01 45 74 11 23	www.revesdenfants.fr
Ti Doudou	01 55 79 06 06	www.tidoudou.fr

government-funded childcare. Space is limited so if you're interested you should register the minute you discover you're pregnant. Your *mairie* also provides *haltes garderies* which are very inexpensive and offer childcare on a part-time basis. For independent babysitters, the American Church (p.17) and the American University (p.122) are both good places to look so check their bulletin boards. Your *concierge* is also a good resource.

Domestic Services

One advantage to living in a building with a *concierge* is that if you need a plumber or an electrician they'll know who to call and will often make the arrangements for you. If you don't have a *concierge* and you have a plumbing problem you should call your landlord before anyone else, unless it's an emergency. Technically your landlord is responsible for repairing anything in the apartment that he owns. Often, however, this is a battle and can take repeated phone calls or letters to finally have that leak fixed. If you find yourself needing the services of a domestic specialist after working hours, wait (if you can) for the next day. Locksmiths in particular are notorious for charging extortionate prices late at night when all you want to do is get inside. In general, everyone charges more for after hours calls. In the case of a locksmith, you might consider calling your local police department for recommendations.

If you do have a domestic problem that requires a specialist make sure that you contact your landlord before you make any plans. Normally the property owner (or manager) will have a roster of plumbers and electricians that they work with and they'll need to sign off on any costs before the work is done.

If you do need to find someone yourself, Paris-based companies RCB Batiment (06 80 75 67 21), Etablissement Moshin (06 80 59 84 66) and Home Improvement Renovation (06 32 62 51 14) all offer English-speaking carpentry, design and renovation services.

DVD & Video Rental

More and more, full-service DVD and video rental shops are giving way to ATM style DVD machines. Online DVD rental has not caught on in France the way it has in other countries and there are still a handful of excellent, albeit struggling, specialist shops which often require an annual membership. Prime Time Vidéo is an excellent DVD and video rental store which specialises in films in English so it's a good place to go if you're looking for the English version of that French film you couldn't understand. Vidéo Fast has a great selection of DVDs for rent and sale while La Onzieme Heure has a vast selection of classic films. FNAC has an excellent selection as well. Increasingly, people are downloading their films (legally) from www.fnac.com, www.amazon.fr and www.mk2.fr.

DVD & Video Rental			
La Onzieme Heure	168 blvd Voltaire	11th	01 40 09 80 89
Prime Time Vidéo	24 rue Mayet	6th	01 40 56 33 44
Vidéo Fast	43 rue de Miromesnil	8th	01 42 65 04 77
Vidéosphere	105 blvd St Michel	5th	01 43 26 36 22

Pets

Paris Pet Parade

There's an enormous pet show each year put on by the French Society for the Protection of Animals (www.spa.asso.fr), and it's an excellent resource for all variety of pet information.

Paris is a famously pet-friendly city and dogs are the kings and queens of the animal world; there are more dogs than children in the city, with the canine count at around 500,000. There are two things which will help you crack through the tough exterior of your average Parisian: love and dogs. If you can't get a reservation in a restaurant, tell the *maitre d'hotel* that it's your first date, your last date or your anniversary you'll likely be seated somewhere. Similarly, the grumpy shopkeeper who never smiles will suddenly fall to his knees if you arrive with a puppy at your feet. Dogs are welcome in restaurants, cafes, boutiques, metros and, probably, in court. This doesn't mean that owning a dog in Paris is easy. The strange irony is that while dogs are welcome in chic restaurants, they're forbidden from many parks.

Without proper papers, by law your pet can be taken away and destroyed so make sure that you take your new pet to a vet immediately after purchase. Any legitimate pet store or breeder will provide all medical certificates necessary to make your pet legal. Your dog must also 'carry' identification in the form of either a tattoo or a microchip inserted under the skin. France has particularly harsh penalties for cruelty to animals and the sale of animals less than eight weeks old is forbidden. Generally landlords allow pets and it shouldn't be a problem moving into an apartment with your dog or cat.

Cats & Dogs

As with all domestic animals, cats and dogs must be licensed and registered at the time of sale. Their tattoo or microchip will serve as their tag. If you do have a dog, consider living within walking distance of a major, dog-friendly park – the 16th near the Bois de Boulogne or in the 12th near the Bois de Vincennes are both excellent for dog walking. Also, there are miles and miles of river to wander. The more refined and manicured the park, the less freedom you'll have, and in many parks dogs must be on a lead at all times and are relegated to certain sections. Dog owners must now pick up their dog's droppings or risk being fined.

Sunday bird market, Île de la Cité

Birds

The Marché aux Oiseaux sets up shop on the Île de la Cité every Sunday. Here you can buy all variety of birds sold by enthusiastic vendors. Also sold here are cages, food, and an assortment of accessories. All pet shops provide a wide variety of the same but with far less personalised service.

Veterinary Clinics

Clinique Vétérinaire	72 rue St Charles	15th	01 45 75 64 03
Clinique Vétérinaire des Docteurs Lahiani	4 rue Théodore de Banville	17th	01 47 66 53 56
Clinique Vétérinaire du Docteur Feraoun	84 rue Chardon Lagache	16th	01 42 88 15 08
Clinique Vétérinaire St Antoine	61 rue Crozatier	12th	01 43 43 17 13

Pet Shops

Buying in a pet shop always brings with it the risk of buying poorly treated, 'factory produced' animals. Alternatively, there are a wide variety of dog and cat breeders throughout France; www.eurobreeder.com is a great place to start. You should also consider giving a recue dog a home. Apart from the SPA (www.spa.asso.fr), a good source of information is at www.30millionsdamis.fr while the society of French dog-breeders is at www.scc.asso.fr.

Vets & Kennels

As with human healthcare, animal healthcare is markedly less expensive in France than in other countries. For a list of vets throughout Paris and France, the Order of Veterinarians can be found at www.veterinaire.fr. Not surprisingly, a wide variety of kennels and dogsitting services are available in Paris. As always, the best place to start is with your *concierge*. Also, your vet should be able to offer good advice. City Canine is recommended and offers information in English and French. Rates average about €50 per night and depend upon the various services you (or your dog) desires.

Pet Grooming/Training

Name	Phone	Web	Type of Service
City Canine	01 45 57 47 06	www.citycanine.fr	Offers spa, boarding, training and daycare.
Dogscool92	06 28 29 23 75	www.dogscool92.com	Offers personalised training and psychological services.
La Tuilerie	01 64 00 15 45	www.la-tuilerie.fr/uk	Offers full kennel service, medical services and welcomes all variety of animals.
Mon Bon Chien	01 48 28 40 12	www.mon-bon-chien-paris.com	Doggy bakery and grooming service.

Taking Your Pet Home

Leaving France with your dog is relatively simple and can be made even more so by applying for a European Pet Passport. Once your animal has been granted his papers you can travel freely among European countries with your pet. To qualify, your dog must have a microchip and a valid vaccine against rabies. Several countries have slightly more stringent requirements so make sure that you check before you go. For comprehensive information on EU pet travel requirements visit www.europa.eu. Make sure you speak to your vet about particular preparations necessary for travelling with your pet, and do so as far in advance as possible.

Electricity

The partially privatised Electricité de France (EDF; www.edf.com) provides the electricity, but the market will soon be entirely open to competing suppliers. Electricity is profoundly more expensive than gas, and when you're looking for an apartment, you should favour the buildings which provide both options.

To have your electricity connected you must provide evidence that you a) exist and b) are the owner or tenant of your property. A passport and any official document associating your name with your address will usually suffice, but the best bet is to present your new residence card along with your bank account information. Call EDF (08 10 01 03 33) or check the phone book for your local agency.

Any appliance you buy in France will be sold with the appropriate plugs and it won't be necessary to purchase an adaptor.

Plugs

France has a 220 volt, 50 hertz electrical supply, with two-pin, round-hole sockets. For details and illustrations of the plugs used in France (and other countries) go to www.kropla.com/electric2.

Water

Water is provided by private companies who've arranged contracts with the city, and is often provided by your building with the minimal cost included in your rent or as a supplemental charge. While the French consume a great deal of bottled water, Parisian tap water is of excellent quality. Recently the City of Paris (and its progressive mayor) launched a campaign to encourage people to drink from their taps rather than buying bottled water. For more information visit www.eaudeparis.fr.

Gas

Mains gas is provided by Gaz de France (08 10 80 08 01; www.gazdefrance.com) and in nearly all cases your gas will already be connected. Buildings share the cost of gas and your monthly charges will include gas along with water and building maintenance fees. Gas is dramatically cheaper than electricity and won't usually cost more than €20 per month.

Sewerage

Paris has an excellent sewer system, with 2,100 kilometres of tunnels. If you'd like evidence of this extraordinary system, visit Paris' very own sewer museum, Les Égouts de Paris (see p.188).

Recycling bin

Recycling

It is against the law to recycle nappies (diapers), plastic bags and wrapping films, oil bottles, small plastic containers, Styrofoam packaging used for meat or poultry, dangerous materials or anything still containing food or liquid.

Rubbish Disposal & Recycling

All rubbish disposal is organised by the city and is done on a daily basis. Property owners pay for this service when they pay their rubbish removal tax, which is called *taxe d'enlèvement des ordures ménageres*. If you're renting, your monthly charges will include rubbish collection along with water and gas. The *concierge* will usually take care of placing the bins (provided by the city) on the kerb when they need emptying. Throughout the city you'll find large, green containers for recycling glass and in most apartment buildings you'll find three separate bins, one each for paper, metal and glass.

103

Telephone

The French telecommunications industry is changing on a seemingly daily basis. New companies are entering the marketplace constantly so new packages and plans are always on offer. Once a government-run company, France's largest telephone company, France Telecom, is now private. You'll find many different companies vying for your business in an increasingly free market but in many cases you'll be obliged to rent a line and the service of that line from France Telecom. Not surprisingly the old giant is, by far, the most expensive, but that's where you should begin. Call 08 00 36 47 75 for their English speaking service, stop into one of their shops throughout the city or visit their website (www.francetelecom.fr) for more information.

In most cases, telephone lines will already exist and you should be able to have them activated within a few hours of signing your contract. All calls from your home are metered and depending upon your plan, local calls may or may not be free. Keep in mind that it is very expensive to call a mobile phone from a landline. Generally though, telephone calls are not expensive and with a burgeoning and highly competitive market, rates are falling constantly. Three-way calling, detailed call-by-call billing, automatic bill payment, voicemail, caller ID and call waiting are all available. If you're receiving harassing telephone calls or simply don't want your name and number listed, ask to be placed on the *liste rouge* which will make all of your personal information unavailable to the public.

Whichever telephone company you end up choosing, make sure that you discuss their various rates with them. Most will allow you significant discounts to specific numbers or countries you call frequently. The cheapest option from home is to purchase pre-paid phone cards from small tourist and cigarette shops; the poorer the neighbourhood, the better the rates. For example, €15 can get you 800 minutes of France to Australia phone calls. Skype is another excellent option and the quality of their service is increasing steadily. Any newsstand in the city will sell a variety of phone cards, but avoid those in very touristy areas.

Mobile Phones

When you arrive in Paris you may be overwhelmed by the sheer volume of mobile phone shops. Phones are marketed aggressively and living here without one will make you a brave and eccentric soul. There are three major carriers and an endless variety of plans, schemes and scams. Your best and safest bet is to go directly to one of the service providers' outlets. You can pay as you go or sign a contract. The different offers change every other minute so

Mobile Service Providers	
Bouygues Telecom	www.bouygues.com
France Telecom (Orange)	www.francetelecom.fr
SFR	www.sfr.fr

check the websites in the table to get started. Without a permanent address in France and official identification you'll be unable to sign a contract and will have to buy your phone outright and pay as you go. Paying as you go is usually more expensive but allows you to be free of any contractual obligations. Even if your phone is stolen, you can keep your number as long as you want and may now change from carrier to carrier without losing your number.

Cheap Overseas Calls		
MCI	08 00 99 00 19	www.mci.com
Pin Plan	na	www.pinplan.com
Telerabais	08 11 65 75 75	www.telerabais.fr

Cheap Overseas Calls

With applications like iChat, MSN, Yahoo and ICQ messenger it is increasingly easy to communicate for free. With a headset and a microphone you can speak to your friends free of charge with all of the above services. Skype provides the best quality and allows you to dial telephone numbers directly.

Free for All

The city of Paris has begun to install 'hot spots' all over the city making the internet entirely free with the goal of free wi-fi service in every arrondissement. See www.wifi.paris.fr for more information.

Internet

Other options **Internet Cafes** p.340, **Websites** p.40

Over the last five years France's broadband network has expanded exponentially and continues to grow. Nearly every major telecommunications company, and now appliance shops, offer 'boxes' which provide full home communication and entertainment packages – phone, cable, internet and wi-fi. Prices are falling fast but service can be spotty so ask around before making any commitments. Noos, one of France's biggest cable and internet providers has suffered enormous financial problems and laid off many of its employees in a massive restructuring.

Most Parisian buildings are now wired for high-speed internet. If, by bad luck, you find yourself living in a non-*dégroupage* zone you'll still be able to get internet service but not at the highest speeds and you'll need a telephone line first. Services and prices change constantly but generally rates are not high. An excellent resource if you're shopping for ADSL, cable, digital television or satellite services is Ariase (www.ariase.com), an independent comparison group. Information is available in English. Also, www.macserviceparis.com offers similar services. Dial-up services are, by far, the most expensive option and you'll find that, in many cases, you're paying not only for the internet service but for the time you spend on your telephone line, even if it's a local call. The best dial up service in France is Free. Generally speaking, unlimited ADSL service, costs around €20 per month. The city has a wide range of internet cafes, the best of which (and certainly the coolest) are the Milk cafes (www.milklub.com) which are open 24 hours a day, seven days a week.

Internet Service Providers	
Alice	www.aliceadsl.fr
AOL	www.aol.fr
Club Internet	www.club-internet.fr
Free	www.free.fr
Neuf	www.neufcegetel.fr
Noos	www.noos.fr
Nordnet	www.nordnet.fr
Orange	www.orange.fr
Tele2	www.tele2.fr
Teleconnect	www.teleconnecfrance.com

Bill Payment

Most bills are paid automatically, but you have a variety of options if you're not comfortable having money taken from your account each month. You may take your bill to any post office where you'll be able to pay with cash or cheque but you will be charged a small fee. Another option is to send a personal cheque and the detachable section of your bill to the billing company, or you may have the amount automatically deducted on a one time basis by filling out the TIP portion of your bill and returning it to the service provider. All of the providers offer full access to your account online where you'll be able to pay your bills and make changes to your account.

Post & Courier Services

With branches located throughout the city, La Poste, the French national postal service, provides a range of services not often associated with post offices throughout the world. In addition to the transportation of letters and packages, La Poste functions as a bank, and is used in this way by many French people. Many branches offer faxing and photocopying services and some offer internet access. Letters sent from France to countries in Europe arrive within a week and to Asia, Australia and the United States you should expect two weeks for arrival. Domestic mail is

Post & Courier Services		
Chronopost	08 25 80 18 01	www.chronopost.com
DHL ▶ p.422	08 20 34 58 21	www.dhl.com
Federal Express	08 20 12 38 00	www.fedex.com/fr
La Poste	36 39	www.laposte.fr
UPS	08 21 23 38 77	www.ups.com

105

remarkably fast and can arrive the next day. Mail boxes are yellow and seem to be on every corner; each box will indicate pick-up times. If you're worried about something not arriving, use Chronopost to send your package. It is La Poste's answer to FedEx and provides fully insurable and traceable packages. Stamps are sold at any post office, via the La Poste website, and at *tabacs* throughout the city. Mail is delivered directly to your building's bank of mailboxes or to your home.

Radio

French radio is excellent. There's an incredible amount of variety and absolutely anything you're interested in is available in one form or another across the dial. FIP and Radio Nova in particular offer incredibly eclectic programming where it's not unusual for Public Enemy to follow Puccini. Some of the best FM radio stations in the city include France Inter (87.8FM), RF1 (89.0), Radio Nova (101.5FM) and FIP (105.1FM). For English language radio, Radio France International (89FM) offers English programming. The BBC World Service can be picked up on 648khz short wave.

Television

Go Digital

Digital terrestrial television has recently been introduced in France, meaning no satellite dish, but you will need a suitable antenna and a decoder. For more information visit www.tvnt.net.

France offers five public television stations offered free of charge. For more than that you'll need to invest in a cable or satellite service. With an antenna you'll have access to TF1, 2, 3, Arté, and M6. Occasionally Canal+ will unscramble their channel and you'll have access to some of its programming but usually the channel is provided only to subscribers. Of these channels, Arté is by far the most interesting and occasionally broadcast programmes in English. TF1, 2, 3 and M6 provide news, films, talk shows and a shocking amount of American cop shows, while France 3 runs high quality films on Sunday nights.

Satellite TV & Radio

There's a widening range of cable and satellite providers in Paris offering a great array of channels and services. Generally, you can expect to pay around €20 per month for basic cable and €50 per month for satellite service. Many services are offered as bundled packages and it is increasingly rare to order cable television without other services included. The variety of channels is breathtaking and you won't have any trouble finding a bouquet appropriate to your interests. With satellite installation, remember that any addition to the outside of your building must be

Satellite & Cable Providers	
Canal+	www.canalsat.fr
Darty	www.dartybox.com
DD	www.ddelec.com
Free	www.adsl.free.fr/tv
Neuf	www.neuf.fr
Noos	www.noos.fr
Numericable	www.numericable.fr
Sky In France	www.skyinfrance.co.uk
TPS	www.tps.fr

cleared by the owner or co-op (and often the city); many buildings in Paris are protected by the city as historical buildings. Most buildings are cable ready; contact one of the cable providers in the table to determine if yours is wired. In most cases, Anglophone bars throughout the city will show major sporting events if you need to get your fix but haven't got the technology – The Moose (16 rue de Quatre Vents 75006, 01 46 33 77 00) is a good bet.

Satellite Radio

Both cable and satellite providers offer digital radio programming and depending upon the service you choose you'll have access to a variety of channels in many languages. Noos cable offers a particularly good radio service.

Dry Cleaners p.74
Divorce Lawyers p.108

Written by residents, these unique guidebooks are packed with insider info, from arriving in a new destination to making it your home and everything in between.

Explorer Residents' Guides
We Know Where You Live

Hôtel Dieu

Fast Food Nation ◀
*The leading cause of
death in France is
cardiovascular disease
(followed by cancer in
second place). With
France facing an
increasing problem
with obesity, a national
campaign encouraging
people to eat well and
exercise more often is
more and more
present. The French
consume more
McDonalds than any
other EU nation.*

General Medical Care

France offers one of the finest healthcare systems in the world and French citizens, residents and even illegal immigrants have the constitutional right to full medical care. In fact, anyone who has been in France longer than three months is entitled to care. French hospitals will treat anyone who walks through their doors, regardless of their financial situations or whether they have medical insurance. Michael Moore's recent film *Sicko* rightly uses the French medical system as a worldwide model. One of the great advantages to living in Paris will be the exceptional and inexpensive medical care you'll enjoy.

The French system allows absolute freedom when choosing medical care. You are not obliged to see a primary care physician, although if you do, costs will be significantly lower. If you choose a *médecin traitant* you'll be reimbursed at a higher rate when you see a specialist referred by that physician. However, you always have the right to a) choose the specialist you want to be referred to and b) change treating doctors at will. Ask around for a referral, and once you've found a doctor you trust and find capable, ask him or her to be your treating doctor. If you have your own private international insurance none of the above will apply to you. However, it is worth considering converting entirely to the French system and stopping the payments on your insurance while you're abroad. That said, while the state insurance provides excellent coverage, many people who have the money to do so, pay for supplemental insurance (*mutuelle*). Dental care is excellent in France but it is worth noting that the state insurance covers very little of the costs of teeth cleaning and that you may have to search to find a dentist who offers the service.

Organ Donation ◀
*About 30% of French
families refuse to allow
their relatives' organs
to be donated for
medical use - the third
highest family refusal
rate in Europe behind
Greece and the UK.*

Government Healthcare

Public healthcare facilities are exclusively run as non-profit organisations and are generally less expensive than private clinics and hospitals. Treatment at public facilities is considered to be excellent and while they may not provide the amenities that private clinics do, you can feel confident that you'll be well taken care of in a public hospital.

Private Healthcare

Private hospitals provide the same services that public hospitals do, but on a smaller scale and in generally newer buildings with slicker facilities. Private hospitals usually provide individual rooms while the public hospitals offer mostly double rooms. The best-known (and most expensive) private hospitals in Paris are the American and British hospitals (p.113). If you choose to use one of these hospitals make absolutely certain that your insurance will cover treatment.

Emergency Services

In case of emergency you should dial one of the following numbers for assistance:
18 – Direct access to both firemen and paramedics.
15 – Calls go directly to a physician and someone will stay on the line with you until help has arrived.
112 – Service provided by the European Union which may be dialled from any telephone within the EU.

Any of the numbers will provide you with the help you need by sending a doctor, ambulance, fire or police to the scene of the emergency. There are two private companies which provide 24 hour medical services: SOS Médecins (01 47 07 77 77) and Urgences Médicales de Paris (01 53 94 94 94).

Every hospital in the city provides emergency room services, but if you have a choice, you should favour the hospitals in less-populated, wealthier neighbourhoods.

Pharmacies

Pharmacies exist in abundance in Paris and are marked by a green cross. There are two 24 hour pharmacies in the city: Pharmacie des Champs (84 avenue des Champs-Élysée, 75008, 01 45 62 02 41) and Pharmacie de la Poste Maarek (26 rue de Paris, 93100, Montreuil). Pharmacies sell a wide variety of products from the homeopathic to the herbal. Pharmacists in France are very well-trained and are often very helpful and willing to provide advice; they are legally able to provide basic first-aid within their pharmacies and recommend over the counter drugs. Most medicines (or their close equivalent) are available in France. You can't, however, walk in and grab a bottle of aspirin from the shelf; all medication is regulated and must be requested from the pharmacist, be it sleeping pills or tablets for indigestion.

Health Check-Ups

Your GP can perform check-ups. All employees require an annual check-up which is provided free of charge by the state. If you require specific tests your doctor will write you a prescription so that the tests can be done in a private lab and both you and your doctor will receive copies of the results. For a full head to toe, comprehensive (and expensive) exam contact the prevention centre at the American Hospital (p.113). The exam is not reimbursed by *assurance maladie*.

Health Insurance

As soon as you begin working in France your employer is obliged to provide you with a social security number. Once you have a social security number you become part of the system and will be covered by the *Secu*, what the French call Social Security. You'll receive a *carte vitale*, which you'll present when you visit your doctor and the pharmacy to have prescriptions filled; at the moment, few doctors have card readers in their offices but nearly every pharmacy does. You will be reimbursed a portion (usually 70%) of what you pay for both doctor visits and prescription drugs. Those who can afford it often buy supplemental insurance, or enrol in their company's supplemental insurance plan, which will cover what social security does not.

Health Insurance Companies		
AGF	01 40 71 68 47	www.agf.fr
AXA	01 43 71 04 04	www.axa.fr
GAN	01 43 87 63 50	www.gan.fr
GMC Henner	01 40 82 44 44	www.henner.com
Opega	01 42 71 94 08	www.opega.fr

Supplemental Insurance

Technically any insurance company (both French and international) can provide supplemental insurance. It's a good idea to enrol with an agency that understands the French system and has offices in Paris. It is possible to be reimbursed by your home insurance company but the delays and amount of paperwork (not to mention translations) required can be overwhelming.

Donor Cards

France has an 'opt-out' or presumed-consent system, whereby unless you've explicitly indicated otherwise, your organs may be used for donation in the event of your death. However, the family still has the right to intervene and prevent organ donation.

Giving Blood

Blood donation is common in France. Throughout the year you'll see advertisements for various blood drives but if you'd like to donate immediately you can contact the Etablissement Francais du Sang (www.dondusang.com) for information or the Federation Francaise pour le don de Sang (www.federation-dondesang.org).

Giving Up Smoking

While Paris has a reputation for being a city full of smokers, their numbers have been steadily diminishing. There are a wide variety of programmes offered by individual doctors, psychologists, psychiatrists, hypnotists, acupuncturists, private clinics and public hospitals. An excellent source for information is the Global Smoke Free Partnership (www.globalsmokefreepartnership.org) while both the American and British Hospitals, as well as all the public hospitals, in Paris offer stop-smoking programmes.

Main Government Hospitals

The Paris hospital system is one of the largest in the world with 38 different hospitals spread throughout the city; the Assistance Publique-Hopitaux de Paris serves the majority of the Parisian community. All hospitals, public or private, must be accredited by the Haute Autorité de Santé, the official French health authority, which holds its hospitals to exceptionally high standards. While some hospital facilities may not appear as sparkling clean and sterile as you're used to, you should be confident that the care you receive in many of the public hospitals is excellent. All of the following public hospitals use the above Assistance Publique-Hopitaux de Paris website (www.aphp.fr).

9 ave Charles-de-Gaulle, 92100 Boulogne-Billancourt
Ⓜ *Boulogne – Jean Jaurès*
Map p.378 B3

Ambroise-Pare

01 49 09 50 00 | www.aphp.fr

Providing 468 beds, Ambroise-Pare is a teaching hospital offering an entire gamut of hospital services including an MRI facility. The hospital recently opened a paediatric and adolescent ward with an excellent reputation. Additionally there's a focus on orthopaedic surgery and cardio-vascular disease.

26 ave du Docteur Arnold-Netter
12th
Ⓜ *Bel-Air*
Map p.412 C2 2

Armand-Trousseau

01 44 73 74 75 | www.aphp.fr

A children's hospital famous for its opthamology department, Armand-Trousseau provides 329 beds to patients from north-eastern Paris. One of the 38 teaching hospitals in the city, the hospital has recently opened a maternity ward providing pre-natal care and plans to become the central pre-natal hospital in eastern Paris – billing itself as a hospital for 'mother and child'. A neuro-paediatric centre is also planned.

46 rue Henri-Huchard
18th
Ⓜ *Porte de Saint-Ouen*
Map p.382 C1 3

Bichat – Claude-Bernard

01 40 25 80 80 | www.aphp.fr

One of the largest hospitals in Paris, the hospital Bichat has over a 1,000 beds and serves as a general hospital that specialises in obstetric surgery. A neurology centre opened in 2004 providing intensive care and post-operative care. Bichat is a full-service hospital serving northern Paris and tends to be busy and sometimes over-crowded.

Dermatologists			
Dr Agathe Adrien	11 chausée de la Muette	16th	01 42 88 00 88
Dr Agnés Desplaces	25 rue Bourgogne	7th	01 47 53 71 14
Dr Laure Dehen	47 rue de Four	6th	01 42 22 56 44
Dr Olivier Brachat	75 rue de Renness	6th	01 45 49 07 15
Dr Sylvie Homareau	63 blvd Victor Hugo	Neuilly-sur-Seine	01 46 41 27 24

**27 rue du Faubourg
Saint-Jacques**
14th
R Port-Royal
Map p.409 D3 **4**

Cochin

01 58 41 41 41 | *www.aphp.fr*

Cochin has 1,152 beds with excellent sports medecine and oncology facilities. Two MRI machines are available as well as a new geriatric ward. The hospital serves children and adults and provides full pre-natal care.

Government Hospitals

Albert-Chenevier	40 rue de Mesly, 94010	Créteil	01 49 81 31 31
Ambroise-Pare	9 ave Charles-de-Gaulle, 92100	Boulogne-Billancourt	01 49 09 50 00
Antoine-Beclere	157 rue de la Porte de Trivaux, 92141	Clamart	01 45 37 44 44
Armand-Trousseau	26 ave du Docteur Arnold-Netter	12th	01 44 73 74 75
Avicenne	125 rue de Stalingrad, 93009	Bobigny	01 48 95 55 55
Beaujon	100 blvd du Général Leclerc, 92110	Clichy	01 40 87 50 00
Bicetre	78 rue du Général Leclerc, 94275	le Kremlin-Bicetre	01 45 21 21 21
Bichat – Claude-Bernard	46 rue Henri-Huchard	18th	01 40 25 80 80
Bretonneau	23 rue Joseph-de Maistre	18th	01 53 11 18 00
Broca	54-56 rue Pascal	13th	01 44 08 30 00
Broussais	96 rue Didot	14th	01 43 95 95 95
Charles-Foix – Jean-Rostand	7 ave de la République	Ivry-sur-Seine	01 49 59 40 00
Charles-Richet	rue Charles-Richet, 95400	Villiers-le-Bel	01 34 29 23 00
Cochin	27 rue du Faubourg Saint-Jacques	14th	01 58 41 41 41
Corentin-Celton	4 parvis Corentin-Celton	Issy-les-Moulineaux	01 58 00 40 00
Emile-Roux	1 ave de Verdun, 94456	Limeil Brevannes	01 45 95 80 80
Fernand-Widal	200 rue du Faubourg Saint-Denis	10th	01 40 05 45 45
Georges-Clemenceau	1 rue Georges-Clemenceau, 91750	Champcueil	01 69 23 20 20
Henri-Mondor	51 ave du Maréchal de Tassigny, 94010	Créteil	01 49 81 21 11
Hospital Europeen Georges-Pompidou	20 rue Leblanc	15th	01 56 09 20 00
Hospitalisation a Domicile	14 rue Vésale	5th	01 55 43 68 00
Hôtel Dieu	1 place du Parvis Notre-Dame	4th	01 42 34 82 34
Jean-Verdier	ave du 14 Juillet, 93143	Bondy	01 48 02 66 66
Joffre-Dupuytren	rue Louis Camatte, 91211	Draveil	01 69 83 63 63
La Collegiale	33 rue du Fer à Moulin	5th	01 44 08 30 00
La Roche-Guyon	1 rue de l"Hôpital, 95780	la Roche-Guyon	01 30 63 83 30
La Rochefoucauld	15 ave du Général Leclerc	14th	01 44 08 30 00
Lariboisiere	2 rue Ambroise - Paré	10th	01 49 95 65 65
Louis-Mourier	178 rue des Renouillers, 92701	Colombes	01 47 60 61 62
Necker – Enfants Malades	149 rue de Sèvres	15th	01 44 49 40 00
Paul-Brousse	12 ave Paul-Vaillant-Couturier, 94804	Villejuif	01 45 59 30 00
Pitie-Salpetriere	47-83 blvd de l'Hôpital	13th	01 42 16 00 00
Raymond-Poincare	104 blvd Raymond-Poincaré, 92380	Garches	01 47 10 79 00
Rene-Muret – Bigottini	ave du Docteur Schaeffner, 93270	Sevran	01 41 52 59 99
Robert-Debre	48 blvd Sérurier	19th	01 40 03 20 00
Rothschild	33 blvd de Picpus	12th	01 40 19 30 00
Saint-Antoine	184 rue du Faubourg Saint-Antoine	12th	01 49 28 20 00
Saint-Louis	1 ave Claude-Vellefaux	10th	01 42 49 49 49
Saint-Vincent de Paul	82 ave Denfert-Rochereau	14th	01 58 41 41 41
Sainte-Perine – Rossini – Chardon-Lagache	11 rue Chardon-Lagache	16th	01 44 96 31 31
Tenon	4 rue de la Chine	20th	01 56 01 70 00
Vaugirard – Gabriel-Pallez	10 rue Vaugelas	15th	01 40 45 80 00

Hôtel Dieu

Hôtel Dieu

1 place du Parvis
Notre-Dame
4th
Ⓜ *Cité*
Map p.399 F3 🝿

01 42 34 82 34 | *www.aphp.fr*

The most centrally located hospital in the city, Hôtel-Dieu is relatively small, providing 349 beds. The hospital is the only facility in the city equipped with a femtoseconde laser used for non-invasive corneal surgery and to treat glaucoma. A major sports medicine centre has also recently opened, providing education, patient care and research. For information contact CIMS by email on cims.htd@htd.aphp.fr

Necker – Enfants Malade

149 rue de Sèvres
15th
Ⓜ *Duroc*
Map p.407 F2 🝿

01 44 49 40 00 | *www.aphp.fr*

The city's foremost public children's hospital offers 393 beds for children and 209 for adults. Founded in 1778 Necker serves as a teaching hospital and has been dedicated to children since 1802 focusing primarily on immunology, human genetics and cell biology.

Pitie-Salpetriere

47-83 blvd
de l'Hôpital
13th
Ⓜ *Saint-Marcel*
Map p.410 B3 🝿

01 42 16 00 00 | *www.aphp.fr*

Once a gun-powder factory, a prison for prostitutes and a holding facility for the criminally insane, Pitie-Salpetriere is the biggest and one of the best teaching hospitals in the city with a vast range of facilities including three MRI machines, a CAT scan unit and a fully renovated haematology unit. Jean-Martin Charcot, considered to be the founder of modern neurology, is a resident professor here. It is also the hospital where both Josephine Baker and Princess Diana died.

Saint-Antoine

184 rue du Faubourg
Saint-Antoine
12th
Ⓜ *Faidherbe Chaligny*
Map p.411 E1 🝿

01 49 28 20 00 | *www.aphp.fr*

Saint-Antoine serves as a general hospital with an excellent gastrointestinal division and provides specialised care in pre and post-natal care. Saint-Antoine is a member of the CancerEst cancer federation and is increasingly involved in cancer care providing chemotherapy and a variety of oncological care. The hospital also serves as an organ transplant centre.

Private Health Centres & Clinics

Dr Anne de la Brosse	11 cité Vaneau	7th	01 45 55 66 00
Dr Anne-Fanny Loew	53 rue de la Chaussée d'Antin	9th	01 48 78 02 31
Dr Bernadette Cosnard-Simon	29 rue Coquillère	1st	01 45 08 90 32
Dr Francis Slattery	32 rue Vignon	9th	01 47 42 02 34
Dr Nancy Salzman	36 rue du Colisée	8th	01 45 63 18 43
Dr Patrice Monin	138 blvd du Montparnasse	14th	01 43 22 41 25
Dr Stephen Wilson	54 rue des Archives	4th	01 48 87 21 10
Dr Tura Milo	93 blvd Saint Germain	6th	01 43 54 22 47

Main Private Hospitals

Aside from the public hospitals, there are two excellent private hospitals available. While these are far more expensive they provide a brand of healthcare that may be more familiar to people coming from countries where hospitals tend to be more clinical in feeling. The care is warmer and more personal, and the facilities generally more modern.

63 blvd Victor Hugo, 92202
Neuilly-sur-Seine
Ⓜ **Pont de Levallois – Bécon**
Map p.378 B2

The American Hospital of Paris

01 46 41 25 25 | www.american-hospital.org

Inaugurated in 1909, The American Hospital of Paris serves both French and international communities and feels more like a country club than a hospital. AHP provides a range of both in and out-patient services including medical imaging, laboratory analysis, assisted procreation and pre-natal diagnostic care. The hospital offers a prevention wing where patients can receive a full check-up. AHP offers international vaccination, breast imaging, sports medicine and vein treatment centres.

3 rue Barbès, 92300
Levallois Perret
Ⓜ **Anatole France**
Map p.378 B2

Hertford British Hospital

01 46 39 22 22 | www.british-hospital.org

The British Hospital serves as a non-profit organisation providing medical care to the English speaking community. Smaller than the American Hospital, Hertford has the distinct advantage of being covered under French social security and is an overall far less-expensive facility. Doctors are primarily French while nurses and mid-wives are British and Irish. The hospital's excellent Centre for Women provides superb neonatal, maternity and paediatric care. The Dermatology Centre also has an excellent reputation.

Other Private Hospitals

Centre Saint Michel	103 blvd St Michel	5th	01 40 51 24 70	www.centre-saint-michel.com
Centre Voltaire	52 rue Léon Frot	11th	01 40 24 11 24	www.centre-voltaire.com
Clinique Alleray Labrouste	64 rue Labrouste	15th	01 44 19 50 00	www.alleray-labrouste.com
Clinique Jeanne d'Arc	11 rue Ponscarme	13th	01 45 83 88 13	www.clinique-jeanne-darc.com

Postnatal Depression
Postnatal depression can occur up to a year after giving birth. Symptoms can include a sense of hopelessness, anxiety, difficulty sleeping and an inability to bond with the child. Around 15% of new mothers suffer from postnatal depression; if you're one of them contact your doctor. In Paris, the Protection Maternelle et Infantile (PMI) provides full postnatal care and can provide help dealing with postnatal depression.

Maternity

Excellent, inexpensive and generous healthcare makes the prospect of having children in France attractive and rarely do pregnant women return to their home countries to give birth. As with all other medical services you can choose between public and private care. Keep in mind that there's a shortage of beds in Paris maternity wards, both public and private, so you should plan well ahead. While legal, home births are not common in France and are generally considered unsafe and even cultish. Anyone in attendance during a home birth is liable under French law if anything happens to the mother or child. Remember that if you're an EU national residing in France you may be obliged to return to your home country to give birth.

Once you know that you're pregnant, your doctor will issue a *déclaration de grossesse* which you'll need to submit to the Caisse d'Allocations Familiales within 14 weeks of your initial examination. The CAF will send you a *carnet de maternité* in which you'll record every step of your pregnancy so bring the book with you every time you visit your doctor. The *carnet* entitles you to 100% reimbursement of maternity costs. This is not, however, always the case in private hospitals.

Delivery will be performed by a midwife or *sage femme* in the maternity ward of a hospital where you'll spend three full days. Epidurals are widely used and are delivered without stigma.

Abortions

Abortion is legal in France up to 12 weeks after conception. Women under 18 may have an abortion without parental consent but they must be accompanied by an adult. Women, regardless of nationality or immigrant status, have the legal right to abortion in France. For more information visit www.planning-familial.org.

Once your child is born you'll have three days to file a *déclaration de naissance* at your local *mairie*, where you'll be given a *carnet de naissance de l'enfant* which will be used to record the health of your baby. For more details see the Birth Certificate and Registration section on p.52.

While a variety of facilities offer maternity services, there is only a limited number which offer a full range of services; if you're planning on giving birth in a public hospital it is recommended that you choose one of those listed below. The care you'll receive at these hospitals will be excellent, but private hospitals and clinics will be more comfortable. That said, they'll also be infinitely more expensive and may not provide the full range of medical services mentioned above.

Government Hospitals

Most government hospitals provide maternity care which is fully reimbursable by social security. Labour wards in public hospitals often require that you bring your own extras like soap and towels and are not known for being nearly as polished as those you might be used to. It's a good idea to find a gynaecologist who serves the hospital you plan to deliver in. Different gynecologists deliver in different hospitals and if you've decided that you'll give birth in a private clinic, for example, make sure that you find a doctor who works there.

Postnatal Care

Your baby will be examined 10 times in the first year, three times in the second and twice in the following two years. Remember that all of these examinations are fully reimbursable by social security. Eight weeks after you have given birth your gynaecologist will examine both you and your baby. Postnatal physical therapy is also provided and paid for by the state.

Maternity Hospitals & Clinics

The American Hospital of Paris	63 blvd Victor Hugo, 92202	Neuilly-sur-Seine	01 46 41 25 25	Private
Antoine-Béclère	157 rue de la Porte de Trivaux, 92141	Clamart	01 45 37 44 44	Public
Cochin	27 rue du Faubourg Saint-Jacques	14th	01 58 41 41 41	Public
The Hertford British Hospital	3 rue Barbès, 92300	Levallois Perret	01 46 39 22 22	Private
La Clinique de la Muette	46-48 rue Nicolo	16th	01 40 72 33 33	Private
La Clinique Saint-Isabelle	24 blvd du Château, 92200	Neuilly-sur-Seine	01 40 88 44 00	Private
Le Centre Hospitalier Intercommunal de Créteil	40 ave Verdun, 94000	Créteil	01 45 17 52 00	Public
Poissy-Saint-Germain	20 rue Armagis, 78105	Saint-Germain-en-Laye	01 39 27 40 50	Public
Pontoise	6 ave de l'Ile de France	Cergy Pontoise	01 30 75 40 40	Public
Robert-Debré	48 blvd Sérurier	19th	01 40 03 20 00	Public
Saint-Vincent-de-Paul	82 ave Denfert-Rochereau	14th	01 58 41 41 41	Public

Maternity Leave

Pregnant women are fully protected by the French government. You are allowed 16 weeks' maternity leave which may be divided as you wish and by law your job must be available to you when you return. You may take up to three years away from work and still have your job guaranteed. If you decide not to return to work at all, you are not required to pay back your employer or the state. Fathers are also entitled to paternity leave. See Employment Contracts on p.56 for more details.

Gynaecology & Obstetrics

As with any other doctor the best way to find a gynaecologist is to ask around and get a reference from friends.

Gynaecology & Obstetrics			
Dr Aline Schiffmann	7 rue Marbeuf	8th	01 47 23 58 04
Dr Anne-Isabelle Richet	109 rue de l'Université	7th	01 45 51 82 32
Dr Pierre Vellay	31 rue St Guillaume	7th	01 45 48 59 93
Dr Roger Chambraud	32 ave Georges Mandel	16th	01 45 53 77 11

Be demanding and don't settle on someone you're not entirely comfortable with. Contraception is readily available in France; you can buy condoms in supermarkets and pharmacies but oral contraception requires a prescription from your doctor. Insurance covers all forms of prescribed birth control.
The government provides fully reimbursable fertility treatments.

Paediatrics

All visits to paediatricians are covered by social security and, as with all other doctors, you have the right to change whenever you like. The basic vaccination schedule is as follows: BCG in the first month; diptheria, tetanus, polio, whooping cough and haemophilus b. after month two; hepatitis B after month three then measles, mumps and rubella after 12 months.

Learning Disabilities

The French are generally dismissive of learning disabilities and while you can find support it will require more work than it would in some other countries. ADHD is not considered a valid syndrome by the majority of French doctors and psychologists. This attitude is changing and there are several French doctors who've recently published books about ADHD in both children and adults. The single best resource for ADHD (TDAH in French) is at www.tdah-france.fr.
Dr Gaillac and Dr Lecendreux (see table) are specialists in ADHD.

Paediatrics			
Dr Annie Claudel-Godet	71 bis rue Philippe de Girard	18th	01 46 07 25 50
Dr Gaillac CMME	100 rue de la Santé	14th	01 45 65 83 67
Dr Jean Barthelemy	29 rue Artois	8th	01 45 62 85 85
Dr Lecendreux	11 rue Bosio	16th	01 42 15 15 75
Dr Richard Mouy	119 rue de Courcelles	17th	01 42 67 67 67

Dentists & Orthodontists

It is possible to get excellent dental care in Paris but it is more expensive than any other basic medical treatment. The French are not fanatical about regular cleanings and licensed hygienists are unheard of. No cosmetic dentistry will be covered by insurance and prices for all dental care vary widely; a dentist trained in the United States working in the 16th for example will be far more expensive than a French trained dentist in the 19th so you should shop around.

Dentists & Orthodontists			
Dr Eric Hazan	185-187 rue de la Pompe	16th	01 47 27 45 35
Dr Julia Levy Cohen	255 rue St. Honoré	1st	01 42 60 03 33
Dr Levy Maguy	9 blvd Richard Lenoir	11th	01 49 29 93 68

Opticians & Ophthalmologists

There are shops selling glasses on almost every corner in Paris. In most you'll find an optometrist qualified to give you a eye test, fit you for glasses and sell you contact

Opticians & Ophthalmologists

Centre de Vision	40 rue Saint Honoré	1st	01 42 33 97 24
Clinique Roosevelt	9 rue Jean Goujon	8th	01 42 25 02 59
Confort-Vision	95 rue de Passy	16th	01 42 24 66 80
Dr Howard Cohn	45 rue Vineuse	16th	01 53 65 68 10
Dr Isabelle Zerah	41 rue de Passy	16th	01 42 24 64 42
Dr Marc Timsit	47 ave Hoche	8th	01 47 66 15 15
Dr Sylvia Platkiewicz	239 blvd Jean Jaurés	B-Billancourt	01 46 21 46 79

lenses, which are readily available. Both lenses and glasses are reasonably priced though contact lens solution, sold only in pharmacies, tends to be more expensive. Lasik surgery is frequently performed by surgeons both in Paris and in other major French cities; costs average between €2,000 and 3,000 for both eyes. For specialised eye care you should consult your ophthalmologist.

Cosmetic Treatment & Surgery

Clinique Esthétique de Paris Spontini	68 bis rue Spontini	16th	01 53 70 59 59
Clinique Petrarque	6 square Petrarque	16th	01 53 70 05 05
Dr Alain Bzowski	6 rue de l'Alboni	16th	01 45 25 44 00

Cosmetic Treatment & Surgery

Plastic surgery is not the subject of popular discussion the way it is in other countries. However, the French are having cosmetic alterations at an increasing rate and there are plenty of facilities available where you can have any operation you'd like. Additionally, there has been a recent wave of high-end spa openings throughout the city, most of which are sponsored by or associated with a major French cosmetic brand. Parisians are major consumers (and producers) of cosmetics and the overwhelming choice of creams, lotions and potions available throughout the city is breathtaking.

Acupressure & Acupuncture

Dr Bernadette Cosnard-Simon	29 rue Coquillière	1st	01 45 08 90 32
Dr Serge Belhassen	130 rue Rivoli	1st	01 42 33 39 59
Ying-Yang Bao	50 rue Disque	13th	01 45 86 79 00

Alternative Therapies

A whole range of alternative therapies is available throughout Paris and they are extremely popular. From acupressure to yoga, the French embrace all varieties of therapies and activities. Incredible spas are springing up throughout the city by the dozen and finding a massage won't take much work. Homeopathic medicine is very popular, as is acupuncture and aromatherapy and as the French become increasingly health-conscious, alternative therapies will only become more prevalent across the city.

Acupressure & Acupuncture

Many French doctors are specialists in both acupuncture and homeopathic medicine so will provide acupuncture sessions in their offices. Accupuncture is reimbursable by French social security. The best way to find a reliable practitioner is to contact your doctor.

Addiction Counselling & Rehabilition

The French health system offers excellent addiction care in clinics and hospitals. There are seven public rehabilitation centres in Paris as well as a large number of specialists treating a variety of addictions. Alcoholics Anonymous has a strong presence offering meetings throughout the city, while Narcotics Anonymous also provides help in English. The Promis clinic has a particularly good reputation throughout Europe.

Addiction Counselling & Rehabilitation

Alcoholics Anonymous	01 46 34 59 65
Centre Monte-Cristo Paris	01 44 29 67 88
Centre Saint-Germain Pierre Nicole	01 44 32 07 90
Debtors Anonymous	01 48 22 16 58
Espace Murger	01 40 05 42 14
La Corde Raide Paris	01 43 42 53 00
La Terasse Paris	01 42 26 01 11
Narcotics Anonymous	01 48 58 38 46
Nicotine Anonymous	06 09 15 46 63
PromisFrance	01 45 04 05 14

Aromatherapy

Aromatherapy			
Centre Heliotrope	43 rue Richelieu	1st	06 25 54 04 52
Kiria	108 blvd St Germain	6th	01 55 42 52 52
Spa Caudalie	228 rue de Rivoli	1st	01 44 58 10 10
Spa Nuxe	32 rue Montorgueil	1st	01 55 80 71 40

Aromatherapy

Aromatherapy treatments are provided by spas and by private massage therapists and are often offered alongside other treatments from facials to pedicures. You will also find aromatherapy oils and other products in boutiques and healthfood shops throughout the city.

Healing Meditation

Meditation classes are offered throughout the city in gyms (usually in association with yoga classes). The Paris Buddhist Center is an excellent resource. Visit www.centrebouddhistparis.org for more information.

Reflexology & Massage Therapy

Other options **Massage** p.239

Reflexology and massage therapy are incredibly popular. As is true throughout the western world, the spa business is an incredibly lucrative one; from absurdly expensive hotel spas to small store fronts in Chinatown you'll find no shortage of massage therapists offering their services. If you're interested in a massage at home visit www.massage-domicile-paris.com for details.

Reflexology & Massage Therapy			
Cinq Mondes	6 square de l'Opéra Louis Jouvet	9th	01 42 66 00 60
Espace Payot	62 rue Pierrre Charron	8th	01 45 61 42 08
Ora Kinemassage	7 rue Daru	8th	01 47 63 94 02
Shiatsu Massage	23 rue Gazan	14th	01 45 88 03 42

Rehabilitation & Physiotherapy

Contrary to popular belief, Parisians are athletic people and competitive sports are a major part of French culture. As a result there are excellent physical therapy resources available in the city. Services are available in both private and public hospitals as well as in individual doctor's offices.

Rehabilitation & Physiotherapy			
American Hospital of Paris PT Wing	63 blvd Victor Hugo Neuilly-sur-Seine	92200	01 46 41 28 90
CIMS (Hôtel Dieu)	1 place du Parvis Notre Dame	4th	01 42 34 87 66
Nollet	23 rue Brochant	17th	01 44 85 19 00

Back Treatment

Massage therapists, acupuncturists and kinesiologists provide therapeutic services to people suffering from back pain and chronic back problems. In France there's a marked difference between a massage therapist and a kinesiologist (Kinésithérapeute), the latter having been better trained and generally focusing on the healing of particular ailments rather than overall relaxation and stress-relief.

Chiropractors are also popular in Paris and there's many working both in English and in French. All of these services are covered in full or part by French social security and, relative to other western

Back Treatment			
Bruno Mouren	60 rue Falsandrie	16th	01 40 72 89 88
Cabinet Chiropratique	17 ave Trudaine	9th	01 40 82 98 68
Centre de Soins du Marais	119 rue du Temple	3rd	01 42 72 62 81
Iona Gray	85 ave Charles de Gaulle	Neuilly-sur-Seine	06 50 19 71 05
Marjorane Dey	24 rue de Charonne	11th	06 66 72 11 18
Matieu Decamps	37 rue de Vouillé	15th	06 13 73 08 24

countries, treatment is inexpensive. If your treating physician refers you to an authorised therapist you will likely be reimbursed at 70%.

Nutritionists & Slimming

Paris is a wonderful city to enjoy food and anything you'd like to eat is readily available, which includes copious fresh fruit and vegetables. However, many expats when they first arrive find the temptation of French pastries too much to resist and quickly gain weight. Pharmacies advertise a whole spectrum of weight loss products but as seductive as these quick fixes may appear you should stay away. If you join a gym you'll often receive a free consultation with a physical trainer and a nutritionist with whom you can discuss your goals.

Nutritionists & Slimming			
Centre Saint Michel	103 blvd St Michel	5th	01 40 51 24 70
Dr Florence Pujol	3 rue Washington	8th	01 40 76 09 36
Dr Gilles Demarque	124 rue de la Pompe	16th	01 45 53 08 57
Dr Pascal Didi	56 ave St Ouen	18th	01 46 27 96 98
Paris Minceur	141 rue Vaugirard	15th	01 47 83 49 77

Culture Shock ◄

Culture shock can precede a bout of depression or intensify the depression you may already be suffering from. Once in Paris, if you find yourself struggling there are many places to seek help and a wide range of therapies, including antidepressants, are all reimbursed by social security.

Counselling & Therapy

While most hospitals in Paris provide psychiatric units, the major psychiatric hospital is the Hôpital Saint-Anne (01 45 65 80 00) in the 14th *arrondissement*. Psychiatrists and psychologists provide private counselling in private practices, clinics and hospitals. Of particular concern to expats is the toll the move can take on your mental health. Many newcomers to Paris are surprised to find the city (and its people) cold and seemingly impenetrable. What was easy to accomplish in your home country may be far more difficult and often for no particular reason. Many new residents find themselves suffering from culture shock which manifests itself in feelings of depression, anger, frustration, hopelessness and regret.

Support Groups

Recently the *Journal du Dimanche* discussed a new condition they've coined as the 'Paris Syndrome', which apparently affects certain Japanese visitors who are so dispirited by the difference between their idea of Paris and its reality that they fall into serious despair. Whether or not 'Paris Syndrome' is legitimate, there is no question that such a mythological city can be disappointing. The following are support groups providing a wide range of services and activities for expats. In general, community and cultural centres are excellent places to meet people with similar backgrounds and interests.

Message – A parenting resource composed of over 1,500 English-speaking families living in Paris. Open to all nationalities. www.messageparis.org

American Aid Society of Paris – A support group providing various forms of aid to Americans living in Paris. Phone 01 43 12 47 90

American Women's Group in Paris – A woman's support group offering a variety of activities for expat women. Website www.awgparis.org

Association of American Wives of Europeans – A non-profit support group created to serve the needs of women married to Europeans. Website www.aaweparis.org

Women of the American Church – A women's group striving to help new expats adapt to life in France. Their 'Bloom Where You're Planted' programme is recommended. Website www.woac.net

Counsellors/Psychologists			
The Counseling Center	01 47 23 61 13	na	Specialising in family and couple therapy
Dr Alexander Lloyd	01 42 22 84 24	na	English speaking psychiatrist
Dr Sylvie Angel	01 47 20 60 99	na	English speaking psychiatrist
ICS	01 45 50 26 49	http://icsparis.ifrance.com	Specialises in international patients
Jill Bourdais	01 43 54 79 25	na	Well-known English speaking psychologist
Paris Therapy Services	na	www.paristherapyservices.com	Lists English-speaking counsellors
SOS Helpline	01 46 21 46 46	www.soshelpline.org	Provides anonymous counselling in English

No More Saturdays
School children in France have traditionally attended Saturday morning classes and taken Wednesday afternoons off, but the government announced that these weekend classes would be scrapped for primary school children in 2008. It remains to be seen whether secondary schools will follow suit.

Education

Paris and the immediate surrounding areas offer an impressive variety of schools catering to the English-speaking community. Residents have the option of sending their children to private English-speaking schools or enrolling them in the French school system. French schools are free for citizens and residents alike but those with international sections may charge tuition. Essentially, there are three general options: International Schools, Bilingual Schools and French Schools that provide international sections. For school-age children the exact documents you will need will depend upon where you're enrolling your child, but in most cases, proof of diptheria-tetanus-polio vaccination and a birth certificate will be all you'll need from your home country. Once you've arrived and have established an address you'll need to provide proof of address when enrolling. Compulsory education begins at age 6 and ends at 16. If you plan to enroll your child you must do so the June preceding the September start of school.

Nurseries & Pre-Schools

French nursery schools, or *écoles maternelles*, accept children from 2 to 6 years of age and are free of charge. To be accepted your child must be 2 years old at the start of school in September and when there are more children than places, older children are given preference. Nearly every French school offers a before and after-school childcare system for which you'll have to pay. While the French schools are uniform in their curriculum, the various international and bilingual schools subscribe to different philosophies.

65 quai d'Orsay
7th
ⓡ **Pont de l'Alma**
Map p.397 E2 **11**

The Bilingual Montessori School of Paris
01 45 55 13 27 | www.montessori-paris.com

Founded in 1980, the Bilingual Montessori School of Paris is a fully accredited school for students aged between 2 and 6 years. The school follows the international Montessori system and provides facilities on three different campuses. The programme is based on the Montessori disciplines of Practical Life, Sensorial, Development, Mathematics and Language.

28 rue Vignon
9th
Ⓜ **Madeleine**
Map p.388 B4 **12**

Les Oursons
01 49 24 05 69 | www.oursons.org

Les Oursons provides a Montessori education to children aged 3 to 6 years. With only 39 students per year, Les Oursons is able to offer highly personalised care. Classes are given in both French and English by an entirely bilingual staff, allowing students to prepare for the next stage of their education in true international style.

40 rue Pierre Guerin
16th
Ⓜ **Jasmin**
Map p.405 D1 **13**

United Nations Nursery School
01 42 88 71 46 | www.unns.net

The United Nations Nursery School, also known as Jardin d'Enfants des Nation Unies, offers an international programme for children aged 2 to 6 years. This is not a bilingual school, but instead focuses on being multi-cultural with French and English both used by teachers without specifically being taught. Class sizes are limited to 18 children, allowing advantageous relationships to develop between pupil and teacher. UNNS puts a strong emphasis on music and art and classes are given in a particularly attractive and quiet setting.

Primary & Secondary Schools

Whether or not your child will have to take an entrance exam or sit for an interview will depend entirely on the school he or she is applying to. Competition is intense between the major international and bilingual schools and each is anxious to have your tuition. The American School of Paris models itself after a large American independent school while the British School of Paris follows, not surprisingly, a British model. All of the major International schools offer the IB program while ASP is the only school to offer the American AP program. Teaching standards are high but each school has its advantages and disadvantages so it is crucial to spend some time on several campuses before you make any decisions. Given the tuition at some schools, you might expect a campus on a par with private schools in your home country but this is not always the case. Private education is expensive everywhere and Paris is no exception. For example, the annual tuition and fees for the 2007-2008 school year at the American School of Paris are as follows:

Application Fee: €760 (non-refundable)

K1: €14,130

K2 – Grade 5: €19,600

Middle School: €22,070

Upper School: €22,070

Capital Assessment Fee: €7,700 (one-time fee)

Bus Fee: €2,420

Security Surcharge: €550

Note that these fees don't include extra-curricular activities. The British School of Paris is slightly less expensive but in the same neighbourhood.

American School of Paris

41 rue Pasteur, 92210
Saint-Cloud
Map p.378 B3

01 41 12 82 82 | *www.asparis.org*

The American School of Paris is an independent, co-educational private school providing a full American curriculum. The school is located outside of Paris in the suburb of St Cloud on a 12 acre campus, which includes a sports field, gym and performing arts centre. The school offers bus service to transport students to and from the campus.

British School of Paris

Chemin du Mur
du Parc 78380
Bougival
Map p.378 A3

01 39 69 78 21 | *www.bsparis.net*

The British School of Paris occupies two different campuses on the outskirts of the city. The Bougival campus is home to a junior school, and a second location in Croissy-sur-Seine also has a junior school as well as the senior school. A British-style education is offered to students aged 4 to 18; 70% of whom are British. BSP offers excellent facilities including a swimming pool, playing fields and gyms. Classes are taught in English. The school provides a daily bus service from Paris and the surrounding areas.

École Active Bilingue

6 ave Van Dyck
8th
M *Courcelles*
Map p.387 E2 **16**

01 46 22 14 24 | *www.eab.fr*

Established in 1954, École Active Bilingue provides a fully bilingual curriculum catering to both French and international students. English is taught both as a native and foreign language with emphasis on cross-cultural development. EAB also has a junior and high school accredited by the Cambridge, Oxford and London Examining Boards, as well as the International Baccalaureate Organisation.

International School of Paris

6 rue Beethoven
16th
M *Passy*
Map p.396 A2 **17**

01 42 27 15 93 | *www.isparis.edu*

The student body of the International School of Paris is composed of children from 41 different countries aged 3 to 18. Classes are small with a strong emphasis on teacher interaction. ISP is the only Anglophone school in central Paris that provides a K-12 education. The school offers the IBO Primary and Middle Years programme as well as the IBO Diploma.

65 quai d'Orsay
7th
R Pont de l'Alma
Map p.397 E2 **18**

Lennen Bilingual School
01 47 05 66 55 | www.lennenbilingual.com
Founded in 1960, Lennen Bilingual School offers a bilingual curriculum for students aged 2 to 11. LBS prides itself on being the only school in Paris that offers such a purely bilingual experience in the primary grades, and the small class sizes and intimacy of the school's three campuses serve to engender a sense of community. Physical education classes are conducted at the American Church of Paris.

rue du Fer à
Cheval, 78175
Saint-Germain-en-Laye
Map p.378 A2

Lycée International American Section
01 34 51 74 85 | www.lycee-intl-american.org
The Lycée International provides coeducational education to 2,600 students from between 13 and 18 years of age. The school integrates students from a variety of countries into the French educational system by providing 11 foreign sections. Both the British and American sections are taught in English and 60% of those who graduate from these sections go on to universities in Anglophone countries, while the remaining graduates attend French universities. Boarding facilities are available.

University & Higher Education
Anyone who has passed their 'bac' or *baccalauréat* is legally entitled to an education at one of France's publicly funded universities. Exceptional students continue with their education 'post-bac', preparing for an entrance exam which, if they do well, will allow them access into one of the prestigious *grandes écoles*. The amount of work required during the *prépas* is extraordinary and only a percentage of those who take the exams at the end will do well enough to continue. It is taken for granted that a degree from a *grande école* will guarantee a certain level of success. It is practically unheard of to find someone in the French government or in a high position of power anywhere in France who didn't attend a *grande école*.

French universities, including the *grandes écoles*, attract foreign students of varying abilities and interests. France is a very popular country in which to study and nearly every major university in the world offers some sort of study abroad programme in cities throughout the country. All of the French universities including the *grandes écoles* are open to international students and courses are, of course, conducted in French.

Further Education
It seems that there's no end to the classes you can take in Paris; as with most cities, there's an endless array on offer. If you'd like to change your life and become a chef you can spend a year or two at le Cordon Bleu (www.lcbparis.com) or any number of

Historic university buildings

other famous cooking schools. At the Women's Institute for Continuing Education, or WICE (www.wice-paris.org), you can become a certified English language teacher. The American University of Paris (see below) offers a whole programme of continuing education courses, as does Parsons School of Design (www.parsons-paris.com).

Universities

**6 rue du Colonel
Combes**
7th
ℝ Pont de l'Alma
Map p.397 E2 20

The American University of Paris
01 40 62 07 20 | www.aup.edu
True to its name, AUP is a fully accredited American-style university in Paris offering 14 undergraduate degrees and five masters programmes. The university has recently partnered with NYU, providing a variety of international exchange opportunities between the two schools. While the school is international in focus, instruction is in English.

45 rue d'Ulm
5th
ℝ Luxembourg
Map p.409 E2 21

École Normale Supérieure
01 44 32 30 00 | www.ens.fr
Consistently ranked as one of the best universities in the world, École Normale Supérieure provides training to researchers, university professors and future high-level political and business leaders. While the school does admit foreign students, ENS is extremely selective and acceptance into the university is difficult. Jacques Derrida and Samuel Beckett are among the many famous professors who have taught at the university.

**27 rue
Saint-Guillaume**
7th
Ⓜ rue du Bac
Map p.398 B3 22

Fondation Nationale des Sciences Politiques
01 45 49 50 50 | www.sciences-po.fr
With a large percentage of foreign students, Sciences Po is a world famous political science university in the heart of Paris. Classes are given entirely in French but the school does admit many students who speak only rudimentary French. Many foreign universities have arrangements with Sciences Po allowing year or semester long courses and most popular among foreign students is the Certificat d'Etudes Politiques, a year-long programme focusing on modern France. The school's Centre for Peace and Human Security (www.peacecenter.sciences-po.fr) has an excellent reputation. Two year programmes are available.

**blvd de Constance,
77300**
Fontainbleu
Map p.373 B2

Institution Européene d'Administration des Affaires
01 60 72 40 00 | www.insead.fr
There are many graduate business schools offering both MBA and French degrees but INSEAD is perhaps the most well-known. With campuses both in Fontainbleu and in Singapore the school offers MBA, Executive MBA and PhD degrees and is affiliated with the Wharton school.

Special Needs Education
While Paris offers excellent schools and universities, there are relatively few resources in English for students with special needs. French schools generally don't have 'special needs' or 'learning differences' sections and those that do offer accommodations do so in French. Within the French system children with special needs are classified as either mentally handicapped, hearing impaired, visually impaired or physically disabled. Depending upon a given student's classification he or she will be placed in an appropriate school, or provided accommodation.
Sharing Professional Resources, Ideas and New Techniques (SPRINT) is a non-profit organisation that serves children with special needs. SPRINT provides a variety of resources in both English and French. Visit www.sprint.france.free.fr or call 01 42 22 90 62 for more information.

Find out all you need to know about living and working in France

Living France magazine is a must for those wanting to get the most out of France

A subscription to *Living France* gives you everything you need to know to make informed decisions

- Real-life stories from those that have made the move
- Epert advice on financial and legal issues
- Tips for living and working in France
- Over 30 pages of fresh property for sale and rent
- 13 issues a year

Available on subscription from as little as **£49** (70 euros*) to France, **£39** to UK for 13 issues by card or Direct Debit.

☎ **+44 (0)1858 438788** Please quote PE07 🖱 **www.subscription.co.uk/livingfrance/pe07**

*Euro equivalent based on the exchange rate at time of going to press, card payments and Direct Debits will be charged in sterling; £49.00 for subscriptions delivered to France.

www.livingfrance.com

PHOTOGRAPH: EVGENIY, DREAMSTIME.COM

Transportation

Other options **Getting Around** p.30, **Car** p.32

Paris enjoys one of the best public transportation systems in the world. Strikes are not uncommon but when it's running nearly every corner of the city and the near suburbs are served by train, bus, tram and metro, which is by far the most popular mode of transportation. The streets are filled with scooters, motorcycles, cars and, increasingly, bikes. Because parking is generally a nightmare in the city, everyone (rich and poor) uses public transportation some of the time. The Île-de-France is served by metro, RER (a regional express train network) and Translien suburban trains. The RATP, the city's transportation authority, runs both metro and bus lines and shares control of the RER with the SNCF, the national railway company, who is in turn responsible for all suburban, national and international trains.

Traffic Updates

For real-time traffic updates throughout France and all things related to driving visit www.bison-fute.equipement.gouv.fr. For radio traffic reports in English, Radio France provides information every 10 minutes on 107.7 FM.

Driving in Paris

Driving in Paris can be a frustrating and exhausting experience. Traffic gets worse and worse, parking is practically non-existent and petrol is expensive at around €1.40 per litre. While it may take five minutes by metro to travel from St-Germain des Prés to the Hôtel de Ville it can easily take 45 minutes in rush hour from the time you pull out of your parking place to the time you pull into another one a few kilometres away. If you're planning on commuting from the suburbs to the city at rush hour you can expect to spend a lot of time in your car. Many people who live in the suburbs keep their cars there and take the train into Paris. Car-pooling, while it might do wonders for Paris gridlock, is just not part of the culture.

Under The Influence

Drivers are considered drunk if their blood/alcohol ratio is equal to or exceeds 0.5 grams per litre. Levels between 0.5 and 0.8 can bring fines of up to €135. Levels in excess of 0.8 bring penalties including two years in jail, the confiscation of your vehicle, the suspension of your drivers licence and a fine of up to €4,500. Driving under the influence of an illegal substance can bring fines of up to €3,000 and three years in prison.

Driving Habits

Parisians are impatient and often fast, reckless drivers. There's a lot of horn-honking, cursing and swerving and if you plan to drive, you'd better do so aggressively. Don't expect smiling drivers waving you ahead or letting you into their lanes. As with most things in daily life, driving is a battle to be won by the most talented, the most creative and the most demanding and, given the wild driving habits of Parisians, there are many accidents.

Non-Drivers

In July 2007 the city of Paris launched its Velib' scheme (p.35), making bicycles available to the public. Throughout the city you can pick up a bike, ride it for 30 minutes and return it to any of the stations spread throughout the city without charge. Along with the launch of Velib', the city has begun an aggressive campaign to promote the use of bicycles and to get people out of their cars. As a result, bikes have become increasingly popular and have started flooding the streets. While this is a good thing for Paris and for the environment in general, there are now more obstacles for drivers. The bikes are popular with tourists who can see the city as an amusement park and are often unaware of the rules of the road. The city has increased the number of cycle tracks, but there's a lot of work to be done. If you're driving be aware that along with motorcycles, pedestrians, other cars and scooters, there will be plenty of cyclists sharing the road with you.

Paris parking

Traffic Rules & Regulations

Unless otherwise marked, the speed limit within the city is 50kph and 130kph on sourrounding expressways. Speed cameras exist throughout the city, for specific locations visit www.securiteroutiere.equipement.gouv.fr. Keep in mind that you're responsible for any fines you incur while operating a car, regardless of whether or not the car is rented or your own. In France the car on the right always has the right of way unless it is explicitly indicated otherwise. You may only pass on the left, though this is a law that is frequently ignored by Parisian drivers.

Parking

When you're considering a parking place, pay careful attention to street signs. Signs marked *payant* require you to either use a parking card (available at *tabacs* throughout the city) or deposit coins into the parking meter. The meter will read your card or accept your money, you'll enter the amount of time you'd like to park, the meter will print a receipt and you display it on the dashboard of your car. In central Paris, parking is occasionally free during holidays and weekends but make sure you always check; there's an army of unsmiling ticket writers wandering the city at all hours ready to present you with a fine. You are allowed to park near your home in *payant* spaces for a reduced rate by applying for a *vignette de stationnement residential* (a residential parking sticker) and these are available at your *mairie*. To pay a parking ticket, purchase a *timbre fiscal* at a *tabac* for the amount of the fine, paste it into the appropriate square of the ticket and send it off.

Petrol Stations

Within the city limits full-blown petrol stations are few and far between. Usually the pumps are built directly into the pavement in front of small store-front garages. The fuel is pumped for you, you pay for the service and you're back on the road. Space is limited and there's just not room for the city block service stations you may be used to. Total, BP, Esso and Shell are the main petrol providers and their stations are all over the city. However, there are few petrol stations in Paris so it's a good idea to know where you're headed before you run out. Petrol is more expensive in Paris than it is in the United States and generally less expensive than it is in the UK. Both diesel (*gazole*) and lead substitute petrol (*essence*) is available.

Vehicle Leasing

Every major vehicle leasing company in the world has an office in Paris so competition is fierce and rates are generally low. Leasing a car is a simple process and requires little in the way of paperwork. You can make reservations on the internet or over the telephone and to lease a vehicle you simply need a driving licence and a credit card. It is often a good idea to check general travel websites such as Expedia for rates. Also online, www.podo.fr is an excellent resource as is www.kayak.com. Rates fluctuate enormously and depend on several factors such as overall supply, season and driver's age, but easyCar

Vehicle Leasing Agents

AutoEurope	08 00 94 05 57	www.autoeurope.fr
Avis	08 20 05 05 05	www.avis.com
Budget	01 58 05 36 00	www.budget.com
EasyCar	na	www.easycar.com
Europcar	08 25 35 83 58	www.europcar.com
Hertz	08 25 86 18 61	www.hertz.com
Renault	01 53 53 61 05	www.renaultusa.com
Sixt	08 20 00 74 98	www.sixt.com

and Sixt both offer consistently low rates. For long-term rentals the best deal by far is with Renault who offers a service specifically geared to expats moving to Europe allowing rentals for up to six months, providing brand new cars, full insurance and 24 hour roadside assistance. For example, a month long rental ranges from €500 to €2,000 depending upon the class of car you choose and daily rentals can be as low as €14 per day with easyCar.

New Motorbike/Scooter Dealers		
BMW	13th	01 45 80 50 31
Ducati	17th	01 58 05 10 20
Harley Davidson	15th	01 48 28 06 74
Honda	3th	01 42 72 29 00
Peugot	9th	01 45 96 09 39
Piaggio	11th	01 43 38 26 26
Scooters Parisien	11th	01 40 30 30 30
Triumph	11th	01 48 04 88 00

Because change is so constant in the travel industry your best bet is to use a comparison website to search for the best deal at the time you're interested in renting.

Company Cars

If you're moving to Paris to work as a high-level executive or as a diplomat it's likely you will be provided with a car service rather than your own car. Because parking is such a hassle, it is

Used Motorbike/Scooter Dealers		
Academy Scooters	11th	01 48 05 19 35
Almet Moto	12th	01 55 25 50 90
Darcos Bastille	11th	01 43 14 26 00
Scoot Minute	11th	01 43 14 00 33

far more convenient to be driven but it is not nearly as common to be provided a driver in Paris as it is in developing nations. Long black limousines are rare; slick black sedans are favoured over the long stretch variety you may be used to seeing.

Buying a Vehicle

While all European car brands are represented in the country, you'll find that most Parisians don't drive big flashy cars. Luxury cars are rare and people tend to favour small, efficient vehicles. Ferraris and the like are generally considered vulgar and, except for in the 8th and in the 16th, big roaring mid-life crisis cars are rarely seen. You'll find the majority of car dealers in the suburbs and in the outer *arrondissements* where there's more space and less traffic. If you're looking for a Porsche, a Ferrari or a Rolls Royce you'll find dealers in the 16th, otherwise companies like Nissan, Toyota and VW have showrooms throughout the city. The new Toyota showroom on the Champs-Élysée is particularly impressive as is the annual Paris auto show (www.mondial-automobile.com). Cars registered in foreign countries are usually brought into France by road or ferry and are not usually registered by French customs. Any vehicle that's been shipped to France will be processes by customs and depending upon the car's value you'll have to pay the appropriate taxes and administrative fees. Additionally, a French mechanic must certify that the car conforms to French standards which can be a long, expensive process.

New Car Dealers

All of the dealerships in the table sell used cars as well as new vehicles. Generally it is far safer to purchase both used and new cars from established dealers, particularly when you don't speak French well or are unfamiliar with the system, but Craigslist, FUSAC and eBay are all popular online sources for used cars, motorcycles and scooters

Car Dealers		
Alfa Romeo/Fiat	17th	01 43 80 55 11
Honda	16th	01 45 00 14 51
Jaguar	19th	01 42 39 20 40
Lamborghini	16th	01 45 08 70 70
Land Rover	19th	01 42 08 77 88
Lexus	17th	01 40 55 40 00
Maserati	16th	01 47 43 00 00
Mazda	17th	01 40 25 40 25
Nissan	16th	01 46 51 80 60
Peugeot	12th	01 44 89 16 10
Renault	8th	01 43 59 35 70
Toyota	15th	01 53 86 80 80

Vehicle Finance

While car dealers, both new and used, offer various financing packages, you'll often get a far better deal at your bank. Dealers require a 30% down payment and the remainder is then paid in monthly or bi-annual payments over three to five years. Interest rates tend to be far higher than what you'll find in the main Paris banks.

Vehicle Finance

Cetelem	08 20 20 91 09	www.cetelem.fr
Credit Municipal de Paris	01 44 61 64 00	www.creditmunicipal.fr
Daimler Chrysler Finance	01 30 80 84 00	www.daimlerchrysler.com
Diac	01 49 32 80 00	www.diac.fr
GAP	01 44 29 05 10	www.gap.fr
Peugeot Finance	01 40 05 66 10	www.peugot.fr

Rates obviously change depending on factors such as the kind of car you're interested in, your age, your income, your position and the duration of your loan. For a €15,000 car, financing ranges from 3.5-5.5 % on a three year loan. Every major bank in France offers automobile loans and the companies in the table are non-bank lending and financing companies.

Vehicle Insurance

Any car on the road in France, without exception, must be covered by unlimited third-party insurance. If you're bringing a car into the country you must maintain an international insurance card proving that your car is insured in France. Temporary insurance policies are available from the customs office at every French entry point. You may not register a car in France without proof of insurance. There are three basic levels of insurance: third-party (*au tiers*) which is the minimum required by law, fire and theft (*tiers complet*) and full coverage (*tous risques*). Other options are available to professional drivers and collectors among others. The cost of insurance depends primarily on your accident and claims record so be certain to provide well-documented evidence of previous coverage. The most well-known automobile insurance companies in France are MACIF, MAAF and GAN. A variety of international insurance companies also exist in France.

Vehicle Insurance

Adinas	01 53 20 03 33	www.adinas.fr
GAN	01 40 61 96 77	www.gan.fr
MAAF	08 20 30 08 20	www.maaf.fr
MACIF	01 55 56 57 58	www.macif.fr
MAIF	01 55 43 44 00	www.maif.fr
MMA	01 53 41 82 41	www.mma.fr
Patrim One	01 42 99 60 11	www.patrimone.com

Registering a Vehicle

As long as you have a permanent residence in Paris and are living in France legally, you have the right to buy a car. When you do, you must register it within 15 days at your local *préfecture*. When you purchase a car from a dealer you'll be given a temporary ownership certificate which is valid for two weeks. The dealer then transmits a request for a permanent proof of ownership called the *carte grise*. If you buy a car from a private seller, he or she is obliged to provide you with a receipt and a clearance, which is a cancelled *carte grise*. If the car is more than 4 years old, the seller must also provide a certificate declaring the condition of the car (this *certificat de controle technique* must be less than six months old). The seller finally must provide you with the original *carte grise* with the name crossed out to indicate that the car has been sold.

Within one month of the sale you must take all of these documents to the *préfecture* where you'll be given a new *carte grise* which you can then take to any petrol station or garage and have licence plates made. When you go to the *préfecture* make sure that you have official identification, proof of residence, the *certificat de cession*, or bill of sale, and a completed registration application. If the car you've purchased is new you'll need to bring the *certificat de conformité*, a certificate proving that the car adheres to present standards.

Traffic Fines & Offences

While Parisians tend to drive like maniacs, park their cars everywhere and generally behave as if there's no law at all, police checkpoints are frequent and traffic fines are common. Seatbelts are compulsory and failure to wear yours if you're driving will result in a €40 fine. Passengers not wearing theirs can be fined €140. When driving you must always carry your driving licence, registration, and proof of insurance. If any of these are missing when you're stopped by the police you're liable to be fined up to €150. Running

127

a red light carries an absolute minimum €300 fine and you may even be called to court. The French authorities can stop you and check your papers whenever they feel inclined. Using a telephone while driving is also illegal and doing so can result in a €150 fine. As for speeding, there are cameras throughout the city and exceeding the speed limit will incur fines of up to €300. A French driving licence has 12 points which may be deducted for breaking various laws and if you lose your 12 points, your licence will be revoked.

Recovery Services/Towing

ABDR	08 00 10 43 05	www.abdr-paris.com
ADA	01 46 55 22 36	www.ada-peugeot.com
Alfauto	01 58 46 10 00	www.alfauto.fr
Auto Guy's Depannage	06 98 81 41 92	www.guysdepannage.com
CHL Depannage	08 00 10 43 05	www.chl-paris.com
Dan Dépann	08 00 25 10 00	www.dandepann.fr
Kablé	01 42 28 33 33	www.kable.fr

Breakdowns

Motorways throughout France are equipped with emergency telephone boxes and, if you breakdown within the city, a payphone, cafe, or restaurant are rarely far. Many car dealers and rental agencies provide 24 hour recovery and towing services. Your insurance company can also provide recovery packages and if you plan to do a lot of commuting it's worth your money to have full coverage.

Traffic Accidents

Traffic accidents are remarkably common in Paris, and France has one of the highest rates of car-related deaths in Europe. Motorcyclists and scooter riders are the most susceptible to fatal accidents. While you should be alert anywhere in the city, pay particular attention when navigating the enormous roundabouts at Etoile, Bastille and Nation.

If you're involved in a traffic accident call the police immediately by dialling 17. If someone has been injured the police will send an ambulance. All parties involved in an accident are required to file an accident report (*constat amiable d'accident*) and you should exchange insurance details. If the accident is minor, the police don't need to be called. Make sure that you keep a copy of the official French accident report form in your glove box; English forms are available from your insurance company. In case of an accident you must fill in the details of the report with the other party or parties involved. Make sure to be precise with the written portion of the report and if you write French badly, you're better off writing in English. Also, if you're unclear about what has been written by another party do not sign the report. The *constat* must be submitted to your insurance company within 24 hours of the accident. It is a good idea to call your insurance agent as soon as possible. Claims are settled by the insurance companies unless there's been an injury, in which case the police will determine responsibility.

Vehicle Repairs

When you take your vehicle in for repairs, make sure that you have your paperwork. A reputable mechanic will not make major repairs on a car that he thinks is stolen, and mechanics are legally obliged to verify that the registration matches the car. Insurance companies will often stipulate

Vehicle Repairs

ASR	18th	01 46 27 33 23
Christian Capus	11th	01 43 07 56 51
Garage Bosquet	1st	01 55 35 30 00
SPEG	16th	01 53 70 18 00
Sud Est	11th	01 43 73 51 78

which garage you should visit but this depends entirely on your insurance coverage, the provider and the circumstances of your repair. Deductibles as well vary enormously and can range from €500–€2,000 and higher depending upon your coverage. The best car dealers will provide full post-purchase service. Paris is not a city built for cars and the constant stop and start traffic, the cobbled streets and the wild drivers will all take their toll on you and your car. You'll see drivers squeezing cars into impossibly small parking spaces by bumping the cars on either end to make room, and no-one bats an eye. If you're living in central Paris with a brand new Porsche, prepare for heartbreak.

Small but indispensable...

Perfectly proportioned to fit in your pocket, this marvellous mini guidebook makes sure you don't just get the holiday you paid for but rather the one that you dreamed of.

Paris Mini Visitors' Guide
Maximising your holiday, minimising your hand luggage

The ultimate destination
for all things Parisian

Paris Cultural Tours • Paris Literary Salons
Paris Lodgings • THE PARIS INSIDER newsletter

FREE at www.paris-expat.com

Exploring

Exploring

City of romance, city of chic, city of light. However you like to think of it, Paris has a habit of reinforcing all its more pleasant cliches. Not content with having more than its fair share of postcard icons, the city has the sort of random beauty that stops you in your tracks.

You want culture? Count on an impressive array of world class museums and cultural events to which scarcely a season goes by without some new addition.

Yet, for all that, you'll still find Paris a touch less frenetic than other major world capitals. With its street corner carrousels, open-air cafes and traditional markets, this is a city that has never quite shaken off its Old Europe pace. In short, it's a delight to explore, which goes some way to explaining why it continues to be one of the world's most visited cities. The city's historic heart beats between the Latin Quarter (p 143). and the Marais (p.139). You won't have to look hard here to find narrow streets and half-timbered houses dating back six centuries or more. Elsewhere, successive kings and emperors have left their stamp of grandeur. But it was Baron Eugene Haussmann who earned Paris its city of light moniker, after he gave it its first street lighting – and a lot more besides. As Prefect of the Seine, he flattened slums and mansions to make way for a mid 19th century vision of modernity. His new boulevards were lined with tall apartments, whose wrought iron balconies and restrained elegance provided a template for city construction long after Haussmann was gone.

Hemmed in by its Périphérique, Paris might seem as though it's in danger of becoming a museum-city. Experienced close-up, you'll find a different reality. New *quartiers* spring up out of wasteland, making inroads into greater Paris. As a city, Paris is constantly reinventing itself. It just happens to be on its own terms.

To grasp Paris as Parisians do, you should think of it in terms of Left Bank and Right Bank. For some visitors, that's a division that only works well when they're travelling downstream along the Seine. If you're one of them, don't despair, for Paris is also a collection of villages. From genteel Passy to multi-ethnic Belleville, there's a sense of identity that's soon apparent to anyone prepared to explore. And, whether your stay is long or short, don't neglect the many gems that lie beyond the Périphérique. Hop on the metro, the bus, the tram or the train; public transport is extensive and great value. Often, though, travelling on foot is most rewarding of all. Getting lost – as you certainly will – is all part of the fun.

Île de la Cité

Check Out The Champs

The Champs Élysée has its critics, but a massive revamp has gone a long way towards putting the oomph back into 'the world's most beautiful avenue.' Inhale the art nouveau elegance of Maison Guerlain, take in some automotive art at l'Atelier Renault, or just join the weekend strollers who never tire of enjoying the avenue's ravishing, tree-lined vista. See p.140.

Canoodle In The Park

What with cycling park attendants and official Wi-Fi hotspots, Parisian parks (p.183) are no longer the stuffy places they once were. The Jardin du Luxembourg is for civilised pleasures, while Bercy and André-Citroën are great places to unleash the kids. Join the joggers on their circuit around Parc Monceau or, if it's romance you want, head hand-in-hand for the hilltop belvedere of Buttes-Chaumont.

Head For The Heights

Notre Dame isn't the only place to get an Eiffel of the city. Paris abounds with vantage points, some thronging with crowds, others surprisingly intimate. If you think Montmartre's views are captivating (and they are), try sampling them from the dome of Sacré Coeur (p.160). Can't face all those steps? Take the lift to the top of the Arc de Triomphe (p.164), and you'll feel like an emperor, or blow away the cobwebs from the 8th floor terrace of Galeries Lafayette (p.291).

Give In To Market Forces

Every *quartier* has one, and every one is different. Whether it's for bargain undies or seasonal indulgences such as *trompettes de mort*, browsing a market is a pleasure that you definitely shouldn't forego. Shop against the grand backdrop of the Eiffel Tower at the Marché de Saxe-Breteuil or head indoors to the Marais' age-old Marché des Enfants Rouges. You'll need to rise at dawn though, in most cases it's all over by lunchtime. See p.295.

Go On A Cruise

Glide under the bridges of the Seine and you're guaranteed another perspective on the city. Most cruises follow a circuit around the Île de la Cité and Île St-Louis, departing from the quays below the Eiffel Tower. For an alternative experience – including an interesting subterranean stretch – take a cruise along the leafy Canal St-Martin. See p.195.

Hit The Beach

Saint-Tropez eat your heart out. During the height of the city's annual summer exodus, a 3km stretch of the Seine's right bank becomes Paris Plage (p.183). The sandy, palm-fringed paradise comes complete with hammocks, deckchairs and day-long activities for recharging the batteries of city-bound beach babes and stay-at-home families. In recent years, the addition of two new beaches, at the Port de la Gare and the Bassin de la Villette, has trebled the fun.

Take Tea At The Top Of The World

…the Institute of the Arab World (p.170), that is. Vertiginous glass lifts soar to the 9th floor of this striking building, where you can linger over a glass of mint tea, enjoy a spot of lunch, or simply enjoy a privileged view on the stately hulk of Notre Dame and the place de la Bastille. Without the trimmings, the views are on the house.

Cheer On The Yellow Jersey

It may be dogged by controversy, but that doesn't stop *le tout Paris* from swarming to the Champs-Élysées to cheer the heroes home. The gruelling 3,350km race draws to a triumphant close in July each year, with honour laps around the Arc de Triomphe. If you happen to be in town then, there's really nowhere else to be. See p.43.

Go To Church

Notre-Dame, Sacré Coeur and the Sainte-Chapelle all deserve their place on any visitor's list, but there are many other superb places of worship to reward your curiosity; take, for example, the mostly 12th century Église St-Pierre-de-Montmartre, tucked away close to Sacré Coeur, or the Église St-Roch, a baroque beauty on the elegant rue St-Honoré. See p.159.

Splash In The Seine

If you only get round to a dip in one of Paris' 35 swimming pools, make it this one. The Piscine Joséphine Baker (p.232) is the city's only floating pool, moored alongside the radically renovated Rive-Gauche. Festooned with bunting, the Baker pool is open to the sky in the heat of summer, when it becomes the focal point for the latest slice of Paris Plage action.

Get The Look

It's not for nothing that Parisians are so routinely well-turned out. Sterling bargains exist for those prepared to sift the rails of the fashion capital's better *dégriffé* boutiques. The same goes for *les soldes*, a twice-yearly affair synchronised with military precision, and capable of making grown women weep for joy. For those in need of formal inspiration, free weekly fashion shows are held at the *grands magasins* of Galeries Lafayette (p.291) and Printemps (p.292).

Step Back In Time

With royal homes such as Versailles and Fontainebleau nearby, it's easy to overlook more modest gems – though modesty, of course, is strictly relative. Several remarkable *hôtels particuliers* (mansions) offer an intimate window on the past. Topping the list are the 19th century home of art connoisseur, Edouard André, now the Musée Jacquemart-André (p.176), and the poignantly beautiful Musée Nissim de Camondo (p.177)

Find Time For A Cafe Pose

Cafes (p.336) are an integral part of Parisian life, and you can linger as long as you like over your espresso (sometimes longer, depending on the waiter's whim). The choice is virtually limitless. Pose outside the ritzy Café de la Paix at Opéra, or ponder the meaning of life within the hallowed walls of les Deux Magots? Then again, why not watch the world go by from the comfort of your local zinc bar? You'll be surprised how quickly you become one of the regulars.

Float Your Boat

Pack a picnic and escape the city limits at one of the city's largest green spaces (p.183). Make a beeline for the Bois de Boulogne, with its stunning ornamental gardens and the children's Jardin d'Acclimatation (actually much more fun than it sounds). Or make a Sunday of it at the Bois de Vincennes, bigger than Boulogne and every bit as pretty. Both have lake with rowing boats for hire.

Take A Hike

If you want to get the real flavour of a *quartier*, the best way is to book a place on one of the many organised walking trips (p.199). Pick a themed tour to take you on the trail of historical or gastronomic Paris, or let locals such as Belleville-based Ça-Se-Visite! show you areas you might not otherwise discover.

Learn Your Chablis From Your Chardonnay

Where better to hone your nose and taste buds? Paris offers wine tasting lessons and courses (p.233) as well as a wealth of wine bars and haute cuisine restaurants to practise in, such as Legrand Filles et Fils (p.350). The city is also within easy reach of some outstanding wine regions including Champagne (p.203) and Burgundy (p.205), but this is a skill that travels so you'll never order a bad bottle again.

Be A Culture Vulture

There are rich pickings on offer if you love museums and galleries. If you don't, well, now's your chance to find out what you've been missing. Aside from the big guns, such as the Louvre (p.174) and Musée d'Orsay (p.171), there's a host of smaller, specialty museums too numerous to list. Whatever your taste, chances are there's something for you.

Meander In The Marais

The Marais (meaning 'marsh') enjoyed a glitzy, aristocratic interlude before slipping into centuries of neglect. Today, it's back on the map as one of the most vibrant spots in Paris. Its historic streets are lined with designer boutiques, trendy bars and restaurants, many of which are just as lively on Sundays when other *quartiers* tend to doze. Start opposite the Hôtel de Ville and follow your fancy. See p.139.

Watch The Iron Lady Dance

The world's favourite monument attracted much criticism when it was built in 1889. Famously, Maupassant claimed to dine at the Eiffel Tower regularly because it was the only place where he was sure to be spared the sight of it. Since 2000, the tower's shimmying night-time light show can be enjoyed from across the city, but from Trocadéro, the sight is transfixing. See p.164.

Haunt The Opera

Paris has two opera houses, but for most visitors, it's the wildly opulent Opéra Garnier (p.167) that's the star. Adorned every inch with polychromatic marble, gilt and mosaics, Charles Garnier's 1875 creation is in a style (or styles) all of its own. If you can't stretch to a performance, be sure at least to peek at the interior –it's pure theatre.

Get On Your Bike

Cycling is a great way to explore, serving up exhilarating new perspectives on landmarks you thought you knew well. There are over 370km of cycle paths and with Vélib', the low-cost rental bike scheme, there's even more incentive to get pedalling. Bike rental points are stationed all across the city, so you can hop on and off at will. The first 30 minutes are free. See p.35.

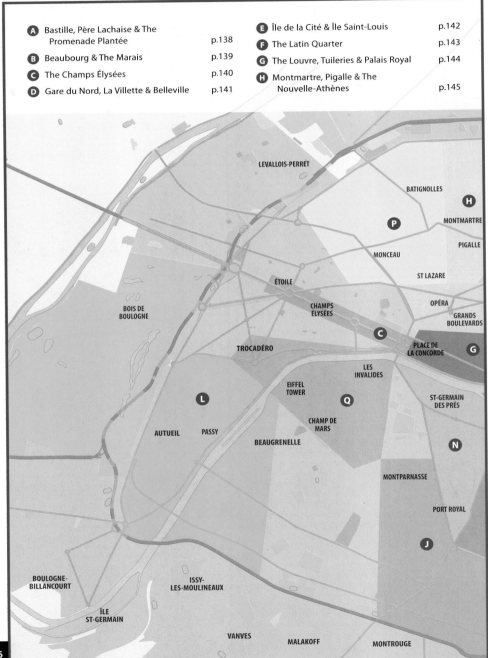

Exploring Overview Map

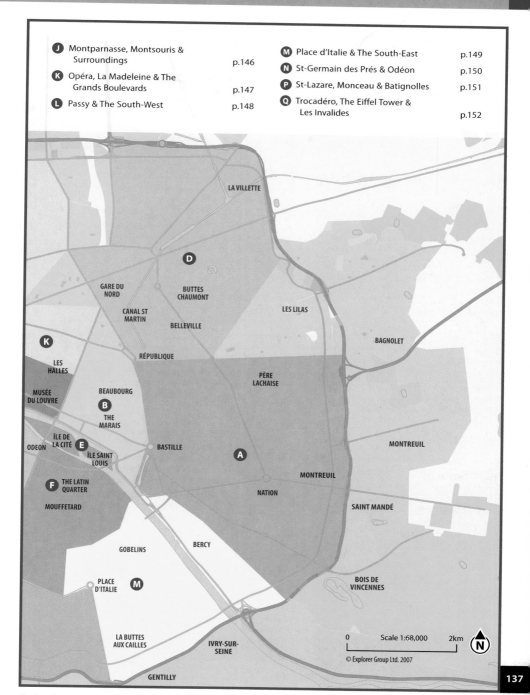

LA VILLETTE

GARE DU NORD

BUTTES CHAUMONT

CANAL ST MARTIN

BELLEVILLE

LES LILAS

BAGNOLET

RÉPUBLIQUE

LES HALLES

MUSÉE DU LOUVRE

BEAUBOURG

THE MARAIS

PÈRE LACHAISE

ÎLE DE LA CITÉ

ODEON

ÎLE SAINT LOUIS

BASTILLE

MONTREUIL

THE LATIN QUARTER

MONTREUIL

NATION

MOUFFETARD

SAINT MANDÉ

GOBELINS

BERCY

PLACE D'ITALIE

BOIS DE VINCENNES

LA BUTTES AUX CAILLES

IVRY-SUR-SEINE

GENTILLY

0   Scale 1:68,000   2km

N

© Explorer Group Ltd. 2007

Map p.401, p.402, p.411
Area Ⓐ p.137

Bastille, Père Lachaise & The Promenade Plantée

The Lowdown
The fashionable set have made inroads into this traditionally working class area.

The Good
Full of character and hidden history, the area offers some fine city walking.

The Bad
You'll need a map to visit Père Lachaise but even then, individual graves can be hard to find. The pretty village of Charonne is little visited because it's awkward to reach.

The Must-Dos
Pay your dues to the dead famous in the most atmospheric of cemeteries; round off a morning's mooch at the Marché d'Aligre with some local hospitality at Le Baron Rouge; get a bird's eye view from the Promenade Plantée.

Port de l'Arsenal

Bastille

You won't find the infamous prison in the place de la Bastille, and don't be misled by the large column in the centre, either: it commemorates an entirely different revolution of July 1830. The spirit of 1789 does live on, though, in the political rallies that generally start or end here on the square. Dominating the space since 1989, the Opera Bastille (p.369) is the city's premier opera venue, though there are still grumbles about its acoustics. The building has been compared to a 'hippopotamus in a bathtub'; still, it's doubtless an improvement on Napoleon's giant plaster elephant, which once adorned the square. At the start of boulevard Richard Lenoir, the regular Saturday arts and crafts market is worth scanning for something original. Nearby, the rues de Lappe et de la Roquette attract a trendy young crowd with their fashionable restaurants, clubs and boutiques. You should also seek out the lively Oberkampf area to the north, for more in the way of a night-time vibe. If you're in the mood for markets, you'll find none livelier than the place d'Aligre which trades daily except Tuesdays, and includes a number of bric-a-brac stalls. The market is just south of the rue du Faubourg St-Antoine, a road that for centuries has been associated with master furniture makers. South of place de la Bastille, the marina of Bassin de l'Arsenal is pleasant to stroll around, and the start point for summer boat trips along the Canal St-Martin.

Père Lachaise

A visit to this rambling necropolis is an outing in itself, and you should set aside a half day to explore its shady lanes and mossy mausolea. North east of Bastille, it stands slightly aloof on its hill, and affords some great views of the living city as well as the dead. The notables are too numerous to list, but they include Chopin and Piaf, Ernst and Balzac, while the tombs of Jim Morrison, Chopin and Victor Noir have become places of pilgrimage in their own right.

At the south-east corner of Père Lachaise is the picturesque village of Charonne, which centres on the 13th century Romanesque church and the cobbled rue St-Blaise. It's as practical to reach by trekking along rue de Bagnolet as it is from metro Gambetta.

The Promenade Plantée

This popular raised walkway, also known as the Coulée Verte, follows the route of the old Bastille–St Maur railway. You can join it from the steps or lift on avenue Daumesnil, just south of the Bastille Opera, or at points along the way. Its 4.5km are imaginatively landscaped with bowers, cascades and sculptures, and offer fascinating vignettes along

the way. The most interesting section takes in the Viaduc des Arts, a community of around 50 artists and craftsmen, snugly housed beneath the old railway arches. Further on, Picpus Cemetery (35 rue de Picpus) makes for a good hour's historical detour. Over a two month period in 1794, 1,036 people were buried in mass graves here after being guillotined on the former place du Trône (off place de la Nation). Many were commoners and their names and occupations are engraved in the cemetery chapel. The main section of the cemetery is reserved for the cream of French high society, among them General Lafayette, over whose tomb the stars-and-stripes flutter. The promenade ends just short of the Porte Dorée, where you'll find the aquarium and the new Cité Nationale de l'Histoire d'Immigration (www.histoire-immigration.fr). The city's biggest green space, the Bois de Vincennes (p.184), is a short walk away.

Map p.400
Area **B** *p.137*

Beaubourg & The Marais

The Lowdown
*An iconic building
dominates an arty
neighbourhood; ancient
streets here have a
contemporary vibe.*

The Good
*Quaint passageways,
hidden courtyards,
museums great
and small.*

The Bad
*Surfacing from metro
Les Halles into the
characterless 70s mall
and gardens.*

The Must-Dos
*Be awed by genius at
the Musée Picasso;
browse, covet or
indulge at the
designer boutiques of
the Marais.*

Beaubourg

Love it or loathe it, the Centre Georges-Pompidou not only defines Beaubourg, for many Parisians, it *is* Beaubourg. Richard Rogers and Renzo Piano challenged all expectations when they opted to turn their building inside-out – escalators, colour-coded utility pipes and all. Three decades on, the concept is no longer unique, but the building still stops you in your tracks. Inside, the Centre's multi disciplined art exhibitions (p.176) continue to ring the changes. Outside, a vibrant mood governs the plaza, a vast, sloping expanse where entertainers of all kinds come to strut their stuff. It's all good fun (but keep an eye on your wallet). On the Centre's southern side, the whacky Stravinsky fountain pays homage to the composer's works, against a backdrop of the Église St-Merry. The streets between here and the Fontaine des Innocents are pleasant to explore before you're caught up in the frenzy of the rue de Rivoli. Nearby, the Tour St-Jacques is more famous as the site of Pascal's experiment with atmospheric pressure than for the church to which it once belonged.

The Marais

Cultured by day, hip by night, the Marais is most visitors' idea of a perfect Paris stroll. Largely spared the Haussmann treatment, and neglected until recent decades, the area oozes history at every turn. Massive double carriage gates reveal glimpses of ancient courtyards, while up-and-coming fashion designers display desirables from snug timber-beamed studios. Some magnificent mansions are now major museums, among them the Musées Picasso (p.177) and Carnavalet (p.170). Throw in a good measure of other curiosities, such as the Cognacq-Jay (p.171), the Musée de la Chasse et de la Nature (01 53 01 92 40) and the Musée de la Magie (01 42 72 13 26), and you can easily fill a weekend or three.

On the rue de Rivoli, the grand Hôtel de Ville (p.165) exerts a gravitational pull on Marais life, hosting popular exhibitions, while its square is the focus for Paris Plage (p.182). Behind the indispensable BHV department store (p.290), the gay scene centres on the rues des Archives and Ste Croix-de-la-Bretonnerie. The cluster of streets around rue des Rosiers has been the Jewish *quartier* since the 12th century, and retains its character still. Set apart a little to the north, the Musée des Arts et Métiers (p.174) is quite unlike other science museums, occupying a 12th century abbey. Towards République, the Marais becomes more working class. Don't skip the remarkable place des Vosges, just short of Bastille. Hardly altered since 1612, it's the city's oldest square. At number 6, you'll find the red brick House of Victor Hugo (p.163).

Les Halles

To Zola, it was a bustling, centuries-old food market that provisioned the whole city. Today's les Halles, a 1970s underground mall, is more or less universally loathed. That's set to change however, with a sweeping architectural revamp due to begin in 2008. It will also transform the gardens, a magnet for unsavoury types.

At their western edge is the circular Bourse, Paris' stock exchange. Nearby, the imposing Gothic church of St-Eustache (p.161) wasn't completed until 1637, which explains its renaissance interior. Among its attributes is an exuberant modern relief of the Les Halles traders. Foodies should make a beeline for lively rue Montorgueil, where several fine old purveyors include Stohrer, in the patisserie business since 1730. Here, Les Halles rubs shoulders with Sentier, home to the rag trade (you may just catch the growl of sewing machines.) On rue Étienne-Marcel, the Tour Jean-Sans-Peur (p.167) is a wonderful survivor from the Hundred Years War. It was built for the Duke of Burgundy, who later lost power as bloodily as he gained it.

139

The Champs-Élysées

Map p.387
Area **C** p.136

The 'world's most beautiful avenue' runs nearly 1.2 miles between Étoile and the place de la Concorde. It traces the old Royal Axis, which led west to the royal residence at St-Germain-en-Laye. In Louis XIV's day, this grand Axis was little more than a glint in the royal eye. By the late 19th century, it had been developed by Paris' burgeoning *haute bourgeoisie*, and was already a popular promenading ground for the fashionable set. After more than a decade in the doldrums, the Champs has largely regained its lustre, thanks to a major facelift and tougher regulations. At weekends, its wide granite promenades and swanky stores are a huge draw for locals and visitors alike.

The Lowdown
High-street names may have lowered the tone, but the city's poshest promenade hasn't lost its pulling power.

The western end is marked by the unmistakable Arc de Triomphe (p.164). As you descend the Champs towards Concorde, the even numbers on the left still represent the more expensive side of the street. It's hard to tell these days, though, as several luxury names have cast in their lot with the odds, and high-street flagships have laid claim to territory on either side. Highlights of a Champs stroll include peeking into the lavish art nouveau interior at Guerlain's perfume boutique and taking the womb-like elevator to the top of Louis Vuitton's handbag emporium (the 'museum' is really a ruse to secure the store's right to trade on Sunday, but the fine views are free). Meanwhile, the cutting-edge showrooms of Citroên, Honda and Renault set out to seduce far more than just car buffs. If you're not ready to splurge on lunch at Fouquet's or nibble macaroons within Ladurée's elegant tearoom, there's always McDonalds – albeit a better-looking version than the one on the high street. The area between avenues Georges V and Montaigne is known as the Golden Triangle; check out the roll-call of couturiers along avenue Montaigne if you want to know why. From Rond-Point des Champs-Elysées the avenue becomes more leafy. Cloistered behind high walls, the Elysée Palace is the official residence of France's president. Opposite, the Grand Palais and the Petit Palais face each other on either side of avenue Winston Churchill. The stunning glass-and-iron Grand Palais (p.157) hosts trade fairs and highly popular temporary art exhibitions. The Petit Palais, also built for the 1900 Exposition Universelle, is a wedding cake of gilt and sinuous lines. Full of treasures, it's a sort of city equivalent of the nation's Louvre, and worth visiting just for the cloistered terrace cafe inside. Nearby, the Pont Alexandre III (named after a Russian tsar) leads over the river to les Invalides (p.166). With its bronze Neptune and cherubs, it's easily one of the city's loveliest bridges.

The Good
A unique perspective, from whichever end of the Champs you stand; stunning Belle Époque architecture, prime terrain for a Sunday stroll.

The Bad
Traffic noise is a constant, while the proportions of the place de la Concorde are completely lost in the volume of cars. Thanks to archaic trading laws, even locals find it hard to know which stores open on Sundays along the Champs. Pickpockets work the area.

At the Champs' eastern end is place de la Concorde. This octagonal square, the city's biggest, has a bloody history. Some 1,300 souls, including Louis XVI and Marie-Antoinette, were guillotined here during the Terror of 1794, before being unceremoniously buried near rue Pasquier. Notable buildings include the opulent Hôtel Crillon (p.25), where the queen took her piano lessons. In the guillotine's place stands a 3,300 year old obelisk, a gift from the Viceroy of Egypt, flanked by statues representing important French cities.

The Must-Dos
Have a night out at one of the many cinemas and round off your evening with a stroll past some of the glitzier stores.

Place de la Concorde

The Champs-Élysées

View from the Parc des Buttes-Chaumont

Map p.390, p.385, p.391 ◄
Area **D** p.137

Gare du Nord, La Villette & Belleville

Gare du Nord & Surroundings

Many people get their first glimpse of Paris when they step out of the Eurostar terminal at the Gare du Nord. Despite ongoing makeovers, the area between this station and the shabbier Gare de l'Est errs on the louche side, and there's no great reason to linger. Just north lies la Goutte d'Or (Drop of Gold). It's a vibrant but poor African *quartier* and so far at least, city plans to create a hotbed of young designer creativity here haven't come to much. Aside from the railway, the other dominating feature is the Canal St-Martin. It transformed city trade when it opened in 1825. Today, it's a real tourist asset and, whether you discover it by boat or on foot, it should certainly figure on your list. The canal extends all the way from boulevard de la Bastille to the place de Stalingrad. Here, beneath an impressive 18th century tollhouse (a leftover from the hated Mur des Fermiers-Généraux) it opens out into the Bassin de la Villette, before continuing as the Canal de l'Ourcq. It's at its most pleasant between the quais Jemmape and de Valmy, a tree-lined stretch with a sprinkling of cafes and niche shops.

La Villette

Surrounded by unlovely housing, the Parc de la Villette (p.185) is best reached by metro if you're not up for a three hour catamaran ride. Either way, its family-friendly attractions are well worth the trek. The funky, thematic gardens might baffle grown-ups, but they're a hit with kids – all the more for features such as the 80 metre long dragon slide. At its northern edge, you'll find La Cité des Sciences et de l'Industrie (p.169), a vast, intelligently run museum with lots of hands-on appeal. Outside, two cinemas and a 1957 submarine vie for your attention. Across the park, the Musée de la Musique (p.173) is also one of a kind. Along with a concert hall and library, the polished concrete building houses a major collection of instruments, most of which you can hear courtesy of the free audioguides. Also within the park is the 6,000 seater rock concert venue, Le Zénith, and la Grande Halle, a classy steel structure dating from 1867, when La Villette supplied meat to the whole of Paris.

Belleville

Rising to the east of the Canal St-Martin, multi-ethnic Belleville and its more upmarket neighbour, Ménilmontant, ooze character. Settled by successive waves of immigrants, Belleville is the Paris that Haussmann left alone. To ensure that it worked both ways, the Baron had sections of the canal covered to provide a strategic defence against the militant working-classes up the hill.

Lower Belleville is a tumult of humanity shopping for halal meat and oriental silk slippers. Uphill, the real village around St-Jean-Baptiste-de-Belleville has a quaintly provincial feel, in sharp contrast to the concrete uglies of nearby place des Fêtes. Keep an eye out for old collective laundry-houses, grand factory facades and secluded workers' cottages, many of which have been snapped up by wealthy professionals. The views from Belleville's modest, vine-covered park give Montmartre a run for its money, but by far the most appealing green space here is the Parc des Buttes-Chaumont (p.185). Built on the site of a former quarry, this is perhaps Haussmann's sole legacy to Belleville. Its rambling paths, lake and fanciful belvedere give it real charm, without the crowds you'll find elsewhere.

The Lowdown
Off the beaten tourist track, Paris populaire *has real gems for those prepared to take a closer look.*

The Good
A 4.5km cruise over and under ground along the Canal St-Martin.

The Bad
The dingy streets by Gare de l'Est could use a makeover – but don't hold your breath.

The Must-Dos
Go for a ramble in La Villette (the 1980s park might be weird, but it all works wonderfully well); bring your own popcorn and blanket to watch a classic movie during La Villette's free Cinema en Plein Air summer season.

141

Île de la Cité & Île Saint-Louis

Map p.399, p.400
Area **E** p.137

Île de la Cité

While some other parts of Paris tend to quieten down during the month of August, the Île de la Cité becomes busier than ever. This is the cradle of Paris, the island settled by the Celtic Parisii and the town the Romans knew as Lutetia. Hausmann's 19th century clean-up operation was radical, but at least it had the effect of focussing the spotlight on two major landmarks: La Conciergerie (p.165) and Notre-Dame (p.167). The island's other must-see attraction is La Sainte-Chapelle (p.160), whose delicate spire soars above its immediate surroundings.

To get a good sense of the island, an attractive approach is the Pont-Neuf. In 1607, it was a novelty, the first bridge to be furnished with pavements where pedestrians could escape a splattering from muddy carriage wheels. It's now the city's oldest bridge. At its mid-point is a statue of a genial-looking Henri IV on horseback. Down some steps is the square du Vert Galant (the name is an allusion to the king's evergreen philandering). It's a pretty garden, shaped like a ship's prow, and you can jump on one of the Vedettes du Pont-Neuf here if the fancy takes you. Back at street level, place Dauphine is a surprisingly peaceful refuge of cobblestones, chestnuts, gently bulging facades and a handful of restaurants. At the square's far end, where the royal Palais de Saint-Louis once stood, is the Palais de Justice. Flanking the quai de l'Horlogerie, the turreted Conciergerie (p.165) is an imposing survivor from the Middle Ages. Outside you'll see the city's first public clock (the original 14th century timepiece has been replaced by a 1585 model). The entrance of La Sainte-Chapelle (p.160) is signposted, though you'll probably spot the queue first.

On place Lépine, there's a thriving flower market, its stalls swelled by birds and pets on Sundays. The Préfecture de Police along quai des Orfèvres is the stuff of legend for Maigret readers, as well as viewers of many a contemporary TV cop show. The rest of the island is dominated by the Cathédrale de Notre-Dame (p.159). In high season, there's little chance of escaping the throngs here (though with a guided tour you'll at least shuffle intelligently). The ascent to the towers often involves a similar wait, but it's soon forgotten when you're gazing out among the gargoyles (not many 19th century embellishments can claim to have added such 'value' to an ancient monument).

Not just the spiritual centre of Paris, Notre-Dame is the road-map hub of France. Look for the bronze star near the west door marking 'kilomètre zéro', the location from which all distances are measured. Also on the square is the Crypte Archéologique where, with a little imagination, you can discover how the Cité settlement grew. Away from the tat-lined thoroughfares, there are glimpses of the past; along rue Chanoinesse, for example, where, in around 1200, Abélard fell for Héloïse (an affair brutally terminated in his castration). At the 'stern' of the island is the claustrophobic Mémorial de la Déportation, honouring the 200,000 French who died in Nazi concentration camps. Inside, its sculpture and inscriptions are fittingly stark.

Île Saint-Louis

If you can't afford to live on the Île Saint-Louis, the next best thing is strolling its streets, browsing the snug antique shops and galleries and indulging in some of M. Berthillon's famous icecream. The island was a swampy, vagabond-ridden area until the 17th century, when the speculator Christophe Marie transformed it with the hôtels particuliers which make up some of the city's most coveted real-estate today. Along the main drag, notice the strange perforated spire of Saint-Louis-en-Île, a later addition to Le Vau's original church, and peek, if you can, at the timber frames of the former tennis court, now an upmarket hotel at number 54. On either side, the quais serve up a feast for mansion-spotters.

The Lowdown

In the heart of the city, these two islands embody the historic and exclusive faces of Paris.

The Good

An afternoon's stroll followed by dinner on the Île Saint-Louis; the uplifting colours of the Sainte-Chapelle's largely original stained glass.

The Bad

The crowds of tourists inside Notre-Dame, even when mass is celebrated.

The Must-Dos

Sharing the sunset with Notre-Dame's gargoyles.

The Latin Quarter

Map p.409
Area **F** p.137

The Lowdown

East of boulevard St-Michel, the Latin Quarter is still very much a centre of academic activity, as well as tourism. It's busy, crowded, historic and vibrant, but the pace slows around Jussieu.

The Good

Stupendous architecture, warren-like streets, centuries of history and plenty of pleasant cafes to watch life go by.

The Bad

The boulevards St-Michel and St-Germain are fairly anonymous and get extremely crowded at rush-hour. Rue Mouffetard and rue de la Huchette can be something of a tourist scrum.

The Must-Dos

Sip coffee amid the bustle of place St-Michel; browse books at Gibert-Jeune or Shakespeare & Co; promenade among Latin-tagged specimens of the Jardin des Plantes; hit the top deck of the Institut du Monde Arabe.

La Huchette & The Sorbonne

The Latin Quarter is not quite what it was. Latin is no longer the lingua franca of Sorbonne students, nor will you find many chain-smoking *intellos* in the cafes of 'Boul'-Mich'. Even so, the lively, narrow streets here are still irresistible for strolling and people-watching. The Fontaine St-Michel has long been the rendezvous of choice for blind dates and student stand-offs. East of here, rue de La Huchette has largely lost its charm to brash, tacky eateries, but the Caveau jazz cellar (p.349) and the Théâtre de la Huchette (p.369) have hardly changed in fifty years. Indeed, Ionesco's absurd play *La Cantatrice Chauve* had its first airing in this theatre in 1957 and is still going strong, with performances every evening from Monday to Saturday. Fronting the river along rue de la Bucherie is the bookshop Shakespeare & Co (p.252). It's not the original, but this reincarnation is still a magnet for expatriates (not least the literary giants of tomorrow who trade a few hours on the till in return for a place to crash). South of here, the Église Saint-Séverin (p.162) is a jewel with sinuous carved pillars and vaulting dating mainly to the 15th century. At the corner of boulevards St-Germain and St-Michel, you can escape the bustle (if not the drone of traffic) in the medieval gardens of the Musée National du Moyen Age (p.175). In a splendid double-act, they're laid around the walls of the ancient Roman baths. It's a stone's throw along rue Champollion to the Sorbonne. The university began its illustrious career in the 13th century, when this college and others hunkering around Montaigne Ste-Geneviève were formed into a guild. Fronting it, place de la Sorbonne is an unhurried square with lime trees and fountains.

The Panthéon

The passion for domes is evident across the city, but the most dazzling of all is that of the Panthéon (p.166), especially on the approach up rue Soufflot. It was commissioned by Louis XV as a basilica to Sainte Géneviève, the teenage Gallo-Roman queen who worked wonders with Parisians' morale when Attila the Hun's armies menaced the city. Thanks to events of 1789, the church has spent most of its life as a temple to the great (or what passed for it at the time). Overshadowed in its corner near Le Bombardier English pub (p.353) stands the far older church of St-Étienne-sur-Mont, begun by François I. This is an area steeped in history. Nearby rue de Clovis reveals a chunk of Philippe-Auguste's city fortifications. And rue Mouffetard probably takes its name from the stench of the Bièvre river, stoked up by the tanneries of les Gobelins. Lined with cheap tavernas and a lively tourist nightspot, this Roman road still has character to spare. At the top end, place de la Contrescarpe boasts two fetching cafes overlooking a pretty fountain. Don't miss les Arènes de Lutèce (p.164), the impressive remains of the Roman arena, just over rue Monge.

Jussieu

Taxidermist workshops pepper the streets in the sleepy *quartier* around the Jardin des Plantes (p.190). France's main botanical garden has grown like topsy since Louis XIV established it as a medicinal garden; it now contains the Grande Galerie d'Évolution, a zoo and more besides. Nearby, behind white crenellated walls is a little corner of North Africa: the Mosque de Paris (p.163). Within the complex, the traditional hammam is open to all; the courtyard tearoom is deliciously cool among the olives in summer, and the restaurant (p.330) is richly exotic. Overlooking the Pont de Sully, the sleek Institut du Monde Arabe (p.170) is another of the area's pleasant surprises. It's very much a public space, with stunning views and a good self-service cafeteria on the roof terrace. When you've taken your fill, you might head down quai St-Bernard to the Jardin Tino-Rossi, to rub shoulders with sculptures by Brancusi, César and Zadkine.

143

The Louvre, Tuileries & Palais Royal

Map p.399
Area **G** p.136

Begun by François I on the site of a medieval fortress, the Louvre (p.174) grew ever more imposing until Louis XIV upped sticks for the fresh air of Versailles. Luckily for us, the Sun King still found time to commission the transformation of the Jardins des Tuileries (p.184), whose curvy stone nymphs and shady cafes make it a favourite spot to saunter or sit. The roar of traffic on place de la Concorde quickly dies away as you enter this chestnut-lined haven with its wide, gravel paths. To the left of this entrance, the Jeu de Paume, once a real tennis court, holds major photographic retrospectives against a backdrop of slick, modern severity. The Musée de l'Orangerie (p.172), roughly opposite, attracts large crowds. Join the Monet pilgrims to see *les Nymphéas* (waterlilies) in the luminous setting they deserve, or promenade onwards along the gravel avenues. Between the two ponds and their pastel-coloured sailboats, you can pull up a heavy chair and watch the world go by, or relax at one of the laid-back cafes on either side – service is erratic, but the prices aren't exorbitant.

The Lowdown

High-brow epicentre of the city, with no less than seven museums and showcases on hand.

The Good

Worth a visit for the Louvre alone but the surrounding museums (the Musée des Arts Décoratifs is particularly splendid) aren't to be missed either. Strollers can escape the traffic in the Tuileries, and the Palais Royal.

The greenery ends at Napoleon's Arc du Carrousel, just about small enough to seem like a dry-run for the two much bigger arches it frames. Opposite, I.M. Pei's glass pyramid was highly controversial when it was unveiled here in 1986. Nowadays, it's widely appreciated, not least by the shoppers in the airy Louvre du Carrousel mall below. If you're Louvre-bound, it's worth buying tickets in advance inside the mall itself, so you can enter at the less crowded entrance on Passage Richelieu, just off the rue de Rivoli. If the prospect of steering a course through some 35,000 works of art overwhelms you, bide your time in admiration of the monumental royal palace that houses them. Onwards through the Louvre precinct, the Cour Napoléon and the Cour Carré make a perfect setting for sunset strolls.

The Bad

The crowds besieging the Louvre and the Orangerie: pre-empt queues by buying advance tickets. Once inside, the Louvre's special exhibitions can be a crowded shuffle.

In a wing of the Louvre, though separately managed, the fabulously revamped Musée des Arts Décoratifs (p.173) charts the ongoing history of (mainly French) taste through a vast array of applied arts. Within the same building, you'll also find the Musée de la Mode et de Textile and the Musée de la Publicité. Though modest compared to the Louvre, these are impressive collections, and you'll still need to pace your visit.

The Must-Dos

Gape at the line-up of arches from place du Carrousel, then relax in the Tuileries.

Kitsch souvenir shops dominate the opposite stretch of the rue de Rivoli, followed by the Antiquaires du Louvre, the place to go if you've a taste for fine antiques and the budget to match. Be sure not to miss the Jardins du Palais Royal, tucked away behind the Conseil d'État and the Comédie Française. Enclosed by elegant, three-tiered arcades, this tranquil space was once the haunt of loose women, gamblers and wild entertainments, welcomed in by the democratically minded (and pleasure-loving) Duc d'Orléans shortly before the Revolution. Parfumiers and antiquarian booksellers have taken their place, while Daniel Buren's humbug-striped columns add a touch of whimsy to the formal surroundings.

Palais Royal

The Louvre

Place du Tertre, Montmartre

Montmartre, Pigalle & The Nouvelle-Athènes

Map p.383, p.389
Area ⒽⒽ p.136

Montmartre

The Lowdown
Delving into the quirky backstreets of Montmartre is one of the highlights of the city.

Perched atop the Butte Montmartre, Sacré Coeur (p.160) is the city's most conspicuous landmark, floating palely into view just when you least expect it. With its artistic heritage and stunning views, the surrounding village attracts tourists by the convoy. But don't let that deter you from exploring the 'real' Montmartre, whose crumbling villas and ivy-clad impasses were the backdrop for Amélie Poulain.

The Good
The vibrant buzz in and around rue des Abbesses.

Leaving metro Anvers, head through the Marché St Pierre, popular with young wannabe designers hunting for textiles. From here, it's an uphill hike through the gardens or a short funicular ride to the basilica of Sacré-Coeur. Begun as a memorial to the losses of the 1870-71 Franco-Prussian War, this Byzantine fantasy wasn't finished until after the first world war. The domed interior is resplendent with mosaics. Outside, you'll find the entrance to the spiral staircase where, for a small fee, you can climb to the city's second highest viewpoint. It's worth running the gauntlet of artists in place du Tertre, if only to compare it with the authenticity as you head towards Caulaincourt. Surrealism fans may not be able to resist the very commercial Espace Montmartre Salvador Dalí close by. Where rue Saules and Saint-Vincent meet, you'll find Montmartre's tiny vineyard, whose un-plummy vintage is celebrated in early October. Also here is the Lapin Agile (p.364), whose cabarets have entertained everyone from Apollinaire to Picasso. Worth visiting for its picturesque appeal alone, the Musée de Montmartre (p.173) was home to the artists Renoir, Dufy, Suzanne Valadon and her son, Maurice Utrillo. rue Lepic, leading down to the village of Abbesses, is pure *Amélie* territory. Trendy 'zincs', one-off shops and a tiled wall declaring love in 300 languages are all reason enough to linger. A short walk west, you can pay your respects to the likes of Berlioz, Degas and the pop diva Dalida at the peaceful Cimitière de Montmartre.

The Bad
The clichés and the crush, all rolled into one at the place du Tertre.

The Must-Dos
Take your time ticking off the landmarks from the esplanade of Sacré Coeur – or better still, from its dome.

Pigalle

Walki-Talki
If you want to take a guided tour of Montmartre without looking like a tourist, visit www.walki-talki.com and download its 'audio walking tour' to your MP3 player. Easy-to-follow directions mean you won't get lost, and you'll learn about the area's history as you go.

Montmartre's seamy neighbour is at the foot of the hill, strung along on either side of a busy thoroughfare of peep-shows and hustler joints. This road is the boulevard de Clichy, which continues east as the boulevard de Rochechouart, an area dominated by hawkers and the cheerful pink checked awnings of the bargain store, Tati. You can still see traces of Pigalle's glory days in the ornate 1890s facades along the street, but despite progressive clean-ups, it remains tawdry. The Moulin Rouge (p.365), birthplace of the can-can, is still going strong at number 82, while galleries of phalluses and vintage voyeurism put a folksy spin on sex at the Musée de l'Érotisme (p.172).

Nouvelle-Athènes

In the lattice of streets east of place Blanche and the church of Ste-Trinité lies the once-bohemian quartier of Nouvelles-Athènes. Delacroix and Dumas lived here, as did Chopin and George Sand. They were among the frequent visitors at painter Ary Scheffer's house on rue Chaptal. Now the Musée de la Vie Romantique (p.173), it's a gem of a museum, with period rooms and a pleasant courtyard which doubles up as a *salon-de-thé*.

Nearby, on rue de Rochefoucauld, the Musée Gustave Moreau (p.176) conjures up the artist's cluttered working environment. A strange and intimate museum, it's decked from floor to ceiling with Moreau's symbolist visions.

Montparnasse, Montsouris & Surroundings

Map p.408
Area ❶ p.136

The Lowdown

*Brimming with cafes
and popular
entertainment,
Montparnasse still has
vestiges of its artistic
heritage. Two very
likeable parks are within
easy striking distance.*

The Good

*The remarkable
Catacombes are worth
saving for a rainy day.*

The Bad

*Along avenue du
Maine, the
architecture is modern
and impersonal.*

The Must-Dos

*Ponder greatness in the
Cimitière de
Montparnasse; lunch
on crêpes and cider in
one of Montparnasse's
many Breton
restaurants; indulge
yourself in the
resplendent 1920s
salon of La Coupole.*

Montparnasse

Montparnasse still trades somewhat on its artistic heyday, though the modern concrete buildings along avenue du Maine might make you wonder why. The 210m Tour Montparnasse (p.191) doesn't help matters either; it's the building Parisians most love to hate. That said, the view from the 56th floor is one of the best in the city. For the rest, this is an attractive, generally bourgeois area, well served with cafes, cinemas and theatres. The latter, including the delightful Comédie Italienne, are ranged along the rue de la Gaîté, where they've been joined by a seedier element. This street leads onto boulevard Edgar Quinet. On Sundays, a lively arts and crafts market is held here.

In the 1920s and '30s, Montparnasse was a cauldron of artistic activity, as writers, painters, sculptors and the avant-garde migrated here from the more expensive Montmartre. Hemingway and Cocteau drank at La Coupole (p.321) on boulevard du Montparnasse. An international mix of artists alighted at La Ruche (see below), a community led by benevolent sculptor, Alfred Boucher.

Spruce Montparnasse Cemetery harbours a famously free-thinking crowd, from veteran resident Baudelaire to Sartre, Simone de Beauvoir, Samuel Beckett and Serge Gainsbourg. The sculptor Zadkine is here, too, and the Musée Zadkine (p.178), along with the Musée Bourdelle (01 49 54 73 73) close by, provide insights into the artistic milieu. But it's not all nostalgia; innovative exhibitions held at the stunning Fondation Cartier (p.156) on boulevard Raspail have put a spring in the step of contemporary art lovers across the city. If you continue east, you'll see the Observatoire, a world first, built for Louis XIV; it is, alas, largely off-limits to visitors. Occupying the southern corner of place Denfert-Rochereau is the entrance to Les Catacombes (p.166), one of the city's more macabre landmarks. A visit through its rambling tunnels of stacked skulls is not for the squeamish, but with all those memento moris, you won't forget it in a hurry.

Back across avenue du Maine, place de Catalogne was designed by Riccardo Bofill in the 1980s (though you wouldn't have guessed it from the imposing classical overtones), and it's agreeable to wander around. If it's open, you should also take a peek at the church of Notre-Dame du Travail, built for the army of construction workers brought in for the Eiffel Tower and the Exposition Universelle. Carry on along rue Vercingétorix if you want to pick up the cycling or walking path leading, eventually, out to leafy suburbs such as Sceaux. The area immediately west of here lacks much in the way of visitor appeal. One exception, though, is the Parc Georges-Brassens (p.186), a modern park which has taken the place of the old Vaugirard abattoir. At weekends, bibliophiles should head for the book fair, held in the old Halle aux Chevaux. Not far away, on passage de Dantzig, you can still see La Ruche, where Boucher rented out studios for absurdly low rents to Modigliani, Chagall and Léger among others. Designed by Gustave Eiffel, the beehive-shaped building was originally a wine pavilion, and it's a genuinely lovely anachronism. If you're in luck, one of the resident artists may let you in to soak up the atmosphere, otherwise, you'll have to settle for a glimpse through the gate.

Montsouris

At the city's southern edge, the Cité Universitaire seems like another country – or possibly several. A large student campus, it dates from the 1920s, and its international aspirations are reflected in an astonishing line-up of architectural styles. The main attraction for visitors, though, is the expansive Parc Montsouris (p.186) across the new tramway that runs along the southern boulevards Maréchaux. The park was created during the Haussmann era when informal gardens in the English style were all the rage. Don't finish up here without taking a stroll up square de Montsouris, a narrow lane full of highly stylised villas and tumbling creepers; look out for the early Le Corbusier house at the end.

Map p.388, p.389
Area **K** *p.137*

Opéra, La Madeleine & The Grands Boulevards

Around Opera

The Lowdown
This is the traditional heart of the city's shopping and business activity.

To the north of the city's traditional commerce and business district, the *grand magasins* of Printemps (p.292) and Galeries Lafayette (p.291) on boulevard Haussmann have been rivals for more than a century. If the world's largest beauty department doesn't appeal, you should still brave the fray at Printemps for a peek at its 6th floor tearoom, crowned by a magnificent, jewel-coloured stained glass dome (p.319). The same applies to Galeries Lafayette, whose cosmetics floor resides beneath tiers of gorgeous, swagged galleries. Keep going to the open terrace on the 7th floor for outstanding views of Montmartre in all its chaotic glory (one floor below, the store's free fashion show takes place every Friday).

The Good
The harmonious period elegance of place Vendôme.

A stone's throw away is the Opera Garnier (p.167). Completed in 1875, it was every bit as controversial as Haussmann's grand projects of the day. The story goes that when its obscure young architect was challenged by Empress Eugénie to define his design, he declared it to be 'Napoléon III style'. Certainly, with its mix of embellishments and colours, there's nothing else quite like it. If that whets your appetite, a tour of the interior won't disappoint. Meanwhile, for those who don't know their Second Empire from their Bourbons, the multimedia show at Paris Story (p.188) on rue Scribe will offer some insights.

The Bad
The scrum of shoppers at the Grands Magasins at peak times such as Christmas and les soldes.

La Madeleine

Grandeur and gourmandise meet at the place de la Madeleine. Dwarfed somewhat by the Église de la Madeleine (p.160), this busy square is populated by upmarket *traiteurs* such as Fauchon and Hédiard, and its splendid art nouveau public toilets merit spending a penny. The colonnaded church looks strikingly like a temple and, in fact, it very nearly was; Napoleon planned to dedicate it to his glory of the Grande Armée. Inside, a stupendous organ makes this a popular place for concert-goers. Outside, the steps yield a grand view across Concorde to the Assemblée Nationale and les Invalides beyond.

The Must-Dos
Window-shop along the ritzy length of rues St-Honoré and Faubourg St-Honoré.

There are Revolutionary echoes in nearby rue Pasquier, where you can visit the 19th century Chapelle Expiatoire (p.164). Dedicated to Louis XVI and Marie-Antoinette, whose remains lay here for decades, it's a tranquil, leafy spot.

Between Madeleine and Concorde, you'll meet rues St-Honoré and Faubourg St-Honoré, arguably the city's most glamorous streets. La Croix, Versace and Galliano are they're all here, along with hip concept store, Colette (p.275). Don't lose your head, though, without visiting the place Vendôme. Flanked by jewellers and the Ritz, this regal square was built by Hardouin-Mansart, the architect of Versailles. In the centre, a towering column commemorates Napoleon's victory at Austerlitz. More than a thousand enemy cannons were melted down for the purpose (though the present column is a replacement, after the original fell during the 1871 Revolution).

The Grands Boulevards

This string of eight boulevards curves from Madeleine to République, passing through the red-light area of boulevard St-Denis en route. Not to be confused with Haussmann's boulevards, they date back to Louis XIV and follow the mediaeval defences of Philippe-Auguste. Off boulevard Montmartre is the prestigious auction house of Drouot (www.drouot.fr), which you can browse freely. Be sure to explore the delightful mid 19th century passages which beckon along the way. Some have been restored to their original splendour, among them Passage Jouffroy, next door to the redoubtable waxworks of Musée Grévin (p.175). Opposite, the Passage des Panoramas ultimately brings you out near the stock exchange, La Bourse, a stately, neoclassical building from 1808.

Map p.395
Area ⓛ p.136

Passy & The South-West

Between the Seine and the Bois de Boulogne (p.184) lies the seriously select neighbourhood of Passy. With the notable exception of the Musée Marmottan (p.176) it's not rich in conventional attractions, but with its provincial atmosphere and architectural flourishes it lends itself to leisurely exploration.

The Lowdown

Old money resides in the west, while across the Seine, sharp landscaping has transformed an industrial wasteland.

Tucked away to one side of Trocadéro, the Cimitière de Passy gives you some idea of the local cachet. Overlooked by the Tour Eiffel, its long-term residents include generals and screen stars, industrialists, couturiers and a good measure of aristocrats. An unpretentious grave unites the painters Manet and Berthe Morisot; Debussy and Fauré are buried here, too.

To get a taste of Passy life, spend a little time in and around the place de Passy. With its spruce church, covered market and cafe terraces, it's strong on village ambience, despite the abundant shopping stores close by.

The Good

With its old world charm, Passy is a pleasure in which to get lost.

Just off rue Raynouard, you'll pass the rue des Eaux and the Musée du Vin (01 45 25 63 26). The street's name recalls Passy's heyday as a therapeutic spa from the 17th century onwards, when many springs bubbled up in the area. Take a trip west to the fountain on square Lamartine if you want to sample the iron-rich water from a water table 600 metres below your feet. Also on rue Raynouard, rather hidden by a high wall, is Balzac's

The Bad

The somewhat cold open spaces of Parc André-Citroën are considered by some to be a landscaping disaster. Decide for yourself.

House (p.162). Harassed by creditors, the writer particularly appreciated the house for its easy rear escape route. Further along the same road, the Maison de la Radio is the home of French broadcasting and, on the corner, the Café à la Fontaine is a favourite spot for celebrity-spotting (assuming you know who to look for, that is).

A late 19th century construction boom in Passy and its southern neighbour, Auteuil, coincided with the ascendancy of Art Nouveau. For admirers of Hecor Guimard and his like-minded contemporaries, these areas offer rich pickings. Just beyond the Maison de la Radio stands one of the most extravagant examples. Castel Béranger (14 rue

The Must-Dos

See the work that gave a name to Impressionism at the Musée Marmottan; linger over lunch on the place de Passy; enjoy a lofty panorama from the Parc André-Citroën's balloon.

Fontaine) launched Guimard's career in 1898, and soon became known disparagingly as Castel Dérangé. It's a private building, though residents are used to passers-by gazing rapt at its gargoyles, dragons, exuberant swirls and scrolls.

For something utterly different, you need look no further than the square du Docteur-Blanche, a few streets west of here. Two very different villas designed by Le Corbusier in the 1920s are a monument to the architect's innovative simplicity. They now form Le Corbusier Foundation (01 42 88 41 53) and the open-plan, airy La Roche villa is open to visitors.

Continue south, and you'll find yourself close to some of the city's most exclusive addresses, many of which, like the knot of streets around boulevard de Montmorency, are gated. This area has several striking *hôtel particuliers*, whose rich 18th century facades you'll spot between here and the place Jean Lorrain. The largely residential areas across the Seine are less colourful than Passy and Auteuil. The area's principal attraction is the large Parc André-Citroën (p.185), built on the site of the former car factory. With its colour-blocked flowers, yawning terraces and squirting jet fountains, it puts a decidedly contemporary twist on the French tradition of formal gardens. For a fee, you can take a short helium balloon ride above the lawns for a view of the scaled-down Statue of Liberty (an early prototype of the full-size version in New York).

Parc André-Citroën

Map p.420
Area **M** *p.137*

Place d'Italie & The South-East

Place d'Italie & Surroundings

The place d'Italie is another of the city's vast star-shaped hubs off which a number of busy roads radiate. There's nothing remarkable here, but a handful of spots nearby merit exploring. At the Manufacture Nationale des Gobelins (p.166), weavers have been making tapestries for royalty and their like for over four centuries. On adjacent rue des Gobelins, you can admire (but not visit) the fairytale turreted Château de la Reine Blanche, a 16th century building which remains something of a puzzle. And, though there's little to see, apart from the monolithic Mobilier National (the repository of all government Ministerial furniture), rue Berbier du Mets traces the course of the old Bièvre river, before the dyers of the Gobelins helped finish it off. South-east of here, between avenues du Choisy and d'Ivry, Europe's biggest Chinatown has infused vibrancy into an otherwise anonymous 1970s development. You'd hardly expect villagey nostalgia round these parts, but south-west of place d'Italie, les Buttes-aux-Cailles offers just that. A fetching nook of flowery lanes and brick-built workers' cottages, it has a smattering of arty shops, cafes and restaurants.

Bercy

Bercy is probably the city's most successful slice of modern urban planning to date. The immense, tree-lined park is divided into thematic gardens which make a feature of existing restored buildings. At its northern end is the turf-clad Palais Omnisports, hosting everything from basketball matches to Marilyn Manson gigs. One of the more striking buildings to border the park is the Cinémathèque Française (p.366), designed by Frank Gehry. With its film seasons and exhibitions, it lends gravitas to the area, against the mainstream entertainment within the Cour St-Émilion mall immediately south of the park. In the 19th century, Bercy was a thriving area for wine importing; its streets lined with *chais* (wine-cellars) and plane trees. A double line of restored *chais* now forms the heart of its modern retail district, while disused railway tracks run the length of the cobbled street. Although the restaurants and shops here aren't extraordinary, it's a pleasure to stroll and the area attracts a convivial crowd at weekends.

Paris Rive-Gauche

Between Gare d'Austerlitz and Porte d'Ivry, this is Paris' newest neighbourhood. The dominating landmark is the Bibliothèque Nationale de France (BNF) (p.190), a fortress-like library of four L-shaped towers, each intended to resemble an open book. The national library hosts occasional exhibitions and there are foreign newspapers available to browse in its reading rooms. Otherwise, it's a rather intimidating structure, which feels almost as out-of-bounds as the sunken 'forest' it encloses. Around the BNF, the apartments of Tolbiac are pleasantly landscaped, but, with few shops, it's a neighbourhood still in search of character. It's a different story along the quayside, though – especially during Paris Plage (p.182), when the family-friendly attractions of the floating Joséphine-Baker pool (p.232) and Le Cabaret-Pirate (p.348) really come into their own. Also here, the Batofar nightclub (www.batofar.org) is a buzzy spot for live music. Bercy is a short walk across the Simone-de-Beauvoir footbridge.

More development is afoot, notably of the Magasins Généraux warehouses near Austerlitz, due to become a '*cité*' of fashion and design in 2008. Meanwhile, Rive Gauche's other outstanding landmark is Les Frigos (www.les-frigos.com), close to the Pont de Tolbiac. The former SNCF cold storage depot was built in the 1920s and its resident artists have a stay of execution – for the time being, at least. You're free to peek inside at the spiral staircase and floor-to-ceiling graffiti. Enthusiasts should make a date for the Portes Ouvertes (Open Doors); see the website for details. You'll find a more slick face of art in rue Louise Weiss, just west of the BNF, where a dozen or so galleries are now well established.

The Lowdown
Past, present and future exist alongside each other.

The Good
Bercy's picturesque chais; its pretty 'jardin potager' and rose mount. The spick-and-span cottages of Butte-aux-Cailles.

The Bad
Parts of Paris Rive-Gauche seem faceless and impenetrable; icy gusts whip around the Bibliothèque in winter.

The Must-Dos
Take a leisurely stroll across the passerelle Simone-de-Beauvoir, Paris' 37th bridge; lounge on the sundeck at the Piscine Joséphine-Baker.

Map p.398, p.399
*Area **N** p.136*

St-Germain des Prés & Odéon

St-Germain

The Lowdown
This is one of the city's most popular areas, for shopping, and cafes, for history.

While you can easily drift here along the boulevard St-Germain, the scenic approach is over the Pont des Arts footbridge from the Louvre. Facing you on the Left Bank, the 17th century domed building is the Institut de France, where the nation's brainiest boffins and bigwigs take their seats among five Academies (the best-known of them, the Académie Française struggles, Cnut-like, to defend the French language from the tide of anglo-saxon words). On weekdays, it's possible to go inside and visit the opulent Bibliothèque Mazarine (01 44 41 44 06), but you'll need ID and photos to apply for a visitor's pass. Close by, the former Mint now houses the Musée de la Monnaie (01 40 46 56 66), a high-tech affair charting French currency from Gallo-Roman times. If this doesn't inspire you, the Musée des Lettres et de Manuscrits (01 40 51 02 25) has much broader appeal; it contains work penned by a pantheon of greats, including Beethoven, Einstein, Ghandi and de Gaulle. It's tucked away behind Hôtel de la Monnaie, though the entrance is on rue de Nesles.

The Good
A smattering of good museums, passages and courtyards to explore – and one of the city's best parks.

This is a lively and attractive area, which gets more fashionable as you thread your way west. There are tempting boutiques along rues Dauphine and Mazarine and a cluster of cafes around the classy food market on rue de Buci. On rues Jacob, Bonaparte and l'Abbaye, interior design shops, antiquarian booksellers and Ladurée's confections all vie for your attention. A host of private galleries on the approach towards the École des Beaux-Arts makes this an art browser's paradise.

The Bad
You'll never walk alone; this is well-charted tourist territory.

Indeed, there's no escaping art in one form or another. There are echoes of the past in the hotel where Oscar Wilde quipped his last (L'Hôtel, p.27); in the little green square where Picasso paid tribute to his friend, Apollinaire with a sculpture of Dora Maar; in the pretty house on rue Furstenburg, where Delacroix lived and worked (p.177). But they're loudest of all at the Café de Flore (p.337) and Les Deux Magots (p.339) on boulevard St-Germain. These two cafes were frequented by Dali, Sartre, Beauvoir, Camus and Hemingway in their time – now a stream of tourists pay for the privilege. Brasserie Lipp (p.319) can claim similar credentials. Nearby, the 11th century St-Germain church (p.162) has seen it all.

The Must-Dos
Lose yourself among the well-dressed boutiques of rue Jacob.

Odéon

A rather older literary hang-out still exists down Passage du Commerce Saint-André, just opposite Odéon metro station. Le Procope (p.323) was Paris' first cafe, a popular meeting place with Voltaire, Rousseau and Diderot. Later, Danton, Marat and Robespierre were regulars while, in a building nearby, Dr Guillotin used sheep to hone the mechanism of his humane new invention. This stretch of boulevard St-Germain is a hotspot for cinema-goers, but the original odeon is the neoclassical theatre which Marie-Antoinette opened – at around the same time revolution was fomenting at Le Procope. Thick with history and beautiful residences, these are pleasant streets to wander among – or enjoy a spree if you've the budget for it. The site of St-Germain's medieval fair on rue Lobineau is now an upmarket shopping arcade, while the fashion boutiques that have colonised the place St-Sulpice *quartier* wouldn't look amiss on avenue Montaigne. Dominating the square, the Église Saint-Sulpice (p.162) was begun in 1646 but took over a century to complete, which may go some way to explaining its two contrasting towers. Inside, you'll find a trio of murals by Delacroix, and an 18th century gnomon which still draws in a few Da Vinci Code pilgrims. Outside, the Fontaine des Point-Cardinaux seems to cock a snook at the bishops perched on its four compass points, none of whom ever got to wear a cardinal's robes. From here, it's a few short steps across the rue de Vaugirard, the city's longest street, to Jardin du Luxembourg (p.184). A haven of greenery, statuary and leisure pursuits, the park is home to the French Senate and the Musée National du Luxembourg, which hosts fine temporary exhibitions.

Map p.388, p.387, p.382
Area **P** p.136

St-Lazare, Monceau & Batignolles

St-Lazare

The Lowdown

Old and new money in a largely residential area fringing on the commercial quartier of the Grands Magasins.

Lacking the glamour of the Champs-Elysées or the artsy charm of Montmartre, this area is generally overlooked by visitors. A stone's throw from les Grands Magasins, St-Lazare was the city's first train station, opened in 1837, though more recently spruced up and fronted by a bronze sculpture of tottering suitcases. For all that, it's a commuter hub rather than an international gateway – unless you count the collection of streets named after European cities which criss-cross behind the station. Today, this area is a curious enclave of sheet music shops and luthiers; otherwise, the *quartier* lacks much in the way of animation. It wasn't always the case. Monet (who immortalised St-Lazare's steam-filled heyday before his beloved waterlilies) was a key member of the Groupe des Batignolles, which included the painters Manet, Renoir, Sisley, Pisarro and Degas. Zola was also a regular at the long gone Café Guerbois where they met up in the 1870s. The result was the birth of the Impressionist movement.

The Good

Fanciful facades, parks and a trio of excellent museums.

Monceau

The Bad

Much of the area is blandly bourgeois and, well, a trifle dull.

The Must-Dos

Dawdle in Parc Monceau and soak up the elegance in the Musées de Camondo or Jacquemart-André.

Not a geranium strays out of place along the balconies of Monceau, where the smart, slightly anonymous boulevards – Courcelles, Villiers, Malesherbes – sum up the Haussmann model to a tee. Until the mid 19th century, the Pleine Monceau was a rural backwater, within which lay the Duc d'Orléans' private gardens. Graced by his 'feudal' ruins and antique temple, they're now the Parc Monceau (p.186), and are at the heart of the quartier. At the north gate, the 18th century Rotonde is a leftover from the Wall of the Farmers-General. The park is framed by *hôtel particuliers*, including the captivating Camondo residence (known as 'the Rothschilds of the East'). It's now a museum (p.177).

Outside the east gate, the Musée Cernuschi (p.171) houses the collection of oriental treasures amassed by Henri Cernuschi, which has swelled massively thanks to more recent acquisitions. But if you only have time to see one magnificent mansion built for a fabulously wealthy collector (or, in this case, two), make it the Musée Jacquemart-André (p.176). On boulevard Haussmann, the home of this 19th century magnate and his artist-wife contains an astonishingly rich collection, including works by Rembrandt and Botticelli.

The area has a few more eccentricities up its sleeve. At 48 rue de Courcelles, an improbable red pagoda was the home of Ching Tsai Loo, a successful Chinese antique dealer, (at the time of writing, Loo & Cie's breathtaking interior was closed for renovations). On rue Daru, there are echoes of Mother Russia in the onion domes of the Alexander Nevsky Cathedral, built in the 1850s for neighbourhood Russians. Around the corner on rue Faubourg St-Honoré, the famous Salle Pleyel concert hall has been sumptuously restored.

Batignolles

A real sense of village still colours the square which spreads out in a semi-circle before the Église-Sainte-Marie-des-Batignolles. The church itself is an elegant, neoclassical affair, built in the 1830s. Stretching out behind it is a Haussmann-era park, landscaped less formally in the *style anglais*. Equipped with a children's mini-kart track and swings, it's a favourite with nannies and their charges from more moneyed Monceau. Along rues des Batignolles and des Dames, antique shops and craft studios have gained a foothold, eventually petering out just short of place de Clichy's working class bustle. Add to that a good sprinkling of trendy restaurants and bars, and you might be persuaded to linger. A short walk west, beyond the rue de Rome, rue de Lévis is home to one of the city's more vibrant markets (p.298), open daily, except on Mondays.

151

Map p.396, p.397
Area **Q** p.136

Trocadéro, The Eiffel Tower & Les Invalides

Trocadéro

The Lowdown
Civic planning at its
most grand; the area
contains some of the
city's most iconic sights
and an abundance of
great museums
and galleries.

Crowning Trocadéro Hill is the creamy-white, art deco Palais de Chaillot, built for the Exposition Universelle of 1937. By day, the broad terrace between the two pavilions throngs with tourists and souvenir hawkers. By night, flanked by the gargantuan statues of Apollo and Hercules, there's no finer spot to admire a shimmering Eiffel Tower. Until recently, Chaillot was starting to seem like a palace without a purpose, thanks to the relocation of the Cinémathèque Française (p.366), and the removal of choice morsels from the Musée de l'Homme to the Musée du Quai Branly. The lavish new Cité de l'Architecture et Patrimoine (01 58 51 52 00) provides a much-needed boost.

The Good
They'll love getting the
postcards back home.

Between here and the place de l'Alma, there's a rich vein of culture. While hardly as comprehensive as the Pompidou Centre, the city's Musée d'Art Moderne (p.172) on avenue du Président-Wilson is nevertheless excellent. Next door, the Palais de Tokyo provides a raw space for contemporary artists to strut their stuff.

The Bad
The wide avenues and
grand official buildings
don't lend themselves
to a casual promenade.

For fashion aficionados, the Musée Galliera (p.175) lays on two or three extravaganzas a year, while the Fondation Yves Saint-Laurent performs its own magic on a smaller scale. Nearby, the Musée Guimet (p.176) specialises in Asian art treasures and has been leased new life by a sensitive modern extension. A corner of place de l'Alma is occupied by the gilt replica of the Statue of Liberty's flame. Since 1997, it's been an unofficial memorial for Princess Diana, whose car crashed in the underpass below.

The Must-Dos
Travel to other worlds
at the Musée Quai
Branly; browse for
gourmet goodies in Le
Bon Marché's food
hall; enjoy the view of
the Eiffel Tower from
the Café de l'Homme
at Trocadéro.

The Eiffel Tower

You may tire of its image on everything from publicity campaigns to tea-towels, but up close the Eiffel Tower (p.164) never fails to impress. Beyond, the regimented flowerbeds of the Champ de Mars were once the parade ground for the École Militaire, built under Louis XV to train soldiers (including, eventually, a young Napoleon). Further along the rather stuffy avenue Suffren are the Y-shaped headquarters of Unesco, cutting edge in 1958 but now looking sorely dated. A spirited market takes place on avenue de Saxe (p.298), and there's further animation to the east on sassy, pedestrianised rue Cler.

Les Invalides

Conspicuous by its golden dome, the Hôtel des Invalides (p.166) was built as a home for Louis XIV's wounded soldiers. Inside, the Musée de l'Armée contains a stupefying collection of weaponry, though the powerful second world war exhibition has broader appeal. Its main claim to fame, though, is Napoleon's tomb, which is deeply impressive if only for its sheer pomp and ugliness.

This area of embassies and government buildings includes the Hôtel Matignon, the home of France's Prime Minister, on rue Varenne. The character alters along rue de Babylone towards Le Bon Marché department store. En route, you'll pass the glorious, crumbling Pagode Cinema (p.366).

It's also an area of outstanding museums. Adjacent to les Invalides, the gardens and mansion of the Musée Rodin (p.178) are a delight. Not in the same league, but still worthwhile, the Musée Maillol (01 42 22 59 58) is north of Le Bon Marché. Further north, the irresistible Musée d'Orsay (p.171) beckons on Quai d'Orsay. Between here and the new Musée du Quai-Branly (p.175), you'll pass the grand loggia of France's lower house, the Assemblée Nationale, the American Church and the kiosk of the Égouts de Paris (p.188). Good for a rainy day, a tour of the city's sewers serves up a fascinating glimpse of the city's moist underbelly.

Views of the Eiffel Tower and Hôtel des Invalides

The Lowdown ◀

*Many towns retain an
individual character.
Easy to reach, they're
worth exploring in
their own right or as
bases for forays in
the countryside.*

The Good ◀

*Fabulously furnished
royal châteaux, some
of which are crowd-
free; popular family
attractions and a
multitude of
other attractions.*

The Bad ◀

*The State Apartments
at Versailles can be
knee-deep in visitors.
Rather than attempt a
whistle-stop trip, build
in time to explore the
quieter reaches.*

The Must-Dos ◀

*Climb the highest
medieval fortified
tower in Europe; take
to the forest at
Fontainebleau or St-
Germain-en-Laye;
relax by the fountains
of Versailles.*

Beyond The Périphérique

North Of Paris

Unemployment and unlovely housing sum up Seine-Saint-Denis' reputation, but it's here that you'll find one of France's key heritage sites. The Gothic Basilique Saint-Denis (p.168) is the burial place of monarchs, a tradition begun in the 7th century. East of here is the emblematic Stade de France (p.191), and at Le Bourget, the Musée de l'Air et d'Espace (p.179), an outstanding museum that will easily fill the best part of a day. All three can be reached on the RER, give or take a bus hop.

Further afield, Auvers-sur-Oise is a must for Impressionist fans. Van Gogh spent his last months here, leaving a legacy of 70 local paintings. The inn where he stayed has been restored and the Château has a good multimedia show. By train, Auvers is an hour's ride from the Gare du Nord, with a direct service in summer. Top-notch equestrian entertainment – and a princely château – make an equally worthwhile outing to Chantilly (p.158). Last but not least, Parc Astérix (p.189) offers a splashing good time in the company of the home-grown cartoon hero (note that the park is not open all year).

East Of Paris

Welcoming more than 12 million visitors a year, Disneyland (p.188) is incontestably the main draw of this area. It's 40 minutes by RER. With queues likely, an early start is best. For a fairytale setting of a different sort, the town of Provins (www.provins.net) has Unesco status for its well-preserved ramparts and underground passages. In summer, it goes to town on medieval pageantry. Count on it taking 90 minutes by train from the Gare de l'Est; less by car on the A4.

South Of Paris

On Paris' doorstep is the Château de Vincennes (p.159), whose stupendous 14th century keep has been restored, with the Saint-Chapelle to follow in 2008. Further out, Fontainebleau (p.158) is a 40 minute drive or an hour by public transport. The château alone is a day-trip, but there's a full weekend's worth here if combined with forest rambles or a visit to Barbizon, the village colonised by Corot and Millet and their circle. Make time, if you can, for a day-trip to Vaux-le-Vicomte (p.159), a château so ravishing it inspired the envy of Louis XIV. Not that it's all about history, though. A short hop from the city, the new Mac/Val (p.179) in Vitry-sur-Seine has put the *banlieue* firmly on the contemporary art map.

West Of Paris

Topping the visiting list is Versailles (p.158); the royal château and grounds keep getting better with each new restoration. At the other end of the architectural spectrum, the business district of La Défense centred on la Grande Arche (p.191) makes a surprisingly good stroll with its eighty-odd sculptures and quirky landscaping. Criticised as cold, it now looks poised for a renaissance, with iconic towers on the way, and more life on the plaza. West of Paris proper, some of the more sought-after suburbs include Sèvres and Boulogne-Billancourt, boasting museums on ceramics (p.179) and 1930s art (p.179) respectively, while the Parc de St-Cloud is wild enough for red squirrels, but near enough to afford a grandstand view of the city. By Rueil, the Château de Malmaison (p.158) tends to be overshadowed by grander affairs. Finally, the upmarket suburb of St-Germain-en-Laye is entrenched in history, and a mere 20 minutes away. The ex-royal château now houses the national archaeology collection (01 39 10 13 00). Outside, Le Nôtre's long terrace offers a very democratic panorama of the capital.

Fashion Boutiques p.123
Financial Advisors p.95

Written by residents, the Barcelona Explorer
is packed with insider info, from arriving
in the city to making it your home and
everything in between.

Barcelona Explorer Residents' Guide
We Know Where You Live

Museums, Heritage & Culture

Paris is sometimes described as a museum city. If that means possessing awe-inspiring monuments, and museums and galleries filled with more art treasures than can ever be shown at one time – well, it's a pretty reasonable claim. For the first timer and the long-term resident alike, Paris offers rich cultural pickings. Between lavish temporary exhibitions at the Louvre, the Orsay and the Arts Décoratifs, and new ventures such as the Pinathèque, the Cité de l'Histoire de l'Immigration or the out-of-town Val/Mac, every season brings something new to discover.

Art Galleries

Other options **Art & Craft Supplies** p.246, **Art** p.246

It may lack the contemporary buzz of New York or London, but art lovers will feel at home in Paris. All the major museums (and many more besides) lay on temporary shows, for which cultivated Parisians turn out in force. An entry fee is charged. When it comes to private galleries, the picture is more complex. Many prestige galleries are in the Marais and St-Germain, with up-and-coming offerings clustered around rue Louise-Weiss (13th). Taking an Art Bus tour (p.200) will give you some good insider leads into the contemporary and alternative scene. Look out, too, for the *portes ouvertes* (open days) offered by communities of artists of all disciplines. Held in spring or autumn, they're a great opportunity to meet artists in their studios and discover the *quartier* at the same time. Most private galleries close on Sunday and Monday and virtually all in August.

261 blvd Raspail
14th
Ⓜ *Denfert Rochereau*
Map p.408 C3 **1**

Fondation Cartier

01 42 18 56 50 | *www.fondationcartier.fr*
Jean Nouvel's strikingly airy glass and steel design has brought a welcome boost to Montmartre's arts scene. Diverse, often internationally orientated multimedia exhibitions do the rest. Recent shows have embraced the hyperrealist figures of Australian sculptor, Ron Mueck and Rock 'n' Roll. The building makes a feature of the 'tree of liberty', a cedar of Lebanon planted by Chateaubriand after the Revolution. Open Tuesday to Sunday, 12:00 to 20:00.

30 rue Beaubourg
3rd
Ⓜ *Rambuteau*
Map p.400 A2 **2**

Galerie Daniel Templon

01 42 72 14 10 | *www.danieltemplon.com*
Enduringly popular, this private gallery has hosted a succession of big names over the years including Lichtenstein, Frank Stella and Andy Warhol. It continues to serve up a diverse menu of established artists such as Larry Bella and Yayoi Kusama, and younger, emerging artists with a distinctive voice. Open Monday to Saturday, 10:00 to 19:00.

5 rue Debelleyme
3rd
Ⓜ *Saint-Sébastien*
Froissart
Map p.400 B2 **3**

Galerie Karsten Greve

01 42 77 19 37 | *www.artnet.com/kgreve-paris.html*
With galleries in Cologne, Milan and St Moritz, the Greve gallery is a big hitter, showing retrospectives from a variety of artists, such as Pierre Soulages, John Chamberlain and Jean Dubuffet. There's also a good play of 'young' talent, including Paco Knöller, Tony Cragg and Sally Mann. Open Tuesday to Saturday 11:00 to 19:00.

5 rue du Temple
3rd
Ⓜ *Hôtel de Ville*
Map p.399 F3 **4**

Galerie Marian Goodman

01 48 04 70 52 | *www.mariangoodman.com*
The Paris counterpart of this New York gallery is enviably housed in a Marais mansion. Its equally impressive programme includes work from Gerhard Richter, Steve McQueen, Chantal Akerman and Pierre Huyghe. Open Tuesday to Saturday 11:00 to 19:00.

156

108 rue Vieille-du-Temple
3rd
Ⓜ **Saint-Sébastien Froissart**
Map p.400 B2 **5**

Galerie Yvon Lambert

01 42 71 09 33 | *www.yvon-lambert.com*
This is a very dynamic private gallery featuring big international names in the main, sky-lit space (Nan Goldin, Jenny Holzer, Andres Serrano), as well as bright new stars such as Douglas Gordon and Jonathan Monk. Open Tuesday to Friday 10:00 to 13:00 and 14:00 to 19:00; Saturday 10:00 to 19:00.

3 ave du Général-Eisenhower
8th
Ⓜ **Champs-Élysées – Clemenceau**
Map p.397 F1 **6**

Grand Palais

08 92 68 46 92 | *www.rmn.fr/galeriesnationalesdugrandpalais*
Built for the 1900 Universelle Exposition, this extravagant palace half way down the Champs-Élysées was conceived as a monument 'to the glory of French Art.' It's managed by the national museums authority and, taken as a whole, its galleries now constitute France's most important venue for international exhibitions. The fabulous glass hall reopened in 2005 after renovation and now hosts, among other things, the annual FIAC art fair. Pre-booking is advised at all times; for visits before 13:00, it's obligatory. Open Monday, Thursday, Sunday 10:00 to 20:00; Wednesday 10:00 to 22:00.

28 pl de la Madeleine
8th
Ⓜ **Madeleine**
Map p.388 B4 **7**

Pinacothèque de Paris

01 42 68 02 01 | *www.pinacotheque.com*
Spread over three floors, this enormous private museum recently opened its doors in the prestigious 8th, where it rubs shoulders with high fashion and gastronomy interests. Behind it is art historian, Marc Restillini, whose mission is to break away from the more traditional and didactic approach to art adopted at the likes of the Musée d'Orsay – and thereby attract a new audience for modern and contemporary creation. So far, things auger well, with a grand Roy Lichtenstein retrospective for openers. Open daily 10:30 to 18:30.

Chateaux

Other options **Historic Houses** p.162

When Louis XIV commissioned Versailles, he intended it to leave all other châteaux in the shade, and so it does, to this day. But all that glitters is not just Versailles, and you should certainly make time to visit some of the other châteaux beyond the city limits. Together and individually, they are unique. From the indomitably fortified Château de Vincennes to Fontainebleau, the palace Napoleon called 'the true home of kings,' you're in for a treat.

Grand Palais

The Complete **Residents**' Guide

Château de Chantilly

BP 70243
Chantilly
Map p.373 B2

03 44 27 31 80 | *www.chateaudechantilly.com*

Purists may not care for Chantilly; much of the creamy Renaissance building is in fact a 19th century reconstitution. That aside, it is delightful. Inside, the main draw is the Musée Condé, a small but superb collection of paintings by Filippo Lippi, Raphael, Poussin and Ingres. Also here is the medieval masterpiece *Les Très Riches Heures du Duc de Berry*. In the park, motor boats cruise the canal network which runs through Le Nôtre's formal gardens and the more romantic English ones. The Musée Vivant du Cheval (p.180) is nearby. It's rather a trek if you don't have a car (30 minutes by train from Gare du Nord to Chantilly-Gouivieux, then a 15 minute walk). If you do, it's only 40km away on the A1. Open daily (except Tuesday): November to March, 10:00 to 17:00; April to October, 10:00 to 18:00.

Château de Fontainebleau

77300 Fontainebleau
Fontainbleu
Map p.373 B2

01 60 71 50 60 | *www.musee-chateau-fontainebleau.fr*

Over its eight centuries, Fontainebleau has seen royal births, marriages, intrigue – even an emperor's abdication. More than anything it has been a royal home, on which a succession of monarchs from Francois I to Empress Eugénie have clearly left their stamp. Highlights include the Grand Gallery with its Renaissance frescos and coffered walnut ceiling, and the elegant mother-of-pearl inlaid boudoir where Marie-Antoinette and her family escaped the gaze of the court. Despite its charms, it's rarely crowded. The gardens are equally delectable, and the forest is visible in the distance. The château is reached by a 45 minute train ride from Gare de Lyon to Fontaine-Avon followed by 15 minutes on bus A. A combined transport plus château ticket is available. Open Wednesday to Monday 09:30 to 17:00 (18:00 in summer).

Château de Malmaison

ave du Château
Rueil-Malmaison
Map p.378 B2

01 41 29 05 55 | *www.musees-nationaux-napoleoniens.org*

It was Joséphine Bonaparte who bought this château in 1799, and it was here that she and Napoleon enjoyed some measure of contentment. When the First Consul wasn't otherwise engaged, Malmaison was the scene of card parties, billiards and theatrical performances. Joséphine remained here after Napoleon divorced her in 1809, continuing to adapt the house to her taste until her death in 1814. Malmaison is small as châteaux go, but ostentatiously swagged and gilded, it's the epitome of First Empire taste. The interior has been restored and displays many possessions, including items of Joséphine's clothing and the canopied bed in which she died. The gardens still contain the summer pavilion where Napoleon liked to work. To reach Malmaison by public transport, take the RER to La Grande Arche de la Défense, then bus 258. Open: October to March, 10:00 to 12:30 and 13:30 to 17:15; April to September, 10:00 to 17:50.

Château de Versailles

Versailles
Versailles
R *Versailles – Rive*
Gauche
Map p.378 A3

01 30 83 76 20 | *www.chateauversailles.fr*

Why the Revolution? If you want an easy answer, look no further than Versailles, the palace Louis XIV built to out-dazzle all rivals, control his courtiers, and escape the unsavoury populace. The state apartments are, for most, the core of the visit – especially following the recent renovation of the Galerie des Glaces, which has returned the lustre and rich hues to the high mirrors and Le Brun's painted ceiling. Guided tours reveal more of the château interior. Le Nôtre's formal gardens are magical. At their far end, Marie-Antoinette's Estate is touchingly intimate. It includes the Petit Trianon, the Jardin Anglais, the Theatre and le Hameau de la Reine, her fantasy thatched village. The château is always busy, but you can limit queuing by buying advance tickets from train stations or online at www.fnacspectacles.com. Open daily (except Monday and public holidays): November to 2 April, 09:00 to 17:30; 3 April to October, 09:00 to 18:30.

Château de Vincennes

ave de Paris
Vincennes
Ⓜ *Château de*
Vincennes
Map p.379 D3

01 48 08 31 20 | *www.chateau-vincennes.fr*

Forget silk upholstery and mother-of-pearl inlay – this is an altogether more muscular kind of château, built to withstand the worst assaults of a 14th century English army. Charles V ruled the country from here, and his 50 metre-high keep, within a formidable curtain wall, was both unassailable and the last word in style. Reopened in 2007 after twelve years of restoration, the keep is remarkably preserved with four-inch thick doors and graceful vaulted ceilings. The 45 minute guided tour includes a film presentation (audioguides supplied free). The reopening of the restored Sainte-Chapelle, begun in 1379 to house holy relics brought back from the crusades, is the next big highlight in the château's calendar. Open daily: May to August, 10:00 to 12:00 and 13:00 to 18:00; September to April, 10:00 to 12:00 and 13:15 to 17:00.

Vaux le Vicomte

Melun
Map p.373 B2

01 64 14 41 90 | *www.vaux-le-vicomte.com*

If you love châteaux, it doesn't get much better than Vaux le Vicomte. Just 55km south-east of Paris, this castle with fairytale looks is set in lavish gardens that roll out towards woodland. Its history is the stuff of fiction. Nicolas Fouquet, Louis XIV's finance minister enlisted Le Vau, Le Brun and Le Nôtre, plus an army of craftsman, to build, decorate and landscape it. The Sun King was so chagrined at being outdone that he promptly jailed its owner on embezzlement charges. Fouquet died in jail; his treasures ended up at Versailles. Vaux le Vicomte was designed on a much more human scale than Versailles, and the result is arguably more beautiful. Candlelight visits and concerts take place in summer; see the website for details. Reach it by train or RER D from Gare de Lyon to Melun, then take a taxi or the weekend Châteaubus in summer. Open 24 March to 11 November and 22 December to 6 January, 10:00 to 13:00 and 14:00 to 18:00 weekdays; 10:00 to18:00 weekends. Closed 25 December and 1 January.

Churches & Cathedrals

France is a secular state, born out of a complex and often bloody religious history. It's a history you'll find written across the capital's churches. Lovers of architecture are in for a feast; how many other cities boast a Gothic cathedral, a neoclassical temple and a machine-age dome within walking distance of each other? What's more, despite the iconoclasm of the Revolution, many Parisian churches display remarkable works of art, objects that wouldn't look out of place in the galleries of the Louvre. For the most part, they remain living places of worship which you're free to explore, providing you show appropriate respect. The cathedrals, basilica and churches in this section represent some of the highlights for visitors, but the selection wouldn't be complete without the Grande Mosquée de Paris (p.163), a beautiful building in its own right, and one which plays an important part in the modern life of the city.

Cathédrale Notre-Dame de Paris

6 Parvis Notre-Dame,
place Jean-Paul II
4th
Ⓜ *Cité*
Map p.399 F4 🄸

01 42 34 56 10 | *www.cathedraledeparis.com*

Built between 1160 and 1345, this Gothic masterpiece turned Paris into an ecclesiastical capital. Hard times came later, notably when Revolutionary zealots decapitated its carved Old Testament kings and made it a temple to Reason. Even Napoleon's coronation here couldn't stop its decline in the 19th century; it took Victor Hugo and the Gothic Revival architect Viollet-le-Duc to do that. The twin towers, rose window and triple doorways of the west front are a triumph of harmony. Inside, the soaring knave is flanked by 37 chapels containing *The Mays* – paintings by Charles Le Brun and others, donated by wealthy guilds each May Day.

On Sunday afternoons, organ recitals are free. The Treasury houses ornate vestments and plates. The crown of thorns goes on show on Good Friday. Complete your visit by climbing the towers (p.167); tickets are sold by the north tower. The Cathédrale is open weekdays 08:00 to 18:45; Saturday, Sunday 08:00 to 19:15.

place de la Madeleine ◀
8th
Ⓜ *Madeleine*
Map p.388 B4 15

La Madeleine

01 44 51 69 00 | *www.eglise-lamadeleine.com*

Rather like the Basilique de Ste-Géneviève (today the Panthéon), this church suffered a crisis of purpose when Revolution struck, and there were even proposals that the part-built church should be used as a marketplace. In 1806, Napoleon commissioned Barthélemy Vignon's design for a Grecian-style temple surrounded by Corinthian columns: to honour the Grande Armée. Napoleon was long dead before the project reached fruition, (the church was consecrated in 1845). The interior is grand but rather gloomy under the domes and polychrome marble. The organ is exceptional; Saint-Saëns and Fauré were both organists here. In the cupola above the altar, Jules-Claude Ziegler's frieze puts a very First Empire slant on the history of Christianity, with Napoleon centre-stage. Open daily 09:00 to 19:00.

6 blvd du Palais ◀
1st
Ⓜ *Cité*
Map p.399 E3 16

La Sainte-Chapelle

01 53 40 60 97 | *www.monuments-nationaux.fr*

The Sainte-Chapelle was built between 1242 and 1248 as a shrine for the crown of thorns and a fragment of the true cross which Louis IX – later Saint Louis – purchased at huge cost from Byzantium (they're now under lock and key at Notre-Dame). Despite being enclosed by the Palais de Justice, it remains one of the city's jewels. The lower chapel, with its rich blue-starred ceiling, was built to accommodate the prayers of servants. Reached by a spiral staircase, the upper chapel for king and court achieves an almost mystical effect, thanks to the 15 metre-high stained glass windows that bathe the space in colour. Remarkably, two-thirds of them are original, and their scenes depict almost the entire bible. The delicate spire you can see outside dates from 1853. A combined ticket includes access to La Conciergerie (p.165) close by. Open daily: March to October, 09:30 to18:00; November to February, 09:00 to 17:00. Closed 1 January, 1 May and 25 December.

35 rue du ◀
Chevalier-de-la-Barre
18th
Ⓜ *Lamarck –*
Caulaincourt
Map p.383 E4 17

Sacré-Coeur

01 53 41 89 00 | *www.sacre-coeur-montmartre.com*

It isn't especially old, nor is its interior universally admired, but the city skyline simply wouldn't be the same without Sacré-Coeur. It was originally commissioned after the bloodshed of the Franco-Prussian War and the Commune of 1871, which looked like small beer after the horrors of the first world war when it was finally consecrated in 1919. The structure was inspired by Istanbul's Hagia Sofia, and the Byzantine theme continues inside with extensive mosaics. Outside, there's a charge to climb the dome between 09:00 and 19:00 (18:00 in winter), but queues are often minimal and the views are as good as they come. Open daily 06:00 to 23:00, last entry at 22:15.

46 blvd Malesherbes ◀
8th
Ⓜ *Villiers*
Map p.388 A2 18

St-Augustin

01 45 22 23 12

Dominating its busy boulevard, the church of St-Augustin has a mildly eclectic air, but the curious red pinnacle that tops the dome gives a clue to its still more unusual construction. It was designed by Victor Baltard, who was responsible for the iron-framed pavilions of Les Halles. Here you can see him in fine 1860s form. Opening hours are irregular, but if you have a chance to cross the stone-clad threshold, the church's iron skeleton is revealed in all its glory.

rue du Jour
1st
Ⓜ **Les Halles**
Map p.399 E1 **19**

St-Eustache
01 42 36 31 05 | www.saint-eustache.org
Work on this imposing church was begun in 1532 but took over a century to complete; the result is Gothic in architecture but Renaissance in decoration. Among the highlights are the elaborate tomb of Colbert, the fine stained glass windows and a naive sculpture added in the 1960s to reflect the great market trading era of Les Halles. Great acoustics with an organ to match make this a popular place for recitals. Open daily 09:00 to 19:30.

2 place du Louvre
1st
Ⓜ **Pont Neuf**
Map p.399 D2 **20**

St-Germain l'Auxerrois
01 42 60 13 96
A church with a long history, the mainly 15th century St-Germain l'Auxerrois was built over a much earlier structure. The bell tower dates from the 12th century, though it was given the Gothic treatment in the 19th. Among the church's treasures are two exquisitely carved Flemish retables, stained glass from the 16th century, and a magnificent canopied wooden bench, designed by Le Brun for Louis XIV. Its proximity to the Louvre made this a very royal church from the 14th century. It's also remembered, infamously, as the church that rang its bell in August 1572 to signal the start of the St Bartholomew's Day Massacre. Open daily 09:00 to 19:00.

Notre Dame

Sacré-Coeur

St-Germain l'Auxerrois

La Sainte-Chapelle

161

3 place ◄
St-Germain des Prés
6th
Ⓜ *Saint-Germain-*
des-Prés
Map p.398 C4 **21**

St-Germain des Prés

01 55 42 81 33 | *www.eglise-sgp.org*

This is the oldest church in Paris. Only a few stones remain from the original Benedictine abbey and basilica built here in around 550, and in which the Merovingian kings were buried. Much else, though, the tower included, dates back to the 11th and 12th centuries. Look out for the tomb of René Descartes – and the early masons' marks near the entrance. Open Monday to Saturday 08:00 to 19:45; Sunday 09:00 to 20:00.

296 rue St-Honoré ◄
1st
Ⓜ *Tuileries*
Map p.398 C1 **22**

St-Roch

01 42 44 13 20

Seen from the street, the baroque facade is misleading: this is a big, church, almost as long as Notre-Dame. Work begun in 1653 by Jacques Lemercier (who was responsible for some galleries of the Louvre), but funds ran dry and it wasn't finished until 1740. Inside, you'll find the tombs of Diderot, Corneille and Le Nôtre, as well as some splendid works of art, not least Michel Anguier's marble Nativity. In 1796, the steps were the scene of a showdown between Royalists and the Conventionalists, led by an ambitious young Napoleon. Two hundred people were left dead and wounded, shot at close range. The rest, as they say, is history. Open daily 08:00 to 19:00.

3 rue des ◄
Prêtres-St-Séverin
5th
Ⓜ *Cluny – La*
Sorbonne
Map p.399 E4 **23**

St-Séverin

01 42 34 93 50 | *www.saint-severin.com*

Begun in the 12th century, but owing much to the 15th, this is one of the Left Bank's oldest – and loveliest – churches. It's famous for its flamboyant Gothic vaulting which culminates in bravura carving in a final 'palm tree' column. A vibrant stained window by the 20th century artist, Jean Bazaine, is also a feature. Free choral recitals sometimes take place in summer. Open daily 11:00 to 19:30.

place St-Sulpice ◄
6th
Ⓜ *Saint-Sulpice*
Map p.398 C4 **24**

St-Sulpice

01 46 33 21 78 | *www.paroisse-saint-sulpice-paris.org*

When it emerges from its restorers' scaffolding, St-Sulpice boasts a fine Italianate portico and two slightly mismatched, though splendid, towers (its construction straddled more than a century from 1646). Just inside are three frescos painted by Delacroix (in a corner of '*Jacob Wrestling with the Angel*' is what looks like the artist's straw hat). Notice also the shell-shaped fonts sculpted by Pigalle, and an 18th century obelisk, part of a gnomon, or astronomical measuring device. Open daily 07:30 to 19:30.

Historic Houses

Other options **Chateaux** p.157

47 rue Raynouard ◄
16th
Ⓡ *Avenue du Pdt*
Kennedy
Map p.395 F3 **25**

Maison de Balzac

01 55 74 41 80 | *www.paris.fr/musees*

The novelist Honoré de Balzac moved to an apartment in this quiet Passy house in 1840 to escape his debts, and quickly established code words to sift friendly callers from creditors. Inside, you'll find the study where he worked on *La Comédie Humaine*, stimulated by endless cups of coffee from his porcelain cafétière. Amid the memorabilia, drafts and letters, there are portraits of friends and his beloved Mme Hanska. One room, devoted to the family of characters that people his novels, is almost a world in itself. There's a small bookshop and garden. Entry to the main museum is free. Open Tuesday to Sunday 10:00 to 18:00.

6 place des Vosges
4th
Ⓜ **Chemin Vert**
Map p.400 C3 26

Maison de Victor Hugo
01 42 72 10 16 | www.paris.fr
For more than a decade, the revered
author of *Les Miserables* rented an
apartment in the Hôtel de Rohan-
Guénemée, the largest house in what
was then known as the place Royale.
Hugo moved here in 1832, shortly
before meeting his life-long mistress,
the actress, Juliette Druouet. On show
are first editions, personal memorabilia
and portraits, as well as the Chinese
salon that Hugo chose for Drouet when
she followed him to Guernsey. Entry to
the main museum is free. Open Tuesday
to Sunday 10:00 to 18:00.

25 rue du
Docteur Roux
15th
Ⓜ **Volontaires**
Map p.407 E3 27

Musée Pasteur
01 45 68 82 83 | www.pasteur.fr
This is not your conventional glimpse
into a great man's life. The guided visit
also takes in a historical science
collection of some 1,000 instruments
and artefacts, and, downstairs, Louis
Pasteur's Byzantine mausoleum, with its

La Mosquée de Paris

floor-to-ceiling symbolist mosaics. But in the apartment where the Pasteurs lived out
the years after the chemist made his greatest breakthroughs, everything is just as
they left it. Among the personal possessions, furniture and photographs, there's a
handsome portrait of the scientist's father, made when Pasteur was barely 20 years
old. Open Monday to Friday 14:00 to 17:30. Closed August and public holidays.

Mosques

2 place du Puits
de l'Hermite
5th
Ⓜ **Place Monge**
Map p.410 A2 28

La Mosquée de Paris
01 45 35 97 33 | www.mosquee-de-paris.org
Paris' main mosque, a dazzling white Hispano-Moorish inspired structure with a green-
tiled Minaret, was built in the 1920s. It's the spiritual centre of the country's mainly
Algerian Islamic community. There's a small admission charge to visit the outer
courtyard and library of the mosque, either under your own steam or with a guide.
Within the complex, there's also a pleasant cafe where mint tea is served on brass trays,
a traditional hammam and a richly polychrome restaurant. Open to visitors daily except
Friday, 09:00 to 12:00 and 14:00 to 18:00. Closed on religious holidays.

Heritage Sites – City
Other options **Museums – City** p.169, **Art** p.246

Paris, one of the most beautiful cities in the world, has spent centuries cultivating its
good looks. Robust medieval buildings have stood the test of time, and even a little of
Gallo-Roman Lutetia survives to tell a tale. Monarchs of the *Ancien Régime* came and
went, leaving their elegant stamp on their city, and Napoleon, in turn, realised some of
his grand ambitions in stone here. From the medieval Tour Jean-Sans-Peur to the Tour
Eiffel, this is a city with more than its share of heritage sights.

163

**place Charles
-de-Gaulle**
8th
Ⓜ **Charles de Gaulle
Étoile**
Map p.386 C3 **29**

Arc de Triomphe

01 55 37 73 77 | www.monum.fr

You can't get far without seeing arches here, but the Arc de Triomphe holds a special place in Parisian hearts. Rising out of a swirling sea of traffic, this is a suitably grand monument to the victories of France's greatest military genius, even if Napoleon didn't live long enough to see its completion. Appropriately enough, it now harbours the Tomb of the Unknown Soldier; take the underpass if you want to admire its martial friezes close up. Alongside the inscribed names of

Arc de Triomphe

battles and generals, there are bas-reliefs all around its surface (the eye-catcher is Rude's impassioned *Le Départ des Volontaires*, better known as *La Marseillaise*). Ascend the monument to appreciate a perspective that runs from the Champs-Élysées to the Louvre, then turn around for an outlook on the daddy of the arches, La Grande Arche de la Défense. The Arc de Triomphe is pivotal to the city's calendar of pomp and ceremony, the dramatic backdrop for the Presidential parade on the Quatorze Juillet and other mass draws such as the Tour de France. Open daily: April to September, 10:00 to 23:00; October to March, 10:00 to 22:30. Closed on public holidays.

rue des Arènes
5th
Ⓜ **Place Monge**
Map p.409 F2 **30**

Arènes de Lutèce

www.paris.fr

Although the 1st to 2nd century arena is one of two important vestiges of the Roman city of Lutetia, there's every chance you'll have it pretty much to yourself, unless the locals have turned up to play pétanque or five-a-side. In its day, thousands gathered here to watch gladiators draw blood or the latest dramatic offering. Some of the terraced seats have survived intact. The remains were buried here for centuries until the construction of rue Monge brought them to light. Open daily: summer, 08:00 to 22:00; winter, 08:00 to 17:30.

29 rue Pasquier
8th
Ⓜ **Saint-Augustin**
Map p.388 B3 **31**

Chapelle Expiatoire

01 44 32 18 00 | www.monuments-nationaux.fr

Partly hidden by trees, this grand but rather lonely chapel in the shape of a Greek cross was commissioned by Louis XVIII in 1826. It stands on the ground where the remains of his brother, Louis XVI and Marie-Antoinette were hastily buried (an ignominy they shared with 3,000 other guillotine victims, including many in the Revolutionary government). The bodies of the king and queen were removed to the Basilique St-Denis. The chapel contains Corot's sculpture of *Marie-Antoinette Sustained By Faith*, while below, a black and white marble altar marks the spot where the bodies were found. There's a small admission fee. Guided tours are available on reservation. Open Thursday to Saturday 13:00 to 17:00. Closed major public holidays.

Champ de Mars
7th
Ⓜ **Bir-Hakeim**
Map p.396 C3 **32**

The Eiffel Tower

01 44 11 23 23 | www.tour-eiffel.fr

Brilliant, graceful, emblematic – even so, the Eiffel Tower provoked a furore when it went up in 1889 (for the Exposition Universelle) on the centenary of the Revolution. Many felt it jarred badly with the existing monuments of the day. Pre-fabricated at Gustave Eiffel's foundry at Levallois-Perret, the tower took only 21 months to assemble, a remarkable achievement for the time. At 276 metres, it was the world's tallest building, and remained so for decades. However, the tower wasn't meant to stay up indefinitely. Staggeringly, by the mid 1920s, it was in such disrepair that a confidence trickster, Victor Lustig, managed to 'sell' it to a scrap dealer. It now welcomes around six million visitors each year. To join them, try coming late in the day when you're more likely to avoid the queues. Tickets are sold at the base; ascent is by hydraulic lift (or stairs to the second floor, if you're game). From here, the 360° view extends up to 50 miles when visibility is good, and you can prolong your visit with a splurge at the Restaurant Jules Verne. The top floor contains Eiffel's cosy office. The first floor becomes a garden terrace in summer, and an ice-rink in winter. Opening times: 1 January to 14 June and 2 September to 31 June, 09:30 to 23:00; 15 June to 1 September, 09:00 to 00:00.

Hôtel de Ville

place de l'Hôtel de Ville
4th
Ⓜ *Hôtel de Ville*
Map p.399 F3 **33**

01 42 76 40 40 | *www.paris.fr*
This city hall building is a 19th century replacement for the one that burnt down during the Commune in 1871. Its substantial exterior boasts some 136 sculptures of famous figures, while the inside is just as fancy, with heavy chandeliers, copious gilding and wood panelling. At the spot where crowds once gathered to watch grisly public executions, Paris Plage (p.183) now draws the masses in summer, along with the winter ice-rink and an array of events in between. Excellent regular free exhibitions are held in the building; it's not unusual to see queues extend around the block. Tours, in French, English, and German, are by appointment. Open Monday to Saturday, 10:00 to 19:00.

La Conciergerie

2 blvd du Palais
1st
Ⓜ *Cité*
Map p.399 E3 **43**

01 53 73 78 50 | *www.monum.fr*
Despite its forbidding aspect, the Conciergerie wasn't always a prison (though one conical tower housed a torture chamber). It takes its name from the Concierge or King's Steward left in place by Charles V when he moved the royal residence. However, its most infamous period was under the *Tribunal Révolutionnaire*, when more than 2,700 condemned prisoners spent their last days here; Marie-Antoinette being the most famous. After making their way through the immense 14th century vaulted hall (the oldest of its kind in Europe) and the bookshop, visitors can peer into her cell. It's a reconstitution, but guarded, cramped and comfortless, it's no less poignant for that. If you intend visiting the Sainte-Chapelle (p.160), plump for a combined ticket. Open daily: March to October, 09:30 to 18:00; November to February, 09:00 to 17:00.

La Crypte Archéologique

place Jean-Paul II
4th
Ⓜ *Cité*
Map p.399 F4 **34**

01 55 42 50 10
Medieval Île de la Cité was largely swept away under Haussmann's redevelopment of the city, but vestiges of shops and streets have been preserved below ground on the plaza in front of Notre Dame. You'll also find some sections of quayside and rampart that date back to the Roman city of Lutecia (Lutèce in French), together with an 18th century orphanage and 19th century sewer. While the resulting hotch-potch can be a little difficult to make sense of, the models of the settlement's development are more enlightening. Open Tuesday to Sunday 10:00 to 18:00.

La Conciergerie

Le Manufacture des Gobelins

42 ave des Gobelins
13th
Ⓜ *Les Gobelins*
Map p.409 F4 🄢

01 44 08 53 49 | *www.mobiliernational.culture.gouv.fr*

In 1667, Colbert brought together ebony carvers, goldsmiths, silversmiths and tapestry weavers to form the *Manufacture Royale de la Couronne*. It took the name of Gobelin from a family of dyers who had set up here around 1440. The factory came to specialise in tapestry alone, and still does – supplying embassies and palaces with masterpieces that take years to create. The gallery in the 1910 factory reopened in 2007 and periodically shows treasures ancient and modern. For a fuller insight, there are regular guided tours (in French) on Tuesdays, Wednesdays and Thursdays. Open Tuesday to Sunday 12:30 to 18:30. Closed 25 December and 1 May.

Le Panthéon

place du Panthéon
5th
Ⓜ *Cardinal Lemoine*
Map p.409 E1 🄣

01 44 32 18 00/01 44 | *www.monum.fr*

Soufflot's neoclassical masterpiece used to dominate the skyline of Paris from its lofty position on the Montagne Sainte-Geneviève. It's still the Latin Quarter's most notable monument. Conceived as a church, it was no sooner completed than the Revolutionary authorities turned it into a necropolis for great men (though not all of those honoured got to stay). It fluctuated between secular and religious use until the 1880s. With its grandiose stone tableaux and painted friezes (some are by Puvis de Chavannes), the choir makes you feel small and, if that isn't enough, a replica of Foucault's Pendulum, suspended from 67 metres up, demonstrates that the planet is relentlessly revolving. At rest in the well-lit crypt are Voltaire, Rousseau, Hugo, Pierre and Marie Curie and Jean Moulin. On fine days, it's worth paying a little extra to climb the dome for great views. Open daily: April to September, 10:00 to 18:30; October to March, 10:00 to 18:00.

Les Catacombes de Paris

1 ave Colonel
Henri-Rol-Tanguy
14th
Ⓜ *Denfert Rochereau*
Map p.408 C4 🄤

01 43 22 47 63 | *www.musees.paris.fr*

From these quarries came the limestone that built Notre-Dame, the Pont Neuf and much more. From 1795, they found a new purpose, as an outlet for the now overflowing cemeteries and charnel houses of the city. It's estimated that the remains of six million people lie here, including those of Robespierre and his henchmen. As you enter, there's a long, winding descent to the tunnels, where skulls, femurs and the rest are tightly and anonymously packed in walls. It's a chilly walk of a couple of kilometres, with macabre memento moris breaking the monotony along the way. There's a €7 entry fee, and a bag search at the end to intercept trophy hunters. Open Tuesday to Sunday 09:30 to 16:00.

Les Invalides

Esplanade des
Invalides
7th
Ⓜ *Invalides*
Map p.397 F3 🄥

01 44 42 40 69 | *www.invalides.org*

Founded as a war veteran's home by Louis XIV in 1670, les Invalides was built by Jules Hardouin-Mansart, of Versailles fame. It's a large complex, comprising two churches, the Musée de l'Armée, the Musée de l'Ordre de la Libération and the Musée des Plans-Reliefs (a collection of scale models of cities begun by Vauban, Louis XIV's military architect). A part of the complex remains a hospital to this day. The gilt Église du Dôme was built for the king's exclusive use. Since 1840, it's been a shrine to Napoleon, whose red porphyry tomb lies surrounded by monumental evocations of greatness and grief. Open daily: April to September, 10:00 to 18:00; October to March, 10:00 to 17:00. Closed first Monday of the month.

Les Catacombes

Opéra Garnier

8 rue Scribe
9th
Ⓜ Opéra
Map p.388 C3 **39**

08 92 89 90 90 | *www.opera-de-paris.fr*
Charles Garnier was a virtual unknown when he landed the plumb job of building a modern opera to embellish the new-look Second Empire city. A string of setbacks (not least the war with Prussia and the Commune) meant that it wasn't finished until 1875. In a style that defies neat definition (other than 'more is more'), it proved to be worth the wait. Inside, the Grand Foyer makes abundant use of multi-hued marble, sculptures and paintings, while the auditorium, sumptuous with its red velvet boxes, boasts a ceiling painted by Chagall in 1964. If you can't fit in a performance, a visit is the next best thing. Open daily 10:00 to 18:00 except during matinées. Closed 1 January and 1 May.

Opéra Garnier

Père-Lachaise

16 rue du Repos
20th
Ⓜ Père Lachaise
Map p.402 A2 **40**

01 55 25 82 10 | *www.paris.fr*
Montparnasse, Montmartre, Passy and Picpus all have their cachet. But none of these offers quite the roll-call of figures you'll find entombed at Père-Lachaise. Chopin, Rossini, Morrison, Balzac, Wilde, Proust, Géricault, Modigliani, Piaf, Sarah Bernhardt… they all lie here within this 116 acre walled necropolis. The cemetery was created in 1804, a much-needed new burial ground after the bloody excesses of the Terror. In a clever public relations coup, the authorities re-interred the remains of Abélard and Heloïse, Molière and La Fontaine here, thereby establishing it as a prestige plot. It's an extremely atmospheric place, with its shaded, cobbled lanes and melancholy sepulchral figures. Pick up a basic map of the divisions at the entrance, or invest in a more detailed one if you're on a mission of pilgrimage. Open Monday to Friday 08:00 to 17:30; Saturday 08:30 to 17;30; Sunday 09:00 to 17:30.

Tour Jean-Sans-Peur

20 rue
Étienne-Marcel
2nd
Ⓜ Étienne Marcel
Map p.399 F1 **41**

01 40 26 20 28 | *www.tourjeansanspeur.com*
Restored and reopened thanks to the graft and determination of a private association, this 27 metre high medieval tower is a mighty leftover from the mansion built by Jean, Duke of Burgundy in around 1409. The 'fearless' Duke seized power after assassinating the Duke of Orleans, but was later murdered by his cousins. You may not fully grasp the intricacies of the Hundred Years War by the time you leave, but the tower's winding, 13th century, stone staircase and magnificent carved vaulting make impressive viewing. Open: November to March, Wednesday, Saturday and Sunday 13:30 to 18:00; April to October, Wednesday to Sunday 13:30 to 18:00.

Towers of Notre-Dame de Paris

rue du clôtre de
Notre-Dame
4th
Ⓜ Cité
Map p.399 F4 **14**

01 5 31 07 00 | *www.monuments-nationaux.fr/*
Due to a lack of foresight in their 12th century design, the towers of Notre-Dame will only take a limited number of visitors at a time, but your patience and the climb are well rewarded. You'll share the extraordinary views with the *Chimères*, the baleful gargoyles added by Viollet-le-Duc in the 19th century. In July and August, visits continue into the evening. If you don't mind queuing, entrance to the towers are free on the first Sunday of the month. Open daily: April to September, 10:00 to 18:30; October to March, 10:00 to 17:30. Closed on major public holidays.

167

Heritage Sites – Out of City

Other options **Museums – Out of City** p.179

If you live in Paris, it's easy to become insular, and, psychologically at least, the Périphérique doesn't help matters. Don't be. Transport links to the suburbs are generally good and there are a number of outstanding sites to lure you beyond the confines of Département 75 for an afternoon or a day-trip. They include not only some of France's finest châteaux (see p.157), but also locations such as Auvers-sur-Oise, Giverny and Barbizon, with their unique artistic heritage. Meanwhile, the World Heritage town of Provins and, right on the city's doorstep, the Basilique St-Denis are serious historical big-hitters, where medievalists will be in their element.

Auvers-sur-Oise

Val d'Oise
Map p.373 B2

01 30 36 10 06 | *www.auvers-sur-oise.com*

Cézanne, Gaugin and other painters of the period found inspiration along the Oise, but the town of Auvers, some 35km north-west of Paris, is particularly famous for its association with Van Gogh. His last two months were spent in a frenzy of painting here, leaving some 70 works, among which number many of his best-known. He died in the Auberge Ravoux and lies buried, alongside his brother, in Auvers' cemetery. The modest room in which he painted is open to visitors. At the edge of the town, there's more in the way of an homage to the Impressionists at the Château d'Auvers (www.chateau-auvers.fr), where displays and an audio-visual show lend insight into their life and times. By road, take the A15 towards Cergy-Pontoise, then the D928. By train from the Gare du Nord, it's an hour's ride changing at Pontoise, with a direct service laid on in the summer.

Barbizon

Fontainbleu
Map p.373 B2

01 60 74 99 99 | *www.fontainebleau-tourisme.com*

Barbizon, 10km north-west of Fontainebleau, gave its name to an artistic movement when a group of early 19th century painters, including Rousseau, Millet and Corot gravitated here, inspired by the unspoiled rock and forest landscape. The inn where they stayed, the Auberge Ganne, and Millet's studio are open to the public, and you can hike the heritage trail which traces their haunts. Barbizon is easily reached by car from Fontainebleau, or along the FB, a picturesque, signed 8km cycling and walking path. Information and maps are available from Fontainebleau Tourist Office.

Basilique Saint-Denis

1 rue de la
Légion d'Honneur
Saint-Denis
Map p.378 C1

01 48 09 83 54 | *www.monuments-nationaux.fr*

According to legend, Saint Denis, a 3rd century martyr decapitated by the Romans, picked up his head and stumbled all the way from Montmartre to this spot, five kilometres north of Paris. He was buried here, and from 7th century Dagobert onwards, so were the majority of French kings and queens. The tradition was revived after the Revolution, when the guillotined monarchs' remains were recovered and re-interred here. This basilica, built between 1137 and 1281 on the site of an earlier church, was the work of Abbot Suger. Magnificent, though not spared some heavy-handed 19th century restoration, it's widely regarded as Europe's earliest Gothic edifice. Equally remarkable is the assembly of seventy-odd sculpted tombs, which include those of Dagobert, François I, Catherine de Medici, Louis XVI and Marie-Antoinette. It's a short walk from metro Basilique St-Denis. Open: April to September, daily 10:00 to 18:15; October to March, weekdays 10:00 to 17:15, Sunday 12:00 to 17:15.

84 rue Claude Monet ◄
Giverny
Map p.373 B2

Giverny: Monet's House and Gardens
02 32 51 28 21 | *www.fondation-monet.com*

Giverny, 80km west of Paris, was the village where Monet chose to spend the last years of his life, perfecting his 'greatest masterpiece' – his garden – and, of course, capturing and re-capturing it on canvas. He lived here from 1883 to 1926. The house and genuinely exquisite gardens are now firmly established on the mass tourist circuit, and get very busy. To drive there, take the A13 to Bonnières, then the D201. Alternatively, it's a 45 minute train ride from Gare St-Lazare to Vernon, followed by a taxi or bus ride. Open April to October, Tuesday to Sunday 09:30 to 18:00.

Seine-et-Marne ◄
Map p.373 B2

Provins
01 64 60 26 26 | *www.provins.net*

Some 90km south-east of Paris, the town of Provins was at the zenith of its power in the 13th century, when it was a capital of the Counts of Champagne. Today, with two kilometres of high ramparts and defensive towers, subterranean passages and ancient churches, it's something of a living museum, as well as a thoroughly pleasant market town. You can easily spend a day strolling among its wood-timbered houses, listed monuments and artisans' shops. Provins works hard to lend colour to its Unesco World Heritage status, organising medieval-themed events such as falconry and jousting. It's best reached by car, taking the A13, then the D231. By train, it's a trek: 1½ hours from Gare de l'Est.

Museums – City
Other options **Art** p.246, **Heritage Sites – City** p.163

At the last count, Paris boasted some 157 museums. They range from private collections on passions as diverse as Edith Piaf and smoking to vast palaces of art and artefacts such as the Louvre and the Musée des Arts Décoratifs. There really is something for everyone. Unsurprisingly, state and city invest enormous sums in conserving and showing their collections and, in the interests of attracting *le grand public*, there's a constant turnover of exhibitions and fresh perspectives.
Typically, museum entry costs around €6-€8, though many museums owned by the City of Paris are free. Of the various sightseeing options, the Paris Museum Pass (www.parismuseumpass.fr) represents the best value – but unless you're set on a frenetic two to six day culture fest, you're unlikely to benefit. Bear in mind, too, that national museums close on Tuesdays and most city museums on Mondays.

Palais de la Porte ◄
Dorée, 293 ave
Daumesnil
12th
Ⓜ *Porte Dorée*
Map p.413 D4 48

Cité de l'Histoire de l'Immigration
01 53 59 58 60 | *www.histoire-immigration.fr*

The first sight that greets you is Alfred Janniot's stunning art deco bas-relief of industrious exotics from France's former colonies. The Palais de la Porte Dorée was built for the Colonial Exhibition of 1931, and its choice as the site of this new museum is deeply symbolic. It highlights the important role played by immigrant populations in France's development over the last two hundred years. The scope is ambitious; cutting-edge displays re-tell the story from a 21st century perspective, drawing on artefacts, documentary footage and first-hand accounts. Open Tuesday to Friday 10:00 to 17:30; Saturday to Sunday 10:00 to 19:00.

30 ave ◄
Corentin-Cariou
19th
Ⓜ *Porte de la Villette*
Map p.385 F2 49

Cité des Sciences et de l'Industrie
01 40 05 80 00 | *www.cite-sciences.fr*

The principal attraction within the Parc de la Villette (p.185), this vast glass and steel hangar of a science and technology museum has as much appeal for adults as for children. Upstairs, in the permanent Explora exhibition, the museum covers everything from biometrics to space exploration and more, with lots of interactive activities ensuring it stays upbeat and accessible. Add to that a planetarium, an aquarium, film shows and an entire Cité des Enfants (which lays on workshops for kids downstairs), and it can all get rather confusing – you might want to invest in an audioguide before setting out. Outside, there are more attractions in the form of the Géode (the silver globe shows films in 180°), the 1957 Argonaute submarine, and the startlingly realistic shows playing at the Cinaxe cinema. Parts of the Cité are free to enter. Buy combined tickets if you're making a day of it. There are cafes within the complex and a well-stocked shop. Open Tuesday to Saturday 10:00 to 18:00, Sunday 10:00 to 19:00.

---

1 rue des
Fossés-St-Bernard
5th
Ⓜ ***Jussieu***
Map p.410 A1 🔟

L'Institut du Monde Arabe
01 40 51 38 38 | *www.imarabe.org*
The Institut was designed by Jean Nouvel, one of the darlings of the architectural scene, who has since furnished Paris with the Fondation Cartier (p.156) and the Quai Branly museum (p.175). His walls of light-adjusting steel and glass apertures are reminiscent of Moorish latticed screens, and the result still cuts quite a dash by the Pont de Sully. The museum on the seventh floor displays Middle Eastern art and scientific treasures, amply revealing the pioneering influence of eastern scientists during the Middle Ages. Within the building, there's a library, a large bookshop and a pleasant cafe serving mint tea. The wonderful views from the roof terrace are a good reason to prolong your visit. Open Tuesday to Sunday 10:00 to 18:00. Closed 1 May.

---

11 place des
Etats-Unis
16th
Ⓜ ***Boissière***
Map p.386 C4 🗓

Musée Baccarat
01 40 22 11 00 | *www.baccarat.fr*
Part of the former *hôtel particulier* of the Vicomtesse de Noailles has been transformed into a showcase for the house of Baccarat, a company that has been producing some of the world's finest crystal since 1764. It's more gallery than museum, but you don't have to be a connoisseur to be blown-away by the masterpieces created for royalty, for the 19th century Expositions Universelles or designed by the likes of Georges Chevalier. The elegant interior comes courtesy of Philippe Starck. Naturally, there's a gift shop and a fabulous restaurant called Cristal Room (p.315). Open Monday, Wednesday, Saturday 10:00 to 18:00.

---

23 rue de Sévigné
3rd
Ⓜ ***Saint-Paul***
Map p.400 B3 🗓

Musée Carnavalet
01 44 59 58 58
www.carnavalet.paris.fr
The Carnavalet is the principal museum on the history of Paris. Its collections fill two exceptional *hôtels particuliers*, one of which was the home of Mme de Sévigné, whose letters vividly capture courtly life under Louis XIV. Don't expect to blitz the museum in one go; you'll certainly bite off more than you can chew. Among the earliest exhibits are the neolithic canoes excavated at Bercy. There are rooms devoted to the Revolution and to the life and times of Madame de Sévigné; there are 18th century artisans' signs, and a wonderful intact art nouveau interior

Musée Baccarat

decorated by Alfred Mucha. You'll even find Proust's bedroom here and, of course, an extensive display of Napoleonic mementoes. A range of children's workshops are offered. Entrance to the museum is free. Open Tuesday to Sunday 10:00 to 18:00.

Musée Cernuschi

7 ave Vélasquez
8th
Ⓜ *Monceau*
Map p.387 F2 **53**

01 53 96 21 50 | *www.cernuschi.paris.fr/*
Within this faintly neoclassical *hôtel particulier* near Parc Monceau is one of Europe's most impressive collections of Chinese art. It was built for Henri Cernuschi, a colourful Milanese banker and philanthropist who threw himself alongside the revolutionaries of 1871, and was arrested for his pains. Partly motivated by the desire to forget his experiences, he set off on an 18 month-long world trip, visiting China and Japan along the way. From Cernuschi's original collection, the museum has

Musée Carnavalet

grown considerably, and now boasts a grand extension. Among the fabulous celadon vessels and Han dynasty funeral figures, the prize exhibit is an 11th century bronze jug in the shape of a tigress. Open Tuesday to Sunday 10:00 to 18:00.

Musée Cognacq-Jay

8 rue Elzévir
3rd
Ⓜ *Saint-Paul*
Map p.400 B3 **54**

01 40 27 07 21 | *www.paris.fr/musees/cognacq-jay*
Not well-known, but a charmer nonetheless, this Marais museum occupies a fine *hôtel particulier* dating back to the 16th century. The museum's focus, however, is the 18th century – the passion of its founder, Ernest Cognacq, who made his fortune from the landmark department store, La Samaritaine. Cognacq's favourite artist, Greuze, is much in evidence, but you'll also see works by Fragonard, Watteau and Boucher, along with Rembrandt and Joshua Reynolds, to name a few. Elegant Louis XV furniture, Meissen porcelain and other decorative *objets* from the era also have pride of place. Open Tuesday to Sunday 10:00 to 18:00. Closed on public holidays.

Musée d'Art et Histoire du Judaïsme

71 rue du Temple
3rd
Ⓜ *Rambuteau*
Map p.400 A2 **55**

01 53 01 86 60 | *www.mahj.org*
Grandly housed in the 17th century Hôtel Saint-Aignan, this fascinating three floor museum is mostly orientated to the Jewish history in France, which it charts through a multitude of artefacts and manuscripts dating from the Middle Ages to the present day. A section of the museum is devoted to the Dreyfuss Affair that split French society over a hundred years ago. Here you can read Zola's famous open letter – *J'accuse* – and Dreyfuss' own letters home from his imprisonment on Devil's Island. Jewish artists are also well represented, with works by Chagall, Modigliani, Lipschitz and others. There's a free audioguide to the permanent collection, and the museum also hosts temporary exhibitions. Open Monday to Friday 11:00 to 18:00; Sunday 10:00 to 18:00.

Musée d'Orsay

1 rue de la Légion d'Honneur
7th
Ⓡ *Musée d'Orsay*
Map p.398 B2 **56**

01 40 49 48 14 | *www.musee-orsay.fr*
Bridging the gap between the Louvre's art collection and the Centre Pompidou's, the Musée d'Orsay concentrates exclusively on art produced between 1848 and 1914, and does so lavishly. The elegant building facing the Tuileries is a converted *Belle Époque* train station, its grand dimensions flooded with natural light. A sculpture gallery occupies the central aisle where the railway tracks once ran. The surrounding galleries

171

unfold more or less chronologically, tracing a route through the Romantics, Symbolists and the Barbizon landscape group, and embracing early photography and decorative arts along the way. The permanently crowded upper floor is devoted to Impressionist and Post-Impressionist masterpieces, among them Van Gogh's *Chambre à Arles* and Manet's *Déjeuner sur l'Herbe*. The gorgeous restaurant dazzles under great crystal chandeliers; there's also a cafe, a bookshop and regular temporary exhibitions. Entry is free on the first Sunday of the month. Open Tuesday to Sunday 09:30 to 18:00.

Musée de l'Art Moderne de la Ville de Paris

11 ave du Président Wilson
16th
Ⓜ *Iéna*
Map p.396 C1 57

01 53 67 40 00 | www.paris.fr

Like the Palais de Chaillot, the grandiose Palais de Tokyo was built for the 1937 Exposition Universelle. In 2006, it opened its doors to reveal the city's own modern art collection with an impressive show of Fauvists, Cubists and a varied programme of temporary shows. Near the entrance, Raoul Dufy's vibrant setpiece, *La Fée Electricité*, fills an entire room. In the Palais' adjacent wing is the new Site de Création – open plan, minimally finished and with acres of space for edgy installations and performances. There's a funky cafe and a bookshop, piled high with the latest must-have arty volumes. Open Tuesday to Sunday 10:00 to 18:00 (Wednesday until 22:00).

Musée de l'Érotisme

72 blvd de Clichy
18th
Ⓜ *Blanche*
Map p.388 C1 58

01 42 58 28 73 | www.musee-erotisme.com

Where does erotica end and porn begin? This eclectic museum doesn't attempt an answer, but its seven floors display everything from ancient fertility symbols to chastity belts, from naughty nuns to Degas' *Scenes from a Brothel*. The upper floors are devoted to modern art; exhibitions change regularly. On the fourth floor, there are fascinating insights into life at exclusive Parisian bordellos such as le Chabanais, whose clientele included the future king of England, Edward VII. Open daily 10:00 to 02:00.

Musée de l'Orangerie

Jardin de Tuileries
1st
Ⓜ *Tuileries*
Map p.398 B1 59

01 44 77 80 07 | www.musee-orangerie.fr

Built as a winter hothouse for the citrus trees that surrounded the Palais des Tuileries, the Orangerie feels lighter and airier than ever, thanks to the extensive use of glass as part of the museum's modern revamp. For most visitors, the real magnet is Monet's cycle of eight Nymphéas (waterlilies), painted towards the end of his life at his garden in Giverny. In the Monet rooms, simplicity is the order of the day, a stroke calculated to set off the shimmering exuberance of Monet's grand oeuvre. If you can tear yourself away, you'll also find works here by Cézanne, Renoir, Modigliani, Matisse, Picasso and others. Advance booking is recommended. The museum has its own bookshop. Open daily (except Tuesday) 12:30 to 19:00 (Friday until 21:00).

Musée de la Marine

Palais de Chaillot
7 place du Trocadéro
16th
Ⓜ *Trocadéro*
Map p.396 B2 60

01 53 65 69 69 | www.musee-marine.fr

Impressively housed in the Passy wing of the Palais de Chaillot, this venerable museum offers visitors a window on maritime history through a collection that dates back to before the Revolution. Don't expect much in the way of new fangled interactive displays here; the thrill comes from pressing your nose against the glass of superb scale miniatures: galleons, frigates, steamships and liners. Look out for Napoleon's imperial barge in fine, original fettle. Another curiosity is the scale model of the first steam-boat, invented by a Frenchman in the 1780s but not, alas, patented. The museum runs regular temporary exhibitions, and the shop stocks a good range of maritime books. The building is also home to the Café de l'Homme, offering extravagant views of the Champ de Mars and the Tour Eiffel. Open daily (except Tuesday) 10:00 to 18:00. Closed 1 May.

Musée de la Musique

Parc de la Villette
19th
Ⓜ **Porte de Pantin**
Map p.385 F2 101

01 44 84 44 84 | *www.cite-musique.fr*

Housed within Christian de Portzamparc's striking concrete structure in the Parc de la Villette (p.185), Musée de la Musique is a feast for music lovers. The interior is understated, so the focus turns on the glass cases of instruments and related artefacts, most of which date from the 17th to the late 19th century. There are also some period setpieces. Towards the end of the permanent collection, non-western music-making puts in a show, though this section is far from comprehensive. Free audio headsets allow you to hear many instruments in action, including some real rarities. During holiday periods, the museum pulls out the stops with live performances. There's a bookshop and cafe within the complex. Open Tuesday to Saturday 12:00 to 18:00, Sunday 10:00 to 18:00.

Musée de la Vie Romantique

16 rue Chaptal
9th
Ⓜ **Pigalle**
Map p.388 C1 62

01 55 31 95 67 | *www.vie-romantique.paris.fr*

Ary Scheffer may have slipped into obscurity, but the green-shuttered villa the Dutch romantic artist lived in is a shrine to the 'little republic of arts and literature' that flourished here in the 1830s. The area became known as the New Athens, partly as a result of the neoclassical architectural touches favoured hereabouts. Scheffer's bohemian guests included Liszt, Chopin and his mistress, the novelist, George Sand. The museum contains a number of her documents, mementos and watercolours, but the period rooms are the main appeal. In summer, the tearoom extends out into the pretty courtyard. The museum is free; there's an admission charge for temporary exhibitions. Open Tuesday to Sunday 10:00 to 18:00.

Musée de Montmartre

12 rue Cortot
18th
Ⓜ **Lamarck – Caulaincourt**
Map p.383 D4 63

01 46 06 61 11 | *www.museedemontmartre.fr*

Just along from Montmartre's tiny vineyard and the Lapin Agile, this pretty white villa with its shuttered windows was home to Renoir, Raoul Dufy, Suzanne Valadon and her son, Utrillo. Drawings, posters and artefacts, including an original 'zinc' evoke the era of *guinguettes* and absinthe. As well as offering a tantalising glimpse into the artistic milieu that flourished here between the 1880s and the first world war, the museum contains exhibits on the redoubtable figure of the Commune, Louise Michel, and the 18th century porcelain factory at neighbouring Clignancourt. Open Tuesday to Sunday 10:00 to 12:30 and 13:30 to 18:00.

Musée de Petit Palais

ave Winston Churchill
8th
Ⓜ **Champs-Élysées – Clemenceau**
Map p.397 F1 64

01 53 43 40 00 | *www.petitpalais.paris.fr*

Small (smaller than the Louvre, at least) and perfectly formed, this is the Ville de Paris' own collection of art treasures, which ranges from early Greek sculptures to late 19th century art. The many exhibits include some fine art nouveau pieces and a smattering of works by Cézanne, Renoir and Bonnard. With its many mosaics and Belle Époque flourishes, the 1900 building is delectable. Round off your visit at the attractive, modern cafe that overlooks the garden. There's a well-stocked book- and gift shop within the museum. Entry to the permanent collection is free. Open Tuesday to Sunday 10:00 to 18:00.

Musée des Arts Décoratifs

107 rue de Rivoli
1st
Ⓜ **Palais Royal Musée du Louvre**
Map p.398 C1 65

01 44 55 57 50 | *www.lesartsdecoratifs.fr*

A 19th century wing of the Louvre unites an ensemble of impressive museums, the latest and most lavish of which is Musée des Arts Décoratifs. The museum charts the history of (mainly French) taste from the Middle Ages to Philippe Starck. If time is limited, make a beeline for the 10 superb period rooms, but don't miss Jeanne Lanvin's art deco salon – in her trademark Lanvin-blue. Also housed here is the Musée de la Publicité, an archive of thousands of posters, TV and cinema adverts that form the basis of its temporary, themed exhibitions. Last, but by no means least, le Musée de la Mode et du Textile conserves a vast wardrobe, elements of which parade into view in the course of its temporary exhibition (check the website for updates). Within the building, the Saut du Loup restaurant is a class act, as is the design shop on the ground floor. Open Tuesday to Friday 11:00 to 18:00 (Thursday until 21:00); Saturday to Sunday 10:00 to 18:00.

Musée des Arts et Métiers

60 rue Réaumur
3rd
Ⓜ *Réaumur –*
Sébastopol
Map p.400 A1 🔢

01 53 01 82 00 | *www.arts-et-metiers.net*

This museum gets off to a flying start with its wonderful setting. Within the ancient priory of St-Martin-des-Champs, it pays homage to technology from the 16th century onwards. Among the flying machines on show is an extraordinary feathered number which, unsurprisingly, never got airborne before being suspended, here, above the staircase. You'll also find cars, early bikes and Lavoisier's laboratory from the 18th century along with all manner of other inventions. On certain days, the museum opens up its gallery of exquisite early automatons and you can see them in action (kids are generally spellbound). There's also a sprinkling of touch-screen computers and a sleek, modern cafe within the building. Look out for the matching metro station, revamped for the museum's bicentenary, and clad in copper to resemble Jules Verne's Nautilus. Open Tuesday to Sunday 10:00 to 18:00 (Thursday until 21:30).

Musée du Louvre

rue de Rivoli
1st
Ⓜ *Louvre Rivoli*
Map p.399 D2 🔢

01 40 20 50 50 | *www.louvre.fr*

The Louvre became a public museum under Napoleon and, with 35,000 works of art and artefacts under its roof and a programme of major temporary exhibitions, it ranks high among the world's great museums. Star attractions include the *Venus de Milo*, Michelangelo's slaves, Géricault's arresting tableau *The Raft of the Medusa* (based on a grisly true shipwreck story), and, of course, Da Vinci's *Mona Lisa*. Such highlights hardly do justice to a permanent collection enshrining everything from Egyptian antiquities to Romantic masters and more, while the grandeur of the former royal palace adds a dimension of its own. To skip the queues, buy your tickets from the machines below ground in the Carrousel du Louvre mall. The exhibits are spread across three wings (Sully, Denon, Richelieu); get your bearings with a colour-coded map available from the information desk. Entry to the permanent collection is free on the first Sunday of the month. Open: Monday, Thursday, Saturday, Sunday 09:00 to 18:00; Wednesday, Friday 09:00 to 22:00. Closed Tuesday.

Musée des Arts et Métiers

Musée du Louvre

Musée du Moyen Age, Thermes de Cluny

6 place Paul-Painlevé
5th
Ⓜ *Cluny – La Sorbonne*
Map p.399 E4 68

01 53 73 78 00 | *www.musee-moyenage.fr*

The national museum of medieval art has one of the best conceivable settings for its exquisite sculptures, tapestries and enamels: a 15th century abbey building, complete with massive masonry fireplaces and Gothic doorways. Its most celebrated treasure is the cycle of six allegorical tapestries known as *La Dame et la Licorne*. Hung in semi-darkened rooms, each is resplendent in its colour and detail; however, the final panel (if, indeed it was intended as such) continues to intrigue scholars most of all. The Hôtel de Cluny was constructed above some 3rd century Roman thermal baths complex, elements of which are displayed within the museum. Even if you are not visiting, you can still marvel at the surviving walls outside among the medieval-themed gardens. The museum lays on free music concerts for visitors on Friday lunchtimes and Saturday afternoons. Open daily (except Tuesday) 09:15 to 17:45. Closed 1 January, 1 May and 25 December.

Musée du Quai-Branly

222 rue de l'Université
7th
Ⓡ *Pont de l'Alma*
Map p.396 C2 69

01 56 61 70 00 | *www.quaibranly.fr*

Opened with a big splash in 2006, this showcase of non-European art and artefacts unites some of the choicest collections of the Musées des Arts d'Afrique et d'Océanie and the Musée de l'Homme (the latter currently exhibits temporarily while it awaits a further metamorphosis). This riverside complex is a show-stopping combination of glass and greenery (some 18,000 square metres of it), designed by renowned architect Jean Nouvel. Once inside, winding footbridges connect the four continents of Oceania, Asia, Africa and America, inviting you to set out on your own journey of exploration. Very much ex-President Chirac's baby, the museum has a huge visual impact, right down to details such as the modern aborigine paintings that adorn the bookshop. There's a garden cafe and a posh terrace restaurant where you can take stock of your travels with panoramic views. Open Tuesday to Sunday 10:00 to 18:30 (Thursday until 21:30).

Musée Galliera

10 ave Pierre 1er de Serbie
16th
Ⓜ *Iéna*
Map p.396 C1 70

01 56 52 86 03 | *www.galliera-paris.fr*

A trio of larger-than-life photos graces the wall of this somewhat overblown 19th century palace, named after the Duchess who lived here. In case you're in any doubt, the Galliera is dedicated to fashion. Its huge collection of almost 100,000 garments and accessories spans three centuries and represents the great names in French couture up to the present day. For conservation reasons, the museum is only open during exhibitions, when a thematic selection is on show. Such events are invariably stylish and intelligently put-together, and normally stay for around four months. Check the museum's website for information.

Musée Grévin

10 blvd Montmartre
9th
Ⓜ *Grands Boulevards*
Map p.389 E3 71

01 47 70 85 05 | *www.grevin.com*

It is pricey at €18, it's kitsch, but it's also lots of fun. This waxwork museum opened in 1882 and was such a sensation that it soon became Paris' most visited site after the Louvre. Times have moved on since then, but it's still an institution that can lay on a bit of a show. One of the highlights isn't wax at all, but the Palais des Mirages, an ingenious lights-and-mirrors setpiece fabricated for the Exposition Universelle of 1900. Aside from the icons and celebs you know well, here's where to test your knowledge of popular French culture. Do you know your Gérard Jugnot from your Gérard Dépardieu? You'll soon find out. Open Monday to Friday 10:00 to 18:30; Saturday to Sunday 10:00 to 19:00.

175

6 place d'Iéna
16th
Ⓜ *Iéna*
Map p.396 C1 72

Musée Guimet

01 56 52 53 00 | *www.museeguimet.fr*

Like the Musée Cernuschi (p.171), this collection of oriental artefacts owes its existence to one man, Émile Guimet, a 19th century industrialist who travelled extensively in Asia. His collection forms a fraction of what is now on show, ranging from exquisite silk kimonos to Javan deities. Inside, Guimet's exotic building opens up like a Chinese box, thanks to a spacious, modern transformation that makes much play of natural light. The museum has its own restaurant and library. Don't miss the Buddhist Pantheon, complete with Japanese garden and tearoom, nearby at number 19 (entry is free). The museum itself is free on the first Sunday of the month. Open daily (except Tuesday) 10:00 to 18:00.

14 rue de
La Rochefoucauld
9th
Ⓜ *Trinité –*
d'Estienne d'Orves
Map p.388 C2 73

Musée Gustave Moreau

01 48 74 38 50 | *www.musee-moreau.fr*

Concerned about the fate of his 'poor little works,' Moreau spent two years preparing the museum he would eventually leave to posterity. The studio and private apartment are ranged over three floors, and nothing has changed since the artist's death in 1868. More than 5,000 of his paintings and drawings are contained here; the result is as arresting as it is cluttered. Brilliant, enigmatic figures stare out of large-scale canvases hung two abreast, and a narrow wrought iron staircase threads its way between floors. There's a small bookshop. Open daily (except Tuesday) 10:00 to 12:45 and 14:00 to 17:15.

158, blvd
Haussmann
8th
Ⓜ *Saint-Augustin*
Map p.387 E3 74

Musée Jacquemart-André

01 45 62 11 59 | *www.musee-jacquemart-andre.com*

Not just a fabulous art collection (though with its brimming rooms of Italian, Dutch and French masters, it's certainly that), the museum offers a fascinating window on life for the upper crust during the 19th century. Built to accommodate their treasures, this was the home of banking heir Edouard André and his wife, the artist Nélie Jacquemart (they met when she painted his portrait). A double spiral staircase leads the way to their 'Italian Museum', where André particularly indulged his taste for Florentine masterpieces by Uccello, Botticelli and Perugini. There are free audioguides, a well-stocked shop and Tiepolo graces the tea-room ceiling. The museum has a programme of activities aimed at adults and children (in French for the most part). Open daily 10:00 to 18:00, including public holidays.

2 rue Louis Boilly
16th
Ⓜ *La Muette*
Map p.395 D2 75

Musée Marmottan-Monet

01 44 22 59 58 | *www.marmottan.com*

The reopening of the Orangerie (p.172) might have stolen a little of the limelight, but the Marmottan is for serious fans of Impressionism. The museum showcases the world's largest collection of Monets, including a painting from 1875, entitled, somewhat vaguely, *Impression, Soleil Levant* (the title was picked up by critics and soon applied to an entire artistic movement). Other Impressionist painters are richly represented, while the collection of works by Berthe Morisot is unsurpassed. There is, however, more for those who want it, including furniture and illuminated manuscripts dating from the 13th century. The building, suitably grand, once served as the hunting lodge of the Duc de Valmy. Open Tuesday to Sunday 10:00 to 17:30.

place
Georges-Pompidou
4th
Ⓜ *Hôtel de Ville*
Map p.399 F2 76

Musée National d'Art Modern

01 44 78 12 33 | *www.centrepompidou.fr*

Focussing mainly on art produced between 1905 and 1950, this major art collection takes up the whole of the 4th and 5th floor within the Pompidou Centre, and has recently undergone a massive revamp in honour of the Centre's 30th anniversary. Among the 58,000 paintings, sculptures and other media are works by Picasso, Matisse and Warhol. Don't worry, though; only a selection of the collection is displayed at any given time, and works are regularly changed to keep perspectives fresh. The Centre's book and gift shop is a good source of gift inspiration, and you can grab a snack at the Café Mezzanine. One floor up from the museum, there are panoramic views from the Restaurant Georges (p.324). Buy your museum tickets on the ground floor – unless you're here during the first Sunday of the month, when entry is free. Open daily (except Tuesday) 11:00 to 21:00. Closed 1 May.

6 rue de Furstenburg
6th
Ⓜ **Mabillon**
Map p.399 D3 🔲

Musée National Eugène-Délacroix
01 44 42 86 50 | www.musee-delacroix.fr
The romantic painter was in ailing health when, in 1857, he moved to this decidedly charming home in order to be nearer to the three murals he was painting at l'Église St-Sulpice. The setting is no less charming now. While Délacroix's most famous works, *Liberty leading the People*, for example, have migrated to the Louvre, the paintings, drawings and memorabilia here afford a glimpse of the man throughout the stages of his life. Among the works, there's a rare self-portrait of the young artist posing as the ill-starred hero of Walter Scott's romantic novel, *The Bride of Lammermoor*. Delacroix's strangely enigmatic *Magdalene in the Desert* has pride of place. Open daily (except Tuesday) 09:30 to 17:00. Closed 1 January, 1 May and 25 December.

63 rue de Monceau
8th
Ⓜ **Monceau**
Map p.387 F2 🔲

Musée Nissim de Camondo
01 53 89 06 50 | www.lesartsdecoratifs.fr
So passionate was the Comte de Camondo about high 18th century taste that he modelled his early 20th century mansion on the Petit Trianon at Versailles and filled it full of treasures. From the Savonnerie carpets to the rock crystal chandeliers, everything was handpicked by Moïse de Camondo to chime with its surroundings. Exquisite as it is, the house overlooking Monceau Park is poignant and personal. Here and there, you'll see framed photographs of Moïse's son, Nissim, who died as a fighter pilot in the first world war, and to whom the house is a memorial. Upstairs, a small exhibition concerns the remaining members of the dynasty who died later in a Nazi concentration camp. There's an informative English audioguide. Open Wednesday to Sunday 10:00 to 17:30.

Hôtel Salé
5 rue de Thorigny
3rd
Ⓜ **Saint-Sébastien Froissart**
Map p.400 B2 🔲

Musée Picasso
01 42 71 25 21 | www.musee-picasso.fr
Behind its neoclassical facade, this 17th century *hôtel particulier* houses the most extensive collection of Pablo Picasso's works in existence: paintings, engravings, ceramics and sculpture. Arranged chronologically, they cover the main periods of a staggeringly prolific artistic life. As a result, visitors get a strong sense of his development, as well as some touching glimpses into his personal life through the portraits of those nearest to him. The mansion itself is a delight, with its ornate walls and magnificent staircase. It was built for a wealthy salt-tax collector – hence its name. Entry is free for under 18s and for all on the first Sunday of the month. Open Tuesday to Sunday: April to September, 09:30 to 18:00; October to March 09:30 to 17:30.

Musée Picasso

Musée Rodin

77 rue de Varenne
7th
Ⓜ **Varenne**
Map p.397 F3 🟥**80**

01 44 18 61 10 | *www.musee-rodin.fr*

Close to les Invalides stands the Hôtel Biron, an 18th century mansion surrounded by a large garden. Auguste Rodin lived here from 1908 until his death in 1917, when the mansion reverted to the state along with the sculptor's work it contained. The house is a wonderful setting for famous works such as *The Hand of God* and *The Kiss*, but also for a wealth of lesser-known works, notably those in clay or plaster – in other words, worked on by the great man himself. Also here are a number of works by Rodin's pupil and mistress, Camille Claudel. You can buy a separate ticket to enter the garden – with many substantial works such as *The Burghers of Calais* and *The Gates of Hell* framed by topiary and shrubs, it's a visit in its own right. There's a boutique and a cafe on the terrace. Open April to September, 09:30 to 17:45; October to March, 09:30 to 16:45.

Musée Zadkine

100bis rue d'Assas
6th
Ⓜ **Vavin**
Map p.408 C2 🟥**81**

01 55 42 77 20 | *www.paris.fr*

Russian born Ossip Zadkine was one of the first sculptors to apply cubism to sculpture, and he lived and worked in this house from 1928 until his death in 1967. It's a tiny museum and the discreet entrance is easily missed. A handful of rooms testify to the apparent ease with which Zadkine moved between media, from gouache to wood and bronze. The works have a sensuous tactile appeal and there are more displayed in the garden. During summer, the museum hosts occasional poetry and literature readings. Entrance to the permanent collection is free. Open Tuesday to Sunday 10:00 to 18:00. Closed public holidays.

Muséum National d'Histoire Naturelle

57 rue Cuvier
5th
Ⓜ **Jussieu**
Map p.410 A2 🟥**82**

01 40 51 91 39 | *www.mnhn.fr*

Set within the fertile grounds of the Jardin des Plantes, this isn't one museum, but three. Taken together, the Galeries de Paléontologie et d'Anatomie Comparée and the Galerie de Minéralogie et de Géologie are world class collections, but can seem a little dry compared with the Grande Galerie de l'Évolution. Here, the fine 19th century, glass-roofed building has been given the modern museum treatment. Educational, upbeat exhibitions (in tone, if not always content) range over biodiversity and man's impact on his environment, and the interior has been quirkily updated to ensure children are engrossed. The star of the show remains the parade of African wildlife on the first floor. Open daily (except Tuesday) 10:0 to 17:00 (until 18:00 in summer). Closed 1 May.

Palais de la Découverte

avenue
Franklin-Roosevelt
8th
Ⓜ **Champs-Élysées –**
Clemenceau
Map p.387 E4 🟥**83**

01 56 42 20 21 | *www.palais-decouverte.fr*

While it can't really compete with the showbiz on offer at the newer science museum at La Villette, the Palais works hard to infuse fun into the serious business of learning about science – and, for the most part, it does a good job. Demos and workshops range from static electricity to chemistry in the art of chocolate-making, and there are good sections on biology and geoscience, along with some excellent temporary shows. There are a number of children's activities on offer, though most are aimed at French speakers. The planetarium remains the star asset. Open Tuesday to Saturday 09:30 to 18:00; Sunday and public holidays 10:00 to 19:00.

Muséum National d'Histoire Naturelle

Museums – Out Of City

Other options **Heritage Sites – Out of City** p.168

There's no disputing that central Paris possesses a huge variety of museums – but it doesn't get to hog all the glory. Head to the outskirts of the city to experience some of the excellent specialist and, in some cases, nationally important museums highlighted below.

place de la Libération
Vitry-sur-Seine
🅡 *Vitry-sur-Seine*
Map p.379 D4

Mac/Val – Musée d'Art Contemporain du Val-de-Marne

01 43 91 64 20 | www.macval.fr

Part museum, part dynamic arts centre, the Mac/Val is the hottest thing to hit the *banlieue* since the 2005 riots. Situated just south-east of the city, it sets out to demystify contemporary art and make it appealing to a far wider audience. The main show draws on an art stash amassed by the Val-de-Marne *department* over the last twenty years. The complex boasts a cinema, an archive centre, a bookshop and a restaurant, with gardens round about. There's a modest €4 fee, and entry is free on the first Sunday of the month. To get there, take RER C to Vitry-sur-Seine, then bus 180. Open Tuesday to Sunday 12:00 to 19:00 (Thursday until 21:00). Closed 1 May, 25 December and 1 January.

Aéroport de
Paris-le Bourget
Le Bourget
Map p.379 D1

Musée de l'Air et de l'Espace

01 49 92 70 62 | www.mae.org

Set aside some hours to explore this absorbing museum in the old passenger terminal at Paris' original airport, north of the city. Its collection spans aeronautics in all its eras, from late 19th century pioneering efforts to Ariane satellite launchers (the latter full-sized models). You can get up close to a Zeppelin gondola, a brace of Spitfires and Concordes, while on the runway there's much more to ogle, including Mirages and a boardable Boeing 747. There's also a planetarium and a touching display on the aviator and much-loved author of *Le Petit Prince*, Antoine de Saint-Exupéry. Sadly, there's no cafe. Get there on RER B to Le Bourget, then bus 152. Open Tuesday to Sunday: April to September, 10:00 to 18:00; October to March, 10:00 to 17:00.

Espace Landowski
28 ave André-Morizet
Boulogne-Billancourt
Ⓜ *Marcel Sembat*
Map p.378 B3

Musée des Années 30

01 55 18 46 66 | www.boulognebillancourt.fr

Tamara de Lempicka is here, but don't expect to see many big names at this museum of the 1930s in Boulogne-Billancourt, a town which boasts some fine buildings from the period. Ranged over three floors, the collection of paintings, sculptures and architectural models gives you a strong sense of the dynamism and optimism of the era, as well as insights into how France's colonial experience influenced artists of the day. There's also a section on the area's industrial heyday, when Billancourt's car manufacturing and aviation industries were booming. Open Tuesday to Sunday 11:00 to 18:00.

place de
la Manufacture
Sèvres
Ⓜ *Pont de Sèvres*
Map p.378 B3

Musée National de Céramique

01 41 14 04 20 | www.musee-ceramique-sevres.fr

If Sèvres was the porcelain of kings, this museum is a kingdom of porcelain – not to mention faïence, terracotta, stoneware, and even glass. Porcelain has been made here since 1756, but only makes up a fraction of what's on show, from ancient anthropomorphic vases to Japanese Satsuma ware. If ceramics fire you up, you'll find this an inspiring collection. South-west of Paris, reach it by T2 tramway or metro. Open daily (except Tuesday and public holidays) 10:00 to 17:00.

179

Musée National de l'Archéologie

place
Charles de Gaulle
Saint-Germain-en-Laye
ⓡ Saint Germain-en-Laye
Map p.378 A2

01 39 10 13 00 | *www.musee-antiquitesnationales.fr*

An extraordinary collection of finds from France's ancient past makes this museum well worth the short trip out of town. Spanning the Stone Age to the 8th century, the galleries are filled with treasures such as Neolithic menhirs (a type of standing stone), wonderful Romano-Gaullish terracotta figurines and the gem-encrusted brooch worn by a Merovingian lady of means. It's attractively and intelligently displayed, and rounded off with a section on archaeological finds from elsewhere in the world. The Château de St-Germain-en-Laye which houses the museum was an important royal residence which fell out of favour in the 17th century and was radically rebuilt in the 19th. Open daily (except Tuesday) 09:00 to 17:00.

Musée Vivant du Cheval

Les Grandes Écuries
Chantilly
Map p.373 B2

03 44 57 40 40 | *www.museevivantducheval.fr*

Chantilly's Great Stables could easily pass for a palace. They were built in the early 18th century to house the horses, hounds and hunting birds of the seventh Prince de Condé, who was convinced that he would be reincarnated as a horse. Restored during the 1980s, they have recently come under the Aga Khan's patronage. The museum combines equine-themed exhibitions with displays of horsemanship. There are two or three demonstrations every day, and a show every first Sunday in the month. The stables are within easy walking distance of the Château and Musée de Condé, Chantilly's other unmissable attraction. Open: November to March, weekdays (except Tuesday) 14:00 to 17:00; weekends 10:30 to 17:00. April to October, weekdays (except Tuesday) 10:30 to 17:30; weekends 10:30 to 18:00.

Festivals

Other options **Annual Events** p.41

The city's calendar isn't dominated by festivals in the traditional sense, but a host of initiatives organised by the state, the Ville de Paris or independently means that there's always something going on.

Cinéma au Claire de la Lune

Various Locations

www.forumdesimages.net

This mid-August film festival sees screenings take place in public squares and parks all over Paris. Free entry.

Festival Chopin à Paris

L'Orangerie, Parc de
la Bagatelle, Bois de
Boulogne
16th

01 45 00 22 19 | *www.frederic-chopin.com*

Taking place in June and July, this festival sees over a dozen recitals in honour of the city's favourite romantic composer. Tickets €17-€34.

Festival d'Automne

Various Locations

01 53 45 17 17 | *www.festival-automne.com*

This is a high profile, high-brow festival presenting contemporary arts from a variety of disciplines. Admission €9-€30. September to December.

Festival Inrocktuptibles

Various Locations

01 42 44 16 16 | *www.lesinrocks.com*

The festival organised under the auspices of the leading French rock magazine, *Les Inrockuptibles* has erred towards trance and techno bands recently. Various venues and ticket prices. Early November.

180

Various Locations ◄

Fête de la Musique
01 40 03 94 70 | *www.fetedelamusique.fr*
An outbreak of music grips Paris (and the rest of France) during the 21 June summer solstice – and it's all free.

Various Locations ◄

Fête du Beaujolais Nouveau
www.beaujolaisgourmand.com
'Le Beaujolais nouveau est arrivé!' Heard mid-November each year, these five words bring Parisians flocking into cafes to sample the new vintage for themselves...and you're welcome, of course, to join in.

Various Locations ◄

Fête du Travail
Trade unions go a-marching and hardly anyone works on Labour Day (1 May), apart from the stall-holders selling sprigs of *muguet des bois* (lily-of-the-valley). Give them for luck on the first day of spring.

Various Locations ◄

Fêtes des Rois
The run-up to Twelfth Night (6 January) sees *patisserie* windows fill with *galettes des rois*, large sweet pies filled with almond paste. Inside, there's a small porcelain *fève*, or charm: the winner becomes king (or queen) and wears the cardboard crown.

rue des Saules ◄
18th

Fêtes des Vendanges de Montmartre
01 30 21 48 62 | *www.fetesdesvendangesdemontmartre.com*
Dressing-up, sing-songs and a parade usher in the grape harvest from Montmartre's tiny vineyard, in the second week of October.

Parc de la Villette ◄
211 ave Jean-Jaurès
19th

Jazz à la Villette
01 44 84 44 84 | *www.jazzalavillette.com*
From the end of August to early September, cool line-ups perform at various venues within the Parc de la Villette; tickets cost between €12 and €30.

Various Locations ◄

Journées du Patrimoine
www.jp.culture.fr
This well-publicised event in September sees all manner of fascinating but normally inaccessible establishments welcome the public for a rare look inside.

Various Locations ◄

La FIAC
01 41 90 47 47 | *www.fiacparis.com*
In late October, the key event in the city's contemporary arts calendar attracts international artists and connoisseurs. The event takes place in the Grand Palais and the Cour Carré du Louvre; admission is €20.

Various Locations ◄

La Nuit des Musées
www.nuitdesmusees.culture.fr
Key museums in Paris (and across France) stay open late and offer free workshops and shows during this one-night bonanza in mid-May

Various Locations ◄

Le Quatorze Juillet
The eve of the anniversary of the storming of the Bastille in 1789 is ushered in with dancing at place de la Bastille. On the day itself, crowds mass along the Champs for the military parade at 10:00. After the evening's lavish firework display over the Champ de Mars, Parisians peel off to their local (ticket only) Sapeurs-Pompiers ball.

Les Puces du Design

Quai de la Loire
Bassin de la Villette
19th

01 53 40 78 77 | www.pucesdudesign.com
A better class of foraging is offered at this three-day modern design 'fleamarket' in October, which attracts niche retailers from across France. Admission is free.

New Year

Various Locations

Festive crowds hit the Champs-Élysées on New Year's Eve. On New Year's Day, *La Grande Parade* sets out with a flashy line-up of marching bands, floats and dancers.

Nuit Blanche

Various Locations

www.paris.fr
Stay up late during this autumn culture-fest (early October), marked by one-off extravaganzas in museums and galleries.

Parc de la Villette

211 ave Jean-Jaurès
19th

01 40 03 75 75 | www.villette.com
From mid-July through August, this film festival features nightly open air screenings (except Tues). Bring a blanket or rent a chair. Free entry.

Paris Jazz Festival

Parc Floral, Bois
de Vincennes
12th

www.parcfloraldeparis.com
Spread over six weeks in June and July, this festival sees balmy jazz-filled evenings in the relaxed setting of the Bois de Vincennes. Admission €5.

Paris Sur Glace

Various Locations

www.paris.fr
The Hôtel de Ville (along with Montparnasse and Stalingrad) spawns a miniature ice rink between December and March. Admission is free but there's a charge for hiring skates. Meanwhile, the Eiffel Tower (p.164) goes glacial on its first floor in December and January.

Paris, Quartier d'Été

Various Locations

01 44 94 98 00 | www.quartierdete.com
This is an eclectic outdoor arts festival from mid-July to mid-August embracing classical and jazz music, dance, theatre and circus. Some performances are free.

Paris Plage

Various Locations

www.paris.fr
Copacabana comes to Paris quaysides, complete with parasols, palm-trees and day-long diversions. See next page. Mid-July to mid-August

Printemps des Musées

Various Locations

www.printempsdesmusees.culture.fr
Selected museums drop their entry fee during this initiative in May.

Printemps du Cinéma

Various Locations

www.printempsducinema.com
For three days in mid-March, all screenings in participating cinemas are only €3.50.

Rock en Seine

Domaine National
de St-Cloud
Saint-Cloud

08 92 68 08 92 | www.rockenseine.com
The city's just-out-of-city rock and indie festival just gets better, with an international and home-grown line-up over three days in late August.

Beaches

Other options **Swimming** p.231

First-time visitors are rarely prepared for *les Grandes Vacances*, when apartments, shops, even neighbourhoods empty, as Parisians pack their bags and head en masse to the coast. There are signs, though, that the tradition is changing – and, if it is, Paris Plage is surely playing a part. Launched by Mayor Delanoë in 2002, the transformation of Seine quayside into beach resort is aimed at families who can't take a holiday away. Paris Plage has proved a huge hit with locals and visitors alike – so much so that two more beaches have been created, turning parts of the remoter 13th and 19th *arrondissements* into fun-packed waterside playgrounds. Dressed with 3,000 tonnes of sand, parasols and palm trees, its razzmatazz and activities cater for all ages – and it's all free. Paris Plage unrolls its togs from late July to late August.

Bassin de la Villette
19th
Ⓜ *Laumière*
Map p.385 D4 🔟

Paris Plage – Bassin de la Villette

www.paris.fr

On the quayside below place Stalingrad, the newest and most northerly of the Paris Plage trio has infused a welcome dash of animation into an area which, until recently, tended to be more shabby than chic. This space sets out to be more family-orientated than the downtown beach. The emphasis here is on water-based activities, with rowing boats, canoes and pedalos setting forth into the mini-marina. Back on dry land, there are painting workshops and pétanque matches laid on. In the evening, the area becomes the setting for riverside *guinguettes* (an outdoor cafe and dancehall).

Paris Plage
Ⓜ *Quai de la Gare*
Map p.411 D4 🔟

Paris Plage – Port de la Gare

www.paris.fr

Spreading out below the four towers of the Bibliothèque Nationale de France in the city's ultra-modern Tolbiac neighbourhood, the kilometre or so of beach here is slightly less crowded but no less convivial. Much of the action takes place in and around the still spanking new Piscine Joséphine-Baker pool (p.232), while the Passerelle Simone-de-Beauvoir is a popular venue for mid-river picnics, extending the holiday spirit into nearby Bercy.

Paris Plage
Ⓜ *Pont Neuf*
Map p.399 E3 🔟

Paris Plage – Louvre

www.paris.fr

The original and most tightly choreographed of the city's man-made beaches is also the most popular. This 3km stretch of summer fantasy fills up quickly; get there well before lunch if you want to stake out your sun-lounger among the multitudes of bronzed bodies. Musicians and dancers are brought in to charm the clusters of picnicking families, while aqua-aerobics workouts are offered in the pool. Elsewhere, there are other organised activities such as volleyball and tai chi, especially around the Hôtel de Ville. By night, under the soft light of Chinese lanterns, the beach attracts promenading couples.

Parks & Gardens

Some cities empty at night. Not so Paris, where many people live in cramped city centre apartments. Parks are therefore well-used and mostly free. What Paris lacks in terms of rolling outdoor space, it makes up for with inventive landscaping, and the multitude of *squares du coin* (local gardens) that are a feature of virtually every *quartier*. Larger parks are popular with joggers and even picnic parties – provided they don't disturb lawns that are *en repos*.

The two Bois (Boulogne and Vincennes) are the places to head when you need to release some energy. Closer to, the formal garden still thrives, with its clipped trees, statues and symmetry. But there are also *jardins anglais* for those who prefer their greenery less regimented. Emerging from wasteland, the latest generation of parks strive to cater for leisure pursuits, as well as laying out some sharp, contemporary styling.

Bois de Boulogne

Porte Dauphine
16th
Ⓜ *Porte Dauphine*
Map p.394 B2 93

01 45 24 30 00 | www.paris.fr

This 2,135 acre park can get crowded on summer weekends, when it seems as though the western half of Paris has come here to unwind. There are parks within the park: the Bagatelle (p.190) and the Jardin d'Acclimatation (p.185); the Pré-Catalan, with its great beech and lawns; the Shakespeare Garden, where the homage to the bard sometimes continues in the open-air theatre. There's even a museum, the Musée National des Arts et Traditions Populaires, a celebration of dying crafts. There's a wealth of activities on offer for those who don't just want to walk or picnic, including two racecourses, a riding school and boating. Criss-crossing the wooded areas, many of the wide avenues are closed to cars at weekends, giving more freedom to rollerbladers and cyclists.

Bois de Vincennes

Porte de Vincennes
Ⓜ *Porte de Vincennes*
Map p.413 F3 94

www.boisdevincennes.com

Occupying almost 2,500 acres to the south-east of the city, this is Paris' largest green space. There's a huge amount on offer among the lawns, lakes and trees, but it's very spread out, and you might want to consider renting a bike, and staggering your visits. Among its attractions, there's a working farm (p.197); a bird reserve, the Parc Floral (p.190); a Buddhist temple and a racecourse. Around the western perimeter you'll find the aquarium (p.192), the zoo (p.192) and the new Cité de l'Immigration (p.169). The big draw to the north is the newly restored Chateau de Vincennes (p.159).

Jardin des Tuileries

rue de Rivoli
1st
Ⓜ *Tuileries*
Map p.398 B1 59

www.paris.fr

This is the quintessential formal French garden. Insulated from the traffic noise, it's an urban haven with its avenues of pollarded chestnuts, circular ponds and statues. It takes its name from the tilemakers' *quartier* which stood here until it was cleared by Marie de Médicis, and the park retains the essential form laid down by Le Nôtre, who landscaped it for Louis XIV. Haul up one of the sought-after metal chairs, and spend an hour reading or tourist-watching. The children's painted sailboats are an institution. The somewhat newer summer Ferris wheel offers grand views over the Champs. Don't miss the wild garden with its life-sized fallen bronze tree.

Jardin du Luxembourg

blvd Saint-Michel
6th
Ⓡ *Luxembourg*
Map p.408 C1 96

www.paris.fr

Right in the heart of the Latin Quarter, this civilised and lively park has such wide-ranging appeal that it can get pretty crowded in summer, especially around the baroque Fontaine des Médicis, where the sturdy chairs are quickly snapped up. The park and the Palais owe their existence to Marie de Médicis, who wanted to recreate the flavour of her native Florence. (The palace now encompasses the seat of the French Senate while temporary exhibitions are held at the Musée de Luxembourg). Chess-players gather under the trees, children can rent dinky boats to launch on the *grand basin*, there are tennis courts, a boules terrain and an apiary. Already rich in statues, the park regularly hosts contemporary art in the grounds. Above all, with its mature trees, grand vistas and pretty *buvettes* (bars serving snacks), this is one of the premier spots to relax in the city. Open daily 07:30 to dusk in summer; 08:00 to dusk in winter.

Le Jardin d'Acclimatation

Bois de Boulogne
16th
Ⓡ Vincennes
Map p.394 B2 93

01 40 67 90 82 | www.jardindacclimatation.fr
Within the Bois de Boulogne, the 49 acre Jardin d'Acclimatation has a bouquet of attractions for tots to pre-teens. In addition to the rides, ponies and 'enchanted river,' there's a puppet theatre, a mini farm, a zoo and an aviary. For older children, there's mini-golf, a diminutive race track and the hands-on Exploradome. The park is served by *le petit train* which steams in from Porte Maillot at weekends and Wednesday afternoons. There's a small admission fee to the park, plus supplements for some attractions. Open daily: June to September, 10:00 to 19:00; October to May, 10:00 to 18:00.

Parc André-Citroên

quai André-Citroên
15th
Ⓜ Lourmel
Map p.405 E2 98

www.paris.fr
This bold, modern park may have earned a place in at least one landscaping hall of shame, but it has breathed new life into the *quartier* where the car factory once stood. Flat and open, there's a densely shaded garden, two enormous hothouses, expanses of lawn and randomly squirting fountains to get soaked in (no one seems to pay any attention to the signs). For a fee, a 'flight' in the tethered balloon (p.198) gives a great view of Paris. Open Monday to Friday 08:00 to dusk; weekends and holidays 09:00 to dusk.

Parc de Belleville

rue des Couronnes
20th
Ⓜ Couronnes
Map p.391 F4 99

www.paris.fr
A pretty community park with vine trellises recalling Belleville's *guinguette* days, and watery cascades in which kids aren't supposed to splash (that, at least, is the official line). The main reason for visiting, though, is the stupendous city view from the top of the steps. Open weekdays 08:00 to dusk; weekends 09:00 to dusk.

Parc de Bercy

rue Paul-Belmondo
12th
Ⓜ Bercy
Map p.411 F4 100

www.paris.fr
Sound-proofed from the traffic by avenues of trees, this modern park exploits inherited features such as the centenarian winecellars and pretty bathhouse. A romantic garden, complete with winding paths, lake and weeping willows gives way to a series of thematic gardens, spruce allotments and a rose-mount. At the park's northern end, leading on to the new Simone-de-Beauvoir footbridge, there's a 'meadow' where kids and dads can kick a ball about with impunity. Open weekdays 08:00 to dusk; weekends 09:00 to dusk.

Parc de la Villette

211 ave Jean-Jaurès
19th
Ⓜ Porte de Pantin

Map p.385 F2 101

01 40 03 75 75 | www.villette.com
Since it was created in 1986, La Villette has been adopted by the young and young-at-heart. It's an expansive park and, allied to the large scale attractions of the Cités de Sciences and Musiques, the Zénith and Cabaret Sauvage, it has something for everyone. Kids love the giant dragon slide and funky Jardin des Voltiges, while the gigantic, half-buried bicycle is there just for its good looks. On either side of the Canal de l'Ourcq, you'll see all kinds of sporting activities, from wooden sabre fencing to capoeira. Open 24 hours.

Parc des Buttes-Chaumont

rue Botzaris
19th
Ⓜ Botzaris
Map p.391 F1 102

www.paris.fr
Not many tourists make it to this rolling park, created on the site of a quarry in the 1860s. A steep climb takes you to the 'belvedere,' a favourite spot for smoochers (on whom the view is rather wasted). In summer, kids appreciate the play area and donkey rides. There's also a grotto and a lake made for romantic strolls, but the bridge known locally as *le Pont des Suicides* is now (understandably) off limits. Open daily: October to April, 07:00 to 20:15; May, August, September, 07:00 to 21:15; June, July, 07:00 to 22:15.

185

rue des Morillons
15th
Ⓜ **Convention**
Map p.416 C1 **103**

Parc Georges Brassens
www.paris.fr

With its lake and clock tower, this relaxed park feels as though it's been here for a half-century or more, not since 1991. Stone horses' heads and a big bronze meat handler hark back to the past, when this site was occupied by the old Vaugirard abattoir. Donkey rides in summer and a puppet pavilion make it a great place for kids, and there's plenty of shady trees and lawn. At weekends, you can browse for second-hand books in the Halle aux Chevaux, tempted by the wholesome odours of the Poilâne *boulangerie* opposite. Open weekdays 08:00 to dusk; weekends 09:00 to dusk.

blvd de Courcelles
8th
Ⓜ **Monceau**
Map p.387 E2 **104**

Parc Monceau
www.paris.fr

Before the Revolution, this charming park belonged to the Duc de Chartres, and it's still graced by his faux Roman columns and mock obelisk. At weekends, immaculate joggers toil by, oblivious to the Arc de Triomphe framed in its gateway, while well-heeled families promenade their infants along the paths. There's a small rink for rollerskating and donkey rides for kids in summer, when students from the nearby university faculties flock to sunbathe on the lawns. The main entrance is marked by an elegant 18th century rotunda, now a public toilet. Open daily: winter, 07:00 to 20:00; summer, 07:00 to 22:00.

blvd Jourdan
14th
Ⓡ **Cité Universitaire**
Map p.419 D3 **105**

Parc Montsouris
www.paris.fr

This fetching park with its paths, hillocks and grotto was part of Haussmann's plan to bring green space to Paris, and it's no coincidence that the informal landscaping is a little reminiscent of London's parks. Rare varieties of trees and the imported turtles which bask on the lake in summer add a touch of the exotic. Opposite the Cité Universitaire, it's popular with students, weekend joggers and families. There are children's swings, an area for ball games and a bandstand where concerts take place now and then. Open weekdays 08:00 to dusk; weekends 09:00 to dusk.

Bois de Boulogne

Jardin des Tuileries

Jardin du Luxembourg

Parc des Buttes-Chaumont

Great things can come in small packages…

Perfectly proportioned to fit in your pocket, these marvellous mini guidebooks make sure you don't just get the holiday you paid for, but rather the one that you dreamed of.

Explorer Mini Visitors' Guides
Maximising your holiday, minimising your hand luggage

Other Attractions

**57bis rue
de Babylone**
7th
Ⓜ **Saint-François-
Xavier**
Map p.397 F4 **106**

La Pagode
01 45 55 48 48
This wonderful listed building was built in 1895 for Monsieur Morin, a director of Le Bon Marché department store, when the passion for all things Oriental was at its height. Exquisitely executed down to the last stick of lacquered wood, the Pagoda was intended as a gift for Madame Morin, though evidently it didn't sufficiently impress; she left him a year later. It became a cinema in 1931. Peek discreetly; better still, take in a film there. Note that not all movies are shown in the *Salle Japonaise*.

1 blvd Poissonière
2nd
Ⓜ **Bonne Nouvelle**
Map p.389 F4 **107**

Le Grand Rex
08 92 68 05 96 | *www.legrandrex.com*
One of the great surviving art deco cinemas, the Rex was opened in 1932 and is still going strong. The 50 minute behind-the-scenes visit, 'Les Étoiles du Rex' includes a presentation on the construction of its cavernous auditorium and a surround-sound effects show in the production room.

**Opposite 93
quai d'Orsay**
7th
Ⓡ **Pont de l'Alma**
Map p.397 D2 **108**

Les Égouts de Paris
01 53 68 27 81 | *www.paris.fr*
A fascinating and only slightly whiffy museum, this is just a taster, so to speak, of the city's 2,100km of underground sewers. The network replicates the city, its channels bearing the names of the streets above. As well as an insight into the heavy duty dredging technology deployed to keep things moving along, there's a display on the history of the sewers, begun under Napoleon but uncharted during the Haussmann era. This dangerous task was the inspiration for Victor Hugo's descriptions of Valjean's subterranean adventure in *Les Miserables*. Open daily (except Thursday and Friday): May to September, 11:00 to 17:00; October to April, 11:00 to 16:00. Closed for two weeks mid-January.

11bis rue Scribe
9th
Ⓡ **Auber**
Map p.388 C3 **109**

Paris Story
01 42 66 62 06 | *www.paris-story.com*
If you've an hour to spare and a hankering for an overview of 2,000 years of Paris history, this multi-media attraction is for you. The panoramic film is narrated by a holographic Victor Hugo (who better?) and incorporates images shot by the Lumière brothers; it's intelligently done and quite beguiling. There's also a scale model of the city, and courtesy internet access, so you can plan the next step of your Parisian adventure. Daily screenings on the hour from 10:00 to 18:00.

Amusement Parks

For many visitors using Eurostar's service from London, Disneyland *is* Paris. The resort celebrated its 15th birthday in 2007 with new rides, new parades and more larger-than-life characters joining the throng. Unlike Disneyland, Parc Astérix isn't open all year round, but the good news is that it's no longer awkward to reach, thanks to a new shuttle service from Paris. The park offers a family jamboree of costumed entertainment, laughs and some impressively hairy rides…and it's cheaper, too. Mickey or Astérix? Why not give both a whirl?

Marne-la-Vallée
Ⓡ **Marne-la-Vallée -
Chessy**
Map p.379 F3

Disneyland Paris
08 25 30 60 30 | *www.disneylandparis.com*
If you have children, a Disneyland trip is obligatory. The resort is vast, but finding your way around is straightforward. It's split into two: the Studios Park, with animation activities, Rock'n'Roller Coaster and Studio Tram Tour through a special

effects film set; and the main park. Here you'll find Fantasyland (the big draw for younger children), Adventureland and Frontierland, offering more in the way of white-knuckle thrills. Add an afternoon parade of cartoon characters and a helping of all-American eats – et voilà. If you're planning a visit, a little preparation goes a long way. Buy your 'passports' beforehand (online or at FNAC and other outlets), and arrive early to get a Fastpass, which enables you to fast-track as queues start to mount. Finally, if you can, visit midweek when the resort is quieter. To get there, take RER A to Marne-la-Vallée/Chessy. By car, it's 32km east on the A14; Exit 14. Opening times: Disneyland Main Park – September to July, Monday to Friday 10:00 to 20:00, Saturday to Sunday 09:00 to 20:00; July to August, daily 09:00 to 23:00. Studios Park – summer, daily 09:00 to 18:00; winter, 10:00 to 18:00.

Elancourt
Map p.373 B2

France Miniature

08 26 30 20 40 | www.franceminiature.com

Spending a few hours here doesn't guarantee you a handle on France's geography, but you will be able to recognise France's most iconic buildings and scenic towns. Located 37km west of Paris, France Miniature makes a thoroughly pleasant day out. Everyone gets a kick out of peering inside the Stade de France at half-time, seeing 'giant' rabbits hop around the Châteaux of the Loire, while tiny TGVs hurry across dramatic scenery and ships steam across the English Channel. Where England should be, there's an excellent adventure park for older children, while a colourful indoor mini-car circuit caters for tots. To get there by car, take the A13, then the A12 to St-Quentin en Yvelines-Dreux, then follow signs to Elancourt. By public transport from La Défense, take the La Vérrière train, then the 411 bus. Open daily: April to November, 10:00 to 18:00; July to August, 10:00 to 19:00. Closed on some September to November dates; see website for details.

Ermenonville
Map p.373 B2

La Mer de Sable

08 25 25 20 60 | www.merdesable.fr

France's first theme park, La Mer de Sable (the Sea of Sand) opened in the 1960s, but with a new broom it's undergone a relaunch, and has added to the existing family-orientated menu of water rides, carrousels and wild west-themed shows. More is promised for 2008 and '09. The park is some 50km north-east of Paris: to drive, take the A1 and Exit 7. By public transport, take RER B to Roissy CDG1, where a shuttle operates. Opening hours are subject to change, and the park is closed on some Mondays and Fridays. Be sure to check beforehand for up to date information.

Plailly
Map p.373 B2

Parc Astérix

08 26 30 10 40 | www.parcasterix.fr

Located 30km north of Paris, Parc Astérix offers plenty of mayhem in the company of France's diminutive cartoon hero. There's also a good dash of stimulation for youngsters, with dolphin shows in the Poseidon Theatre, character parades along the Via Antiqua and ludicrous legionnaires providing more entertainment down at the Arena. Though large, the park is manageably divided into historical sections, with the perfect comic-strip Village Gaulois at the heart of it all. The serious thrills are on the Tonnerre de Zeus and the Goudurix rollercoasters, but there are also plenty of tamer and splashier flume rides to please younger children. If you're driving, take the A1 (Lille) and exit after junction 7. There's now a direct daily shuttle leaving the Carrousel du Louvre at 08:45. The Christmas opening hours were new for 2007, so check ahead to make sure of timings. Open: April to June, daily 10:00 to 18:00; July to August, daily 09:30 to 19:00; September to 7 November, Wednesday, Saturday, Sunday 10:00 to 18:00; 22 December to 6 January, 10:00 to 18:00.

Botanical Gardens

Route de Sèvres à
Neuilly, Bois de
Boulogne
16th
ℝ *Porte Dauphine*
Map p.394 B2 93

Jardin de la Bagatelle

Within the Bois de Boulogne, the Jardin de la Bagatelle is a horticultural treat. Although every season has its appeal, June is the month to see the spectacular show of roses for which the park is famed (there are over 1,000 varieties). Add to that whimsical bridges, a Chinese pagoda and peacocks roaming at liberty across the lawns, and you have the ideal setting for a genteel Sunday outing. There's a tea room, too. The gardens take their name from a bet wagered between the Comte d'Artois and Marie-Antoinette, who reckoned it would all take three months to build. The Count won; it took 64 days. The 18th century Trianon and Orangerie host musical events, including the annual Chopin Festival. Open daily 09:30 to dusk.

57 rue Cuvier
5th
Ⓜ *Jussieu*
Map p.410 B2 112

Jardin des Plantes

01 40 79 54 79 | *www.mnhn.fr*

The city's main botanical gardens – and a lot more besides – started life as a royal medicinal garden in 1635. Encompassing the Grande Galerie d'Évolution and its neighbours, a small zoo and several cafes, it will easily swallow up an afternoon's visit. Although the hothouses and other elements are gradually being renovated, the gardens are lovely to wander, with avenues of Russian plane trees, alpine and kitchen sections and carp-filled ponds planted with exotic specimens. Local joggers have adopted the *labyrinthe* for its shady uphill paths, and the expansive lawn is a great place to sunbathe and enjoy the grandiose vista on the scientific buildings. Entrance to the main garden is free; there's an entrance fee for other attractions. Open daily: winter, 08:00 to 17:30; summer, 08:00 to 20:00.

esplanade du
Château de Vincennes
Bois de Vincennes
Ⓜ *Château de*
Vincennes
Map p.379 D3

Parc Floral de Paris

01 43 28 41 59 | *www.parcfloraldeparis.com*

A short walk or bus ride from metro Château de Vincennes, this 76 acre park offers great variety throughout the year. Tulips in spring and an autumn dahlia show result in spectacular seas of colour. Among the other micro-gardens, there's a hydroculture 'living wall,' a bonsai garden, a butterfly garden and a nature reserve - which, along with the adventure playground, the little train and the miniature golf circuit make this a great park for kids. There are also restaurants and table-tennis. In June and July, the Paris Jazz Festival is held here. Open daily 09:30 to dusk.

Landmarks

quai François
Mauriac
13th
Ⓜ *Bibliothèque*
François Mitterrand
Map p.411 D4 114

Bibliothèque Nationale de France

01 53 79 53 79 | *www.bnf.fr*

The flagship of the new 13th, the Bibliothèque Nationale de France (or the BNF as it is also known) was the last of President Mitterand's *Grands Travaux*. Dominique Perrault's design takes the form of four towers intended to resemble open books. A national archive amounting to some 13 million books, journals, music scores, photographs, manuscripts and whatnot are contained within, and much of the library is accessible to the public. The central feature, a sunken forest of trees transplanted from Fontainebleau, is just for the birds. Open Monday 14:00 to 20:00; Tuesday to Saturday 09:00 to 20:00; Sunday 12:00 to 19:00.

Bibliothèque Nationale

1 parvis de
la Défense
La-Défense
Ⓜ *La Défense –*
Grande Arche
Map p.378 B2

La Grande Arche de la Défense

01 49 07 27 27 | *www.grandearche.com*

Completed in 1989, the 110 metre-high Grande Arche crowns the historical axis that extends from the Cour Carré of the Louvre to what is now Paris's main out-of-town business district, west of the city. Its architect, Otto van Spreckelsen was virtually unknown outside his native Denmark when his winning design for this 'Arch of Fraternity' was selected. Glass-capsule lifts transport you up to the terrace where there are screenings of a documentary film on the Arche's concept and the gargantuan feat of engineering it represents. There's a bar-restaurant, too, though it's not especially inspiring. Best of all are the unbroken perspectives along the axis, and the sweeping views of city and surrounding countryside. Open daily: April to September, 10:00 to 20:00; October to March, 10:00 to 19:00.

Saint-Denis
Ⓡ *Stade de France –*
Saint-Denis
Map p.378 C2

Stade de France

08 92 70 09 00 | *www.stadefrance.fr*

Parisians are justifiably proud of the Stade de France, just north of the city (not least because *les Bleus* won the football World Cup here in 1998). The state-of-the-art stadium has a capacity of 80,000 and an apparently levitating roof, though whether that whets your appetite for a one-hour guided visit is a moot point. Summer sees it transformed into a beach resort, and you can ski here in winter.

33 ave du Maine
15th
Ⓜ *Montparnasse*
Bienvenüe
Map p.408 A2 **117**

Tour Montparnasse

01 45 38 52 56 | *www.tourmontparnasse56.com*

Loathe it or love it (for there are surely those who do), the 1970s Tour Montparnasse dominates southern Paris, its 210 metres of steel and smoked glass visible from faraway Montmartre. A ride to the panoramic gallery is fun to take, especially at night when the city is transformed. Lifts take less than a minute to whoosh you to the 56th floor. From there, you can see just about everything (except the Tour Montparnasse, of course, which for some makes it the best view in Paris). Open daily: April to September, 09:30 to 23:00; October to March, Sunday to Thursday 09:30 to 22:30, Friday, Saturday 09:30 to 23:00.

Natural Attractions

With the symbolic exception of the Seine, natural attractions are not Paris' strong suite. Vantage points have been built on or landscaped, and even the superficially relaxed Parc Saint-Cloud has a thoroughly formal layout. But if you're prepared to venture further, the 42,000 acre Forest of Fontainebleau (www.fontainebleau-tourisme.com) is genuinely scenic with its ravines, rock formations and verdant forest. It also has an extensive network of paths suitable for walking or cycling, as well as good opportunities for climbing.

To the north, the 160,000 acre Vexin regional park (www.pnr-vexin-francais.fr) is similarly well endowed. During summer months, the region facilitates visits with a special bus connecting the RER stations of Cergy-Préfecture and Pontoise with some of the principal beauty spots.

Aquariums & Marine Centres

An inland capital isn't the obvious place to look for salt water aquariums, yet the city does its best to deliver. The venerable aquarium at Porte Dorée now has competition from the more central CinéAqua, whose curious mix of fish and flicks can be a fun indulgence on Trocadéro Hill; doubtless there's room for both. But if you simply must give the kids their fix of pirate-infused aquatic entertainment, make a day of it and head out of town to Sea Life.

CinéAqua

5 ave Albert De Mun
16th
Ⓜ *Iéna*
Map p.396 B1 118

01 40 69 23 90 | *www.cineaqua.com*
And you thought aquariums were simply about fish? On the site of old Trocadéro Aquarium, once the world's largest, this modern offering sets out to break the mould by marrying serious marine life displays with animated backdrops, three cinema screens and a restaurant. The aquatic element traces a circuit of eleven different zones, from the Seine estuary to French Guiana, and includes a touch pool. Stir in plenty of eco-activities and children's workshops and the result is startling and fun – if pricey. There are sharks, too. Open daily 10:00 to 20:00.

Palais de la Porte Dorée – Aquarium Tropical

293 ave Daumesnil
12th
Ⓜ *Porte Dorée*
Map p.413 D4 119

01 44 74 84 80 | *www.palais-portedoree.org*
With its fabulous moulded panels, the palais near the Bois de Vincennes is an art deco delight, built for the 1931 Exposition Coloniale. This is a traditional aquarium, home to all the rainbow-coloured specimens you might expect. Of the dozing crocodiles, some came here in 1948 and are expected to live out a century – possibly by virtue of conserving their energy. Open daily (except Tuesday) 10:00 to 17:15.

Sea Life Val d'Europe

Centre Commercial
Val d'Europe, 14
cours du Danube
Serris (Marne-la-Vallee)
Ⓡ *Val d'Europe*
Map p.373 B2

01 60 42 33 66 | *www.sealife.fr*
Located within the Val d'Europe shopping village, this neighbour of Disneyland is aimed squarely at children rather than grown-ups. Tank deco tends towards the kitsch, but the collection of aquatic life, including sharks, rays, seahorses and green moray eels and more, is genuinely impressive, with interactive screens and touch pools for inquisitive fingers. Count on a little under an hour to reach the attraction if taking the RER to Val d'Europe. Open daily 10:00 to 17:30.

Zoos & Wildlife Parks

Ménagerie du Jardin des Plantes

57 rue Cuvier
5th
Ⓜ *Jussieu*
Map p.410 B1 120

01 40 79 37 94 | *www.mnhn.fr*
Created in 1794 and stocked with the ex-royal beasts from Versailles, and other animals from fairs, this is one of the oldest zoos in the world. Admission is €7. It's not large, taking a five and a half hectare chunk of the Jardin des Plantes, but it's a respectable collection which specialises in endangered species including orangutans and red pandas. On the same theme, don't miss the unique merry-go-round outside in the Jardin des Plantes. Open daily 09:00 to 17:30.

Parc de Thoiry

Thoiry
Map p.373 B2

01 34 87 53 76 | *www.thoiry.tm.fr*
If you have a car, this African safari park alongside zoo, gardens, labyrinth and four-centuries-old château offers a grand day out. Buy a combined ticket if you intend to visit more than the safari park alone (and note that you can't visit the safari park on foot!). The Parc de Thoiry is 45km west of Paris. Take the A13, then the A12, then the N12, direction Dreux. Open summer, 10:30 to 18:30; winter, 11:00 to 17:00.

Zoo de Vincennes

53 ave de
Saint-Maurice
Map p.413 E4 121

01 44 75 20 00
Hard to miss with its 65 metre-high Grand Rocher, this large landscaped zoo is home to over 200 species, including many primates, birds and mammals, and boasts a miniature train which does the whole circuit. Sections are currently undergoing renovation, a fact that's reflected in the reduced entrance price. Open daily 09:00 to 18:00.

Other Attractions

Mémorial de la Déportation

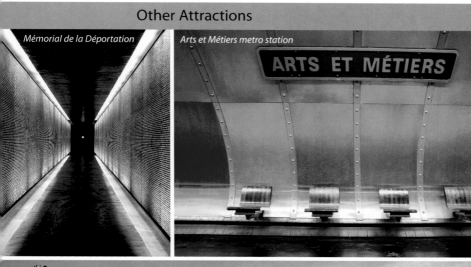
Arts et Métiers metro station

ARTS ET MÉTIERS

Grande Galerie de l'Évolution, Jardin des Plantes

La Grande Arche de la Défense

Place de la Concorde

Tours & Sightseeing

Unsurprisingly, Paris has a wealth of tour options geared to helping you get the most out of your stay. If time is limited, a guided breeze on a bike or open-top bus can be just the thing to get a handle on the city. You'll also find a wide range of out-of-town sightseeing tours listed later in this section.

For a dash of novelty, consider touring the city by Segway (p.200), exploring its lesser-known attractions by electric bike (see below), or taking a spin in a classic Citroên 2CV (p.200). Less informative, but very appealing for out-of-town visitors, boat cruises serve up romantic views from the Canal St-Martin as well as from the Seine. Heritage is well served, too. Among the notables, Paris Walks (p.200) has been providing excellent close-ups on the city for over a decade, while Paris Muse (p.198) offers lively and intimate tours within art galleries and museums. If your French is good enough, the programme run by the Centre des Monuments Nationaux (p.197) is well worth tapping into. And, whether your stay is long or short, don't overlook the other options. Specialists such as Edible Paris (p.200), Ô Château (p.201) and Chic Shopping Paris (p.199) are on hand to reveal their insights into the art of *savoir-vivre*. Where better than in the city that perfected it?

Tour companies in Paris are well regulated and the guiding profession is tightly controlled by law. Only officially licensed guides are authorised to accompany groups into museums, monuments and galleries. For visits out and about, it's not compulsory for guides to have a formal diploma, though it won't hurt. Tours can be booked directly with the operators, in many hotels and at the Paris Convention and Visitors Bureau (p.23). If you're taking a cross-border excursion to a neighbouring country such as Belgium or the UK, remember to check any visa requirements with the tour company or your embassy.

Bicycle Tours

24 rue Edgar Fauré
15th
Ⓜ Dupleix
Map p.396 C4

Fat Tire Bike Tours

01 56 58 10 54 | *www.fattirebiketoursparis.com*

The sister company of City Segway Tours (p.200) and Classic Walks (p.199), Fat Tire runs four-hour bike tours encompassing all the main sights and providing upbeat and interesting insights along the way. No reservations are needed and tours still run if it's rainy. Departure is from the southern pillar of the Eiffel Tower. Night-time tours are a fun alternative; they're slightly more expensive and last up to an hour longer.

place Vendôme
1st
Ⓜ Opéra
Map p.388 C4

Paris Charms & Secrets

01 40 29 00 00 | *www.parischarmssecrets.com*

Broadly speaking, it's a bike tour - but not as you know it. These nippy, battery-powered bikes take the toil out of hills, enabling groups to cover over 20 kilometres with a minimum of effort, and bringing a number of lesser-known sites into the fold. The bikes are easy to use and the guides are well-versed. Groups number up to 20 bikes, setting out from the place Vendôme. Daytime tours set off at 09:30 and 14:30, and last around four hours; evening tours leave at 20:00 and last three hours.

Boat & Yacht Charters

Other options **Dinner Cruises** p.318

Various Locations

Chris River Yacht Charter

06 66 52 18 66 | *www.geocities.com/parisprivateyachtcruise*

Exclusive Seine river cruises are the deal here, on a 30ft luxury motor yacht which comes fully crewed and serves up gourmet snacks and champagne along the way. Cruises take two to five passengers and cost between €179 and €395 per person. Itineraries and boarding piers vary. Book two days in advance. Cruises operate May to October.

194

Boat Tours

Bateaux-Mouches

Port de la Conférence, Port de l'Alma
8th
R *Pont de l'Alma*
Map p.397 D2

01 42 25 96 10 | *www.bateaux-mouches.fr*
The formulaic sightseeing cruise accompanied by a whistle-stop eight-language commentary may not stoke your engine, but the veteran Seine-cruise company also offers dinner, lunch and, for a price, romantic cruises for those with an excuse to splash out. Times and costs vary according to tours; see the website for details.

Batobus

Porte de la Bourdonnais
7th
M *Bir-Hakeim*
Map p.396 C2

08 25 05 01 01 | *www.batobus.com*
With eight stops at strategic locations along the Seine, the Batobus describes itself as a river-boat shuttle service. It's true that some locals use the boats to commute, and annual passes are available for €55, but the main function is sightseeing. Operating hours vary according to the season, with the first boats setting sail at 10:00 or 10:30, and running up to 21:30 in the summer months. Frequency is every 15 to 30 minutes. Tickets are available at every stop. A popular tourist option is the Paris à la carte ticket which can be used in conjunction with L'Open Tour buses (p.196).

Canauxrama

Bassin de la Villette, 13 quai de la Loire
19th
M *Jaurès*
Map p.385 E4

01 42 39 15 00 | *www.canauxrama.com*
Canauxrama offers cruises with commentary along the city's other waterway, the Canal St-Martin, built under Napoleon to facilitate access to the Seine from the eastern side of Paris. Lasting around 2½ hours, cruises pass through some of the city's up-and-coming areas, under bridges and through four double locks. You'll also glide through stretches of tunnel, brightened up these days by Keïchi Tahara's luminous installation. The same company also organises other options, including a day-long excursion past the city's industrial southern fringes to the leafy countryside along the Marne. Book ahead. Timings and costs vary.

Paris Canal

Bassin de la Villette, 19-21 quai de la Loire
19th
M *Jaurès*
Map p.385 E4

01 42 40 96 97 | *www.pariscanal.com*
Like Canauxrama, Paris Canal offers sightseeing cruises along the Canal St-Martin, but the route also takes in a stretch of Seine and the Canal de l'Ourcq. It's a leisurely affair, with boats departing from the Quai Anatole France below the Musée d'Orsay and arriving in the Parc de la Villette two and a half hours later. There's a commentary in French and English. The company also offers a full day's Marne cruise in July and August. Book ahead. Cruises operate daily at 09:30 from the Musée d'Orsay; 14:30 from Parc de la Villette. Additional sailings during high season.

Bateaux-Mouches

195

Port de Suffren
7th
® *Champ de Mars*
Tour Eiffel
Map p.396 B2

Vedettes de Paris

01 47 05 71 29 | *www.vedettesdeparis.com*

There's canned commentary on the one-hour sightseeing cruise, which leaves every hour from below the Eiffel Tower. The company also offers lunch, dinner and children's cruises for 'little sailors' (French commentary). It's worth keeping an eye on their website for special deals which may include discounts on attractions such as CinéAqua and the Musée du Vin. Operating daily every hour: Easter to Oct, 10:00 to 22:00; November to February, 11:00 to 18:00.

square du
Vert Galant
1st
Ⓜ *Pont Neuf*
Map p.399 D3

Vedettes de Pont-Neuf

01 46 33 98 38 | *www.vedettesdupontneuf.com*

Handily located at the jetty just below Pont Neuf, these boats ply a pleasant one-hour circuit up and down the Seine. With a discount if you book online, this is the cheapest of all the Seine sightseeing cruises. Departures are every 30 to 45 minutes in high season, every 45 minutes in winter. Don't disembark without picking up your Official VPN medal. Daily cruises: March to October, 10:00 to 22:30; November to February, 10:30 to 22:00.

Bus Tours

Other options **Walking Tours** p.199

If this is your first visit to the city, bus tours can be a good way to introduce you to the essential sights – and they may come into their own if you're entertaining visitors from back home.

2 rue des Pyramides
1st
Ⓜ *Pyramides*
Map p.398 C1

Cityrama

01 44 55 60 00 | *www.pariscityrama.com*

A number of daily sightseeing tours are on offer in air-conditioned double-decker buses, with multi-lingual commentary. All the major tourist attractions are covered. Tours last from one and a half to four and a half hours, and start from €18. The company also offers a variety of excursions further afield to destinations such as Mont St-Michel (p.201). Reservation only.

13 rue Auber
9th
® *Auber*
Map p.388 B3

See the sights on a bus tour

L'Open Tour

01 42 66 56 56 | *www.paris-opentour.com*

These hop-on, hop-off open buses pretty well have the city covered with their four circuits. There's a multi-lingual commentary along the way. Combined passes with Batobus (p.195) are available.

Les Cars Rouges

17 quai de Grenelle
15th
Ⓜ *Bir-Hakeim*
Map p.396 A4

01 5 39 59 53 | *www.carsrouges.com*

Big, red, hop-on, hop-off buses ply a standard two and a quarter hour tour covering the main monuments. There's a multi-lingual commentary and the ticket is valid over two days. Starting at 09:30, departures are every eight to 15 minutes in summer; 10 to 20 minutes in winter. The last departure is at 18:00 from Trocadéro.

Paris Vision

214 rue de Rivoli
1st
Ⓜ *Tuileries*
Map p.398 C1

01 42 60 30 01 | *www.parisvision.com*

Large air-conditioned bus and minibus tours are available, as well as soirées around town. The company also offers a range of day-long sorties to the Loire valley and other destinations. Paris Vision organises walking tours too.

Farm & Stable Tours

Other options **Horse Riding** p.223

Académie du Spectacle Equestre

Château de Versailles
Versailles
Map p.378 A3

08 92 68 18 91 | *www.acadequestre.fr*

The royal stables built by Jules Hardouin-Mansart for the Sun King's 600 horses are now home to an elite 30 or so, under the choreography of dressage-supremo, Bartabas. The majority are cream-coloured Lusitanians, but the 'cavalry' includes black Arab thoroughbreds and even a Shire horse. These superb creatures are put through their dressage paces on Saturday and Sunday mornings in *les Matinales des écuyers*. The main showpiece, *La Reprise Musicale*, takes place on Saturday evenings and Sunday afternoons. Both spectacles are followed by a tour of the stables. Book ahead. Closed August.

La Ferme de Paris

rue du Pésage
Bois de Vincennes
Map p.379 D3

01 43 28 47 63 | *www.boisdevincennes.com*

This 10 acre slice of rustic life emerged from an agrarian research facility founded in the 1860s by one Georges Ville. More recently, it's been turned into an educational urban farm, complete with small plots of crops, an orchard and animals. Pens have glass panels and there's a children's activity room. Tucked away behind the hippodrome, it's a 15 minute hike from the Bois if you don't have your own transport. Open weekends and public holidays: April to September, 13:30 to 18:30; October to March, 13:30 to 17:00.

Helicopter/Plane Charters

Hélifrance

Le Bourget Airport
Le Bourget
Ⓡ *Le Bourget*
Map p.379 D1

01 45 54 95 11 | *www.helifrance.fr*

Feeling flush? If you've ever dreamt of having the city at your feet, this is the one for you. The 25 minute, €135 Sunday flight from Le Bourget Airport gives you an exhilarating bird's eye view of Paris, its geometry and its landmarks. You can combine it with a flight over Versailles or, if you want to go the whole hog, the company offers all this plus an hour's visit to the Musée de l'Air et l'Éspace at Le Bourget (This last package departs from the Paris Héliport at Issy-les-Moulineaux). Reservation only.

Heritage Tours

Centre des Monuments Nationaux

blvd Morland
4th
Ⓜ *Quai de la Rapée*
Map p.410 B1

01 44 54 19 30 | *www.monuments-nationaux.fr*

If your French is up to it, and nothing but the whole truth will do, the *Visites Conférences* organised by the Centre des Monuments Nationaux, offer some of the most informative insights to be had. They range from highly focussed tours of a single monument or building such as the Assemblée Nationale to all-day coach excursions out of the city. Most tours cost €8 and don't require advance booking. Pick up the programme from your local *mairie* or check the website.

Various Locations ◀

Paris Muse

06 73 77 33 52 | *www.parismuse.com*

This is an educational service tailored to English-speakers, providing in-depth art tours for groups of four or less within some of Paris' most notable museums, including the Louvre, the Musée d'Orsay and the Musée Picasso. The company also caters for children and family visits. Led by academically trained art historians, most tours last from 90 minutes to two hours, and start from around €70. Reservation only.

Hot Air Ballooning

Parc André-Citroên ◀
15th
Ⓜ *Lourmel*
Map p.405 E2 98

Aeroparis

01 44 26 20 00 | *www.aeroparis.com*

Found in the heart of the Parc André-Citroên, this is one of the largest tethered balloons in the world. The sphere itself is the height of a 12 storey building. The Eutelsat-sponsored balloon is filled with 5,500 cubic metres of helium, and can hold up to 30 adults in its open air gondola. It quietly rises 500 feet or more up into the sky, to prove that the best view in Paris is not from the Eiffel Tower, but rather somewhere else looking at it.

4 rue du Magasin ◀
28320 Bailleau-
Armenonville
Map p.373 B2

Air-Pegasus Montgolfières

02 37 31 01 96 | *www.air-pegasus.com*

This company operates a range of balloons, including the *Pégase XII* which is big enough to accommodate 16 passengers for an unforgettable dinner flight. Other options include a flight just for two people – perfect for popping the question. This is the sort of ballooning that begs for a castle sleepover; flights leave from one of eight bases at châteaux to the south-west of Paris, and overnight stays can be arranged. Take your pick from venues including the Château d'Esclimont, the stunning 13th century Château de Maintenon, and the Château de Villiers-le-Mahieu.

24 rue Nationale ◀
41400 Montrichard
Map p.373 B2

France Montgolfières

02 54 32 20 48 | *www.franceballoons.com*

Taking off from Moret-sur-Loing (less than an hour's drive from Paris), this hot air balloon ride will see you gliding 3,000 feet above the famous Fontainebleau forest. Don't be surprised if, during these just-over-an-hour-flights, the balloon dips down to skim over a river or two. Note that if you do not have a car, you can easily access the meeting place by train from the Gare de Lyon and the organisers will come to pick you up at the train station.

Private Tours

65 rue Pascal ◀
13th
Ⓜ *Les Gobelins*
Map p.409 F4

Paris International VIP Services

01 43 31 81 69 | *www.paris-tours-guides.com*

Paris International VIP Services specialises in delivering private tours; it has ten years' experience and is accredited with the Paris Office of Tourism. According to your needs and interests, they'll deliver a bespoke itinerary, a guide and/or interpreter, a chauffeured car and make any other bookings or arrangements necessary for a successful visit.

Shopping Tours

Other options **Shopping** p.242

Various Locations

Chic Shopping Paris

06 14 56 23 11 | www.chicshoppingparis.com

CSP's tours are led by bilingual Parisians with insider knowledge of the hotspots. A wide variety of shopping themes are available, from baby wear to outlet fashion or gourmet produce. Prices start at €100 per person for a tour of around four hours, excluding refreshments. Groups are limited to five people or less.

Various Locations

Shopping Plus

01 47 53 91 17 | www.paris-gourmet.com

This company has been offering tours for Francophiles since 1990. There are three shopping options available: fashion (focussing on the Golden Triangle), Antiques (a foray into the Carée Rive Gauche) and Interior Design (in and among the *bonnes addresses* of the Left Bank). Tours are limited to 10 people. A day tour costs €230; lunch and a coffee break are included.

Walking Tours

1 rue Robert Houdin
11th
Ⓜ *Belleville*
Map p.391 D4

Ça-Se-Visite!

01 48 06 27 41 | www.ca-se-visite.fr

The multi-ethnic, working class *quartiers* of eastern Paris were, until recently, well off the visitor trail. Locally run Ça-Se-Visite! has done much to change that, offering lively urban walks around the area's hidden courtyards, artists' studios and historic streets. If your French is up to it, take your pick from a wide choice of regular walks, locally led and packed with anecdotes. The Saturday 'Belleville Past and Present' walk is offered in English to groups of eight people, by arrangement.

Walking in Paris

24 rue Edgar Fauré
15th
Ⓜ *Dupleix*
Map p.396 C4

Classic Walks

01 56 58 10 54
www.classicwalksparis.com

The company's classic tour is a hefty hike of three and a half hours, but the time flies by in the company of a locally based expatriate with lots of facts and anecdotes to share. Covering virtually all of Paris' major landmarks, this is an excellent orientation to the city as a whole. Classic Walks also runs more focused walks, for example, on Montmartre, the French Revolution and the second world war. Times and prices vary so call or check for details. In most cases, reservations are optional rather than necessary. Most tours start out from the company's offices in the 15th.

Various Locations ◄ | ## Paris Walks

01 48 09 21 40 | www.paris-walks.com

The 'original' Paris Walks offers a diverse programme of tours led by local expats. Guides are chatty and informed, and the *quartier*-centred tours are a great way to deepen your acquaintance with a particular neighbourhood. Themed tours change regularly. Recent offerings have included gourmet chocolate tasting, Edith Piaf and literary Paris tours, while longer out-of-town packages are also available. Most tours last two hours. Check the website for the current programme and rendezvous points. In most cases, there's no need to book and tours run daily, rain or shine, between March and October.

Other Tours

12 rue Chabanais ◄
2nd
Ⓜ *Pyramides*
Map p.398 C1

4 Roues Sous 1 Parapluie

06 67 32 26 67 | www.4roues-sous-1parapluie.com

This young company offers tours from the comfort of the quintessential French vehicle, the Citroên 2CV. Outings range from a 90 minute sweep-around-the-sights to a tailor-made excursion lasting several hours. You name the pick-up spot. Chauffeur-driven, the cars take a maximum of three passengers, so the personal touch is virtually guaranteed. NB: umbrellas *(parapluie* in French) are not part of the package; the name is how Pierre Boulanger summed up his iconic car!

52 rue Sedaine ◄
11th
Ⓜ *Voltaire*
Map p.401 D3

Art Bus

01 47 00 90 85 | www.art-process.com

The Art Process agency runs this once-monthly minibus tour of all that's new and happening in Paris' contemporary art scene. Typically, a circuit may take in commercial collections, artists' studios, art centres and alternative art spaces, and there are frequent opportunities to meet artists, gallery owners or art directors of key institutions. It's a bilingual (French and English) affair, takes four to five hours and costs €35. Places are limited; so book ahead. If you can't make the date, there's an art limo service, too. Tours depart at 11:00 on the third Saturday in the month.

24 rue Edgar Fauré ◄
15th
Ⓜ *Dupleix*
Map p.396 C4

City Segway Tours

01 56 58 10 54 | www.citysegwaytours.com

American-run, this arm of Fat Tire Bike Tours (p.194) is based on the curious-looking, self-balancing 'Human Transporter' – or Segway. Standing upright on your wheels, you glide effortlessly around in a small, guided convoy. The Segways are very user-friendly and require no special skill or effort on the part of rider. A range of city and out-of-town tours is offered, including a night-time Paris tour. Generally, they last four to five hours. Tours operate from 15 February to 30 November, departing at 09:30, 14:00 and 18:30.

Various Locations ◄

Edible Paris

www.edible-paris.com

Paris-based food writer and restaurant critic Rosa Jackson provides customised, self-guided itineraries for foodies. Prices start at €200 for a one day itinerary, which includes a personalised selection of shopping addresses, cafes, brasseries and restaurants with reservations. Ms Jackson also offers guided tours for up to six people, going behind the scenes of some of her favourite food shops and the best local markets. Tailor-made to suit individuals' particular interests, these tours last three hours and cost €250.

Ô Château

100 rue de
la Folie Méricourt
11th
Ⓜ *Goncourt*
Map p.400 C1

08 00 80 11 48 | *www.o-chateau.com*

Young Parisian entrepreneur and sommelier Olivier Magny organises tours to a number of vineyards and châteaux across France. They're in English and the approach is very informative and upbeat. The company also offers basic wine tastings from the Wine Loft near the Marais: prices from €20 for a basic introduction. See p.233 in the Activities section for further details.

Tours Outside Paris

A number of companies provide tours beyond Paris by coach or, for a more personal visit, by minibus. Key destinations are the Châteaux of the Loire (typically you'll visit three, including Chenonceau and Chambord) or Reims for a champagne house visit and a good look around the cathedral. Tours to the Normandy Landing beaches ring the changes but usually feature the outstanding Memorial Museum at Caen. Mont-St-Michel makes a long day trip, but it's also a favourite. In addition to these staples there are also excursions further afield, to Provence, Bruges or London.

Cityrama

2 rue des Pyramides
1st
Ⓜ *Pyramides*
Map p.398 C1

01 44 55 60 00 | *www.pariscityrama.com*

Cityrama's big double-decker air-conditioned coaches (and more expensive air-con minibuses) range far and wide over the French countryside. Packages range from half-day trips to Giverny to four-day guided tours of Normandy and the Loire Valley Châteaux, with accommodation, meals and tickets included. Guides speak a variety of languages, but they always include English. The coach tours depart from rue des Pyramides; minibuses pick up and drop off on request. The company also organises excursions using TGV and Eurostar.

Paris Euroscope

27 rue Taitbout
9th
Ⓜ *Chaussée d'Antin*
– La Fayette
Map p.389 D3

01 56 03 56 81 | *www.euroscope.fr*

This company's out-of-town offerings range from a half-day Chartres visit to four-day combined trips around the Normandy beaches, Mont-St-Michel and the Châteaux of the Loire, with stays in two or three-star hotels. Tours are by air-conditioned minibus, with a driver-guide. English, German, Spanish, Italian and Portuguese are offered.

Paris Vision

214 rue de Rivoli
1st
Ⓜ *Tuileries*
Map p.398 B1

01 42 60 30 01 | *www.parisvision.com*

A good range of day tours and short breaks are offered by Paris Vision. Transport is by air-conditioned coach or pricier minibus and accompanied by a guide interpreter. Within the Parisian region, they combine destinations such as Fontainebleau, Barbizon and Vaux-le-Vicomte, and make interesting forays into the Seine Valley. Further afield, there are thematic trips to Burgundy, Champagne, Britanny and an excursion over the border to Bruges. The company also offers walking tours.

Other Tour Operators

Artventure et Culture	01 42 06 94 71	www.artventures-paris.com
Driver Guide France	06 82 87 60 60	www.driverguidefrance.com
Easy Dream	06 82 87 60 60	www.easy-dream.com
France Tourisme	08 20 34 37 62	www.francetourisme.fr
Guidatours	01 39 02 05 18	www.guidatours.com
Paris Authentique Sabine	01 30 47 39 36	www.paris-authentique.com

Weekend Breaks

One of the pleasures of living in Paris is the ease with which you can escape to somewhere entirely different… and still be wowed by what's on offer. In little more than two hours you can be hitting the beach, be sampling champagne at its source, or deep in Château country. One thing to note: if you're travelling in August, most of Paris will be, too.

Canal Cruise
Between April and October, you can take a 50 minute cruise along Amiens' canals. Boats leave from 14:00 onwards.

Amiens

Amiens was more or less flattened during the Battle of Picardy in 1918, when somewhere in the region of 12,000 shells thundered down on the city. The 'less' is important though, because somehow, the Cathédrale de Notre-Dame was spared. Built in record speed during the 13th century, it's reckoned to be one of the purest examples of Gothic monumental art. It's also one of the biggest – it could hold Paris' Notre-Dame over. From the square, you can't fail to pause in awe at its facade, but the city lays on a splendid summer light show just to clinch the deal. Besides the cathedral, Amiens is a solidly likeable city. It's a good base for visiting the battlefields of the Somme, but there's enough to fill a weekend if you don't. Near the cathedral, the medieval *quartier* of St-Leu, with its little marina and colourful houses, has a real holiday feel. To the east of here are Les Hortillonages, a tranquil expanse of 'floating gardens' criss-crossed by mini-canals. The Musée de Picardie is worth the visit, too; inside the splendid Second Empire building, there are frescos by Puvis de Chavannes, Italian masters and a surprising selection of 20th century art. Served by a direct train service, Amiens is 137km north of Paris.

Seasonal Highlights
From April to September, the town lays on a nightly son-et-lumière *show and in* October, it plays host to a major traditional arts and crafts fair, Les Artisanales de Chartres.

Chartres

Only 88km south of Paris and with a regular train service, Chartres could be a suburb, if it weren't surrounded by the flat farmland of the Beauce. Why come here? Principally for the cathedral, quite simply one of the finest examples of Gothic architecture in Europe, but also for a whiff of provincial life, a smattering of good local restaurants and a relaxed pace. The cathedral has remained largely unaltered in structure since it was built in the late 12th and 13th centuries, and the sculptures at the Royal doorways are outstanding. Inside, the original labyrinth is a rarity as is the carved stone screen, but the stained glass in 'Chartres blue' is the star turn. The glass-working tradition lives on in a number of studios around the city. Stunning examples of the art are often on show at the Centre International du Vitrail, a (strictly metaphorical) stone's throw from the cathedral. The old town has some fine old medieval buildings linked by steep lanes known as *tertres*. Hire an audioguide from the tourist office to accompany you as you wander.

Châteaux Bus
From Blois, there are three daily bus excursions to the Châteaux of Cheverny and Chambord during summer. Buy tickets on the bus outside the train station.

The Châteaux Of The Loire

The Loire valley has all the ingredients of a longer holiday; good food, great wines, lush, rolling countryside and stunning châteaux. For something in the way of a taster, the historic town of Blois, 184km south-west of Paris, makes a starting point. The château here was the main royal residence until Henri IV's reign, and it has witnessed its share of intrigue and assassination. The building unfolds like an architectural picture book, with flourishes like François I's octagonal staircase along the way. It's authentically furnished to boot. Located 16km south-east of Blois, the Château de Cheverny is the most sumptuously furnished of all the Loire châteaux. The inspiration for Marlinspike Hall (Tintin's home-from-home), the château is privately owned. (The master of the house, a direct descendant of the first one, still goes stag-hunting with a 70 strong pack of hounds). Cheverny's Orangerie has its own distinction; the Mona Lisa was safely stashed here during the second world war. If time is limited, head instead for Chambord, 20km east of Blois. Creamy, turreted, spired and domed, the château is a gorgeous Renaissance affair with a double helix stone staircase said to be Da Vinci's work. Above all, Chambord is François I's château (even if he didn't actually spend much time here); you'll see the big man's emblematic salamander carved throughout. Finally – and it's a close call, Chenonceau is more ravishing still. Built and adapted for a succession of women (among them Diane de Poitiers and Marie de Médicis), it's a breathtaking creation, further distinguished by the gallery of arches spanning the river Cher. Chenonceau is a 45 minute drive south of Blois.

Enghien-les-Bains

Take a Stroll
If you don't have time for anything else in Enghien-les-Bains, there's simple pleasure to be had in strolling around the lake and admiring some of the town's more eccentric spa architecture.

It's only 14km north of Paris, but this rather engaging resort town has enough to justify a visit of a day or more if you're in need of relaxation and a little diversion. It owes its popularity to the casino, and the thermal waters that, somewhat bizarrely, exempt the town from Paris' no-casino law. The lakeside casino itself has been newly restored from top to bottom, and the *tenue correcte* dress rule is strictly maintained. Progress in the form of a number of slot machines may have taken its toll on its 19th century glamour, but you can still play roulette and blackjack in atmospheric surroundings, and until the wee small hours. A new deluxe spa complex offers a royal flush of beauty treatments, a fitness suite, pool and health cures. The town's theatre hosts regular events, including the four-day Jazz Festival at the end of June.

Honfleur, Deauville & Trouville

Shrimp Fever
Autumn sees Honfleur gripped by shrimp fever during the annual Fête de la Crevette. There's lots going down, not least the hapless crustaceans.

At the mouth of the Seine, the postcard-pretty town of Honfleur has inspired many artists – and a good many gallery-owners who mop up the trade from weekending Parisians. Honfleur has a quartet of interesting museums, an old town full of half-timbered houses, and an excellent Saturday market selling *produits du terroir*. But it's the 17th century dock (Le Vieux Bassin) that's the focus. It's flanked by narrow houses, many of which are now restaurants and bars with a quayside view of the bobbing boats. West of Honfleur, Trouville and Deauville face each other over the Touques river but are worlds apart. Trouville, too, has a 17th century port, but it's a working affair with a daily fish market. There are quaint back streets, and a long, sandy beach – the same one Monet painted. Glamorous Deauville has been putting on the ritz since the early 20th century, when the Duc de Morny turned it into a swanky resort with a racecourse, a casino and top-end hotels. The town hasn't lost its nostalgic appeal; a hardwood boardwalk still skirts the beach, and the vivid beach huts are a fixture. So is the enormous neo-Louis XIV casino, which attracts a sleek crowd as one of the major casinos in Europe. The town hosts the glitzy American Film Festival in September. Be warned that tens of thousands descend on the town during holiday season; if you haven't booked ahead, your chances of staying are slim. The Normandy Riviera is just under 200km from Paris, and you can get there by train.

Reims & Champagne Country

Getting There
Reims is 130km north-east of Paris, and 45 minutes by TGV. Epernay is just over an hour by train.

Reims has taken to calling itself 'the city of a thousand smiles' and, between champagne and historic charm, you'll find plenty to cheer you here. The city's Gothic cathedral was the traditional coronation place of French monarchs and its exterior is adorned with thousands of statues, including some famously jolly angels. (Nearby, the Palais du Tau museum shelters more original sculptures damaged during first world war shelling). Cathedral tours are conducted in season, or you can hire an audioguide from a selection at the tourist office: among the trails, there's now one covering the city's impressive art deco heritage. But champagne alone is quite enough to justify a jaunt here. Some 300 million bottles of bubbly are produced in Reims and the neighbouring town of Epernay every year. Not all champagne houses offer tours; notable ones that do include Moët & Chandon and Mercier in Epernay, and Pommery in Reims. Descending into the chilly, damp cellars, you'll discover the fascinating process involved in making the tipple of toffs, and tours conclude with a tasting. It's easy to make your own arrangements; alternatively, Reims Tourist Office (www.reims-tourisme.com) now offers champagne tour packages.

Weekend Break Hotels

64 blvd Henry
Vasnier
Reims
Map p.373 B2

Château les Crayères

03 26 82 80 80 | *www.lescrayeres.com*

Set in its own 17 acre park close to the centre of Reims, this 19th century château has 20 rooms in all, including a suite and a separate three-room cottage. Rooms are luxuriously furnished, some decked in *toile de Jouy*, others in a more restrained elegance. The restaurant enjoys a reputation for gourmet cuisine.

85 rue Général du
Gaulle
Enghien-les-Bains
Map p.373 B2

Grand Hôtel Barrière

01 39 34 11 34 | *www.grand-hotel-enghien.com*

With 45 rooms and seven suites, the Grand errs on the intimate side of grand, and it's just the place for some out-of-town pampering. It's all tastefully styled, with wood-panelled reception areas and a lighter touch in the rooms. Then there's the prime lakeside location, with the casino nearby and with direct access to the spa complex. If you must mix business with pleasure, it's well set up for meetings and functions.

22 place des Épars
Chartres
Map p.373 B2

Grand Monarque

02 37 18 15 15 | *www.bw-grand-monarque.com*

A former coaching inn dating to the 17th century, this comfortable hotel is in the centre of Chartres, close to the cathedral. The furnishing is traditional, but the 55 rooms and five suites have been refurbished and all have broadband Wi-Fi access. Paintings adorn the walls of the smart restaurant, and the chef leads gastronomic cookery courses.

27 rue
Rabelais
Amboise
Map p.373 B2

Hôtel le Clos d'Amboise

02 47 30 10 20 | *www.leclosamboise.com*

Set in its own extensive formal gardens, the 16th century mansion was originally built for a clergyman to the court. The hotel has 17 rooms, all individually and elegantly styled. The old stables have been restored to accommodate a modern gym and you can cool off on summer days in the pool in the gardens. Conveniently located close to Amboise town and château, the hotel is a romantic base for forays into the Loire valley.

44 rue des
Capucins
Honfleur
Map p.373 B1

La Maison de Lucie

02 31 14 40 40 | *www.lamaisondelucie.com*

An 18th century house in the centre of Honfleur has been transformed into this delightfully intimate retreat. The five rooms and two suites have parquet floors and are furnished with a delicate touch. There are antiques in the timber-beamed lounge and below stairs there's a spa. On warm days, breakfast is served on the pretty garden terrace.

17-19 place au Feurre
Amiens
Map p.373 B1

Mercure Amiens

03 22 22 00 20 | *www.mercure.com*

Nothing swanky here, but a pleasantly refurbished hotel with a fine 18th century facade and a convenient city-centre location. It's close to the cathedral and only a five-minute walk from the bars and restaurants of the quartier St-Leu. The bar has a peaceful outdoor terrace and Wi-Fi internet access is available to guests.

Bellevue
Champillon
Epernay
Map p.373 B2

Royal Champagne

03 26 52 87 11 | *www.royalchampagne.com*

En route for Reims, Napoleon stayed in this former coaching inn. It's now a luxuriously appointed 25 room hotel with a gastronomic restaurant and a well-stocked cellar. The setting's the clincher, though; the Royal Champagne is on a hill and there are stunning panoramic views over the vineyards. It's located mid-way between Reims & Epernay.

Holidays from Paris

Between the airports of Roissy and Orly, Paris has world destinations pretty well covered, but the majority of Parisians still take their holidays within France or nearby. Factor in a handful of low-cost airlines and an excellent rail service (you can always hire a car at your destination), and it isn't hard to see why this is the case. After all, why go long-haul when there are so many attractive destinations closer to? If you intend to take your holiday in August, remember that most Parisians do too. Be sure to book ahead, or you may find there's no room at the inn. The following is a selection from the huge range of interesting holiday destinations inside and outside France.

Train time: *2 ½ hours*
Best time to visit:
Year round

Alsace

The new TGV route to Strasbourg has opened up this hilly region on the German border. Apart from the heritage, charm and character of the capital, you can follow your taste buds through picturesque half-timbered towns on the Route du Vin. The northern Vosges mountains and the Gérardmer lake add the appeal of summer water sports and winter skiing.

Flight time: *2 hours*
Best time to visit:
Year round

Berlin

Germany's vibrant capital is still very much in transformation, with exciting new buildings replacing drab, Communist-built blocks, and a rich cultural scene including three major opera houses and outstanding museums and galleries. A surprisingly green city, it also offers much in the way of shopping, restaurants, nightlife and overall buzz; in short, its contrasts make it an excellent mini-break destination from Paris. Best time to visit: year round, but November-March can be bleak months.

Train time: *2 ½+ hours*
Best time to visit:
April to October

Britanny

Britanny's dramatic coastline is punctuated by long, sandy beaches and picturesque fishing ports such as Quimper. Add to that a very distinctive local character which is still evident in the traditional religious processions (*pardons*) as well as in Breton cuisine and music. Some of France's most monumental prehistoric sites are to be found here, and they're not to be missed.

Flight time: *2 hours*
Best time to visit: *April to September*

Budapest

The Hungarian capital is almost as beautiful as Prague, but its bubbling naturally mineralised thermal spas give it an extra edge. If you can tear yourself away from being expertly pummelled by the poolside, you can explore Lake Balaton, Central Europe's largest lake, the Eger-Tokaj wine area or go riding on the Hungarian Plain.

Travel time: *1 ½ hours*
Best time to visit:
Year round

Burgundy

The international renown of the Burgundy vineyards brings wine-lovers and foodies flocking to the area around Dijon and Beaune, both centres of outstanding history and architecture. East of here, you can burn off the calories in the densely forested Franche-Comté. It's a magnet for outdoor sports enthusiasts, with great opportunities for hiking, caving, canoeing and cross-country skiing.

Flight time: *1 ½ hours*
Best time to visit:
Spring for the flora; otherwise, year round.

Corsica

The island of Napoleon's birth has bewitching mountain scenery, sandy beaches and some graceful, slightly faded towns of character. The interior is unusually lush for a Mediterranean island, and much of it is protected. For walkers, the big draw is the famously challenging GR30 route, but touring by car or train also has great appeal. All in all, it's one island you should try hard to visit.

Flight time: *1.5 hours to Nice*
Best time to visit: *Year round*

Côte d'Azur

One way or another, it's easy to get there; Nice is served by flights and a car-train service if you want to bring your own wheels. The rest is the stuff of legend; palm-tree lined towns that glitter at night, fashionable arty havens like St-Tropez, and delightful beaches which are very, very popular in summer. Inland, exploring the precarious mountain villages of Provence makes for highly scenic touring, and to the west, the splendid Roman city of Arles is also a must-see.

Flight time: *2 hours*
Best time to visit: *Year round*

Italy

If the French are not 'Mediterranean' enough for you, meet their outgoing neighbours. Great food, mind-blowing history, picturesque fishing villages, sandy beaches – you can make what you like of an Italian holiday. There are lots of packages available, but there are also direct flights to major cities if you're touring by hire-car or rail. The French have a soft spot for Sicily, with its elegant ruins and jewel-like bays; combine it with trips to the surrounding Aeolian Islands if you can.

Train time: *3 hours*
Best time to visit: *Easter to September*

La Rochelle & the Côte d'Argent

Seaside fun is the big draw along this stretch of Atlantic coast. Most visitors flock to the Île d'Oléran, France's second largest island, and the mega-dunes of the Côte d'Argent further south. The historic port of La Rochelle has a rich history and plenty of charm. Inland, Bordeaux's 18th century city centre merits a visit, while the Futuroscope theme park near Poitiers pulls in a family crowd from all over the country.

Train time: *2.5 hours*
Best time to visit: *Year round*

London

The handy Eurostar service from the Gare du Nord has nurtured France's fascination with its strange neighbour across the water. London is a popular mini-break destination which combines mild exoticism (double-decker buses, traditional pubs) with a huge number of attractions. Take a 'flight' on the London Eye, take in the monuments from a river cruise or hit some of the splendid free museums; visitors are spoilt for choice.

Flight time: *3 hours*
Best time to visit: *September to June*

Morocco

For beach relaxation and exotic ambience, a stay in a riad makes Morocco a popular destination with families and couples. The tourism boom means that there's a wide range of budget options. Beyond the bustling souks of Marrakesh and Fez, you can explore prehistoric cave paintings, go camel trekking or go climbing in the Atlas mountains.

Train time: *2 hours to Caen*
Best time to visit: *Year round*

Normandy

Don't underestimate Normandy; it's packed with heritage, and you won't squeeze it all into a weekend's visit from Paris. From the remarkable 11th century Bayeux tapestry to the floating harbour at Arromanches and the D-Day Landing beaches,

Travel Agencies

Jet Tours	08 25 30 20 10	www.jettours.com
Kuoni	08 20 05 15 15	www.kuoni.fr
Look Voyages	01 45 15 31 70	www.look-voyages.fr
Nouvelles Frontières	08 25 00 07 47	www.nouvelles-frontieres.fr
Pierre et Vacances Maeva	08 92 70 21 80	www.pv-holidays.com
Selectour	08 92 23 30 02	www.selectour.com
SNCF	08 92 30 83 08	www.voyages-sncf.com
Thomas Cook	08 26 82 67 77	www.thomascook.fr

there's history at every turn. There are tours from Paris, but the area is ideal for touring by car – that way you can stop at pretty thatched-roof villages, and savour the countryside, the castles and the Calvados at your own pace. On no account miss Normandy's crowning glory, the ancient abbey of Mont-St-Michel, standing aloof on its rock.

Train time: *2 hours*
Best time to visit:
Year round

The Rhône Valley & the Alps

This area draws gastronomic and outdoor adventurers alike. Historic, sophisticated, Lyons is an out-and-out gourmet capital, while the Beaujolais, Rhône and Drôme vineyards offer ample tasting opportunities. The majestic Ardèche gorge is a favourite with canoeists and climbers. To the east of the region, the winter ski stations get a second wind in late June, when the hikers arrive, notably to tackle the tour du Mont Blanc.

Flight time: *2 hours*
Best time to visit:
Year round

Spain

For many French holiday-makers, Spain means the heavily developed resorts of the Costa del Sol, but there are also direct flights to the buzzing capital of Madrid, as well as delectable Seville, with its dazzling Moorish architecture and tapas culture. Low-cost flights have made Barcelona a deservedly popular city-break spot with those in the know. Explore Gaudi's creations and the Gothic quarter, sample the shopping, Catalan cuisine and the nightlife, and you'll have more than enough for a long weekend.

Flight time: *2.5½ hours*
Best time to visit:
September to June

Tunisia

Tunisia offers an uncomplicated, relaxing holiday formula along the southern Mediterranean coastline. In addition to sun-worship, well-developed resorts offer diving, sailing, windsurfing and golf, while archaeological sites such as the ancient city of Carthage are easily visited.

Marrakesh

Corsica

Alsace

207

Jump over the daily grind.

Fly over nagging thoughts.

Glide into your own space.

Cut through monotony.

Ski Dubai. Leave it all behind.

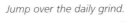

ESCAPE EVERY DAY

SKI DU

an unforgettable snow ex

Activities

Activities

Sports & Activities

Parisians don't tend to think in terms of circuit training and chin ups; they walk so much that they've already done their daily workout by the time they've snagged their first *pain au chocolat*. In the past, Parisians have eschewed the gyms to 'make sport': skiing, tennis, and football (soccer), but with the introduction of McDonalds and the internet expanding everyone's gluteus maximus, the French have started visiting a hoard of excellent new gyms. Pilates classes, martial arts studios and more have begun to crop up and there's a swimming pool in every *arrondissement*. Despite all this change, the past is not overlooked; montgolfier (ballooning), pétanque, and jeu de paume are older than the finest aged wines and can still be found tucked into this or that corner. The French may be French, but they do a fabulous job of integrating other cultures into their activities, with horseball from Argentina, 'le foot' (rugby) and cricket from the UK, Péteca from Brazil and volleyball from America, just to name a few. Golf has finally made its real presence known to the French and although most of the best courses are within sprinting distance of the *périphérique*, those looking for a hole-in-one can visit the facility within the Hippodrome d'Auteuil in the 16th.

With all the indoor, outdoor, extreme and seasonal sports that thrive in Paris, the inhabitants haven't forgotten to go zen. Cafe sitting is a must-do every day, parks are as prevalent as the museums, those hankering for a massage won't be short of choices and there are always Hammams for anyone who has spent the day hopping over poodle droppings, or elbowing their way through the Louvre to get close to Mona.

Quiet Time

The French take long holidays with most of May, all of August and many long holiday weekends seeing an exodus of Parisians. Providing the staff don't take off, these might be good times for the shy to start their gym visits.

Activity Finder

Accrobranche

42 rue Bancel
Melun
Map p.373 B2

Aventure Aventure

01 60 04 26 37 | *www.aventure-aventure.com*

Let your inner Tarzan (or Jane) out by swinging from tree to tree; this activity is ideal for anyone who's been stuck in the museums for too long. You'll be hooked up to all sorts of safety cables and the rest is up to your courage and muscles (and vertigo... some spots are almost 60 feet high). With several courses from which to choose, all progressive in difficulty, even small children can swing as long as they are accompanied by an adult. Cross a swinging rope bridge, scale rope ladders, work your way from tree trunk to tree trunk. It's worth remembering that trees are slippery when wet, and winter months require reservations as some days are not available.

Aerobics

Other options **Dance Classes** p.218

65 quai d'Orsay
7th
Ⓡ *Pont de l'Alma*
Map p.397 E2 🔳

The American Church in Paris

01 40 62 05 00 | *www.acparis.org*

The American church is a breath of fresh air for those who've had just a little too much of that Parisian *je ne sais quoi*. All sorts of English spoken classes are offered, but the Aerobics American Style will help your stomach muscles come to terms with those extra Ladureé macaroons to which you've become so addicted. The Sweat and Sculpt is choreographed cardio combined with severe leg work and after one class of this you'll be ready for that macaroon again. The instructors are friendly English speakers and attract an international crowd so, no matter how much it hurts, you'll be in good company.

Art Classes

Other options **Art & Craft Supplies** p.246, **Art Galleries** p.156

11 rue Saint Maur
11th
Ⓜ *Voltaire*
Map p.401 E2 🔳

Paris Loisirs Culturels

01 43 70 70 26 | *http://p.dizian.free.fr*

Those with artistic ambitions can work with oil-based paints, acrylics or watercolour at this atelier in the Bastille. On the first Sunday of the month, classes are also taken off site to the major museums, such as the Louvre and the musée d'Orsay, where striving to thriving artists can study with the work of the real grand masters, such as Renoir and Monet, around to encourage. Beginners and more experienced students are taught; by both English and French teachers so future artists can work on their language skills too. This is an amicable crowd that will inspire you to become part of the Parisian art scene. Sessions (three hours) are by appointment only and cost €25 and the atelier is open Monday to Saturday.

20 rue Voltaire
Rueil-Malmaison
Map p.378 B2

Paul Flury Workshops

01 42 87 37 69 | *www.flury-sculpture.com*

If you want to work with your hands, come to Paul Flury. You can carve wood and stone, mold plaster, learn the techniques of glass sculpting, solder tin, work with scrap metal, do just about anything in bronze and, of course, sculpt clay. Everything is at your fingertips in this professional studio just outside Paris. Jewellery making is also taught for those who prefer to wear their creations. You can be a beginner, but your French needs to be advanced to truly benefit from the high standard of teaching. For true artists, a class under Paul Flury is as close as you'll come to getting next to Alexander Caulder.

Astronomy

La Salle des Planches
Place des Planches
Orsay
Ⓡ Le Guichet
Map p.373 B2

Association Astronomique de la Vallée
http://aav.free.fr

Adapt your eyes to the darkness and study celestial geography with fellow astronomers at this club in Paris. All people who share the interest of astronomy and have the passion to search the vault of the skies are welcome. Many members have significant websites while others are simply amateur star worshippers. Regardless as to whether you enjoy finding Ursa Major or doing extensive maths to figure out the magnitude of a star, you'll be invited on trips to observatories with others of your star-gazing ilk. Many languages are shared here, celestial being the main one.

Badminton

12 rue du Cers
Eragny
Map p.373 B2

Speedminton
06 03 52 01 59 | www.speedminton-eragny.com

The relatively new sport of speedminton is played at Speedminton Club at Eragny/Oise, 15 miles north of Paris. This is a sport that can be played both day and night and just about anywhere, indoors or out. A cross between badminton, tennis and squash, it doesn't require a net, but the rules are competition precise and the 'speeder' (a shuttlecock on speed) is designed to go up to 175 miles an hour. The speeders, rackets and rubberized belts used to form the square court boundaries, can be purchased as florescent and lighted equipment, turning the game into Blackminton. The speed of the speeder and the fact that this can be played at night on a rooftop, mountain or cliff edge puts this activity firmly in the category of extreme sports.

Baseball

Various Locations

Les Patriots de Paris
www.patriotsparis.com

In the Bois de Vincennes during summer and in the Croix-Nivert Gymnasium in the 15th *arrondissement* in the winter, you'll find the only club in Paris that offers both baseball and softball for both sexes. This club also sports a lively social calendar and you'll be welcomed with open arms as the club is trying to propagate the sport in France. Come join a team, get your pitching arm warmed up for a no-hitter and show your team-mates how to really pulverise the opposing side.

Basketball

quai Branly
7th
Ⓜ Bir-Hakeim
Map p.396 C2 ₃

Le Parc du Champ-de-Mars
01 40 71 75 60 | www.paris.fr

Join a pickup game of basketball in the long park in front of the Eiffel Tower, the Champ-de-Mars. Although the games are informal the players are abundant, as this is one of the more populated areas of Paris. You'll be playing with many French speakers, of course, but don't be surprised to find that Japanese, Americans, Spaniards and Brits get in on the game too. In summer play early in the morning or later in the day; the Eiffel Tower doesn't exactly provide strong shade.

Basketball in the Parc du Champ-de-

Beauty Training

Other options **Beauty Salons** p.237

16 rue du Perche
3rd
Ⓜ **Saint-Sébastien Froissart**
Map p.400 B2 4

École de Maquillage Artistique

01 42 72 73 02 | www.avantscene75.com

Learn how to do commercial makeup (so you can get a job after you earn your diploma in cinema or television), how to paint the faces that strut the catwalks at fashion week, how to deal with makeup transformations, wigs and chignons. Technology, chromatology, psychology and the history of cosmetics are just some of the subjects you'll learn at this very creative French speaking school. After graduating, you'll have the knowledge to say 'Non, ce n'est pas possible. Vous n'avez pas des cheveux de Jennifer Aniston'.

176 blvd St-Germain
6th
Ⓜ **St-Germain des Prés**
Map p.398 C3 5

shu uemura

01 45 48 02 55 | www.shuuemura.com

If you have a predisposition to shu uemura products, head over to the boutique on boulevard St-Germain in the 6th to get a makeup lesson, where you learn that simplicity is the best way to bring your real beauty out. The staff will teach you how to add the extra wows by adding some of the frills from their eyelash bar or just upping the shimmer factor. The women behind these counters are particularly agreeable, and can offer helpful hints for men, make up and skincare, all set in modern Japanese, minimalist surroundings.

Beekeeping

rue de Tournezy
Bois-le-Roi
Map p.373 B2

Bois-le-Roi

01 64 81 33 31 | www.boisleroi.ucpa.com

Honey (*miel*) is right up there with *chocolat chaud* when it comes to little daily pleasures for the French. What most people don't know is that even in the Jardin du Luxembourg there's a beekeeping area but, to take a real course in beekeeping, head to the Bois-le-Roi, south of Paris, and learn all about collecting honey, the different flowers the bees visit and even the biology of the bee. Courses run on Saturdays and are in French, however other attendees are happy to translate.

Billiards

111 rue St Maur
11th
Ⓜ **Parmentier**
Map p.401 E2 6

Blue Billard

01 43 55 87 21

This spacious upscale billiard hall would feel like a home away from home were it not filled with so many Frenchmen. You can sit at the bar surrounded by posters of BB King and the Blues Brothers, or have your drinks served at your pool table. The billiard room, replete with 18 tables of blue velvet, is decorated with large, rough wood beams and a wooden staircase up to a mezzanine; everything is well-lit by a skylight during the day. The second floor houses a restaurant, and a lunch special gets you two hours of pool with your meal for under €10.

84 rue de Clichy
9th
Ⓜ **Place de Clichy**
Map p.388 B2

Cercle Clichy Montmartre

01 48 78 32 85

Elegance isn't something you normally associate with billiard halls but this stunning space in the 9th might change your mind. With 16 tables, including five for French billiards, you can practise your game then take part in the daily tournaments; taking part costs between €4.80 and €11.70 per hour.

213

Birdwatching

Other options **Environmental Groups** p.219 60

Wild birds are protected at the Allée Royale in the eastern Bois de Vincennes (p.184), as well as the western park, the Bois de Boulogne (p.184). First set up to protect the endangered bullfinch peony and grisette warbler, these ornithological reserves became successful enough to be equipped with panels to help bird viewers identify the birds flocking before them. Ornithological visits can be set up by the LPO (Ligue pour la Protection des Oiseaux; 01 53 58 58 38, www.lpo.fr) and CORIF (Centre Ornithologique Île-de-France; 01 48 51 92 00, www.corif.net) or simply take your binoculars and enjoy the variety of birds. Shovelers and long-tailed ducks, shelducks, tufted ducks, peregrine falcons, European sparrow hawks, ring-necked pheasants, ring-necked Parakeets, Eurasian coots, grey cuckoos, green woodpeckers, turtle doves, long-eared owls, tawny owls, grey wagtails, skylarks, chiffchaff and more can all be spotted.

Fontainbleu
Map p.373 B2

Fontainebleau Forest

The rare Dartford Warbler has found its home within the 25,000 hectares of the forest of Fontainebleau. Along with this species, bird lovers can also spot wrynecks, hoopoes, nightjars, woodlarks, redstarts, pied flycatchers, red-backed shrikes, European bee-eaters, Eurasian honey-buzzards and great spotted woodpeckers, and that's just to start. For every day birds check for the bark-camouflaged, Bonelli's warblers to be nesting on the famous sandstone boulders of this forest, as they'll lay their eggs directly on the rocks. If you bring your kids along, they might be more fascinated by the colourful strutting peacocks in the Chateau's garden. A baguette goes a long way to making these descendents of Louis the IX's peacocks happy.

Boxing

Various Locations

Fédération Française de Savate

01 53 24 60 60 | www.ffsavate.com

Unlike English boxing, French boxing (or *savate*) allows blows with the hands and the feet, with absolutely no room for below the belt cheating. The regulations are strict, but the movements are intense; a direct hit, an uppercut, a hook and a swing from the hands. Choose your sparring partner by the colour of their gloves: if you're a beginner, go for the blue; if you're intermediate, go for the reds; and by all means, unless you're a master, steer clear of those boxing with yellow gloves. See the website for details of the many clubs in Paris offering the sport.

Camping

Other options **Outdoor Goods** p.273

allée du Bord de
l'Eau, Porte Dauphine
16th
Ⓜ *Porte Maillot*
Map p.394 B2 🄅🄓

Bois de Boulogne

01 45 24 30 00 | www.paris.fr

This campsite really is in Paris. Open all year round, it's a true find for those who want a lot of room for not many euros. There are multiple equipped (and roomy) caravans, some with air conditioning, and hoards of sites to pitch a tent. Dogs are allowed, kids are allowed to run free and there's a grocery store with adapters and fresh fruit available. Amenities include laundry facilities, a pizza place, a restaurant (open for breakfast, lunch and dinner), a games room and a swimming pool, plus a private shuttle to the nearest metro stop, Porte de Maillot. This is fine living in the great outdoors at the heart of the Bois de Boulogne woods.

rue Berthelot, 78000
Versailles
Map p.378 A3

Huttopia Versailles

01 39 51 23 61 | www.huttopia.com

Alongside a lake, in the heart of the Rambouillet forest, just 20 minutes from Paris and five minutes from the Palace of Versailles are the little wooden bungalows called Roulettes. Inside is everything you need; bathrooms, showers, kitchens, accessories, and beds. For those who want less comfort, there are ridge tents designed for families, and bivouacs for those who just want to get down and dirty. B&B packages are available, as are many activities including bike hire, hiking, table tennis, badminton, board games and swimming in the on-site heated pool.

Canoeing

Other options **Outdoor Goods** p.273

88 rue de
Saint Martin
Voulangis
Map p.373 C2

Canoe-77

06 07 87 97 84 | www.canoe-77.com

At the Base nautique de la Villette in the 12th *arrondissement*, next to the Parc de la Villette, you can rent row boats, canoes, canoe-kayaks and get busy paddling in a large basin. You'll be lucky to get the rental for more than an hour so an alternative is to head 20 minutes south of Paris to Moret and go on a canoe excursion that can last anywhere from an hour to a weekend. The longer the ride, the prettier, and you'll glide past the beautiful village of Grez on Loing. The scene is pastoral, especially around the old mill and, if you have the time, go all the way to the end, right before Saint Mammés, where the river runs wild.

Capoeira

Various Locations

École de Capoeira Angola de Paris

06 20 69 21 45 | www.angola-ecap.org

The history of capoeira is almost as interesting as the sportive dance itself. In a nutshell, it is derived from slaves who were thrown together with different cultures and strangers, and who had no way to communicate or rebel other than through dance. Music is crucial because an audience forms a circle (roda) and plays at different tempos to help spur the participants on. The participants feign hitting each other while they dance; imagine break dancing and martial arts, and you'd just about have a visual of what the players are doing inside the circle. Paris has been passionate about capoeira for years now, and clubs have cropped up everywhere, but this is the club of choice for those in the know. Venues vary, so check the website or ring for details.

Chess

38 rue des Amandiers
20th
Ⓜ *Père Lachaise*
Map p.402 A1 **7**

Tour Blanche Échecs

01 39 12 54 31 | www.tourblanche.asso.fr

You're in Jardin du Luxembourg, playing a peaceful game of chess, when it starts to rain – what to do? Take it inside to Tour Blanche Échecs (White Rook Chess), next to Père Lachaise in the 20th *arrondissement*. The club prides itself on its conviviality and camaraderie as well as its history (it was inaugurated the day after the liberation of France in 1945), but it's also more than just a neighbourhood hangout – this club plays to win at several national levels and holds a well-attended annual tournament. Recently the club opened a chess school for ages from 6 years and up, and several chess camp, for veterans as well as beginners so you can improve your game and your French at the same time.

Climbing

Fontainbleu
Map p.373 B2

Fontainebleau Forest

These are some of the best rounded sandstone boulders in the world. The forest is loaded with orange and blue circuits, plus four highball red circuits. Everyone, from beginners to those who are virtuosos at topping out, should start at Roche aux Sabots at Trois Pigeons, then advance to the southern part of the forest with the toughest climbs. The unique grading-system starts at 1 and goes up to 8. To spend the weekend, hit the free bivouac at Bas Cuvier but for those who want more comfort, stay at charming Hôtel de Londres (01 64 22 20 21), directly across from the famous chateau and ask for a room with a view.

Cookery Classes

Hotel Ritz Paris
1st
Ⓜ Opéra
Map p.398 B1 **10**

École Ritz Escoffier

01 43 16 30 50 | www.ritzparis.com

Most of us only dream about staying at the Hotel Ritz so it's amazing that the cooking school here is within budget and open to anyone of just about any age or level of cooking. Don a chef's Toque hat and take the various courses offered, but bear in mind they'll be in French with some English translation. Learn how to groove courgettes, prepare fish for the *portefeuille* and make a mean puff pastry. You'll also learn how to master wines, cocktails, and, believe it or not, even arrange flowers, because to the French, food is the art of life. At the end of the day you take home your own little diploma.

18 ave de la Motte
Picquet
7th
Ⓜ École Militaire
Map p.397 E3 **9**

La Cuisine Marie de Blanche

01 45 51 36 34 | www.cuisinemb.com

One of the best cooking classes of all for expats is run by Princess Marie-Blanche de Broglie. Not only has she taught chefs to cook, but even Princess Diana learned to boil *de l'eau* here. Learn how to master *poulet aux langoustine*s and *les poisons* or have a go at making *clafoutis en amandine, tarte à la crème de figues* and all sorts of other fabulous pastries. You'll also learn how to understand over 400 French cheeses, as well as how to choose wine, and for those who want *les enfants* to earn their keep, children aged 6 and up can take inexpensive classes.

Cricket

13 Grande rue
Arnouville les Mantes
Map p.373 B2

Chateau de Thoiry

01 34 87 55 70 | www.thoirycricket.com

The playing fields at Chateau de Thoiry and Cricket Club, less than an hour from Paris and founded in 1990, are considered the most glorious in France. In addition, this club's professionalism is second to none, winning the inaugural European club championship in 1992 and the prestigious Saint Astier sixes tournament in 2002. Anyone can join as long as they love the game and are willing to make at least 32 runs for the final wicket – or be agreeable enough to make the afternoon tea. Membership also comes with the perk of having access to the safari park all year long, where elephants, camels, lions, tigers and bears reside.

British Boozer

So you can't play at The Cricketer (41 Rue Mathurins, 01 40 07 01 45), but you will need to know where to go to watch the sport. This pub is so British you'd swear you were in England, instead of a stone's throw from Galaries Lafayette and Printemps in the 8th. There are two widescreens with cricket matches, Beamish to be downed and a so-so variety of different foods, including Tex-Mex tacos, tandoori chicken and fish n chips.

Is getting lost your usual excuse?

Whether you're a map person or not, this
pocket-sized marvel will help you get to know
the city like the back of your hand – so you
won't feel the back of someone else's.

Amsterdam Mini Map
Fit the city in your pocket

Cycling

Other options **Cycling** p.234,
Sports Goods p.281

The RATP system has taken a stand
against pollution by making bicycle
transportation easy in the city.
During all but peak hours, bikes are
allowed on the RER as well as Line 1,
and bus lanes are now also bike
lanes. RATP's Roue Libre service (08

Cycling in Paris

10 44 15 34, www.rouelibre.fr) is the largest bike rental company in the city, offering a
variety of bikes for adults and children, along with other accessories and helmets. Take
guided bilingual group tours if you're too chicken to pedal around the Arc de Triomphe
solo. Both the Bois de Boulogne and the Bois de Vincennes also offer well-maintained
bike trails. Paris à Vélo C'est Sympa! (www.parisvelosympa.com) in the 11th offers tours
including Paris at Dawn, Paris Nocturne, Heart of Paris, and Paris Contrasts, in addition
to bike and tandem rentals. Paris Vélo Rent A Bike (www.paris-velo-rent-a-bike.fr) in the
5th rents bikes out, suggests routes and offers guided tours including Les Grands
Monuments, La Rive Gauche and Balade au bois de Vincennes. See also Bicycle Tours
on p.197 in the Exploring chapter, and p.30 for details of the Vélib bike rental scheme.

Dance Classes

Other options **Music Lessons** p.226

25 rue Boyer
20th
Ⓜ **Gambetta**
Map p.392 A4 **10**

Centre Momboye

01 43 58 85 01 | www.momboye.com

Mali, Senegal, Guinea and Cameroon all brought dance over to France, and Parisians
were quickly hooked on the evocative rhythms of the different countries. Centre
Momboye takes what came from the old country and teaches the art of gestures via
drumming. Learn the Bolowi, the acrobatic dance from the Ivory Coast, and others
from the same region, such as the Boloye and Kotou, both dances of rejoicing. The
Dundumba, the Guinea strong man's dance, as well as the Senegal Sabar air dance, are
among other dances learned here. The teachers are exceptionally nice and they'll
humorously work with those who are weak in all but the English tongue.

102 blvd du
Montparnasse
14th
Ⓜ **Vavin**
Map p.408 B2 **39**

La Coupole

01 43 20 14 20 | www.lacoupoleparis.com

In the lower level of brasserie La Coupole (made famous by Hemingway, Sartre and
Man Ray), dance under the twinkling lights and be in good company working your way
around the tiny dancefloor. Try not to get elbowed in the eyeball by couples who have
been coming here for years on Tuesday nights to salsa, and by newbie foreigners who
flock to try out the paso and tango on other nights. Full orchestras don white suits and
play big band goodies and on some nights French DJs come to mix hip hop, disco and
garage music. In other words, there's really no idea of what to expect, except to have a
good time and you might even find the (dance) partner of your life.

83 blvd MacDonald
19th
Ⓜ **Porte de la Villette**
Map p.385 F2 **11**

Mandunga

01 40 36 68 67 | www.mandunga.fr

Música tropical, otherwise known as Salsa, can be found at Mandunga, where you can
dance on a two-level floor inside or, in warmer months, outside on the veranda.
Whether you enjoy mixed-style or Cuban salsa you'll learn sexy moves and meet

incredibly nice people who share their love for this steamy dance. Located in La Villette, many of these classes are taught by El Salserito, the professed professor of Salsa, who teaches you how to work with techniques without forgetting the electrifying and sultry mood. Even children hit the scene on Sunday afternoons. Word of warning: hold on to your date or you might lose them in this huge establishment.

Dog Training

Other options **Pets** p.101

Various Locations

Danielle Mirat

01 39 80 76 58 | www.communicanis.com

This behaviour specialist trains the master, as well as the dog, enabling aggressive, destructive, barking, ferocious dogs to be turned into adorable pooches. It's not an overnight process – it takes a while to train the master. All great respect is given to the dog and there will be no harmful techniques used. Mirat is also the first person you should visit while trying to decide how to choose the right animal for you, keeping in mind your way of life, your leisure capability and your character.

Various Locations

Du Loup à l'Agneau

01 44 93 96 69 | www.duloupalagneau.fr

Yann Lucas will train your dog and you in French, but the dog doesn't mind; dogs speak dog language. You'll learn how to lead without hurting the animal or having frustrations, and how to resolve any conflicts with your dog with the resolution being that most of these conflicts arise from the master not being a proper leader. Under the tutelage of this dog whisperer your dog will begin to change in some areas immediately and as a plus, Yann boards and walks dogs, but he only accepts two at a time, so reservations are a must.

Environmental Groups

Other options **Voluntary & Charity Work** p.56

22 rue des Rasselins
20th
Ⓜ **Porte de Montreuil**
Map p.403 A4

Greenpeace France

01 44 64 02 02 | www.greenpeace.org/france

If you were a Greenpeace activist before, there's no reason to stop now that you're in France. These are serious activists, and you'll be blockading French tuna fishermen in Marseille before you know it. You can get involved on many levels; make a donation, join the local chapter, volunteer in the mailing room of the Paris office and, if you're confident in your French, you can work one of the information tables at a market or festival. From a social point of view, Greenpeace is also a great way to meet like-minded people while making a difference.

9 rue Dumenge,
69317 LYON
Map p.373 C2

Sortir du Nucléaire

04 71 76 36 40 | www.sortirdunucleaire.org

This English-friendly anti-nuclear lobby is a network of over 700 French environmentalist groups. Although the majority of their current publications are in French, you'll find their most important documents posted in English on their bilingual website, including a form that allows you to indicate just how to get involved. Most campaigns involve disseminating information or getting in contact with the authorities in some manner, in addition to joining protests and rallies, so if your letter writing skills aren't up to scratch you can still take action. For more information on what activities work best for you, get in touch with André Larivière, their international contact, at lariviere@sortirdunucleaire.fr.

219

Fencing

19 blvd Jourdan
14th
Ⓜ *Porte d'Orléans*
(Général Leclerc)
Map p.419 D3 12

Paris Université Club Escrime

06 11 87 23 03 | www.puc-escrime.over-blog.com

Situated in a building called the 'Espace Sud' Maître Christian Tisseyre will give you a short but hearty welcome. This fencing club at the PUC is one of the largest and the best in Paris; they fence all three weapons (épée, foil, saber) as well as practice artistic fencing, and the teams for each weapon all compete in Division 1 in France. In recent years the club has produced several members for the Équipe de France (France's international team) as well as Brice Guyart, an Olympic gold medallist. This club welcomes foreign fencers, including English speakers, and offers popular beginner programmes. *En garde!*

First Aid

6 rue Larrey
5th
Ⓜ *Censier Daubenton*
Map p.410 A2 13

Protection Civile de Paris

01 43 37 01 01 | www.protectioncivile.org

The Protection Civile de Paris organizes around 1,000 courses of all different types of first aid each year, making it the largest in the Parisian region. In France, the level-one course called the AFPS (Attestation de Formation aux Premiers Secours), is taught to a general audience and anyone can sign up. The time requirement is only two days, and you'll learn CPR, how to deal with choking, heavy bleeding, sicknesses, trauma and more, so it's a valuable use of your time if you have a free weekend. Due to the need to communicate effectively with both the victim and medical professionals, some proficiency in French is required.

Fishing

Other options **Boat & Yacht Charters** p.194

Grab a beret, a fishing rod and a *carte de pêche* (a mandatory fishing licence available at any town hall) and head to the banks of the Seine at Île Saint Louis to cast your line. Rules state that you mustn't start fishing until half an hour before the sun rises and you must stop half an hour after it goes down. You'll want to comply too; fishing is monitored heavily in Paris. See www.lapecheenregionparisienne.com for more details. For serious fishermen who need serious equipment, must-visit stores include Au Coin de Pêche (ave de Wagram, 17th, 01 42 27 28 61) and La Maison de la Mouche Dubos (blvd Henri IV, 4th, 01 43 54 60 46).

Fishing by the Seine

Flower Arranging

Other options **Gardens** p.263, **Flowers** p.260

Hôtel de
Crillon-Concorde
8th
Ⓜ *Concorde*
Map p.388 A4 **2**

La Belle École

01 47 04 50 20

Classes are taught at the gilded Hôtel Crillon, where not one of your five senses will be left undisturbed. Smells, sights, touch, hearing and even taste (with the popular fruit bouquets) are all around. There are many different courses from which to choose; focus on monochromatic or multicoloured arrangements, learn how to go wild or decorate for the holidays. You'll come away understanding not only how to place flowers in an arrangement, but how to pick the right flowers and how to keep them fresh, longer.

Football

17 blvd Jourdan
14th
Ⓡ *Cité Universitaire*
Map p.419 D3 **15**

Paris Université Club Foot

06 20 67 77 09 | www.pucfoot.com

Die-hard football (soccer) fans from all ages and levels come to have a go at PUC. The club sports a policy of team spirit, where all members help each other to technically progress. Practiced at the Stade Dalmasso in historic Montparnasse, this club welcomes lovers of the game, who have come to play for the past 100 years.

Golf

place du Château,
45330 Augerville-la-
Riviere
Map p.373 B2

Château d'Augerville

02 38 32 12 07 | www.chateau-augerville.com

Located 25km from Fontainebleu, this 18 hole, par 72 course is set within mature woodland covering 110 hectares. Designed by Olivier Dongradi, the course offers a number of challenges including water hazards. Midweek green fees start at €29 in low season, rising to €54 for a weekend round in high season. A host of other activities are offered at the château, including shooting and quadbiking.

Route de
Montmorency,
95330 Domont
Map p.378 C1

Golf de Domont

01 39 91 07 50 | www.golfdedomont.com

Set within the Montmorency forest 20km north of Paris, this 18 hole, par 71 course can be technical, with no two holes the same. The 15th enjoys beautiful views across one of the course's two lakes, and there's also a driving range, a pitch and putt area and two putting greens. Coaching is available, and the clubhouse has a restaurant and bar.

Route d'Orléans,
77300
Map p.373 B2

Golf de Fontainbleu

01 64 22 22 95 | www.golfdefontainebleau.org

Located in the Fontainbleu forest, this 18 hole, par 72 golf course offers narrow fairways bordered by mature trees, ferns and lilac and is one of the oldest greens in France. It was ranked by readers of *Golf European* as the best in the country in 2001 and continues to offer excellent facilities in beautiful surroundings.

60 rue du 19 janvier
Garches
Map p.378 A3

Golf de Saint-Cloud

01 47 01 01 85 | www.golfsaintcloud.com

This private club, formed in 1911, is rich in tradition, and has hosted the French Open 14 times. There are two 18 hole courses – the 5,945m, par 71 *parcours vert*, and the 4,824m, par 67 *parcours jaune*. The club is only open to members and their guests, except for July and August when non-members can play. Closed Mondays.

221

Golf Disneyland

Allée de la Mare Houleuse, 77700 Magny le Hongre Magny le Hongre Map p.373 B2

01 60 45 68 90 | www.disneylandparis.com/fr/golf

Golf purists may not approve, but the facilities here at Golf Disneyland are more than adequate. The Ronald Fream designed course consists of three nine-hole courses which can be played separately or combined to form a longer challenge. There's a 35 bay driving range, and a putting green in the shape of Mickey's head. A bar and restaurant await in the clubhouse, and you can even stock up on equipment in Goofy's Pro Shop.

Golf du Bois de Boulogne

Hippodrome d'Auteuil 16th Map p.394 B4 16

01 44 30 70 00 | www.golfduboisdeboulogne.com

A little closer to home then the other courses listed here, Golf du Bois de Boulogne is situated in the middle of the Hippodrome d'Auteuil in the 16th. It's not a full-blown course, but a practice area allowing golfers to perfect their swing. There's also a 'crazy golf' area with bunkers and greens. This is a public facility open to non-members, although membership is available, allowing reduced entry fees.

Les Bordes

Les Bordes Saint Laurent-Nouan Map p.373 B2

02 54 87 72 13 | www.lesbordes.com

Designed by Robert von Hagge, the 18 hole course of Les Bordes was formerly a hunting estate of Baron Marcel Bich, the maker of the Bic pen. The challenging 7,062 yard, par 72 woodland course is considered to be one of the finest in France and has won *Golfjournal*'s Travel Oscar for Best European Golf Course. Check out the Rodin replica statues lining the driveway as you enter, including one of the writer Balzac striking his forehead with the heel of his hand in exasperation, as if he's missed a putt.

Paris Golf & Country Club

121 rue du Lieutenant-Colonel de Montbrison Rueil-Malmaison Map p.378 B2

01 47 77 64 00 | www.pariscountryclub.com

This nine-hole, par 35 course is set within the Hippodrome de Saint-Cloud racecourse, 2km to the west of the Bois de Boulogne. In addition to the course, with its share of bunkers and water hazards, there's a large 200 berth driving range, separate pitch and putt areas, two putting greens, and zones to practice chipping and bunker play. The golf course is open from 08:00 to 21:00 in the summer, and 08:30 to 18:30 in winter. The club also offers other sports including tennis, volleyball, basketball, football and swimming.

Paris International Golf Club

2 ave du Golf, 78280 Guyancourt Map p.378 A4

01 30 43 36 00 | www.golf-national.com

Surrounding the historic Chateau of Versailles is the famous Albatros course at Le Golf National designed by Hubert Chesneau and Robert Von Hagge. As a cross between a target course and a links course, this is a clay based, lengthy (over 7,000 yards) par 72. It is not only recognised as one of the top courses in Europe, but has also hosted the French Open. There are three courses from which to choose, but most people make a bee-line for the championship Albatros, because it is here where the challenge awaits.

Vaucouleurs

Rue de l'église Civry la Forêt Map p.378 B2

01 34 87 62 29 | www.vaucouleurs.fr

Situated west of Paris, Vaucouleurs offers two very different courses to golf enthusiasts; Les Vallons is a real links course 5,638 metres long with a par of 70, while La Rivière, par 73 and 6,138 metres is typical for this part of France. With a bar, restaurant and pro shop on-site this is the perfect countryside course and will suit golfers of all abilities to a tee.

Hang Gliding

Bondoufle
Map p.373 B2

Les Voyageurs du Ciel

01 60 66 47 47 | *http://ulmdelta.free.fr*

Situated outside the Périphérique in Bondoufle is the École Delta of the Voyageurs du Ciel club. The 65 feet buttes are used to practice gliding, and are perfect for the beginner. The trainers, who have more than 25 years of experience, are happy to speak English, so no need to recall how to say 'help' in French. Start with the four-hour 'discovery session' which will familiarise you with the equipment, takeoff procedures, and have you gliding (albeit just a few inches off the ground) in no time. If that whets your appetite, go for the five-session camp where you'll learn all the practical and theoretical knowledge you need for your first *grand vol*, or big flight. Afterwards, you'll probably decide to join the club, at which point, you can watch and learn how gliders are made. The club also offers microlight (ultralight) training at its site in Le Fay, 40km to the south-east of Fontainebleau.

Horse Riding

Other options **Farm & Stable Tours** p.197

rue Clos de la
Bonne, 77760
Recloses
Map p.373 B2

Centre Equestre de Recloses

01 64 24 21 10 | *www.cheval-en-foret.com*

Annie Durieux and Sandra Urban would make anyone feel good about being on a horse, so if this is your first time, you're in great hands and if you're accomplished, you're at a great place. Located near Recloses (just south of Paris), this school provides jaunts through the woods, training courses including jumping, short sessions, long sessions and continual sessions, little rides through the quaint village of Recloses and excursions to other parts of France. The one thing you will leave knowing, for sure, is to how to properly care for a horse, because Annie and Sandra are amenable, professional horse lovers above all.

Horseball

Route Muette
à Neuilly
16th
Ⓜ Porte Dauphine
Map p.395 D1 **17**

Centre Hippique Touring Club de France

01 45 01 20 88 | *www.chtcf.com*

Rumour has it that the game was developed long ago by Argentineans who galloped along the Patagonian desert and tossed about a live duck inside a leather pouch. Fact has it that in 1970, the French civilised the game and claimed it as their own. Horseball consists of two teams on horses, each with their own net, and a ball that resembles a basketball with leather handles. Each team has 10 seconds to pick up the ball while the horse is galloping at full speed, then passing the ball to make the net in time to score. It's a bit of a mix between rugby and basketball but is actually a very safe sport that many kids play and it's fairly easy to grasp with just one good lesson. Horseball even counts country musician Shania Twain as a fan.

Ice Hockey

Other options **Ice Skating** p.224

8 blvd de Bercy
12th
Ⓜ Bercy
Map p.411 E3 **18**

Club des Français Volants de Paris

01 40 02 60 16 | *www.francais-volants.org*

There's no reason to leave your hockey skates behind just because the Champs-Élysées isn't known for icing over. Paris has its own ice hockey (hockey sur glace) team, the Français Volants. The club has its home in the breathtakingly modern and grass-

223

topped 17,000 seat stadium at Bercy and is always on the lookout for new members. Gender is of no concern; as long as you are over 3 years old, you can play. The Français Volants also fields competitive teams, which can be found weekday evenings at Porte 28: Patinoire Sonja Henie at the Bercy omnisports complex. After working up a sporting appetite, Bercy Village is loaded with great restaurants.

Ice Skating

Other options **Ice Hockey** p.223

8 blvd de Bercy
12th
Ⓜ Bercy
Map p.411 E3 18

Bercy
01 40 02 60 60 | www.bercy.fr

Take the futuristic Meteor metro line 14 from the Opera to Bercy Village's cour St-Emilion and look for the Palais Omnisports de Paris-Bercy. It's a pyramid shaped building, with grass serving as the outer walls, and inside you'll find competitive sports, as well as climbing, football and equestrian events. There's also the Dote d'une Patinoire – the ice skating rink – which is big even by Paris standards and has an incredible lighting and sound system. Bercy is yet to be discovered by tourists, so you'll be sharing the ice with a few French.

Jeu de Paume

74 ter rue Lauriston
16th
Ⓜ Boissière
Map p.386 B4 20

Jeu de Paume Squash Club
01 47 27 46 86 | www.jdpsquash.com

Jeu de Paume was the oldest club for the popular 16th century namesake sport and is now the only remaining place to play. Jeu de Paume (also known as 'real tennis') is a cross between squash and tennis. You start with a racket and a net, but any ball served must touch the roof before it falls into play. After that, expect a lot of wall and roof rebounding and a lot of fun. You don't have to be a member to play the game but you have to pay each time you play if you're not a member. The pros do speak French… even though they're English. If you're lucky enough to discover the pleasure of this game and the members of the club, remind yourself that you're not only playing a sport, but you're taking part in a cultural inheritance. For those who don't know how to play, you can take lessons, and there's a much-needed sauna waiting for afterwards.

Jorkyball

21/23 rue du
Petit Albi, 95891
Cergy Pontoise
Ⓡ Cergy – Saint-Christophe
Map p.373 B1

Jorkyball vs Pro
01 30 31 06 91 | www.jorkyball-vs-pro.com

Take four people, two on each team, a very small cage with some markings and a ball and you've got Jorkyball. The sport prohibits any bodily contact and is a cross between soccer and squash, but without the use of the head or hands. A match consists of three sets of seven goals and, as with soccer, there's a goal net at each end. However, you can't pass the centre line without the ball, take the ball out of the penalty line or bounce the ball off your head... this is a game about footwork, speed and a lot of forethought. Jorkyball is a game perfect for kids or adults. It's an intense sport, but one that doesn't require a lot of running!

Kids' Activities

Paris is packed with parks, museums and unexpected discoveries designed to delight *les enfants*. In the great outdoors, Jardin d'Acclimation (p.185) boasts a wealth of fun-filled activities for kids. There's a carousel, rides, a small train that's been around since

1880, a mammoth rope tent, toboggan slides, a pony club, a circus, a practice range for golf with lessons, different types of gardens and lots of places to eat.

Jardin des Tuileries (p.184) is the ideal destination after you've lugged your kids around the Louvre. You'll find a circular basin where children float colourful toy wooden sailboats, see puppet shows, ride ponies and a carousel, not to mention the nearby striped Colonnes de Buren at Palais Royale.

In the vast Cité des Sciences (p.169) you and the kids can experience a true park-museum hybrid. From the Park de la Villette that has the giant buried bicycle sculpture to a giant dragon slide, to the interactive facilities inside the museum, the 3D video planetarium, the pilot simulator in the cinaxe, and the Geode with the giant 3,200sqft hemispheric screened movie, the whole family will be occupied for days. Plan the day around a Canal St Martin cruise which brings you up to the Ourcq canal.

After all that fresh air, Les Catacombes de Paris (p.166) provide the perfect eerie antidote. This dark cavernous underground tomb is exactly where your kids will want to go after they've seen the Eiffel Tower. There are hoards of skulls and bones, carefully stacked centuries ago by Carrières and there's a reverence that even children seem to understand without being told. Afterwards, circle back around to the front door of the Catacombes and cross the street to have a *café* at Le Rendez Vous Denfert, overlooking the reproduction of the regal Lion of Belfort Statue, designed by the Statue of Liberty designer Frederic Bartoldi.

Knitting

37 ave de l'Opéra
2nd
Ⓜ *Opéra*
Map p.388 C4 **21**

Café-Tricot at Brentano's
01 42 61 52 50 | www.brentanos.fr

Just walking into Brentano's near the old Opera in Paris, you might be tempted to remortgage your house to buy books. But knitters beware, it only gets worse. Head downstairs to the lower level, find a little spot to squeeze into during knitting night and pull out your knitting needles. You'll soon be spinning a bilingual yarn with others just like you. Even though the knitting circle is free, you might just spend your metro fare on all those delightful knitting books surrounding you, but at least you can whip up a scarf to keep you warm on the walk home.

Language Schools

38 ave de l'Opéra
2nd
Ⓜ *Opéra*
Map p.388 C4 **22**

Berlitz
01 44 94 50 00 | www.berlitz.fr

Berlitz offers fast, solid language courses, but one of the best things about taking classes here are the other students; they come from all over the world, so you get to see how others adapt to the language. If your head starts to hurt, just take a break to look out the window at the famous Opèra to get rejuvenated for the next round of conjugating verbs. And conjugate your verbs you will; this is very structured learning.

29 rue de Lisbonne
8th
Ⓜ *Europe*
Map p.387 F2 **23**

Institut Parisien de Langue et de Civilisation Françaises
01 40 56 09 53 | www.institut-parisien.com

Intensive courses, one-on-one courses, group courses, tailor-made courses and effective conversation courses effective are all offered, along with courses on culture, business language and history. And, if that's not enough, you're just a few blocks off the Champs-Élysées, which means that after you've learned your *avoirs* and *êtres*, you can reward yourself with some retail therapy – conducted in your newly acquired language, of course.

225

Libraries

Other options **Second-Hand Items** p.278, **Books** p.251

10 rue du
Général Camou
7th
Ⓜ *Pont de l'Alma*
Map p.396 C2 24

American Library in Paris
01 53 59 12 60 | www.americanlibraryinparis.org

Paris has its own system of municipal lending libraries through which anyone may borrow books free of charge but, quite problematically for English speakers, the vast majority of the books are in French. Help is at hand at the American Library in the 7th *arrondissement*, known to be the biggest American library in Europe. Whether you're a member or just a one-time visitor, you might want to check out their Evenings with the Author series on Wednesdays. Take a peek into the library with a €12 day pass (but at this price you might want to spring for the €15 one-week membership), or if you are in Paris for longer, you might want to look into the range of membership options on their website.

Martial Arts

87 rue de Vaugirard
6th
Ⓜ *Vaugirard*
Map p.408 A1 25

Taïki Club
01 45 40 92 03 | www.taikiclub.com

Tucked away in a gym in the 6th *arrondissement* of Paris, this Shotokan-style karate club has been the Champion of Paris in technique for 20 consecutive years, as well as the Champion of Île-de-France in competition in 2006. Taïki Karate takes new students and members, of experience levels and all ages, starting from 4 years. If you have no experience or training in karate you can try a free lesson or, for those under 14, one whole month's worth of training free with professor Daniel Naussy, a certified member of the Japan Karate Association.

Motorsports

90 rue
d'Aguesseau, 92100
Boulogne-Billancourt
Ⓜ *Billancourt*
Map p.378 A3

Avenir Consult Compétition
01 55 60 09 11 | www.stage911.com

This is a real racing school, with professional drivers who show you how to navigate racing cars. Start with a training course that teaches the importance of braking, trajectories and more, and then hit the road. After 15 turns at the wheel of a Porsche, you'll get to power up and try the Ferrari F355 Challenge. Then it's onto the five mile circuit course Val d'Or, near Versailles, where you can have your real moment under the Mario Andretti sun. Professional racers spend a half day with you to teach you what horse power really means, and you even go home with a diploma. If your French is iffy, asking for an English speaking instructor is a must.

Music Lessons

Other options **Music, DVDs &
Videos** p.272, **Singing** p.230,
Dance Classes p.218

5 rue des Batignolles
17th
Ⓜ *Rome*
Map p.388 B1 26

Learn & Fun
01 42 94 85 31
www.learnandfun.com

Pleasure is the aim at Learn and Fun, where serious guitar lessons are taught in an unserious manner. The atmosphere is convivial and the instructors will make you want to spring

Musicians by Place des Vosges

from your chair, heading out the door strumming and singing. For those who can't tune their voice, these boys won't let you leave without learning how to tune your guitar. Classes are held in small groups so if your French isn't really up to par, ask for a one-on-one in English. Oh, and one more thing, if you want to start off playing your favourite song, this is the place that will let you start with 'Hey Jude' instead of do-re-mi.

80 rue Daguerre
14th
Ⓜ Raspail
Map p.408 B4 **27**

Paris Accordeon

01 43 22 13 48 | *www.parisaccordeon.com*

If you're a music lover, how can you not learn how to pump out 'La Vie en Rose' through the bellows while in Paris? Lessons are available either on diatonic or chromatic accordions, but for authenticity, a diatonic accordion is the French squeezebox of choice. You can rent or buy, then give it a day lesson (in French only) and see how it goes. Once you can coordinate your right hand to play the keyboard, and your left hand to manipulate the bass harmony keys, you'll be so chuffed with yourself that you'll want to learn it all.

Paintballing

36 rue de Saussure
17th
Ⓜ Malesherbes
Map p.381 F4 **28**

Universal Paintball Terrain

01 48 88 07 97 | *www.universal-paintball.com*

Don your *anti-buée* protective mask, snatch up your biodegradable, multicoloured paint capsules, get snug with your semi-automatic air compressed Lanceur and get ready to hammer. The grounds here are dug up, carved out, hacked away and jam-packed fun. The Labyrinth is full of multiple bushes and shrubbery so it's every man for himself, while The Fort is strategic and The Valley is loaded with superb ambush spots and bunkers. You can also find Boost-Air (upon advanced request), play fast, easily-spotted Hyberball, and Universal Paintball has also started a circuit of extreme xball if shooting people with paint in the normal way just isn't enough.

Parachuting

Aérodrome de
Dieppe, 76550 Saint
Aubin sur Scie
Map p.373 B1

Air Libre Parachutisme

06 07 72 09 88 | *www.airlibre-parachutisme.com*

Unless you want your derriere to land on the point of the Eiffel Tower, if you're interested in parachuting it's best to head out of town to Saint Aubin sur Scie, approximately two hours north of Paris. Start in the instruction room where you learn everything you need, including how to pack the parachute and, perhaps crucially, how to say no if you decide not to jump at the last minute. Then it's off to the Cessna Soloy 207 for you, to be rigged, suited up and dared to have the time of your life. And after, there's a bar, where you might just want to order a large drink.

Pétanque

If running around Paris has you a bit fatigued, try playing a game that requires you to stand still; pétanque. The name comes from the Provençal 'pés tanqués' or 'stuck feet' and players on two opposing teams each have a set number of metal balls which they toss towards a smaller ball called a cochonnet

Pétanque by the Eiffel Tower

(jack). The player's feet must remain on the ground within a small circle while throwing, and a team wins a round by placing the ball closest to the cochonnet. One of the advantages of the game is that it can be played on almost any surface, although the best pitches are often made from small gravel as seen in many parks across Paris. Good places to look for pick-up games include the Champ de Mars (p.212), the Jardin du Luxembourg (p.184) or, best, Arènes de Lutèce (p.164).

Photography

6 rue du Pas de
la Mule
3rd
Ⓜ *Chemin Vert*
Map p.400 C3 29

Photography Workshop in Paris
06 33 65 51 19 | www.davidphenry.com

The very amenable David Henry, an internationally renowned photographer, teaches one-on-one courses on how to take photos that capture the moment. Regardless if you want to take the classic shot of the Eiffel Tower or an off-beat picture of a Parisian dog, his lessons encompass all the important elements that will help ensure that you'll not only have the most original photos, but you'll never look through a lens the same way again. One session runs from four to six very creative hours.

8 rue Jules Vallès
11th
Ⓜ *Charonne*
Map p.401 F4

Spéos
01 40 09 18 58 | www.speos.fr

Learn to develop a distinct photographic signature of your own by going under the professional tutelage of these instructors who have worked for Louis Vuitton, Anne Cartier-Bresson, Galeries Lafayette, Printemps, Reuters and more. Summer workshops are available, as are longer courses, and all courses are tailored to turning you into a professional photographer. This is serious training as opposed to aim and click and you'll be immersed in texture, light reflection and studio work, along with aesthetics and photo styling.

Picnicking

Le Bon Marché's grocery store, La Grande Épicerie, is where you should head to snap up some great salads, prepared dishes, cheeses, and fruit. Alternatively, visit one of the many street markets (p.298) for fresh picnic fodder. Then hop on the metro to your favourite park, pick a spot and prepare to picnic Parisian style. The Parc des Buttes Chaumont (p.185) is possibly the most beautiful park in town, and one of the least crowded too.

In Parc de la Villette (p.185) during the months of July and August, you can rent a lawn chair or bring a blanket to sit and watch films on a giant screen at Cinema en Plein Air. Ben & Jerry's gives free ice cream on certain film nights, and those who rent lawn chairs often get discounts for future tickets. Arrive early to find a place to spread out, and expect the film to start late, as summer nights in Paris don't get dark until well after 21:30. This is a perfect place to share a night-time picnic with food purchased from any Parisian market.

Rollerblading & Rollerskating

place Raoul Dautry
14th
Ⓜ *Montparnasse*
Bienvenüe
Map p.408 A2 30

Pari-Roller
www.pari-roller.com

This is unadulterated street skating at its free-for-all best, and most of the participants are out for the wild ride. Join over 10,000 people every Friday night as they blast off from Montparnasse, go for almost 20 miles around the uneven paved streets of the city, and then end up back at the start around 01:00. Full protection is a must; these are serious skaters. For those just learning the heel stop and stagger stance techniques, Sunday afternoons at Place de la Bastille won't be quite so daunting. You'll get to slowly roll with bikers, skateboarders, runners and see Paris in full safe daylight.

Rowing

15 blvd Marcel Paul, 93450
L'Île-Saint-Denis
Map p.378 C1

Rowing Club
01 42 43 61 95 | www.rowing-club.fr

This is a friendly crowd that will make a non-rower want to take up the oars. Join a team or learn from scratch, via any type of boat that amuses you. Every boat is covered here, from the two person skiff, all the way up to the eight-seater with a coxswain. Lessons are intense, as these members want you to be the best skiffor and skiffeuse possible. This is as

Rollerblading near the Grand Palais

much a community as a rowing club, so expect organised excursions, barbecues, competitions, festivals and plenty of time spent behind the oars.

Rugby

17 ave Pierre de Coubertin
13th
Ⓡ *Cité Universitaire*
Map p.419 E4 🟦**31**

Paris Université Club (PUC)
01 44 16 62 69 | www.puc-rugby.com

The French love rugby, and although most play in the South of France, that doesn't mean you can't form a scrum in the City of Light. Regardless of your skill level, you'll find a team at Rugby PUC, the largest rugby club in Paris, played at Stade Charlety in the 13th *arrondissement*. The club is made up of teams of amateurs who love the game with a passion. Plus, it's the only French club directed by its players: 500 players divided into 19 teams (including one female), all committed to winning championships. La Troisieme Mi-Temps is unparalleled in Paris so the instructors are concerned with performance, building confidence, striving to lessen field brutality while helping rugby grow into an even bigger Paris pastime.

Worth a Try

The sister pub to the famous watering hole in Dublin, Kitty O'Shea's (p.355) is so Irish that it's kitsch, but if it's rugby on the big screen and Guinness in the gut that you need, you have come to the right place. Expect to meet just about anyone who speaks English, as well as some thirtysomething French and, of course, the Irish team can be found when they're in town.

Running

Paris has everything for the runner; long, even tracks for the injury-prone, beautiful paths through the city or gorgeous runs around the Bois de Boulogne. Less serious runners are best on loose gravel paths at the Jardin du Luxembourg in the 6th but if you're after hilly terrain for that cross country feel, head to Parc des Buttes-Chaumont in the 19th; or for the dirt tracks go to Bois de Vincennes in the 12th. For the marathon trainer, it's probably best to head to the southern suburban Parc de Sceaux (where you can also play tennis, soccer, rugby and even fish) with its hectares of great dirt paths cutting a swath through lines of majestic trees... then hit the crepe stands for a hefty carb intake.

229

Scouts & Guides

65 rue Glacière
13th
Ⓜ *Glacière*
Map p.419 E1 32

Les Scouts et Guides de France

01 44 52 37 21 | www.sgdf.fr

Scouting (or *le scoutisme*) has been in France for 100 years. However, it has had a turbulent and even sectarian history; many disparate organisations have carried the scouting flag and this one, at 138,500 members, is itself a fusion of two organisations with Catholic overtones. The Scouts and Guides do all the traditional scouting activities such as camping and backpacking, but the emphasis in France appears to be more on civic engagement and social interaction rather than the traditional outdoorsy focus.

Singing

Other options **Music Lessons** p.226

41 auai Victor
Hugo, 94500
Champigny-sur-Marne
Ⓡ *Champigny*
Map p.379 D3

La Guinguette de l'Île de Martin-Pêcheur

01 49 83 03 02 | www.guinguette.fr

This little establishment is always ready for a festival. It thrives off nostalgia for the hundreds of *guinguettes* that used to line the Seine and the Marne; these outdoor cafes served *guinguet* (a sour white wine) and food to the workmen of the area, all to the tune of traditional French music and dancing. Come to sing and dance and experience the revival of this old tradition. The music is mostly French chanson with a lot of accordion and guitar, but you can also hear jazz, swing and rock. In addition to the seating under festooned trestles, you can also find a place in the spacious restaurant or simply eat at the crêperie to its side. Saturday nights are the busiest and the best, so future Edith Piafs should reserve.

Skateboarding

The Trocadéro (map p.396 A1) in the 7th is probably the best venue in the Paris skateboard world and has hosted the World Cup in the past. Not only are there super views of the Eiffel Tower, but you'll also find great flat surfaces with wide steps and different levels. You can also cross the river to the Champ de Mars in front of the Eiffel Tower; this is where skateboarders first started to hit the City of Light, and it's really the perfect place to have someone snap a photo of you doing a 180 frontside ollie. Around the Fontaine des Innocents at Les Halles (map p.399 F2), you'll find exceptional curbs around the fountain, but do expect a non-skateboard crowd too. Mekanism (www.mekanismskateboards.com) offers high-end, specialised French skateboards designed on limited edition decks by up and coming artists.

Social Groups

Other options **Support Groups** p.118

8 rue de Belloy
16th
Ⓜ *Boissière*
Map p.386 B4 33

The British & Commonwealth Women's Association

01 47 20 50 91 | http://bcwa.paris.online.fr

If you're British, married to a Brit or even if you just want to be a Brit this is where you go after you've had one of those particularly bad Paris days when the taxi driver ignores you and the woman at Monoprix snarls at you for not weighing your veggies. Forget your troubles and pick up a game of Scrabble or Mah Jong here, or dig into some Needlepoint, or even see a chick flick. Still not interested? Then there's yoga, Pilates, scrapbooking, or you can play bridge or enjoy the library. The main point is that you're away from the men and the French... and you know what they say about both: can't live with them, can't live without them!

20 blvd du
Montparnasse
15th
Ⓜ *Duroc*
Map p.408 A1 34

WICE

01 45 66 75 50 | www.wice-paris.org

WICE is the most diverse Anglophone social group in Paris. All genders and nationalities are welcome (they used to be called Women's Institute for Continuing Education, but have since changed to their acronym in order to welcome everyone). They offer courses in art history, languages but it is the creative writing department that made them famous, boasting programmes for travel writing, erotic writing, blog writing, and more. In keeping with their literary theme, they have a bilingual book group and produce their own literary journal. If writing isn't your thing, you can become involved with community hikes, meetings and opportunities to volunteer in just about any interest of your choice. They also have a cyber-group online where you can go to ask questions about living in Paris.

Special Needs Activities

Other options **Special Needs Education** p.122

44 rue Louis Lumière
20th
Ⓜ *Porte de Bagnolet*
Map p.403 D2 35

Fédération Française Handisport

01 40 31 45 00 | www.handisport.org

Historically France has virtually ignored the disabled but now there is a very developed system of handicapped sports, and the Parisian region in particular has a wide array of 'handisports'. There are over 120 clubs in Île-de-France that boast sports as diverse as basketball, fencing, tennis and sailing, to name a few. The downside is that the system is decentralised and federal; the most the national organisation can do is direct you to clubs in your area that might offer the sport you wish to pursue. Two highly clubs recommended in Paris central are Paris Jean-Bouin (01 47 43 94 92) for tennis and Entente Sportive Handi Paris (01 47 89 46 62) for fencing and swimming.

Squash

14 rue Achille
Martinet
18th
Map p.383 D3 36

Squash Montmartre

01 42 55 38 30

Forget that there's a miniature motor raceway track inside this sports club, the real story is squash, with a restaurant and bar for after a good game. Located north of Sacré-Coeur just over the Montmarte Hill, you'll get a good warm up before you even step foot in the quarter court. You may well see some famous squash players at this sporting hotspot; there aren't that many places in Paris to play squash so everyone heads here for a game – and these four glazed courts have huge windows that allow you to watch and be watched.

Swimming

4 rue Louis Armand
15th
Ⓜ *Balard*
Map p.405 E1 37

Aquaboulevard

01 40 60 10 00 | www.aquaboulevard.com

The mammoth Aquaboulevard is almost 23,000 square feet, making it the biggest water park in Europe. You'll find 11 enormous toboggans, including the 80 metre Aquaplouf, a 84°F pool with rolling waves, a water mushroom fountain, manmade geysers, water cannons, swimming lessons, fun water toys, palm trees, a sauna, jacuzzis, restaurants, a hamman and cinemas. Forest Hills (p.236), Europe's largest fitness club, is also on site providing facilities for tennis, squash, racquetball, badminton, ping-pong, and as well as a gym so you can get your body ready for the (faux) beach.

Bibliothèque
François Mitterrand
13th
Map p.411 D4 **38**

Piscine Joséphine-Baker

01 52 61 46 50

Josphine Baker, the actress and civil rights leader, always did make a splash so it was appropriate when the new *piscine* in the 13th was built, that it be named after her. The top slides back on this pool, exposing swimmers to the sky above and the Seine below and all around. Paris' newest swimming pool is a floating barge of aqua. Water is pumped in from the Seine, clarified, chlorinated, then swum in, cleaned out and put right back into the river. Most swimmers don't speak English, so remember to duck if you hear someone yell 'Attention!' because a cannonball may be coming your way.

Hotel Ritz Paris
1st
Ⓜ *Opéra*
Map p.398 B1 **10**

Ritz Health Club

01 43 16 30 60 | www.ritzparis.com

Certainly the most beautiful place to backstroke in all of France is the *piscine* at the health club in the Ritz Hotel. With marble Corinthian columns surrounding the whirlpool, you'll feel as if you're in ancient Rome. The pool has jet-streams, as well as underwater sound for complete relaxation. After a good swim, walk up the stairs under the fluted columns to the Mezzanine bar, order a fruit cocktail (the orange and carrot juice is a bit of heaven) and have a light lunch.

Table Tennis

25 ave de la
Porte d'Ivry
13th
Ⓜ *Porte d'Ivry*
Map p.421 D3 **40**

Paris 13 TT

01 45 85 19 50 | www.paris13tt.org

Paris 13 TT, with over 300 members, professes to be the largest club in Paris, and by table count alone, they're probably right; the club sports a room with 24 tables, with each table separated by tournament-style dividers. The table tennis school offers summer camps for the younger crowd, private lessons for the desperate and competitions for all levels. The club is known to be inclusive and accessible to those who speak little French so joining up is a great way to integrate yourself into the culture, as well as to improve your game.

Tennis

Jardin du
Luxembourg
6th
Ⓡ *Luxembourg*
Map p.409 D2 **41**

Municipal Courts

01 43 25 79 18

Paris has 41 municipal tennis centres, with a variety of outdoor and covered courts with assorted playing surfaces. The most popular courts (six in all) are located in the Jardin du Luxembourg. Far from city noise, all you'll hear is the squeaking of the tennis shoes, the ball popping and the occasional grunt from a frustrated player. To play you'll need a *carte Paris tennis* pass, which also allows you to reserve a court and get discounted lessons from instructors who often speak English. Visit www.paris.fr for more information. While online, do reserve the court of your choice, because if you just show up you'll most likely only be allowed 30 minutes of court time.

121 rue du
Lieutenant-Colonel
de Montbrison
Rueil-Malmaison
Map p.378 B2

Paris Golf & Country Club

01 47 77 64 00 | www.pariscountryclub.com

About 10 minutes west of the Arc de Triomphe are 21 courts (asphalt and synthetic) for the player who wants to join a club and profit from the benefits of being a member of the French Federation of Tennis. The young teaching staff of pros are at the ready to give lessons, but the real benefits of joining the club are that you'll also have access to the nine-hole golf course, chlorinated pool, fitness centre, swanky club house and the snazzy restaurant for when you're ready to take off those sweat bands.

Volleyball

The Paris Plage urban beach (p.183) is shipped in and set up along the Seine from mid July to mid August, and most of the sand is taken up by three volleyball courts. There are tournaments and competitions that take place but there are also plenty of casual games. To find your nearest club, and for details of the national organising body, visit the website of the Fédération Française de Volley-Ball: www.volley.asso.fr.

Water Polo

Piscine Hébert, 2 rue des Fillettes
18th
Ⓜ **Marx Dormoy**
Map p.378 D2

Club Montmartre Natation Sauvetage
01 48 44 47 17 | www.amns.fr

It's time to score a goal, make a dry or a wet pass, but no splashing the opposing team; this isn't rough neck water polo from the past, but civilised play. Don a tight bathing suit, a bathing cap, pay €200 for the year and jump on in. Regardless of your sex, you're invited to play in the Hébert swimming pool.

Waterskiing

1 allée du bord de l'eau
16th
Ⓜ **Pont de St Cloud**
Map p.378 B2

Ski Nautique Club de Paris
01 47 71 76 01

Take Juliette Binoche's lead in *Les Amants du Pont-Neuf* and waterski on the romantic, yet toxically sludgy Seine. In the suburbs of Paris, find the welcoming Ski Nautique Club de Paris, where you can ski, ski barefoot or wakeboard. The water is generally calm, and the skiing takes place between the Pont de Suresnes and the Pont de Sèvres, with a grand view of the Arche de la Défense. Visitors, novices and competitors are all welcome and, of course, you can also join the club.

Wine Tasting

6 rue de Bourbon le Chateau
6th
Ⓜ **Mabillon**
Map p.399 D4 44

La Dernière Goutte
01 43 29 11 62 | www.ladernieregoutte.com

Stop in this shop to buy booze, join free wine tastings on Saturdays or even to meet a featured wine grower who will educate you in the joys of vinos. The store is small but the atmosphere is lovely, and American-born Juan Sanchez knows how to pick excellent estate-bottled. Need food with your wine? Head down the block to La Dernière Goutte (p.233) in the 6th, also owned by Sanchez and his partner.

100 rue de la Folie Méricourt
11th
Ⓜ **Goncourt**
Map p.400 C1 45

Ô Château
08 00 80 11 48 | www.o-chateau.com

Olivier Magny, the 'Jamie Oliver of wine', isn't just a wine expert, he's a humorous wine expert with not a sniff of the pretentious about him. At Ô Château you don't have to feel intimidated that you aren't fluent in wine knowledge. Magny, who is a visiting sommelier at Hôtel de Crillon, not only chooses unique wines, but enhances each tasting with such fantastic knowledge that you'll never order undrinkable wine again. Different options are offered, including tastings that involve cheese for that truly French experience, customised tastings and even romantic tastings on top of the Eiffel Tower. Santé!

Ô Château

Cycling

Various Locations

Tour de France
www.letour.fr

The Tour de France is certainly the best-known bicycle race in the world, and the only major race followed by a non-cycling audience. It's a three week long journey through France, and occasionally neighbouring countries, that's split into 20 one-day individual race stages. Look for distinctive jerseys that the cyclists are required to wear and are awarded after each stage: the *maillot jaune* (the yellow jersey) is worn by the leader; the *maillot vert* (green) is worn by the rider who has won the greatest number of points, which are awarded according to placement at each stage; and the *maillot vert* is a 'sprint' competition. Finally, the *maillot à pois rouges* (red polka dots) is awarded to the best climber on the mountainous stages. The race has a unique tradition; a rider is generally permitted to lead the race through his hometown or on his birthday.

Golf

Various Locations

Open de France
www.opendefrance.fr

The Open de France first teed off in 1906, making it the oldest professional golf tournament on the continent and has been a member of the European Tour ever since it was inaugurated. With a prize fund of €4 million in 2006, it's clearly in the top echelon. And names like Massy, Braid, Ballesteros, and Montgomerie are all winners. The 2007 Open was hosted at the 7,202 yard Le Golf National, where the champion Graeme Storm, managed to make it to the top by conquering some of the hardest holes, bunkers and water hazards in Europe.

Horse Racing

Route des Tribunes
Bois de Boulogne
16th
Map p.394 C1

Le Prix de l'Arc de Triomphe
01 44 30 75 00 | www.france-galop.com

One fine spring day in April of 1857, Emperor Napoleon III and his wife floated lazily down the Seine in their private yacht to watch a race in the newly constructed Hippodrome de Longchamp, and today you can still see why this was a favourite haunt during the Second Empire. This 57 hectare horse racing facility, with four interlaced tracks of varying lengths, has retained the charm and verdure that became the subject of a few Manet paintings. Today, the biggest draw to the course is the annual Prix de l'Arc de Triomphe, which is the premier end-of-the-season (beginning of October) middle-distance race in Europe, featuring champions from all over the world. The track is a mile and a half long, with upward and downward sloped sections, and an exciting finish line, with a €1.5 million purse for the winning horse.

Tennis

Stade Roland Garros,
2 ave Gordon
Bennett
16th
Map p.404 B1 47

French Open
01 47 43 48 00 | www.fft.fr

The French Open, also known as the Tournoi de Roland-Garros, is one of the four annual Grand Slam tournaments. It's a two-week tournament that begins in May and ends in June and is also the premier clay court tournament in the world. Clay courts slow down the ball and allow for a higher bounce, factors which contribute to this tournament's reputation as the most physically demanding in the world. The Roland-Garros at Stade de France is a unique tournament, and it is advisable to reserve tickets well in advance.

Life in the fast lane?

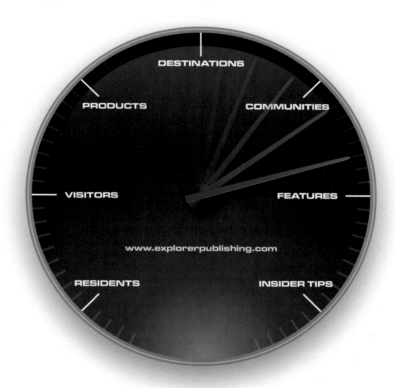

Life can move pretty quickly so make sure you keep in the know with regular updates from **www.explorerpublishing.com**

Or better still, share your knowledge and advice with others, find answers to your questions, or just make new friends in our community area

www.explorerpublishing.com – for life in real time

Gyms

Body Gym

*157 rue du Faubourg
Saint-Antoine
11th
Map p.401 E4 48*

01 43 42 42 33 | *www.bodygymparis.com*

This gym in the 11th has a good selection of fitness equipment, and numerous classes are offered in the large fitness room. Activities include Body Pump, step, stretching classes, Pilates and salsa dancing courses. There's a juice and snack bar and even a sunbed for when you're looking a bit pasty.

Club Med Gym

Various Locations

www.clubmedgym.com

Club Med operates 22 gyms in Paris, including 10 with swimming pools. Between them the gyms offer 50 activities, including Body Pump, aerobic workouts and dance classes. Yoga and Pilates classes are available, and most clubs also have a sauna. For location details see the website.

Club Montmartrois

*60 rue Ordener
18th
Map p.383 F1 49*

01 42 52 50 50 | *www.club-montmartrois.fr*

Established in 1966 this is definitely the old kid on the block, but don't let the age put you off. You'll find all the equipment you would expect to see in a modern gym, and a host of classes and activities are offered. If you're scared of commitment, you can try out a class for €10 before signing up. The company also operates two other gyms under the Club M brand, at 50 rue Duhesme in the 18th (01 42 54 49 88) and 87, blvd Vincent Auriol in the 13th(01 45 70 77 36).

Forest Hill

*4 rue Louis Armand
15th
Ⓜ Balard
Map p.411 D1 50*

01 40 60 10 00 | *www.forest-hill.com*

Forest Hill, along with its sister-water park, Aquaboulevard, is almost an institution in Paris. You can take dance classes, play table tennis, indoor and outdoor tennis, squash, racquetball, badminton, lift weights, take aerobics and cardio training classes, swim and relax in a hamman, sauna, jacuzzi and solarium. You could live here and, in fact, there's even a hotel connected with this centre as families come from miles around. This isn't your neighbourhood gym, but other than charm, it is lacking in nothing.

L'Usine

*8 rue de la
Michodière
2nd
Ⓜ Opéra
Map p.388 C4 51*

01 42 66 30 30 | *www.usineopera.com*

If you're one of those types who go to the gym to see and be seen, than L'Usine Opera is the number one place for you. Celebrities pump weights, cycle, row, run on the treadmill, get private coaching, take lessons in yoga, Pilates, boxing and anything cardio that burns calories for the waiting paparazzi. And you too can run with the celebs. You'll get a great workout here, starting with your biceps when you pull nearly €1,500 out of your pocket to become a member. To be fair, you are paying for the very best in state-of-the-art equipment, so get your trainers on.

Vit'Halles

Various Locations

01 42 77 21 71 | *www.vithalles.fr*

These eight flashy gyms across Paris boast everything you would expect and more, including Les Mills classes, a spa, weight rooms and personal training. Vit'Halles offers a day pass for €20 or various memberships, and is particularly popular with expats looking to get buff while indulging in the favourite Parisian pastime of people watching.

Beauty Salons

Other options **Perfumes & Cosmetics** p.274, **Beauty Training** p.213

350 rue Saint Honoré
1st
Ⓜ *Tuileries*
Map p.398 C1 52

Darphin Centre de Beauté
01 47 03 17 70

Rue St Honoré offers the best of everything and Darphin, one of the world's most renowned plant-based skin care companies, has opened a spa there. Follow the cobblestone courtyard where Joséphine married Napoleon and open the door. These five rooms are where you go for long sessions of deep phyto-draining masks, warm massages using essential oils, reflexology, finger-pressuring facials, and the feeling that all is good in the world. You come here to experience complete harmony.

Hairdressers

9 rue Guénégaud
6th
Ⓜ *Pont Neuf*
Map p.399 D3 53

Autour de Christophe Robin
01 42 60 99 15 | *www.colorist.net*

When we think of beauty, we tend to think of Parisian women, and Catherine Deneuve embodies this seductive species. Christophe Robin is her hair colourist of choice and now he has staked his claim on the charming rue Guénégaud. The atmosphere is comforting and chic; from a high-tech wire staircase to cute cow statues, there's humour to be found, along with a great head of hair. You can also get skin care, manicures, medical pedicures, and a 50 minute osteopathic treatment. This is indulgence at its best.

Health Spas

Other options **Massage** p.239

112 rue du
Faubourg Saint-
Honoré
8th
Ⓜ *Miromesnil*
Map p.387 F3 54

Anne Sémonin Atelier de Beauté
01 42 66 24 22 | *www.anne-semonin.de*

It's really no wonder that some of the most refined and sophisticated hotels in the world use Anne Sémonin products in their bathrooms. Neither is it a surprise to find the newest Anne Sémonin spa inside The Hôtel Bristol, one of Paris' most famous luxury hotels. Her treatments are renowned for being cures for jetlag and, after leaving, who's to argue? There are the usual spa offerings available but the facials are the main attraction; the Eye Contour Treatment helps ditch the dark under eye circles and the Revitalization Treatment is volcanic mud-induced euphoria.

62 avenue des
Champs-Élysées
8th
Ⓜ *Franklin D*
Roosevelt
Map p.387 E4

Institut Guerlain
01 45 62 52 57 | *www.guerlain.com*

Synonymous with luxury, Guerlain has successfully cornered the spa market with this tiled haven on the Champs-Élysées, which first opened 90 years ago. Designed by Andrée Putman in 2005, the spa's interior gleams with mosaic and glass but don't fear, there's substance as well as style available. Using the famed products, many treatments are on offer to lift you from exhausted expat to relaxed resident; choose from personalised facials, make up lessons and harmonising massages or even go for a full day experience.

62 rue Pierre Charron
8th
Ⓜ *George V*
Map p.387 D4 57

L'Espace Payot
01 45 61 42 08 | *www.payot.com*

The swimming pool at L'Espace Payot is a technically-lighted dream. Slip into a deep periwinkle water, with its massaging pulse places and aquatic music, or simply hit the aromatherapeutic jacuzzi. For those who feel the need to work out first, there's a personal trainer to help bend you with yoga, shape you with Pilates,

237

and sculpt you with muscle strengthening. A hairdresser, manicurist and pedicurist are also at the ready to pamper you. After all of that, fresh fruit juice and light snacks await you at the Payot bar.

La Bulle Kenzo

1 rue du Pont-Neuf
1st
M *Pont Neuf*
Map p.399 E2 **55**

01 45 61 42 08 | *www.labullekenzo.com*
Situated in the fashion label's flagship store, this futuristic spa will transport you from the busy streets to blissed-out luxury. Using coloured lights, state-of-the-art equipment and a healthy dose of humour (check out the website), this spa sets the modern standard in Paris. Choose from unique massages and facials or even take a siesta, but if it's your mind that needs therapy, then opt for 45 minutes of lying down and 'expressing yourself to your heart's content'.

Marc Dugast

11 rue Lobineau
6th
M *Mabillon*
Map p.399 D4 **56**

01 53 10 13 30 | *www.marcdugast.com*
It's all here; everything you've ever wanted to do with your appearance but didn't know you could do it in one place. Marc Dugast has developed a system that can turn you into a stylish Parisian overnight. Morphobeauté tweaks, cleans, exfoliates and clarifies your skin; Morphobien-être kneads, massages and more to your body; Morphorelooking sorts your rotten taste in clothes and Morphcoiffure creates salon-perfect hair. Before you know it, you're walking out the door, strutting your stuff on the Champs-Élysées looking French enough that the pickpockets will leave you alone.

The Spa

Four Seasons
Hôtel George V
8th
M *Alma – Marceau*
Map p.387 D4 **1**

01 49 52 70 00 | *www.fourseasons.com/paris*
Step back in time at this classically opulent hotel. The Spa is adorned with 18th century prints but there's nothing historic about the treatments on offer; from a chocolate body scrub to the Polynesian lagoon water facial, the experienced staff will pamper you to the point of passing out. Luxurious to the end, there's a private VIP room with a whirlpool, sauna, steam bath, two massage beds and music stations. If you're lucky enough to be staying at the hotel, you can have in-room massages to save you the bother of walking around in your robe.

The Spa, Four Seasons George V

Massage

Other options **Health Spas** p.237, **Reflexology & Massage Therapy** p.117

Various Locations

Cocoon

www.cocoonez-moi.com

There is nothing more relaxing than a massage, apart from a massage at home. The masseuses (male or female, at your request) at Cocoon come over, set up and chill you out with a choice of treatments, including Thai, reflexology, Shiatsu and their signature Cocoon Massage, a cross between Western and Eastern techniques, with four hands doing exquisite things to your muscles and spirit. The Vital Breath therapy is the ultimate in reducing tension; you not only learn to breathe again but after this, you can tackle the Chatelet metro at rush hour, no problem!

Pilates

41 rue de Richelieu
1st
Ⓜ Pyramides
Map p.399 D1 59

élément

01 40 20 42 62 | www.elementparis.com

élément is owned by a convivial crowd who teach yoga, massage and gyrokinesis (a yoga/tai-chi class that uncrunches your spine) but they're most well-known for their Pilates classes. It's been rumoured that élément first brought the workout to Paris, and it's obvious that they've got it down to a science. After bending, shaping and stretching, get a salt scrub and seaweed wrap, or go for some acupuncture.

39 rue du Temple
4th
Ⓜ Hôtel de Ville
Map p.400 A2

Le Studio Pilates de Paris

01 42 72 91 74 | www.studiopilatesdeparis.com

This studio was started by Phillipe Taupin, who introduced the method to France and was trained by the direct successor of Josef Pilates. Private and semi-private, as well as group mat classes, are available in English and French. With highly qualified teachers who are dedicated to improving your technique, you're guaranteed to see and feel results.

Yoga

5 rue Morand
11th
Ⓜ Parmentier
Map p.391 D4

Ashtanga Yoga

01 45 80 19 96 | www.ashtangayogaparis.fr

This intimate space is flooded with natural light and overlooks a Japanese zen garden to ensure total relaxation and concentration. With classes throughout the week you can discover Ashtanga in a group; or come for a private class - you can even gather some friends and attend together. The owners, Linda and Gérald, speak both French and English and you can find out more at their comprehensive website.

17 rue du
Faubourg Montmartre
9th
Ⓜ Grands Boulevards
Map p.389 E3 60

Bikram Yoga

01 42 47 18 52 | www.bikramyogaparis.com

Bikram has a total of 26 different postures, as well as two breathing exercises, so you can excel in the Half Moon, Tree, Spine Twisting, Half Tortoise or even the Wind Removing Position. The main difference between regular yoga and Bikram is the fact that you'll do these exercises in 105° heat. Don't forget your water because you'll lose lots of fluid during the 90 minute sessions. The heat will help you to get into poses you might not be able to achieve in a regular yoga environment and the more you sweat, the more toxins leave your body. You can rent a mat at the studio.

239

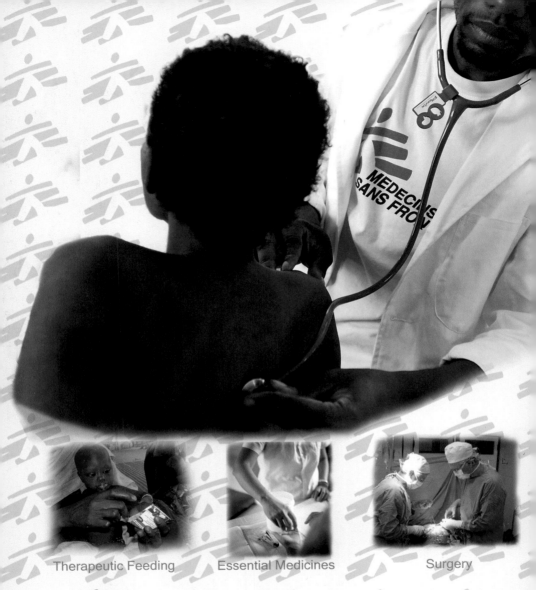

Therapeutic Feeding   Essential Medicines   Surgery

MEDECINS SANS FRONTIERES
أطبـــاء بـــلا حـــدود

Providing emergency medical
relief in over 70 countries.

help us help the helpless

Shopping

Shopping

Ah, Paris. City of light. A destination for lovers. The capital of…shopping? That's right, alongside romance and refinement, this is a city known for its fabulous retail culture. Here you will find the full range of shopping experiences, from department store chic to local shopping malls, open air markets and fantastic independent boutiques.

Fashion forward shoppers will love exploring the Marais and St-Germain, arty-types can find all manner of independent galleries up around Montmartre, lovers of luxury should make their way to the chichi avenue Montaigne while those seeking a different perspective can journey to the ethnic centre of Belleville in the 20th *arrondissement*, or Chinatown in the 13th.

Wherever in the city you are drawn to, it is worth keeping in mind the timing of Paris' two big sale periods before making any rash purchases. Over six weeks at the end of January and June, the whole city moves in to official sale mode. Reductions of up to 75% on all end-of-season stock makes for some amazing bargains with tourists flying in from all over the world to get in on the act.

Sales aside, the cost of living in Paris – though less expensive than that of London and New York – is by no means cheap. How expensive it is exactly depends largely on the neighbourhood which you choose to call home; you'll find that property, food, restaurants and bars are all more costly in well-to-do *arrondissements* like the 8th and the 16th compared to some of the city's eastern quarters such as the 19th and 20th. Prices on items such as white goods, electronics and homewares compare favourably with other European countries but unfortunately, the great deals to be found in Hong Kong and Singapore do not generally apply in Paris.

As for store assistants, be prepared to be meeted and greeted to within an inch of your tolerance. Expect a *bonjour* and *au revoir* and, in between, many questions regarding whether you need help, some special product, a skirt in another colour or size... you get the picture. So much attention can be disconcerting for those just wanting a quiet browse, however, simply letting staff know you would just like to be left to a look usually cuts off any over-enthusiastic advances.

Paris has two main rates of VAT tax. The base rate stands at 19.6%, with a reduced rate of 5.5% that mainly applies to cultural and food products. Some products, like medicines, face no tax costs at all.

From high fashion to health food, Paris has your retail requirements covered so get ready to test that credit card to the max. Bon shopping!

What & Where To Buy – Quick Reference

Alcohol	p.245	Electronics/Appliances	p.259	Lingerie	p.268	Shoes	p.279
Art	p.246	Eyewear	p.259	Luggage & Leather	p.269	Souvenirs	p.281
Art & Craft Supplies	p.246	Flowers	p.260	Medicine	p.270	Sports Goods	p.281
Baby Items	p.248	Food	p.261	Mobile Telephones	p.271	Stationery	p.282
Beachwear	p.249	Gardens	p.263	Music, DVDs & Videos	p.272	Tailoring	p.284
Bicycles	p.250	Gifts	p.264	Musical Instruments	p.272	Textiles	p.284
Books	p.251	Hardware & DIY	p.265	Outdoor Goods	p.273	Toys & Games	p.285
Camera Equipment	p.253	Health Food	p.265	Party Accessories	p.273	Wedding Items	p.286
Car Parts & Accessories	p.253	Home Furnishings	p.265	Perfumes & Cosmetics	p.274		
Clothes	p.254	Jewellery & Watches	p.267	Pets	p.277		
Computers	p.258	Kids' Items	p.268	Second-Hand Items	p.278		

Online Shopping

Just as with the rest of the world, Paris has become enamoured with the world of online shopping. Just start up your home computer to organise purchase and delivery of groceries, music and CDs, furnishings, paintings, home appliances, or even artist materials. Practically every site will deliver, with some, like FNAC, offering free postage within France. Others will charge delivery under a certain dollar purchase while others will still charge delivery based on weight and your chosen method of freight: over-land courier services are naturally less expensive than air freight. When the time comes to pay, have your credit card at the ready – these are universally accepted. Some companies will also accept money transfers from Paypal accounts.

Goods from international locations are generally not subject to rigorous inspections from French customs officials and, unlike Australia which bans import of many food types, there is very little that cannot be imported. As with most countries, rare and endangered animals and firearms are obvious exceptions.

Online Shopping	
www.amazon.fr	Books, CDs, computer programmes, games and videos.
www.darty.com	White goods and home electrical appliances.
www.fnac.com	Computers and computer equipment, cameras and telephones.
www.laredoute.fr	Absolutely everything available from fashion and beauty to furnishings and computer games.
www.ooshop.com	Carrefour's online grocery shopping and delivery service.
www.sephora.fr	Make up and beauty products for men and women.

Refunds & Exchanges

Shoppers have significant rights when it comes to refunds and exchanges in France, so it is worth making yourself aware of them. At the most basic level, many shops will have signs in-store advertising their refund and exchange policies. If not, it pays to ask at the cash register at the time of purchase what your rights are when it comes to exchange of goods. Legally, customers who have bought products with a pre-sale defect that is undeclared, and which renders them unuseable, have rights to a replacement, or a partial or total refund. If a defective product causes damage then the trader is responsible for the damage caused by the goods.

Even during sales, traders are required to replace or refund goods with hidden defects. The only exception is when the goods have been acknowledged by the store to be faulty prior to sale. It is legal for traders to make goodwill gestures and give additional guarantees by saying 'If you're not satisfied bring it back for a full refund'. If these promises are made in any advertising in-store, in the public domain or even on receipts, they must be adhered to. If not, the trader is liable for misleading advertising.

Consumer Rights

As with the rest of Europe, there are laws protecting the rights of consumers. The website www.citizensadvice.org.uk has links to the French consumer rights site with translation available in English. This is a free service which provides free and independent advice so is worth considering should you have specific questions, or have encountered service or consumer activities that you believe infringed your rights. Another site is www.eej-net.info, which provides information on consumer rights in France and Germany. This also has an English-language option. If things do go awry take steps to contact the vendor personally to try and rectify any problems. If this fails, contact the Direction Générale de la Concurrence, Consommation et de la Répression des Fraudes (DGCCRF) at www.minefi.gouv.fr/dgccrf, or L'Union Fédérale des Consommateurs (UFC) at www.quechoisir.org to register your complaints. Even simply warning the shopkeepers that this is your next step may be enough to resolve any issues.

243

Shipping

Being one of the world's premier shopping destinations, shipping goods internationally presents little problem in Paris. For small items the government-run postal service, La Poste (www.laposte.fr), can often be the best. Packages are available for secure, express, air or regular mail deliveries to all countries and continents. Keep in mind that as the package weight gets heavier the post becomes less economical; sending a single bottle of wine to Australia from Paris may set you back as much as €50. In these cases sending in bulk through larger courier companies may prove a cheaper option. The well-known international shipping companies, FedEx (www.fedex.com), DHL (www.dhl.fr) and UPS (www.ups.com) operate within France at prices comparable to those in the UK and the US. Many art galleries and furnishing stores can help organise shipping (for an extra charge) so it is worth asking before buying. Prices vary considerably depending on the boutique, and most are happy to give quotes before you seal any deals.

How To Pay

As in most international destinations, shoppers have a wide range of payment options at their disposal. The euro is accepted everywhere, but bear in mind that paying in large denominations for small items is frowned upon. Cash is also often the only form of accepted payment at markets and street stalls. When it comes to credit cards, standard rules apply, with Visa and MasterCard widely accepted, and American Express and Diner's Club slightly less so. Those with a European bank account can also debit directly from their account using EPS, which allows users to tap their pin code into an electronic handset in lieu of signing a receipt. International debit cards, however, are not accepted. Don't make the mistake of relying on payment in alternate currencies and travellers' cheques, which will be refused across the board with few exceptions. French cheques, however, are a different story and unless a sign is posted stating a policy of refusal, they will be accepted in all situations. *Ticket restos*, essentially subsidised restaurant vouchers offered by French employers, can be used in all Paris restaurants displaying a sticker of acceptance.

Bargaining

Marché aux Puces de St-Ouen

If you find the thrill of the barter equal to the excitement of the purchase, Paris is definitely not the city for you, so get a flight to Marrakech. Attempting to talk down prices in retail and department stores will, on the whole, win you nothing but disdain. Exceptions can be found in some smaller, independent art galleries where multiple purchases may result in a small markdown: be polite, not pushy. A charming manner can also earn dividends with vendors at the weekly food markets that pop up on different days throughout Paris, where small offerings of extra produce are not uncommon.

Desperate for the opportunity to test your skills of persuasion? The permanent flea markets (Marché aux Puces, p.296) on the city's outskirts are jammed with antique and second-hand merchants willing to play the game. However bargains are not what they once were – floods of tourist buses spilling foreign visitors into the markets have resulted in a rise in prices and a decrease in real haggling. Where big ticket items are concerned, cars – both new and used – offer the best opportunities for negotiation, but don't expect to knock off more than about 5% from the original price.

Alcohol

Other options **On the Town** p.342, **Drinks** p.308

The French love for the grape is legendary and unparalleled. Needless to say you won't need to look far to find a place to buy alcohol. Supermarkets and grocers (*epiceries*) join speciality wine, champagne and beer stores in selling a huge variety of beverages. Not to mention the enormous array of bars, *tabacs*, restaurants and even *boulangeries* that serve alcohol at all hours. But no matter where the purchase is made, buyers can be sure of one thing – sound advice is always on hand. Knowledge of wine is a point of cultural pride, and rarely will you stumble across an alcohol vendor unable or unwilling to offer a knowledgeable opinion. Neither is price a stumbling block: of course costs for a single bottle can reach into the hundreds but for most there is good drinking to be had for as little as €10.

Specialist wine retailer Nicolas is a good first port of call with branches all over the city. Les Caves Auge is the oldest wine seller in Paris, however Lavinia has perhaps the biggest selection, in addition to a wine bar and restaurant (though prices can be slightly inflated). Galeries Lafayette (p.245) also has a great general selection in its wine cellar located at Lafayette Gourmet on boulevard Haussmann, while La Derniere Goutte in the heart of St-Germain sells French and international wines, holds frequent tastings and caters to English-speakers. Specialised retailers also abound: fans of Bordeaux will find all they need at La Maison des Millesimes, a wine merchant selling only Bordeaux-region wines that is also open Sunday, while Le Nez Rouge houses a good selection of foreign wines alongside many smaller, lesser-known French producers. Arômes et Cépages has its focus firmly fixed on wines of the organic variety.

Neither will beer drinkers find themselves left out in the cold. At Beer Specials in the 11th you can discover beers from Belgium, Portugal, Poland, Scotland and even China. Those interested in the brewing process can find out more at Biere de Brie farm and brewery near Paris where visitors can also sample the product. Supermarkets sell a wide range of international and domestic beers starting from around €6 for a six-pack. For spirits, La Maison du Whisky stocks an extensive range of Scottish, Irish, American and Japanese whiskies, with sales staff that know their tipple. Ryst Dupeyron is a family store which has sold Armagnac, the French liqueur, for generations and has bottles dating to the mid 19th century. Vintage port and rare whiskies can also be found here. Vodka, gin, tequila, mixers and other spirit are available at general supermarkets and grocers, where a standard bottle of spirits is likely to set you back about €15.

When it comes to restrictions on alcohol, there are few. While the legal drinking age is set at 18, enforcement is almost unheard of. Courtesy of a culture which permits tastes of wine with dinner for children as young as 10 years old, France doesn't suffer from problems of under-age drinking to the same extent as other Anglicised nations.

Alcohol

Aromes et Cépages	3rd	01 42 72 34 85	www.aromes-et-cepages.com
Beer Specials	11th	01 48 07 18 71	na
Biere de Brie	Courpalay	01 64 25 76 05	www.biere-de-brie.com
Corade Whisky Specialists	15th	01 53 68 96 55	na
De Vinis Illustribus	5th	01 043 36 12 12	www.devinis.fr
Galeries Lafayette	Various Locations	01 42 82 34 56	www.galerieslafayette.com
La Dernière Goutte	6th	01 43 29 11 62	www.ladernieregoutte.com
La Maison des Millésimes	6th	01 40 46 80 01	www.jackswines.com
La Maison du Whisky	8th	08 20 16 01 80	www.whisky.fr
Lavinia	1st	01 42 97 20 20	www.lavinia.fr
Le Nez Rouge	15th	01 47 34 87 40	www.le-nez-rouge.com
Les Caves Auge	8th	01 45 22 16 97	na
Nicolas	Various Locations	01 41 73 55 55	www.nicolas.com
Ryst Dupeyron	7th	01 45 48 80 93	www.ryst-dupeyron.com

Art

Other options **Art Classes** p.306, **Art Galleries** p.156, **Art & Craft Supplies** p.246

Alongside food and fashion, it is art that makes up the third piece in the Holy Trinity of Parisian passions. From street portrait sketchers along the Seine and amateur painters vending their canvases in the place du Tertre, to international artists displaying in galleries, finding pieces to your taste and budget is as simple (and as difficult) as narrowing down the vast array of choice. When it comes to artistic styles, there is everything on offer including traditional, modern, contemporary and emerging art.

For the best atmosphere visit the city's known art quarters, where you will find multiple galleries within a few blocks. These include St-Germain des Prés in the 6th *arrondissement* (www.artstgermaindespres.com) and Montmartre in the 18th (www.art-montmartre.com). For a really comprehensive overview of exhibitions, artists, photographers and galleries in each *arrondissement* log on to www.paris-art.com, an endless resource listing literally hundreds of events, addresses and artists.

Purchase of art is as simple as walking in to a gallery and pulling out a cheque book: no middleman is needed. As for prices, these vary from €50 for a piece in the place du Tertre to the priceless works of art for sale in galleries at Le Louvre des Antiquaires. Those seeking advice will find it with art buyers such as Arzao, a company specialising in personalised art shopping trips and private auction visits. For private portraiture in painting and photography there is an enormous number of artists available for hire. Kathy Burke is an American portrait artist based in the Marais, or you could contact French artist Francoise Garret. Of course these are just two names out of the many available, so check your phone book or galleries for further recommendations. When it comes to photography, there is a large number of commissionable portrait artists: David Brenot specialises in photojournalistic portrait style, South African Caronine Garbutt shoots children, babies and pregnant women while Dana Maitec shoots moody, studio works.

Art

Arzao	18th	06 23 15 42 56	www.arzao.com
Bayadere	10th	01 42 09 20 55	www.bayadere.com
Caronine Garbutt	Various Locations	06 10 98 43 05	www.caroninegarbutt.com
Dana Maitec	13th	01 45 85 29 04	www.maitecart.com
David Brenot	Various Locations	06 83 86 07 94	www.davidbrenot.com
Francoise Garrett	12th	01 43 41 15 31	www.francoisegarret.com
Kathy Burke	4th	01 42 71 11 75	na
Le Louvre des Antiquaires	1st	01 42 97 27 27	www.antikaparis.com

Art & Craft Supplies

Other options **Art Classes** p.306, **Art** p.246, **Art Galleries** p.156

Even art and craft supplies take on a hip edge in Paris, where you'll find beautiful, highly specialised stores. Take, for example, the boutique Michel Charbonnier, the city's only dedicated origami store. Cross-stitch enthusiasts will find their Nirvana at Les Bonheur des Dames and Des Fils et une Aiguille. Phidar, with nine outlets around Paris, stocks gorgeous yarns in wool and acrylic blends alongside easy-to-read and fashionable patterns (in French). Online ordering is also available. Amateur artists can order everything they need from Boesner, an enormous warehouse outside the city stocking professional artist materials and free delivery of online and in-store purchases over €120 is offered. For dedicated artist boutiques within the city bounds Maison Gattegno and Esquise, both in the 6th *arrondissement*, are two addresses worth noting.

Work Visas p.54
Weekend Breaks p.155

Written by residents, the Dublin Explorer is packed with insider info, from arriving in the city to making it your home and everything in between.

Dublin Explorer Residents' Guide
We Know Where You Live

For generalist stores, department store BHV has an entire floor dedicated to art supplies. Falling under the one company umbrella, Créa, Rougier & Plé and Graphigro really rule the market when it comes to art and craft mega-boutiques. There are five stores across the city headed under the various banners – one Créa, one Rougier & Plé and three Graphigro addresses; your best bet for browsing or when a wide range of stock is needed. For courses and tuition in painting, sculpting, ceramics, drama and even music request a brochure from ADAC Ville de Paris, a group organising workshops in studios across Paris. *Frimousse* magazine and *Le Paris des Tout-Petits* (available at kiosks) contain extensive information on upcoming workshops. The local town hall (*mairie*) in each *arrondissement* will also run adult learning courses, including those focussed on the arts. Ask for the booklet, *Cours Municipal d'Adultes*.

Art & Craft Supplies

ADAC Ville de Paris	8th	01 42 33 45 54	www.adacparis.com
BHV	4th	01 42 74 90 00	www.bhv.fr
Boesner	Champigny-sur-Marne	01 55 97 17 70	www.boesner.com
CREA	6th	01 53 63 60 00	www.crea.tm.fr
Des Fils et une Aiguille	2nd	01 49 26 09 34	na
Esquisse	6th	01 43 26 06 86	www.esquisseparis.fr
Graphigro	Various Locations	01 43 48 23 57	www.crea.tm.fr
Les Bonheur des Dames	Various Locations	01 45 23 06 11	www.bonheurdesdames.com
Loisirs & Création	Various Locations	01 53 33 27 50	www.loisirsetcreation.com
Maison Gattegno	6th	01 55 42 79 00	www.maisongattegno.fr
Michel Charbonnier	1st	01 39 59 09 14	www.curiositel.com/ana/origami
Phidar	Various Locations	na	www.phidar.com
Rougier & Plé	3rd	01 44 54 81 00	www.crea.tm.fr

Baby Items

Other options **Toys & Games** p.285

Having seen an explosion in the national birth rate over the past few years, Paris is well-equipped when it comes to all things enfant.

In a city justifiably known for its exquisite children's fashion, parents face a mind-boggling array of choice. At the top-end, Bonpoint and Tartine et Chocolat are two brands specialising in frills and flounce, creating adult-like styles (think baby boy shirts and beautifully tailored dresses in miniature) at very grown-up prices: a cashmere new-born can set you back €80. Designer babies will be taken care of at Le Bon Marché, where baby brands include offerings from Burberry and Dior. Petit Bateau, well-known internationally, offers a mid-range option and more casual styling with a huge range of good quality cotton onesies, singlets and mini T-shirts in a range of colours from €10. Those seeking a more urban look will find fewer options, thanks to the French fascination with classic kid's fashion. Try Le Marchand d'Étoiles, a relative new brand selling modern and quirky designs from boutiques in the 7th and 9th *arrondissements*. Prices range from €15 to €30. Okaidi, with nine stores in Paris, also specialises in original and colourful clothing. Less expensive basics can also be found at Baby Gap and H&M. Six Pieds Trois Pouces and Pom d'Api, both with multiple locations in Paris, sell an eclectic range of beautiful footwear for newborns to teenagers up to 16 years.

When it comes to equipment, megastore Sauvel Natal in the 15th *arrondissement* offers an enormous range of goods, from cots and prams (including Maxi Cosi, Bugaboo and Peg Perego), to toys, bottles, sterilisers and anything else you may need for your new arrival. Due to its massive purchase power prices here are often less than smaller boutiques. One exception to this rule, however, is La Do Re, a small independent store selling the full range of clothing and equipment at great prices. Service here is personal and well-informed with staff happy to order in stock for a wide range of brands. Better-known company Aubert has multiple outlets around Paris offering coordinated furnishings, clothing and equipment. The store produces extensive catalogues, online purchase options, mail order and gift services. Those on short stays or not eager to accumulate baby goods can hire equipment, car seats and even breast pumps from Natal Services. The store promises same-day delivery within the Ile de France on all goods ordered before 15:00.

When it comes time for nourishment, supermarkets stock a large range of baby foods and formulas with smaller selections available in pharmacies. Blédina and Nestlé are the top brands, producing pureed baby food, soup and cereal mixes and fruit drinks, though they do contain sugar, salt and some additives. Hipp, a German brand available at Le Bon Marché, G20 and Champion supermarkets, provides an organic alternative as does Babybio, an organic line found in many health stores. Carrefour also stocks its own organic brand, Carrefour Bio.

Baby Items

Aubert	Various Locations	01 40 39 90 71	www.aubert.fr
Bonpoint	Various Locations	01 40 51 98 20	www.bonpoint.com
Carrefour	Various Locations	01 43 53 86 00	www.carrefour.fr
Champion	Various Locations	01 53 73 00 60	www.champion.fr
G20	Various Locations	na	www.supermarchesg20.com
La Do Re	15th	01 42 50 26 47	www.ladore.com
Le Bon Marché	7th	01 44 39 80 00	www.lebonmarche.fr
Le Marchand d'Étoiles	Various Locations	01 42 84 42 02	www.marchand-etoiles.com
Natal Services	15th	01 58 09 89 00	www.natalservices.fr
Natalys	Various Locations	na	www.natalys.fr
Petit Bateau	Various Locations	01 48 87 27 10	www.petit-bateau.com
Pom d'Api	Various Locations	01 45 48 39 31	www.pomdapi.fr
Sauvel Natal	15th	01 42 50 47 47	www.sauvel.com
Six Pieds Trois Pouces	Various Locations	01 45 44 03 72	www.6pieds3pouces.com
Tartine et Chocolate	Various Locations	01 45 56 10 45	www.tartine-et-chocolat.fr

Beachwear
Other options **Sports Goods** p.281, **Clothes** p.254

Though there's not a speck of sand to be seen for miles except, of course, when the *plage* (p.183) hits town come summer, Paris does a brisk trade in beachwear all year around. Eres, a dedicated lingerie and bathing suit chain, has multiple outlets and specialises in high-fashion styles. The luxury lingerie and swimsuit store La Perla also has boutiques across the city for those who never let a tight budget get in the way of fashion. Men also have their pick of exclusive swimwear at Vilebrequin, specialists in bright, patterned board shorts and swimming trunks. Surf stores like Quiksilver and Oxbow (available for purchase online) provide slightly less expensive – and less flashy – options. For women, Etam and Princesse Tam-Tam are two well known chains selling great styles at mid-to-lower range prices.

Department stores Le Bon Marché, Galeries Lafayette, Citadium and Printemps are all top destinations when it comes to beachwear for both adults and children. There are dozens of brands to choose from, ensuring there is little danger shoppers will fail to find an appealing style or fit at a price point they can afford. H&M, Gap and Zara provide a cheaper option, however unlike the department stores the offering of swimsuits in these chains is seasonal. Maternity fashion boutiques such as Formes will stock maternity swimwear, so too the larger baby goods stores such as La Do Re in the 15th *arrondissement*. La Do Re also sells UV protective suits for kids.

Beachwear			
Citadium	9th	na	www.citadium.com
Eres	Various Locations	01 47 42 28 82	www.eres.fr
Etam	Various Locations	08 25 00 38 26	www.etam.com
Formes	Various Locations	01 49 26 00 66	www.formes.com
Galeries Lafayette	Various Locations	01 42 82 34 56	www.galerieslafayette.com
Gap	Various Locations	01 53 32 82 10	www.gapfrance.fr
H&M	Various Locations	01 55 34 96 86	www.hm.com/fr
La Do Re	15th	01 42 50 26 47	www.ladore.com
La Perla	Various Locations	01 43 12 33 60	www.laperla.com
Le Bon Marché	7th	01 44 39 80 00	www.lebonmarche.fr
Oxbow	Various Locations	na	www.oxbowworld.com
Princesse Tam Tam	Various Locations	01 42 86 52 46	www.princesstam-tam.com
Printemps	Various Locations	01 42 82 57 87	www.printemps.com
Quiksilver	Various Locations	01 44 82 79 99	www.quiksilver.com
Vilebrequin	Various Locations	01 42 22 75 83	www.vilebrequin.com
Zara	Various Locations	01 40 13 70 17	www.zara.fr

Bicycles

The last few years has seen a surge in construction of bicycle lanes across Paris, sparking a corresponding rise in cyclist numbers and courtesy of the city's chaotic traffic, it has now become a favoured mode of transport. Helmets are required by law and, given most bike lanes are shared by buses and taxis, wearing one is a good idea. Cyclists are also subject to the same road rules as motorised vehicles: running traffic lights or riding on footpaths will result in fines. Bike theft is common, so a good bike lock is essential.

New road, mountain and BMX bikes and biking equipment for children and adults are available in chain sport equipment stores Decathlon and GO Sport, as well as specialist retailers. Prices on new bikes vary according to make and model, ranging from as little as €150 to as much as €2,000. Accessories are generally inexpensive: foot-controlled bike pumps cost as little as €10, with bike locks available for between €2 and €30. Those looking for a budget buy on a previously owned bike must try Paris à Velo, a bicycle rental company which sells its stock of bikes in autumn.

When it comes to repairs La Maison du Velo is the boutique of choice, however its popularity means repairs can take some time courtesy of the backlog of customers.

Bicycles			
Cycles Laurent	11th	01 47 00 27 47	www.cycleslaurent.com
Decathlon	Various Locations	01 45 72 66 88	www.decathlon.fr
GO Sport	Various Locations	01 44 74 38 38	www.go-sport.com
La Maison du Velo	10th	01 42 81 24 72	www.lamaisonduvelo.com
Paris à Vélo	11th	01 48 87 60 01	www.parisvelosympa.com

Professional cyclists or those with quality road bikes requiring repair prefer Cycles Laurent in the 9th *arrondissement* and the store also stocks one of the most comprehensive ranges of bicycle brands for sale in Paris. It's worth noting that neighbourhood bike shops may refuse to repair cheap bikes bought at the chain stores, preferring to service their own customers.

Books

Other options **Second-Hand Items** p.278, **Libraries** p.226

Foreign language is no barrier to finding good reading material in Paris for the expat and tourist community, thanks to a strong network of new and second-hand English bookshops. The best collection of contemporary new titles and international magazines is to be found at WHSmith. Though by no means the only outlet, the store offers unparalleled range. What it doesn't have staff will order, a practice commonly adhered to among the city's other booksellers. The one thing to keep in mind is prices: due to import costs on English-language books prices are slightly higher than you would normally expect to pay. Most boutiques dealing in new books offer online purchase and delivery. Foragers can head straight to the *bouquinistes* positioned along the Seine around Pont Neuf, where permanent vendors deal in all thing paper: from old and interesting second-hand books, to collector's magazines and posters. More second-hand treasures can be found at The Village Voice, a fantastic resource for used books – in English – in St-Germain. The yearly Salon du Livre (www.salondulivreparis.com) at the exhibition centre at Port de Versailles runs in March, where hundreds of publishers display all manner of unique and interesting titles. Daily readings and author's signings are also a highlight.

83 quai de Valmy
10th
ⓂＭ *Jacques Bonsergent*
Map p.390 B3 **1**

Artazart

01 40 40 24 00 | *www.artazart.com*
On the Canal St Martin in the bohemian 10th, Artazart's bright orange exterior is a good indicator of the eclectic mix of design and art titles located within. Shelves are stocked with standard architectural, photographic and design-oriented magazine and texts, continuing along the spectrum to specific titles covering typefaces and such specialist topics as the art of Japanese paper folding. Those with dainty sensibilities may also need to avert their eyes from some of the more startling magazines and books on display.

37 ave de l'Opéra
2nd
Ⓜ *Opéra*
Map p.388 C4 **21**

Brentano's

01 42 61 52 50 | *www.brentanos.fr*
Labelling itself as the American bookstore in Paris, Brentano's has been in operation since 1895 specialising in literature from the United States. Departments include art and crafts, classic non-fiction, children's books, graphic novels, non-fiction, language, and exam aids. There's also a kid's club and regular author readings.

224 rue de Rivoli
1st
Ⓜ *Tuileries*
Map p.398 B1 **2**

Galignani

01 42 60 76 07
Offering a mix of French and English titles since 1810, Galignani is a half-way point between the commercial offerings of WHSmith and the design-leanings of Taschen. In a beautifully arranged shop with wood-panelled walls, the stock spans everything from culinary titles and literature to international magazines, business and biographies. The boutique specialises in English-language translations of French literary classics, from the works of Balzac to Zola. If not in store, titles can be ordered.

22 rue St Paul
4th
Ⓜ *Saint-Paul*
Map p.400 B4 **3**

The Red Wheelbarrow

01 48 04 75 08 | *www.theredwheelbarrow.com*
With its bright red front hiding an interior where ordered chaos rules, the Red Wheelbarrow is crammed with an enormous selection of diverse literary offerings. Appealingly chaotic, the store is renowned for its amiable and well-read staff, on hand to offer reviews and advice. Stock includes bilingual French-English children's books, a large French-interest selection, poetry, drama, literary criticism and thrillers. Owners Penelope and Abigail hold regular author readings and creative writing competitions.

251

37 rue de la Bûcherie
5th
Ⓜ **Saint-Michel**
Map p.399 E4 **4**

Shakespeare & Co
01 43 25 40 93
www.shakespeareco.org
Housed in an historic, charmingly dilapidated apartment on the Left Bank opposite Notre Dame, Shakespeare and Co was established by American, George Whitman, in post-war Paris in 1951. A veritable treasure trove of rare and interesting books, the store also offers a place to stay for establishing writers, an ideal Whitman instigated at the

Shakespeare & Co

shop's inception. Henry Miller and Anäis Nin were once in residence but today the book shop runs a regular writer's group along with a host of readings. Check the monthly schedule on the website for details. Open every day from noon until midnight.

2 rue de Buci
6th
Ⓜ **Mabillon**
Map p.399 D4 **5**

Taschen
01 40 51 79 22 | *www.taschen.com*
This outlet of the well-known German book company is on a bustling pedestrian street just off boulevard St-Germain. The boutique is justly known for its extensive collection of photographic and coffee table books.

24 rue Mayet
6th
Ⓜ **Falguière**
Map p.408 A1 **6**

Tea & Tattered Pages
01 40 65 94 35
This is a treasure trove of more than 15,000 used books in English. Take stock of the overflowing shelves, grab a title and take to the shabbily pretty tearoom separated by a beaded curtain at the rear of the shop. Linger over an array of American and British treats (you won't be hurried out the door) enjoy the company of the resident parrot. There's also a loyalty card on offer to regulars.

6 rue Princesse
6th
Ⓜ **Mabillon**
Map p.398 C4 **7**

Village Voice
01 46 33 36 47 | *www.villagevoicebookshop.com*
There are around 18,000 books to be found at the Village Voice, which opened in 1982 between place St Sulpice and place St-Germain des Prés. A two-storey space that is well-frequented by both English-speaking expats and French Anglophones, the focus is fixed firmly on literature, culture and politics. Check the website for listings of upcoming evening readings. It's worth noting that the shop stocks of the Sunday edition of *The New York Times*.

248 rue de Rivoli
1st
Ⓜ **Concorde**
Map p.398 B1 **8**

WHSmith
01 44 77 88 99 | *www.whsmith.fr*
This outlet of the British book chain is set over two floors on rue Rivoli and houses reading material on every conceivable topic, both fiction and non-fiction. Also available is an extensive range of imported magazines and current newspapers from the US, the UK, Australia, Italy, Spain and further afield. Prices are slightly higher than you would find in the countries of origin thanks to freight charges. The bilingual team of staff is knowledgeable and helpful, offering to track down or order any title where possible. Open Sundays.

Camera Equipment

Other options **Electronics & Home Appliances** p.259

Just as with computers and home electronics, amateur Parisian photographers and happy-snappers looking for well-priced camera equipment generally head to one of the chain electronic stores. FNAC, Darty, Surcouf, Conforama and Carrefour each stock a wide range of camera equipment and accessories. Prices are not what you would find in any of the larger cities known for their discounts, however these stores will sign off Duty Free slips where appropriate.

Camera Equipment			
Cameras-Pari.Com	Online Only	na	www.cameras-paris.com
Carrefour	Various Locations	01 43 53 86 00	www.carrefour.fr
Cirque	3rd	01 40 29 91 91	www.lecirque.fr
Conforama	Various Locations	01 42 33 78 58	www.conforma.fr
Darty	Various Locations	08 21 08 20 82	www.darty.com
FNAC Micro	5th	01 44 41 31 50	www.fnac.com
Pixmania	13th	na	www.pixmania.com
Sony	Various Locations	01 44 05 05 05	www.sony.com
Surcouf	Various Locations	08 92 70 76 00	www.surcouf.com

For specialists and would-be professionals seeking very technical equipment or more knowledgeable advice there exist a couple of other options. Cirque is one of the best among these, offering a full range of still and video cameras for professionals and amateurs. The store will also undertake repairs. Online, Cameras Paris sells an eclectic range of new, used and vintage equipment, such as folding and box cameras. International camera specialists, Pixmania, also sell a vast range of equipment at very competitive prices and the company offers a price-matching guarantee, promising to refund the difference on any equipment found advertised cheaper on any other online site within seven days. Clients can buy online or head to its Paris branch in the 13th *arrondissement*.

Car Parts & Accessories

Depending on the make and model of your car, motorbike or scooter there is a long list of workshops providing parts and accessories. Most workshops, however, are located outside the borders of the périphérique in surrounding suburbs of Paris. Norauto and Euromaster are both chains with multiple outlets in the wider region of the île de France. Sport Auto, Turbos Moteurs Migne and Alliance Paris Est are just three locations doing a brisk trade in spare parts, but of these, only Alliance Paris Est is within Paris' city limits. IMS deals in new and spare parts for both private and commercial vehicles. Car enthusiasts will need to note the address for MMC, specialists in the sale and provision of parts for collectors and sports cars while motorcycle owners will want to remember Hein Gericke, an outlet of the world-famous German chain stocking helmets, leathers, shoes and other motorbike accessories. Carrefour is a good generalist option for parts and accessories, offering products at good prices.

Car Parts & Accessories			
Alliance Paris Est	12th	01 53 17 37 37	na
Euromaster	Various Locations	01 42 84 23 46	www.euromaster.fr
Harley Davidson, Bastille	3rd	01 48 04 02 17	www.harleydavidson-paris-bastille.com
Hein Gericke	Various Locations	01 60 88 97 37	www.hein-gericke-store.com
Hutchinson Worldwide	8th	01 40 74 83 00	www.hutchinson.fr
IMS	Persan	01 69 36 38 80	www.ims-auto.com
MMC	16th	01 45 25 35 35	www.mmc-paris.com
Norauto	Various Locations	08 20 85 85 85	www.norauto.fr
Sport Auto	Pierrelaye	05 61 02 96 02	www.perso.orange.fr
Turbos Moteurs Migne	Lons	05 59 72 91 50	www.turbos-moteurs-migne.com

253

Figuring out your size isn't rocket science, just a bit of a pain. Firstly, check the label – international sizes are often printed on them. Secondly, check the store – they will often have a helpful conversion chart on display. Otherwise, a UK size is always two higher than a US size (so a UK 10 is actually a US 6. To convert European sizes into US sizes, just subtract 32 (so a European 38 is actually a US 6). To convert European sizes into UK sizes, a 38 is roughly a 10, but some countries size smaller so you'll have to try on to be sure. Italian sizing is different again.

Clothes

Other options **Tailoring** p.284, **Beachwear** p.249, **Lingerie** p.268, **Shoes** p.279, **Sports Goods** p.281

From the razzle-dazzle of the seasonal prêt-a-porter and couture shows to the sheer numbers of clothing boutiques around the city, it's patently clear that the fashion industry wields enormous economic and cultural power in Paris. This presence is a boon for the style-conscious, who will never want for choice, be they lovers of high-end punk, cheap and cheerful high street styles or sleek designer dresses. What follows is a small sampling of the city's offerings neatly packaged into a few general groupings. Paris' department stores and shopping malls have not been included here, neither markets. Look to the end of this chapter for more on those options.

Budget & Warehouse

For real bottom-dollar fashion grab your car keys or metro map and be prepared for a day's excursion: though there are various stock shops for clothing brands in Paris, the larger factory outlets, called *usines centres* are all located outside the metropolitan area. This is where you'll find the greatest selection and the very best prices because clothing brands deliberately keep sale of much of their cheap stock outside the city to reduce the economic impact on full-price stock. Usine Centre Villacoublay, Marques Avenue Île-Saint-Denis, La Vallee Outlet Shopping Village and Usine Centre Paris Nord 2 all stock men's and women's brand label clothing at discount prices. A little farther afield is Troyes; 150km east of Paris this is the capital of the French clothing industry and – with some 150 textile firms around the city – has an enormous selection of factory outlets open to the public. Brands available include Aigle, Burberry, Timberland, Kenzo, Armani, Nike and Cerruti. A coach service runs from Bastille to Troyes' centres each Saturday. Look to www.eva-voyages.com for information.
In Paris there are many designer label stock-shops selling second-hand or last season's fashions. Buy cheap Et Vous at Et Vous Stock, Sonia Rykiel's end of line clothing at SR Store, discount Cacharel at Cacharel Stock and chic reduced price pieces in St-Germain's Surplus A.P.C. For the full list see *Le Paris des Touts Petits* or *Le Guide des Magasins d'Usine*, both of which can be purchased on www.amazon.fr. Finally there are the *ventes privées*, or private sales. Held in discreet locales around Paris, this is where designers sell off old stock at drastically reduced prices. A word of warning, however; these sales are accessible by invitation only. You must be on the distribution or member's list of the private sale companies (or brands) or be sponsored by a member. Some sales are open to all, with news of the times and locations usually generated by word of mouth, so keep an ear out. Alternatively, log on to www.venteprivee.com, www.espacecatherinemax.fr or www.espace-ngr.com to get the inside information.

Vintage

With its six stores clustered in the one street, Reciproque is the first port of call for men and women when it comes to great vintage buys. Each of the multiple shop-fronts is dedicated to its own category, spanning women's evening wear, women's casual, menswear, accessories and coats. Le Mouton à Cinq Pattes is another vintage chain with multiple outlets selling a great selection of second-hand designer labels. A great indie find is Quidam de Revel, offering a hand-picked selection from such designers as YSL, Cardin and Hermes, with jewellery from Georg Jensen among others. As you would expect for a boutique in the Marais, which is a magnet for amateur collectors of vintage clothing, prices are a little higher here than elsewhere. Alternatives, also in the Marais, is more of a jumble; men will find some great jackets and suits from designers such as

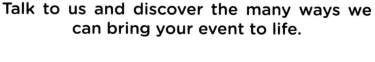

Paul Smith and Kenzo while women can get stuck in to such designers as Prada and Dries Van Noten. Trend store Kiliwatch falls somewhere between second-hand and vintage. Though the super hip boutique just off rue Etienne Marcel sells new trend brands, the largest portion of the store is given over to 'vintage' pieces. Clothes are not really designer label but they are chosen for their style impact so it's great for those who want something between high-end vintage and just general second-hand fodder.

Clothes

Abaco	Various Locations	01 48 87 86 86
Abou d'Abi Bazar	3rd	01 42 77 96 98
AG Spalding & Bros	4th	01 42 71 33 32
Agnes.B	Various Locations	01 45 08 56 56
Alternatives	4th	01 42 78 31 50
Antik Batik	Various Locations	01 44 78 02 00
APC	Various Locations	01 42 22 12 77
Barbara Bui	Various Locations	01 40 26 43 65
Bonnie Cox	18th	01 42 54 95 68
Brontibay	4th	01 42 76 90 80
Cabane de Zucca	1st	01 44 58 98 88
Cacharel	Various Locations	01 40 46 00 45
Cacharel Stock	14th	01 45 42 53 04
Carhartt	Various Locations	01 40 02 02 20
Chanel	Various Locations	01 53 05 98 95
Cheap Monday	4th	01 44 54 94 14
Christian Lacroix	8th	01 42 68 79 00
Comptoir des Cotonniers	Various Locations	01 42 76 95 33
Diesel	Various Locations	01 42 36 55 55
Dior	Various Locations	01 40 73 73 73
Et Vous	Various Locations	01 55 80 76 10
Et Vous Stock	2nd	01 40 13 04 12
Father & Sons	Various Locations	01 34 51 02 53
French Touche	17th	01 42 63 31 36
Griff Troc	8th	01 42 25 86 07
Gucci	Various Locations	01 56 69 80 80
Hugo Boss	Various Locations	01 45 62 57 57
Isabel Marant	Various Locations	01 49 29 71 55
Jack Henry	Various Locations	01 42 21 46 01
Kenzo	Various Locations	01 42 61 04 14
Kiliwatch	2nd	01 42 21 17 37
La Vallee Outlet Shopping Village	Serris (Marne-la-Vallee)	01 60 42 35 00
Lafayette Homme	9th	01 42 82 34 56
Le Mouton à 5 Pattes	Various Locations	01 43 26 49 25
Les Prairies de Paris	7th	01 40 20 44 12
Lonchamp	Various Locations	01 43 16 00 16
Louis Vuitton	Various Locations	08 10 81 00 10
Louison	12th	01 43 44 02 62

Luxury Labels

It's safe to say that every major international luxury brand boasts at least one outlet in Paris. Dior, Gucci, Yves Saint Laurent, Louis Vuitton, Christian Lacroix, Chanel, Kenzo… draw breath, the roll call just keeps on rolling. Head to the streets where these glittering showrooms cluster: primarily this takes in avenue Montaigne, rue Faubourg St-Honoré and its continuation, rue St-Honoré, rue des Saint-Peres, avenue George V, the Champs-Élysées near the Arc de Triomphe (where you'll find the temple to Vuitton), and the intimate space of the Palais Royal, just behind the Louvre. Both men's and women's collections are to be found so don't forget your gold credit card, and be prepared to spend big.

Classic French Look

Reproduction of that effortless French style is certainly made easier by knowledge of where Paris' most stylish women go in search of their wardrobe. From the A of Agnes B to the Z of Zadig & Voltaire, local brands are renowned for their flattering cuts, body-skimming (never body-hugging) fabrics and softly neutral colour palettes. Comptoir des Cotonniers is great value for trend buying, where you can expect to pay between €70 and €200 for great tops, trousers and dresses that are better quality than high street buys but less expensive than designer gear.

Maje, Et Vous, Sandro, Berenice, Vanessa Bruno and Zadig & Voltaire are all slightly more expensive, however the cuts, quality and styles justify the price tags: think quietly chic, well-tailored and subtly sexy. If you want that certain je ne sais quoi, this is where to get it. Isabel Marant – famed for her drapey cuts – and Barbara Bui are both one more step up the price ladder. Somewhere between designer and boutique, these are great places to buy during sale times for those that cringe at spending upward of €500 on an exquisitely tailored cropped leather jacket with embroidered detailing. At Antik Batik you'll find a complete style change; this brand is renowned for its Indian-inspired, beaded and glittery fabrics cut in beautifully modern pieces. It's a particularly great boutique when it's time to stock the summer wardrobe.

For men there is a similarly mind-boggling array of choice. Start at APC for well-cut basics in quality fabrics. Pick up leather pea-coats, needle-cord jeans and shirts that sit as well on the body as they do on the hanger. Cacharel is great for relaxed suiting: think lots of linen and a Mediterranean-casual aesthetic that will have you blending with the St Tropez crowd. Agnes B's menswear line, Agnes B Homme, also does a good job of outfitting those seeking that well-cut, casual Euro vibe. Father & Sons and Melchior are both a little more mainstream but are well-priced and good choices for casual shirts and jackets that could go from work to weekend. And then there's Jack Henry. Though created in New York, this is a brand with a distinct European feel. Cuts are slim and edgy with an urban sensibility that is more unique than Diesel. The label also has a great women's line.

Clothes (cont)

Madame André	1st	06 19 97 06 30
Madelios	1st	01 53 45 00 00
Maje	Various Locations	01 42 36 36 75
Maris Luisa	1st	01 47 03 48 08
Marithe et Francois Girbaud	Various Locations	01 44 54 99 01
Marques Avenue Ile-Saint-Denis	L'Île-Saint-Denis	01 42 43 70 20
Melchior	Various Locations	01 42 71 81 11
Miss Sixty	Various Locations	01 45 08 19 49
Noir Kennedy	4th	01 42 74 55 58
Printemps de l'Homme	9th	01 42 82 50 00
Quidam de Revel	3rd	01 42 71 37 07
Réciproque	Various Locations	01 47 04 30 28
Replay	Various Locations	01 42 33 16 00
Sandro	Various Locations	01 40 39 90 21
Shinzo	2nd	01 42 36 40 57
SR Store	14th	01 43 95 06 13
Surplus A.P.C.	6th	01 45 48 43 71
Usine Centre Villacoublay	Velizy-Villacoublay	01 39 46 45 00
Usines Centre Paris Nord 2	Roissy	01 48 63 07 67
Vanessa Bruno	Various Locations	01 42 61 44 60
Yves Ssaint Laurent	Various Locations	01 43 26 84 40
Zadig & Voltaire	Various Locations	01 40 70 97 89

Accessories

No outfit is complete without the right accessories. The ladies can start at Griff Troc in the 8th *arrondissement*, where you can find vintage handbags and accessories from Chanel, YSL, Prada, Celine and Gucci among other big-name international luxury names. At the other end of the spectrum is French Touche where a myriad of little-known French artists and designers sell trinkets and creative accessories. When it comes to handbags go to Louison for its metallic-leather pouches, Abaco for the brand's elegant boho, pigment-dyed bags or Brontibay for its relaxed totes with contrast leather handles. Or go French classic at Lancel and Longchamp, both French brands well-known for their gorgeous handbags in beautiful leather. Mac Douglas boutique in the 14th sells ultra chic clutches for as little as €35 while La Sartan sells cute leather totes from its all-blue boutique starting from €20.

For men, try A.G. Spalding & Bros for leather bags, wallets and totes as sporty as they are stylish. Hugo Boss is great for classics like leather belts and sleek wallets, while Kenzo's colourful leather and textile man-bags are created with the stylishly adventurous in mind. Printemps de l'Homme (ground floor) and Lafayette Homme (ground floor) also have a fantastic collection of men's accessories from labels like Mulberry, Paul Smith, Hugo Boss and Mandarina Duck.

Urban & Denim

The streets around Les Halles are packed with great urban fashion boutiques, but there are a few brands which rate a special shopping mention. Italian labels Diesel and Replay have a couple of great outlets, particularly the stores on rue Etienne Marcel and Replay even has an outlet for super cool kids. Miss Sixty – famed for its ultra skinny jeans and sexy style – is also nearby. Carhartt has great denim cuts for men alongside stylish jackets in heavy cotton and denims. More directional is the fashion on offer from April 77, a French brand churning out the best in rock star style; think drainpipes for men and women, cropped jackets with zip detailing and distressed T-shirts. Find a good range at the boutique, Noir Kennedy. Along the same lines is Cheap Monday, a jeans-meets-fashion brand from Sweden that is now making an international impact. It has its own store on rue Sevigne, alongside rack space at Noir Kennedy and Kiliwatch. Baggier cuts are the trademark of Evisu, a Japanese designer denim label you can pick up at Shinzo (among other Parisian locales.) For avant-garde denim go straight to Marithe et Francois Girbaud. The French label produces streetwear in high-tech fabrics using laser cutting and welding, churning out some highly original pieces not for the self-conscious.

Boutique Shopping

Multi-label boutiques are another way of getting your shopping fix, offering a range of interesting brands under the one roof and they are a great choice if you only have time for one stop. At Madame André find Japanese silk-screened totes, pick up blowsy peasant tops at Les Prairies de Paris or head to Abou d'Abi Bazar to try on Isabel Marant, Tara Jarmon and Stella Forest. Maria Luisa in rue Cambon is known for her eclectic picks: expect to find pieces from Collette Dinnigan, Christian Lacroix and London's Julien MacDonald among others. Boutique Bonnie Cox in the shadow of Montmartre is a great place to scout for new designer names. For men, Cabane de Zucca is the outlet for Japanese designer Issey Miyake's streetwear label, stocking clothing and accessories for men (and women). Just off the elegant place de la Madeleine, Madelios offers more than 100 upscale brands to guys seeking that city chic look so well done by Hugo Boss and Ralph Lauren. You'll find both those labels here, alongside Armani and Lanvin in one of the biggest dedicated menswear boutiques in Paris.

Computers

Other options **Electronics & Home Appliances** p.259

From PCs at FNAC to iBooks at the city's dedicated Macintosh stores, finding the latest in computer technology is not a difficult task. But finding a great bargain? Now that's another matter entirely. Though by no means substantially more expensive than computer technology in the US or UK, the low costs of Singapore and Hong Kong are not to be found within Paris' many computer stores.

Computers		
Antares Multimedia	01 34 51 05 50	www.antares-multimedia.com
Apple	01 49 23 89 89	na
Carrefour	01 43 53 86 00	www.carrefour.fr
Darty	08 21 08 20 82	www.darty.com
FNAC	08 25 02 00 20	www.fnac.com
Surcouf	08 92 70 76 00	www.surcouf.com

Chain stores FNAC and Darty stock a fairly wide range of both PCs and Macs at decent prices, however service in both instances leaves something to be desired. Staff shortages and busy stores means those seeking knowledgeable advice may be in for a long wait. PCs can also be found at Carrefour stores. When it comes to repairs, be prepared for a decent wait: computers bought at generalist electronic stores will need to be returned to the maker for assessment and repair, resulting in delays that can stretch as long as eight weeks. And be attentive with guarantees; standard warranties usually run no longer than 12 months with an option to purchase more time at extra cost. Consider this a wise investment, as the costs of repair outside warranty can be prohibitive – like DVD players and music systems, repairs often cost nearly as much as the original purchase price. Guarantees will not cross international borders in most instances, so if you plan on taking your new computer out of the country prepare to send it back to France should anything go awry.

Electronics & Home Appliances

Other options **Computers** p.285, **Camera Equipment** p.253

While buyers can select from the full range of major international brands, prices for electronics and appliances are no cheaper than what you would expect to pay in the UK or the US. There remains, however, a sliding scale of prices. BHV, Darty, Conforama and Surcouf offer some of the best deals in Paris. All four companies stock most major brands – from Miele and Westinghouse to Smeg and GE – at prices ranging from as low as €100 for a simple washing machine to €1,000 and up for stylish, large capacity ovens and refrigerators. Auchan and Boulanger are two chain stores offering similarly great prices and ranges, though neither have outlets within the city limits.

Electronics & Home Appliances			
Auchan	Various Locations	08 10 28 24 26	www.auchan.fr
Bang & Olufsen	Various Locations	01 56 26 07 50	www.bang-olufsen.com
BHV Ivry Entrepôts	Ivry-sur-Seine	01 49 60 44 00	www.bhv.fr
Bose	Various Locations	01 30 61 33 10	www.bosefrance.fr
Boulanger	Various Locations	01 56 86 10 40	www.boulanger.fr
Conforama	Various Locations	01 42 33 78 58	www.conforma.fr
Darty	Various Locations	08 21 08 20 82	www.darty.com
E Dehillerin	1st	01 42 36 53 13	www.e-dehillerin.fr
FNAC Micro	5th	01 44 41 31 50	www.fnac.com
La Niche by BHV	4th	01 42 74 90 00	www.bhv.fr

Thankfully, both offer online order and delivery services. Brand specialists like Bose, Sony and Bang & Olufsen also have multiple outlets in the city for those seeking higher-end stereo, television and home entertainment systems. Cooking enthusiasts may want to head to E.Dehillerin, a specialist kitchen store dealing in appliances as well as cooking and baking utensils.

Hunting down second-hand goods is simple, courtesy of various expatriate websites and journals. As non-furnished Parisian apartments are rented without basic household appliances, there exists a significant trade in used goods as expatriates take their leave. Look to the classifieds section online at www.angloinfo.com, pick up a copy of *FUSAC* at any of the English-language bookstores, or research the French journal *De Particulier à Particulier*, released every Thursday and found at news kiosks. BHV also runs its own warehouse just outside Paris – BHV Ivry Entrepôts – selling shop-soiled, sale white goods and electrical appliances that often need little more than a good clean. A high standard of after-sales service is to be found across the board, with delivery also available from the larger boutiques and chain stores for a small extra fee. Given that most of the larger white goods must be hauled up stairs by delivery men, tipping is a nice idea. Those for whom Paris is not a long-term stay may want to consider the international compatibility of appliances and electronics before they spend big. Compatibility is not a problem between Europe and the UK, however British and European goods require use of expensive adaptors in order to function in the US due to a different voltage.

Eyewear

Other options **Sports Goods** p.281

The optical industry is big business in France; government subsidies mean even fashion prescription frames warrant a reimbursement should your health insurance cover eye care. Needless to say the industry has decided to profit from this generosity, with the city's many optical boutiques falling in to three distinct categories: independent boutiques selling some fantastically unusual designer frames (Voyeurs, Optique St Honoré or Marc le Bihan); big chain stores offering great service and discounts (Grand Optical and Alain Afflelou); and department stores stocking a wide range of internationally recognised brands.

259

Few outlets will carry out eye testing on site, as the law dictates all tests must be performed by a qualified ophthalmologist. Tests cost around €45 and are refundable through the social security system for residents. Optical boutiques, however, provide plenty of other services including after-sales service, repairs and custom-building of both prescription and sunglasses. Grand Optical and Alain Afflelou will also run the occasional buy-two-get-a-third-pair-free offer on prescription sales.

Eyewear			
Alain Afflelou	Various Locations	01 43 59 87 99	www.alainafflelou.com
Alain Mikli	Various Locations	01 45 49 40 00	www.mikli.fr
Espace Optical	9th	01 40 82 77 88	www.espaceoptical.com
Grand Optical	Various Locations	01 40 06 92 73	www.grandoptical.com
H&M	Various Locations	01 55 34 96 86	www.hm.com/fr
Marc Le Bihan	Various Locations	01 42 36 22 32	na
Oakley O Store	1st	01 44 88 22 22	www.ostoreparis.com
Optique St Honoré	1st	01 42 86 88 01	na
Réciproque	Various Locations	01 47 04 30 28	www.reciproque.fr
Solaris	Various Locations	01 45 26 64 09	www.solaris.fr
Voyeurs	7th	01 45 49 30 44	na
Zara	Various Locations	na	www.zara.fr

Sales of sunglasses, while no match for prescription glasses, are also growing in France thanks to the abundance of fashion styles available in a wide array of stores. The dominant big fashion brands such as Gucci, Dior, Chanel and Marc Jacobs are available in both independent boutiques, speciality chain stores such as Solaris, and department stores. Prices start at around €100 and head upward of €500 for exclusive frames from high fashion brands like Chanel and Hermes. Those looking to economise might try H&M or Zara, where stylish frames come with a less startling price tag. For a custom look, head to Oakley's store on rue du Pont Neuf, where buyers can put together their own pair of sunglasses, selecting from a range of frame and lens combinations. True fans of vintage should make their way to Réciproque in the 16th, where an entire boutique is dedicated to luxury, vintage accessories, including sunglasses.

Flowers

Other options **Gardens** p.263

Saying it with flowers is made easy in Paris thanks to the plethora of chain and boutique florists – and the prices won't make Cupid wince. In season and floral arrangements are relatively economical; in spring tulips are particularly good value, selling for as little as €5 a bunch. Supermarket florists can provide surprisingly good quality offerings at a price significantly less than you would expect to pay at floral boutiques. There, florists provide amazing service and beautiful arrangements – but at

Flowers			
Aquarelle	Various Locations	na	www.aquarelle.com
Au Nom de la Rose	Various Locations	08 92 35 00 07	www.aunomdelarose.fr
Auarelle	Various Locations	08 20 82 04 50	na
Hervé Gambs	Various Locations	01 70 08 09 08	www.hervegambs.com
Interflora	Various Locations	08 10 35 38 77	www.interflora.fr
Lachaume	8th	01 42 60 59 74	na

a price. For a more lasting thought, floral boutiques also commonly sell indoor plants. Thanks to the miracle of freight, beautiful blooms are available all year round; however it can be worth ordering ahead in the lead up to occasions such as Valentine's Day. Major operators, Interflora, provide an online service throughout France and internationally, while other French groups such as Au Nom de la Rose (rose specialists), and Aquarelle also provide a comprehensive online delivery service. Aquarelle even runs its own *ateliers* teaching flower arrangements. Locating independent florists in your neighbourhood is as simple as taking a stroll around the block and the sheer number of boutiques suggests flowers are an essential part of

Marché aux Fleurs, Île de la Cité

everyday Parisian life. Le Marché aux Fleurs on the Île de la Cité also provides a convivial market atmosphere in which to buy some gorgeous floral gifts.

For truly special arrangements head to Lachaume, master florists since the 19th century on rue Royale. Hervé Gambs, where artificial flowers are transformed into gorgeous decorative arrangements, is also a possibility for posies that are made to last.

Food

Other options **Health Food** p.265

Food, glorious food. Paris is a gourmet paradise, home to an endless number of eye-opening fine food stores, each more fantastic than the last. For everyday needs there is a good number of supermarkets (p.301), hypermarkets (p.292) and health food stores (p.265), but the real joy is to be found in scouting out the specialist stores and specialist food markets for delicious new flavours and finds.

Bakeries

The local baker, or *boulanger*, is undoubtedly one of the most important people in each neighbourhood. Bread plays a huge part in daily life, not to mention the luscious pastries which tempt from each *boulangerie* window display. Addresses worth a special visit? Eric Kayser for his breads with fruits or nuts, Poilane for the sourdough, Le Boulanger de Monge for organic breads, Bechu for its gorgeous pastries, Jean-Pierre Cohier for the best baguettes in Paris and Patisserie Stohrer for cakes that impressed Queen Elizabeth II, to name but a few.

Butchers

Those that like their meat shrink-wrapped will get something of a shock at their local butcher, where whole chickens, skinned rabbits and entire pigs are on display within the glass meat cases. The French like to know where their cut of meat is coming from. Butchers will cut and pre-prepare meat to your specifications, or for a real treat buy one of the rotisserie chickens many *boucheries* cook in a glass case at the shop's front; truly delicious. Jean-Paul Gardil, a butchers on the Île St-Louis, is worth a visit for its fairytale feel and reputation for outstanding quality. Adventurous types might want to try a horse steak from Boucherie J.D. in rue Montorgueil, a well-known butcher specialising in the sale of horse meat.

Cheese

Kraft has no market hold in France, the country famed for its production of some 365 different types of cheese. To get a taste head to your local *fromagerie*, where most vendors will offer you a slice of whatever takes your fancy before purchase. And don't be afraid to ask for advice; cheese is highly seasonal and *fromagers* are usually generous with their knowledge of what is best eaten when. For a real cheese experience head to Marie-Anne Cantin for luscious unpasteurised cheeses, Alléosse for farmhouse camembert and certain rare offerings, or Barthelemy for the house special, boulamour, a small ball of *fromage blanc* that is studded with dark and golden raisins.

Chocolate

It's perhaps no coincidence that some of the best chocolate houses in Paris are the most universally well-known. Jean-Paul Hevin, Patrick Roger and La Maison du Chocolat are each known for their beautifully rich truffles, Pierre Herme – while more a pastry genius than a *chocolatier* – makes some fabulously rich chocolate desserts and at Debauve & Gallais you can taste the treats from the official chocolate makers to the Kings of France.

Ethnic Foods

Have a hankering for a cuisine other than French? Around the metro stop La Chapelle in the 10th *arrondissement* you will find the streets lined with Indian grocers, while the area surrounding rue des Petit-Champs is crammed with Japanese *épiceries*. For rare spices try Goumanyat in the 3rd. Allicante specialises in rare olive and flavoured oils from Morocco, Greece and Liguria, Le Stübli bakes some fantastic German cakes (don't miss the classic Black Forest), Noura sells sticky Lebanese pastries and savoury goodies in the 16th, while the Maison d'Afrique deals in all delicacies African. And that's just a teeny taste of the vast selection of ethnic food stores to be found.

Grand Epiceries

At these fine food superstores you will find everything you need to enjoy a true gourmet experience; from fine chocolates and candied fruits to deluxe ready meals, elegant biscuits and exotic fruits. Fauchon, Lenotre and Hediard all have stunning flagship stores on the place de la Madeleine. La Grande Epicerie at Le Bon Marché on the Left Bank is a food experience all its own with international and French gourmet fresh and packaged goods all vying for your attention.

Speciality Foods

No food speciality is too expensive or obscure in Paris to warrant its very own boutique. At La Maison de la Truffe you can find the finest selection of fresh and preserved truffles before heading just a few doors up to snatch up salty caviar at Caviar House & Prunier (specialists in French caviar). Boutique Maille offers choice of more than 30 varieties of mustard with flavours like blue cheese or apricot. Icecream fans must visit Berthillon, France's famed icecream house, for a rich and creamy take-home pack. And while foie gras may be increasingly politically incorrect

Food shopping

outside of France, here it still signifies the ultimate in gourmet luxury. Pick up your taste at the Comtesse du Barry, a chain of boutiques specialising in traditional foie gras, confits and cassoulets.

Markets

Good quality fruit and vegetables are easily picked up in the local supermarket, however, experiencing Paris' open-air produce markets is as much a cultural experience as it is a chance to buy some of the freshest and finest food around. Head to the Marché Place Baudoyer in the Marais, an afternoon market held each Wednesday with a fantastic free-range egg stand alongside stalls selling fresh paella and delicious *charcuterie*. The Marché Mouffetard is very well-known and for good reason; colourful and vibrant, it offers one of the most atmospheric experiences. On Thursdays and Saturdays pick up your groceries with a view of the Eiffel Tower at avenue de Saxe, where you'll find beautifully arranged olives, paté and cheeses. See page 295.

Food		
Alléosse	17th	01 46 22 50 45
Allicante	11th	01 43 55 13 02
Barthelemy	7th	01 45 48 56 75
Bechu	16th	01 47 27 97 79
Berthillon	4th	01 43 54 31 61
Boucherie J.D.	2nd	01 42 36 32 11
Boutique Maille	8th	01 40 15 06 00
Caviar House & Prunier	8th	01 47 42 98 98
Comtesse du Barry	Various Locations	01 43 80 33 34
Debauve & Gallais	7th	01 45 48 54 67
Eric Kayser	Various Locations	01 44 07 09 23
Fauchon	8th	01 42 61 45 46
Goumanyant	3rd	01 44 78 96 74
Hediard	8th	01 43 12 88 88
Jean-Paul Gardil	4th	01 43 54 97 15
Jean-Paul Hévin	Various Locations	01 55 35 35 96
Jean-Pierre Cohier	17th	01 42 27 45 26
La Maison du Chocolat	6th	01 45 44 20 40
La Grande Epicerie, Le Bon Marché	7th	01 44 39 81 00
La Maison de la Truffe	8th	01 42 65 53 22
Le Boulanger de Monge	5th	01 43 37 54 20
Le Stübli	17th	01 42 27 81 86
Lenotre	Various Locations	01 45 02 21 21
Maison d'Afrique	18th	01 42 54 78 22
Marie-Anne Cantin	7th	01 45 50 43 94
Noura	16th	01 47 23 02 20
Patisserie Stohrer	2nd	01 42 33 38 20
Patrick Roger	6th	01 43 29 38 42
Petrossian Paris	7th	01 44 11 32 22
Pierre Herme	6th	01 43 54 47 77
Poilane	6th	01 45 48 42 59

Gardens

Other options **Hardware & DIY** p.265, **Flowers** p.260

And on the seventh day Paris… gardened. While much of the rest of the city takes Sunday to rest, local garden centres do a brisk trade in all things green and floral. Though living space is tight, a quick look skyward at any apartment building will reveal balconies and window boxes overflowing with geraniums, ivy and all manner of flora. Apparently even those enamoured with city living occasionally feel the need to flex their green thumbs.

For a real market experience, the grouping of plant nurseries at the Marché aux Fleurs on the Île de la Cité is a sight to behold. Numerous vendors operating out of permanent greenhouses sell everything from seeds and seedlings to full-grown trees and hot-house orchids. Garden equipment, pots, bags of soil and fertiliser is also available. Advice is freely given, though most often in French. The market experience continues across the Seine where further garden boutiques display their wares along the quai de la Mégisserie and quai de Gesvres, selling the full range of plant life alongside outdoor furnishings.

For a less expensive option, the discount department store chain, Carrefour, incorporates an expansive gardening section at its 13th *arrondissement* address. BHV department store, just opposite the Hôtel de Ville in central Paris, is also a good economical option for garden and outdoor furnishings. Decorative items, nursery plants and outdoor and leisure products can be tracked down at Truffaut, a specialist garden centre that has 18 outlets across the city. Discount chain Castorama, with multiple locations in the Île de France region, offers great buys in garden furnishings, plants and even pools and spas. When it comes to landscaping and independent boutiques, Boutique Vilmorin on the quai de la Mégisserie offers landscaping services alongside flora and equipment. Le Jardin de Victoria in the 15th will create and maintain gardens, taking on yearly maintenance

Territoire in the 8th

contracts for both individuals and corporate enterprises. For those with smaller outdoor spaces to fill, Jardin d'Edgar is a boutique nursery selling bonsai, ornamental plants and trees for small balconies and gardens.

Gardens			
Boutique Vilmorin	4th	01 42 33 61 62	www.vilmorin-jardin.com
Carrefour Jardins	13th	01 43 53 86 00	www.carrefour.fr
Castorama	Various Locations	01 53 42 42 42	www.castorama.fr
Jardin d'Edgar	4th	01 56 24 42 44	www.aujardindedgar.fr
La Niche by BHV	4th	01 42 74 90 00	www.bhv.fr
Le Jardin de Victoria	15th	01 47 83 23 20	www.jardin-de-victoria.com
Truffaut	Various Locations	01 53 60 84 50	www.truffaut.com

Gifts

Searching for gift shops in Paris is like shooting fish in a barrel: the list of categories and addresses is never-ending. The city has an enormous retail culture with myriad speciality shops selling exclusive categories of goods: bear fans will be delighted by L'Ours du Marais; indulge your loved-one's passion for taxidermy at Deyrolle; Les Archives de la Presse deals in collectible magazines and catalogues; browse whimsical toys and home accessories at Territoire; Colette has a great range of limited-edition and trend pieces for the fashion-conscious; give the gift of beautiful practicality at Madeleine Gely, the oldest (and most luxurious) umbrella and parasol boutique in the capital; pick up something for the kids at Le Ciel est a Tout le Monde; or drop by Hediard or Lenotre and pick up some goodies for the food-lover in your life. The department stores (p.290) are also great for a huge general gift selection.

It is worth remembering that gift giving etiquette is well-established in France, with popular choices including a cup and spoon for christenings and crystal ware for weddings. Even an invitation to dinner requires the thoughtful choice of a bottle of wine or flowers.

Gifts			
Colette	1st	01 55 35 33 90	www.colette.fr
Deyrolle	7th	01 42 22 30 07	www.deyrolle.fr
Galeries Lafayette	Various Locations	01 42 82 34 56	www.galerieslafayette.com
Hediard	Various Locations	01 47 20 44 44	www.hediard.fr
L'Ours du Marais	4th	01 42 77 60 43	www.oursdumarais.com
Le Bon Marché	7th	01 44 39 80 00	www.lebonmarche.fr
Le Ciel est a Tout le Monde	Various Locations	01 48 78 93 40	www.lecielestatoutlemonde.com
Lenotre	Various Locations	01 45 02 21 21	www.lenotre.fr
Les Archives de la Presse	3rd	01 42 72 63 93	www.lesarchivesdelapresse.com
Madeleine Gely	7th	01 42 22 17 02	na
Marechal	1st	01 42 60 71 83	www.limogesmarechal.fr
Printemps	Various Locations	01 42 82 57 87	www.printemps.com
Territoire	8th	01 42 66 22 13	www.territoire.com

Hardware & DIY
Other options **Outdoor Goods** p.273

Apartment living may not be conducive to DIY, but there exists more than just one or two large chains catering to hardware and DIY needs. There is little need to fuss around with specialist stores, thanks to the expansive selections available in the well-known hardware megastores. First stop may be the basement of department store BHV, renowned for its enormous selection of hardware, painting and DIY materials. Staff are on hand to help you navigate the labyrinthine space which is best avoided on weekends if possible. Generalist stores Bricorama, Leroy-Merlin, Mr.Bricolage and Castorama also provide a great selection of tools, materials, paints and kits in multiple centres across Paris and the wider Île de France. After-sales service is offered by each, with telephone hotlines set up to offer advice and answer questions. For small, local hardware and DYI needs look for shops bearing the sign *quincaillerie*. These are hardware stores selling everything from taps and piping to hammers, nails, paint and gardening equipment.

Hardware & DIY			
Bricorama	Various Locations	01 45 86 56 56	www.bricorama.fr
Castorama	Various Locations	01 53 42 42 42	www.castorama.fr
IKEA	Roissy	08 25 82 68 26	www.ikea.fr
La Niche by BHV	4th	01 42 74 90 00	www.bhv.fr
Leroy-Merlin	Various Locations	01 44 54 66 66	www.leroymerlin.fr
Mr Bricolage	Various Locations	01 40 02 02 04	www.mr-bricolage.fr

Health Food
Other options **Food** p.261

The concept of 'health food' is still a relatively new one in France but some specialist stores do exist. Naturalia is a chain of health food stores with 32 branches around the city offering gluten-free, lactose-free and organic pre-prepared foods, alongside healthy snacks, organic vegetables, vitamins, food supplements, and organic baby products and cosmetics. Bio (organic) cooperatives can also be found dotted around Paris' 20 *arrondissements*, operating as organic and natural food grocery stores. These outlets are a bonus for those with food allergies or following strict vegan or vegetarian diets, as most restaurants can not be relied upon to accommodate special dietary requirements. Supermarkets and pharmacies will also stock a limited range of health foods, however much of this product is produced with the dieter – not the health food fan – in mind. For those seeking a dedicated health food supermarket, Les Nouveaux Robinson has three locations on the outskirts of Paris, stocking a huge range of organic produce, cruelty-free cosmetics and even organic clothing.

Health Food		
Biocoop Grenelle	15th	01 45 77 70 14
Biocoop Lemo	11th	01 48 05 02 09
Biocoop Paris	17th	01 42 26 10 30
Biocoop Paris Glaciere	13th	01 45 35 24 36
Canal Bio	19th	01 42 06 44 44
Les Rouveaux Robinson	Various Locations	01 41 10 94 10
Naturalia	Various Locations	01 55 80 77 81

Home Furnishings & Accessories
Other options **Hardware & DIY** p.265

First impressions carry significant weight in style-conscious Paris, and the home interior is no exception. Luckily the city offers a vast array of furnishing and decoration options for all budgets at prices which are comparative with the UK and the USA. Habitat is perhaps the largest of the mid-range stores, stocking contemporary furniture and accessories for the entire home at prices young couples can afford. An affordable range of options can also be found among the designer brands on show at both Galeries Lafayette Maison and Printemps Maison. Pier Imports carries ethnic-style accessories and furnishings for slightly fewer euros. Dealing exclusively in bathroom furnishing and fittings, Bathroom Bazaar offers a one-stop shop for all things *salle de bain*, however those on a budget may be better off at BHV.

Leading the pack when it comes to chic are Lignes Rosset and Roche Bobois, both with multiple stores in the city. Prices here range from more than €1,500 for sideboards and sofas. Roche Bobois has three or four different arms to its franchise, each specialising in a different interior style including French provincial and modern. More unique are the boutiques along the Viaduc des Arts, a central gathering space for independent artisans. There you will find expensive furnishing stores specialising in made-to-measure pieces using luxurious materials but this isn't the only space where bespoke furniture is an option. Many independent furnishing salons focus on client-ordered pieces; in the 15th *arrondissement*, Ateliers St Paul specialises in creating cabinets, kitchen fittings and staircases to order, while at Eclat de Vie custom-made wood furnishing walks hand-in-hand with the store's interior design service. Placards et Miroirs in the 5th *arrondissement* will also custom design cupboards and mirrors alongside provision of standard stock.

Antique and reparation stores are quite common. In the 11th *arrondissement*, La Chaiserie du Faubourg is known for repairs and re-upholstering of chairs and lounges, while a cluster of stores selling antiques and performing reparations are congregated in the Village St Paul and the Village Suisse.

Heading out of town, there are quite a few large discount houses for those seeking real value for money. IKEA is justifiably popular for its flat-pack, do-it-yourself offerings, while the mall in Cergy-Pontoise, Art de Vivre, brings together a large number of

Home Furnishings & Accessories

Art de Vivre	Cergy Pontoise	01 34 21 83 00	www.artdevivre95.com
Atelier 154	13th	06 62 32 79 06	www.atelier154.com
Babble Circus	7th	01 45 55 07 28	www.babblecircus.free.fr
Bathroom Bazaar	Various Locations	01 45 48 29 29	www.bathbazaar.fr
BHV	4th	01 42 74 90 00	www.bhv.fr
Caravane	Various Locations	01 44 61 04 20	www.caravane.fr
The Conran Shop	7th	01 42 84 10 01	www.conranshop.fr
Domus	Roisny-sous-Bois	01 48 12 18 60	www.domusparis.com
Eclat de Vie	Luzarches	01 30 29 91 95	www.eclatdevie.fr
Galeries Lafayette	Various Locations	01 42 82 34 56	www.galerieslafayette.com
Greenfields	4th	01 40 27 94 93	www.greenfields.fr
Habitat	Various Locations	01 55 37 75 00	www.habitat.net
IKEA	Roissy	08 25 82 68 26	www.ikea.fr
In Lease	Lille	01 76 63 74 14	www.in-lease.com
La Chaiserie du Faubourg	11th	01 43 57 67 51	na
Les Puces de St-Ouen	St-Ouen	01 40 12 32 58	www.marchesauxpuces.fr
Lignes Rosset	Various Locations	01 45 48 54 13	www.lignes-roset.tm.fr
Marché aux Puces de la Porte de Vanves	14th	na	www.pucesdevanves.typepad.com
Pier Import	Various Locations	01 40 29 04 99	www.pierimport.fr
Placards et Miroirs	5th	01 46 33 60 09	www.placardsmiroirs.com
Printemps Maison	9th	01 42 82 50 00	www.printemps.com
Roche Bobois	Various Locations	01 49 54 01 70	www.roche-bobois.com
Viaduc des Arts	12th	na	www.viaduc-des-arts.com
Vibel	Various Locations	01 42 93 08 08	www.vibel.com
Village St Paul	4th	01 48 87 69 27	www.parislemarais.com
Village Suisse	15th	01 40 51 37 52	www.levillagesuisseparis.com

reasonably priced stores in the one locale. Relatively new, Domus is another multi-brand furnishing mall on the outskirts of Paris which also offers an interior design service. Paris' flea markets – the Marché aux Puces de la Porte de Vanves and Les Puces de St-Ouen – are two further centres overflowing with great furnishing deals for buyers with a good eye and a knack for bargaining.

Children need not feel left behind thanks largely to the impressive array of furnishing and decor stores specialising in eclectic designs. Two of these are Babble Circus in the 7th and the numerous Vibel franchise boutiques around the city. Both businesses offer colourful designs and themed bedroom sets.

Highly specialised boutiques also rate a mention, not least the boutique Greenfields. Available for viewing by appointment only, Greenfields stocks a stunning range of Waterford Crystal home accessories, including stunning crystal chandeliers. In the 13th *arrondissement*, Atelier 154 presents an amazing collection of furnishings inspired and created by industrial products. Caravane, meanwhile, offers a range of over-sized sofas and accessories from India, Uzbekistan and Morocco. Lastly, those seeking temporary furnishings will find everything they need with In Lease, an international company specialising in the lease of furnishings and accessories for people with temporary living situations.

Jewellery, Watches & Gold

The cluster of jewellery boutiques found around the moneyed neighbourhoods of the 1st and 8th *arrondissements* is no coincidence – who better to frequent these boutiques than the city's affluent classes? Place Vendôme is bling central, where just about every international luxury jeweller can be located, each display window more magnificent than the last. Gasp over the latest designs from Cartier, Mikimoto, Van Cleef & Arpels, Bvlgari and Chaumet, the official jeweller to Napoleon. Away from the recognisable big names but still costing big money are the boutiques Bilbault JP and Perinet Michel, both on the rue St-Honoré.

Bijoux Anciens-Eve Cazes in the 8th sells a stunning array of antique jewels and watches at eyebrow-raising prices.

Don't have a fortune to spend? Youthful, contemporary looks in silver are on show at Clio Blue at very reasonable prices. Éric et Lydie specialise in delicate designs with a retro edge, working frequently with stained, antique-look metals. Prices are in the mid-range. For statement jewellery with a bohemian aesthetic head to Monies, while Devana in the Marais specialises in design of ethnic-influenced pieces in sterling silver showcased

Jewellery, Watches & Gold				
Agatha	Various Locations	01 43 59 68 68	www.agatha.fr
Antoine Camus Jewellers	16th	01 45 20 00 87	www.antoinecamus.fr
Atelier Julien Créations	3rd	01 42 77 33 60	www.ajcreations.com
Bijoux Anciens-Eve Cazes	8th	01 42 65 95 44	www.evecazes.com
Bilbault JP	1st	01 42 60 14 38	na
Bvlgari	Various Locations	01 55 35 00 50	www.bulgari.com
Camille & Lucie	1st	01 42 96 88 26	www.camille-lucie.com
Cartier	Various Locations	01 42 18 43 83	www.cartier.fr
Cécile & Jeanne	Various Locations	01 4 26 68 68	www.cecilejeanne.com
Chaumet	Various Locations	01 44 77 26 26	www.chaumet.com
Clio Blue	Various Locations	01 42 61 31 13	www.clioblue.com
Devana	3rd	01 42 78 69 76	na
Éric et Lydie	2nd	01 40 26 52 59	na
Gas	2nd	01 45 08 49 46	na
La Licorne	3rd	01 48 87 84 43	na
Les Ateliers Tamalet	9th	01 45 23 47 47	na
Mikimoto	1st	01 42 60 33 55	www.mikimoto.fr
Monies	1st	01 40 20 90 01	www.monies.dk
Montre Service	Various Locations	01 43 21 12 10	www.montreservice.fr
Perinet Michel	1st	01 42 61 49 16	na
Tiffany & Co	Various Locations	01 40 20 20 20	www.tiffany.com
Top Time	1st	01 42 72 50 00	na
Van Cleef & Arpels	1st	01 53 45 35 50	www.vancleef-arpels.com
Wempe	8th	01 42 60 21 77	www.wempe.de

in a dramatic boutique replete with live python. Costume jewellery is also big business in Paris, ranging on the scale from the cheap, fun offerings of charm bangles, faux-gilt and chunky earrings from chain store, Agatha, to the pretty necklaces and bracelets inlaid with coloured crystals and semi-precious stones at GAS. Camille and Lucie on the rue Rivoli specialise in costume jewellery at great prices while La Licorne focuses on unique costume pieces from the 1920s and '30s, with numerous offerings in bakelite and jade. The boutique will also undertake jewellery repairs, as will Antoine Camus Jewellers in Passy.

Finding jewellers willing to create custom designs is not difficult; Atelier Julien Créations in the 3rd *arrondissement* and Les Ateliers Tamalet in the 9th are both good starting points and both offer services in English. For watches, Top Time on rue de Rivoli has an enormous collection of more than 2,000 watches and weather forecasting devices while nearby on rue Royale is Wempe, the century-old luxury watch and jewellery brand. For repairs and services try Montre Service, with stores across the city. The department stores also stock a huge range of international name brands at both low-to-mid and mid-to-high price targets.

Kids' Items

Age is not a prohibiting factor when it comes to being fashionable in Paris, good news for young trend-setters trying to convince parents that they really don't have a thing to wear. Du Pareil au Meme is a chain store which sells inexpensive, brightly coloured clothing for children up to 14 years and new collections are released several times a year. La Compagnie des Petits and Catimini operate along similar lines but remember that sizing is on the small side at these shops. Gapkids is another good economical choice, selling stylish but well-priced basics but for clothing with a little more quirk try Miki House. The business has three shops in Paris selling unique and chic clothing. Okaidi and Sergent Major also veer from traditional styles to present outfits with a point of difference. Pamp'lune in the 18th is another great find, selling original designs that would prove just as stylish on grown-ups. For frills and flounce, Bonpoint and Tartine et Chocolat lead the pack,

Kids' Items		
Bonpoint	Various Locations	01 40 51 98 20
C&A	9th	01 53 30 89 33
Catimini	8th	01 53 76 21 51
Cryillus	7th	08 03 81 38 13
Du Pareil au Meme	1st	01 42 36 07 57
Gapkids	8th	01 56 88 48 00
H&M	Various Locations	01 55 34 96 86
La Compagnie des Petits	6th	01 42 22 48 93
Miki House	1st	01 40 20 90 98
Okaidi	5th	01 42 17 45 94
Pamp'lune	18th	01 46 06 50 23
Sergent Major	3rd	01 53 01 86 86
Tartine et Chocolate	Various Locations	01 45 56 10 45

however prices can be shocking so be prepared. If both parents and kids need some new duds and you are short of time try shopping at C&A, Cyrillus and H&M, all of which stock clothes for the whole family.

Lingerie

Other options **Clothes** p.254

Lingerie is big business in the city of romance, where stylish underwear is deemed just as important as fashionable outerwear. Not particularly enamoured by fetish styles, lingerie boutiques appear to subscribe to the notion that classically elegant sex appeal will win hearts over garish outfits. And for those seeking sex kitten-style glamour, the city's lingerie boutiques have your needs covered.

Supermarkets stock basic cotton briefs and bras in single and multi-packs at rock-bottom prices. For something a little more fashionable (though still affordable), lingerie chains Etam and Princesse Tam-Tam house a great range of options; everything from peek-a-boo lace sets to the more sensible and sturdy. As with swimwear, La Perla boutiques specialise in delicate and sexy pieces with a high-fashion price tag. For a 1950s aesthetic head to one of the city's two Fifi Chachnil boutiques where you'll find fluffy, feminine designs in a boudoir-style setting.

For multiple labels under one roof Le Bon Marché offers a gorgeous selection of designer and mid-range brands, including Christian Dior and Yves Saint Laurent, in an atmosphere that is pure glamour-puss luxe. Service here is at a premium, so don't be surprised should your sales lady follow you to the change cubicle for a no-holds-barred fit and measure. A recent redesign of Printemps' lingerie department has also made it essential viewing for shoppers. Agent Provocateur is available exclusively here. Galeries Lafayette also offer 80

Lingerie

Anita Oggioni	7th	01 45 49 27 61	na
Cadolle	Various Locations	01 42 60 94 94	www.cadolle.fr
Etam	Various Locations	01 44 76 73 73	www.etam.com
Fanny Liautard	8th	01 42 86 82 84	www.fannyliautard
Fifi Chachnil	Various Locations	01 42 61 21 83	www.fifichachnil.com
Galeries Lafayette	Various Locations	01 42 82 34 56	www.galerieslafayette.com
Grandiva	17th	01 46 22 00 44	www.grandiva-aliceb.com
La Perla	Various Locations	01 43 12 33 60	www.laperla.com
Le Bon Marché	7th	01 44 39 80 00	www.lebonmarche.fr
Princesse Tam Tam	Various Locations	01 42 86 52 46	www.princesstam-tam.com
Printemps	Various Locations	01 42 82 57 87	www.printemps.com
Sabbia Rose	7th	01 45 48 88 37	na

brands alongside a manicure bar and occasional courses in striptease – ask the store for details. Fit and measure is part of the service at all three department stores.

High-end, luxury boutiques Sabbia Rose, Fanny Liautard and Cadolle will hand-make lingerie in specific styles and colours for enthusiastic clients. Of these, however, it is Cadolle that is justifiably the most well-known; Marguerite Cadolle measured lingerie for Mata Hari in the 1920s and her granddaughter, Poupie, continues to run the business today. Pick from 400 styles of bras and be prepared to attend multiple fittings. Bras can cost up to €300 and boned corsets twice as much. Ready-to-wear lingerie at lower cost (bras for around €80) is carried in the ground-floor boutique. Now an institution, there are three boutiques providing different functions – couture, ready-to-wear and perfumes – around Paris.

Grandiva specialises in luxury lingerie for full-figured women, taking private appointments two days a week. Online, head to www.vivelesrondes.com, where an extensive online catalogue of brands catering to larger sizes is at your finger tips.

France is decidedly liberal when it comes to advertisement of underwear and boutique window-displays – it's not unusual to view posters of topless models or mannequins in particularly spectacular get-up – so the puritanical may want to shield their eyes.

Louis Vuitton

Luggage & Leather

Whether it's Louis Vuitton and a trip on the QE2, or Samsonite and a Ryanair skip to Glasgow, finding the right luggage and leather accessories is easy in Paris.

Albertson's Maroquinerie in the 9th *arrondissement* stocks quality leather goods at wholesale prices, selling everything from leather cigar holders to gloves and briefcases, and bulk purchases are available. Les Halles has a plethora of bazaar-style stores carrying Samsonite, Antler, Quiksilver and other brands at budget prices. The quality is

decent though perhaps not as long-lasting as some of the better-known brands. A step down is the luggage and leather sellers at the various moveable markets that pop up around the city. Try the market on Wednesday and Saturday mornings on avenue President Wilson in the 16th. Care needs to be taken in these situations, however, as luggage and leather goods bought at market stalls obviously come without a guarantee. Lancel, Longchamp and Lamarthe are firm French favourites for the stylish traveller not afraid to spend a little, while popular modern brand Mandarina Duck also has multiple outlets around the city. Tumi also offers mid-to-high range prices on classic luggage and men's and women's accessories. AG Spalding & Bros in the Marais caters to the sporty and design-conscious guy with a great selection of masculine wallets and briefcases. For the best deals head to Printemps and Galeries Lafayette during the two sale periods, falling at the end of June and the end of January. Here you will find the full range of luggage and leather goods at up to 70% off as the sales draw to a close. High-fashion brand Hermès stocks extraordinarily fashionable cases, handbags and leather accessories at exorbitant prices. Goyard on rue St-Honoré has been in operation since 1853 and with a stunning array of luxury travel cases – including old-fashioned cases with draws and hanging space for luxury cruise travel – is worth a visit just to experience the glamour of handmade luggage. Similar luxury is on display at Atelier du Bracelet Parisien, specialists in leather craftsmanship, including wallets and other handmade goods.

Lovers of leather clothing should make a call to Loewe, an exclusive Spanish leather house on avenue Montaigne specialising in sexy leather bodysuits, python jeans and bustier-style leather tops. Don't have that kind of spending limit? The flea markets at Porte de Clignancourt (Le Marché aux Puces de St-Ouen, p.296) do a brisk trade in leather jackets and pants at a *prix moins cher*.

Luggage & Leather

AG Spalding & Bros	4th	01 42 71 33 32	www.spaldingbros.com
Albertson's Maroquinerie	9th	01 48 24 32 16	na
Atelier du Bracelet Parisien	1st	01 42 86 13 70	www.abp-paris.com
Galeries Lafayette	Various Locations	01 42 82 34 56	www.galerieslafayette.com
Goyard	1st	01 42 60 57 04	www.goyard.fr
Hermes	Various Locations	01 40 17 47 17	www.hermes.com
Lamarthe	Various Locations	01 42 97 45 72	www.lamarthe.com
Lancel	Various Locations	na	www.lancel.com
Les Puces de St-Ouen	St-Ouen	01 40 12 32 58	www.marchesauxpuces.fr
Loewe	8th	01 53 57 92 50	www.loewe.com
Longchamp	Various Locations	01 43 16 00 16	www.longchamp.com
Louis Vuitton	Various Locations	08 10 81 00 10	www.louisvuitton.com
Mandarina Duck	Various Locations	01 43 26 68 38	www.mandarinaduck.com
Printemps	Various Locations	01 42 82 57 87	www.printemps.com
Tumi	Various Locations	01 45 79 70 30	www.tumi.com

Medicine

Other options **General Medical Care** p.108

Like *boulangeries*, pharmacies can be found on just about every street corner, distinguishable by the flashing neon green cross above the doorway. They are independent businesses governed by the Ordre de Pharmaciens. Having trained for seven years, pharmacists are qualified to give medical advice, so it's worth heading to the nearest pharmacy – not the doctor – for minor illnesses. Pharmacists can administer first aid and, if necessary, can direct you to the nearest hospital or call emergency services. They will also carry lists of nurses, doctors, paediatricians and medical laboratories in your area.

When it comes to medications, French law is quite restrictive regarding the distribution of drugs; non-prescription drugs in other countries may be by prescription only in France, and other medications like paracetamol (available in supermarkets in the UK and US) are only available in French pharmacies. Should you forget your prescription, pharmacists can call your doctor and will accept telephone confirmation.

Medicine

Grande Pharmacie Daumesnil	12th	01 43 43 19 03
Pharmacie Les Champs Dhéry	8th	01 45 62 02 41
Pharmacie Perrault/Europeene	9th	01 48 74 65 18

Out-of-stock medications can also be ordered promptly with delivery usually promised the same day or within 24 hours. Prescriptions are sold at a recommended retail price set by Social Security, however pharmacists are qualified to substitute name brands for cheaper, generic options of the same form. They will also accept unused drugs which are handed over to aid organisations for use in developing countries. It's also worth remembering that should your pooch or kitty become ill, the pharmacist is able to sell medication for pets on prescription from a vet.

Most adhere to standard store opening hours (Monday to Saturday 09:00 to 20:00), but there are three 24 hour, seven-day chemists dotted around the city: Les Champs Dhéry on the Champs-Élysées, the Grande Pharmacie Daumesnil in the 12th and Pharmacie Perrault/Europeenne at place de Clichy in the 9th. The website www.goparis.about.com provides a comprehensive online directory in English of other outlets open outside normal hours.

Mobile Telephones

Other options **Telephone** p.104

There are three mobile networks covering Paris: Orange, SFR and Bouygues. Each network offers its own chain of stores selling phones and plans, alongside The Phone House and France Telecom boutiques. As mobile phone specific shops these are the best places to head, each offering a range of plans and services in dozens of locations throughout the city.

Mobile Telephones

Asten	17th	01 55 37 30 50	na
Bouygues	Various Locations	06 60 61 46 14	www.bouyguestelecom.fr
France Telecom	Various Locations	08 00 10 07 40	www.francetelecom.fr
George V Telecom	8th	01 47 20 30 40	na
Orange	Various Locations	08 00 10 07 40	www.orange.fr
The Phone House	Various Locations	08 25 07 80 00	www.phonehouse.fr
SFR	Various Locations	06 10 00 19 00	www.sfr.fr

When it comes to billing there are two options: monthly *forfeit* which is priced to your specifications and is directly debited from your account, or pay as you go accounts – known as *sans abonnement* – useful for those not wanting to commit to the one or two year contracts most phone companies would have you sign. A basic phone will come free with any contract, however more sophisticated sets can be bought and put on the plan; a fully-integrated device offering phone, email and camera costs around €100. No matter which of the large brand's you choose prices are all reasonably aligned and the quality of after-sales service is high across the board. Guarantees come with contracts but check the time period as these differ.

For broken phones out of guarantee there exist various mobile phone repair shops, including Asten in the 17th *arrondissement* which also hires mobile phones for those on short-term stays. Or call the boutique George V Telecom, which will deliver mobile phones to Paris hotels 24 hours a day. Visitors on international networks can buy French SIM cards starting from around €35 for the card and a minimum amount of talk time. Top ups are sold at phone shops and *tabacs*.

Music, DVDs & Videos

Music aficionados find no shortage of shopping options in Paris, where both mainstream lovers and vinyl collectors can find their own piece of instrumental heaven. For conventionalists, international chain Virgin Megastore lives up to its moniker with a multi-storey complex on the Champs-Élysées selling the entire range of musical categories alongside listening stations, a bustling cafe, an enormous DVD selection and continual price reductions on older titles. The store will also occasionally host signings and appearances of well-known names in music and film. The specialist French electronics and music store FNAC has multiple outlets, with the Champs-Élysées location (a block up from Virgin) being the best bet for music and DVDs. Like Virgin, the selection is vast, with interactive stations and a small cafe. In both cases you'll find knowledgeable staff, however it's worth noting that titles of English-release movies often differ in France.

Those searching for something specific should know both before asking. The independent music store scene is thriving: 12 Inch Record Shop on rue de Turbigo specialises in vinyl and collectors editions,

Music, DVDs & Videos

12 Inch Record Shop	2nd	01 40 13 90 00	www.12inch.fr
Black Label	11th	01 40 21 92 44	www.blacklabel-records.com
FNAC	Various Locations	08 25 02 00 20	www.fnac.com
Toolbox	11th	01 48 05 80 16	na
Virgin Megastore	Various Locations	01 49 53 50 00	www.virginmegastore.fr

Toolbox in the Oberkampf district stocks tribe, hardtek, ragga jungle and more, while Black Label is a magnet for drum and bass enthusiasts. Though there is no single area where music stores congregate, both the 11th and the 13th are home to many, courtesy of the student-heavy demographics. For a full and extensive listing of shops, look to www.vinylunity.com, where stores are listed alphabetically by city.

Musical Instruments

Other options **Music Lessons** p.226, **Music, DVDs & Videos** p.272

There are dozens of shops dealing in musical instruments, song books and instrument repairs around Paris so there's bound to be one for you. For guitars, Lead Guitars in the 9th sells both new and vintage acoustic, electric, classic and jazz guitars, providing guarantees of between six months and five years depending on the brand and condition of the instrument. The store also permits clients to sell instruments through the store, displaying guitars in the boutique and on the website for one month before either the instrument must be collected or the price dropped. At Centre Chopin, take your pick from the biggest names in new and special occasion pianos. The boutique also stocks musical accessories – music stands, instruments cases and speakers – alongside a selection of world music instruments: think ethnic drums, maracas and wooden xylophones. Feeling Musique in the 8th has a great selection of brass instruments and is one of the leading distributors of wind instruments in France; choose from the trumpet and trombone to flutes, saxophones and more. Those seeking good second-hand buys can go online to www.instrument-musique.vivastreet.fr, the site

Musical Instruments

Centre Chopin	20th	01 43 58 05 45	www.centre-chopin.com
Curiositel	na	na	www.curiositel.com
Feeling Musique	8th	01 45 22 30 80	www.feelingmusique.com
Instrument Musique	na	na	www.instrument-musique.vivastreet.fr
Lead Guitars	9th	01 42 81 46 01	www.leadguitars.fr

offering an expansive selection of used instruments for sale. Lastly, www.curiositel.com showcases a seemingly unlimited listing of boutiques selling, repairing and custom-making all forms of musical instrument. With an hour set aside to research, both amateur and professional musicians can find a shop catering to their specific needs.

Outdoor Goods

Other options **Hardware & DIY** p.265, **Sports Goods** p.281, **Camping** p.214

Perhaps unsurprisingly, comprehensive outdoor goods stores can be tricky to locate, which makes Au Vieux Campeur – a chain of outdoor stores with 23 outlets scattered around the 5th – such a great find. Each boutique has its own speciality, be it mountain climbing gear, running equipment, hiking shoes, camping goods and sports nutrition or men's and women's thermal underwear. The website has a comprehensive list of all store locations, specialities, opening hours, delivery services, catalogues and product information. Staff are extremely knowledgeable and content to spend significant amounts of time ensuring all your questions are answered. If you are serious about outdoor activities these are the only addresses you'll need. Be warned that weekends are chaotic so, if you haven't time to spare, aim for a mid-week visit.

Outdoor Goods		
Au Vieux Campeur	01 53 10 48 48	www.au-vieux-campeur.fr
Decathlon	01 45 72 66 88	www.decathlon.fr
GO Sport	01 44 74 38 38	www.go-sport.com
Hawaii Surf	01 46 72 07 10	www.hawaiisurf.com
Quiksilver	01 44 82 79 99	www.quiksilver.com

Offering a more generic range of goods are the chains Decathalon and Go Sport, where buyers can find both equipment and clothing for selected outdoor sports. Specialists in both winter and summer board sports, Quiksilver and Hawaii Surf both have multiple locations around Paris with staff equipped to dispense sound advice. Hawaii Surf also offers an online buying service. For independent retailers head to Bastille where a small cluster of boutiques can be found.

Party Accessories

Other options **Party Organisers** p.363, **Parties at Home** p.363

Throwing anything from an elegant dinner party to a lively kid's bash is made easy in Paris courtesy of the great number of caterers, party accessory boutiques and the odd party-hire company operating within the city. Party accessory specialist, Tutti Frutti, has multiple outlets around Paris selling everything from streamers, garlands and balloons to themed table dressings and novelty objects for birthdays, Christmas and everything in between. The company will also offer advice on ideas for decoration and party-favours. Internet-based company Fetes-par-Fetes offers a similarly expansive selection for online purchase and delivery; buy over-sized clown feet or tableware for Halloween and St Patrick's Day.

Party Accessories			
Cinescene	18th	01 42 23 08 20	www.cinescene.fr
Fetes-par-Fetes	Online	na	www.fetes-par-fetes.com
Galeries Lafayette Gourmet Catering	9th	01 40 23 53 52	www.galerieslafayette.com
Gymboree	15th	01 40 71 61 60	www.gymboree-france.com
La Boutique des Produits Ferrari	1st	01 42 61 26 12	www.lesproduitsferrari.fr
La Grande Epicerie, Le Bon Marché	7th	01 44 39 81 00	www.lagrandeepicerie.fr
La Traiteur du Marais	4th	01 42 36 05 35	www.traiteur-marais.com
Options	Les Mureaux	01 34 92 20 00	www.options.fr
Stella Production	17th	01 43 80 44 94	www.stella-production.com
Sushi on the Skin	1st	06 75 27 20 85	na
Thanksgiving	4th	01 42 77 68 28	www.thanksgivingparis.com
Tutti Frutti	Various Locations	01 42 55 60 15	www.tuttifrutti.com

273

Supermarkets will also stock the basics in paper or plastic crockery, balloons, streamers and toy whistles. For larger celebrations, Options, a party rental company based outside Paris, hires out elegant table settings and furnishings, while Stella Production provides musicians and singers for hire spanning the spectrum from swing to soul. A little more flashy is La Boutique des Produits Ferrari, a Paris-based business offering Ferraris for hire with drivers for special occasions. For the kids, Gymboree in the 15th offers a birthday party service for children from six months to 6 years while Cinescene performs circus numbers and children's entertainment at private parties.

Catering is also a cinch, with a range of choices depending on budget. At the top end of the scale is La Traiteur du Marais specialising in high class and VIP events while Sushi on the Skin provides catering services for private yachts, jets and home evening meals. A little more low-key is Thanksgiving, an American speciality store great for southern BBQ and Thanksgiving dinners. Galeries Lafayette and La Grande Epicerie at Le Bon Marché are also good sources for general catering needs. For special occasion cakes try your local *boulangerie*, the vast majority of which take advance orders.

Perfumes & Cosmetics

In a city where even a Sunday morning visit to the *boulangerie* requires an acceptable level of dress and styling – no jogging bottoms, please – the beauty industry is correspondingly large in size and presence. Centres for beauty treatments are a dime a dozen, ranging from budget to hyper-luxe; from specialist boutiques like nail chain L'Onglerie, to the generalist budget branches of Body Minute waxing, hair removal and tanning salons. Not to mention the dedicated perfume houses specialising in the mix of personalised scents, or cosmetic boutiques where perfectly coiffed women are on hand to offer advice and application of makeup. Nothing is too specialised; Frank Vidoff runs a salon dedicated to the art of blonde colouring, while pedicurist Bastien Gonzales at Hôtel Costes is sought-out by foot fetishists for his amazing pedicure treatments and self-named product line (book far in advance). Nor have men been left out in the cold with a selection of über exclusive men's beauty boutiques opening to cater for the growing demand in male grooming.

When it comes to general purchasing, supermarkets offer a basic range of well-known brands such as Nivea creams and Chanel cosmetics. Specialist beauty superstore Marionnaud is a great place to search out a wide selection of well-known brands, while Yves Rocher sells an extensive range of plant-based products from its own line in stores across Paris. For a treat for both the nose and eyes visit the Comme des Garçons perfume shop in the 1st where the scents are almost as impressive as the cutting edge interior design. Naturally, the city's biggest department stores also offer huge range, with entire floors dedicated to showcasing extensive ranges of both French and international cosmetic and perfume brands.

Perfumes & Cosmetics

Bastien Gonzalez, Hôtel Costes	1st	08 77 83 72 07	www.bastiengonzales.com
Body Minute	Various Locations	na	www.bodyminute.com
The Body Shop	Various Locations	na	www.thebodyshopinternational.com
Comme des Garçons	1st	01 47 03 15 03	na
Frank Vidoff	7th	01 42 22 66 33	www.frankvidoff.com
Galeries Lafayette	Various Locations	01 42 82 34 56	www.galerieslafayette.com
L'Onlgerie	Various Locations	na	www.l-onglerie.fr
Le Bon Marché	7th	01 44 39 80 00	www.lebonmarche.fr
Marionnaud	Various Locations	na	www.marionnaud.fr
Printemps Beauté	Various Locations	01 42 82 57 87	www.printemps.com
Yves Rocher	Various Locations	na	www.yves-rocher.fr

Various Locations

Annick Goutal

01 45 51 36 13 | *www.annickgoutal.com*

Famous for her floral and subtle perfumes, Annick Goutal obtained a large celebrity following (Madonna is a fan) before passing away a few years ago. Her legacy carries on in her Paris boutiques, where perfumes, eaux de toilette and a large range of body lotions, oils and soaps stock the beautifully presented shelves. Gorgeously scented candles have also proven to be popular purchases.

Various Locations

By Terry

01 44 76 00 76 | *www.byterry.com*

For women who like their shoes to come from Louboutin and their suits from Chanel, By Terry offers the last word in couture cosmetics. After years spent working as the creative director for Yves Saint Laurent cosmetics, Terry de Gunzburg established By Terry, her salons specialising in personalised cosmetics. At her Vero-Dodat store in the 1st, clients are lead upstairs to a luxurious velvet-curtained salon where they will encounter a team of chemists and colour stylists on hand to create made-to-measure lipsticks, foundations and other makeup essentials. Products take between one and four weeks to prepare. For those without the patience or the funds for customised makeup, Terry also offers a ready-to-wear collection.

213 rue St-Honoré
1st
Ⓜ **Tuileries**
Map p.398 C1 **11**

Colette

01 55 35 33 90 | *www.colette.fr*

This now well-known trend store is one of the only locales in Paris where you can lay your hands on a large range of Kiehl's products, stacked on minimalist shelves on the ground floor entry. The only downside – aside from the inflated prices – is nudging past wide-eyed tourists and local scenesters who flock to the boutique every day of the week.

Various Locations

Editions de Parfums Frédéric Malle

01 45 05 39 02 | *www.editionsdeparfums.com*

Selecting a perfume from the myriad scents lining one of the coolly sparse interiors of your nearest Frédéric Malle store has never been so easy. Simply visit the website, fill in the online questionnaire and Monsieur Malle (son of the creator of Dior perfumes) will personally recommend a scent he deems perfect for you. Of course that would mean failing to visit the *perfurmerie* in person, missing out on the joys of delicately sniffing each scent which is atomised in its own perfume chamber; a clever idea that keeps the remnants of each perfume from lingering in store and overwhelming the chic space.

Editions de Parfums Frédéric Malle

Comme des Garçons

275

Various Locations

La Sultane de Saba
01 45 00 00 40 | *www.lasultanedesaba.com*
Lovers of the scents and sensibilities of the East will become fast fans of La Sultane de Saba's Parisian boutiques. Featuring earth-tones, tiling and heavily scented air, expect to be greeted with a mint tea and sticky Moroccan pastry as you wait. Take a hammam, book a wax and enjoy a manicure, massage or pedicure before stocking up on the brand's lusciously scented products to take home, from a honey and ginger skin mask to a caramel and rose body scrub. Scented candles and beautifully beaded kaftans are also on sale. Products are reasonably priced from around €10 and up.

31-33 rue des
Blancs Manteaux
4th
Ⓜ *Saint-Paul*
Map p.400 A3 🔢

Les Bains du Marais
01 44 61 02 02 | *www.lesbainsdumarais.com*
Both men and women flock to this exotic steam bath and beauty complex in the Marais, where the tired and weary can enjoy a steam bath in Moroccan-styled rooms. Single visits cost €35, with access to the sauna, relaxation salon and slippers, towels and dressing gown included. Make a day of it and avail yourself of the services of the in-house masseuse, beauty therapists and hairdressers before retiring to the restaurant for a refreshing mint tea. Prices range from €20 for a bikini wax to €70 for a 60 minute oil massage. Regulars seeking to make a small saving can also purchase multiple hammam visits which are €315 for 10, or €630 for 20.

Various Locations

M.A.C.
01 45 48 60 24 | *www.maccosmetics.fr*
Service is a big part of the M.A.C. experience, and with more than 150 lipstick colours you will undoubtedly require knowledgeable assistance. The sheer magnitude of products on offer is at once daunting and exciting. It is also beneficial – those with special skin needs or Asian or African-American complexions can select from a range that caters to almost every skin type. Lipsticks and lip balms start from around €15, with multiple eye-shadow packs ranging from €20 to €40 depending on size.

11 rue de la Jusienne
2nd
Map p.399 E1 🔢

MYXT
01 42 21 39 80
Former makeup artist Damien Dufresne is the man behind this makeup salon, a favourite with in-the-know fashionistas, models and actresses alike. Faithful only to the idea of quality, Damien selects what he believes to be the best products from the best makeup brands, selling eye shadow from Il Makiage alongside select products from Paris-Berlin and Trucco. Those in need of a quick eyebrow tidy up can drop in for a quick shape without prior booking too.

5 rue La Boétie
8th
Ⓜ *Saint-Augustin*
Map p.388 A3 🔢

Make Up Forever
01 53 05 93 30 | *www.makeupforever.fr*
This is the boutique to seek out when specialist makeup help is required. A professional makeup brand for everyday situations, this is a company well-versed in providing the products that others don't: think waterproof body foundation for long beach days alongside products with specially formulated colours, pigments and finishes for black skin.

49 rue Bonaparte
6th
Ⓜ *St-Germain*
des Prés
Map p.398 C4 🔢

Mary Quant
01 43 25 03 96 | *www.maryquant.co.uk*
The English designer who, alongside many others, claims credit for design of the mini-skirt, is now better known for her range of vibrantly coloured nail varnishes. The flamboyant Donatella Versace is said to be a fan. Prices start from a low €5 for varnishes.

48 rue des
Francs Bourgeois
3rd
Ⓜ *Saint-Paul*
Map p.400 A2 19

Nickel

01 42 77 41 10 | *www.nickel.fr*

The first dedicated spa for men in Paris, Nickel takes the self-consciousness vibe out of male grooming. The minimalist boutique offers waxing, facials, manicures, pedicures and massage designed specifically with male 'beauty' needs in mind. Packaging is far from girly, with product names like 'anti-hangover'. There are now two salons in Paris, with the opening of a spa in Printemps de l'Homme. Locations also include New York and London.

14 rue Rambuteau
3rd
Ⓜ *Rambuteau*
Map p.400 A2 20

Patyka

01 40 29 49 49 | *www.patyka.com*

A luxury brand waving the organic flag, Patyka is a specialist in gorgeous alcohol free perfumes, skin care and body products. A visit to the brand's own boutique is an experience in itself; beautifully coiffed women test the sleekly packaged product lined-up on wooden shelves that lend the boutique a distinct flavour of old-world elegance. Patyka's organic mantra has the brand steering clear of synthetic ingredients. Prices vary, with a bottle of their best-selling Huile Absolut Organic Serum hovering around the €40 mark.

Various Locations

Sephora

01 53 93 22 50 | *www.sephora.fr*

The grand dame of the beauty world, Sephora stores are famed for their unparalleled selection, amazing free makeup tests and great service. With multiple locations around Paris, it is nonetheless the enormous Champs-Élysées shop that offers the best experience; many a girl group has wondered in for free product testing at midnight on a Friday night following one too many cocktails. Stocking makeup, beauty, bath and hair care products, perfume and accessories for both men and women, this is a one-stop shop. The only downside is battling your way to the cash register.

Pets

Other options **Pets** p.101

Parisians are serious pet owners. Dogs and cats are more often than not pedigree and bought at exorbitant prices from reputable breeders and pet specialists. The latter you will find among the plant vendors along the quai de la Megisserie; conditions are decent though slightly cramped so visiting the litters of beautiful puppies in wire cages can be a little disturbing. There are also numerous websites dealing in sale of animals: try www.chien.com or www.chatdumonde.com to find the dog or cat of your dreams. There is some movement toward adopting animals, with billboards occasionally posted on the metro by

Feathered friends

277

animal rescue organisations promoting their work. You can adopt an animal at www.animal-services.com.

Whichever avenue of pet ownership you choose it is required that owners tattoo or microchip their dogs and have them regularly vaccinated (there are no dog licences in France). Have your dog tattooed at the Fichier Central des Chien Tattoués (01 49 37 54 54). Remember that owners of 'defence' dog breeds – mastiffs, pitbulls, boerbulls, rottweilers, Staffordshire terriers and Tosa breeds – must declare them at their *mairie* or *préfécture* and must purchase civil responsibility insurance. The dogs must also be muzzled and on a lead when in public.

Pets			
Animalis	12th	01 53 33 87 35	www.animalis.fr
CaniCrèche	3rd	01 42 71 59 09	www.canicreche.fr
La Ferme Tropicale	13th	01 45 84 24 36	www.lafermetropicale.com
La Niche by BHV	4th	01 42 74 90 00	www.bhv.fr
Mon Bon Chien	15th	01 48 28 40 12	www.mon-bon-chien-paris.com
Taxi Dog	Various	01 53 27 04 85	www.taxi-dog.net

Finding out about dog friendly parks is as easy as calling the *mairie* hotline on 08 20 00 75 75. As for special pet services, there are plenty. Taxi Dog will transport both yourself and your best friend around Paris. Order organic dog food online and have it delivered from www.zooplus.fr, drop it off to doggie daycare at CaniCrèche, spoil them with a present from La Niche by BHV (the department store's dedicated pet boutique) or take your animal for a grooming at Animalis in the 12th. Mon Bon Chien in the 15th is a specialist canine bakery and accessories shop where you'll find doggie sweaters and fancy dress costumes. Fans of reptiles must visit La Ferme Tropicale, where you can even buy centipedes.

Second-Hand Items

Other options **Books** p.251

Paris is one city where second-hand doesn't mean second best. Where fashion is concerned, second-hand stores, known as *depot-ventes*, attract a large following among wily shoppers seeking the many vintage bargains to be found among racks of clothing, shoes and accessories for men, women and children. The biggest of these is Réciproque with seven separate boutiques clustered on rue de la Pompe in the 16th *arrondissement*: each showcases a different speciality, from objects and homeware to handbags, scarves and women's evening wear. Le Mouton à 5 Pattes has two outlets selling designer vintage and previous year's collections for adults, while La Clef des Marques stocks a good range of second-hand athletic wear and swimsuits.

True bargain-hunters will love Guerrisold, a chain store selling mass-market second-hand men's and women's clothing from the '70s and '80s. There are several outlets around Paris, each store sorting stock according to garment type. Paris also has a good selection of permanent sale shops selling the previous season's stock of well-known brands; buy Et Vous at Et Vous Stock or reduced cost Bonpoint cashmere onesies and gorgeous children's party dresses at the children's sale shop, Bonpoint Fin de Series. A little way outside Paris at Ivry-sur-Seine, BHV Ivry Entrepôts offers a warehouse of shop-soiled and sale furniture, electrical appliances and white goods at good discount prices (about 30% off). The opportunity for bargain buys here is good, with many items simply needing a decent clean-up. The warehouse is accessible by RER. There are regular neighbourhood car boot sales around the city, though locating times and dates can be difficult. The solution is to head to the Marché aux Puces de la Porte de Vanves. Open every weekend, this is a large second-hand and antique market and the only one in existence in inner Paris.

Disposing of your own second-hand goods can, in fact, be more difficult than buying them. Depot-ventes will buy used clothing, however they are very choosy. Many

Parisians simply leave unwanted clothing and furniture on the street to be taken away by others or picked up by the city's cleaning crews. The Croix Rouge (www.croix-rouge.fr) will gratefully accept clothing and goods, just call to arrange collection. Check the website for details. When it comes to classifieds, FUSAC is one of the highest-read English-language classified magazines and can be picked up at boutiques and bookstores across the city. WHSmith always has a plentiful stock. For French-language classifieds browse *De Particulier à Particulier*, a weekly journal available at news kiosks every Thursday selling second-hand furnishings, cars as well as general knick-knacks.

Second-Hand Items

BHV Ivry Entrepôts	Ivry-sur-Seine	01 49 60 44 00	www.bhv.fr
Bonpoint Fin de Series	7th	01 45 48 05 45	na
Et Vous Stock	2nd	01 40 13 04 12	na
Guerrisold	9th	01 45 26 38 92	na
La Clef des Marques	1st	01 47 03 90 40	na
La Croix Rouge	Various Locations	01 47 05 57 40	www.croix-rouge.fr
Le Mouton à 5 Pattes	Various Locations	01 43 26 49 25	www.mouton-a-cinq-pattes.info
Marché aux Puces de la Porte de Vanves	14th	na	www.pucesdevanves.typepad.com
Réciproque	Various Locations	01 47 04 30 28	www.reciproque.fr
WHSmith	1st	01 44 77 88 99	www.whsmith.fr

Shoes

Other options **Beachwear** p.249, **Sports Goods** p.281, **Clothes** p.254

With hundreds of shoe stores in Paris catering to all tastes, sexes and ages there is no need to strut the streets in shoddy footwear. Department stores Printemps and Galeries Lafayette offer the best general selection of both evening and day footwear in town for men, women and children. Le Bon Marché is a close runner-up, with a slightly smaller but more expensive collection of brands.

For urban cool you can't beat the shoe shops at Les Forums des Halles (p.300). Start at Tube and make your way around the surrounding boutiques. Or try the website, www.shoes-up.com, a shoe company which lists the best places to buy stylish sneakers in Paris. International brands like Camper and Paraboot can all be found with styles for both men and women. For problem feet head to some of the specialist stores dealing in stylish orthopaedic offerings, Lucien Hasley in the 17th *arrondissement* among them. Though there isn't a particular street famed for its shoe boutiques, you will find plenty of stylish stores around St-Germain, the Marais and Etienne Marcel districts.

Men

English company Church's is the first port of call for men looking for beautiful handmade leather shoes. Though expensive (loafers are upward of €300), these are classic and long-lasting. The company also makes beautiful custom shoes. Still on classic luxury, Fausto Santini designs beautiful leather styles with an emphasis on width for comfort and a Japanese minimalist aesthetic. More eclectic are the offerings at Jean-Baptiste Rautureau, a particularly flamboyant brand whose designs reach from pink crocodile-skin cowboy boots to pointy-toed, square-heeled white leather brogues. A little lower down the price rung but still fashionable is Free Lance for men, while Stephane Kelian also has a great men's line.

279

Women

Where to start? 58M on rue Montorgueil is as good a place as any. Prices are steep but the fashion is fabulous: grab a pair of super stylish Marc Jacobs' heels among other high end brands. Free Lance and Venise sell boots and evening shoes at reasonable-to-expensive prices in multiple stores across Paris, while Repetto does a brisk trade in variations on the classic ballet slipper. Heading in to the higher price points is the handcrafted, classic leather footwear of Robert Clergerie, the masculine styling of German shoe designer Karena Schuessler, and the dressy femininity of Sergio Rossi's beautiful creations. Stephane Kelian is justly famed for his woven leather shoes and sexy boots. On the bargain front try the Boot Shop, selling designer-look boots at a good price. Kabuki After is a designer shoe sale shop selling last season's Miu Miu and Prada at fantastic mark-downs. For drag queen fashion head to Michel Perry to find skyscraper heels and trend shoes that border on fashion caricature. Or go for broke with a pair of Christian Louboutin's red-soled heels (from around €500), a firm favourite of the international celeb set.

Children

Spending a lot of money on children's shoes makes little sense, which is why parents love the discount stores La Halle aux Chaussures, Petit Petons, Till, and Il Court, le Furet, all with multiple locations around the city. Other options include Pom d'Api for budding little fashion-lovers, Six Pieds Trois Pouces for a great range of trend and classic brands, and Bonpoint but be prepared to pay for the latter. At Tavernier you will find gorgeous little sneakers. For those that don't mind shelling out the big bucks, go to Le Bon Marché where you will find luxury label children's shoes at prices to make you wince.

Shoes

58M	2nd	01 40 41 02 40	na
Bonpoint	Various Locations	01 40 51 98 20	www.bonpoint.com
Boot Shop	6th	01 46 33 60 73	na
Camper	Various Locations	01 45 48 22 00	www.camper.com
Christian Louboutin	Various Locations	01 42 36 05 31	www.christianlouboutin.fr
Church's	Various Locations	01 40 20 94 67	www.church-footwear.com
Fausto Santini	6th	01 45 44 39 40	www.faustosantini.it
Free Lance	Various Locations	01 45 48 14 78	www.freelance.fr
Galeries Lafayette	Various Locations	01 42 82 34 56	www.galerieslafayette.com
Il Court, le Furet	17th	01 43 80 28 08	na
Jean-Baptiste Rautureau	4th	01 42 77 01 55	na
Kabuki After	2nd	01 42 36 44 34	na
Karena Schuessler	1st	01 53 29 93 93	na
La Halle aux Chaussures	Various Locations	01 42 74 35 32	www.lahalleauxchaussures.com
Le Bon Marché	7th	01 44 39 80 00	www.lebonmarche.fr
Lucien Hasley	17th	01 45 22 77 67	na
Michel Perry	1st	01 42 44 10 07	www.michelperry.com
Paraboot	Various Locations	01 45 49 24 26	www.paraboot.com
Petit Petons	Various Locations	01 42 84 00 05	na
Pom d'Api	Various Locations	01 45 48 39 31	www.pomdapi.fr
Printemps	Various Locations	01 42 82 57 87	www.printemps.com
Repetto	2nd	01 44 71 83 12	www.repetto.com
Robert Clergerie	Various Locations	01 45 48 75 47	www.robertclergerie.com
Sergio Rossi	Various Locations	01 42 84 07 24	www.sergiorossi.com
Six Pieds Trois Pouces	Various Locations	01 45 44 03 72	www.6pieds3pouces.com
Stephane Kelian	Various Locations	01 42 61 60 74	www.stephane-kelian.fr
Tavernier	5th	01 47 07 21 90	na
Till	Various Locations	01 42 22 25 25	na
Tube	1st	01 40 39 99 00	na
Venise Collection	Various Locations	01 47 63 03 43	na

Souvenirs

The problem in Paris is trying to escape the souvenir shops rather than finding them – especially around the major tourist landmarks. Around the Eiffel Tower and Sacré-Coeur prepare to be propositioned by the multitudes of merchants illegally selling miniature replicas for as little as €1 a piece. Remember that it's very easy to bargain your way to a better deal.

Official boutiques line the rue de Rivoli, vending everything from tea towels, chocolates, mugs, scarves and posters all with various souvenir prints. Prices are reasonable (you can walk away with a Parisian memento for as little as €5) though quality can be questionable and the mark up considerable. You'll find a similar range of tokens at both Charles de Gaulle and Orly airports and kiosks in the major train stations across the city. Museums are the best bet in regards to tracking down quality souvenirs. Commonly on offer are coffee table books, CDs, artist biographies and reproduction posters alongside the usual assortment of keyrings and less useful paraphernalia. The Carrousel du Louvre (p.300) at the Louvre offers an enormous selection in its various boutiques.

Souvenirs			
Au Pain Bien Cuit	8th	01 42 65 06 25	na
Carrousel du Louvre	1st	01 43 16 47 10	www.louvre.fr
Galeries Lafayette	Various Locations	01 42 82 34 56	www.galerieslafayette.com
Hermes	Various Locations	01 40 17 47 17	www.hermes.com
Jean-Paul Hévin	Various Locations	01 55 35 35 96	www.jphevin.com

Perhaps surprisingly some of the more interesting mementos can be found in boutiques not typically considered souvenir shops: *chocolatier* Jean-Paul Hévin creates miniature chocolate Eiffel Towers; a speciality *boulangerie*, Au Pain Bien Cuit on boulevard Haussmann bakes Eiffel Tower-shaped baguettes which can be eaten or preserved; Hermes sells classic scarves and Galerie Lafayette has a new specialist souvenir space on the sixth-floor which it claims to be the largest dedicated souvenir store in Paris.

As for customs restrictions, these exist mainly in regards to produce and alcohol. Most nations outside the EU will not allow you entry with cheeses and items such as foie gras unless vacuum sealed (and some don't permit them at all), while limits on alcohol also apply.

Sports Goods

Other options **Outdoor Goods** p.273

Sunday morning at the Bois de Boulogne, Paris' largest park, is a sight to behold with runners, cyclists and rollerbladers all battling for space on the myriad of paths winding

Souvenirs of Paris

through the woods. It is the one morning a week where Parisians bow at the temple of exercise. Though not known for their dedication to maintaining the body beautiful through hard work and sweat, the city's residents are, nonetheless, well catered for when it comes to athletic apparel and sporting equipment.

Chains Decathalon and Go Sport are two of the largest sellers of general sporting equipment. Both stock products for swim, gym, weight-lifting, cycling, martial arts, tennis… the list is extensive. Electronic home gym equipment – treadmills, rowing machines and elliptical trainers – are also for sale. It's worth remembering that staff here are, by-and-large, unable to offer specific, knowledgeable advice. Those seeking very specialised or high-end equipment may want to frequent some of the more specialised stores to be found. On avenue de la Grande Armée, Planet Jogging

Sports Goods			
Adidas	Various Locations	01 58 62 51 60	www.adidas.com
Boutique PSG Champs- Élysées	8th	01 56 69 22 22	www.psg.fr
Everlast	10th	01 42 08 44 00	www.everlastboxing.com
Golf Laza	15th	01 40 59 80 40	na
Golf N Swing	Le Pecq	01 30 08 70 20	www.golfnswing.com
Golf Plus	Various Locations	01 45 74 86 28	www.golfplaza.fr
Nike	8th	01 42 25 93 80	www.nike.com
PC American Sport	15th	01 45 75 37 00	na
Planet Jogging	17th	01 45 72 40 00	www.planetjogging.com
Roller Station Bastille	3rd	01 42 78 33 00	na
Sport USA	15th	01 45 67 59 16	na
Tramplex	Seine-et-Marne	01 64 38 63 60	www.tramplex.fr

stocks everything a running enthusiast needs and staff can also provide information on fun-runs operating throughout Paris. Adidas and Nike both have dedicated stores offering fashionable outfitting for tennis enthusiasts, joggers and gym junkies while boxing enthusiasts will find the full range of clothing and accessories at Everlast. Golfers needing equipment, clothing and accessories should head to Golf Laza and Golf Plus while Golf N Swing outside Paris at Le Pecq is the sole distributor of the Tom Wishon Golf technology system and has an on-site workshop specialising in computer-aided swing analysis. American baseball and football equipment can be found at PC American Sport and Sport USA, both in the 15th. Roller Station caters to rollerblade and rollerskating enthusiasts from three boutiques across Paris, including one near Bastille in the 3rd.

You can find replica team clothing at most sporting good stores, including Adidas, Nike and the Paris St-Germain football team flagship store on the Champs-Élysées.

Stationery

Office Depot is the first port of call for business and standard stationery requirements. The number of stores across Paris is innumerable, prices are low, fidelity cards are available and the range of goods – from pens to printer paper – is expansive. More limited ranges of basic stationery at very reasonable price points are available in all newsagents and supermarkets. But why shop standard when Paris offers such a great number of boutique, unique and designer *papeteries*? L'Ecritoire in the Marais stocks an amazing range of wax seals,

Stationery			
Calligrane	4th	01 48 04 31 89	na
Cassegrain	Various Locations	01 42 60 20 08	www.cassegrain.fr
Espace Ecriture	4th	01 44 61 01 18	na
L'Ecritoire	4th	01 42 78 01 18	www.lecritoire.fr
Marie Papier	7th	01 43 26 46 44	www.mariepapier.fr
Melodies Graphique	4th	01 42 74 57 68	na
Mont Blanc	Various Locations	01 44 20 07 70	www.montblanc.com
Office Depot	Various Locations	01 53 35 02 10	www.officedepot.fr
Relma	6th	01 43 25 40 52	www.relma.fr
Rougier & Plé	3rd	01 44 54 81 00	www.crea.tm.fr

quirky envelopes and inks while Marie Papier in the 6th specialises in stunningly beautiful handmade paper and stationery, offering a custom service for businesses and

When you're lost what will you find in your pocket?

Item 71. The half-eaten chewing gum

When you reach into your pocket make sure you have one of these miniature marvels to hand… far more use than a half-eaten stick of chewing gum when you're lost.

Explorer Mini Maps
Putting the city in your pocket

special occasions. Espace Ecriture in the exclusive place des Vosges has a stunning collection of antique letter-boxes and tables alongside glass pens and goose and swan quills selling for around €15. Relma is another treasure trove of goods including decorative papers and book binding materials. French company, Cassegrain, is one for lovers of luxe with its collection of leather diaries, journals and blotters, wallets and fine pens, while international luxury goods label, Mont Blanc, is justly famed for its exquisite (and expensive) pens and assorted accessories.

Tailoring

Other options **Clothes** p.254, **Textiles** p.284, **Tailors** p.99

Lusting over the latest Lanvin without the credit limit to back it up? Tailors, known as *retouchers*, occupy hole-in-the-wall boutiques in every neighbourhood and will undertake all manner of services, from taking up a too-long hem to making three-piece suits from professional patterns. There are a few tips to remember: bring your own material, even buttons and zips; they can copy clothing without patterns; and prices depend on the tailor. Also consider that standards of quality do vary, so seek local advice on the most experienced *retouchers* in your local area where possible. For special occasion items such as formal gowns, wedding dresses or suiting it can be a good idea to seek out specialists. Bespoke by Bryaub create beautiful made-to-measure men's suits and shirts. More costly are the services offered by the made-to-measure suiting at luxury boutique, Hermés, and the historic Charvet boutique, one-time suit maker to Emile Zola and John F Kennedy among others. At Atelier de Style en Aiguille, Marie Demarty will help you design the wedding dress of your dreams for as little as €800 for a custom creation. Her team also designs and makes men's suits and children's wedding clothing. A little pricier are the services of Nathalie Durieux at her self-named boutique and Mireille Brunel at Mercerie d'un Soir, both of whom specialise in made-to-measure wedding gowns.

When it comes to the home, tailors will happily whip up table accessories and linens, however made-to-measure curtains are best done by specialist curtain stores. Like tailors, there are a few locale boutiques in most neighbourhoods. Unlike tailors, these stores will stock an enormous range of curtain fabrics and dressings, fabric catalogues and measuring services. Printemps Maison on boulevard Haussmann has a great soft-furnishings floor which is worth seeking out, if only to browse the beautiful materials.

Tailoring			
Atelier de Style en Aiguille	na	01 46 02 14 98	www.robedemariee.net
Bespoke by Byraub	5th	01 43 95 00 18	www.bespoke.blog.lemonde.fr
Charvet	1st	01 42 60 30 70	na
Hermes	Various Locations	01 40 17 47 17	www.hermes.com
Mercerie d'un Soir	7th	01 45 48 26 13	na
Nathalie Durieux	7th	01 42 22 04 05	www.nathalie-durieux.com
Printemps Maison	9th	01 42 82 50 00	www.printemps.com

Textiles

Other options **Souvenirs** p.281, **Tailoring** p.284

Historically, Sentier in the 2nd *arrondissement* has been the centre for textile sales in Paris and today that tradition continues. On rue de Sentier and rue d'Aboukir you will find dozens of boutiques selling an enormous range of fabrics at both wholesale and retail prices. Spread over five storeys, the Marché Pierre in the 18th is a great alternative for well-priced textiles; here you will find every possible colour, weave and quality while Bouchara is a more expensive option with a less extensive range. All of these locations offer material for both clothing and interiors, though specialist interior fabric stores do exist; try Dominique Picquier or Angely. When it comes to quality, all boutiques will sell their fabrics with labels stating the material's content and place of manufacture.

There are dedicated stores for trims and buttons, Entrée des Fournisseurs among them, and at Mokuba you will find literally hundreds of ribbons in every size and colour. Le Rouvray is a quilt shop specialising in fabrics from America and it also offers lessons in quilting.

Textiles

Angely	2nd	01 42 61 63 20	www.angely-paris.com
Aux Fils de Temps	7th	01 45 48 14 68	na
Bouchara	9th	01 42 80 66 95	www.bouchara.com
Dominique Picquier	3rd	01 42 72 39 14	www.dominiquepicquier.com
Entree des Fournisseurs	3rd	01 48 87 58 98	www.entreedesfournisseurs.com
Le Rouvray	5th	01 43 25 00 45	www.lerouvray.com
Marché St Pierre	18th	01 46 06 92 25	na
Mokuba	2nd	01 40 13 81 41	www.mokuba.fr

Toys & Games

If having children hasn't already resulted in the enthusiastic embrace of a second childhood, an afternoon touring the city's toy stores should swiftly change this. Irresistible are the games hand-crafted in wood at Au Nain Bleu, a specialist toy store since 1836. Buy interactive games, robots and see permanent magic shows at Musée de la Magie. And at Nature et Decouvertes budding scientists and environmentalists can indulge an interest in the planets and stars, wildlife and the sea with toys made from environmentally friendly materials. Dedicated Disney fans can brave the hordes on the Champs-Élysées, however there are numerous other large stores stocking everything from mechanised toys to puzzles and educational games, Fnac Eveil et Jeux and the warehouse-sized Toys R Us outlets among them. Si Tu Veux, a stand-alone store in Galeries Vivienne, the 19th century shopping arcade, has toys as well as dressing up gear and birthday accessories. If you need a treat, Variantes is one for the grown-ups, stocking a great range of unique games you may not find elsewhere.

Toys & Games

Au Nain Bleu	8th	01 42 65 20 00	www.aunainbleu.com
Chantlivre	7th	01 45 48 87 90	na
Disney Store	8th	01 45 61 45 25	www.disneystore-shopping.disney.co.uk/fr
Fnac Eveil et Jeux	Various Locations	08 92 35 06 66	www.eveiletjeux.com
Joueclub	na	05 56 69 69 00	www.joueclub.com
La Grande Récré	16th	01 42 30 52 02	www.lagranderecre.fr
Les Cousins d'Alice	14th	01 43 20 24 86	na
Musée de la Magie	4th	01 42 72 13 26	www.museedelamagie.com
Nature et Découvertes	Various Locations	01 47 03 47 43	www.natureetdecouvertes.com
Si Tu Veux	2nd	01 42 60 59 97	na
Toys R Us	Puteaux	01 47 76 29 78	www.toysrus.fr
Variantes	6th	01 43 26 01 01	www.variantes.com
Vilac	Various Locations	na	www.vilac.com

Wedding Items

Here comes the bride. And she can be… off-the-rack, all-in-white, made-to-measure or authentic-vintage. From franchise boutiques to couture design salons, you will have no trouble finding all you need for the big day. Those seeking a walk-in, walk-out purchase will find a great selection at L'Empire du Mariage, stockists of a range of bridal dress brands, children's bridal outfits, and cocktail attire. A similar array is available at the myriad Point Mariage boutiques, though the nearest to Paris is located at Coignieres, 40 minutes' drive from the city. This place is worth the trip for those seeking budget options (dresses from as low as €99) and one-stop-shopping; the bride, groom, wedding party and children are all catered for from head to toe.

For wedding gowns and cocktail dresses with a little more detail, Hervé Mariage offers a large selection with prices ranging €400 for special sale stock to gowns priced at more than €2,000. For a truly unique bridal gown, Suzanne Ermann creates gorgeously quirky dresses available off-the-rack. Colour copies can be made on command. Or make an appointment at the boutique Sonia L. The prestigious boutique carries a range of designer gowns, menswear, outfits for the bridal party, shoes, accessories and even photo albums.

Those seeking made-to-measure gowns will face a similar array of choice. Award-winning French wedding gown designer Max Chaoul creates designer weddings dresses from €3,500, while Mireille Brunel at Mercerie d'un Soir designs ball dresses and wedding gowns to your taste, budget and specifications. At the boutique of society milliner, Philippe Model, brides and bridal parties can find beautiful, individual hats along with bridal shoes. In the vintage department, Ragtime is an Aladdin's cave of antique French fashion including a beautiful selection of vintage wedding dresses. Sizes are on the small side but alterations can be made in-house at the boutique where possible.

Department stores Printemps, Galeries Lafayette and Le Bon Marché are all good generalist stores given their extensive ranges of shoes, gowns, accessories and clothing. Each centre also offers a fantastic wedding registry service: there really is little reason to look elsewhere. The same can be said of Cassegrain and Marie Papier when it comes to customised invitations, both boutiques offering the last word in elegance. Confused by choice? Visit the Salon du Mariage et de la Fete (www.salonmariagefete.com) at the Espace Champerret exhibition centre, held each November, for a great overview of everything and anything wedding.

Wedding Items			
Cassegrain	Various Locations	01 42 60 20 08	www.cassegrain.fr
Cymbeline	Various Locations	01 64 78 56 50	www.cymbeline.com
Galeries Lafayette	Various Locations	01 42 82 34 56	www.galerieslafayette.com
Hervé Mariage	11th	01 43 14 70 55	www.hervemariage.com
L'Empire du Mariage	Various Locations	01 48 78 71 49	www.empiredumariage.com
Le Bon Marché	7th	01 44 39 80 00	www.lebonmarche.fr
Marie Papier	7th	01 43 26 46 44	www.mariepapier.fr
Max Chaoul	Various Locations	01 43 25 44 02	www.maxchaoulcouture.com
Mercerie d'un Soir	7th	01 45 48 26 13	na
Philippe Model	1st	01 42 96 89 02	na
Point Mariage	Various Locations	02 43 49 62 78	www.pointmariage.com
Printemps	Various Locations	01 42 82 57 87	www.printemps.com
Ragtime	1st	01 42 36 89 36	na
Sonia L	9th	01 42 81 03 10	www.sonia-l.com
Suzanne Ermann	Various Locations	01 43 56 06 06	www.suzanne-ermann.com

Places To Shop

Department stores, independent boutiques, factory outlets, hypermarkets, shopping malls – the list of places to shop in Paris is as diverse as you would expect from a cosmopolitan city famed for its style. From lunch break blitzes to whole days spent abusing the credit card, this is a shopper's paradise.

Streets/Areas To Shop

The only stumbling block with bringing together a list of Paris' best places to shop is deciding where to draw the line: take it as a given that the following offers just a taste of what the city has to offer. Much of the fun is in discovering the hidden locales which appeal to your individual taste. As for transport, driving within the city can be a frustrating experience so in all cases, make the most of the extensive and well-kept metro and bus systems. Of course if all those shopping bags drag you down, you can always hail a cab!

8th
Ⓜ **Franklin D. Roosevelt**
Map p.397 D1 23

Avenue Montaigne

Polish up your Louboutin heels, grab your Vuitton clutch and throw on that Marni dress – a stroll along the tree-lined avenue Montaigne is no time for haphazard fashion statements. One of the chicest spots in Paris, the avenue is home to both luxury clothing and jewellery labels alike; check out the latest at Prada and Dior before taking a blinding peek at the goodies in Fred Leighton. Break for lunch at L'Avenue (01 40 70 14 91) where Brad Pitt, Drew Barrymore and Sarah Jessica Parker all love to drop by, before sipping an exquisite cocktail in the bar at the Plaza Athenee (p.348) once evening descends. La Maison Blanche (01 47 23 55 99) restaurant just up the block is a fabulous, if rather expensive, spot for dinner, with a stunning view taking in the Eiffel Tower. Can't afford the indulgence? Spend an afternoon window shopping among the city's über-polished bourgeoisie crowd.

9th
Ⓜ **Saint-Augustin**
Map p.388 B3 24

Boulevard Haussmann

It's not just the *grand magasins* of Galeries Lafayette and Printemps that call this 9th *arrondissement* address home; further toward the Arc de Triomphe homeware enthusiasts will find more than a few boutiques to hold their interest. Lighting stores, dedicated sofa retailers, custom furniture businesses and interior design specialists can all be located on the stretch between avenue Friedland and the metro stop Havre-Caumartin. Atmosphere, however can be a little lacking. This is really a business district so don't come looking for quaint streets, an eclectic mix of people or romantic eateries. However, if you are here in the evening dinner, at Bistrot du Sommelier (97 blvd Haussmann, 01 42 65 24 85) comes highly recommended.

6th
Ⓜ **Odéon**
Map p.399 E4 25

Boulevard St-Germain

So obvious a choice it almost doesn't warrant inclusion. Nonetheless, no guide of Parisian shopping streets is complete without the mention of the famed boulevard St-Germain. Perhaps it says something that – even though tourists flock here in their millions each year – it is still a space Parisians themselves are happy to claim. Near its beginnings on the border of the 7th *arrondissement* you can shop at Sonia Rykiel (01 40 49 00 84), enjoy an over-priced coffee at Le Deux Magots (p.339) or wander the narrow alleys running off the boulevard which houses chic boutiques and interesting eateries when the press of the crowds becomes too much. Further down toward the 5th *arrondissement* the boulevard takes on a slightly less glossy feel. Here you'll find cheaper kebab shops, less glossy (and less appealing) boutiques and a more student-heavy crowd.

287

Quai de Valmy

10th
Ⓜ **Louis Blanc**
Map p.390 B2 🔢

The tranquil, tree-lined canal isn't the only feature attracting trend setters to this slightly shambolic quarter of Paris. On the quai de Valmy lovers of colourful, eclectic clothing head to the fuchsia and green shop front of Antoine et Lili (01 42 05 64 98), renowned for its neo-hippie fashions. Also on the radar? Stella Cadente (01 42 09 27 00) and her gorgeous chiffon dresses and nearby Ginger Lyly (rue Beaurepaire, 01 42 06 07 73) for its sassy one-off pieces by local designers. When hunger strikes head across the canal to Hôtel du Nord (01 40 40 78 78) on quai de Jemmapes; made famous by the French movie of the same name, the former historic hotel is now a favoured hipsters eat-and-greet space serving up great mod *bistrot* fare.

Rue Charlot & Rue de Poitou

3rd
Ⓜ **Filles du Calvaire**
Map p.400 B2 🔢

You can barely walk a metre along these two streets without discovering yet another boutique whose patrons clearly worship at the temple of design. Justifiably labelled 'the chicest addresses in the Marais', expect to encounter über-styled locals and fashionable tourists staying at Hôtel du Petit Moulin (01 42 74 10 10), with its Christian Lacroix-designed interior. Pick up a floral-inspired bag from designer Dominique Picquier's self-named space (p.285) or peruse the eclectic mix of Scandinavian antiques and paintings at Anders' Hus (27 rue Charlot, 01 42 72 00 49). Need a quick bite? Try Bio Moi on rue Poitou (01 42 78 03 26) or, for something a little more special, Le Pamphlet (38 rue Debellyme, 01 42 73 39 24). And all this against a backdrop of ancient streets.

Rue de Grenelle

7th
Ⓜ **Varenne**
Map p.398 A3 🔢

Stretching from the Eiffel Tower in the 7th *arrondissement* to the border of the 6th, rue de Grenelle is an interesting mix of bustling residential interest, chic boutiques and Parisian colour. Home to the aristocracy in the 1800s, the quarter now houses a mix of well-to-do Parisians and long-time-local American expats attracted by the chic vibe. Closer to the Eiffel Tower you'll find the lively pedestrian market street of rue Cler where fashionable families doing the weekly shopping mix with tourists eager to experience a little Parisian authenticity. At the other end is a clustering of great boutiques around rue du Bac and rue des Saint-Peres, including Prada, Catherine Malandrino, YSL, Diane von Furstenberg and M.A.C makeup. Oh, and Le Bon Marché with its *épicerie* and glamorous fashions is just a two-minute walk.

Rue du Roi de Sicile, Rue des Francs Bourgeois & Rue des Rosiers

3rd
Ⓜ **Saint-Paul**
Map p.400 B3 🔢

This intersecting triangle of streets in the heart of the Marais – the city's original Jewish neighbourhood – reveals all you'll need to know about what is one of the hippest *quartiers* in Paris. On rue des Rosiers you'll find a multitude of Jewish *épiceries*, bakeries, falafel outposts and, among them, the avant-garde boutique L'Eclaireur (01 48 87 10 22), where adventurous and knowledgeable fashion types go for the great collection of brands, including Yohji and Maharishi. Next take a stroll along Roi du Sicile for edgy street duds or head to rue des Francs Bourgeois to discover a mix of well-known and boutique-name brands. Recognised as the heart of the city's gay district, men's fashion features highly. Once night descends grab a drink at The Lizard Lounge (p.350), just off rue du Roi de Sicile. The quarter's maze of winding, cobbled streets is in stark contrast to the ultra-mod outfits of the area's stalwarts. It's a great, vibrant scene and one of the only areas of Paris open on Sundays.

Rue Etienne Marcel, Rue Montorgueil & Rue Montmartre

2nd
Ⓜ **Étienne Marcel**
Map p.399 E1 🔢

Et Vous, Diesel, Replay, Barbara Bui, Miss Sixty... the list of hot boutiques lining rue Etienne Marcel and rue Montmartre extends as a who's who of the chic-street fashion world. The quarter's expensively street-styled set wouldn't shop anywhere else. Around the corner on rue Montorgueil discover one of the oldest market streets in Paris, now an interesting mix of old and new: from the horse meat butcher at number 72 to the minimalist Italian cafe, Santi, at number 49.

Rue Lepic & Rue des Abbesses

18th
Ⓜ **Abbesses**
Map p.382 C4 **31**

In the shadow of Sacré-Coeur, away from the tourist hordes, discover romantic Paris in the hilly, narrow streets of this lively Montmartre quarter. A favoured location of the bohemian and artistic sets, the area is vibrant with galleries, boho boutiques, relaxed bars and a colourful Sunday street market. Particularly well-known for its produce, *boulangeries*, *fromageries* and *traiteurs* are all worth a visit. Finish shopping and explore the last vineyard in Paris before taking in the Moulin de la Galette – the windmill once painted by Renoir.

Rue Mouffetard

5th
Ⓜ **Censier Daubenton**
Map p.409 F2 **32**

Home to the young and stylish, rue Mouffetard is universally considered one of the most ancient and lively of all Parisian streets. Sunday mornings are particularly colourful, with the street's produce market in full swing and hordes of funky Parisians brunching and chatting up a storm. Bars, too, are worth a visit: stop in for *un verre* at The 5th Bar (01 43 37 09 09) before throwing back some oysters at L'Huitre et Demie (01 43 37 98 21). This is the Latin Quarter at its relaxed, fun and invigorating best.

Rue Oberkampf

11th
Ⓜ **Parmentier**
Map p.401 D1 **33**

An influx of hip students and cool cats has inspired establishment of some of the quirkiest boutiques and kitschest bars in and around this bustling street. The locals prefer a slightly dressed-down, boho aesthetic, so leave your mainstream sensibilities behind and discover a new view of Paris: less romantic, more noughties with a definite indie edge. Drop in to Café Charbon (109 rue Oberkampf, 01 43 57 55 13) for an espresso in a setting that is pure bohemian bistro before moving on to check out a myriad of original boutiques. Around the corner on rue Moret you'll find a great selection of stores selling '30s and '40s beaded handbags and frocks. At night the many pumping bars make this is a great place to come for a cocktail and a hefty dose of cool.

Rue Poncelet

17th
Ⓜ **Ternes**
Map p.386 C2 **34**

Between the German *patisserie* Stubli (01 42 27 81 86), the gourmet hot dog stand of Epicurya (01 48 88 98 07), and the cool art deco surrounds of Le Dada cafe, rue Poncelet is precisely the type of permanent, open-air market street which attracts food-focussed locals and tourists alike. Buying fresh produce from the amiable vendors is loads of fun. The beautiful fruits, cakes, savoury nibbles and scent of fresh-cooked paella will whet your appetite while the lively chat and bustling market-day feel will stimulate your sense. A fun morning out in an *arrondissement* of Paris which many dismiss as an area of little interest.

Rue Saint Louis en Île

4th
Ⓜ **Pont Marie**
Map p.400 A4 **35**

Together with the Île de la Cité, the Île Saint-Louis is one of the oldest areas of Paris. As such, the main street running the length of the latter provides an amazingly atmospheric backdrop to the selection of gourmet food stores, gift shops and selection of art galleries and restaurants which fill these centuries-old buildings. The cobble-stone street is especially beautiful in winter, when the warm lights from such restaurants as Le Fin Gourmet (01 43 26 79 27) and Mon Vieil Ami (01 40 46 01 35) beckon. If you are in time for tea, make a stop at the beautiful La Charlotte de l'Isle (01 43 54 25 83) for tea and cake before peering in the gallery windows or stopping at Berthillon (p.336) for a luscious scoop of icecream.

289

Department Stores

Other options **Hypermarkets** p.292

The concentration of fantastic department stores in central Paris is no accident. Courtesy of the exploding population that followed Baron Haussmann's total redesign and reconstruction of Paris in the mid 19th century, commerce took a front seat. Aristide Boucicaut was the first with the department store concept, building Le Bon Marché on the Left Bank in 1852, setting the model for large, multi-brand stores which would later be built across the rest of Europe and America. Thanks to the city's economic well-being Boucicaut's idea proved a roaring success. Soon to follow? Construction of BHV, Printemps, Samaritaine and Galeries Lafayette between 1856 and 1895. Of those Samaritaine is the only one no longer in operation, having shut down in 2005 after being condemned as a fire risk. Today the department stores stock an enormous range of international and French brands, restaurants and client shopping and information services. The healthy competition that prompted their construction all within a short space of time still exists today, with the store managements' enthusiastic attempts to secure new brands, offer discounts and create dynamic shopping environments helping to keep attracting the floods of shoppers who continue to surge through the doors each year.

BHV

14 rue de Temple ◀
4th
 Hôtel de Ville
Map p.399 F3 🔟

01 42 74 90 00 | *www.bhv.fr*
Built in 1856, BHV (le Bazar de l'Hôtel de Ville) is precisely that – a bazaar-style store offering great deals on all manner of product. The homely stepsister to the city's other fashion department stores, BHV is where the people of Paris come for inexpensive home furnishings and accessories, bed linens, bathroom fittings and all-manner of hardware requirements. But despite its long standing history BHV offers very little in the way of glamour; the building is as utilitarian as the product. So, too, the cafe: though offering decent salads, sandwiches and snacks, those seeking something really tasty are better off visiting one of the dozens of eateries in the surrounding few blocks. Services, however, are a strong point. The department store offers quotes on simple household works and renovations, diagnostic services on internet issues, and there is even a separately housed medical sales boutique selling home aids, health and hygiene products and medical instruments. There is nearby underground parking but considering BHV's central location just opposite the Hôtel de Ville (city hall) and right on the rue de Rivoli, metro and bus is a good option.

Citadium

50-56 rue Caumartin ◀
9th
Ⓜ *Havre-Caumartin*
Map p.388 B3 🔢

www.citadium.com
Tucked behind Printemps and Galeries Lafayette in the 9th *arrondissement*, Citadium is a four-storey paradise for lovers of street and sport fashion. From Vans and Converse to Le Coq Sportif and Puma, Citadium safely covers every conceivable mainstream urban fashion statement. You will also find a small range of sporting equipment. Two restaurants take up space on the top floor.
Don't drop by if it is service you are seeking; staff numbers are few, making tracking down sizes and specific preferences an exercise in patience. Register queues, too, can stretch long on weekends with the store's youthful client-base snapping up the latest-edition sneakers or cargo-style Carhart pants. But what it lacks in service it makes up for in atmosphere: the store runs regular brand promotions on the ground-floor, alongside the occasional concert. Sign up to the newsletter on the store's website to receive the latest news.

80 rue de Passy
16th
Ⓜ La Muette
Map p.395 F3 **42**

Franck et Fils

01 44 14 38 00

Something between a department store and a megastore, Franck et Fils is where the well-heeled fashionistas in the 16th *arrondissement* come to rack up their credit when an excursion to Le Bon Marché or Printemps just seems like too much trouble. What used to be a rather haphazardly run local enterprise has since been bought by the luxury fashion mega-group LVMH, resulting in better service and range. Prices, naturally, have stayed in the mid-to-high range. Alongside labels such as Christian Dior, La Perla, Bobbi Brown cosmetics, Celine and Donna Karan, the store also houses its own hat *atelier*; tours to watch the hat construction are available when booked in advance. Due to its scaled-down nature, shoppers will generally find fewer services here than at the city's larger department stores; there are no stunning rooftops restaurants *a la* Printemps or child-friendly departments as at Galeries Lafayette. You will, however, find nearby underground parking and plenty of great neighbourhood eateries within shouting distance.

Various Locations

Galeries Lafayette

01 42 82 34 56 | *www.galerieslafayette.com*

Though there are now two Galeries Lafayette locations in Paris alone, it is the complex at 40 boulevard Haussmann to which people refer when speaking of 'Galeries'. Though the last to be built in the mid 1800s rush which saw construction of the city's other department stores, Galeries by no means plays second-fiddle; it attracts the largest number of tourists to its multiple buildings. Most stunning architecturally is the main building, with its central atrium extending the full seven storeys, topped by a dome of mosaic glass that allows coloured light to flood through. Amazing, themed window displays are also worth seeing, if only once. In summer, head to the rooftop cafe and terrace for the decent food and stunning view over Paris. Galeries holds frequent fashion shows, offers shopping advice free of charge and will also perform in-house clothing alterations for a small charge. Over in the gourmet department, food-lovers can browse and eat at any of the many food stalls or enjoy a more formal dining experience at Le Chenevert. Less formal eateries are present on the sixth and fourth floors. There is underground parking and great access by public transport. One of the RER stops even comes to rest in the basement of Galeries Lafayette's main building. Tourists can also make the most of the English-speaking welcome service on the ground floor.

Galeries Lafayette

24 rue de Sèvres
7th
Ⓜ *Sèvres Babylone*
Map p.398 B4 🄸🄸

Le Bon Marché

01 44 39 80 00 | *www.lebonmarche.fr*

Watch the beautifully clothed shoppers streaming in the doors and you'll soon realise Le Bon Marché represents the best of department store luxury. Attempt to count the number of gold visa cards whipped out of Vuitton wallets at the myriad luxury brand counters, from Balenciaga and Burberry to Galliano and Gaultier. Smaller and more intimate than either Galeries Lafayette or Printemps, Le Bon Marché was the city's first department store and exudes an atmosphere of genteel chic. Services are highly personalised from the phones in the lingerie change rooms which allow you to call an assistant with no fuss, to the store's service offering package delivery to Parisian hotels. The ground floor houses a dedicated men's department while the elegant basement stocks luxury clothing and toys for children. As for the rest? Women's shoes, handbags, lingerie, perfume, prêt-a-porter – you name it, Le Bon Marché stocks it. Oh, and let's not forget La Grande Epicerie (p.261), the famed food section selling exotic fruits, delicious pastries and breads alongside an enormous range of international foods and decadent ready-made meals. Or assuage your appetite at any one of four cafes and restaurants. Underground parking is adjacent but the area is well serviced by metro and buses, incentive if ever there was to avoid driving these congested streets.

Various Locations

Printemps

01 42 82 57 87 | *www.printemps.com*

Like Galeries Lafayette, Printemps also now exists in multiple locations across Paris and France. It is the boulevard Haussmann store built in 1865, however, that is still the most impressive in terms of architecture and array of goods. Once better known for homeware, an expensive renovation in the 1990s converted Printemps into one of the main centres for Parisian fashion; the department store is incredibly sleek with the prices to match and includes one of the largest beauty floors in the world. Laid out over three building – Printemps men, fashion and home – its hallmark is the amazing art nouveau glass cupola in the main fashion store. Printemps is known for its sale of luxury and trend labels, however store management has been equally wise in retaining high-street labels to attract a younger, less-moneyed crowd: peruse the collection of designers like Helmut Lang, check out the beaded creations of Ventilo or stick with Zara or Mango. Choice is limitless, as are services. Alongside a free image and consultancy service, parents can also make use of a free short-stay nursery for children between the ages of 2 and 9 years old. Foodwise, Printemps excels. There is a Ladurée cafe, a *boulangerie* concept created by Alain Ducasse in the home store, a free-service restaurant on the ninth floor, an organic restaurant in the beauty department, sushi on the fashion floor, a wine bar designed by Paul Smith in the men's store and a sublime designer brasserie under the cupola of the main building on the sixth floor. Bon appetite.

Hypermarkets

Various Locations

Auchan

08 10 28 24 26 | *www.auchan.fr*

The best way to define Auchan, one of the biggest of France's hypermarket chains, is by stating that what it doesn't sell isn't worth knowing. Offering delivery and installation on goods alongside a variety of warranties, Auchan is favoured by those seeking great budget buys. Like E.Leclerc, there are no branches to be found within metropolitan Paris, however you won't have to travel deep in to the suburbs in order to hit the closest outpost. Go for food, clothing, car parts, jewellery, garden equipment and, well, everything but the kitchen sink. Though, now that you mention it, you may even chance upon one of those.

Various Locations ◀

Carrefour

01 43 53 86 00 | *www.carrefour.fr*

Taking the concept of the multi-purpose store one step further than Monoprix, Carrefour's hypermarkets really are a one-stop shop: electronics, food, sporting goods, financial and travel services, fuel stations, pharmacies, mobile phones and gift registry services are all available through its outlets. Located both within the city and outside metropolitan Paris, the French company is difficult to beat when it comes to pricing, courtesy of the company's enormous buying power. Customers can even find regular deals concerning tickets for concerts and shows, as Carrefour offers reductions on ticket prices for purchases over a certain sum, but it's best to see the store for details at the time of purchase as conditions change. As with all of today's large French supermarket chains, online ordering and delivery is just part of the package.

Various Locations ◀

E.Leclerc

08 10 87 08 70 | *www.e-leclerc.com*

Just like Carrefour, E.Leclerc is an impressively large retail chain selling an extraordinary array of goods and services through its multitude of hypermarkets. Unlike Carrefour, however, this is one company which is yet to move inside the city limits of Paris. Dotted just outside the périphérique in Clichy and Levallois among other suburban locations, E.Leclerc sells more than 3,000 different products at prices around 15% below what you can expect to pay in other stores. Buy clothing, food, organic goods, electronics, music, optics and even white goods. The only negative is losing yourself among the vast number of shopping aisles. Even for those without easy access to transport, these stores provide great bargains where a huge generalist shop is necessitated.

Independent Shops

The independent shopping scene in Paris is very healthy indeed, with new boutiques popping up in all the most fashionable areas of the city. Though some undoubtedly have a short lifespan, there are many that go the distance. Knowing where to find the hottest and chicest new boutiques is simply a matter of becoming familiar with Paris' up and coming neighbourhoods. In the past few years this has meant the 10th, 18th, 13th and 11th *arrondissements*. There is also a great concentration of indie shopping spots around the north Marais, into the 3rd. Go forth and shop.

20 rue Bonaparte ◀
6th
Ⓜ **St-Germain des Prés**
Map p.398 C3 49

Aesop

01 44 41 02 19 | *www.aesop-europe.com*

With its sleek counters and steel colour palette, Aesop's new Paris boutique looks more like an industrial design space than a high-class skincare emporium. Skincare is indeed the focus of the Australian company famed for its derision of miracle cures; the company mantra actually places intellectual curiosity as the best *preservateur* of youth. French architect Jean-Francois Bourdet designed the ultra chic space in St-Germain which attracts the beautiful and the beauty-conscious in droves.

45 rue de l'Arbre Sec ◀
1st
Ⓜ **Louvre Rivoli**
Map p.399 E2 50

Artoyz

01 47 03 09 90 | *www.artoyz.com*

Just in case you thought toys were just for kids, head to rue de l'Arbre Sec to discover just what it is which sustains the very grown-up Japanese toy phenomenon. Ultra designer, ultra kooky and ultra cool, collecting these über-designed figures has become a widespread urban trend. The boutique stocks Manga toys alongside Frank Kozik's famed smoking rabbit, magazines, fashions, books and hip key chains. The downstairs gallery space regularly displays the works of selected artists.

25 rue des Filles du Calvaire
3rd
Ⓜ *Filles du Calvaire*
Map p.400 C1 **51**

Balouga

01 42 74 01 49 | www.balouga.com

For the budding Philippe Starck in the family, Balouga has opened its dedicated designer children's furniture gallery among the hip adult boutiques of the Marais. All sleek curves, funky materials and well-recognised design names (think vintage Jean Prouve and contemporary designs from Jasper Morrison among others), the first floor space displays the modular pieces while the upstairs, 1950s inspired bedroom provides a little extra inspiration. Quite clearly it's never too early to let a little design into life.

7 quai Malaquais
6th
Ⓜ *Pont Neuf*
Map p.399 D3 **52**

Dries Van Noten

01 44 27 00 40 | www.driesvannoten.be

It's been more than two decades in the making, but Belgian designer Dries Van Noten has finally opened his first Paris boutique in the beaux-arts district of St-Germain. All Murano chandeliers, Mongolian patterned rugs, marble touches and Asian lacquered furniture, the boutique fits right in with its antique-store neighbours. Here, between rooms styled alternatively as a salon and a library, you can discover his beautifully cut clothing sewn from the richest of fabrics. Throw on your best bib and tucker before coming here to browse.

3 rue de Fleurus
6th
Ⓜ *Saint-Placide*
Map p.408 C1 **53**

Georges de Providence

01 42 84 48 79

Three diverse fashion labels take pride of place at this store, mixing together a quirky melange of jewellery, furniture and curiously chic men's and women' clothing: take your pick from Kitsune's eclectic menswear, La Prestic Ouiston's cleverly reworked vintage pieces and Robert Normand's amusing designs for women. The mix of funky vintage furniture and contemporary pieces bought by the interior designers who set up the boutique adds the final inspired touch.

Various Locations

Jamin-Puech

01 40 20 40 28 | www.jamin-puech.com

More than 15 years ago, handbag designing super-stars Isabelle Puech and Benoit Jamin took it in to their heads to search for materials rarely before seen in the leather industry. This endeavour, alongside the twosome's amazing design talent, has resulted in creation of their uniquely beautiful bag label. And with the opening of their fourth, minimalist boutique in the chic rue Cambon, there is now one more space for new fans to discover these beaded, stitched, fabulously adorned handbags. Tip: devotees and those in the know go to Jamin-Puech Inventaire in the 10th – it's the only boutique that carries bags from past collections, as well as samples and one-offs.

56 rue de Seine
6th
Ⓜ *Mabillon*
Map p.399 D4 **55**

Kusmi Tea Shop

01 46 34 29 06 | www.kusmitea.com

Tea has been given a modern makeover with the opening of Kusmi Tea's sleek new boutique in the heart of St-Germain and the red and white interior colour scheme shows off the silver cylinders of tea to best effect. But it's what's inside those stylish tins that really draw the crowds; green, black and organic are just a few of the blends on offer, though it is the Russian flavours which really stand out. With a spicy overtone, they are best drunk with a little added sweetness. Take the tea home or try it in one of the upstairs tea rooms and you'll soon discover why the tsars made this their royal tea of choice.

La Librairie de la Mode

22 rue Pierre-Lescot
1st
Ⓜ **Étienne Marcel**
Map p.399 F1 **56**

01 40 13 81 50 | *www.modeinfo.com*

Looking for a fashion mag to flick through on your next lunch hour? Head to La Librairie de la Mode just a couple of paces from Les Forums des Halles. A mecca for fashion industry professionals and fashion junkies alike, the specialist style bookstore contains more than 1,000 titles on design, fashion, trend, and colour forecasting. Specialist staff are on hand to help select the best publications to suit your requirements. The racks also house an enormous selection of international fashion publications. If WHSmith doesn't cover your fashion mag needs, then this is the place to head.

Ménage à Trois

9 rue Clauzel
9th
Ⓜ **Saint-Georges**
Map p.389 D2 **57**

01 48 78 44 80 | *www.menage-a-trois.fr*

Opened by three friends who spawned their creative collaboration when working together at the Hôtel Amour, a favourite Parisian hang-out, this new boutique combines a love for vintage, kitsch design and fashion. The trio have put together a killer cocktail of a boutique on an off-kilter street in the 9th *arrondissement*. Spiralled 70s carpet, black walls, leather surrounds, porcelain cheetahs and mirror art give an idea of the fashion sense here. You'll find lots of florals, heavily glitzed bat-wing tops, bold coloured leather, Argentinean strings, major sunglasses, clothes for hire and wild prints, so it's a fun address to keep checking in with.

Surface to Air II

68 rue Charlot
3rd
Ⓜ **Filles du Calvaire**
Map p.400 B1 **58**

01 49 27 04 54 | *www.surface2air.com*

Rue Charlot in the north Marais has become home to yet another super cool store with the opening of Surface to Air's second boutique. Run by a groovy collective that dabbles in art and video directing and production of *Vice* magazine among other endeavours, the new boutique stocks edgy fashion from labels like Blaak and Cathy Pill while also stocking its own range of men's and women's underwear. The second line of LA fashion designer Rick Owens can also be found on the racks. The clientele is as funky as the boutique itself.

Markets

Street markets are a way of life in Paris. The city boasts dozens of food, clothing, furniture and flower markets – both temporary and permanent – spread across the 20 *arrondissements* and surrounding suburbs. Finding them is as simple as logging on to the city's official website, www.paris.fr. Click the link 'Les Marchés Parisiens' for details of the markets in each *arrondissement*. Those seeking the full experience can make the most of the array of market tours on offer. See p.201 for a selection of companies offering tours in Paris.

It's worth keeping in mind that markets are not always where you will find the best deals, particularly when it comes to food. Organic and farmed produce brought in from rural areas can often cost more than supermarket stock. Still, the experience and quality is often worth the extra cost. Where else could you taste *charcuterie* from Alsace, cider from Normandy and foie gras from the south-west while picking up a bunch of fresh cut flowers and perhaps an artisan pair of earrings? Only at a Parisian market.

Carreau du Temple

rue Eugene-Spuller &
rue du Petit-Thouars
3rd
Ⓜ **Temple**
Map p.400 B1 **61**

A 19th century covered market hall, the Carreau du Temple provides a grand backdrop to what is essentially a specialist clothing market. Fans of leather clothing flock here to find the garment of their dreams, choosing from a vast range including fitted leather pants to stylish blouses. The market is positioned within the heart of the *quartier* Sentier, the city's original garment district, so there's plenty more boutiques to browse nearby once you've scouted the best of the clothing on offer.

295

Marché aux Fleurs

Île de la Cité, place
Louis Lepine
4th
Ⓜ *Cité*
Map p.399 E3 62

Though there are well-known flower markets at both place des Ternes in the 17th *arrondissement* and place de la Madeleine in the 8th, it is the Marché aux Fleurs on the historic Île de la Cité which really lays claim to the title of best flower market in Paris. Stall after stall of cut-flowers and potted plant life colour both the place Louis Lepine and the banks of the Seine opposite, where further boutiques take up residence. Rub shoulders (literally) with locals and tourists alike in this lively Parisian quarter as you squeeze along the crowded aisles.

Marché aux Puces de St-Ouen

Porte de
Clignancourt
St-Ouen
Ⓜ *Porte de*
Clignancourt
Map p.383 D1 63

01 40 11 77 36 | *www.marchesauxpuces.fr*

With some 1,000 fashion vendors and more than 2,500 antique and second-hand bric-a-brac and furnishing stores, the Marché aux Puces de St-Ouen provides a universe of flea-market finds for savvy shoppers and persistent bargain hunters. The combination of shouting vendors, shrewd art dealers and excited visitors makes wandering the many aisles a great experience though heed a couple of warnings. Firstly, the onslaught of tourist buses means prices have skyrocketed and truly great bargains can be difficult to come across. Secondly, this is a pick-pocket's paradise so be very careful.

Marché aux Timbres

Cnr ave Marigny
& ave Gabriel
8th
Ⓜ *Champs-Élysées –*
Clemenceau
Map p.387 F4 64

Impassioned stamp collectors will experience nothing but sheer delight at the Marchés aux Timbres, a pocket-sized market specialising in the sale and purchase of collector's edition and rare stamps. Vendors are friendly as is the contingent of regulars, lending the market a really relaxed and informal air. You'll find the stalls are the haphazard, lean-to variety barely sheltered by slightly grubby canvas awnings. Feel free to look around, admire and chat, but refrain from touching any of the stamps or cards on display.

Marché de Vanves

ave Marc Sangnier
& ave George
Lafenestre
14th
Ⓜ *Porte de Vanves*
Map p.417 E2 65

www.pucesdevanves.typepad.com

The only flea market inside the city limits of metropolitan Paris, Marché de Vanves specialises in small *objets d'art*, textiles, great second-hand clothing and handbags, and the odd sprinkling of interesting furniture. Being more local than Marché aux Puces de St-Ouen (you won't find any tourist buses lined up out front here) means foragers can still find some fantastic finds at really good prices. The atmosphere is very relaxed, as are the opening hours: though it advertises its hours as up until 15:00, many vendors will pack up at lunchtime, so it's worth making an early-morning trip.

Marché des Batignolles

Terre-plein des
Batignolles
17th
Ⓜ *Rome*
Map p.382 A3 66

Newer and more intimate than the organic market on boulevard Raspail in the 6th, the organic produce market attracts foodies from across Paris with its fantastic offerings and atmosphere of relaxed bonhomie. Recommendations include the fruit and veg from the house of Giboulot, cheeses from La Table du Roy, pastries from the stand Gustalin and luscious crème fraiche brought down from Normandy by Henri Martin.

Marché Raspail

Cnr rue de Rennes
& rue du
Cherche-Midi
6th
Ⓜ *Rennes*
Map p.408 B1 67

This is the market for food-lovers who enjoy a little star-spotting alongside their Sunday morning shopping. One of the most well-known food markets in Paris, Marché Raspail attracts French celebs from the big and small screen alongside gastro tourists and local gourmands. Though much of the produce is exceptional there are some especially great vendors to look out for; try the comté from the *fromagerie* Sumière, pick up your fruit and veg at Conard and grab some sweet and savoury nibbles – samosas, various cakes and terrines – from 'Madame Annie'.

Scenes from the markets

Markets

1st			
Saint-Honoré	pl du Marché Saint Honoré	Wed & Sat	Wed 15:00-20:30, Sat 07:00-15:00
2nd			
Bourse	pl de la Bourse	Tue to Fri	12:30-20:00
3rd			
Enfants Rouges	39 rue de Bretagne	Tue to Sun	08:30-13:00 & 16:00-19:30; Fri-Sat 20:00
4th			
Baudoyer	pl Baudoyer	Wed & Sat	Wed 15:00-20:30, Sat 07:00-15:00
5th			
Maubert	pl Maubert	Tue, Thu & Sat	07:00-14:30
Monge	pl Monge	Wed & Sun	07:00-14:30
Port Royal	nr the Val de Grace Hospital, blvd de Port-Royal	Tue, Thu & Sat	07:00-2.30
6th			
Raspail	blvd Raspail btn rue du Cherche-Midi & rue de Rennes	Tue & Fri	07:00-14:30.
St-Germain	4-8 rue Lobineau	Tue, Sat & Sun	08:30-13:00. & 16:00.-19:30; Sun 08:30-13:00
7th			
Saxe-Breteuil	ave de Saxe	Thu & Sat	07:00-14:30
8th			
Aguesseau	pl de la Madeleine	Tue & Fri	07:00-13:30
Europe	1 rue Corvetto	Tue, Sat & Sun	08:00-13:00 & 16:00-19:00; Sun 08:00-13:00
9th			
Anvers	pl d'Anvers	Fri	15:00-20:00
10th			
Alibert	rue Alibert near Hôpital St-Louis	Sun	07:00-15:00
St-Martin	31-33 rue du Château d'Eau	Tue, Sat & Sun	08:30-13:00. & 16:00.-19:30; Sun 08:30
St-Quentin	85 bis, blvd Magenta	Tue, Sat & Sun	08:30-13:00. & 16:00.-19:30; Sun 08:30
11th			
Bastille	blvd R Lenoir btn rue Amelot & rue Saint-Sabin	Thu & Sun	07:00-14:30
Belleville	blvd de Belleville	Tue & Fri	07:00-14:30
Charonne	btn rue de Charonne & rue A Dumas	Wed & Sat	Wed, 07:00-14:30; Sat, 07:00-15:00
Pere-Lachaise	blvd de Menilmontant, btn rue des Panoyaux & rue des Cendriers	Tue & Fri	07:00-14:30
Popincourt	blvd R Lenoir btn rue Oberkampf & rue J-P Timbaud	Tue & Fri	07:00-14:30
12th			
Beauvau	pl d'Aligre	Tue, Sat & Sun	08:30-13:00 & 16:00-19:30
Bercy	pl Lachambaudie	Wed & Sun	Wed, 15:00-20:00. Sun, 07:00-15:00
Cours de Vincennes	btn blvd Picpus & rue Arnold Netter	Wed & Sat	07:00-14:30
Daumesnil	blvd de Reuilly btn rue de Charenton & pl F Eboue	Tue & Fri	07:00-14:30
Ledru-Rollin	ave Ledru-Rollin btn rue de Lyon & rue de Bercy	Thu & Sat	07:00-14:30
Poniatowski	blvd Poniatowski btn ave Daumesnil & rue Picpus	Thu & Sun	07:00-14:30
Saint Eloi	36-38 rue de Reuilly	Thu & Sun	07:00-14:30
13th			
Alesia	rue de la Glaciere & rue de la Sante	Thu & Sun	07:00-14:30
Auguste-Blanqui	blvd Blanqui nr pl d'Italie	Tue, Fri & Sun	07:00-14:30
Bobillot	btn pl Rungis & rue de la Colonie	Tue, Fri & Sun	07:00-14:30
Jeanne d'Arc	pl Jeanne d'Arc	Thu & Sun	07:00-14:30
Maison-Blanche	ave d'Italie btn 110 & 162	Thu & Sun	07:00-14:30.
Salpetriere	pl Salpetriere, blvd de l'Hôpital	Tue & Fri	07:00-14:30
Vincent-Auriol	blvd Vincent Auriol btn 64 & rue J d'Arc	Wed & Sat	07:00-14:30

298

Markets

14th

Brune	ave G Lafenestre & rue Gal Séré de Rivières	Thu & Sun	07:00-14:30
Edgar-Quinet	blvd Edgar Quinet	Wed & Sat	07:00-14:30
Mouton-Duvernet	pl Jacques Demy	Tue & Fri	07:00-14:30
Villemain	btn ave Villemain & rue d'Alesia	Thu & Sun	07:00-14:30

15th

Cervantes	btn rue Bargue & rue de la Procession	Wed & Sat	07:00-14:30
Convention	rue Convention btn rue A Chartier & rue de l'Abbe Groult	Tue, Thu & Sun	07:00-14:30
Grenelle	btn rue Lourmel & rue du Commerce	Wed & Sun	07:00-14:30
Lecourbe	btn rue Vasco de Gama & Leblanc	Wed & Sat	07:00-14:30
Lefebvre	ave de la Pte de Plaisance, ave A Bartholomé & rue A Theuriet	Wed & Sat	07:00-14:30
Saint-Charles	rue St-Charles btn rue de Javel & rond-point St-Charles	Tue & Fri	07:00-14:30

16th

Auteuil	pl Jean Lorrain	Wed & Sat	07:00-14:30
Gros-La-Fontaine	rue Gros, rue La Fontaine	Tue & Fri	07:00-14:30
Passy	pl de Passy	Tue, Sat & Sun	08:30-13:00 & 16:00-19:30; Sun 08:30-13:00
Point du Jour	ave de Versailles from rue Le Marois to rue Gudin	Tue, Thu & Sun	07:00-14:30
Porte Molitor	pl de la Porte Molitor	Tue & Fri	07:00-14:30
President Wilson	ave du Pdt Wilson btn rue Debrousse & pl d'Iena	Wed & Sat	07:00-14:30
Saint-Didier	rue Mesnil & rue St Didier	Tue, Sat & Sun	08:30-13:00. & 16:00.-19:30; Sun 08:30

17th

Batignolles	96 bis rue Lemercier	Tue, Sat & Sun	08.30-13:00 & 16:0 -19:30; Sun 08:00
Berthier	blvd de Reims, nr Square A Ulmann	Wed & Sat	07:00-14:30
Ternes	8 bis rue Lebon	Tue, Sat & Sun	08:30-13:00 & 16:00-19:30; Sun 08:30-13:00

18th

Barbes	blvd Chapelle nr Hôpital Lariboisière	Wed & Sat	07:00-14:30
La Chapelle	10 rue l'Olive	Tue, Sat & Sun	08:30-13:00 & 16:00-19:30; Sun 08:30
Ney	blvd Ney btn rue J Varenne & rue C Flammarion	Thu & Sun	07:00-14:30
Ordener	btn rue Montcalm & rue Championnet	Wed & Sat	07:00-14:30
Ornano	btn rue Mt-Cenis & rue Ordener	Tue, Fri & Sun	07:00-14:30

19th

Crimée-Curial	rue de Crimée btn 236 & 246	Tue & Fri	07:00-14:30
Jean-Jaures	ave Jaures btn rue de l'Ourcq & rue des Ardennes	Tue, Thu & Sun	07:00-14:30
Joinville	cnr rue Joinville & rue Jomard	Thu & Sun	07:00-14:30
Place des Fêtes	pl des Fêtes	Tue, Fri & Sun	07:00-14:30
Porte Brunet	ave de la Pte Brunet	Wed & Sat	07:00-14:30
Porte d'Aubervilliers	ave de la Porte d'Aubervilliers	Wed & Sat	07:00-14:30
Riquet	42 rue Riquet	Tue to Sun	08:30-13:00. & 16:00-19:30; Sun 08:30-13:00
Secretan	33 ave Secretan	Tue to Sun	Tue-Thu 08:30-19:30, Fri-Sat 08:30-20:00
Villette	blvd de la Villette btn 27 & 41	Wed & Sat	07:00-14:30

20th

Belgrand	rue Belgrand, rue de la Chine & pl Piaf	Wed & Sat	07:00-14:30
Mortier	blvd Mortier btn ave de la Pte de Menilmontant & rue M Berteaux	Thu & Sun	07:00-14:30
Pyrenees	rue des Pyrenees btn rue de l' Ermitage & rue de Menilmontant	Thu & Sun	07:00-14:30
Reunion	pl de la Reunion	Thu & Sun	07:00-14:30
Telegraphe	rue du Telegraphe	Wed & Sat	07:00-14:30

Shopping Malls

The shopping mall concept hasn't particularly grabbed the imagination of Parisian shoppers. This is not surprising given the grandeur of the city's department stores and the excitement to be taken from window shopping along the streets. Perhaps the architecture of the shopping malls is also to blame; aside from the interest generated by browsing in the basement of the Louvre, there is little to endear the city's few malls to the buying public. In fact, most malls do not adhere to the concept in the American sense; though you will find restaurants and some children's facilities, these are not areas to spend the day, eat and meet friends. The same can be said of the factory centres outside of Paris. As with the department stores, weekends are incredibly busy so are best avoided if possible. Mall hours align with independent shops – normally 10:00 to 20:00.

Carrousel du Louvre

99 rue de Rivoli
1st
Ⓜ *Louvre Rivoli*
Map p.399 D2 **36**

01 43 16 47 10 | *www.louvre.fr*

It seems almost sacrilegious to consider housing a shopping complex in the basement of one of the world's greatest museums, but that is exactly what has happened. There are 50 boutiques here specialising in fashion, music, beauty, games and hobbies alongside restaurants, parking and an exhibition space. Being part of the Louvre, services here are fantastic; services include wheelchair and pram hire, postal services, baggage storage and information booths in multiple languages. And while some shops adhere to normal Sunday closing policy, the Virgin Megastore, at least, is open for business.

Les Forums des Halles

101 Porte Berger
1st
Ⓡ *Châtelet-Les*
Halles
Map p.399 F2 **37**

01 44 76 96 56 | *www.forumdeshalles.com*

In existence since 1137, Les Forums des Halles must be one of the oldest shopping malls in the world. Of course there have been a few changes since then. Formerly the city's main food market, this combined indoor and outdoor mall now boasts a 50 metre pool, gardens, two cinemas, 24 hour parking and 19 restaurants. There are also prams available for use, information points and baby change rooms. Shoppers will find an enormous range of shops specialising in everything from fashion, homeware and beauty to jewellery, electronics, optics and games. The cinemas and some restaurants are open Sundays. As for clientele, this has become a central meeting point for the city's youth. The atmosphere is vibrant if the area a little grubby. Les Halles does attract some unsavoury elements so beware of pickpockets and avoid late-night visits.

Passy Plaza

53 rue de Passy
16th
Ⓡ *Boulainvilliers*
Map p.395 F3 **38**

01 40 50 09 07 | *www.passyplaza.com*

A neighbourhood shopping mall in the well-to-do, expat-heavy streets of Passy, this complex is a rather intimate, two-level space boasting just 26 shops within the covered, art deco style gallery. The stores, however, are anything but boutique. Among the list is Gap Kids, H&M, Zara, Grand Optical and Comptoir des Cotonniers, large chains all. There is also a supermarket, Inno, on the basement level. Services include two levels of parking, mall security, a cafe, baby changing facilities and toilets. The centre is open everyday except Sunday until 19:30, though the parking remains open until 21:30.

Usines Center Paris Nord 2

134 ave de la
Plaine de France
Gonesse
Ⓡ *Parc des*
Expositions
Map p.379 D1

01 48 63 20 72 | *www.usinescenter.biz*

More a business park than a mall, this is nonetheless a great spot to come for those seeking a collection of bargain stores and factory outlets in one location. It is a budget buyer's paradise and you'll find IKEA, the shoe company Les Halles aux Chaussures, homeware store Pier Import, lingerie by Darjeeling, Villeroy & Boch, snow gear at Rossignol and children's wear at Jacadi among countless other stores. Visit the website for the full list of brands selling out-of-season and end-of-line stock at incredibly cheap prices. As a purpose-built outdoor shopping complex there are almost 2,000 parking spaces, car washing facility and good disabled access. When it comes time to eat, be prepared for fastfood. The centre is open seven days a week: Monday to Friday 11:00 to 19:00; Saturday and Sunday 10:00 to 20:00.

Supermarkets

Other options **Hypermarkets** p.292

Paris may possess a strong food market culture but supermarkets have gained greatly in popularity as modern families seek a speedy, one-stop shopping destination. Produce is of a high standard, though not what you may find when frequenting your independent butcher, grocer or bakery. Pricing among the chains is quite consistent, though there are some chains, such as Leader Price, known for their bottom-dollar price points. Expect to find more than just food stuffs: the concept of the supermarket has expanded to now include stationery, magazines, alcohol, online services, delivery, photocopying, shoe repair, sale of kitchen appliances, tailoring, catering, and in some instances, own-brand clothing. For frozen goods head to Picard (see below).

Other Supermarkets

Casino	Various Locations	01 56 26 17 00	www.casino.fr
Franprix	Various Locations	01 64 21 50 89	www.franprix.fr
Leader Price	Various Locations	08 00 35 00 00	www.leader-price.fr

You will find supermarkets located on city streets, not in shopping malls. Free parking in nearby carparks is sometimes included on presentation of a supermarket receipt so ask at the check-out as you leave. Toilet facilities are not present. Supermarkets are closed on Sundays – if you need an emergency supply of goods, head to your closest *epicerie*, a grocer-cum-corner store which is often open Sundays.

Various Locations
Monoprix
08 10 08 40 00 | *www.monoprix.fr*

Part supermarket, part multi-purpose store, Monoprix is one of the city's most recognisable supermarket chains, selling the entire range of items from fruit and vegetables to its own-label clothing, stationery, beauty products and small-scale kitchen appliances. Selected stores also provide photocopying services, photo development, tailoring, shoe repair and pick up of SNCF train tickets. There are multiple branches in each *arrondissement* ranging in size from the full-service hypermarkets like the type found on the Champs-Élysées to smaller produce-focussed stores in local side streets. Neither in-store cafes nor facilities for children form a part of the brand's ethos, however online ordering and delivery is available. The website contains extensive information on the full range of products and services.

Various Locations
Picard
08 20 16 00 39 | *www.picard.fr*

This specialist frozen foods supermarket is a home cook's best friend. Stocking everything from gourmet ready meals, to frozen meats, fish, vegetables, desserts, fruits and icecream, Picard provides a complete selection of foods for all occasions. Prices represent good value for money and with around 100 stores located around Paris finding your closest outlet means checking online. Online purchasing and delivery is available for purchases over €20, just take a look at the catalogue for a full range of products. The chain also produces its own magazine with recipes. As for food quality, it really does vary; the vegetable-stuffed puff pastries are divine, but some frozen fruits lose flavour and texture when defrosted. Produce – meats and fish – is generally of a pretty high standard, while traditional cakes such as *financiers* and *madeleines* are surprisingly tasty.

301

The world has much to offer.
It's just knowing where to find it.

If you're an American Express® Cardmember, simply visit
americanexpress.com/selects or visit your local homepage, and click on
'offers'. You'll find great offers wherever you are today, all in one place.

selects

THE WORLD OFFERS. WE SELECT. YOU ENJOY.

Going Out

Traditional French restaurant

Going Out

Paris conjures up so many different images for its devotees, but one that everyone agrees upon is the city's love affair with food. Whether it's the open-air markets or dining out, the French grow up with an appreciation for farm-fresh produce, meats and dairy from the bounty of France's varied natural landscapes. Consequently, Parisians take their restaurants seriously and going out is a national pastime. Leisure time is fiercely valued and whiling away hours at a sunny cafe, a two-hour business lunch or meeting friends for *un verre* after work are all parts of daily life. In Paris, food and social drinking are often intertwined. A meal can often start out with an *aperitif*, with the dinner accompanied by white and red wine pairings, and then be settled by a *digestif*. Some cafes will not serve alcohol unless food is ordered as well, while others will provide a tiny bowl of olives or nuts to accompany a drink. It's not unusual to be at a cafe and notice that the only guests consuming alcohol without food are expats. Foreigners and locals can be found in the same social scenes although the language barrier can be intimidating for those who are non-French speakers. Whereas Anglophones tend to socialise with strangers when going out, Parisian culture is more reserved. Since the day's activities tend to start later than in other countries, lunch and dinner times are pushed out as well so most restaurants close for the afternoon, but cafes stay open all day and into the evening. Dining out during the week is common and places will receive guests until 22:00, while on Fridays and Saturdays, late night dining locales will seat as late as 23:30. A law was recently passed banning another of France's national pastimes, smoking. Lighting up in restaurants and cafes is forbidden (effective 1 January, 2008); those who try to sneak a Gauloise are threatened with a €75 fine, and the government has offered to pay a portion of the expense for smoking cessation therapy.

To Dine Or Dance?

In a city where wining, dining, and dancing till dawn are an essential part of the culture, it is no surprise that all of your hedonistic desires can often be satisfied by visiting one single location. A vast number of venues throughout Paris are known for their world class restaurants that either turn into a late night cocktail scene, or have an adjoining club or lounge. Often one might enjoy more glowing notoriety than the other, whether it's the restaurant for its famous chef or stylish decor, or the club for its prized reputation as an 'it' place to be, but they generally stand on equally impressive ground and bask in mutual glory. The following is a list of establishments which offer both restaurant and club or lounge: Hôtel Costes (p.345), Black Calvados (p.360), Plaza Athénée (p.318), Kong (p.346) Le Murano (p.349), Aqua (Ozu restaurant) (p.360), Alcazar (p.344), Pershing Hall (p.326), Mood (p.316), Impala Lounge (p.311), Baxo (p.314), La Coupole (p.321) and Cabaret (p.361).

Eating Out

Foodies travel from all corners of the globe to dine in the epicurean magnet of Paris. As Julia Child brought French cuisine into the home during the 1960s, the world's fascination with gastronomy increased the spotlight on Paris' restaurants. Today the abundance of top-rated chefs is mind-boggling, with celebrity chefs such as Alain Ducasse, Joel Robuchon, Pierre Gagnaire, Hélène Darroze and Guy Savoy offering exquisite culinary adventures.

While there is no shortage of Michelin-starred locales in France, the trend is to eschew the rigid pressures of the rating systems. Chefs are concentrating on their original passion – sharing a love of cuisine with their guests. A variety of 'accessible' restaurants providing more affordable indulgences includes Spoon, Food & Wine (01 40 76 34 44) from Ducasse, Gagnaire's Gaya (01 45 44 73 73), Senderens (01 42 65 22 90) and Les Cocottes (01 45 50 10 31) on Christian Constant's restaurant row.

The beauty of living in a city revered for its cuisine is that chefs who have trained under the greats go out on their own and the best from other countries are drawn here. As a result, lucky diners are treated to a wide variety of international restaurants offering affordable and authentic creative cuisine. Most neighbourhoods are home to a mix of ethnic styles, although there are two Chinatowns filled with a bevy of Asian spots; one at place d'Italie and the other around Belleville. Many places are closed all day Sunday and Monday, but as the brunch concept grows an increasing number open on Sunday afternoons. Eating *petit déjeuner* (breakfast), *déjeuner* (lunch) and *dîner* (dinner) is considered an integral part of the daily routine, with snacking between meals mostly reserved for children. Breakfast occurs between 07:00 and 09:00 and typically consists of a coffee and a croissant or bread with butter and preserves. *Boulangeries* are a flurry of activity in the morning as commuters stop by for a steaming croissant on their way to work.

Restaurants typically seat lunch and dinner guests from 12:00 to 14:30 and 19:30 to 22:00. A customary method for ordering meals is the *formule*, a fixed-price menu made up of a combination of an *entrée* (appetiser), *plat* (main course) and a dessert. Higher priced dishes are also available *à la carte*. French wine is served everywhere, and usually the house *pichet* (pitcher) is quite drinkable and inexpensive. Tap water in France is perfectly potable; order *une carafe d'eau* unless you prefer bottled *gazeuse* (sparkling) or *plat* (still) water. During warmer months the streets are lined with outdoor diners *en terrasse*,

305

although during July and August restaurants tend to reduce their hours or close entirely, since many Parisians are away on holiday. Some places in the touristy areas remain open since the locals are replaced by visitors. Buffet and all-you-can-eat (*à volonté*) restaurants are rare. An exception is Flam's Lombard (62 rue des Lombards, 01 42 21 10 30) in the 1st *arrondissement*, which serves unlimited Alsatian flammekueche, an open-faced flat bread with savoury toppings. Dinner parties erupt all over town on the third Thursday of November to celebrate the Beaujolais Nouveau release, and during the December holiday season reservations at restaurants are essential.

Hidden Charges

Normally restaurant charges are pretty straightforward with no hidden surprises; if bread is served it is included in the price of your meal. But be careful when asking for water. Unless *une carafe d'eau* or *un verre d'eau* is specified, meaning a free pitcher or glass of tap water served without ice, the waiter is likely to serve a bottle that once opened will be added to your bill. If there's already a bottle of water on the table, know that you'll be charged if it is opened.

Local Cuisine

In one sense the culinary tradition of Paris is the famed style of *haute cuisine*; bringing the regional specialities of France to gastronomic heights through rare ingredients, elaborate sauces and complicated, time-consuming recipes. The 8th *arrondissement*, and in particular the 'Golden Triangle' bordered by the Champs-Élysées, avenue Marceau and avenue Montaigne, is flush with Michelin-starred addresses. Taillevent (p.323), named after the author of one of France's oldest known cookbooks dating from 1379, and Alain Ducasse at Plaza Athénée (p.318) serve the epitome of *haute cuisine* with exacting preparation and the highest levels of service. With *formules* running at €200 to €300 and higher, this obviously falls into the 'grand occasion' dining category. The roots of *haute cuisine* lie in France's varied agricultural landscape, so in another sense Parisian cuisine is an anthology of the other regions of France. From the mountains to the sea and temperate to brisk climates, the culinary array is shaped by the country's natural diversity.

Child Friendly

Parisians dote on their children, but while cafes may welcome families into the evening, some restaurants are resistant. A family favourite is the Hippopotamus chain (www.hippopotamus.fr), offering a Hippo Kids menu with colouring books, crayons and balloons. They also serve steaks and mains to please the parents. La Poussette Café in the 9th (6 rue Pierre Sémard, 01 78 10 49 00, www.lepoussettecafe.com) is designed for parents with young children, featuring a 'garage' for *les poussettes* (strollers), highchairs, bibs and changing tables. There are menus for 4, 6 and 9 month olds, and light fare for the adults. Toddlers enjoy the story telling and puppet shows, and birthday parties are also fun.

Food products must follow strict standards in order to be considered an authentic representation of one of the more than 400 regions and receive an AOC (Appellation d'Origine Contrôlée) certification. The restaurant L'AOC (p.321) uses only endorsed ingredients in their expert cuisine and is a not-to-be-missed opportunity to explore France's abundant styles. Neighbouring Germany has heavily flavoured the dishes of the Alsace-Lorraine region, as discovered in the hearty sausages and sauerkraut paired with floral rieslings and gewurztraminers. Normandy excels with scallops and mussels in addition to dairy and apple products like cider, calvados and tarte normande. Sweet crêpes and savoury buckwheat galettes originate from Brittany; Breizh Café (p.320) serves the real thing made from organic grains. This area and the Marennes-Oléron basin on the Atlantic coast are the oyster capitals; for a taste of the freshest *fines de claires* in town, Huîtriere Régis (p.331) stands out. The Périgord region further south is home to Cognac and fowl-based dishes such as terrines, magrets and foie gras. Domaine de Lintillac (p.320) features everything imaginable from the Périgord, all made with duck. In Bordeaux, specialities of roasted lamb and steaks with bordelaise sauce blend beautifully with the district's stellar wines, while central France hosts the Champagne, Bourgogne and Loire Valley regions which also have spectacular vineyards and fragrant melons, strawberries, cherries and blackcurrants for kir and other liqueurs. Goat's cheese and andouille sausage are traditions of the Loire; Dijon mustard, escargots and the buttery epoisses cheese reign in Bourgogne. The Alpine area is home to the monks of Chartreuse, whose liqueur is a 400 year old secret recipe made from 130 herbs. Switzerland's influence is noted too with the cheese raclettes and fondues; Les Fromages de Pierre (p.323) is a cheese lover's paradise showcasing traditional variations. The gastronomic city of Lyon is particularly known for its garlicky pepper sausage and hearty Rhône Valley cuisine; Aux Lyonnais in the 2nd (32 rue St Marc, 01 42 96 65 04) offers fine examples under the helm of Ducasse. The Mediterranean spirit of Provence is embodied through the lush vegetables, garlic, lavender, olive oil and seafood which perfectly complement the region's spicy wines and *pastis apéritif*. Ratatouille and bouillabaisse stews as well as pissaladière, Nice's pizza-like tart with onions, anchovies and olives, are typical dishes. The menu at Chez Janou (p.320) features Provençal interpretations in a sunny, laid-back setting.

Cafes, Bistrots, Brasseries & Restaurants

It can be difficult for a newcomer to know what to expect from each of Paris' different types of dining establishments. Part of the confusion has evolved because there are many exceptions to each of the traditional definitions. Generally the distinction has to do with the scope of food plus the time of day and atmosphere in which it is served. Cafes have a casual ambience and offer inexpensive cold sandwiches and salads. Historically a *bistrot* serves a small selection of simple, hot meals at lunchtime and in some instances, at dinner. The term 'bistrot', Russian for 'quick', was popularised in 1814 when the Cossacks occupying Paris would pound on the bar's zinc countertop and shout 'bistro' to command speedy service. In the past a *brasserie*, French for 'brewery', made its own beer and served food from the Alsace region. Over time it has come to mean a large, beautifully decorated place with a bustling ambience and which serves traditional French cuisine throughout the day and often late into the night. A restaurant, on the other hand, usually closes mid-afternoon and serves meals at a more

Kids welcome

leisurely pace. In this chapter, restaurants are listed first and include *brasserie* and *bistrot* settings. The Cafes & Coffee Shops section then follows, listing lovely places to linger over a coffee or glass of wine. Since in reality the services offered by a cafe can vary, many recommendations also serve warm meals in a relaxed atmosphere.

Restaurant Timings

Restaurants characteristically have two separate shifts for lunch and dinner. Lunch service begins at midday, with guests accepted until about 14:30. Most places then close and reopen about 19:30 for supper. The French tend to eat later in the evening, with 21:00 or 22:00 being a popular time to eat after having an aperitif at a cafe nearby. Restaurants typically seat diners until 22:00 during the week and 23:30 on weekends.

Once settled-in though, you're welcome to linger; many places stay open until midnight during the week and 02:00 on Fridays and Saturdays. Street vendors stay open late as well, especially around areas with lots of bars and clubs such as Bastille, République and Montparnasse. On Sunday and Monday many places are closed or have limited hours, and to allow everyone to enjoy a well-deserved vacation, restaurants often shut down for several weeks in July and August. *Les fermetures exceptionnelles*, or closures outside the normal schedule, are also common on public holidays and the week after Christmas.

Web Reviews

The French love to dine out and luckily they're eager to tell you about their experiences. Popular websites allowing diners to nominate and rate local restaurants include www.fra.cityvox.fr, www.lefooding.com, www.lesrestos.com, www.oubouffer.com, www.pagesrestos.com and www.restoaparis.com. Check out the French section of www.egullet.com, too – it has English-language threads that comment on press reviews and industry changes in Paris' restaurant scene.

Delivery

Parisian professionals often work until 20:00, so it's easy to understand why when dinner time rolls around they are fond of going out or eating restaurant food at home. Many neighbourhood establishments are also *traiteurs*, meaning they offer prepared food for you to take away. Home delivery from hundreds of restaurants in the metropolitan area can be ordered online through Alloresto (www.alloresto.fr, 01 40 03 62 33). The delivery fee is €1, and orders can also be placed in advance for dinner parties or business lunches. SushiShop (p.328) delights diners with its seven metro area locations offering free delivery of fresh, prepared-to-order handrolls, sushi and sashimi for lunch and dinner until 23:00. Les Dîners de Bérénice (www.lesdinersdeberenice.fr, 01 46 38 86 42) delivers well-priced meals, wine, and even tableware and flowers to Paris and the suburbs. Customers can select pre-planned menus or dishes customised to individual tastes and they also offer themed meals for the holidays or a special date.

Drinks

Other options **Alcohol** p.245

Drinking alcohol is closely intertwined with socialising and meals, so nearly every block has a cafe, corner store or supermarket where wine, beer and often spirits are available. France's legal drinking age is 16, although younger children drink wine with their family dinner. In restaurants a bottle of wine begins around €17 while an individual glass or a draft beer, *un pression*, is at least €5. Mixed drinks are pricier with a €10 minimum depending on the venue. Cocktail bars are a staple of the party scene, ranging from the legendary Harry's Bar (p.345) to the ephemeral cool of the Hôtel Costes (p.345). France is an oenophile's paradise; Willi's Wine Bar (p.352) and the tasting room inside the Lavinia (p.245) wine shop are notable for their vast selections. Restaurants serve coke for about €3.50 and a popular juice option is *un citron* or *orange pressé*, freshly squeezed lemon or orange juice served with sugar and a pitcher of water to mix to taste.

Wine Bars

Unlike regular bars and clubs, wine bars boast a wide selection of wines and champagnes from all over the world, and often have bottles for purchase. Food is

Mini Marvels

Explorer *Mini Visitors' Guides* are the perfect holiday companion. They're small enough to fit in your pocket but beautiful enough to inspire you to explore. With detailed maps, visitors' information, restaurant and bar reviews, the lowdown on shopping and all the sights and sounds of the city, these mini marvels are a holiday must.

308

generally served to complement your choice of wines, with simple menu items including cheese, charcuterie platters, foie gras and small salads. At the increasingly popular restaurant/wine bar hybrid, a full course meal is served with particular attention paid to selecting the appropriate wine to suit each course. Recommended wine bars include Willi's Wine Bar (p.352), La Belle Hortense (p.346), Wini June (p.352), Le Wine and Bubble (p.352), Au Père Louis (p.344), Le Mange Disque (p.349) and Lavinia (p.245). For wine restaurants, pay a visit to La Cave Gourmand – le Restaurant de Mark Singer (p.325), Chateaubriand (p.324), Mori Venice Bar (p.326) or Severo (p.333).

The Yellow Star

The natty yellow star seen to the right is our way of highlighting places that we think merit extra praise. It might be the atmosphere, the food, the cocktails, the music or the crowd, but any review that you see with the star attached is somewhere that we think is a bit special.

Hygiene

The DGCCRF (Direction Générale Concurrence, Consommation et Répression des Fraudes) is the consumer protection agency that regulates food safety and heath code compliance. Although most places are safe, some *traiteurs* prepare the platters of food displayed in their glass cases off-site so the kitchen's cleanliness standards can be a gamble.

Seasonal Specials

During holidays such as Valentine's Day, Christmas and New Year's Eve restaurants create special seasonal menus. A specifically French celebration occurs annually on the third Thursday in November when the Beaujolais Nouveau vintage is released; chefs create wine pairing menus and restaurants and cafes all over town are brimming with revellers. Some places host dinners to celebrate the American Thanksgiving in November, but be sure to reserve at least a couple of weeks in advance as spaces are taken quickly. Check out *Fusac*, the English-language magazine for expats, to find participating restaurants.

Food from around the world is available

Street Food

It seems there is at least one vendor selling food on nearly every street in Paris. Most commonly found are the independent shops offering kebabs, pizzas, and sometimes hamburgers with fries, but the traditional French crepe stands are plentiful too in the more touristy areas around the Eiffel Tower, St-Germain des Prés and Sacré-Coeur. Occasionally confectionery or spiced nut vendors set-up shop with many varieties for sale by the scoopful. Individuals stake a spot on the pavement with a grill to roast chestnuts during the autumn and winter; of course this is the season when the chestnuts are falling off the trees into the streets, so their cleanliness can be questionable. In most cases the hygiene standards will be acceptable for street food, but of course common sense should always prevail.

Tax, Service Charges & Tipping

A service charge of about 15% and the standard value-added tax (VAT) rate of 19.6% are built into the price of each menu item. The service charge is not the same as a tip and is not paid directly to the server. Since waiting tables is a respected profession in France, staff are paid well and do not rely on tips to make up the majority of their salary as in other countries. Most of the time, the bill will indicate *service compris*, meaning the service charge is included in the total; this is always the case for fixed-price menus. If it is not added to the bill, the receipt will read *service non compris* or *service en sus*. A token of appreciation is still welcomed, although not expected, if you have received exceptional service or you're part of a large group. Called a *pourboire* (drinking money) it can range from rounding up to the nearest euro for a drink or light meal to leaving €10 to €20 for a large party or at a fine dining establishment. A *pourboire* cannot be added onto credit card payments and must be given in cash.

Cooking Classes

The spirit of gastronomy in Paris often inspires residents to create their own gourmet feasts and cooking classes exist for all levels allowing recreational chefs to sharpen their skills. A World in a Pan (www.worldinapan.com, 06 03 05 10 27) offers English-language international cuisine classes by native home chefs who welcome you into their residences. Themed culinary adventures combine cooking and culture; for example, after creating (and consuming) dishes served by Monet to his guests, students visit the Impressionist Marmottan Museum. Other topics range from Balzac to 'Boboism'. Alain Cirelli Evénements Culinaires (www.evenements-culinaires.fr, 01 48 78 77 13) provides French-language cooking instruction for amateurs and professionals in students' homes or at the school. Courses are taught by world-renowned chefs who've passed through the kitchens of l'Ambroisie, Lucas Carton, Taillevent, Impala Lounge (p.311) and Brasserie Printemps (p.319); topics covered include three-star recipes and children's lessons for little chefs.

Vegetarian Food

France has not traditionally been known for its vegetarian-friendly fare, but as more restaurants focus on providing health-conscious options it's becoming much easier to dine meat-free. Most places have something suitable on the menu, although a French *bistrot* can become monotonous after a dozen *chèvre* salads. Luckily Paris' rich assortment of ethnic spots and fusion locales provides tasty alternatives. Korean restaurant L'Arbre du Sel (p.328) has a daily vegetarian *formule* and Living B'Art (p.316) uses free-trade and equitable commerce ingredients in their hearty dishes. There are also 100% vegetarian or vegan joints such as La Victoire Suprême du Coeur (p.334) where the garden-fresh creations are all non-GMO. Maoz in the Latin Quarter (01 43 26 36 00) is a favourite student cheapie offering falafel-stuffed pitas with all-you-can-eat salads.

Independent Reviews

The restaurants, cafes, bars and clubs in this Going Out section have been independently reviewed by a hungry and thirsty bunch of Paris-based writers. The aim of the reviews is to give an informative and unbiased view of the outlets. If any review has led you astray, or your favourite venue is missing from these pages, drop us a line at info@explorerpublishing.com and we'll take a look in time for next year's edition.

Restaurant Listing Structure

To review every eating and drinking venue in Paris would be a lifetime's work and would fill countless volumes, so this Going Out section presents a cross section of the city's recommended outlets. Restaurants have been categorised by cuisine, and are listed in alphabetical order.

African

**143-145 rue
Léon-Maurice
Nordmann**
13th
Ⓜ **Glacière**
Map p.409 E4 **1**

Entoto

01 45 87 08 51 | www.entoto.fr

Entoto is France's oldest Ethiopian restaurant, originally founded 25 years ago. Today, the gracious, warm-hearted Marie and an amazing team of women seamlessly keep it all going. It's appropriately named in honour of the monasteries in the Entoto Mountains, as the food is truly divine. A colourful 'palette' of ragouts is artfully served on a large pancake of injera, the customary tangy, spongy bread. For authentic dining, bits of the flavour-soaked bread are torn to scoop-up aromatic stews that meld lamb, poultry, beef or root vegetables with subtle spices of berbere, mitmita, coriander and cardamom. To further indulge, tedj, a fermented honey wine, is homemade along with an Ethiopian chocolate cake. A cosy, family environment with handicrafts, instruments and artwork makes Entoto a mid-priced adventure for vegetarians or carnivores to reserve for any occasion. Open every evening from 19:00 to 22:30.

2 rue de Berri
8th
Ⓜ **George V**
Map p.387 D4 **2**

Impala Lounge

01 43 59 12 66 | www.groupe-bertrand.com/impala

The rich walnut decor with African artefacts, tribal-beat techno and jazz, and an unusually-spiced menu have kept this crossroad of culture a hot spot for many years. Just off the Champs-Élysées, the intriguing, mid-priced dishes include ostrich steaks, sautéed kangaroo and mafé, a peanut and antelope stew from Senegal. Alternating Sundays feature a live gospel or jazz brunch for an international, smartly-dressed crowd. Natural textures, animal skins and carved masks create an exotic journey drawing guests not just for the culinary adventure but for the nightlife, filled with supposed virility-inducing cocktails and jams from the world-renowned musicians on Impala's signature CDs. Open Sunday to Thursday 12:00 to 02:00; Friday and Saturday 12:00 to 05:00.

American

17 rue des Écoles
5th
Ⓜ **Cardinal Lemoine**
Map p.409 F1 **3**

Breakfast in America

01 43 54 50 28 | www.breakfast-in-america.com

Route 66 has been extended to Paris with this ol' fashioned diner. Craig Carlson set up shop with a boomerang-patterned counter from Philly, an iconic Cubs football helmet and photos of movie diner scenes from *Taxi Driver* and *When Harry Met Sally*. You won't hear Supertramp in the background, but a diverse mix of American folk, rock n roll, jazz, and country. The Sunday brunch, bottomless cups of coffee and non-stop breakfasts featuring pancakes, scrambled eggs, bacon and fries are plentiful favourites. The student lunch specials are a big draw for expats too, as the BLTs, patty melts and burger assortments are tasty wonders. Just like in America, the friendly servers work for tips, so don't forget to show your appreciation. Check out the second location at 4 rue Mahler in the 4th (01 42 72 40 21). Open every day 08:30 to 23:00.

20 rue Ponthieu
8th
Ⓜ **Saint-Philippe du Roule**
Map p.387 E4 **4**

PDG

01 42 56 19 10

PDG's entrance reads 'The Greatest Hamburgers in Town' – a pretty confident claim that fortunately delivers deliciously on its promise. The secret is the combination of top-quality beef, ripe tomatoes and, crucially, the buns. Frédéric Lalos, voted France's best bakery worker, created these delectable sesame-seed coated creations especially for PDG. Crunchy on the outside, tender and springy on the inside, they're the burgers' crowning glory. Served with homemade golden crisp steak fries and zippy coleslaw, remember it's a gourmet burger which explains the slightly above-average cost.

Pastrami filled bagels, grilled chicken salads and a copious Sunday brunch are other all-American favourites of the mostly French clientele. French posters of American movies contribute to a spirited ambience and the live music on Thursday and Friday evenings sees friendly owner/waiter/singer/comedian Pierre Lannadère on the mic. Good times abound in the 6th too at 5 rue du Dragon (01 45 48 94 40). Open Monday to Sunday 12:00 to 15:00 and 19:00 to 23:00.

Arabic/Lebanese
Other options **Moroccan** p.330

27 ave Marceau
16th
Ⓜ *George V*
Map p.387 D4 **5**

Noura
01 47 23 02 20 | *http://noura.com*

For a high-quality gourmet Lebanese food fix, Noura goes way beyond the standard hummus and tabouleh; healthy, mid-priced plates are beautifully presented and offer guests tastes of many regional specialities. The wood-fired grill dishes are especially recommended, like the lamb and chicken shawarma or the kellege grillé, Lebanese bread stuffed with halloumi cheese, tomatoes and mint. Fatayers, flaky pastries with spinach and pine nuts are popular too. For dessert, sweet and nutty bite-sized morsels are artfully arranged. Noura offers friendly non-stop service in simple, modern surroundings suitable for a business lunch or a late-night get-together with family and friends. Lebanese foodstuffs and takeaway meals are available in addition to catering for small and large events. Check the website for other locations. Open Monday to Sunday 12:00 to midnight.

Argentinean
Other options **Latin American** p.329

15 rue Paul Bert
11th
Ⓜ *Faidherbe Chaligny*
Map p.401 F4 **6**

Unico
01 43 67 68 08 | *www.resto-unico.com*

Two Argentinean-born residents of Paris, an architect and a photographer, have created this stylish new Bastille hotspot frequented by the in-crowd. The 70s spirit of this former butcher's shop is preserved through the retro counter, umber wall tiles and harvest gold pendant lamps, while the slabs of beef hanging on the meat rack are an icon of the space's prior life. Food fans have been raving about the flavourful pampas beef cooked in a charcoal grill imported from Argentina, especially the lomo with spicy chimichurri sauce and the stuffed empanadas accompanied by a regional Malbec wine. The filling, upscale dinner is best appreciated at the community dining table, and advance reservations for this non-smoking restaurant are a must. Open midday to 14:30 and 20:00 to 22:30. Closed Sunday and Monday.

Belgian

4 rue Saint Denis
1st
Ⓜ *Châtelet*
Map p.399 F3 **7**

Au Trappiste
01 42 33 08 50

One of life's little pleasures in Paris must be *moules frites* and with one of the best assortments in town, this jeans-and-kid-friendly Belgian *brasserie* offers a lively chance to check them out. The lodge-like decor aims to conjure up a trappist monastery through warm, honeyed wood tones and faux stained glass

Unico

windows; the second floor offers plenty of seating and a nice view of the neighbourhood. Heaping platters of *moules* (mussels) are served with aromatic, steaming sauces and broths. The classic moules marinières dish is prepared with white wine, garlic, and onions; other variations are made with crème fraîche or provençal style. The *frites* (fries), crisp and potatoey, are best with the traditional spicy mustard. Other menu options include grilled sausages with sauerkraut or crêpes. The predominantly Belgian beer selection is well-cultivated with well over a hundred bottled types and a couple of dozen on draft. Open Sunday to Thursday 11:00 to 02:00; Friday and Saturday till 04:00.

British

46 rue des Martyrs
9th
Ⓜ *Saint-Georges*
Map p.389 D2 8

Rose Bakery
01 42 82 12 80

Hungry and happy Brits rejoice upon discovering this made-fresh alternative to the fish and chips found in Paris' numerous 'English' pubs. Always friendly, Rose Carrarini (of the recently published *Breakfast, Lunch, Tea: The Many Little Meals of Rose Bakery*) and husband Jean-Charles create daily menus with dishes like kedgeree (a Scottish recipe with rice and fish), bangers and mash and English cheeses with homemade chutney. Along with baked goods such as scones, shortbread and carrot cake, everything usually sells out by 14:30 – meaning there's a morning rush for the most popular options. Afternoon tea and weekend brunch bring in a family crowd, while the lunch rush sees professionals in this cheery but somewhat crowded spot. Fruits and vegetables are sourced from Bio-Alizé, and the foodstuffs section has hard-to-find organic items like Neal's Yard cheeses, Clipper teas and a variety of Whole Earth products. Open for lunch and weekend brunch, Tuesday to Saturday 09:00 to 1900; Sunday 10:00 to 17:00.

Chinese

170 rue Saint Martin
3rd
Ⓜ *Rambuteau*
Map p.399 F2 9

Ba-Shu
01 48 87 87 38

For fiery, authentic Szechuan cuisine, this is the only place in town. The native speciality of Chengdu is 'hot pot', a rainbow of healthy vegetables, marinated meat and fresh fish individually dipped fondue-style into bubbling broths. Szechuan flavours are distinctively different to those from other regions of China as discovered with the variety of peppers and in other healthy selections like the fish stews and spicy sautées. Friendly service and a cosy, casual decor invite good friends and family to linger over the zesty cuisine that is best paired with an icy Tsingtao beer. With inexpensive menus at lunch and dinner, Ba-Shu is surely an address to keep for a unique culinary adventure.

95 ave Niel
17th
Ⓜ *Pereire*
Map p.386 C1 10

Chez Ly – Palace de Chine
01 40 53 88 38

This brilliant pearl in the 17th is a real treasure. The elegant Asian decor with warm wood walls, intimate lighting and fragrant flowers creates a stylish yet comfortable setting to showcase the culinary creativity of Quoc Lan Ly and his genteel spouse Sy Chit Ly. Inventive, organically sourced fusions of Chinese cuisine with French touches make for mouthwatering temptations, while splashes of Cambodian, Thai and Vietnamese styles pepper the generously portioned menu too. A noted speciality is the sake-marinated foie gras encrusted with lotus and poppy grains. Other delicacies include the Hong Kong style Cantonese duck and spicy scallops with basil. In a neighbourhood known for costly gastronomy, Chez Ly holds its own with reasonably priced lunch and dinner *formules* as well as a la carte options. Open every day 12:00 to 14:30 and 19:30 to 23:00.

311

Davé

12 rue de Richelieu
1st
Ⓜ *Palais Royal Musée*
du Louvre
Map p.399 D1 **11**

01 42 61 49 48

Paris' hottest fashion designers, models and entertainment moguls vie for the best tables at this Chinese and Vietnamese restaurant, although it's really more about checking everyone out, gossiping and meeting legendary host Davé, rather than the food. In fact, most never even consult a menu – or the high-end prices – they just let Davé know what they want and he takes care of them. Of course in the carb-free fashion world it's all about the veggies including broccoli and bok choy with tofu. For 25 years members of this elite 'club' have included the likes of Helmut Newton, Karl Lagerfeld, Tom Ford, John Galliano, Marc Jacobs, Leonardo DiCaprio, Gwyneth Paltrow and Stella McCartney, and photos of Davé's famous fans line the embroidered crimson walls. Reservations are based on fashion clout, and during Fashion Week become dearer than your new pair of Manolos.

Pema Thang Restaurant du Tibet

13bis rue de la
Montagne Ste
Geneviève
5th
Ⓜ *Maubert-Mutualité*
Map p.409 F1 **12**

01 43 54 34 34 | www.pemathang.net

Translated as 'lotus field', Pema Thang is the partner of a like-named guest house near the Dalai Lama's home in the Himalayan Mountains. Not quite Chinese and not quite Indian, Tibetan cuisine combines the best influences of each for healthy vegetarian and meat dishes. Some moderately sized favourites include steamed vegetable dumplings, a spicy lamb curry, and bhoethouk, a nourishing broth with noodles, coriander and vegetables. Warm tea with yak butter, a traditional drink, is graciously served as is a refreshing honey lassi. The Dalai Lama's photo greets all who enter this well-priced closely-seated haven, encouraging Tibet's gentle spirit throughout the restaurant, from the smiling welcome to the tranquil decor. A second location is in the 3rd at 204 rue du Parc Royal (01 42 72 45 66). Open Monday to Saturday 12:00 to 14:30 and 19:00 to midnight (Monday, evening only).

Zen Zoo

13 rue Chabanais
2nd
Ⓜ *Quatre-Septembre*
Map p.389 D4 **13**

01 42 96 27 28 | www.zen-zoo.com

The signature of this cheerful, low-key restaurant (and the only place in Paris to get it) is the silky, milky zhenzhou bubble tea, made with plump tapioca 'bubbles' larger than salmon eggs and with tea varieties like black, green, coconut, sesame, taro and banana. Authentic and plentiful Taiwanese food is simmered-up with inexpensive daily *formules*: stir-fries like spicy pork with mushrooms and cabbage are paired with healthy side dishes. Desserts like the taro and azuki tart, green tea cake and kumquat cheesecake are exotic favourites. Kid-friendly, Zen Zoo is a colourful playground for the tastebuds and is always crowded with Asian and French locals as well as visitors. Takeaway and catering is also available. Open Monday to Saturday 11:30 to 23:30 (only tea in the afternoon).

Contemporary

Baxo

21 rue Juliette Dodu
10th
Ⓜ *Colonel Fabien*
Map p.390 C3 **14**

01 42 02 99 71 | www.baxo.fr

With all the style but none of the attitude, this smart newcomer to the restaurant scene is a collaboration between three genuinely nice guys – Cedric, Jean-Pierre and Sylvain. They have created an unpretentious, light-hearted space that merges attentive service with inventive, reasonably priced meals and music from the hottest DJs in Europe. Baxo welcomes international gay and straight friends for lunch and dinner at lively communal tables set in a modern, loft-like ambience or on the private, candlelit patio. Popular dishes include the duck simmered with peaches, and whisky flambéed shrimp. Sunday brunch, followed by a 'tea dance', is the most recent addition to Baxo's line up. On the weekends, music director and top DJ NickV brings in globally acclaimed artists to get the evening crowd pumped to dance.

Cristal Room Baccarat

11 pl des États-Unis
16th
Ⓜ léna
Map p.386 C4 **51**

01 40 22 11 10 | www.baccarat.fr

From the moment they glide down the red carpet embedded with countless glittering lights, visitors to the Baccarat showroom designed by Philippe Starck feel as glamorous and precious as the crystal on display. The Cristal Room Baccarat restaurant turns the drama up a notch further, with theatrical interiors that contrast rough-hewn brick walls

Cristal Room Baccarat

with pearlescent finishes and twinkling chandeliers. Thierry Burlot, former chef at the Emporio Armani Café, draws upon his Bretagne heritage to create upscale, inventive dishes based on regional ingredients such as the pigeon with carrots, mint and rose petals; the sea bream with sugar snap peas and apricots; and the rotisserie-cooked lobster with oven-roasted tomatoes. Since opening, this has remained one of Paris' most desirable hotspots with the well-heeled glitzy set. Stop by for an afternoon tea, but reserve a few days in advance for lunch and dinner inside, or for the signature picnic on the garden terrace. Open Monday to Saturday 12:00 to 14:00 and 19:30 to 21:45.

Cuisine & Confidences

**33 pl du Marché
St Honoré**
1st
Ⓜ Tuileries
Map p.388 C4 **16**

01 42 96 31 34

The sprawling Cuisine & Confidences on this trendy plaza provides a breath of fresh air welcoming families and buttoned-up bankers, with the friendly co-proprietors creating a modern yet comfortable ambience with generous, well-priced plates. Healthy and tantalising creations pepper the menu including cumin-marinated tuna with shrimp and an apple and foie gras crumble. Brunch on Saturdays and Sundays is a family affair, with a sweet and savoury spread that keep diners satisfied for the day. A nice touch are the red blankets provided to ward off the chill when there's a breeze on the terrace. With a second address on the same square plus their expansion next door, securing a table is never a problem.

Hôtel Amour

8 rue de Navarin
9th
Ⓜ Saint-Georges
Map p.389 D2 **17**

01 48 78 31 80 | www.hotelamour.com

This is a see-and-be-seen spot for Paris' denizens of cool. A new addition to Thierry Costes' repertoire, Hôtel Amour is located in a quirkily designed by-the-hour hotel, in homage to the racy reputation of its Pigalle neighbourhood. A hotchpotch of vintage furniture by Charlotte Perriand and Jean Prouvé mixed with flea-market finds and bare-boned walls creates an eclectic, underground club vibe, while the courtyard garden gushes with greenery and a fountain. The surprisingly well-priced, simple cuisine features meals such as the 'green plate' of zucchini, peas, fava beans and mozzarella marinated in a fruity olive oil. Sunday brunch is packed with bed-headed bobos and offers an a la carte menu of items like pancakes, eggs, pastries and hamburgers. There's no reservations, so expect to grab a quick drink at the bar while waiting. Open daily 12:00 to 23:30.

La Famille

**41 rue des
Trois Frères**
18th
Ⓜ Abbesses
Map p.383 D4 **18**

01 42 52 11 12

In the true spirit of Montmartre, the jovial, inventive team at La Famille likes to break the rules. Chef Jaume Morera continues the restaurant's tradition of untraditional wizardry through what he calls 'deconstructive cuisine'– restructuring the ingredients of classic recipes to create distinctive taste experiences and presentations. Guests choose from a mid-priced *formule* or the higher-priced tasting dinner of six tapas plus a few surprises.

315

Some of La Famille's 'inside-out' dishes include kebabs of paella-stuffed calamari, sorbet made from peas and a three-part lemon tart of meringue, crème and shortbread. Shaking things up at the bar is the mad-scientist Houssin; be sure to ask for one of his new generation dry-ice cocktails. The tables are few and the fans are many, so reservations are recommended. Open Tuesday to Saturday 20:00 to 02:00.

15 rue la Vieuville
18th
Ⓜ **Abbesses**
Map p.389 D1 **19**

Living B'Art

01 42 52 85 34 | *http://livingbart.free.fr*

With well-priced, honest food with a side of philosophy, Living B'Art promotes evenings of cultural exchange through art exhibits, spellbinding gypsy jazz, literary discussions and theatrical presentations. Only fair-trade or equitable commerce ingredients are used in the simple yet flavourfully creative meals, served at long community tables. Charcuterie plates, vegetable-stuffed tarts, hearty soups and unique garden salads satisfy all diners, while the dense, decadent chocolate cake tops it all off. The sunny Sunday brunch is a favourite with the local artsy crowd, but this small, comfortable *atelier* fills quickly every night so booking ahead is a good idea. Open Wednesday to Friday 12:00 to 15:00 and 19:00 to midnight; 12:00 to midnight at weekends.

53 rue Jean-Pierre Timbaud
11th
Ⓜ **Parmentier**
Map p.401 D1 **20**

Menza

01 47 00 57 49 | *www.menza.fr*

Think of Menza as an art gallery of creative cuisine; the cool, minimal interiors allow the vivid colours and aromas of the imaginatively composed dishes to take centre stage at this gay-friendly, chic little gem. Chef Alexis Godet, who spent time in the kitchen of Alain Ducasse, knows how to strike just the right balance of flavours with his well-priced, healthy menu that brings out the best qualities of the seasonal fare. Seafood dishes such as the tuna tartare with lime and passion fruit are light and refreshing, while the pineapple gazpacho with mint granita and red berries is simply ingenious. The friendly service welcomes late-night diners with the last seating on the weekends at 23:30. Reservations are advised.

114 ave des Champs-Élysées
8th
Ⓜ **George V**
Map p.387 D3 **21**

Mood

01 42 89 98 89 | *www.mood-paris.fr*

Whatever you're in the mood for, be it love or a little harmless flirtation, this swanky Franco-Asian salon is the place to meet and greet. Designer Didier Gomez has created spicy and sexy moods within the interiors. Upstairs, the larger-than-life geisha photos, floating Noguchi lamps and shimmering silvery silks are a glamorous backdrop for chef Jacky Ribault's intriguing combinations like dim sum with scallops, prawns and foie gras. Downstairs, the crimson and gold vermeil opium den ambience features intimate and social tables for late-night dining and cocktails. In the back, ruby velvet drapes conceal beds for lounging to the live music and DJs spinning every weekend. Mood's gracious and gorgeous servers also offer a zen and jazzy buffet brunch on Sundays with an abundant variety of wok and breakfast items. Open daily 10:00 to 04:00.

37 rue Quincampoix
4th
Ⓜ **Rambuteau**
Map p.399 F2 **22**

Ozo Restaurant

01 42 77 10 03 | *www.ozoresto.com*

With the motto 'natural and unexpected food', this well-priced healthy spot around the corner from the Pompidou Centre allows diners to become culinary artists. Rather than sticking to the conventional system, the owners have created an original three-step process for designing generous, individually tailored dinners. Each guest chooses a meat or seafood item such as sirloin or shrimp, and a light sauté seasoning such as mango with roasted eggplant or campania with cherry tomatoes and savoury herbs. Lastly, diners select from an appetising array of side dishes such as green pepper and arugula salad

316

with parmesan icecream or quinoa tabouleh. Trading bites is encouraged by the gracious staff to discover the many taste possibilities. The spacious terrace as well as the interior's zinc columns and textured stone walls provide a modern yet intimate welcome for the late-night, creative crowd that has spread the word about dinner and Sunday brunch at Ozo. Open for dinner from 19:30 and Sunday brunch 11:00 to 16:30.

28 rue de la
Tour d'Auvergne
9th
Ⓜ **Cadet**
Map p.389 D2 23

Spring

01 45 96 05 72 | freshsnail@free.fr

An overnight sensation, Chicagoan chef Daniel Rose is shaking up the establishment and winning them over all at the same time. Within a few months of opening, Spring had become the most sought-after table in town with its pared-down 'one man chaud' approach, as coined by *Figaroscope* when awarding Rose their highest rating. His philosophy of 'taking charge of the unknowns' means that he does everything from taking reservations and food shopping to cooking the menu that changes daily. With only 16 seats in the restaurant's minimalist interior it's impossible not to have a view of the action in the open kitchen, but ask for the 'ledge' table to catch the details. With Michelin's award of a Bib Gourmand, Rose's moderately-priced and imaginative cuisine intuitively pairs classic ingredients in untraditional ways. Whether it's with a group of friends or for a fun date, be sure to book well in advance. Open for dinner Tuesday to Friday, and lunch also on Thursday and Friday.

27 rue du Colisée
8th
Ⓜ **Saint-Philippe du**
Roule
Map p.387 E4 24

Toi

01 42 56 56 58 | www.restaurant-toi.com

This homage to the 70s has orange, gold and plum walls hung with black and white lithographs from films like *The Godfather* and *Pulp Fiction*. Chef Guillaume Leprêtre's continental cuisine features vibrant fruits and vegetables of the season complementing lobster, truffles, fresh fish and steaks in inventive recipes. Each night features a theme: jazz, magicians, clairvoyants or fashion shows with world-renowned DJs on weekend nights. Trendy Toi attracts fashionistas and celebrities like Hugh Grant and Patrick Bruel who come for a happy hour rendezvous, late-night dining and music mixes that guarantee a fun frolic with friends or a date. Open daily non-stop, the side-by-side tables mean elbow-to-elbow dining; there's always a crowd for the mid-priced menus, cocktail lounge and Sunday brunch. Reservations are recommended.

11 blvd Montmartre
2nd
Ⓜ **Grands Boulevards**
Map p.389 E4 25

Victoria Station

01 42 36 73 90

Forget the Eurostar; this restaurant offers instant transportation not just to London, but back though time to the early 20th century. Outfitted with authentic dining cars acquired from London's Victoria Station in the 1940s, the restaurant's decor has ruby velvet banquettes, fringed lampshades and brass luggage racks that add to the adventurous spirit. Ask to sit in the second dining room for a more complete immersion into the locomotive theme. This is a fun, casual spot for families and groups of friends to enjoy the well-priced menu featuring wood-fired pizzas and grilled meats. The pizza au chèvre with goat's cheese, ham and crème fraîche is a customer favourite. They don't take reservations, so be prepared for the occasional short queue.

Victoria Station

Deli

23bis rue des Rosiers
4th
Ⓜ *Saint-Paul*
Map p.400 B3 26

Micky's Deli

01 48 04 79 31

For those times when nothing but hot pastrami on rye will do, Micky's comes to the rescue. Serving only kosher cuisine under orthodox rabbinic supervision, this inexpensive family-oriented Jewish deli is located on rue des Rosiers in the Marais, the historic heart of Paris' Yiddish community that sadly has become increasingly gentrified in recent years. Thank goodness this spot has held out with its social New York deli atmosphere serving filling plates like the onion roll with charcuterie, poppy seed bagel stuffed with chicken and the 'Micky', an American-style burger with ground beef and pastrami. Although closed Friday evening and Saturday, it's one of the rare places open for lunch and dinner on Sundays. So stop your kvetching and get over to this tasty joint for some lip-smacking indulgence. Open Sunday to Thursday 11:30 to 15:00 and 19:00 to 23:30; Friday 11:30 to 14:30. Second location in the 16th at 33 rue de Greuze (01 45 05 47 70).

Dinner Cruises

Other options **Boat & Yacht Charters** p.194

pte de la
Bourdonnais
7th
Ⓜ *Bir-Hakeim*
Map p.396 C2 27

Bateaux Parisiens

01 46 99 43 13 | www.bateauxparisiens.com

Watching Paris' spectacular landscape slip by while drifting down the Seine is undeniably romantic in its own right; but paired with exceptional cuisine it is an unforgettable experience. As the sun sets over the monuments and the evening lights begin their twinkle, a slow waltz on the dance floor accompanied by live musicians adds to the glamour. Chef Yves Gras creates a variety of all-inclusive, high-end *formules* with dishes like a vegetable and truffle pastry, foie gras, scallops with fennel and baba au rhum. Special holiday dinners and theme nights for visitors and locals alike are offered throughout the year. Smart-casual dress and reservations are essential for this modern, glass-enclosed vessel departing twice every day in front of the Eiffel Tower. Lunch cruises depart at 12:45 and return at 14:30; dinner cruises depart at 20:30 and return at 23:00. The boat can also be chartered for private functions.

French

25 ave Montaigne
8th
Ⓜ *Alma – Marceau*
Map p.397 E1 9

Alain Ducasse au Plaza Athénée

01 53 67 65 00 | www.plaza-athenee-paris.com

Curated by Ducasse with chef Christophe Moret, the emphasis on purity and faultless preparation brings the classical elements of *haute cuisine* into a contemporary realm. The cloud of 10,000 shimmering crystals floating overhead blends modern and traditional sophistication in an ambience which interior designer Patrick Jouin calls 'magic and poetry'. For the gourmands who venture into this three-starred journey it is an indulgence of the highest magnitude while the impeccable service and culinary perfection guarantees lifelong memories. Open for lunch Thursdays and Fridays 12:45 to 14:15 and dinner Monday to Friday 19:45 to 22:15.

6 rue Coquillière
1st
Ⓜ *Les Halles*
Map p.399 E1 29

Au Pied du Cochon

01 40 13 77 00 | www.pieddecochon.com

If you've ever wondered where to satisfy that 3am craving for oysters or French onion soup, look no further. Just next to St Eustache church, this institution in Les Halles has been serving tourists and locals 24 hours a day for over 60 years. With its bordering-on-kitsch decor, traditional brisk waiters and always-packed terrace of family and friends, it's a lively slice of late-night Paris. In the style of a grand *brasserie*, heaping platters of oysters, crab, shrimp and lobster are served on beds of ice. Plus of course, the namesake is on the menu – grilled pigs' feet with béarnaise sauce. Au Pied du Cochon also coordinates a 'chauffeur' service for those who who've pigged-out a little too much. Open 24 hours a day, seven days a week.

Aux Anysetiers du Roy

61 rue Saint-Louis en l'Île
4th
Ⓜ Pont Marie
Map p.400 A4 **30**

01 56 24 84 58

This intimate restaurant on Île St Louis is located in a picture-perfect 17th century building classified as a historic monument. The name celebrates the organisation traditionally charged with making the king's aniseed liqueur, or *pastis*, from Provence. During its colourful cabaret past it was named Au Petit Bacchus, and for several decades it has served classic French cuisine with Provençal touches to local romantics, visitors and historical celebrities like Dali, Bardot and Jerry Lewis. Rabbit glazed with mustard, duck with a honey and raisin sauce, onion soup and boeuf bourguignon are featured on the well-priced *formules* and a la carte menus. With carved stone friezes, royal coats of arms, stained glass and snugly-placed wooden tables, the medieval decor transports diners to the restaurant's origins. Reservations are advised at weekends.

Brasserie Lipp

151 blvd St-Germain
6th
Ⓜ St-Germain des Prés
Map p.398 C4 **31**

01 45 48 53 91 | *www.brasserie-lipp.fr*

Along with neighbours Les Deux Magots (p.339) and Café de Flore (p.337), Brasserie Lipp completes the St-Germain des Prés 'holy trinity' from the Belle Époque era. This celebrated establishment is one of Paris' original upscale Alsatian-style *brasseries* and continues to feature regional sausages and pork with sauerkraut along with a large selection of beers. Visionary figures have been intertwined with this legend since its beginning in 1880, such as literary masters Proust and St-Exupéry; political bigwigs Pompidou, Mitterrand and Chirac; and cinema stars such as Harrison Ford, Woody Allen and Robert Altman. The high-powered business and political ambience remains noticeably present, but everyone's snugly packed-in so don't plan on divulging any top-secret insider information. There's always a lively gathering at the Lipp, so reservations are strongly recommended. Orders taken from 10:00 to 01:00 every day.

Brasserie Printemps

66 blvd Haussmann
9th
Ⓜ Havre-Caumartin
Map p.388 B3 **32**

01 42 82 58 84 | *www.groupe-bertrand.com*

Pure magic awaits you under the awe-inspiring stained-glass dome created in 1923 for the top floor of the department store Printemps Haussmann. The interior was redesigned in 2006 by Didier Gomez with art deco motifs and modern lines. Centred around the dome's 'floating pearl' is a seafood bar serving oysters and lobster. On a par with the glittering ambience is the seasonal French cuisine by top-notch chef Alain Cirelli. Whether it's the ladies who lunch, a midday business gathering or international visitors, all appreciate the high-quality yet moderately-priced *brasserie* fare with a twist. The veal piccata and roasted sea bass are favourites, as is the afternoon tea accompanied by handmade sweets. Occasionally wine tastings are hosted by noted producers of the Pays d'Oc; just give them a call to sign-up. Open Monday to Saturday 09:00 to 19:00 (Thursday evenings until 22:00).

Brasserie Printemps

Breizh Café

01 42 72 13 77 | *www.breizhcafe.com*

109 rue Vieille du Temple
3rd
Ⓜ *Saint-Sébastien Froissart*
Map p.400 B2 🔳

Sure there's crêpe stands on every corner, but they simply can't compare to the authentic preparations of this inexpensive, family-friendly Breton *bistrot*. Although new to Paris, owner Bertrand Larcher has a location in native Cancale plus several in Japan. Delicate and lacy crêpes (sweet) and galettes (savoury) of organic buckwheat are filled hot off the griddle and served on the region's rustic pottery. The traditional square fold creates a frame for the colourful ingredients; the classic Bretonne is a creamy concoction of eggs, ham, mushrooms and cheese bursting with flavour. For dessert, crêpes made with Bretagne's famous buttery, salted caramel can be topped with fruit compotes or caramel icecream. Choose from over 15 artisanal ciders or calvados to accompany your meal; the award-winning Tsarkaya oysters are also a rare find from the region. Open non-stop for lunch and late dinners, this place has a cheery setting that's sure to please.

Chez Janou

2 rue Roger Verlomme
3rd
Ⓜ *Chemin Vert*
Map p.400 C3 🔳

01 42 72 28 41 | *www.chezjanou.com*

A quick trip to easy-going Provence is just the antidote to the hustle and bustle of Parisian city life. If that's not an option, the next best thing is a getaway to Chez Janou right around the corner from place des Vosges. Over 80 types of pastis and a wide range of high-quality yet affordable Rhône Valley wines are available to accompany the Mediterranean cuisine. Since 1912 this neighbourhood favourite has attracted both residents and visitors for its healthy Provençal influenced dishes such as chilled ratatouille, anchovy spread and olive tapenade served with crusty bread, or the shrimp sautéed in pastis. The garden-like terrace, with its trellis of climbing vines and jazz music, makes for a cheery spot to unwind with family and friends.

Chez Papa

206 rue La Fayette
10th
Ⓜ *Louis Blanc*
Map p.390C1 🔳

01 42 09 53 87

'Papa' Bruno welcomes customers all over town with his chain of restaurants featuring food from the Auvergne. Inexpensive *formules* and large servings attract hungry families, students, tourists and frugal French for the filling south-western specialities. Cassoulet Papa, a white bean stew with sausage, and the leafy ham salad with blue cheese and browned potatoes are popular. Chilli ristras hung from the ceiling, oak plank walls and heavy rustic tables create a casual countryside atmosphere that, along with the friendly late-night service, keeps the place packed. Open every day 12:00 to 01:00.

Domaine de Lintillac

10 rue Saint Augustin
2nd
Ⓜ *Quatre-Septembre*
Map p.389 D4 🔳

01 40 20 96 27 | *www.lintillac-paris.com*

Take a gander at this casual country charmer specialising in duck from the Périgourd region. Foie gras lovers have found their home at this reasonably-priced gem welcoming families and friends. The ducks are raised and prepared at the namesake's estate, with the tender meat and foie gras then cooked at the restaurant in an array of temptations; the cassoulet, magret, and boudin sausages are recommended, and the foie gras glazed with honey-imbued sauternes is a huge success. Wine is inexpensive too with champagne under €40 so it's a great place to indulge. Each cosy table is covered by a checked cloth and has a toaster for warm and crunchy bread with the foie gras. The menu offers a small selection for non-duck lovers too. Open Monday to Friday 12:00 to 14:15; Monday to Wednesday evenings 19:00 to 22:15 and Thursday to Saturday evenings 19:00 to 23:00. Dinner is served in two shifts and reservations are a must. Additional locations and boutiques at 20 rue Rousselet in the 7th (01 45 66 88 23) and 54 rue Blanche in the 9th (01 48 74 84 36).

L'AOC

The Eiffel Tower
7th
Ⓜ Bir-Hakeim
Map p.396 C3 **32**

Jules Verne
01 45 55 61 44 | www.restaurants-toureiffel.com

Popular legend has it that self-proclaimed critic of the Eiffel Tower, Guy de Maupassant, ate lunch in its restaurant every day because it was the only place in Paris he couldn't see the landmark. Instead of a view of the tower, a 360° panorama of the timeless cityscape and tranquil Seine is the crowning glory of Paris' iconic monument. A new chapter was written into the history of the Jules Verne restaurant in 2007, as under the helm of Alain Ducasse the 'modern classic' French cuisine has risen to even greater heights. The big splurge dining options include a six-course tasting menu in the evenings or a lunch *formule*; a la carte selections are available too. Offering a private elevator and valet service, indulging in Jules Verne is always a well-dressed occasion for the most romantic of dates. A minimum two-month advanced reservation is required to join the leagues 324 metres above the sea. Open seven days 12:15 to 13:30 and 19:15 to 21:30.

14 rue des Fossés St-Bernard
5th
Ⓜ Cardinal Lemoine
Map p.410 A1 **40**

L'AOC
01 43 54 22 52 | www.restoaoc.com

Sophie and Jean-Philippe Lattron welcome locals and visitors as family into their sunny home. Jean-Philippe's discerning eye for high-quality meats comes from his expertise as a master butcher, a passion learned from his father, a horsemeat specialist. Self-taught in the kitchen, he selects the best AOC (Appellation d'Origine Contrôlée) ingredients for this *bistrot carnivore*. Fragrant aromas waft from the rotisserie into the gold-coloured dining rooms filled with antique sideboards and family heirlooms. AOC is known for *triperie* (organ meat) but less adventurous mid-priced specialities like the succulent pork loin or suckling ham are divine with the dripping-roasted potatoes. Earthy homemade terrines come with an onion and raisin compote whose recipe Sophie's mother gave to Jean-Philippe. The cafe sweetly seals the deal with *amuses bouches* of cinnamon rice pudding and caramel chocolate mousse.

4 rue Taine
12th
Ⓜ Dugommier
Map p.412 A3 **38**

L'Inédit Café
01 43 43 21 80

This is a real find for delicious French food at extremely reasonable prices. The traditional recipes are made with fresh, quality ingredients and come from a kitchen that truly knows what it's doing. The old-fashioned grilled steak with thyme *brûlé* (lit at the table) perfumes the air with a wonderful earthy aroma, while the succulent salmon with sweetly tart sauerkraut is essential eating. The outdoor dining is a pleasure in this quiet neighbourhood. Inside, the tumbled stone walls and dark wood create a warm, leisurely air perfect for dining with a date, family or friends. With most main courses under €10 and desserts such as the warmed chocolate cake all at €5, it's no wonder the tables fill quickly for lunch and dinner. The young team provide generous cocktails for the after-work crowd, and a Sunday brunch that is a real community draw.

102 blvd du Montparnasse
14th
Ⓜ Vavin
Map p.408 C2 **39**

La Coupole
01 43 20 14 20 | www.lacoupoleparis.com

An elegant example of Paris' tradition of *grandes brasseries*, La Coupole has been a fixture in Montparnasse since 1927. Art deco mouldings and mosaics complement the beautifully preserved pillars painted with frescos by pupils of Matisse and Léger, while the underground dancehall that once hosted Joséphine Baker today hosts

321

world-renowned DJs and salsa nights. Over the years luminaries such as Sartre, Picasso and Gauguin (with his Javanese mistress) have indulged in the moderately priced classic cuisine, notably the lamb curry that has graced the menu since the beginning, and the sparkling silver platters of fresh shellfish. Reservations can be made online and, as this remains a popular destination for both international visitors and locals, are recommended.

1 rue Théophile Roussel
12th
Ⓜ *Ledru-Rollin*
Map p.401 D4 **41**

Le Baron Rouge

01 43 43 14 32

A neighbourhood tradition just next door to the Marché d'Aligre, this busy spot is an inexpensive place where you can fill up your heart's content on tangy oysters, earthy regional charcuterie and bio wine straight from the barrel. Customers crowd around the bar and the upturned wooden barrel that serves as a table, eventually overflowing onto the street and down the block. With oysters arriving fresh from the Bassin Arachon in the Aquitaine region, customers pair them with wines made at small family vineyards and then fill up a jug (their own, or one borrowed from the bartender) to be consumed at home. The rustic decor adds to the family-friendly vibe both at lunch and in the evenings.

33 rue Lepic
18th
Ⓜ *Blanche*
Map p.382 C4 **42**

Le Basilic

01 46 06 78 43

Journey through the winding cobblestone streets of Montmartre to discover this intimate, ivy-covered nook dating back to 1830. A former inn, the original hand-carved walnut bar, bookcases and expansive stone fireplace have been retained to create a perfect setting to enjoy a well-priced traditional French meal in a non-smoking environment. Try the tender steak with foie gras or snappy gingerbread encrusted lamb; for dessert, the silky crème brûlée spiked with vanilla bourbon is a favourite. Perfect for a romantic candlelit date or a relaxed lunch, locals as well as tourists reserve a table to appreciate Le Basilic's quintessential French charm.

Lac Inferieur
Bois de Boulogne
16th
Map p.394 C1 **43**

Le Chalet des Îles

01 42 88 04 69 | *www.lechaletdesiles.net*

Without a doubt one of Paris' most romantic dining experiences, Le Chalet des Îles can only be accessed by ferry across Le Lac Inferieur in the Bois de Boulogne. In 1880, this Swiss chalet was bestowed upon Empress Eugenie by Napoleon III. Following a fire, it was rebuilt in 2001 into the exquisitely lush garden cottage it is today. Outdoor terraces are alive with greenery and charm, while inside, French toile, murals of hunting parties, and plush seating by the fireplace create a cosy, elegant welcome. Classic French cuisine with contemporary touches is the perfect partner for the setting. Mid-priced lunch *formules* are available during the week, and reservations are always a good idea. The restaurant is also available for private parties.

33 ave du Maine
15th
Ⓜ *Montparnasse Bienvenüe*
Map p.408 A2 **44**

Le Ciel de Paris

01 40 64 77 64 | *www.cieldeparis.com*

With a view that takes your breath away, dining on the 56th floor of the Montparnasse Tower is an unforgettable, on-top-of-the-world experience. It's hard to compete with the dazzling 360° panorama of Paris' monuments, but the high-end traditional French cuisine of Jean-François Oyon shines brightly as well. The lobster ravioli and simmered steak with truffle sauce are perennial recommendations. Whether it's a breakfast or lunch business meeting or a special occasion dinner, there are fixed-price menus available. Book dining reservations in advance to bag the best views, but don't hesitate to stop by for afternoon tea or a glass of champagne and listen to the jazz piano while soaking up the twinkling skyline. Open every day 08:30 to 23:00.

Le Procope

01 40 46 79 00 | *www.procope.com*

Le Procope is reputed to be the oldest cafe and restaurant in Paris, having first opened its doors in 1686. When the Comédie-Française moved next door in 1689, it became the hub for actors and audience members as well as literary and political leaders from the French Revolution; Rousseau, Voltaire, Danton and Marat were legendary patrons. The world's first encyclopaedia was written here and Benjamin Franklin even polished up the American constitution over a *café* or two. Today it continues to draw tourists as well as literati and intellectuals who gather around spectacular shellfish platters – extravaganzas of oysters, mussels, langoustines, scallops and crab. Meat options abound too, and the Philosophers' Menu serves calf brains from the original recipe of 1686. A living museum laden with oil paintings and antiques, dining here is unforgettable.

Le Soufflé

01 42 60 27 19 | *c_rigaud@club-internet.fr*

Little fluffy clouds of love await those fortunate enough to dine at Le Soufflé; with a golden brown top yet delicate and light inside, many savoury and sweet styles are available. Of course the emmental and comté cheese soufflé is a perennial favourite, but the wild mushroom or salmon with sorrel are mouthwatering contenders. The fixed-price menus with three varieties are reasonably priced for the quality, especially if you order the Grand Marnier soufflé for dessert – the bottle is left on the table to consume as desired. It's best to make reservations with a romantic date or friends so everyone can trade tastes. Open for lunch and dinner.

Les Fromages de Pierre

01 45 54 12 26 | *www.lesfromages-depierre.com*

Fromage-a-philes take note, you have found your destiny. This restaurant offers dozens of cheese varieties from all of France prepared in every way for nearly any dish imaginable. Les Fromages de Pierre specialises in classic Alpine fondues as well as an incredible tartiflette made with potatoes, bacon, and reblochon cheese. Tasting platters with an array of five to 20 styles can be complemented with wines bringing out the best flavours of each. The dessert sampler is extra-special, with seven or eight *bouchées* (bites) of chocolate and perhaps roquefort or chèvre sorbets... sweet little bits of heaven. Although a bit out of the way, this lively place fills quickly with a casual, friendly crowd, so it's best to reserve online a day in advance to be sure of a spot. Open Monday to Friday 12:00 to 14:30 and 19:30 to 22:00; Saturday 20:00 to 22:00.

Taillevent

01 44 95 15 01 | *www.taillevent.com*

The name of this legendary *haute cuisine* establishment pays tribute to a French father of gastronomy, Taillevent, who in 1379 authored France's oldest known cookbook and served as chef to many kings during medieval times. Today, under the expert helm of chef Alain Solivérès, the recipes are different but still fit for royalty. Although some consider the 2007 loss of their third Michelin star to be a scandal, the cuisine and ambience remain of the highest calibre. The classic French cuisine has subtle concessions to modernity; you'll find roasted duck with ripe cherries as well as lobster sautéed in Thai basil. In the 19th century Emperor Napoleon III was a frequent dinner guest at this timelessly elegant former residence of the Duke de Morny; the museum-quality contemporary art collection and unparalleled service contribute to an extraordinary culinary experience. Plan ahead for this one as reservations well in advance are essential. Open Monday to Friday for lunch at 12:15 and dinner at 19:15.

Indian

Ratn

9 rue La Trémoille
8th
 Alma – Marceau
Map p.397 D1 **49**

01 40 70 01 09

Ratn is a delightful spot for indulging in India's highest-quality gastronomy. Based on traditional Moghul recipes cooked for royalty, the offerings provide an authentic trip though the varied flavours and cooking styles of the region. A gracious welcome is provided by Sanjay, whose Delhi-born father, Chaman Lal Bhalla, is credited with popularising 'gourmet' Indian cuisine in Paris during the 1970s and training many chefs who went on to open their own spots in town. The mid-priced menu has lunch and dinner *formules* that emphasise quality over quantity. Fit for a maharajah, the tandoori chicken, lamb saag and the homemade cheese grilled with peppers are made with freshly ground spices and well-sourced ingredients. Rich jewel-toned colours and detailed, carved wood accents create a spirited ambience for dining with friends and family.

Sabraj

175 rue
Saint-Jacques
5th
 Cluny – La Sorbonne
Map p.409 E1 **50**

01 43 26 70 03 | www.restaurantsabraj.com

Every bit of this 14th century dining room has been meticulously decorated with the vibrant colours, rich woods and silky textures of Mumbai. Rose petals scattered on candlelit tables and the quiet melodies of sitar strumming create a romantic ambience to taste the traditional specialities cooked in the earthen tandoor oven. As well as tandooris, Sabraj offers a wide assortment of naan breads, biryanis and curries in varying degrees of spiciness. Low-priced lunch and dinner *formules* bring in a casual, budget-minded student crowd from the nearby Sorbonne as well as neighbourhood guests from the Panthéon area. At times there's a wait for one of the tightly placed tables, so reserve online or by phone if you're in a hurry. Open everyday 12:00 to 14:30 and 19:00 to 23:30.

International

Chateaubriand

129 ave Parmentier
11th
 Goncourt
Map p.390 C4 **51**

01 43 57 45 95

Chateaubriand has quickly become *très* chic on Paris' dining scene. The adventurous culinary blends of Basque chef Iñaki Aizpitarte (formerly of La Famille, p.315) yield surprises of unlikely ingredients coming together in inventive ways. The €40 *prix fixe* tasting menu features five courses that change daily, such as corn with fresh pistachios or rockfish and beetroot in squid ink. The inexpensive lunch *formule* shows a more *bistrot*-style influence, although creative dishes such as a penne with mussels and chorizo still pepper the *formule* and a la carte menu. Impressive organic wines are featured with high-calibre knockouts from Pommard and St Joseph. The polished elegance of the dark woods, creamy linens and blackboard of offerings form a sophisticated ambience for Chateaubriand's well-heeled culinary aficionados. No reservations are required at lunch, but three to four day advance dinner reservations are a must.

Georges

19 rue Beaubourg
4th
 Rambuteau
Map p.399 F2 **52**

01 44 78 47 99 | www.centrepompidou.fr

This 6th floor hotspot from Thierry Costes, Paris' maven of cool, sits atop the modern art museum in the Pompidou Centre. It offers an eye-popping view of the city's skyline and a futuristic postmodern decor by Dominique Jacob and Brendan McFarlane that blends the museum's industrial architecture with aluminium pods housing the kitchen and VIP room. The upscale international cuisine is accented with Asian touches like the caramelised duck with cubes of fresh coconut, and coriander spiced tuna. It's not just tourists who dine here; high-style Parisians reserve for a business lunch or dinner with

324

friends, while stopping by in the late hours to socialise over a cocktail and chill out to the ambient sounds from the house DJ. Be sure to let the doorman know you have a reservation. To avoid confusion, remember that the restaurant's private elevator is just to the left of the museum's main entry.

32 rue de Picardie
3rd
Ⓜ Temple
Map p.400 B1 53

Guillaume

01 44 54 20 60

The restaurant Guillaume is truly a collaborative effort by the family and friends of its down-to-earth namesake: art from his mother's house, dining tables from his aunt's, and friends who decorated the walls and are proud to serve Belgian Chef Xavier Thierry's *cuisine du monde*. Inventive without being pretentious, the generous and modestly-priced dishes change seasonally; examples include a sea bass ceviche with peaches, medium-rare beef served sushi-style with wasabi, and squid with tahini sauce and chorizo. Independent vineyards provide reasonable organic wine selections. The top two floors, an art gallery curated by Guillaume's cousin, bask in a brilliant luminosity filtered through skylights; if you're interested in attending an opening just leave your email address. Lovely for a romantic date, dinner with friends or even a high-power meeting, this is an address to reserve.

**10 rue du
Général Brunet**
19th
Ⓜ Botzaris
Map p.392 A1 54

La Cave Gourmande – le Restaurant de Mark Singer

01 40 40 03 30

Foodies the world-over make a pilgrimage to this tree-lined neighbourhood near Parc Buttes-Chaumont just to delight in Philadelphian Mark Singer's accessible *haute cuisine*. The honesty of *bistrot* fare is combined with his self-dubbed style of 'opportunity' – fanatically sourcing the best of the best from highly-specialised producers according to seasonal availability and whatever interesting, unusual ingredients can be located. The results provide intriguing culinary adventures that satisfy both Singer's creative passion and the cosmopolitan guests' indulgence in the extraordinary. His Robuchon and Michelin backgrounds are evident as everything wild – truffles, boar, venison, lobster, and oysters – finds its way to his lean team for the astonishingly well-priced lunch and dinner menus and wine carte. Exceptional vineyards culled from more than 3,000 bottles allow for ideal pairings and hard-to-find treasures; he once surprised Johnny Depp with a Romanée Conti. For a truly special occasion, reservations are recommended and required on Saturdays. Open Monday to Friday 12:00 to 14:30 and 19:30 to 22:30; Saturday 19:30 to 22:30.

107 rue de Rivoli
1st
Ⓜ Tuileries
Map p.398 C1 55

Le Saut du Loup

01 42 25 49 55 | *www.lesautduloup.com*

Finally, a museum restaurant that doesn't serve stale, prehistoric relics better suited to the archives. Even with a spectacular terrace nestled among the springtime blossoms of the Jardin du Carrousel and a view of the Louvre, Jardin des Tuileries and Eiffel Tower, the creative cuisine of chef Pascal Bernier further elevates the awe-inspiring ambience. The foie gras accented with anise, scallops with a cinnamon soufflé and rhubarb tiramisu are just the beginning of his imaginative menu. Le Saut du Loup is a refined yet comfortable setting for an upscale business lunch, dinner with friends or a romantic date. If it's a rainy day, the first floor dining room and bar provide the best views.

27 quai Branly
7th
Ⓜ Alma – Marceau
Map p.396 C2 56

Les Ombres

01 47 53 68 00 | *www.lesombres-restaurant.com*

This flat-out stunning new addition to the Parisian landscape is on the 5th floor rooftop of the Musée du Quai Branly and offers an unparalleled view of the Eiffel Tower and its surrounds. Jean Nouvel, architect of both museum and restaurant, has seamlessly integrated *les ombres*, or shadows, of the omnipresent icon into the dining room and terrace, down to designing the plates and cutlery. This *chef d'ouevre* has met his match with *chef de cuisine* Arno Busquet, whose time under the auspices of Joël Robuchon is most evident. His philosophy underscores that of the museum, as it celebrates world cultures by integrating intriguing and often fair-trade ingredients into classical cuisine. Seasonal, tasting and a la carte big-budget menus are available. Perfect for a special occasion, important meeting or a very romantic date, reservations are essential at dinner.

Pershing Hall

49 rue Pierre Charron
8th
Ⓜ **George V**
Map p.387 D4 57

01 58 36 58 36 | *www.pershinghall.com*
The stunning decor, designed by genius Andrée Putman, is reason enough to visit Pershing Hall. Modern lines and beaded walls perfectly offset the classical architecture and Paris' version of the Hanging Gardens of Babylon, a breathtaking wall covered by 250 types of foliage reaching up to clouds. It's an incomparable space for enjoying the international cuisine, afternoon tea or an evening cocktail. Late nights this hothouse turns into one of the best clubs in town featuring leading DJs; Hôtel Costes' Stephane Pompougnac compiled Pershing Hall's concept CDs and Putman even sings on them. The well-heeled cosmopolitan crowds are loyal devotees and have made Pershing Hall an *incontournable* (reliable favourite) on the dining and social scene.

Ze Kitchen Galerie

4 rue des Grands Augustins
6th
Ⓜ **Saint-Michel**
Map p.399 D3 58

01 44 32 00 32 | *www.zekitchengalerie.fr*
High ceilings and snow white-walls hung with rotating exhibits of vivid art create a modern air in William Ledeuil's hotspot just a few doors down from Picasso's old studio. The singular decor is an elegant backdrop for his inspired palette of flavours assembled from his travels in Thailand, Vietnam and Japan. Named Chef of the Year by *Gault Millaut* in 2006, the charming Ledeuil and his friendly international team create a Discovery Menu each month, a smattering of seven dishes featuring inventive juxtapositions of Asian spices with seasonal ingredients. The chic and cosmopolitan come for both lunch and dinner to this spot close to the Seine, so reservations are a must.

Italian

Other options **Mediterranean** p.329

Amici Miei

44 rue Saint-Sabin
11th
Ⓜ **Chemin Vert**
Map p.400 C3 59

01 42 71 82 62
Pizza lovers come from all over town to indulge in this perfect wood-fired pie. Over 20 varieties of pizza offer either red or white sauce and have a thin, crunchy crust that is loaded-up with toppings. L'Amici Miei, the house special, is a filling number made with white sauce, ham, cherry tomatoes, basil, and buffalo mozzarella. Additional Mediterranean favourites include the fresh octopus salad and the linguine with clams. Beige stone walls and dark wood tables create a casual, family ambience. Since they don't take reservations or credit cards and the brisk service is always packing the crowds in, bring cash and join the queue – die-hard fans agree it's worth the wait. Open 12:00 to 14:30 and 19:00 to 23:00. Closed Sunday and Monday.

Mori Venice Bar

2 rue du Quatre Septembre
2nd
Ⓜ **Bourse**
Map p.389 D4 60

01 44 55 51 55 | *www.mori-venicebar.com*
Philippe Starck's vision of bringing to Paris the 'pure Venetian' cuisine he savours at his homes in Burano has come alive through a partnership with the ever-gracious Massimo Mori of the famed Emporio Armani Café. Murano glass table settings and

finely woven textiles infuse a classic Venetian glamour into Starck's postmodern canvas showcasing the high-end regional specialities. The heartbeat of the restaurant is Venice's celebrated tradition of the 'bàcaro' – smiling friends toasting with an amarone around a bar laden with cicchetti – savoury hot and cold antipasti appetisers. The chef, along with most of the staff, hails from the city and knows how to create a generous serving of linguine with clams that transports you to the Lido. A corporate and press power-lunch spot as well as a celebrity haunt for the likes of Zidane and Belmondo, it's advised to reserve online a couple of days in advance.

Pizzeria d'Auteuil

81 rue la Fontaine
16th
**Ⓜ Michel-Ange –
Auteuil**
Map p.405 D1 61

01 42 88 00 86

There's almost always a queue to snag a seat with the regulars at this inexpensive neighbourhood joint. One bite and you'll know why. It's certainly a contender for the best pizza in Paris with its thin, crackery crust, vine-ripe sauce and loads of cheese and fresh toppings. The stagione is to die for with mushrooms, olives and an artichoke 'flower' in the middle. With ham, mozzarella and tomatoes sourced from Italy, the appetisers and pasta are *magnifico* too. Grilled vegetables with intensely sweet flavours and salty slivers of ham make the antipasti and prosciutto plate a winner, and you'll be full for weeks with the rigatoni amatriciana with bacon and peppery pecorino. The reasonably-priced barbaseco wine is a steal too. With an old-school Italian decor from the 1950s and tables so tight you'll need to watch your elbows, it's a lively affair. Open 19:00 to 22:00 for dinner only; reservations advised.

San

27 blvd du Temple
3rd
Ⓜ Filles du Calvaire
Map p.400 C1 62

01 44 61 73 45 | www.sanristorante.com

Every detail of San celebrates the Italian arts; crisp and modern interiors with plush red dining chairs, films projected on the restaurant's pure white walls like Fellini's *La Dolce Vita*, dark and moody vocals of Paolo Conte, and of course, inventive interpretations of classic northern Italian cuisine. Sociable young waiters welcome everyone with a smile and create a lively setting for laughing with friends and family on the terrace. San serves 20 styles of pizza pie, like the namesake San made with a red pesto base of sun dried tomatoes, buffalo mozzarella, scamorza and spicy sausage. For dessert, the pannacotta with green anise and cherries is a heavenly treat. Since opening in 2006, San's reasonably priced menu and creative style keep the jeans-clad locals from the République and Marais coming back for seconds. Open Tuesday to Saturday 12:00 to 14:30 and 19:30 to 23:00.

Sardegna a Tavola

1 rue de Cotte
12th
Ⓜ Ledru-Rollin
Map p.411 D1 63

01 44 75 03 28 | sardegnaatavola@wanadoo.fr

Even the dreariest of Paris days melts away upon entering Antonio Simbula's authentic Sardinian home. Golden walls displaying traditional pottery, photos of wizened mountain shepherds and pepper and basil bunches inspire the sun-drenched spirit of the Mediterranean to come alive. Urbane Italian and French locals linger for hours around handmade wood tables, drinking vermentino from Riedel stemware and savouring every exploding flavour in the fresh cuisine made from seasonal ingredients sourced from the island. Sardegna a Tavola claims to be the world's only restaurant serving a ewe's milk pecorino made by a specialised, tiny mountain producer. The sublime ravioli stuffed with figs and melted pecorino is sweet yet earthy, while the butter-soft red tuna, customarily eaten at summer beach parties, is served on the crackery pani carasau shepherd bread. Reserve a couple of hours with friends or colleagues and let Antonio guide you on a relaxed lunch or dinner tour through the best of Sardinia. Open 12:00 to 14:30 and 19:30 to 23:00; closed all day Sunday and Monday lunchtime.

Japanese

Novotel Tour Eiffel
61 quai de Grenelle
15th
Ⓜ *Bir-Hakeim*
Map p.396 A4 64

Benkay

01 40 58 21 26 | *www.novotel.com*

Exhibiting a spectacular panorama of the Seine, Maison de la Radio and Paris' Statue of Liberty, this rooftop restaurant in the Novotel won't let you down. Many claim this upscale haven has the best authentic, gourmet Japanese cuisine in town, expertly prepared before your eyes. The kimono-sporting master chefs artfully create sushi as well as shabu shabu (hot pot) and teppanyaki on the tableside iron griddles. A favourite with top politicians and the press, this is a big-budget indulgence for a business lunch or romantic date. The airy, honey wood interiors take a back seat to the spectacular view and colourful plates graciously served by Benkay's welcoming team. Whether for the lunch *formule* or an a la carte dinner, reservations are required. Open every day lunch and dinner 12:00 to 22:00.

24 rue de la Tour
16th
Ⓜ *Passy*
Map p.396 A2 65

Comme des Poissons

01 45 20 70 37

The secret's out about this favourite sushi spot for Japanese expats. Native Parisian friends and work colleagues adore it too, packing into this tiny shoebox with minimal decor and service, to delight in just-off-the-hook fish. Master chef Kino San's slicing and dicing wizardry is a delight to watch from the counter as he prepares sashimi, maki and sushi with ocean delicacies like blue fin tuna, salmon, shrimp, octopus and smoked eel. Healthy accompaniments are on offer too, with miso soup and the cucumber salad with seaweed. Regulars often request a surprise meal from the chef as he never fails to create something delicious and unusual. Reservations are a must as die-hard sushi fans keep this reasonably priced destination full at lunch and dinner. Takeaway is available, and occasional cooking classes (in Japanese) are a fun draw too.

38 rue de Ranelagh
16th
Ⓜ *Rue de la Pompe*
Map p.395 F4 66

SushiShop

08 25 56 88 88 | *www.sushishop.fr*

SushiShop offers a handsome, modern setting with community tables to discover the traditional and inventive Japanese combinations. The mango tango rainbow roll has the fresh fruit mixed with shrimp and cucumbers; the nevada temaki is a nori cone overflowing with shrimp, avocado and mint and there's also a wide variety of fresh sushi and sashimi. Inexpensive mix-and-match lunch and dinner plates are filling and popular with professionals as SushiShop offers grab-n-go items as well as prepared-to-order handrolls, sushi and sashimi. With seven shops in metropolitan Paris and online ordering, free delivery is available throughout town.

Korean

138 rue de Vaugirard
15th
Ⓜ *Falguière*
Map p.407 F2 67

L'Arbre de Sel

01 47 83 29 52 | *www.arbredesel.com*

Lightly crispy seafood galettes, bibimbap with vibrant vegetables and exotic lotus flower roots, an invigorating homemade kimchi relish and an alcohol-free cinnamon and ginger *digestif* are just a few of the tasty and colourful delights to be discovered in this most welcoming Korean restaurant near Montparnasse. Using no MSG or chemical additives, the purity of the daily-sourced ingredients shines though in the healthy and authentic specialities. The fresh decor is enhanced by exhibits of local art, while the charming owners and well-priced, generous lunches and dinners keep the locals raving about this newcomer to the neighbourhood.

Latin American

Other options **Argentinean** p.312, **Mexican** p.330

13 rue Beautreillis
4th
Ⓜ *Bastille*
Map p.400 B4 **68**

Calle 24

01 42 72 38 34 | *mechy@voila.fr*

Hot Havana rhythms and ripe Caribbean cuisine add up to a spicy night in Paris. Just a couple of blocks from the Bastille area, the tiny Calle 24 offers an immersion into Cuban culture. Percussion-laden mambo and salsa beats put everyone in a mood for dancing, while the ceiling bears colourful posters and the rustic stone walls display rotating collections of Cuban artists. Chef Mechy brings the flavours of his Havana hometown to Parisians through tasty tapas, hot plates and desserts available individually or as a reasonably priced *formule*. Customer favourites are the cod fritters with sweet potatoes, spicy calamari, eggplant stuffed with manchego, and sautéed plantains. The strong mojito, caipirinha and Cuba libre cocktails go down easily during happy hour, and the rich coffee really merits a try. Whether for a fun date or with a group of amigos, at Calle 24 there is always a fiesta in the making.

9 rue Lacépède
5th
Ⓜ *Jussieu*
Map p.410 A2 **69**

El Picaflor

01 43 31 06 01 | *www.picaflor.fr*

Lourdes and Lalo Justo warmly invite you to their 'cuisine carnival', a celebration of the international influences that have shaped Peru's healthy gastronomy. Seafood, sweet potatoes, strawberries and quinoa are all commonly found in dishes from the Andes Mountains. During the week, fixed menus in all price ranges offer the chance to try specialities like a fish escalope with lime and onions, or a duck ceviche with coriander sauce. The Peruvian style lomo beef is also especially recommended, but be advised to consult the online menu to order certain favourites a day in advance for a minimum of four guests. With live music on the weekends, El Picaflor's cobbled archways, colourful textiles and snugly spaced tables all contribute to a jovial Latin welcome for a loyal community of international customers.

Mediterranean

Other options **Italian** p.326, **Spanish** p.332

27 rue du Roi de Sicile
4th
Ⓜ *Saint-Paul*
Map p.400 A3 **70**

L'Alivi

01 48 87 90 20 | *www.restaurant-alivi.com*

It's a different pace of life on the sunny Mediterranean isle of Corsica. Although there are influences from the Côte d'Azur and Tuscany, L'Alivi's cuisine is a uniquely Corsican style. The convivial restaurant's strong point is the a la carte menu displaying the island's wide range of culinary styles: wild boar stew, stuffed goat and rabbit with balsamic reduction, foie gras with figs and the crispy eggplant with broccoli are typical dishes that benefit from the island's temperate gardens. Seafood abounds, with the langoustine risotto especially noted. Walls of rough-hewn rocks, colourful vintage posters and a sunny, quiet terrace create a chilled-out atmosphere for friends or colleagues to gather over a glass of a spicy regional wine, enjoy the well-priced menu and drift off, just for a while, to dream of turquoise-blue waves and powder-soft sands. Open Monday to Friday 12:00 to 14:30 and 19:00 to 23:00; Saturday and Sunday 12:00 to 23:30.

5 rue Herold
1st
Ⓜ *Palais Royal*
Musée du Louvre
Map p.399 D1 **71**

Lémoni Café

01 45 08 49 84 | *www.lemonicafe.fr*

For health-conscious food-lovers who don't want to sacrifice flavour, Café Lémoni has delicious solutions. Made in the Crétois (from the island of Crete) Mediterranean cooking style, the predominantly vegetarian meals use fresh seasonal produce that is

329

dry-cooked without butter or cream to retain all of its vitamins. Inexpensive *formules*, sociable service at the counter and a crowded but cheerful atmosphere in crisp, clean citrus tones have led a fashion-conscious artsy crowd to adopt this lunch-only locale. Some of the nutrition-packed selections include a gratin of sweet potatoes and carrots, roasted salmon with vegetables, and tabouleh mildly spiced with curry. Lémoni has tasty guilt-free desserts as well, like the raspberry banana pannacotta with almond milk and the chocolate mousse made without butter. Whether for takeaway or dining-in, families and business friends pop in for light and tasty lunches throughout the week.

Mexican

30 rue des Bernardins
5th
Ⓜ **Maubert-Mutualité**
Map p.399 F4 **72**

Anahuacalli

01 43 26 10 20 | www.anahuacalli.com

This is the real deal. For 10 years Cristina Prum and her warm-hearted staff have been welcoming Latin American expats and Parisians into their sunny casa to experience authentic, moderately priced Mexican cuisine that is light years away from Tex-Mex fare. Natives swear that the nopalito (cactus) salad is as fresh as grandma's and the slow-simmered pork with a mellowed annatto sauce is not to be missed. For a real treat try the special dessert of flambéed bananas with a dulce de leche caramel glaze – the recipe is courtesy of the chef's aunt. The high-quality margaritas slide down easily, while the cosy golden glow accented by carved wooden sunflowers invites guests to linger and laugh with friends. Anahuacalli offers take-out too, but be sure to book a day ahead if you're planning to join Cristina's fiesta. Open every day 19:30 to 23:00 and Sundays for lunch.

Moroccan

Other options **Arabic/Lebanese** p.312

69 rue des Gravilliers
3rd
Ⓜ **Arts et Métiers**
Map p.400 A1 **73**

404

01 42 74 57 81

This magical and mysterious late-night rendezvous is a sensual feast, with dramatic lights and shadows scattered over the 16th century cobbled walls and snugly placed tabletops leading to a private, candlelit courtyard. Fragrant aromas waft from the open kitchen, whetting the appetite for the filling couscous and tagines with grilled meats and vegetables served in handmade pottery by gracious waiters. Saturdays and Sundays, the Berber Brunch features menus like the Oriental, with a spicy galette of eggs and potatoes, minted chèvre, oranges dusted with cinnamon and sweet mint tea. The Mazouz family, owners of neighbouring bar Andy Wahloo (p.344) plus Momo and Sketch in London, has hosted well-funded fashionistas and media crowds here for nearly 20 years. Reservations are essential – book the VIP 'loft' to take it all in. Open Monday to Sunday 12:30 to 15:30 and 20:30 to midnight.

9 rue Saint-Hilaire
5th
Ⓜ **Place Monge**
Map p.410 A2 **74**

La Mosquée

01 43 31 38 20 | www.la-mosquee.com

Vibrant mosaics and murals, gingerbread wood details and pointed arches provide eye candy everywhere you turn in this open, airy wonder. But that's what La Mosquée is about; delighting the senses of the international guests on the highest level. The tastebuds are tantalised by the well-priced restaurant's aromatic North African tagines as well as with the tea room's sweetly intense mint infusions, while the body is soothed by the hammam's gommage and massage treatments. There's even a souk to bring the pleasures of La Mosquée into your home. The *formule*-with-a-twist provides an opportunity to indulge in everything, although each can be experienced individually too. The restaurant's speciality is the Couscous Royal with lamb, chicken, kefta and merguez. Over 70 homemade honeyed pastries and apple-fragranced shisha pipes enjoyed on the sprawling patio create a very happy ending for your Arabian night.

36 rue Rodier
9th
Ⓜ **Saint-Georges**
Map p.389 E2 **75**

Wally Le Saharien
01 42 85 51 90

Venture into Monsieur Wally's friendly souk-like restaurant for an enchanted evening filled with culinary adventures and mystical ambience. Fragrant spices perfume the air as a rich mix of textiles, delicately carved chairs with intarsia patterns, and tribal artefacts provide the perfect setting to experience the signature 'dry' couscous with slow-cooked lamb and zesty merguez sausage. While lunch offers a la carte options, at dinner only the fixed tasting menu is available (€39) which features additional generously proportioned Berber specialities such as pastilla, a pastry filled with pigeon, vegetables and aromatic spices. For dessert, a jewel box of sweets handmade by the bakery next door is accompanied by flavourful mint tea. Word-of-mouth has made this a destination for food lovers worldwide so advance reservations or take-out are advised, particularly on Saturday evenings when the musical textures of the darbouka hand drums and naï flutes weave an air of mystery and romance.

Seafood

69 rue de Seine
6th
Ⓜ **Mabillon**
Map p.399 D3 **76**

Fish La Boissonerie
01 43 54 34 69

This former *poissonerie* (fish shop) has a new life serving, as you might guess, a wide range of fresh seafood. Colourful mosaic tiles and fun fish sculptures create a friendly, low-key vibe. With co-owners from New Zealand and the US, Fish has become a popular destination for English-speaking expats. As they also have a wine store a few doors down (La Dernière Goutte, 01 43 29 11 62), it's a guarantee that the restaurant's selections will be delicious enough to drink like a fish. Chef Matthew Ong has designed a mid-priced menu that combines the season's freshest seafood with healthy vegetables and spices. The saffron risotto with shrimp and mascarpone is dynamite, and when they're available the mussels are a treat. Meat eaters have not been ignored, with several options for them too. Family-friendly, and great for a relaxed group of friends, reservations are recommended as the limited tables fill-up fast.

3 rue de Montfaucon
6th
Ⓜ **Mabillon**
Map p.399 D4 **77**

Huîtrerie Régis
01 44 41 10 07

The twinkling-eyed Régis welcomes his guests as friends into this 14 seat cabana in St-Germain des Prés. The magical oysters are sourced from Marennes Oléron in partnership with culturist Claude Garnier, who owns restaurant Huîtrerie Garnier in the 16th (117 avenue Mozart, 01 40 50 17 27). Although available species vary by season, France's fastest oyster shucker in 2004 is a whiz with the assorted fines de claires, spéciales de claires, pousses en claires and belons. Plump and meaty with mineral and citric flavours, they are available by the dozen or in *formules* perfectly paired with the respected Daniel Crochet's flinty sancerre. Shrimp or a scallop terrine are on the menu for non-oyster addicts. Open non-stop with no reservations from noon to midnight, Tuesday to Sunday, they are worth the wait.

Le Congrès Auteuil

01 46 51 15 75 | www.rest-gj.com

With its intimate corners perfect for wheeling and dealing, this is a well-known hub for discreet meetings among business clients and politicians. The downstairs bar is a place to grab a drink on the way home, while the quiet, curved room upstairs offers picturesque views of the historic village of Auteuil. Just remodelled, touches of the chestnut Belle Époque decor and the sweeping staircase remain but with modernised updates. Le Congrès is especially reputed for mid-priced, fresh seafood, although other filling selections are available too. In their tennis-whites, BCBG (*Bon Chic Bon Genre*)

Hamaika

thoroughbreds from the neighbourhood often stop by after a match at the Rolland-Garros stadium. Reservations are recommended, particularly during the French Open.

Spanish

Other options **Mediterranean** p.329

Hamaika

01 40 28 91 15

Walking into Hamaika feels like entering a family's rustic cabin tucked away in the mountains; the cosy dining room is lined with wide planks of reclaimed wood displaying framed art, photos, books and knickknacks, while the Basque-style tapas menu is written on a blackboard spanning an entire wall. Well-portioned, mid-priced tasty titbits such as Serrano ham, fish soup, grilled prawns and crème catalane are enjoyed by the relaxed, lively crowd. Basque and Spanish music add to the energetic vibe, and the warm, sincere service has made Hamaika a favourite with friendly neighbourhood revolutionaries and regulars. Open Monday to Friday 12:00 to 14:30; Tuesday to Saturday 20:00 to 23:30.

La Pirada

01 47 00 73 61 | www.pirada.com

¡Es muy caliente en La Pirada! Not only are the tapas spicy and saucy but so is the lively crowd that dines in this cheerful, mosaic-tiled restaurant. Capturing the sociable spirit of the sun-drenched Iberian culture, the speciality at this late-night (05:00 on weekends) well-priced fiesta is the wide range of tapas. The Iberico ham, manchego cheese and grilled calamari are favourites, while the paella is often enjoyed with the juicy fresh sangria or a rich rioja wine. Partnered with El Bierzo Spanish grocer (01 43 20 41 52) and the candlelit Amira bar across the street, smiling patron Dominique Granger throws a vibrant party every night while guitarists serenade boisterous amigos. Sunday brunch buzzes too with locals and visitors sharing the breakfast-style tapas.

Steakhouses

Other options **Argentinean** p.312, **American** p.311

Le Relais de l'Entrecote

01 49 52 07 17 | www.relaisentrecote.fr

Steak frites is the only item on the menu at this mid-priced Paris institution, but with a dinner this divine you'd never want to order anything else. Just let your waitress know how you'd like your beef cooked – *saignant* (rare), *bleu* (nearly rare), *à point* (medium) or *bien cuit* (well done) and then get ready for a little bit if heaven. The melt-in-your-mouth steak is accompanied by a sublime savoury sauce, a secret family recipe that many have unsuccessfully tried to crack, and perfectly golden fries that are light and crunchy. Try the house red from the owner's vineyard in Tarn to round out a memorable meal. No reservations are accepted here, or at their second location in the 6th (01 45 49 16 00), so come early to avoid waiting. Open for dinner from 20:00.

122 ave de Villiers ◄
17th
Ⓜ *Pereire*
Map p.380 C4 82

Meating

01 43 80 10 10 | *www.restaurant-meating.com*

Paris' only New York style steakhouse specialises in serving the finest beef from the best regions in the world: black angus from America, hemford prime from Ireland and styles of chalosse, blonde d'Aquitaine, pyrenees and pauillac from France. The prime rib and NY strip are the house specialities, although seafood options like grilled red tuna or roasted scallops are available too. Caesar salad, oysters and of course cheesecake are other NY steakhouse traditions on the mid-priced menu, and the extensive wine list is perfectly matched for the cuisine. Honey-toned wood walls, large black-framed mirrors and spacious candlelit tables create a handsome, upscale atmosphere. Open for lunch and dinner, reservations are strongly advised.

8 rue des Plantes ◄
14th
Ⓜ *Mouton-Duvernet*
Map p.418 B1 83

Severo

01 45 40 40 91

For 20 years maestro William Bernet has been welcoming in-the-know carnivores who concur that Severo has the best steak in Paris. Bernet uses the expertise from his days as a butcher to personally select and age the tender, thick slabs of Limousin beef. In addition to succulent faux filet, bavette and entrecote cuts, other mid-priced offerings include a tartare, crunchy fries, and a tomato salad made from 10 varieties. The dark polished mahogany, white linens and balloon wine glasses lend a classical elegance while the wall-length blackboard listing 200 handpicked *varietals* underscores the integrity of the cuisine. Down the block, newcomer Bis de Severo features a Japanese chef adding ultra-fresh seafood to the generous menu. Both places are tiny, so reservations are imperative.

Thai

49 rue de Belleville ◄
19th
Ⓜ *Belleville*
Map p.391 E3 84

Lao Siam

01 40 40 09 68

Those in the know make the trek out to Paris' second Chinatown at Belleville for low-priced but high quality authentic Thai and Laotian specialities. It's definitely about the food, as the no-frills ambience and service belies the treasure to be discovered on the menu. Favourites include the salad douce made from shrimp, banana flowers and shredded coconut and the fish with coconut milk. The torteau à la diable, soup with a whole crab, is for the truly adventurous. And, of course, nothing goes better with spicy Thai than a Singha beer. Lao Siam is pretty well-known for a secret spot so expect to wait for a table. Open every day 12:00 to 15:00 and 19:00 to 23:30.

35 rue du Banquier ◄
13th
Ⓜ *Gobelins*
Map p.410 A4 85

T'chok Dy

01 43 36 01 83

This is a true gem serving inexpensive and traditionally prepared Siamese specialities. Popular with professionals at lunch and local residents at night, the cheerful Thai family who run this restaurant makes sure their guests are comfortable. A modern decor with rich walnut tones and soothing fountains creates a stress-free ambience, and the deliciously spiced dishes are served family-style so that everyone can share. House favourites include the juicy green papaya salad, shrimp pad thai, lemongrass and coconut chicken soup and the delicate daurade fish with spicy-sweet chu-chi curry. You'll be hooked no matter what you try.

Vegetarian

41 rue des
Bourdonnais
1st
Ⓜ *Châtelet*
Map p.399 E2 86

La Victoire Suprême du Coeur

01 40 41 93 95 | www.vscoeur.com

Traditionally Paris' fine cuisine has not offered many options for non-meat eaters, so vegetarian and vegan diners – and their carnivorous friends – will be overjoyed to discover the inspired, healthy menu at La Victoire Suprême du Coeur. Savour the roasted mushrooms with blackberries, handmade pasta or green tea icecream with hazelnut cream, all created with fresh, non GM ingredients. Although no alcohol is served, there is a large drink selection including fruit lassis and carrot-ginger juice. Featuring the artwork of spiritual teacher Sri Chinmoy, the sunny decor and attentive service contributes to a vibrant, friendly atmosphere that nourishes your body and soul.

4 rue Lacépède
5th
Ⓜ *Jussieu*
Map p.410 A2 87

Le Jardin des Pâtes

01 43 31 50 71

Since 1984 these affable gardeners have been 'growing' the freshest and most interesting pasta in town; all of the grains used in the homemade pasta are organic, grown without chemical weedkillers or pesticides. Wheat, rice, barley, rye, buckwheat and chestnut pastas are made fresh onsite and used in creative pasta dishes. A favourite from the inexpensive menu is the rice pasta with sautéed vegetables, ginger and tofu; the wheat pasta with mozzarella, tomatoes, eggplant and peppers is popular too. Meat options are also available, as well as organic beers and juices. A bright, airy ray of sunshine seems to fill this cosy restaurant as the white tumbled stone walls, abundant greenery and slatted garden-style furniture create a tranquil atmosphere for chatting with friends and family over a leisurely meal. A second location in the 13th is at 33 boulevard Arago (01 45 35 93 67).

Vietnamese

80 rue Monge
5th
Ⓜ *Place Monge*
Map p.409 F2 89

Foyer du Vietnam

01 45 35 32 54

This tiny, low-key joint packs a powerful, peppery punch. Several styles of savoury phos, bô-kho, and bô-bun with nems are just the beginning of the authentic cuisine served in this very welcoming hangout for Vietnamese patrons and students. The crab sautéed to order and mushrooms stuffed with shrimp are also highly popular but be sure to try the artisanal Vietnamese icecream quê huong in cinnamon, fig, coconut and ginger flavours for dessert. The Foyer du Vietnam stays busy all the time with the extra friendly service and extremely reasonable prices. Lunch and dinner *formules* average around €10, with an additional discount for students. Know though, that this is no student cafeteria fodder, but the real deal served with traditional Vietnamese warmth. Open every day (except Sunday) 12:00 to 14:00 and 19:00 to 22:00.

15 rue de Bassano
16th
Ⓜ *Iéna*
Map p.386 C4 90

Kambodgia

01 47 23 31 80 | www.kambodgia.com

The dramatic decor of this south-east Asian gem is a cross between an intimate tea house and an opulent opium den. The latticed mahogany walls are lined with hundreds of tiny drawers for medicinal herbs and spices, while ornate statues and candlelit tabletops cast an air of mystery. Whether on a date or with friends, you're sure to savour the mainly Vietnamese and Cambodian fare like ginger fish wrapped in banana leaves, caramelised pork with coconut sauce or the many styles of dim sum and barbecue. Madame You Sin's desserts of green tea macarons or ginger pear crisp are also recommended. With a reasonably priced lunch *formule* and mid-range a la carte dinner menu, Kambodgia is a sure-fire escape to a realm of earthy delights.

Cafes & Coffee Shops

Cafes can be a leisurely gathering place for friends, a corner to read a good book or an office for meetings. Hours are generally from 08:00 to midnight non-stop so customers linger for hours over one drink, and remember that standing at the counter is cheaper than sitting at a table. From bohemian styles like Le Loir dans la Théière (p.339) to upscale spots like Angelina (below), families can also enjoy sandwiches and salads at cafes across the city. Forget your standard American-style ordering; in Paris un café or un express is a short espresso, une noisette has a splash of milk, and un grand café or un grand crème means a larger cup. In the evenings, cafes turn into hangouts where friends rendezvous for a wine or beer. With 30 locations in the city, Starbucks (www.starbucks.fr) has invaded Paris, but French-owned Columbus Café (p.338) got a head start.

226 rue de Rivoli
1st
Ⓜ **Concorde**
Map p.398 B1 **91**

Angelina
01 42 60 82 00 | *www.groupe-bertrand.com*
Just across from the Jardin des Tuileries (p.184), this is a real slice of Parisian luxury. Home to what many claim to be the best hot chocolate in Paris, it serves steaming pitchers of melted African dark chocolate served alongside a silver bowl brimming with frothy, unsweetened Chantilly cream. The polished marble and sparkling mirrors create an elegant ambience in this 1903 landmark, which was once favoured by Coco Chanel and Marcel Proust. Today it's filled with tourists as well as smartly-dressed locals who come for the famous Chocolat Africain and splendid pastries like the Mont Blanc, a meringue filled with chestnut crème and Chantilly. Open daily non-stop, Angelina is known for the somewhat pricey, yet copious, servings and it also offers an assortment of breakfast and lunch choices.

**29-31 rue Saint
Louis en l'Île**
4th
Ⓜ **Pont Marie**
Map p.400 A4 **92**

Berthillon
01 43 54 31 61 | *www.berthillon.fr*
While in theory you could visit this casual salon de thé for a spot of Earl Grey, in reality that is never the reason Parisians flock to this legendary purveyor of dreamy delights. Since 1954, three generations of the Berthillon family have created all-natural icecreams and sorbets without preservatives or artificial flavours. Exotic mouthwatering choices like cinnamon, gingerbread, pear-and-caramel, liquorice, mango, tiramisu and chocolate-mandarin are just the beginning of the ever-changing flavours available in tiny scoops or larger tubs. Families and friends can enjoy the outside tables on tiny Île Saint Louis and watch lines of excited customers debate what are the best selections to try. Many Parisian restaurants and cafes also serve this decadent dessert, which is particularly welcome when the shop shuts down for the month of August. Open Wednesday to Sunday 10:00 to 20:00.

52 rue Fabert
7th
Ⓜ **La Tour Maubourg**
Map p.397 E2 **93**

Café d'Esplanade
01 47 05 38 80
Situated directly across from Les Invalides (p.166), Café d'Esplanade is another striking alliance of the Costes brothers' backing and Jacques Garcia's design flair. The influence of its historical neighbour can be seen in the cannonball-and-chainlink chandeliers as well as the revisited classical colonnades flanked by 'columns' of upright cannons. Favoured by the area's politicians, government officials and journalists, this swanky, late-night bistrot also offers an airy terrace during the warmer months. The signature dish is the club sandwich with bacon or smoked salmon, though the chicken nems with Thai basil and the tender Château Béarnaise steak are permanent favourites on the seasonal, upwardly-priced menu. Suits and ties abound Mondays to Fridays, but the weekends bring a relaxed, slower-paced crowd. Open every day of the year 08:00 to 01:30.

172 blvd St-Germain
6th
**Ⓜ St-Germain
des Prés**
Map p.398 C4 94

Café de Flore

01 45 48 55 26 | *www.cafe-de-flore.com/indexa.htm*

This is the famous rival of Les Deux Magots (p.339) and these cafes have grown up side-by-side throughout the many famous artistic, political and philosophical periods that have shaped Parisian culture. Café de Flore has hosted many greats; Trotsky, Sartre, Signoret, Hemingway, Capote, Bardot, Dali, Bacall, De Niro… and the list of stars and French intellectuals who call this home continues to grow today. Of course there's also a large group of tourists who stop by, but an afternoon of watching the world go by over *un café* or pastis does make for an interesting spectator sport. A light menu of omelettes, salads and club sandwiches is served, and theme nights with theatrical readings and philosophy debates keep the creative spirit alive. Open daily 07:30 to 01:30.

15 rue Lepic
18th
Ⓜ Blanche
Map p.382 C4 95

Café des Deux Moulins

01 42 54 90 50

This now famous cafe in Montmartre was used as the film set where Audrey Tatou portrayed the good-hearted waitress Amélie Poulain, and has since become a must-do for nostalgic fans. There's still some locals with a newspaper at the copper-topped bar, and the movie-themed touches don't overwhelm the authentic 1950s design. The menu has a couple of *Amélie* items like the crème brûlée d'Amélie Poulain and the light breakfast gouter d'Amélie, but luckily fame hasn't gone to their heads with reasonable prices and friendly service. The cafe is open 07:00 to 02:00 every day with brunch always available.

**156 rue du
Faubourg Saint-
Martin**
10th
**Ⓜ Gare de l'Est
(Verdun)**
Map p.390 B2 96

Café K

01 46 07 15 15

This relaxed spot is a favourite with in-the-know jazz lovers. Every night brings some of Paris' best musicians, with piano, guitar, bass and vocals to entertain locals of all ages. Varying musical styles, such as acoustic *manouche* (gypsy jazz), draw crowds of liberal, artistic regulars who appreciate the high-quality vibes and the low-cost menu. Just east of Gare de l'Est, it's definitely off the beaten path but still quite convenient. During warmer days and late nights, the large patio is filled non-stop with animated Gauloise-smoking Parisians, while the friendly and unpretentious staff welcome everyone into the simple but spacious interior. A great wine selection and strong cocktails loosen everyone up for a mellow good time.

Café d'Esplanade

Café de Flore

Café Marly

93 rue de Rivoli
Cour Napoléon
1st
Ⓜ *Palais Royal*
Musée du Louvre
Map p.399 D2 97

01 49 26 06 60

In the Richelieu wing of the Louvre (p.174), this Costes brothers' enterprise continues to be a see-and-be-seen spot in the Parisian cafe world. With a terrace looking out onto the IM Pei-designed Pyramid and the antiquities of the Louvre within sight, it is a setting that truly immerses you in the essence of French history and beauty. Fashionistas like Karl Lagerfeld and members of the press check each other out over a coffee and upper-end *bistrot* fare in the stately crimson and gold decor. Remember high style and dress are de rigueur, so plan ahead if you'll be touring the museum at the same time. Dining reservations are recommended, but stop by for an elegant coffee or aperitif and a taste of French sophistication.

Café Very

Jardin des Tuileries
1st
Ⓜ *Tuileries*
Map p.398 B1 59

01 47 03 94 84

Nestled inside the Jardin des Tuileries, Café Very provides a romantic setting to savour a coffee or light tartine during a stroll through the park. Comfortable and jeans-friendly, pleasant servers welcome lovebirds and families for a leisurely afternoon of relaxation. The mid-range menu (including special prices for children) offers fresh salads and exquisite desserts, all served in idyllic surroundings. Hours vary by season; it is open late in the summer but during the winter closes in the early evening. There is a second location under the name Dame Tartine in the 4th (2 rue Brisemiche, 01 42 77 32 22).

Columbus Café

25 rue
Vieille du Temple
4th
Ⓜ *Hôtel de Ville*
Map p.400 A3 99

01 42 72 20 11 | *www.columbuscafe.com*

France's answer to Starbucks, Columbus Café baristas whip up a variety of flavours and sizes of coffees, teas, chocolate and fruit drinks, as well as offering pastries and inexpensive cold sandwiches. Especially popular are the muffins, with a new flavour introduced every month. Open non-stop morning to night, they serve take-out coffees which are a relatively new concept in France, but the family-friendly, casual setting also has tables and terraces for a quick bite and free Wi-Fi. The government permitted Columbus to expand throughout France before allowing competitor Starbucks to open its doors, so independent locations as well as outlets in FNAC shops are scattered around the city. Now it's just a matter of translating, 'double half-soy non-fat decaf frappuccino with foam' into French.

La Galerie des Gobelins

25 ave Montaigne
8th
Ⓜ *Alma – Marceau*
Map p.397 E1 28

01 53 67 66 00 | *www.plaza-athenee-paris.com*

Leagues ahead of your everyday cafe, this is undeniably Paris' most plush and memorable spot for afternoon tea. Oui, you go there for the fragrant house blend served in a sterling silver teapot, the dainty petits fours and the twinkling harp music, but really it's about soaking up the old-fashioned glamour of the Plaza Athénée and watching the couture-clad beauties sashay around the Louis XVI fauteuils. You can't help but feel pampered and oh-so-chic after an afternoon of star gazing. Open daily 08:00 to 01:00.

Le Café Corrazza 1787

12bis rue de
Montpensier, 11-12
Galerie Montpensier
1st
Ⓜ *Palais Royal*
Musée du Louvre
Map p.399 D1 101

01 42 60 13 52

Named after its 1787 founder, Signor Corrazza, this location has hosted upscale guests within the park-like courtyard of the Palais Royal for over 200 years. This was a key gathering spot for the extreme-left philosophical and political intellectuals who stirred up the French Revolution, such as Michelet and the Goncourt brothers while General Napoléon Bonaparte was reputed to be an icecream aficionado who frequented for the famous maraschino cherry variety. Today they serve not only mid-priced Italian fare like antipasti and bruschetta, but also recommend a range of couscous dishes. On warmer days, fashionable Parisians stop by after popping in to Marc Jacobs to linger over a drink or meal and soak up tranquil views at tables dotting the perimeter of the gardens. During the winter, the amber coloured lights and brick walls offers a warm refuge for busy shoppers.

Le Loir dans la Théière

3 rue des Rosiers
4th
Ⓜ *Saint-Paul*
Map p.400 B3 **102**

01 42 72 90 61

Curl up in one of the many mismatched chairs to sip a steaming mug of jasmine tea and discuss life with the artistic folk who have made this inexpensive, cosy joint an institution in the Marais. 'The Dormouse in the Teapot' is a reference to Alice in Wonderland, and the array of concert flyers, wall murals and antique toys mixed in with the relaxed service certainly does create an ethereal, dream-like atmosphere. An old-fashioned sideboard displays the homemade strawberry tarts and apple crumbles baked fresh that morning, with a small menu offering light salad and omelette lunch options. No laptops are allowed in this anti-establishment hideaway, so settle-in for some carefree conversation and liberally portioned brunch on Saturdays and Sundays.

Les Deux Magots

6 place St-
Germain des Prés
6th
Ⓜ *St-Germain*
des Prés
Map p.398 C3 **103**

01 45 48 55 25 | *www.lesdeuxmagots.fr*

Intellectuals of the Left Bank have debated politics, philosophy and literary merit for around 100 years at this legendary institution. Gide, Malraux and Hemingway have all been regulars, while Jean Paul Sartre with Simone de Beauvoir would write for hours inside this competitor of Café de Flore (p.337). The literary award 'Le Prix des Deux Magots' originated out of this original culture of scholarly curiosity. Today it still attracts elements of this local crowd, albeit closely mixed-in with a good deal of casually-dressed tourists. Traditional *bistrot* fare of tartines, mixed salads and croque monsieurs are available as well as a monthly-changing menu of warm cuisine. In truth though, the true beauty of this scandalously priced cafe lies in soaking up the history and indulging in some intriguing people-watching over *un café* or glass of wine. Open every day 07:30 to 01:00.

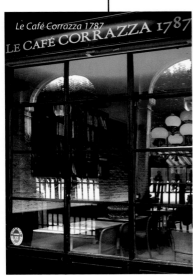

Le Café Corrazza 1787

Les Deux Magots

339

30 rue du
Bourg-Tibourg
4th
Ⓜ Hôtel de Ville
Map p.400 A3 104

Mariages Frères

01 42 72 28 11 | www.mariagefreres.com

Henri Mariage said 'the fragrance of adventure and poetry endlessly pervades each cup of tea' and since the 18th century the Mariage family has imported spices and tea, serving royalty and the well-to-do families of France. Today, the ceremonial art of the afternoon tea can be appreciated by all at the *salons de thé* in Paris offering hundreds of exotic *mélanges* from all over the world. Shelves lined with countless tins of fragrant tea blends adds to the nostalgic setting where Parisian friends and visitors gather for a mid-priced lunch of salads, tiny sandwiches and luscious desserts. Each location also has a museum of the history of tea as well items for takeaway. Weekend brunch brings in the family crowd and girlfriends on a shopping break. Other addresses: 13 rue des Grands-Augustins in the 6th (01 40 51 82 50) and 260 Faubourg St-Honoré in the 8th (01 46 22 18 54).

2 place Gustave
Toudouze
9th
Ⓜ Saint-Georges
Map p.389 D2 105

No Stress Café

01 48 78 00 27

Good vibes are what it's all about. Chill out and soak up the positive energy – and satisfying food – at this perennial hang-out of the neighbourhood theatre and artist crowds. Before a show, enjoy a reasonably priced calamari and prawn stir-fry or indulge in an ever-popular cheeseburger; afterwards pop over for *un verre* of wine or a cocktail. The brightly coloured wall murals, mismatched cushions and crystals in the chandeliers all set the tone for the Thursday to Saturday evening 'appetisers' of tarot card readings and massage therapy. A mellow Sunday brunch on the sunny, spacious terrace located right on St-Georges plaza is the perfect way to spend a leisurely afternoon catching up with good friends.

1 rue des Fossés
Saint-Bernard
5th
Ⓜ Jussieu
Map p.410 A1 106

Ziryab

01 53 10 10 16 | www.imarabe.org

For a breathtaking view of Notre Dame and the Right Bank along the Seine, the relatively quiet rooftop terrace above the Institut du Monde Arabe offers several tables with umbrellas to enjoy an afternoon tea. Aromatic mint leaves swirled in delicately painted glasses or a sparkling kir royal accompanied by an assortment of dainty, honeyed pastries make for a lovely break in the day. The building's intricately patterned and light-reactive steel shutters designed by architect Jean Nouvel, as well as the cultural exhibits, are worth seeing in their own right. Check out the viewing room adjacent to the terrace for a panorama that stretches beyond the Eiffel Tower.

Internet Cafes

Hundreds of cafes, pubs and restaurants offering free Wi-Fi are listed on www.wi-fihotspotlist.com and www.journaldunet.com. Anglophone places include Breakfast in America (p.311) and Frog and Princess (p.354) as well as most McDonald's, Starbucks and Columbus Cafés (p.338). Some hi-tech old-fashioned cafes are Café Marguerite in the 4th (1 place de l'Hôtel de Ville, 01 42 72 00 04), Le Buci in the 6th (52 rue Dauphine, 01 43 26 67 52) and Café Madeleine in the 8th (1 rue Tronchet, 01 42 65 21 91). Milk Internet Hall has six locations open all hours with swarms of internet and gaming computers priced according to the time of day and duration (on average €3 per hour). Visit www.milklub.com for details of locations.

Bakeries

The French truly have perfected the art of breads and sweet pastries. Traditionally a *boulangerie* sells only bread items and a *pâtisserie* sells only sweet treats. Today the majority of bakeries are a combination of the two. The iconic baguette has many sizes; from thinnest to thickest they are the ficelle, baguette, flûte, pain, and pain poilâne (the thick-crusted round loaf). *Croissants aux beurres* are made with 100% butter, while *croissants ordinaires*, made with margarine, are lighter and flakier in texture. The holidays bring specialised bakery traditions. At Christmas the *bûche de noël* is a rolled cake filled with cream and decorated to look like a log chopped for the holiday fire. During Epiphany season from 6 January until Mardi Gras, bakeries display *galettes des rois*, or a 'king's cake' with a *fève* hidden inside; traditionally a bean, today it is a plastic baby or tiny toy, and whoever finds it in their cake wears the crown of the king. Bakeries have long queues during the lunch hour as they are a popular, inexpensive way to take-out a quick lunch of a *croque monsieur* (ham and cheese) sandwich, charcuterie-stuffed baguette or large salad. Parisians disagree over which bakeries are the very best, but favourites include Le Pain Quotidien in the 1st (18 pl Marché St Honoré, 01 42 96 31 70, and several other locations in Paris); Paul (various locations; www.paul.fr); Maison Kayser in the 5th (14 rue Monge, 01 44 07 17 81); Bread & Roses in the 6th (7 rue de Fleurus, 01 42 22 06 06); Pain d'Epis in the 7th (63 ave Bosquet, 01 45 51 75 01); Le Nôtre in the 16th (44 rue d'Auteuil, 01 45 24 52 52, see www.lenotre.fr for other locations) and Grillon d'Auteuil, also in the 16th (56 rue d'Auteuil, 01 42 88 05 79). For famed macaroons to write home about head to Ladurée in the 8th (16 rue Royale, 01 42 60 21 79) or Pierre Hermé in the 6th (72 rue Bonaparte, 01 43 54 47 77).

Brunch		
404	3rd	01 42 74 57 81
Angelina	1st	01 42 60 82 00
Baxo	10th	01 42 02 99 71
Breakfast in America	5th	01 43 54 50 28
Café des Deux Moulins	18th	01 42 54 90 50
Cuisine & Confidences	1st	01 42 96 31 34
Hôtel Amour	9th	01 48 78 31 80
Impala Lounge	8th	01 43 59 12 66
L'Inédit Café	12th	01 43 43 21 80
La Pirada	11th	01 47 00 73 61
Le Loir dans la Théière	4th	01 42 72 90 61
Living B'Art	18th	01 42 52 85 34
Mariages Frères	4th	01 42 72 28 11
Mood	8th	01 42 89 98 89
No Stress Café	9th	01 48 78 00 27
Ozo Restaurant	4th	01 42 77 10 03
PDG	8th	01 42 56 19 10
Rose Bakery	9th	01 42 82 12 80
Toi	8th	01 42 56 56 58

Brunch

Over the past few years the concept of brunch has become *très branché* (fashionable) as Parisians have fallen in love with rolling out of bed into a laid-back afternoon detoxing and dining with family and friends. Usually the brunch menu is only available on Sundays, but a handful serve it on Saturdays too. Restaurants expand their menus beyond the traditional croissants and baguettes, with some advertising fixed-price American style brunch with ham and cheese omelettes, fluffy scrambled eggs, thick bacon, freshly squeezed juice, and – a rarity in Paris – bagels. Brunch is not cheap and usually costs €20 to €25 per person, but some places such as Cuisine et Confidences (p.315) offer lower-priced children's plates as well tiny tables and chairs.

Fruit Juices

Other options Cafes & Coffee Shops p.336

It seems juice bars are popping-up all the time as the concept grows in popularity with healthy minded Parisians. Some spots are designed for lunch-on-the-go while others offer seating at a bar or table. Guests at Bob's Juice Bar (15 rue Lucien Sampaix, 06 82 63 72 74) near Canal St Martin share a community table to enjoy soups, salads, juices and smoothies with the option of spirulina or guarana supplements. With locations at Odéon, Bastille and Montorgueil, Wanna Juice (www.wannajuice.com) uses no added sugars and only fresh fruit to make 'remedies' such as the Jetlag Joker and extracted juices like the Sunny Ginjaninja with apples, carrots, oranges and ginger. They also serve an inexpensive *formule* including a smoothie and a soup, salad or sandwich. Paradis du Fruit (www.leparadisdufruit.fr, 08 26 10 04 08) has nearly 20 addresses serving hot meals as well as juicy concoctions.

341

On the Town

Wine at lunch, an apero, more wine at dinner, digestif, cocktails – despite their mantra that moderation is key, the French unapologetically revolve their days around drinking. Hedonistic tendencies run high in a city where you can find your drink of choice at any hour, in the streets or tucked away in a dark bar, without any judgment being passed. A forever decorous culture, most French avoid total inebriation, which in turn improves their staying power and often keeps the night going well into the next morning. Change is not easily accepted by the French, and the nightlife scene is just another aspect where this is apparent, although the last decade has seen a minor shift. The proliferation of bars and clubs throughout the city allows you to discover whatever best fits your mood and lifestyle. Oberkampf and Ménilmontant dominate the edgy, alternative bars and clubs, taking over the formerly trendy Bastille area while the Latin Quarter is primarily student bars and expat pubs, with a mix of travellers, international students, and French people hoping to improve their English. St-Germain has maintained a few upscale establishments to draw the fashion crowd to the Left Bank. Paris has finally brought some life to its greatest asset; the waterways. The Seine, formerly utilised for sleepy boat tours, is now lined with *péniches* full of trendy young Parisians sipping cocktails and enjoying the lazy days of summer, and the bobo (bohemian bourgeois) chic dominate the bars along the tree-lined Canal St Martin. The Marais is forever gay (but always welcoming of others) and the Champs-Élysées has the market on über-glam, Asian theme, bordello style and super select clubs where the beautiful people play. No matter what your party predilection, Paris has something to meet your needs.

Theme Nights

The French adore a festive soirée and any excuse to reduce the price of drinks, with ladies' nights, 80s nights, discos, blondes, brunettes and quiz night just to name a few. Most of the bars and pubs with regular theme nights advertise them inside, and you can keep up to date by visiting their own websites, or www.soiree-paris.com and www.2night.fr. The Irish, English, Australian, and American bars are where you are most likely to find the quiz nights, typically on Sundays. Student night is one theme quick to catch on regardless of the bar's origin and, similarly, many bars are not averse to celebrating the fairer sex by offering cheaper drinks on ladies' nights. Females looking for exquisite royal treatment shouldn't miss the all-inclusive and deliciously scandalous ladies' nights hosted by Regine's (p.362), Queen (p.358) and Pink (p.361).

Door Policy

From effortless to arduous, Paris nightlife poses varying levels of challenges. While you can easily glide into a bar or pub without missing a beat, some lounges maintain their elitist privilege to pick and choose their clientele from behind red ropes. Some establishments depend on guestlists, while others rely on the trained eye of their doormen to permit entrance to their regulars and other worthy partygoers. The smaller the group the better, and guys are more desirable when coupled with a lady. Some bars close at 02:00, but since many stay open until 04:00 or 05:00, prime arrival time is between midnight and 01:00. You can improve your chances of getting in and avoiding queues by arriving early.

Dress Code

In one of the leading fashion capitals of the world, there is an unspoken rule that appearance and respect go hand in hand. The French revere self presentation above most other things, so to avoid sticking out as a tourist, a safe bet would be to dress up rather than down. Bars and pubs tend to be more casual, whereas lounges and clubs are a veritable fashion show of each season's hottest trends. Gentlemen, nice shoes are a must; sneakers and sandals are grounds for instant rejection at the door. In the winter feel free to wear your best coat to a club, where you can check it for a small fee, but be cautious in a bar where 'coat check' is a pile on a chair – you might not see yours again.

Not big, but very clever…

Perfectly proportioned to fit in your pocket, this marvellous mini guidebook makes sure you don't just get the holiday you paid for but rather the one that you dreamed of.

New York Mini Visitors' Guide
Maximising your holiday, minimising your hand luggage

Bars

Other options **Nightclubs** p.360, **Pubs** p.353

62 rue Mazarine
6th
Ⓜ **Odéon**
Map p.399 D3 107

Alcazar Mezzanine Bar

01 53 10 19 99 | www.alcazar.fr

With a modern, minimalist feel, this DJ bar upstairs from Terrence Conran's Alcazar restaurant is the epitome of a chic Parisian lounge. Despite its somewhat small size, the light open spaces and balcony looking down on the diners below gives the impression of being bigger than it is. The crowd tends to be a late 20s to 30s contingent of well-dressed professionals and pretty little things, and is one of the favourites amongst the international crowd. The stylish decor combined with the laid-back atmosphere and snacks available upstairs make it the ideal cocktail venue.

69 rue Gravilliers
3rd
Ⓜ **Arts et Métiers**
Map p.400 A1 108

Andy Wahloo

01 42 71 20 38 | www.myspace.com/andywahloo

Overturned paint can seats, mismatched tables, ornate chandeliers, lanterns, bottles and tins adorn the walls of this creatively kitsch bar. Small with limited seating, the place can get quite full with the mixed crowd of fashionable loungers that filter in for the cocktails and to chill out to ambient Arabic Rai music. When warm weather hits, everyone fights for space out in the back terrace for an almost authentic summer escape. Taking you on a Moroccan pop art journey, this is the perfect place to start the night before heading out to the next venue.

38 rue Monsieur
Le Prince
6th
Ⓜ **Odéon**
Map p.409 D1 109

Au Père Louis

01 43 26 54 14

A truly authentic Left Bank experience, Au Père Louis offers a traditional Toulousain restaurant next door to its immensely popular wine bar. There is never a dull moment at the wine bar, and by the end of the week it is fully packed with the crowd celebrating the arrival of the weekend. Predominantly frequented by locals, you feel the authentic French flair through the clientele and the decor, with exposed stone walls and original beams. Large old wine barrels serve as tables to perch your wine upon, and if space permits you can sit around them on tall wooden stools.

3 rue Tournelles
4th
Ⓜ **Bastille**
Map p.400 C3 110

Bar Fleur's

01 42 71 04 51 | http://fleuretvodka.free.fr

Day or night you can satisfy all of your floral needs at this shop, but let the scent of the flowers draw you into the store and pause for a moment to enjoy its dual appeal – the bar. Luscious champagne and vodka cocktails, traditional or infused with flower essences are the perfect complement to the bright and beautiful shop, complete with monthly art exhibitions by local artists. This original concept is something truly unique, offering a tranquil environment to relax and enjoy some of the most fragrant cocktails to ever touch your lips.

35 place du Marché
St Honoré
1st
Ⓜ **Pyramides**
Map p.388 B4 111

Barlotti Lounge

01 44 86 97 97 | barlotti@buddhabar.com

Upstairs from a stylish Italian restaurant, this fabulous little cocktail bar boasts the best bellinis in Paris, with an exotic variety to choose from that goes beyond your traditional recipe. The cosy and intimate decor, with dark wood panelling, big couches and candles on every table, plus low-key music and impeccable service make this the location for a date or a relaxing drink with friends. Right in the heart of the city and open every night of the week until 02:00, it's the perfect place to have an amazing cocktail by itself, before or after dinner, or as a prelude to a night on the town.

Concorde Atlantique

Porte de Solférino
opp 8 quai Anatole
France
7th
Ⓜ *Assemblée*
Nationale
Map p.398 A2 **112**

01 47 05 71 03 | *www.concorde-atlantique.com*
The wonders of the Seine have finally been capitalised upon, and the champagne swilling youth can put their sea legs to the test without feeling like they are trapped on a clichéd cruise. Docked just off the place de la Concorde, this rocking little terrace is the summer's answer to a Riviera escape for those willing to choose murky green over crystal azure. But what could be better than being packed on a funky boat deck with a smattering of the hippest Parisians while drinking and listening to music as the sun sets?

De La Ville Café

34 blvd Bonne
Nouvelle
10th
Ⓜ *Bonne Nouvelle*
Map p.389 F4 **113**

01 48 24 48 09
This is another shining example of Paris' debauched past resurfacing in the form of an ancient bordello turned modern-day hotspot. The distressed walls and grand staircase, which separate it into three levels, give an eclectic industrial chic vibe, and as the night draws in, trendy crowds arrive to enjoy the famous minty mojitos before heading to the nearby clubs. The bar also boast a large outdoor terrace, ideal in warm weather, but also heated in the winter to allow the brave some fresh air. Prices are below your trendy nightlife average, and you can get a wide range of food.

Harry's

5 rue Daunou
2nd
Ⓜ *Opéra*
Map p.388 C4 **114**

01 42 61 71 14 | *www.harrysbar.fr*
Hardly a new discovery, Harry's New York bar has a reputation that precedes itself and it has come to enjoy its local and tourist appeal. Birthplace of the bloody mary, many dedicated drinkers believe a trip to Paris is not complete without a visit to Harry's to pay homage at this temple of inebriant ingenuity. Dark wood panelling and memorabilia tracing back to its opening in 1911 makes it a cosy den resembling a collegiate club more than a classy lounge, offering a laid back environment for those seeking a drink and the famous hot dogs. The downstairs piano bar has seen its own fair share of history in the making, and continues to offer live music Tuesdays to Saturdays from 22:00.

Hemingway Bar Hôtel Ritz

15 place Vendôme
1st
Ⓜ *Tuileries*
Map p.398 B1 **115**

01 43 16 30 31 | *www.ritzparis.com*
One of the world's best bars with one of the world's best bartenders, this is an essential stop in your tour of literary and luxurious Paris. The undeniably chic Ritz is the ideal locale for a homey cocktail haven; large stuffed chairs, the old-fashioned bar and library panelled walls create a warm setting for the fancy patrons to mix, mingle, and imbibe. Though a bit pricey, you get your money's worth with impeccable service and some of the best drinks in the city. Largely an Anglo meeting spot for an evening cocktail, the Hemingway also hosts a fine contingent of single women out to treat themselves and perhaps hoping to find a little bit of that alleged Parisian romance.

Hôtel Costes

239 rue St Honoré
1st
Ⓜ *Tuileries*
Map p.398 B1 **116**

08 26 10 12 86 | *www.hotelcostes.com*
The Costes is the unequalled Parisian haunt for the trendy lounge lizards and jet-set. A glance around the room will confirm time has not diminished its panache, and you can still find a room full of models and supremely chic fashion types. The luxury and grandeur of the interior with the rich velvets, reds, wood and seductive lighting are quintessential Paris, and the DJ achieves ambient perfection with his mixes to get everyone in the mood. Come early and indulge in an exquisite meal in the lobby restaurant or in the atrium, which has started a revolution as the Costes brothers take over the city with their venues. On warm nights take advantage of the lovely terrace cafe.

1-5 psg Ruelle
18th
Ⓜ **La Chapelle**
Map p.384 A4 117

The Ice Kube
01 42 05 20 00 | www.kubehotel.com

Cover up and chill out, this new concept bar is not for feeble bodied boozers. Half an hour is all you are allowed in this glacial bar tucked away in the retro pop Kube Hotel, so racing against the clock is the name of the game as you are forced to warm yourself from the inside to battle the -5°C temperature. Despite the giant parkas, mittens, and optional boots which are provided, the game is decidedly easier when the attentive bartender keeps you warm with deliciously flavoured Grey Goose Vodkas. The deal is €38 for all you can drink for 30 minutes – the same price as two cocktails elsewhere. It's a perfect way to start your evening, with an experience that falls outside usual the nightlife box.

Cocktail Bars
Though wine and the occasional glass of bubbly remain the lifeblood of the French culture, the influx of trendy bars and lounges has inspired a wave of cocktails to take over the menus. While Harry's and the Hemingway Bar (both p.345) are perhaps the most legendary, mix it up at Le Fumoir (p.349), Kong (p.346), Le Plaza Athénée (p.318), Hôtel Costes (p.345), or L'Echelle de Jacob (p.346), just to name a few. Though the prices can be a bit lofty, so are the standards of the venues. With chic yet cosy decor and good music, they make a happy medium between the hype of a club and the low-key vibe of a local cafe or bar.

1 rue du Pont Neuf
1st
Ⓜ **Pont Neuf**
Map p.399 E2 118

Kong
01 40 39 09 00 | www.kong.fr

Most famous to visitors as the setting of Carrie's awkward lunch with the ex in *Sex and the City*, and known to Parisians simply as the cocktail bar and sushi restaurant with the great view in the Kenzo building, Kong is in fact both of these things. Most importantly this place offers a breathtaking view from its fifth storey windows and futuristic kitsch décor by the ubiquitous Philippe Starck. Very small, it fills up fast and on weekends tends to feel more like a club than a lounge, with enthusiastic dancing on tables as space becomes limited and inhibitions become a distant memory. Come early to avoid the fickle doormen and to secure a precious seat so you can enjoy your cocktails with the slightly older but fun, international crowd.

10-12 rue Jacob
6th
Ⓜ **Mabillon**
Map p.399 D3 119

L'Echelle de Jacob
01 46 34 00 29

This is a homey place to enjoy a drink with friends, wishing that home was in fact, equally stylish and frequented by hip people. One of the few upscale cocktail bars in the area, this small place fills up quickly with a mix of trendy Parisians and internationals that come to savour some of the best martinis in town without the hype of the Champs-Élysées clubs. A tall staircase, presumably Jacob's ladder for which the bar is named, leads to a second level with tables that can accommodate bigger groups. Until recently this was a weeknight hotspot but popularity seems to have drifted to the weekend, with music starting low-key and pumping up, along with the crowd, as the night goes on.

**31 rue Vieille
du Temple**
4th
Ⓜ **Saint-Paul**
Map p.400 A3 120

La Belle Hortense
01 48 04 71 60

Capitalising on two of the most important pastimes in Paris, wine and literature, comes La Belle Hortense, where the clever owner realised that a drink and good book go so well together. The small bar feels like your second home, where you can come and peruse the multi-language library and settle into the secluded back room to indulge in your selection. The front room is more lively where the patrons can socialise and the personable bartender keeps glasses full, beautiful little canapés coming, and plays an eclectic mix of music from his iPod. Beyond charming, this is Paris at its best.

La Bellevilloise

La Bellevilloise

19-21 rue Boyer
20th
Ⓜ **Gambetta**
Map p.392 A4 **121**

01 46 36 07 07
www.labellevilloise.com
La Bellevilloise combines the visual and musical arts in its various spaces, including a club, loft and atrium cafe. It appeals to all your needs for a creative and culturally full day or, as they would hope, night in one creatively designed place. The charming outdoor terrace is a vibrant place for supporters of the arts to convene when the fickle weather abides; sit among the greenery, take in the sights and sounds and savour the charm of this artistic environment in one of the most culturally rich *quartiers* of Paris.

La Fleche d'Or

102bis rue
de Bagnolet
20th
Map p.402 C2 **122**

01 44 64 01 02 | www.flechedor.fr
On the funkier side of eastern Paris, 'The Golden Arrow' is an aesthetically interesting venue where you can see just about any kind of live music. A defunct train station plus over-zealous art students gives a unique appeal that certainly warrants a visit. One of the most popular alternative musical venues due to its calendar, decor and ambience, it attracts a wide range of patrons from across the spectrum that aren't afraid to wander this far east in search of musical talent. Offering electronica and hip hop to rock, indie, jazz, even Celtic and beyond, the scene is laid-back and this is one place where you won't have to worry about dress code. There is also a restaurant open from 20:00 to midnight specialising in salads and platters named after various countries.

La Maroquinerie

23 rue Boyer
20th
Ⓜ **Gambetta**
Map p.392 A4 **123**

01 40 33 35 05 | www.lamaroquinerie.fr
Just next to the similarly inspiring La Bellevilloise (see above), La Maroquinerie has swept into Belleville with its literary cafe, offering readings and discussions with authors. Also on offer is its intimate concert hall featuring varied rock, folk, and indie bands, for a true collective of creative and artistic minds. Offering a refreshing alternative to the typical nightlife scene, literary and musical Paris come alive here exactly as so many expats envision it to be. The restaurant and bar are open during concert hours, though the meal prices may not appeal to the starving artist. Come early to secure some of the limited seating for a concert and enjoy the convivial atmosphere.

La Palette

43 rue de Seine
6th
Ⓜ **Mabillon**
Map p.399 D3 **124**

01 43 26 68 15
For a culture that balks at change, La Palette is a safe haven where the decor, menu, and crotchety old waiters don't threaten to budge. Nor can anyone remember exactly why people love coming so much – this simple cafe with little round tables and chairs inside and out is like so many other cafes around the city. But any youthful Parisian hipster knows that when the sun is shining it's time to meet and greet at the Palette terrace, battling for any remaining seats, or sitting on laps if all else fails. Don't expect to have to make any big decisions with drinks as choices are limited, as is the selection of food if you come for a meal. But, despite the ambiguity of the appeal, it's worth a visit as an iconic part of Paris drinking culture.

347

78 rue Vieille
du Temple
3rd
Ⓜ **Saint-Sébastien**
Froissart
Map p.400 B2 125

La Perle
01 42 72 69 93

Navigate the narrow cobblestone streets and pass the boy bars to witness this beautiful crowd spilling over onto the pavements. Whether it's the name that established itself as a precious locale, or the rumours that the bartenders spike their drinks with absinthe, La Perle is a hotspot where you are sure to see some of the most interesting and unusual trends in fashion. Come early if you hope to get a seat, otherwise fight your way through the smoke and the crowd to find a nice vantage point to scope out the tragically trendy.

10 rue de l'Odéon
6th
Ⓜ **Odéon**
Map p.399 D4 126

Le Bar Dix
01 43 26 66 83

This small, somewhat nondescript hang-out could use a good rifle through a design magazine but is still is a long-time St-Germain favourite for its simplicity and authentic feel. Tattered though it may be, the charms of this basement bar are undeniable, making it clear why generations of local students continue to flock here soaking up their weight in jugs of homemade sangria (which is all anyone seems to drink) and playing eclectic mixes on the ancient jukebox.

75 rue de Seine
6th
Ⓜ **Mabillon**
Map p.399 D4 127

Le Bar du Marché
01 43 26 55 15

This a Parisian institution that has become a mainstay in trendy cafe culture, but the real reason for its popularity cannot quite be determined. Perhaps it is due to the ideal pavement seating on rue du Bucci in St-Germain, allowing for that highly regarded Parisian pastime of people watching. Or perhaps it is due to the silly uniforms donned by the waiters, their overalls and caps making you feel a bit sorry for them, no matter how cute and charming they may be. Or perhaps it is simply because one day someone, somewhere decided that this would be the new place to be, and the trendy Parisians have kept the word on the street, as is so often the case. No matter what the reason, 'Le Marché' remains a great place to get a drink with a fun crowd. On warm nights be ready to wait (or fight) for a table outside.

Hôtel Plaza Athénée
8th
Ⓜ **Alma – Marceau**
Map p.397 E1 9

Le Bar du Plaza Athénée
01 53 67 66 00 | www.plaza-athenee-paris.com

It is no wonder that the hotel that brings you the best of dining with Alain Ducasse (p.318) will also deliver a formidable venue that takes cocktailing to new heights. You will be entranced by the exquisite design, with the sleek, ice-like bar and then pulled into the furthest part of the room where leather club chairs and artwork create a warm contrast. Delicious colourful cocktails and champagne glasses dance in the hands of the chic and beautiful as they mill around the room. As a prelude to a night at the nearby clubs or by itself, the Plaza never fails to disappoint.

Port de la Gare
quai François
Mauriac
13th
Ⓜ **Quai de la Gare**
Map p.411 D4 129

Le Cabaret Pirate
01 44 06 96 45 | www.guinguettepirate.com

One of Paris' hidden treasures, this old Chinese junk boat is docked on the Seine out in front of the Bibliothèque François Mitterrand and provides a bizarre sliver of Hong Kong fusion. The less than sturdy plank and pungent sea smells requires a hearty nautical spirit to embark upon the journey, though it is well worth the trip. Offering a full restaurant inside the kitsch boat, you can savour a full meal followed by drinks and the wide variety of live shows they present, with everything from jazz, funk and world music, to rock, indie and folk or reggae and Afro-Cuban beats. In the summer the terrace opens up around the boat, intermingling the Paris Plage with the cabaret festivities.

Le Caveau des Oubliettes

52 rue Galande
5th
Ⓜ Cluny – La
Sorbonne
Map p.399 E4 130

08 26 10 12 87

One of the greats on the St-Germain and Paris live music scene, this bar takes you on a journey back in time to a drinking den of the middle ages. Hang out in the upstairs room, where you can watch the action going on downstairs on a TV, or to get closer to the music, descend the precarious stone staircase into the little adjoining caves – one for the bar and one for the performances. The secluded caves, with exposed natural stone and low, arched ceilings, tiny tables and the small bar, come alive with the energy of the musicians and the crowd. Unlike some of the other jazz clubs in the area, des Oubliettes also features a lot of bands playing varied types of music including indie, folk, rock and covers, mixed in with the incredible jazz and blues jam sessions.

Le Fumoir

6 rue de l'Amiral
de Coligny
1st
Ⓜ Louvre Rivoli
Map p.399 D2 131

01 42 92 00 24 | www.lefumoir.com

On warm days, the terrace at this trendy cocktail bar is an ideal place to relax with a drink, watching the people pass by. Inside, sit by the busy bar and see why it was named the prime place to pick up a banker; notorious for having cute men galore, happy hour takes on a whole new meaning here. Or escape it all and relax in the back room perusing the magazines and books from the library as you sip a coffee or cocktail, and treat yourself to one of their delectable desserts. Food is served all day, including light salads and pastries in between lunch and dinner. There's also an outstanding fixed menu for Sunday brunch.

Le Mange Disque

58 rue de la
Fontaine au Roi
11th
Ⓜ Goncourt
Map p.391 D4 132

01 58 30 87 07

The original idea of a simple record store evolved into the marriage of a *disquaire* and wine bar to result in Le Mange Disque, where they certainly do not eat records as the name suggests. Instead indulge in a nice selection of cheese and charcuterie plates, tartines, and small menu items to accompany the wine. With mismatched tables, chairs, and comfy couches, friendly staff, and equally amiable clientele you feel like you are at an apartment party. Amazing artwork by local artists is displayed around the space and adds to the eclectic decor, with the mood depending on the DJ and event. Since they serve only wine, it gives a nice mellow high while enjoying the music before going out to your next venue.

Le Murano

13 blvd du Temple
3rd
Ⓜ Filles du Calvaire
Map p.400 C1 133

01 42 71 20 00 | www.muranoresort.com

Set apart from the pack, this urban resort stands just at the edge of the Marais near République. The super sleek white space of the lobby has leather couches and a sizzling fire, creating an impressive entrance while the long bar has colourful stools where you can sample delicious cocktails and 100 different types of vodka from test tubes. Despite the somewhat remote location, Le Murano has worked its appeal to become a top Parisian hotspot, with an upbeat vibe and a trendy crowd without the pretension. The restaurant is equally impressive, and guests of the hotel enjoy the luxury of three swimming pools.

Le Point Ephémère

136-200 quai Valmy
10th
Ⓜ Château Landon
Map p.390 B2 134

01 40 34 02 48 | www.pointephemere.org

Catering to the new class of canal dwellers, this large venue satisfies every requirement for a fun, edgy, and cultural evening. The truly unique space is a welcoming base for creative spirits and those who appreciate it can take part in the myriad of events offered. Live rock bands and DJs keep the patrons dancing nightly, and regular art exhibitions held in the gallery attract the more visually inclined. Let the large warehouse take you back to the grunge era with its vast concrete space, decorated with creative artwork, no-frills furniture, and simple selection of inexpensive drinks served in plastic cups. The prime canal-side outdoor seating makes the Ephémère a warm weather favourite, and don't forget to leave your legacy on the bathroom walls.

20 rue du Croissant
2nd
Ⓜ Bourse
Map p.389 E4 **135**

Le Port d'Amsterdam
01 40 39 02 63 | www.leportamsterdam.com
Go through the door and you are transported a world away from the civility of Paris and into the high intensity party scene with all the magic that Amsterdam has to offer… well, maybe not all of it. But it's the only real Dutch bar in Paris, and you can drink a lot of real Dutch beer and eat real Dutch snacks with some really crazy Dutch people. The strong international contingent partake in the obligatory late night table dancing so you can expect dressing up for parties and special occasions, as this festive crowd never misses an opportunity to celebrate. Monday is student night with happy hour all night long and there are cheap drinks to be had for non-students on Fridays and Saturdays 22:00 to 23:00.

2-4 rue du Sabot
6th
Ⓜ St-Germain des Prés
Map p.398 C4 **136**

Le Théâtre
01 45 48 86 47 | contact@theatrebar.fr
This newcomer has the potential to draw some of the social sleek back to the somewhat abandoned Left Bank. It is relatively large by Parisian standards, with a theatrical mezzanine that puts it somewhere between a club and a cocktail bar. But where cosiness is lost, sexiness and intimacy are won by the red tones, candles, velvet motif walls and a mirror on the ceiling. The dramatic can flaunt their moves on stage to a repertoire of favourites you probably haven't heard in years – and if you happen to hit it off with one of beautiful patrons, isn't saying you met at the theatre so much more appealing?

1 rue de la Banque
2nd
Ⓜ Bourse
Map p.399 D1 **137**

Legrand Filles et Fils
01 4 26 07 12 | www.caves-legrand.com
Soon after opening in 1880 as an *épicerie*, the Legrand family began to cultivate what has become one of Paris' most diverse selections of international wines. The torch was passed to new owners in 2000, who have authentically restored the boutique while integrating a wine bar alongside the Galerie Vivienne, an intimate pedestrian arcade designed in 1823. Although every wall of Legrand is filled floor-to-ceiling with wine bottles, the majority of their collection is stored in an underground cave. Charcuterie and cheese plates, wines by the glass or a bottle from the extensive collection (with a €15 corkage fee) can be enjoyed at the bar until 19:00. In the evenings it turns into a classroom with various lessons and tastings upon reservation. Across the Galerie, Legrand has a shop offering wine books and accessories.

Legrand Filles et Fils

18 rue Bourg-Tibourg
4th
Ⓜ Hôtel de Ville
Map p.400 A3 **138**

The Lizard Lounge
01 42 72 81 34
www.cheapblonde.com/lizard
This small Marais establishment has a rather distinct American vibe, but has long established itself as the universal expat hangout. Touted for its authentic Anglo bar fare, hearty

brunches, and the friendly staff with a heavy hand pouring 'lethal' cocktails, expats and travellers tend to congregate here to find like-minded people. The mezzanine level is an ideal vantage point to relax and peruse the scene below, while the basement is where things can get heated, with a DJ and a second bar contributing to the convivial atmosphere. The student vibe makes this one of the friendlier places in Paris, and the mix of travellers passing through for a few nights and fresh faced eager expats makes this one of the better places to meet people.

3 rue de Ponthieu
8th
Ⓜ *Franklin D*
Roosevelt
Map p.387 E4 **139**

Mathis Bar
01 53 76 01 62

This is yet another stylised den with the brothel decor instilling a debauched spirit. Le Mathis is hardly a new kid on the party block but it has been maintaining its discreet hipster status with admirable tenacity. Notorious as a favourite cocktail hangout for the PR and film industry, the limited plush velour couches fill quickly, but they generally welcome anyone as long as you are appropriately attired, so arrive early to secure a spot. Tiny and typically fashionable, this is an intimate bar to enjoy a pricey but delicious cocktail before heading to the clubs just down the street.

105 rue Amelot
11th
Ⓜ *Saint-Sébastien*
Froissart
Map p.400 C2 **140**

Pop In
01 48 05 56 11

With its no frill feel, the Pop In is making waves in east Paris for its unapologetically relaxed atmosphere and astoundingly good bands that pop on through. Definitely more shabby than chic, the artsy crowd feels right at home hanging out and making friends, enjoying the rock, indie and folk bands as well as the disarmingly un-Parisian prices of the drinks. A fair amount of Anglophones tend to make their way through here, mixing it up with the local crowd, and they regularly organise different theme nights like gay night, making it a wonderful, open and diverse place where everyone can feel comfortable.

4bis rue Neuve
Popincourt
11th
Ⓜ *Parmentier*
Map p.401 D1 **141**

Rosso Café
01 49 29 06 36 | *www.lerosso.com*

Walk into this bar on a quiet residential street where your everyday wanderings wouldn't normally take you, and you get the impression that you have stumbled upon a new hidden treasure. It maintains a more underground vibe than its main-drag neighbours, but the small place gets quite full with locals and the occasional Anglo of the artsy-intellectual variety. The result is a lively scene with a complete lack of pretension. The music is the perfect complement for the scene and crowd, blaring from an aptly situated boom box behind the bar. As the name suggests, red engulfs the space, both inside and out. As a bonus, the excellent cocktails are well-priced – it's one of the few places in Paris where cranberry juice can be found – and the bar staff aren't bad either.

10 rue Feydeau
2nd
Ⓜ *Bourse*
Map p.389 D4 **142**

Truskel
01 40 26 59 97 | *www.truskel.com*

This 2nd *arrondissement* dive is a haven for the sceners who don't like the scene, with an international mix of all ages to come to enjoy the cheap drinks and live rock bands. The gritty appearance of the bar elicits images of sleazy boozers, but in fact it caters to much of the fashion and music world looking for an alternative watering hole where pretension and airs are frowned upon. Some great bands visit, and it can be found surprisingly full until the late hours of the morning pretty much any night of the week. The ratio of men to women always seems to be in the women's favour, so ladies can always expect plenty of undivided attention here, whether they want it or not.

351

Willi's Wine Bar

13 rue des
Petits Champs
1st
Ⓜ **Bourse**
Map p.399 D1 **143**

01 42 61 05 09
www.williswinebar.com

The legendary Willi is one of the founding fathers of the Paris wine bar scene, and as terminally un-chic as the name may be, this 1930s style bar is a legend. Offering a wide selection of wines from various regions by the glass or by the bottle, Willi's was one of the first to introduce the idea of integrating the wine bar with a full menu restaurant, where people can select the appropriate wine to go with their meal. English is commonly heard around the bar due to the fact it has become a favourite place to indulge in France's finest libation for many visiting and residing Anglophiles.

Wine & Bubble

3 rue Francaise
1st
Ⓜ **Étienne Marcel**
Map p.399 F1 **144**

01 44 76 99 84

This is the place for connoisseurs aiming to delight in an entire bottle, amateurs looking for a guided glass, buyers seeking to stock an empty cellar, and everyone in between. As the name suggests they boast a fine selection of France's favourite tipples, so whether you like your glass still or with a bit of fizz you will find an appropriate choice, and the knowledgeable and friendly staff can help in the process. The modern interior decor maintains a snug atmosphere with comfy chairs downstairs and the mezzanine with wine bottles lining the walls. On warm days the tiny street outside is transformed into a terrace. A small, simple selection of fine cheeses and meats with bread are the perfect complement, and if a certain bottle particularly meets your fancy you can pick one up on your way out from their well-stocked shop.

Wini June

16 rue
Dupetit-Thouars
3rd
Ⓜ **Temple**
Map p.400 B1 **145**

01 44 61 76 41

Classy chic meets Empirical charm in this tiny gem of a wine bar. Walk into a wonderland and enjoy the eclectic antique furniture, dancing flames from the various candles, and beautiful flowers accenting the tables. Opened in the summer of 2006, it is easy to see why this bar enchants everyone that walks through its doors and sips its fine selection of wine from Baccarat glassware. The presentation is impeccable, with luscious little

Ladies' Nights	
Le Wagg	Thursday
The Long Hop	Tuesday
Pink Paradise	One Friday a month
Queen	Wednesday
Regine's	Thursday

canapés offered in the early evening, and attention is paid to every detail, even down to the toilets where they have not forgotten to hang a painting and position flowers in crystal vases. It is more expensive than your average wine bar, but that is the price you pay to drink out of crystal at this luxurious and charming treasure.

Pubs

Other options **Bars** p.344

2 pl du Panthéon
5th
Ⓜ *Cardinal Lemoine*
Map p.409 E1 156

The Bombardier

01 43 54 79 22 | *www.thebombardier.com*

This is perhaps the most English of all the English pubs in Paris, with authentic and cosy wooden tables and benches, service at the bar only and little, if any, attempt at speaking French made by the staff. It is no wonder that so many English feel right at home here. It also has one of the best locations in Paris looking right out onto the magnificent Panthéon, which you can enjoy from the terrace when the weather's right. The nearby universities keep the student quotient high, but this doesn't deter the older crowd with an affinity for beer and the regularly scheduled activities, like Sunday quiz night.

13 rue d'Artois
8th
Ⓜ *Saint-Philippe du*
Roule
Map p.387 E3 146

The Bowler

01 45 61 16 60

Quite simply, The Bowler is a pub like any other; nothing more, nothing less. But just off the glitzy glamorous Champs-Élysées sometimes it's nice to have your basic wooden barstool kind of pub that doesn't feel the need to pull out all the stops, and this is exactly the consensus of the local neighbourhood Irish and Englishmen that frequent this establishment. The ideal place for a drink between the boys, The Bowler tends to host a slightly older crowd, and keeps them entertained with billiards, darts, sports broadcasts, quiz nights on Sundays and Curry Night. It's low key during most traditional peak hours, but it can become fairly bustling during happy hour and sporting events.

8 rue de Berri
8th
Ⓜ *George V*
Map p.387 D3 147

Bugsy's

01 42 68 18 44

This animated bar advertises itself as 'the original Chicago speakeasy' and it almost succeeds in transporting you to the 1920s, with black and white photos of gangsters and American actors on the walls. With a local contingent of predominantly English, Irish and Americans, English is certainly the dominant language here and you will feel a world away from Paris. The waiters are warm and welcoming, the cocktails receive a most favourable reception, pints of Guinness go down like water, and they are said to have some of the best burgers in Paris. Come early for lunch to avoid the crowd. Happy hour is from 18:00 to 20:00 and marks the unofficial commencement of the evening's festivities.

18 rue St Denis
1st
Ⓜ *Châtelet*
Map p.399 F3 148

Café Oz

01 40 39 00 18 | *www.cafe-oz.com*

This cavernous Australian pub in the heart of Les Halles has a tendency to get a bit raucous. With a mix of travellers, expats and French men looking to pick up on freshly imported foreign women under the pretence of hoping to improve their English, weekends at Oz can certainly become a bit of a meat-market. Weeknights can be laid-back and true to its pub roots there's live music Sunday and Monday, but Thursday to Saturday come prepared as you walk into a frat party meets spring break in Paris. The music is a lively and fairly predictable repertoire of top 40 and bar classics, inspiring a good showing of table dancing as the night goes on, dramatically raising the temperature of the room. You can also visit its much smaller, but not much less crowded or rowdy, sister bar in the Latin Quarter, located at 184 rue St Jacques in the 5th.

12 rue de Mirbel
5th
Ⓜ **Censier
Daubenton**
Map p.409 F2 149

Connolly's Corner
01 43 31 94 22 | *www.connollyscorner.fr*

The colourful and eye-catching artwork covering the outside of this bar gives an alternative edge that doesn't quite match up with your image of a typical Irish pub. But step inside on any given afternoon and the laid-back environment is just what you would expect, and the perfect place to grab a drink after hitting up the nearby Mouffetard markets. The students in the area keep Connolly's happily in business, and the place gets lively and crowded for their darts tournaments and live music on Tuesdays, Thursdays, and Sundays. This is one place in Paris where casual attire is strictly required and suits are most definitely not welcome. Staff are notorious for cutting ties off and hanging them from the ceiling, so consider yourself warned – but you will get a free drink for it.

15 rue Clément
6th
Ⓜ **Mabillon**
Map p.399 D4 150

Coolin
01 44 07 00 92 | *www.coolinbarparis.com*

With its ideal setting snugly tucked beneath the beautiful arches of the Marché St-Germain, the vast wooden warmth of the Coolin welcomes all who pass through its doors. On warm days, the terrace is a picture perfect spot to soak up some sun and enjoy the calm street with a beer and a burger. Evenings take a turn for a much livelier atmosphere, with the English and Irish tendencies for a raucous time taking over. Happy hour is from 17:00 to 20:00, but things tend to get started a little later in the evening, true to Parisian form, when the party-goers are just getting started. Every Sunday there is live music starting at 17:00.

110 blvd de Clichy
18th
Ⓜ **Blanche**
Map p.388 C1 151

Corcoran's
01 42 23 00 30 | *www.corcoranirishpub.com*

In one of Paris' saucier districts of Pigalle, Corcoran's has established itself as the favoured post-performance watering hole for the lovely Moulin Rouge dancers. It's a lively and convivial hangout where lots of expats convene for a pint, a meal, or for a game of billiards, darts, or to watch either a match on TV or one of the live bands that come through. The original Corcoran's in St Michel (28 rue St André des Arts, 01 40 46 97 46) boasts an equally festive Irish atmosphere with jovial drinking, home cooked meals, sporting events, and live music on Wednesdays and Sundays.

9 rue Princesse
6th
Ⓜ **Mabillon**
Map p.398 C4 152

The Frog & Princess
01 40 51 77 38 | *www.frogpubs.com*

The most popular of the chain of Frog pubs, the Princess brings the best of English pub life to the Left Bank. The music is a loud mix of your typical bar favourites, and gets everyone in the mood to move, attempting to dance despite being packed shoulder to shoulder in the large space. The lively and upbeat atmosphere will stop any grumpiness, even when you've just had the special Frog micro-brewed beer sloshed on you or a goofy tourist has stepped on your toes. Long tables set the scene for socialising, and a well blended mix of locals and Anglophile expats make this a great place to let loose with a fun-loving convivial crowd. Every Tuesday is student night. You can also check out their more low-key sister bars The Frog and Rosbif in the 2nd (116 rue St Denis, 01 42 36 34 73), The Frog at Bercy Village in the 12th (25 cour St Émilion, 01 43 40 70 71) or The Frog & British Library in the 13th (114 ave de France, 01 45 84 34 26).

11 rue du Pot de Fer
5th
Ⓜ **Place Monge**
Map p.409 F2 153

The Hideout
01 45 35 13 17 | *www.hideout-bar.com*

A purportedly Irish pub, The Hideout in the Latin Quarter has a loyal following of customers who revel in the easygoing, fun vibe and some of the lowest prices in Paris. Its widespread popularity spawned a second location across the river in the 1st at

Châtelet (46 rue des Lombards, 01 40 28 04 05) boasting the same super happy hours lasting from 16:00 to 21:00 plus seven huge screens for all those sports fans. The two locations share the same name and kindred thriftiness, but the spirit differs vastly. The 1st *arrondissement* locale remains a haunt for alternative locals or sports fans and the occasional passing tourist, while this Latin Quarter den remains the longstanding student bar for mixed internationals. Take your pick.

8 rue Nevers
6th
Ⓜ **Pont Neuf**
Map p.399 D3 154

The Highlander
01 43 26 54 20 | www.the-highlander.fr

Down a narrow passage you come upon the oldest Scottish pub in Paris, where you can sample their 25 different whiskies, or the less inclined can stick to beer and shots. You feel as if you have stepped away from France for a moment, as English becomes the primary language among the bar staff and patrons, who are generally Anglophile expats mixed in with the occasional local Parisian. The atmosphere is laid-back most nights, and the downstairs can be reserved for private parties – bring your own festivity accoutrements, including your own choice of music. No matter what floor you're on you can stay till the sun comes up. Basketball fans should note that this is one of the few places in Paris to show American sporting events.

10 rue des Capucines
2nd
Ⓜ **Opéra**
Map p.388 C4 155

Kitty O'Shea's
01 42 96 02 99 | www.kittyosheas.com

Sometimes, after a long day of battling the fashionistas in the shops on rue St Honoré, you just want to get a drink where you can relax and someone's going to know your name. That's just the kind of place Kitty O'Shea's is, and that's exactly why it has become the longest standing and most beloved Irish bar in Paris. With a mix of local Parisians and the neighbourhood expats, Kitty's offers everything from your typical night at the pub to a plethora of events. Legendary as a sporting hub, the pub draws all the sports fans each year for the Six Nations rugby tournaments. There is also a trivia night every Wednesday, a traditional Irish band every Sunday, a guest band once a month, and occasional theme parties, all contributing to making it a lively and loveable hotspot.

46 rue de la Montagne St-Geneviève
5th
Ⓜ **Cardinal Lemoine**
Map p.409 F1 157

Le Violin Dingue

'The Mad Violin' is an appropriate translation for this late night Latin Quarter bar – it is renowned for orchestrating a bit of madness. Sitting just behind the looming Panthéon, it is a favourite stop-off point when the rest of the bars have shut, but the night doesn't quite feel finished. Despite having two levels, the first for drinking and socialising and the downstairs for dancing, the 'Dingue' offers little space and fills quickly with a very interesting mix of mostly students and expats that have had their fair share of the potent cocktails. Reminiscent of an American fraternity party, this is probably the closest thing you'll come to a typical college bar in Paris.

25-27 rue Frederic Sauton
5th
Ⓜ **Maubert-Mutualité**
Map p.399 F4 158

The Long Hop
01 43 29 40 54

Large and spacious with a big outdoor terrace for those warm summer days, this English pub with an American feel hosts a wide range of cultures and generations. Enter during the day to a relaxed atmosphere and you are likely to see a mixed crowd and hear a number of languages. As night falls, things heat up when the DJ comes on and the partying youth emerge, with a mix of tourists, expats and local students. For those less interested in dancing, enjoy a pint while playing billiards or darts. Drinks prices are reasonable, especially if you happen to be female and catch the Tuesday Ladies' Night. Weekends are the most fun and can turn into a pick-up haunt, so you should have no trouble pulling here, but unaccompanied men are not welcome, so find a friend.

355

The Mazet

61 rue St Andre
des Arts
6th
Ⓜ Odéon
Map p.399 D4 159

01 43 25 57 50

A favourite stop for fans of The Doors, The Mazet is allegedly the site of Jim Morrison's last hurrah before his death. Though it's officially an English pub and has a vast English speaking staff and clientele, it maintains a more European feel than a lot of the other pubs in the same category, with a greater mix of French locals and students passing through. Live bands offer great entertainment, and there's also a DJ on Friday and Saturday nights when the pub stays open until 05:00. The overall vibe is upbeat with a fun crowd, and reasonably priced drinks only sweeten the deal.

O'Sullivans

92 blvd de Clichy
18th
Ⓜ Blanche
Map p.388 C1 160

01 42 52 24 94 | *www.osullivans-pubs.com*

There are two bars in Paris by the same name and they could not be more different. The one thing they do have in common is the fact they never fail to deliver a great time. O'Sullivans By The Mill, perched high up in Pigalle just next to the famous Moulin Rouge feels and looks more like a club than the Irish pub it claims to be, with vast open spaces and a back room dedicated entirely to the DJ. The friendly and outgoing staff are largely Anglophone expats, and the crowd is a mix of internationals and locals always ready for fun. Open till the sun comes up, this is a favourite late night stop before catching the metro home. The sister bar at Grands Boulevards (1 boulevard Montmartre, 01 40 26 73 41) is much more like a local pub, but has the same energetic and fun-loving crowd and lively party atmosphere. Every night you'll find the best of expats looking for a taste of home, tourists enticed by the smell of fun, and locals looking to practise their English.

Pub St-Germain

17 rue de l'Ancienne
Comédie
6th
Ⓜ Odéon
Map p.399 D4 161

01 56 81 13 13

This 'pub' is in fact a stylish three-storey cocktail establishment with a late night restaurant. The decor is refined and majestic with comfortable couches, interesting chairs and romantic lighting achieved by various lamps and candles. The spacious room can accommodate large groups, and is also an ideal place for couples. Music highlights the ambience, and the wonderful selection of cocktails makes this a great place to enjoy a drink with friends or to get a bite to eat late at night. Happy hour runs from 18:00 to 20:00.

Drink Driving

France's policies on drink driving are tough. The blood alcohol tolerance level is 0.5 mg/ml, which for an average person is around two glasses of wine. A driver can be given a breath test if they are stopped by the police. If the blood alcohol content (BAC) is between 0.5 and 0.8 mg/ml penalties include a fine and points on their driving licence. A BAC above 0.8 mg/ml could mean a lost licence (for up to three years), a fine of several thousand euros, and even up to two years in jail. Accidents, especially those involving fatalities, bring much more severe punishments. Restaurants and bars should be happy to call for taxis, as they can be fined if their guests are arrested for drink driving. Taxis are reasonably priced and stands exist wherever nightlife is plentiful. Another option is Allo Chauffeur (08 20 20 06 12, www.allochauffeursvp.com), a driving service that takes clients home in their own car. Alternatively, the Noctilien night buses extend to the outskirts of Paris from the main hub at Châtelet. During special celebrations such as La Nuit Blanche and New Year's Eve, certain metro lines stay open all night with reduced schedules and stops.

Quiz Nights

The Bowler	01 45 61 16 60	Sunday
The Hideout	01 45 35 13 17	Sunday
The Highlander	01 43 26 54 20	Sunday
Kitty O'Shea's	01 42 96 02 99	Wednesday
Le Bombardier	01 43 54 79 22	Sunday

Gay & Lesbian

Since Parisians generally abide by a live-and-let-live policy, the gay community has found Paris to be a great place to live, love, and proudly fly their flag. Le Marais, in the 3rd and 4th *arrondissements,* is the epicentre of the gay community. You can find anything from a cosy corner bar or stylish lounge, to a sleazy sex bar where you can fulfil your every fantasy and the word 'taboo' doesn't translate. While options for lesbians were formerly rather limited, in the last few years there has been an increase in bars, clubs, and restaurants specifically for lesbians. In keeping with the tradition of open-mindedness, the majority of bars and clubs are extremely welcoming of the straight community too.

8 rue des Ecouffes
4th
Ⓜ *Saint-Paul*
Map p.400 A3 163

3W Kafé
01 48 87 39 26 | *www.3w-kafe.com*
In place of one of Paris' most notorious lesbian bars, Les Scandaleuse, comes 3W, which stands for 'women with women'. The new look is much more modern, chic, and feminine, with a pretty purple bar, comfy red couches and the perfectly accented lighting. The crowd and the staff have matched the upgrade, but the overall warmth may not be on a par with some of the other establishments which perhaps gives it that certain Parisian charm. There is a basement with a DJ and regular theme nights, including fortune-telling every Monday and singles night the first Thursday of the month.

42 rue Vieille
du Temple
4th
Ⓜ *Saint-Paul*
Map p.400 A3 164

Amnésia Cafe
01 42 72 16 94 | *www.amnesia-cafe.com*
Offering the best of both worlds, you can come here during the day to relax, listen to some chilled music, enjoy the upbeat staff and take in some eye candy. Things pick up in the evening with a lively and friendly crowd that is predominantly male, though women are most welcome. The main room and mezzanine are more relaxed for mixing and mingling, and those looking for a more upbeat party can descend to the basement after 21:00 to dance to a variety of music including disco, pop, 80s and more.

15 rue des Archives
4th
Ⓜ *Hôtel de Ville*
Map p.400 A3 165

Cox
01 42 72 08 00 | *www.coxbar.fr*
As the trendification of the Marais continues and the lines between gay and straight blur, it's no surprise the subtly named Cox is standing strong as exclusively gay. The tiny inside bar has standing room only during happy hour, and the sea of big, burly men overflows onto the pavement. Notorious for its decor, Cox undergoes a complete makeover and changes its look each season.

4 rue Chabanais
2nd
Ⓜ *Pyramides*
Map p.389 D4 166

La Champmesle
01 42 96 85 20 | *www.lachampmesle.com*
While the lesbian bars are more spread out and away from the gay hub of the Marais, places like this long-standing institution on the circuit enjoy the benefits of being just a few blocks from the beautiful Opéra Garnier. With dim lighting and exposed stone and wood, this is a great place to meet for a fun and lively evening. On Thursday and Saturday evenings there are singers and live performers, and on Tuesdays you can have your fortune told by a psychic. Each month they host art exhibitions by local artists.

12 rue des
Haudriettes
4th
Ⓜ *Rambuteau*
Map p.400 A2 167

Le CUD
01 42 77 44 12 | *www.cud-bar.com*
Chances are, if you haven't already been swept off your feet you'll retreat to this late night establishment with hope in your heart. The tiny first floor bar offers a bit of reprieve when you need to come up for air from the real action down below. Descend the spiral staircase, checking whatever amount of clothing you wish before entering this wall to

357

wall haven of nocturnal partiers and prowlers. The stone caves, with two bars, can make you lose all track of time as you dance the night away with the sexy and vivacious crowd. This is an exclusively gay bar, but accompanied women are welcome.

Le Duplex

25 rue Michel le Comte
3rd
Ⓜ *Rambuteau*
Map p.400 A2 168

01 42 72 80 86 | www.duplex-bar.com

If you're more into conversation than shameless cruising, check out the oldest gay bar in the neighbourhood, where you can find a more intelligent gathering of patrons. Small, smoky, and inviting, Le Duplex has an artsy and laid back vibe that is rare and most welcome in the Marais. Exhibitions by local artists make for an eclectic and interesting decor that supplements the ambience. The friendly bartenders joke and chat easily, so whether you are here with someone or alone you'll never be stuck for conversation.

O'Kubi Caffe

219 rue Saint Maur
10th
Ⓜ *Goncourt*
Map p.390 C3 169

01 42 01 35 08 | www.okubicaffe.com

This girl bar has set up shop away from the rest of the pack near the Canal St Martin and place St Marthe, where the ambience of the venue is in keeping with the surroundings as popular, lively and bohemian. Art and photo exhibitions decorate the space, and DJs beautify the airwaves of this predominantly lesbian but gay and hetero-friendly bar and restaurant. The owners, staff, and crowd are friendly, with drink and food prices to match.

PM Café

20 rue du Plâtre
4th
Ⓜ *Hôtel de Ville*
Map p.400 A2 170

01 42 72 43 70 | pm_cafe@hotmail.com

This little cafe is a gem tucked away in the heart of the Marais, avoiding all the madness of the main drags and offering a bit of a reprieve. Thus is the intention and the meaning behind the PM – you can interpret it how you like; 'Paris Marais', 'evening' or 'Pause du Marais'. The lavish gold and red velvet decor is the perfect setting in which to relax any time of day, enjoying a coffee, milkshake, or one of their delectable cocktails. The staff and clientele are friendly, giving this the feeling of a true neighbourhood establishment, predominantly gay, but as always welcoming to all. Things pick up in the evenings, especially on the weekends and for special soirées.

Queen

102 ave des Champs-Élysées
8th
Ⓜ *George V*
Map p.387 D3 171

08 92 70 73 30 | www.queen.fr

The most legendary gay dance club in Paris – actually, the most legendary club in Paris – proves again that the queens really know how to party. This monstrosity is always packed with scantily clad clubbers gyrating to the beats of the night's theme: disco on Monday, house on Tuesday, and varied on Wednesday Ladies' Night and Saturday's Metrosexual party. The club proudly flies its flag of many colours and over the years it has become more and more mixed, with an influx of tourists, local youths and a hetero contingent overtaking the gay scene. It will always hold a special place in Paris' heart as the gay club, even when it's not that gay anymore. Entrance is €15 to €20 with one free drink.

Raidd

23 rue du Temple
4th
Ⓜ *Hôtel de Ville*
Map p.400 A2 172

01 48 87 80 25 | www.raiddbar.com

This is a one-of-a-kind temple to campdom. Where else can you have your drinks served by the half-naked ensemble of the Village People while naked men shower as you dance to a lip-syncing drag queen, before descending to the 100% men, 100% sex basement? Over the top? Raidd is indeed known for going above and beyond the call of the party gods, but that's what makes it the liveliest joint this side of boystown. The bartenders are painfully good looking and woo everyone that utters the word 'cocktail.' Girls are welcome to savour the eye candy upstairs, but the basement is strictly men only.

Written by residents, the Geneva Explorer is packed with insider info, from arriving in the city to making it your home and everything in between.

Geneva Explorer Residents' Guide
We Know Where You Live

Nightclubs

Holding their own against international rivals on the nightlife circuit, the Paris clubs are where the social elite come out to see, be seen, and play hard. While the number of distinguished clubs remains relatively few, the rise in elite establishments such as Black Calvados (below), Le Baron (below), and Neo (p.361) ensures select clientele and the best parties. Places like Cabaret (p.361), VIP (p.362), and Queen (p.358) may have seen better days as the city's hotspots, but today they enjoy a different glory as celebrated tourist favourites. Many clubs are packed any night of the week until 06:00. With all these people inside it is no wonder that the door is so hard to get through, so until you have managed to make your face and name known on the Paris club scene, your best bet is to ride the coattails of someone who already has. The most select clubs don't charge a cover, but you can expect to pay between €10 and €20 at some others for entrance; this sometimes includes a drink ticket.

5 ave Albert de Mun
16th
Ⓜ Iéna
Map p.396 B1 **173**

Aqua
01 40 69 23 90 | www.cineaqua.com
CinéAqua is a unique concept that offers a stunning aquarium, concerts, a cinema, Japanese restaurant Ozu, and by night a pulsating nightclub called Aqua – all in one unbelievable location. The originality of the entire complex extends to the club itself, whose stylish interior and fashionable crowd is enough to lay the foundation for a great night out. Dancing beside the enormous and majestic aquarium, with beautiful and exotic sealife, sums up what is truly captivating about this venue.

40 ave Pierre
de Serbie
8th
Ⓜ George V
Map p.387 D4 **174**

Black Calvados
01 47 20 77 77 | www.bc-paris.fr
Some of the biggest names in the nightlife business (including Chris Cornell of Soundgarden and Audioslave fame) pulled together to reinvent the legendary Calvados of the 60s and 70s. The inspired result is Black Calvados, or BC, which instantly became *the* place to be, attracting celebrities and the city's party elite. The restaurant upstairs, with its glammed up pseudo-American cuisine, is the perfect start to the night before you head downstairs. With black stainless steel, smoked mirrors and glowing cube tables, the small club has certainly achieved the modern, rock'n'roll vibe they were going for. It's also one of the few clubs in Paris where you can hear rock music.

15 rue Princesse
6th
Ⓜ Mabillon
Map p.398 C4 **175**

Castel
01 40 51 52 80
Castel is one of the few truly private 'members only' clubs in Paris, bringing a bit of much-needed panache to the nocturnal happenings of St-Germain. An elite enclave tucked away amid the rowdy pubs of rue Princesse, it may not enjoy the hype of its glory days, but it maintains a high standard of friendly patrons. Members have access to private areas of the three-storey mansion, while visitors can dine in the restaurant, drink in the lounge or let loose in the basement club with a DJ that will keep you dancing until dawn. You don't actually need to be a member to enter; you just need to look like you should be.

6 ave Marceau
8th
Ⓜ Alma – Marceau
Map p.397 D1 **176**

Le Baron
01 47 20 03 01 | www.lebaron.jp
An influx of B-list French celebrities and the social elite has made it possible for the surly bouncers to turn away patrons with the ever transparent excuse of *'C'est privée'* – which means you're just not getting in tonight. The remnants of its saucier days as a bordello remain, with red lights galore. The crowd laps up the edgy attitude, returning night after night to see world-class DJs and live performances. Find a *habitué* (regular) to get you in and experience an essential part of the most fashionable nightlife Paris has to offer.

Le Cabaret Club

2 pl du Palais Royal
1st
Ⓜ Palais Royal
Musée du Louvre
Map p.399 D2 177

01 58 62 56 25 | www.cabaret.fr

It's clear to see why 'Le Cab' once seduced Paris' social elite. Even the looming presence of the Louvre near the entrance cannot detract from the luxurious and stylish interior, with sensual coloured lighting, plush seating, and secluded alcove seating. The heyday has passed and it's not what it once was, but it still remains a popular spot with tourists and a few moneyed locals. There is also a restaurant before the clubbers come in, and the food is pricey and average, but diners are guaranteed free entrance to the club after. Arrive early to avoid queues as the door can be difficult, or visit the site for mailing list and guest list information. The cover price varies, but is generally €20 and includes a drink ticket.

Le Paris Paris

5 ave de l'Opéra
1st
Ⓜ Pyramides
Map p.398 C1 178

01 42 60 77 02 | www.leparisparis.com

Put a gritty basement dive behind velvet ropes with discerning doormen, throw in some great music and you suddenly have a hotspot. Despite the rather grimy ambience of this former gentleman's club, Le Paris Paris has become an über-sceney locale for the fashion, art and music crowds, with occasional celebs thrown into the mix. Tending to be more punk than chic, the overall attitude matches the environment. The music varies greatly, with top electro DJs, europunk and rock bands, 80s nights, live karaoke bands, and the legendary iPod battles that are making waves around the world. Check the website for whose list to get on for which night, or get there early and hope you make the cut.

Neo

23 rue de Ponthieu
8th
Ⓜ Saint-Philippe du
Roule
Map p.387 E4 179

01 42 25 57 14 | www.neoclub.fr

Neo is like the cool table in your high school cafeteria – if your high school's cool table had booze, models, and the occasional celebrity. But one thing's for sure, it's where everyone wants to be, and everyone is glad to be there. Small, dark, and select, nothing is particularly outstanding about this place except that it's where the beautiful people come to party, and it always delivers on a good time. The music is often an eclectic blast from the past and seems to be the same mix time after time, but nonetheless it inspires the masses to move. Whether you've got a bottle at a top table, or are getting down on the floor, the mix of Parisians and expats makes this a perfect place to mingle and party.

Nouveau Casino

109 rue Oberkampf
11th
Ⓜ Parmentier
Map p.401 E1 180

01 43 57 57 40 | www.nouveaucasino.net

Nouveau Casino has maintained its allure by rebelling against all things mainstream, even when putting on events that are seemingly trendy, such as the occasional fashion show. Dark and austere from its former days as a cinema, except for spots of colour and two magnificent chandeliers, the decor is perfectly aligned with the cutting edge music. Hear everything from rock to rap, with some of the best DJs and live bands supporting the venue's mission to represent innovative musical expression. The split levels allow you to rock out on the first floor dancefloor and sidle up to the bar, or enjoy the lounge area on the second floor and relax at the couches and tables. Check the website for listings and concert times.

Pink Paradise

49-51 rue
de Ponthieu
8th
Ⓜ Saint-Philippe du
Roule
Map p.387 E4 181

01 58 36 19 20 | www.pinkparadise.fr

For those of you looking for the saucier side of Paris without feeling like you're on a tourist trip, head to this post-club hotspot where men and women convene around the all-baring beauties. Whether you want to enjoy the ladies on stage or just continue your night of drinking and dancing, Pink is the obvious fun and sexy late-night answer to the

361

question 'where to next?'. The club also offers one of the city's best Ladies' Nights – Pink and the City – one Friday a month. For €35 you get a buffet dinner and cocktails, a fashion and beauty lesson, plus a pole dancing lesson followed by a sexy strip show. The newly opened Pink School also offers pole dancing lessons for only €25.

Regine's

49-51 rue de Ponthieu
8th
Ⓜ **Saint-Philippe du Roule**
Map p.387 E4 **181**

01 43 59 21 13 | *www.regine-paris.com*

The iconic woman after whom this club is named not only ran the first discotheque in the world, but established her fame for being the 'Queen of the Night'. Regine's still stands strong today, with its retro-glam decor of plush red seating and mirrored ceilings and walls. The trendy clientele is diverse, with a broad spectrum of nationalities and ages and a friendly mix of young professionals and elite internationals. For a deluxe, saucy night not to be missed, every Thursday Regine's hosts 'Au Bonheur des Dames,' more commonly known as Crazy Ladies' Night. This evening is strictly reserved for ladies and everything is free from 21:00 to 23:00 including entrance, buffet dinner, drinks, and the hottest male strippers in Paris. Needless to say, the anxious men are tearing down the red ropes outside to be let in at 23:00.

Rex Club

5 blvd Poissonière
2nd
Ⓜ **Bonne Nouvelle**
Map p.389 E4 **183**

01 42 36 10 96 | *www.rexclub.com*

This unassuming club takes on no pretences or frills, nor does it expect such from its patrons, who can come as casual as they please without fear of judgment which is a real rarity in Paris. Here, the focus is on the music and the dancing. Some of the best DJs from around the world come to spin here, skilfully blaring predominantly house and techno music at an unfathomable volume while their fans go crazy dancing until dawn. There's not much room to sit down if you tire out, so wear comfortable shoes and make sure you've built the stamina to go the distance in the dancing marathon.

Showcase

Under Pont Alexandre III
8th
Ⓜ **Champs-Élysées – Clemenceau**
Map p.397 F1 **184**

01 45 61 25 43 | *www.showcase.fr*

This hotspot is under the Pont Alexandre III, but for those who can't get their head around the idea of a club under a bridge, it is actually inside the length of the bridge. The same magnificent stone arches you see from the outside become part of the disco wonderland as you lounge in black leather chairs marvelling at the occasional glint of the Seine through the exposed stone and metal. The impressive space is beautifully designed, and the allure of dancing the night away under a bridge explains why this quickly became one of Paris' most popular clubs. It certainly wins the location award. But despite the long queues and rumours of being *très* select, the clientele ranges so widely you would be hard pressed to fathom the bouncers' criteria for selection. Just come well-dressed and be prepared to wait for a bit.

VIP Room

76 ave de Champs-Élysées
8th
Ⓜ **George V**
Map p.387 D4 **185**

01 56 69 16 66 | *www.viproom.fr*

Though nowadays this club generally caters to celebrities during its fashion week parties and special events, it adheres to its name with a flashy facade and glamorous bravado. A hefty sum was invested to give a much needed facelift and put it back on the nightlife map. It now features long leather couches, glass tables and columns, a waterfall and giant screens. The music is a mix of your basic club sounds though the design of the place leaves little room for dancing, resulting in most of the late-night footwork being done on top of the nearest empty surface. The bathrooms are a marvel of modern design, but a force to be reckoned with after one too many cocktails.

Parties At Home

To be welcomed into a Parisian's home for a party is both an honour and a potentially awkward experience (at first). The invitation alone speaks volumes of how you have etched away at French resistance to allow new people into their social circles. Now you're left with what can be an enjoyable night plus a study of the local rules and etiquette. Show up looking fabulous and bearing gifts and you'll be sure to get off on the right foot. It is customary to bring the host a bottle of wine or other alcohol, unless it is for a dinner party when they will typically have already chosen their wines, in which case bring flowers or chocolate. The next quandary is to *bise* or not to *bise*? It is polite to introduce yourself and give kisses on both cheeks all around the room, unless the room is dauntingly full at your time of arrival, in which case you should simply say hello as you enter and kiss on an individual basis as you are introduced.

Party Organisers

Other options **Party Accessories** p.273

Whether you are looking to put on an intimate dinner, celebrate some nuptials or throw an epic party that will make a lasting impression, there is someone out there that can help you create the perfect event. With the Parisian flair for sophistication and festivities and the help of professional party organisers, you are guaranteed a refined and impeccable soiree that will allow you to enjoy your evening without thinking about the hard work behind the scenes. From small private affairs to large scale events, you can find a company to take care of everything including choosing the venue, invitations, design, food, and more. If the food is all you need for your gathering, there are a number of good caterers throughout Paris (see below).

Caterers

Paris has a wide variety of catering providers, ranging from those better suited to a small dinner party to those capable of servicing upscale private and corporate celebrations. Many restaurants are also *traiteurs* allowing customers to order platters and special dishes in large quantities. Normally these places are reasonably priced but do not deliver, while other restaurants such as Wally le Saharien (p.331) offer a chef who will cook in your home for a private party. Catering company Le Figuier (08 11 00 30 02, www.lefiguier.fr) delivers French and international-style boxed lunches, sweet or savoury appetiser trays, wine and hot meals. For full-service catering, Paris Traiteurs (01 71 11 33 21, www.paris-traiteurs.com) is a network of caterers offering set menus or custom world-cuisine menus, along with reception hall coordination, equipment rental and entertainment for hire. They have catered functions for many of the leading businesses in Paris.

Party Organisers & Caterers

À Table	08 26 95 69 56	www.atable.com	Based in Versailles but serving all of Île de France; offers everything from simple breakfast to full buffets
Curty's	01 53 92 80 80	www.curtys.com	Focused on design and presentation, also offers event organisation
La Traiteur du Marais	01 42 36 05 35	www.traiteur-marais.com	Very stylish caterer for upmarket and VIP events
Les Fetes Surprises Évenement	01 43 71 10 86	www.lesfetessurprises.com	Company specialising in the creation and organisation of private or business events of any size
Parisian Events	01 74 70 05 64	www.parisianevents.com	Small American-owned company providing consultations for weddings, parties and special events
Rebellis	06 07 16 85 08	www.rebellis.com	Larger creative firm with event-planning for business events, weddings and private functions
Sibel Pinto	06 65 27 21 76	www.sibelpinto.com	Caters for home and office gatherings with Mediterranean cuisine
Thanksgiving	01 42 77 68 28	www.thanksgivingparis.com	This small shop in the Marais, offering hard-to-find American food products, has a catering service

Cabaret & Strip Shows

Cabaret exists today as the quintessential Parisian experience for visitors. Two forms of cabaret exist; the most popular involving a full evening comprising dinner, drinks, and topless dancers performing choreographed routines. The other form less explored by tourists is a more artistic expression of the French *chanson* and very particular sense of humour, which will certainly be lost on you if you do not understand the language. The former, however, is one of the most highly sought after forms of entertainment for tourists – the less conservative ones that is. The shows have a Las Vegas-style quality, with grand costumes and choreography, so despite the dancers being topless, the spectacle maintains its Parisian class and is far from a seedy strip show.

Au Lapin Agile

22 rue des Saules
18th
Ⓜ *Lamarck –*
Caulaincourt
Map p.383 D4 186

01 46 06 85 87 | *www.au-lapin-agile.com*
Au Lapin Agile has been a bit of an institution for about 150 years, drawing locals and curious visitors to enjoy the entertaining performances and to get a glimpse of old Montmartre. It is less glamorous than the other venues with no dinner option, just an ancient, dimly lit room with lampshades, paintings on the walls, wooden tables, benches and a bar. There is a piano in the middle of the room, and performers entertain with a variety of musical and comedy acts. You will certainly not miss out on any of the charm, but may appreciate the content more if you understand some French. You can come and go as you please anytime between 21:00 and 02:00. Entry is €24, which includes one drink, additional drinks are €7.

Crazy Horse

12 ave George V
8th
Ⓜ *George V*
Map p.387 D4 187

01 47 23 32 32 | *www.crazyhorse.fr*
As the name implies, the Crazy Horse is the place where the girls can let a little bit looser, with performances that are a perfect combination of slightly raucous mixed in with a bit of magic and comedy to complement their skilful stripteases. The theatre is small, creating an intimate atmosphere with the selective group of women, who have truly perfected the art of seduction. Dinner packages with nearby participating restaurants for before or after the show can be arranged when making reservations. Seating is first come, first serve, so arriving early is advised.

Le Paradis Latin

28 rue
Cardinal Lemoine
5th
Ⓜ *Cardinal Lemoine*
Map p.409 F1 188

01 43 25 28 28 | *www.paradislatin.com*
While creating one of the most iconic landmarks in history, Gustave Eiffel took the time to give Paris this little cabaret gem set away from pack on the Left Bank. It has a very lively show with acrobatics, wonderful lighting effects, great choreography, and proclaims itself to be the most Parisian of all the great cabarets. Dinner and a show costs from €117 to €170; champagne and a show is €82.

Lido

116bis ave des
Champs-Élysées
8th
Ⓜ *George V*
Map p.387 D3 189

01 40 76 56 10 | *www.lido.fr*
Located on one of the most famed and magnificent avenues in the world, it is no wonder that the Lido maintains its reputation as one of the most extravagant shows in Paris. Home to the famous Bluebell girls, and showcasing breathtaking scenes and costumes, it has all the glitz and glam of a Las Vegas act. Prices for dinner and the show start at €140, or opt for the show only, with a half-bottle of champagne for €90 to €100. There's a matinee option on Tuesday and Sunday costing from €80 to €125.

Moulin Rouge

Michou

80 rue des Martyrs
18th
Ⓜ Abbesses
Map p.389 D1 **190**

01 46 06 16 04
www.michou.fr

If you're looking for a bit of colour in your life, treat yourself to an unforgettable alternative cabaret experience, warmly greeted by the perpetually blue-clad owner Michou. Frequented mostly by locals, you will better appreciate the nuances and humour if you understand French, but the entertainment value of this eccentric and fun drag show will certainly not diminish regardless of what gets lost in translation. Dinner and show €99 (book in advance).

Moulin Rouge

18 blvd de Clichy
18th
Ⓜ Pigalle
Map p.389 D1 **191**

01 53 09 82 82 | www.moulinrouge.fr

Since its debut in 1889, the Moulin Rouge has remained the most famous cabaret venue in the world, made only more so by the Hollywood film. Its trademark red windmill has been welcoming visitors from around the world for years, drawing them into a world reminiscent of the first saucy Parisian can-can experience. Be warned that the influx of tourism can detract somewhat from the authentic sexy appeal and turn it into a bit of an amusement park attraction. Dinner and show €145 to €175 (depending on menu choice); show only €99 (includes a half-bottle of champagne).

Casinos

Birthplace of roulette, possibly blackjack, and famous for its poker rooms and tournaments, France is indeed a gambler's paradise. Though they may lack the glitz and glamour that draw the masses to the true gamblers' paradise of Las Vegas, the eight casinos in Paris are certainly stylish. Gambling is legal when sanctioned by the Justice Ministry, but the casinos do face certain restrictions, which have led to the growing popularity of online casinos in France. However, this has not impacted the casinos' popularity with international clientele or those who enjoy the social interaction of the gambling experience. Perhaps the most popular establishment with travellers, due to its location on the Champs-Élysées, is the Aviation Club de France which offers a wide range of games and services.

Casinos			
Association Cercle Eldo	3rd	01 42 77 48 68	Multicolour, poker, stud poker
Aviation Club de France	8th	01 45 62 26 88	Baccarat, backgammon tournaments, blackjack, poker, stud poker
Cercle Anglais	2nd	01 47 42 29 63	Banque a tout va, chemin de fer, poker, stud poker
Cercle Central	9th	01 42 85 28 45	Multicolour, poker, stud poker
Cercle Clichy Montmartre	9th	01 48 78 32 85	Multicolour, poker, stud poker, billiards
Cercle Gaillon	8th	01 45 62 08 33	Blackjack, french roulette, poker
Cercle Haussmann	2nd	01 47 42 67 82	Backgammon tournaments, banque a tout va, chemin de fer, multicolour, poker, stud poker
Cercle Wagram	17th	01 43 80 65 13	30-40, baccarat, blackjack, boule, chemin de fer, craps, poker

365

Cinemas

Paris has a great passion for film which allows for a wide range of traditional and original cinematic entertainment. Renowned for a unique and distinct style, French cinema is extremely popular, appreciated as much as US and UK films, for which you have to wait a few months after the original release. For non-French films, be sure that they are being played in VO (*version originale*), the original language with French subtitles. VF films (*version francais*) are dubbed into French without subtitles. The least expensive films are the matinees played before noon, but some cinemas only discount the first film of the day. Tickets can be anywhere from €5 to €10. Some of the larger cinemas, like the UGCs and the Gaumont, have basic food concessions but many of the smaller ones do not offer anything. The best offer is the MK2 Bibliothèque in the 13th (128-162 ave de France), a new cineplex where you can get a sandwich, salad, dessert, drink, and film voucher for €13.

There are a number of alternative choices to the movie going experiences, from debates and jazz at L'Entrepôt, to regular showings of the *Rocky Horror Picture Show* at Studio Galande and a film in an old Japanese pagoda at La Pagode. CineAqua has a movie theatre, world-class aquarium, Japanese restaurant, concerts, and nightclub all in the same fun-filled complex under the Jardin de Trocadéro. Serious film aficionados should check out the Cinémathèque Française, a film museum, library, and research centre in a Frank Gehry-designed dwelling that also sponsors daily screenings. Summer is the time for open-air festivals, with one at Parc de la Villette in July through until August, showing films from around the world, including many in English. In mid-August, the Cinéma au Claire de la Lune event sees films screened in parks and public squares around the city. You can check listings in the weekly *Pariscope* which comes out each Wednesday and can be bought at any newsstand, or by checking online at www.allocine.com. You can reserve online for some of the larger cinemas to save time queuing, but do so cautiously because sometimes the machines to claim tickets require a European bank card with a microchip.

Cinemas

Name	Phone	Website	Map
CineAqua	01 40 69 23 23	www.cineaqua.com	p.396 B1
Cinéma Studio 28	01 42 54 18 11	www.cinemastudio28.com	p.383 D4
Cinémathèque Française	01 71 19 32 00	www.cinematheque.fr	p.411 E3
Forum des Images	01 44 76 62 00	www.forumdesimages.net	Various
Gaumont	na	www.cinemasgaumontpathe.com	Various
L'Entrepôt	01 45 40 07 50	www.lentrepot.fr	p.408 A4
La Pagode	01 45 55 48 48	na	p.397 F4
Le Grand Action	01 43 29 44 40	www.legrandaction.com	p.409 F1
Le Grand Rex	08 92 68 05 96	www.legrandrex.com	p.389 F4
Le Lucernaire Forum	01 45 44 57 34	www.lucernaire.fr	p.408 C2
Le Max Linder Panorama	08 92 68 50 52	www.maxlinder.com	p.389 E4
Les Ecrans de Paris	na	www.lesecransdeparis.fr	Various
MK2	08 92 89 28 92	www.mk2.com	Various
Studio Galande	01 43 54 72 71	www.studiogalande.fr	p.399 E4
UGC	08 92 70 00 00	www.ugc.fr	Various

Comedy

French comedy can be difficult to appreciate as a foreigner, even with a solid grasp of the language. They pride themselves on cutting witticisms, dark and elegant irony, or the hilarity of simple and zany situations. Their delivery and content is very culture-specific, and they all find it very amusing, but it may be lost on someone accustomed to a different style of humour. Paris has a number comedy acts showing throughout the city, in the form of stand-up, or integrated into cabaret and theatre acts. If your French is outstanding you may appreciate some of the more local venues like L'Ane Rouge in the 17th (3 rue Laugier, 01 43 80 79 97) or La Grande Comédie in the 9th (40 rue de Clichy, 01 48 74 03 65). Otherwise, to satiate your anglocentric sense of humour, the production company Laughing and Music Matters regularly hosts some of the best English speaking stand up comedians from around the world at a few venues throughout Paris, like La Java in the 10th (105 rue du Faubourg du Temple, 01 42 02 20 52). Check out www.anythingmatters.com for details.

Fashion Shows

As a reigning fashion capital, some might find that every day in Paris is an endless couture parade, where the smallest streets can be transformed into a catwalk. You stare, you try imitating, and you want to shop. Occasionally you notice more model types in the street and Cristal popping in the clubs; you feel the buzz in the air, and you know that it is once again that time of year that so many Parisians live and die by – Paris Fashion Week. Days on end are dedicated to the demonstration, critique, and appreciation of the creation of clothing, where the fashion-conscious eagerly discover what stylistic gems the designers have bestowed upon them for the next seasons. With different dates for each collection, Fashion Week generally falls in June or July for spring/summer men's and autumn/winter women's couture, September for spring/summer women's ready to wear collections, and then again in January or February the next season. Tickets are extremely hard to come by for the top designers and are reserved for journalists, stylists, and the who's who of the fashion industry. It can be possible to get tickets to some of the lesser known shows by sending requests to the designers' press offices. Just explain who you are and why you want to attend the show. Information for show dates and press office details can be found on www.modemonline.com.

Take The Mic

For budding musicians in search of an audience, Thomas Brun organises open mic nights at The Highlander every Wednesday. See p.368 for contact details.

Live Music

Conductor Leopold Stokowski said that 'a painter paints his pictures on canvas, but musicians paint their pictures on silence'. Paris is a virtual monument dedicated to those who captured their vision on canvas, and when you are tired of the deafening silence of art, let the nocturnal painters fill that silence with a different kind of magic. Live music is a vibrant part of the Paris nightlife scene, with every style to meet your desires pulsating from cosy caves, local bars, large amphitheatres, churches and cathedrals, and in the open air. Some of the biggest names in the music industry come through Paris's large concert halls, or you can discover hidden talents trying to emerge from clouds of smoke in dimly lit rooms.

Summer is the time when the city comes alive again and you can enjoy a number of festivals, parades, and benefit events such as Solidays for AIDS awareness on the first weekend in July (www.solidays.org), and everything from techno at the Techno Parade on the third Saturday in September (www.technopol.net) and the two-day Rock-en-Seine festival at the end of August (www.rockenseine.com) to world music throughout the summer for Quartier d'Eté (www.quartierdete.com). One of the most celebrated events, on June 21st every year, is Fête de la Musique; (p.41) when music resonates throughout the city, inspiring a bacchanalian atmosphere as people weave through the sounds playing in the bars, cafes, and streets. Also popular, the Paris Jazz Festival in May celebrates the spirit of jazz and showcases artists throughout the city, in keeping with a tradition of appreciation that has attracted international musicians for years. It is this very recognition of the aesthetic of the music not so freely granted in other countries that makes the Parisian jazz scene so widely popular. Some venues have become world famous (at least in the jazz world) for having seen some of the greats on their stage, others are dark and smoky hopefuls for history in the making, but no matter how big or small, they are all part of a thriving and vital musical culture. Keep up to date by picking up a copy of *Pariscope*, which you can buy at any *kiosque*.

Live Music Venues

Major Concert Venues

Bataclan	11th	01 43 14 00 30	www.le-bataclan.com
L'Elysée Montmartre	18th	01 42 23 46 50	www.elyseemontmartre.com
Olympia	9th	08 92 68 33 68	www.olympiahall.com
Palais Omnisports de Paris – Bercy	12th	01 40 02 60 60	www.bercy.fr
Zenith	19th	01 44 52 54 56	www.le-zenith.com

Classical Concert Venues

La Sainte Chapelle	1st	01 53 40 60 97	www.lasainte-chapelle.monuments.nationaux.fr
Salle Pleyel	8th	01 42 56 13 13	www.sallepleyel.fr
The American Church	7th	01 40 62 05 00	www.acparis.org
Théâtre des Champs-Élysées	8th	01 49 52 50 50	www.theatrechampselysees.fr

Jazz Clubs

7 Lezards	4th	0148 87 08 97	http://7lezards.com
Balle au Bond	6th	01 43 40 02 10	www.laballeaubond.com
Café Universel	5th	01 43 25 74 20	www.myspace.com/cafeuniversel
Caveau de la Huchette	5th	01 43 26 65 05	www.caveaudelahuchette.fr
Duc des Lombards	1st	01 42 33 22 88	www.ducdeslombards.fr
La Fenetre	11th	01 40 09 70 40	na
Le Caveau des Oubliettes	5th	01 46 34 23 09	na
Le Franc Pinot	4th	01 46 33 60 64	na
Le Houdon	18th	01 42 62 21 34	na
Lionel Hampton Jazz Club	17th	01 40 68 31 42	www.jazzclub-paris.com
New Morning	10th	01 45 23 51 41	www.newmorning.com
Swan Bar	6th	01 44 27 05 84	na

Independent Venues

China Club	12th	01 43 43 82 02	www.chinaclub.cc
Harry's	2nd	01 42 61 71 14	www.harrysbar.fr
The Highlander	6th	01 43 26 54 20	www.the-highlander.fr
House of Live	8th	01 42 25 18 06	na
La Cigale	18th	01 49 25 81 75	www.lacigale.fr
La Fleche d'Or	20th	01 44 64 01 02	www.flechedor.fr
La Scène	11th	01 48 06 50 70	www.la-scene.com
Le Cabaret Pirate	13th	01 44 06 96 45	www.guinguettepirate.com
Le Divan du Monde	18th	01 40 05 06 99	www.divandumonde.com
Le Paris Paris	1st	01 42 60 64 45	www.leparisparis.com
Le Point Ephémère	10th	01 40 34 02 48	www.pointephemere.org
Le Réservoir	11th	01 43 56 39 60	www.reservoirclub.com
Nouveau Casino	11th	01 43 57 57 40	www.nouveaucasino.net
Pop In	11th	01 48 05 56 11	na
Showcase	8th	01 45 61 25 43	www.showcase.fr
Truskel	2nd	01 40 26 59 97	www.truskel.com

Opera

Though opera as a musical form has often been swiftly brushed aside by many as elitist, increased exposure and accessibility has led to mounting popularity in the last few years. Opera appreciation runs high in Paris, due largely to the fact that the city boasts two of the most magnificent opera houses, the classic and luxurious Palais Garnier (p.167) and the ultra modern Opéra Bastille. You can also find occasional performances in other venues around Paris, like the Théâtre des Champs-Élysées or the Théâtre du Châtelet. While the lifestyles of the rich and famous in the days of yore may have involved fur coats and bottles of champagne in their box at the opera, today sees a very different picture. While some nights remain expensive and tickets may be difficult to come by, the popularity of the opera has forced the extravaganza down from its pedestal to a more reasonable form of entertainment. You can try buying reduced price tickets on the day for certain shows at one of two theatre kiosks located at place de la Madeleine in the 8th *arrondissement* or Esplanade de la Tour

Opéra Garnier

Montparnasse in the 14th (visit www.kiosquetheatre.com for available tickets – in French). Last minute tickets are also sometimes available at the box office half an hour before the showing for as little as €6 or €7, but visibility is limited to nonexistent.

Opera

Opéra Bastille	01 40 01 19 70	www.operadeparis.fr
Opéra Comique	08 25 00 00 58	www.opera-comique.com
Opéra Garnier	08 92 89 90 90	www.operadeparis.fr
Théâtre des Champs-Élysées	01 49 52 50 50	www.theatrechampselysees.fr
Théâtre du Châtelet	01 40 28 28 40	www.chatelet-theatre.com

Theatre

The French flair for the dramatic has led to the proliferation of theatrical venues throughout Paris. From small and intimate to lavish and impressive, you can be entertained in the setting of your desire pretty much any night of the week, with a wide array of different styles. Ticket prices range anywhere from €10 to close to €100, depending on the establishment and popularity of the production, but you get a lot of them at a reduced price for students or 50% off when bought the same day of the performance. Most of the theatres rotate their seasonal programmes with various opera, dance, orchestra, vocal, and theatrical artists from around the world. Many of the theatre performances are in French, particularly in the smaller venues, which cater mostly to locals, but certain venues, like the Théâtre de Nesle, Odéon Théâtre, and Sudden Théâtre, will usually have at least one production in English each season. A wonderful experience, even if you don't understand French, is the open-air production of Shakespeare performed at the Théâtre de Verdure in the Bois de Boulogne. You can find the listing of all shows performances in Paris each week in the *Pariscope*, which you can buy at any *kiosque*. Check www.parisvoice.com for other listings in English.

Theatre

La Comédie-Française	1st	01 44 58 15 15	www.comedie-francaise.fr
Les Abbesses	18th	01 42 74 22 77	www.theatredelaville-paris.com
Molière – Maison de la Poesie	3rd	01 44 54 53 00	www.maisondelapoesie-moliere.com
Odéon Théâtre	6th	01 44 85 40 40	www.theatre-odeon.fr
Sudden Théâtre	18th	01 42 62 35 00	www.suddentheatre.fr
Théâtre de l'Européen	8th	01 42 65 07 09	www.theatremadeleine.com
Théâtre de la Huchette	5th	01 69 03 29 97	www.theatrehuchette.com
Théâtre de la Ville	1st	01 42 74 22 77	www.theatredelaville-paris.com
Théâtre de Nesle	6th	01 46 34 61 04	www.galeriedenesle.com
Théâtre de Verdure du Jardin Shakespeare	16th	01 40 19 95 33	na
Théâtre du Rond-Point	8th	01 44 95 98 21	www.theatredurondpoint.fr
Théâtre du Vieux-Colombier	6th	01 44 39 87 00	http://vieux.colombier.free.fr

369

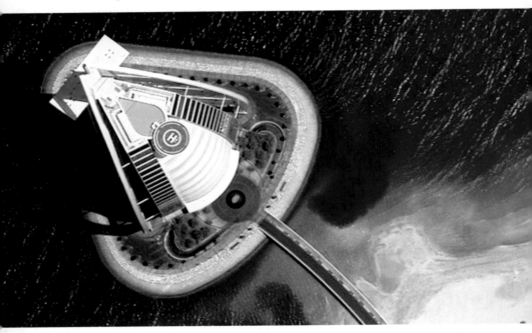

Maps

Maps

User's Guide

This section features detailed maps to help you get your bearings when you first arrive, and give you an idea of where we're talking about in the main chapters of the book. There's a France overview map on p.373 and an overview of Paris and the surrounding areas on p.378. Everything within the Périphérique is then covered in the large-scale maps (scale 1:10,000) starting on p.380 – turn to p.376 for the sheet index. Starting on p.374 there's an index of the main streets in Paris, with a grid reference pointing you to the right page. Note that many of the streets will extend over several grids, and over numerous pages too.

We've included the main hotels from the General Information chapter (p.24 onwards) along with schools, hospitals, shopping centres, museums, heritage sites and parks. See the legend below for an idea of which is which. We've also put on the metro stations (look out for the red circles with an M inside) and RER stations (the red circles with an R) and inside the back cover there's a metro map.

More Maps

Need More?

We understand that this residents' guide is a pretty big book. It needs to be, to carry all the info we have about living in Paris. But, unless you've got the pockets of a clown, it's unlikely to be carried around with you on day trips. With this in mind, we've created the *Paris Mini Map* as a more manageable alternative. This packs the whole city into your pocket and once unfolded is an excellent navigational tool. It's part of a series of Mini Maps that includes cities as diverse as London, Dubai, New York and Barcelona. Wherever your travels take you, you'll never have to ask for directions again. Visit our website, www.explorerpublishing.com for details of how to pick up these little gems, or nip into any good bookshop.

Beyond these maps and our own very nifty **Paris Mini Map** (see right for details) there are a number of street directories to be found in Paris' bookshops and newsagents. Massin produces a range of map products including the little blue Paris Pratique which has one page for each arrondissement. They also publish a bigger atlas with in-depth maps for the surrounding areas too. The Paris Poche metro map can be picked up at any station.

Online Maps

There are a few websites that have searchable maps of Paris: Google maps is worth a look, but the navigation can be a bit tricky; the 3D landmarks on www.viamichelin.com make searching for the major attractions easy. Hardcore map fans tend to like Google Earth (download from http://earth.google.com) for its satellite images, powerful search facility and incredibly detailed views.

Map Legend

H	Hotel	**OPÉRA**	Area name
	Education	*Porte des Lilas*	Junction name
	Park/Garden		Highway
+	Hospital		Major Road
	Shopping		Secondary Road
	Heritage/Museum		Other Road
	Industrial Area		Tunnel
	Agriculture	**R**	*RER*
	Pedestrian Area	**M**	*Metro*
	Built up Area/Building		Country Border
	Land		Steps
	Petrol Station	**E**	Embassy
	Church	**i**	Tourist Info
			International Airport

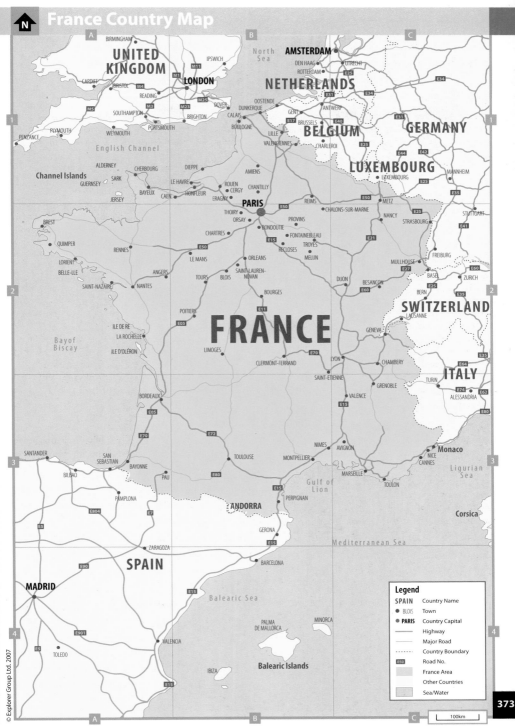

373

Street Name	Map Ref
8 Mai 1945, Rue du	p.381 E1
Albert 1er de Monaco, Ave	p.396 B2
Alésia, Rue d'	p.417 F1
Alexandre III, Pont	p.397 F1
Algérie, Blvd d'	p.392 B2
Ampère, Rue	p.381 D4
Amsterdam, Rue d'	p.388 B2
Anatole France, Ave	p.380 A2
Anatole France, Quai	p.398 A2
Andre Citroën, Quai	p.405 F1
André Joineau, Rue	p.392 C1
Arago, Blvd	p.409 D4
Aristide Briald, Ave	p.418 B4
Aristide Briand, Rue	p.398 A2
Arquebusiers, Rue des	p.400 C3
Arrivée, Rue de l'	p.408 A2
Aubervilliers, Rue d'	p.384 C3
Auguste Blanqui, Blvd	p.419 E1
Auteuil, Rue d'	p.404 C2
Avron, Rue d'	p.402 C4
Bagnolet, Rue de	p.402 B3
Balard, Rue	p.405 F3
Barbès, Blvd	p.383 F4
Bastille, Blvd de la	p.410 C1
Batignolles, Blvd des	p.388 B1
Belgrand, Rue	p.380 B1
Belleville, Blvd de	p.391 E4
Belleville, Rue de	p.391 E3
Belliard, Rue	p.382 C2
Benjamin Franklin, Rue	p.396 A2
Béranger, Rue	p.400 B1
Bercy, Blvd de	p.411 E3
Bercy, Rue de	p.411 D2
Berryer, Rue	p.387 D3
Berthier, Blvd	p.380 C4
Bessières, Blvd	p.382 A2
Bineau, Blvd	p.380 A4
Bir Hakeim, Pont de	p.396 B3
Bois, Rue des	p.392 B2
Boissy d'Anglas, Rue	p.388 A4
Bosquet, Ave	p.397 E2
Bourdon, Blvd	p.410 C1
Bourdonnais, Ave de la	p.397 D3
Branly, Quai	p.396 C2
Breteuil, Ave de	p.397 F4
Brune, Blvd	p.418 B3
Camille Desmoulins, Rue	p.415 D1
Carrousel, Pont du	p.398 C2
Championnet, Rue	p.383 D2
Champs Élysées, Ave des	p.387 D4
Chapelle, Blvd de la	p.390 A1
Chapelle, Rue de la	p.384 B2

Street Name	Map Ref
Charenton, Rue de	p.401 D4
Charonne, Blvd de	p.402 B4
Charonne, Rue de	p.401 E4
Château Landon, Rue du	p.390 B1
Chàteau, Rue du	p.408 A4
Châteaudun, Rue de	p.389 D2
Chemin Vert, Rue du	p.401 D2
Cité, Rue de la	p.399 F3
Clichy, Ave de	p.382 A3
Clichy, Blvd de	p.388 C1
Clichy, Rue de	p.388 C2
Commandant L'Herminier, Rue du	p.413 E1
Commerce, Rue du	p.406 C1
Concorde, Pl de la	p.398 A1
Concorde, Pont de la	p.398 A1
Constantinople, Rue de	p.388 A2
Convention, Rue de la	p.393 E1
Corentin Cariou, Rue	p.385 F2
Courcelles, Blvd de	p.387 E2
Courcelles, Rue de	p.387 E2
Courteline, Ave	p.413 D2
Crimée, Rue de	p.385 E3
Curial, Rue	p.385 D2
Danielle Casanova, Rue	p.388 C4
Daumesnil, Ave	p.411 E2
Davout, Blvd	p.403 D2
Denfert Rochereau, Ave	p.408 C4
Départ, Rue du	p.408 A2
Diderot, Blvd	p.411 E1
Dijon, Rue de	p.411 F4
Docteur Arnold Netter, Ave du	p.412 C2
Douaumont, Blvd de	p.381 E2
Edouard Vaillant, Ave	p.380 B2
Elie Faure, Rue	p.413 E1
Emile Zola, Ave	p.417 D3
Ernest Renan, Ave	p.416 A1
Ernest Renan, Rue	p.417 D3
Ernest Roche, Rue	p.382 A2
Étienne Marcel, Rue	p.399 E1
Exelmans, Blvd	p.404 C2
Faidherbe, Rue	p.413 F3
Faubourg Poissonnière, Rue du	p.489 F1
Faubourg St Antoine, Rue du	p.401 D4
Faubourg St Denis, Rue du	p.390 A1
Faubourg St Honoré, Rue du	p.388 A4
Faubourg St Jacques, Rue du	p.409 D4
Faubourg, Rue du	p.387 E3
Flandre, Ave de	p.385 E3
Foch, Ave	p.386 A3
Fontaine, Rue	p.388 C1
Four, Rue du	p.398 C3
François Mauriac, Quai	p.411 E4

Street Name	Map Ref
François Mitterrand, Quai	p.421 F2
Francois Ory, Rue	p.418 B4
Frémicourt, Rue	p.406 C1
Frères Voisin, Blvd des	p.415 E2
Friedland, Ave de	p.387 D3
Gabriel Péri, Rue	p.415 E4
Gallieni, Ave	p.403 E2
Gambetta, Ave	p.402 A1
Gambetta, Blvd	p.415 F2
Gare, Quai de la	p.410 C3
Garibaldi, Blvd	p.414 C3
Garigliano, Pont du	p.405 D3
Gaston Tessier, Rue	p.385 D2
Général de Gaulle, Ave du	p.413 E2
Général Leclerc, Ave du	p.415 F2
George V, Ave	p.387 D4
Georges Mandel, Ave	p.395 F1
Gervex, Rue	p.381 D4
Glaïeuls, Rue des	p.392 C2
Gobelins, Ave des	p.410 A4
Gourgaud, Ave	p.380 C4
Gouvion St Cyr, Blvd	p.386 B1
Grande Armée, Ave de la	p.386 A2
Grands Augustins, Quai des	p.399 E3
Grenelle, Blvd de	p.407 D1
Grenelle, Port de	p.396 A4
Guébriant, Rue de	p.393 D3
Guersant, Rue	p.386 B1
G V de Suède, Ave	p.396 B2
Guy Môquet, Rue	p.382 A3
Halévy, Rue	p.388 C3
Haureleuille, Rue	p.399 E4
Haussmann, Blvd	p.487 E3
Henri Barbusse, Rue	p.393 E1
Henri Farmann, Rue	p.405 E4
Henri IV, Blvd	p.400 B4
Henri Martin, Ave	p.395 F1
Hoche, Ave	p.415 E2
Ibsen, Ave	p.403 D1
Iéna, Ave d'	p.386 C3
Iéna, Pont d'	p.396 B2
Invalides, Blvd des	p.397 F3
Issy les Moulineaux, Quai d'	p.405 D4
Italiens, Blvd des	p.389 D4
Jean Jaurès, Ave	p.391 D1
Jean Moulin, Ave	p.417 F3
Jean Zay, Rue	p.408 A3
Jemmapes, Rue de	p.390 C4
Joseph Kessel, Rue	p.411 E4
Jules Ferry, Blvd	p.415 D2
Kellermann, Blvd	p.419 F3
Kléber, Ave	p.386 B4

Street Name	Map Ref
La Boétie, Rue	p.387 E3
La Fayette, Rue	p.389 D3
La Feuillade, Rue	p.399 D1
Lagny, Rue de	p.413 F1
Lannes, Blvd	p.395 E1
Lavoisier, Rue	p.403 E4
Lecourbe, Rue	p.407 D2
Lefebvre, Blvd	p.416 B1
Legendre, Rue	p.381 F4
Lénine, Ave	p.393 F1
Léon Frapie, Rue	p.393 D3
Léon Gaumont, Ave	p.403 E4
Liberté, Blvd de la	p.393 F2
Liége, Ave de	p.413 F2
Londres, Rue de	p.388 B2
Louise Thuliez, Rue	p.392 A2
Macdonald, Blvd	p.385 F2
Madeleine, Blvd de la	p.388 B4
Magenta, Blvd de	p.389 F1
Maine, Ave du	p.408 A3
Mal Gallieni, Ave du	p.397 F2
Malakoff, Ave de	p.386 A3
Malaquais, Quai	p.398 C3
Malesherbes, Blvd	p.381 E4
Malte Brun, Rue	p.402 B1
Manin, Rue	p.391 E1
Marceau, Ave	p.386 C3
Marx Dormoy, Rue	p.384 B4
Mégisserie, Quai de la	p.399 E3
Ménilmontant, Blvd de	p.401 F2
Menilmontant, Psg de	p.401 E1
Michel Ange, Rue	p.404 C2
Michelet, Quai	p.380 A1
Mirabeau, Rue	p.405 E1
Molitor, Rue	p.405 D2
Monge, Rue	p.409 F1
Montaigne, Ave	p.397 D1
Montebello, Quai de	p.399 F4
Montmartre, Blvd	p.388 A4
Montparnasse, Blvd du	p.408 A1
Montreuil, Rue de	p.402 B4
Mozart, Ave	p.395 D4
Murat, Blvd	p.404 B2
Navier, Rue	p.382 B2
Neuilly, Rue de	p.380 C1
Neuve Tolbiac, Rue	p.420 B2
New York, Ave de	p.396 B2
Ney, Blvd	p.382 C2
Niel, Ave	p.386 C1
Noisy Le Sec, Rue de	p.393 E3
Notre Dame de Lorette, Rue	p.389 D2
Notre Dame Des Victoires, Rue	p.389 E4

Street Name	Map Ref
Oberkampf, Rue	p.401 D1
Opéra, Ave de l'	p.398 C1
Ordener, Rue	p.383 D3
Ornand, Blvd	p.383 E2
Orsay, Quai d'	p.397 E2
Paillet, Rue	p.409 E1
Pantin, Rue de	p.393 F2
Pasquier, Rue	p.388 B3
Pasteur, Ave	p.393 D2
Paul Doumer, Ave	p.396 A2
Pépinière, Rue de la	p.388 A3
Pereire (Sud), Blvd	p.381 E4
Périphérique, Blvd	p.381 E2
Philippe Auguste, Ave	p.402 A4
Pierre Bonnard, Rue	p.402 C3
Pierre Brossolette, Ave	p.415 E3
Pierre de Coubertin, Ave	p.419 E4
Pierre Grenier, Ave	p.414 A2
Poissonnière, Blvd	p.389 E4
Poniatowski, Blvd	p.412 C4
Port Royal, Blvd de	p.409 E3
Porte d'Asnières, Ave de la	p.381 D3
Porte d'Auteuil, Ave de la	p.404 A1
Porte d'Italie, Ave de la	p.420 A2
Porte d'Orléans, Ave de la	p.418 B3
Porte de Bagnolet, Ave de la	p.402 B3
Porte de la Villette, Ave de la	p.385 F1
Porte de Montmartre, Ave de la	p.383 D1
Porte de Sèvres, Ave de la	p.405 F4
Porte du Pré St Gervais, Ave de la	p.392 C1
Pré St Gervais, Rue du	p.392 A2
Président Wilson, Rue du	p.380 A1
Pyramides, Pl des	p.398 C1
Pyrénées, Rue des	p.402 B1
Raphaël, Ave	p.395 D4
Rapp, Ave	p.397 D2
Raspail, Blvd	p.398 B4
Récamier, Rue	p.398 C4
Reille, Ave	p.418 C2
Reims, Blvd de	p.381 D3
Rennes, Rue de	p.398 C4
Republique, Ave de la	p.400 C1
République, Blvd de la	p.404 A4
Reuilly, Rue de	p.411 F1
Richard Lenoir, Blvd	p.400 C3
Richard Lenoir, Rue	p.401 E3
Riquet, Rue	p.384 B3
Rivoli, Rue de	p.398 B1
Rochechouart, Blvd de	p.389 F1
Rome, Rue de	p.388 A1
Rouget de Lisle, Rue	p.415 D1
Royale, Rue	p.388 A4

Street Name	Map Ref
Sadi Carnot, Rue	p.393 E4
Saints Péres, Rue des	p.398 C3
Sébastopol, Blvd de	p.399 F2
Secrétan, Ave	p.391 D1
Ségur, Ave de	p.397 E4
Sérurier, Blvd	p.392 A1
Sèvres, Rue de	p.398 B3
Simon Bolivar, Ave	p.391 D2
Soult, Blvd	p.413 D3
St Antoine, Rue	p.400 C4
St Bernard, Quai	p.410 B1
St Denis, Blvd	p.390 A4
St Fargeau, Rue	p.392 C3
St Florentin, Rue du	p.388 B4
St Germain, Blvd	p.398 B3
St Honoré, Rue	p.398 C1
St Jacques, Blvd	p.409 D4
St Jacques, Rue	p.409 D3
St Lazare, Rue	p.388 B3
St Mandé, Ave de	p.412 C2
St Martin, Blvd	p.390 A1
St Michel, Blvd	p.409 D2
St Ouen, Ave de	p.382 B2
Stalingrad, Quai de	p.414 A2
Strasbourg, Blvd de	p.390 A3
Suchet, Blvd	p.395 D2
Suffren, Ave de	p.397 D4
Temple, Rue du	p.400 B1
Ternes, Ave des	p.386 B2
Tolbiac, Pont de	p.411 E4
Tolbiac, Rue de	p.419 E2
Tour, Rue de la	p.389 E2
Tournelle, Quai de la	p.400 A4
Tourville, Ave de	p.397 F4
Vanne, Rue de la	p.418 B4
Vaugirard, Rue de	p.407 D3
Verdun, Ave de	p.414 A4
Versailles, Ave de	p.405 E2
Victor Cresson, Ave	p.415 D3
Victor Hugo, Ave	p.386 B3
Victor Hugo, Blvd	p.381 F1
Victor Hugo, Rue	p.415 E2
Villas, Ave de	p.397 F4
Villette, Blvd de la	p.391 D3
Villiers, Ave de	p.380 B4
Villiers, Rue de	p.380 A4
Voltaire, Blvd	p.400 C1
Voltaire, Quai	p.398 B2
Voltaire, Rue	p.403 F3
Vouillé, Rue de	p.407 D4
Wagram, Ave de	p.381 D4
Winston Churchill, Ave	p.397 F1

N

380-381

LEVALLOIS-PERRET

BOULEVARD PERIPHÉRIQUE

382-383

BATIGNOLLES

MONTMARTRE

La Seine

A14

386-387

ÉTOILE

CHAMPS
ÉLYSÉES

388-389

MONCEAU

PIGALLE

ST LAZARE

OPÉRA

GRANDS
BOULEVARDS

BOIS DE
BOULOGNE

394-395

396-397

TROCADÉRO

La Seine

EIFFEL
TOWER

LES
INVALIDES

398-399

PLACE DE
LA CONCORDE

ST-GERMAIN
DES PRÉS

AUTUEIL   PASSY

CHAMP DE
MARS

BEAUGRENELLE

404-405

La Seine

406-407

408-409

MONTPARNASSE

PORT ROYAL

E05 BOULEVARD PERIPHERIQUE

414-415

ISSY-
LES-MOULINEAUX

ÎLE
ST-GERMAIN

416-417

E05

BOULEVARD PERIPHÉRIQUE

418-419

VANVES

MALAKOFF

MONTROUGE

E05

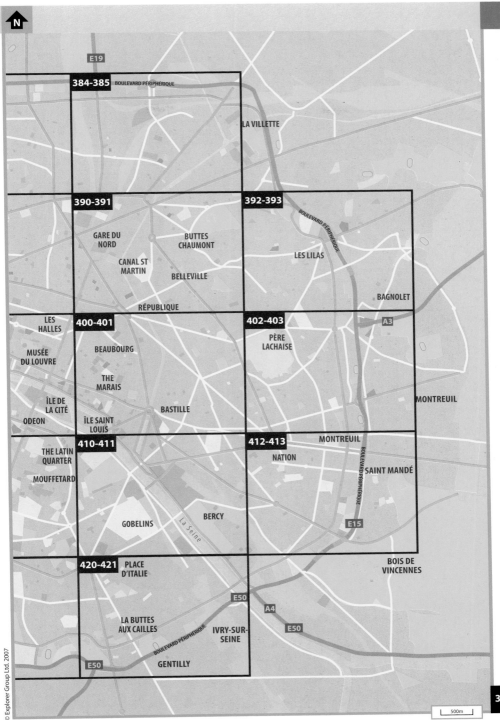

E19

384-385 BOULEVARD PÉRIPHÉRIQUE

LA VILLETTE

390-391

GARE DU
NORD

BUTTES
CHAUMONT

CANAL ST
MARTIN

BELLEVILLE

RÉPUBLIQUE

392-393

BOULEVARD PÉRIPHÉRIQUE

LES LILAS

BAGNOLET

LES
HALLES

400-401

BEAUBOURG

MUSÉE
DU LOUVRE

THE
MARAIS

ÎLE DE
LA CITÉ

BASTILLE

ODEON

ÎLE SAINT
LOUIS

402-403

PÈRE
LACHAISE

A3

MONTREUIL

410-411

THE LATIN
QUARTER

MOUFFETARD

GOBELINS

BERCY

La Seine

412-413

NATION

MONTREUIL

BOULEVARD PÉRIPHÉRIQUE

SAINT MANDÉ

E15

420-421

PLACE
D'ITALIE

BOIS DE
VINCENNES

LA BUTTES
AUX CAILLES

E50

IVRY-SUR-
SEINE

A4

E50

BOULEVARD PÉRIPHÉRIQUE

E50

GENTILLY

500m

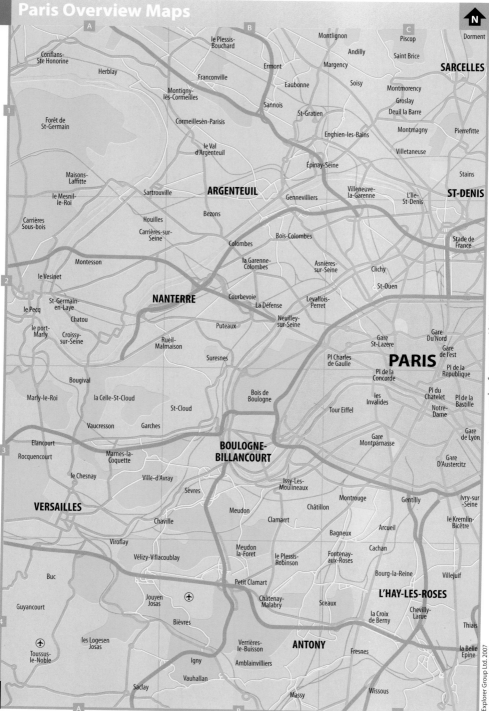

le Plessis-Bouchard

Montlignon

Piscop

Dorment

Conflans-Ste Honorine

Andilly

Saint Brice

Herblay

Ermont

Margency

SARCELLES

Franconville

Eaubonne

Soisy

Montmorency

Montigny-lès-Cormeilles

Sannois

St-Gratien

Groslay

Deuil la Barre

Forêt de St-Germain

Cormeillesen-Parisis

Enghien-les-Bains

Montmagny

Pierrefitte

le Val d'Argenteuil

Épinay-Seine

Villetaneuse

Maisons-Laffitte

Stains

le Mesnil-le-Roi

Sartrouville

ARGENTEUIL

Gennevilliers

Villeneuve-la-Garenne

L'Ile-St-Denis

ST-DENIS

Carrières Sous-bois

Houilles

Bezons

Bois-Colombes

Stade de France

Montesson

Carrières-sur-Seine

Colombes

la Garenne-Colombes

Asnières-sur-Seine

Clichy

le Vesinet

St-Germain-en-Laye

Courbevoie

Levallois-Perret

St-Ouen

le Pecq

Chatou

La Défense

Neuilly-sur-Seine

Gare St-Lazare

Gare Du'Nord

le port-Marly

Croissy-sur-Seine

Puteaux

NANTERRE

Rueil-Malmaison

Gare de l'est

Suresnes

Pl Charles de Gaulle

PARIS

Pl de la Republique

Bougival

Bois de Boulogne

Pl de la Concorde

les Invalides

Pl du Chatelet

Pl de la Bastille

Marly-le-Roi

la Celle-St-Cloud

St-Cloud

Tour Eiffel

Notre-Dame

Vaucresson

Garches

BOULOGNE-BILLANCOURT

Gare Montparnasse

Gare de Lyon

Elancourt

Marnes-la-Coquette

Gare D'Austercitz

Rocquencourt

Ville-d'Avray

Issy-Les-Moulineaux

le Chesnay

Sèvres

Montrouge

Gentilly

Ivry-sur-Seine

VERSAILLES

Chaville

Meudon

Châtillon

Clamarrt

Arcueil

le Kremlin-Bicêtre

Viroflay

Bagneux

Cachan

Vélizy-Villacoublay

Meudon la-Foret

le Plessis-Robinson

Fontenay-aux-Roses

Bourg-la-Reine

Villejuif

Buc

Petit Clamart

L'HAY-LES-ROSES

Jouyen Josas

Châtenay-Malabry

Sceaux

la Croix de Berny

Chevilly-Larue

Guyancourt

Bièvres

Thiais

les Logesen Josas

Verrières-le-Buisson

ANTONY

Fresnes

la Belle Epine

Toussus-le-Noble

Igny

Amblainvilliers

Saclay

Vauhallan

Massy

Wissous

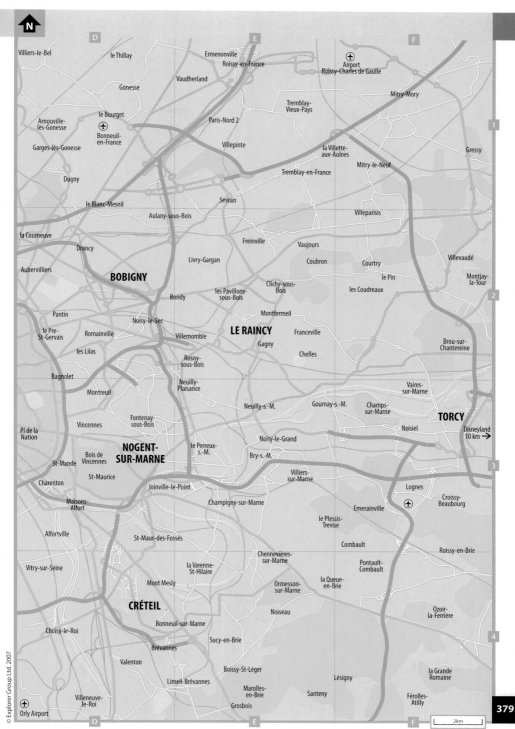

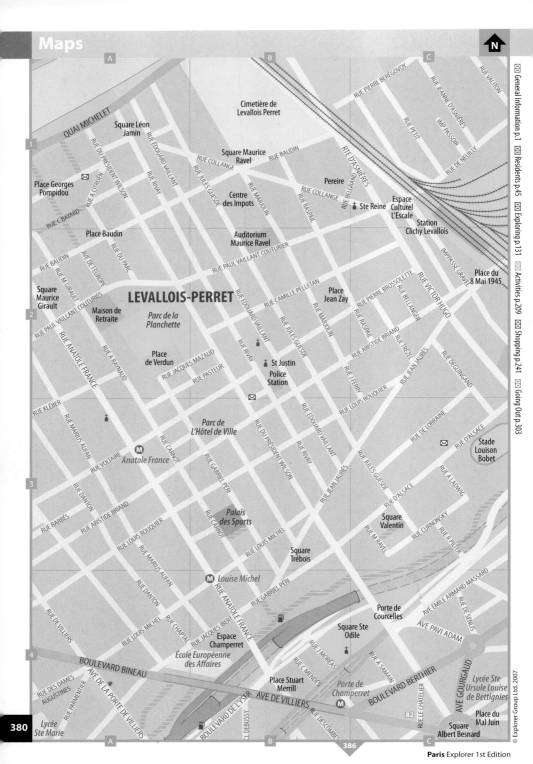

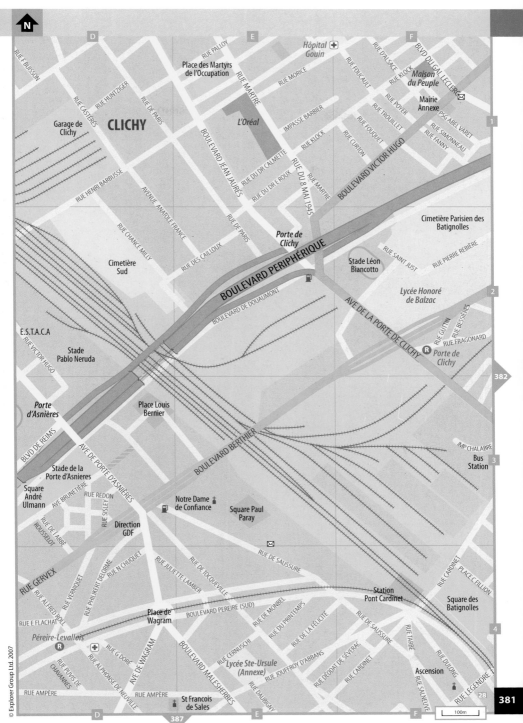

RUE F BUISSON
RUE HUNTZIGER
RUE CASTERÈS
RUE DE PARIS
RUE PALLOY
RUE MARTRE
Place des Martyrs
de l'Occupation
RUE MORICE
Hôpital
Gouin
RUE FOUCAULT
RUE D'ALSACE
RUE KLOCK
BLVD DUGAL LECLERC
Maison
du Peuple
Garage de
Clichy
CLICHY
L'Oréal
RUE DU DR CALMETTE
BOULEVARD JEAN JAURÈS
IMPASSE BARBIER
RUE POYER
RUE TROUILLET
Mairie
Annexe
PSG ABEL VARET
RUE SIMONNEAU
RUE FANNY
RUE HENRI BARBUSSE
RUE DU DR E ROUX
RUE KLOCK
RUE CURTON
RUE FOUQUET
BOULEVARD VICTOR HUGO
RUE SIMONNEAU
AVENUE ANATOLE FRANCE
RUE CHANCE MILLY
RUE DE PARIS
RUE DES CAILLOUX
RUE DU 8 MAI 1945
RUE MARTRE
Porte de
Clichy
Cimetière Parisien des
Batignolles
Cimetière
Sud
BOULEVARD PERIPHÉRIQUE
RUE SAINT JUST
RUE PIERRE REBIÈRE
Stade Léon
Biancotto
E.S.T.A.C.A
RUE VICTOR HUGO
BOULEVARD DE DOUAUMONT
Stade
Pablo Neruda
AVE DE LA PORTE DE CLICHY
Lycée Honoré
de Balzac
RUE GUTTIN
RUE BESSIÈRES
RUE FRAGONARD
R Porte de
Clichy
382
*Porte
d'Asnières*
Place Louis
Bernier
BLVD DE REIMS
AVE DE PORTE D'ASNIÈRES
BOULEVARD BERTHIER
IMP CHALABRE
Bus
Station
Stade de la
Porte d'Asnières
Square
André
Ulmann
AVE BRUNETIÈRE
RUE REDON
RUE SISLEY
Notre Dame
de Confiance
Square Paul
Paray
RUE DE L'ABBÉ ROUSSELOT
Direction
GDF
RUE DE SAUSSURE
RUE GERVEX
RUE ALFRED ROLL
RUE VERNIQUET
RUE PHILIBERT DELORME
RUE N CHUQUET
RUE JULIETTE LAMBER
RUE DE TOCQUEVILLE
PLACE C FILLION
RUE CARDINET
Square des
Batignolles
Station
Pont Cardinet
RUE E FLACHAT
Place de
Wagram
BOULEVARD PEREIRE (SUD)
RUE DE MONBEL
RUE DU PRINTEMPS
RUE DE LA FÉLICITÉ
RUE DE SAUSSURE
RUE TARBÉ
Péreire-Levallois
R
RUE G DORÉ
AVE DE WAGRAM
BOULEVARD MALESHERBES
RUE CERNUSCHI
RUE JOUFFROY D'ABBANS
RUE DÉODAT DE SÉVERAC
RUE CARDINET
RUE SAI NEUVE
RUE DULONG
RUE LEGENDRE
Ascension
RUE PUVIS DE CHAVANNES
RUE ALPHONSE DE NEUVILLE
RUE AMPÈRE
RUE AMPÈRE
RUE DAUBIGNY
*Lycée Ste-Ursule
(Annexe)*
St Francois
de Sales
28
381

N

SAINT-OUEN

PASSAGE LE COLSÉE
RUE LA FONTAINE
RUE MOREL
RUE ARAGO
RUE FRUCTIDOR
RUE TOULOUSE LAUTREC
Porte de St Ouen
RUE DU DR BABINSKY
RUE E VAILLANT

RUE FLORÉAL

Square Henri Huchard

1

Jardin Émile Borel

Stade Max Rousie

RUE ANDRÈ BRECHET

Hôpital Bichat-Claude-Bernard

RUE H BRISSON

Cimetière Parisien des Batignolles

RUE PIERRE REBIERE

RUE L LOUCHEUR

Porte Pouchet

École Nat de Commerce

BOULEVARD BESSIÈRES

BOULEVARD NEY

Villa St Ange

Porte de St-Ouen

BOULEVARD BESSIÈRES

Square Jean Leclaire

RUE JEAN LECLAIRE

AVE DE SAINT OUEN

RUE LEIBNIZ
RUE BELLIARD

2

RUE NAVIER

RUE ERNEST ROCHE

RUE BERZELIUS

RUE DE EPINETTES

RUE POUCHET

RUE LANTIEZ

RUE A BRIERE

RUE F GEMIER

RUE VAUVENARGUES

RUE GEORGETTE AGUTTE

Ste Geneviève de Grandes Carrières

RUE BARON

Square des Épinettes

RUE LAGILLE

RUE M DERAISMES

Square Boulay Level

RUE DE LA JONQUIERE

St Joseph des Epinettes

RUE P BODIN

RUE BOULAY

RUE A COLLETTE

RUE J CARTIER

RUE CHAMPIONNET

Centre de Rééducation Fonctionnelle

381

RUE EMILE LEVEL
RUE BERZELIUS
RUE POUCHET

RUE GAUTHEY
RUE SAUFFROY
RUE DES MOINES

RUE LACAILLE

Guy Môquet

RUE VAUVENARGUES

BATIGNOLLES

RUE MARCADET

Square Carpeaux

Clinique Marcadet

RUE CARDINET

RUE DES APENNINS

RUE DAVY

RUE LEGENDRE

AVE DE SAINT OUEN

RUE D'OSLO
RUE COYSEVOX
RUE JOSEPH

RUE CARPEAUX

3

Brochant

AVE DE CLICHY

RUE LACROIX

RUE DU DR HEULIN

RUE LAMARCK

RUE ETEX

VETEX

Place Nattier

RUE EUGÈNE
RUE F ZIEM
RUE DAMRÉMONT

Marché des Batignolles

RUE LECOMTE

RUE DES MOINES

RUE LEGENDRE

RUE DAUTANCOURT

Lycée St Michel

RUE LAMARCK

Hôpital Bretonneau

RUE STEINLEN

RUE CAULAINCOURT

Clinique Nollet

St Michel des Batignolles

Descente du St Esprit

RUE FAUVET

RUE DE LA BARRIÈRE BLANCHE

Clinique Dautancourt

RUE NOLLET

RUE CLAIRAUT

RUE LEGENDRE
RUE LECOMTE
RUE JACQUEMONT

La Fourche

RUE ETIENNE JODELLE

Cimetière de Montmartre

RUE DE MAISTRE

RUE TOURLAQUE

4

Place du Dr Felix Lobligeois

RUE TRUFFAUT

RUE LAMANDE

RUE BRIDAINE

RUE LEGENDRE

RUE NOLLET

Jardin Ernest Charisson

RUE HÉLÈNE

RUE LEMERCIER

RUE P GINIER

Lycée Technologique Auguste Renoir

RUE CAVALLOTTI

Terrass Hôtel

RUE DURANTIN

RUE LEPIC

RUE J DE MAISTRE

Ste Marie des Batignolles

RUE BOURSAULT

RUE TRUFFAUT

Mairie

RUE DE BIZERTE

RUE DES DAMES

AVE DE CLICHY

La Condamine

AVE RACHEL

AVE CAULAINCOURT

RUE FOREST

RUE LEPIC

General Information p.1 | Residents p.45 | Exploring p.131 | Activities p.209 | Shopping p.241 | Going Out p.303

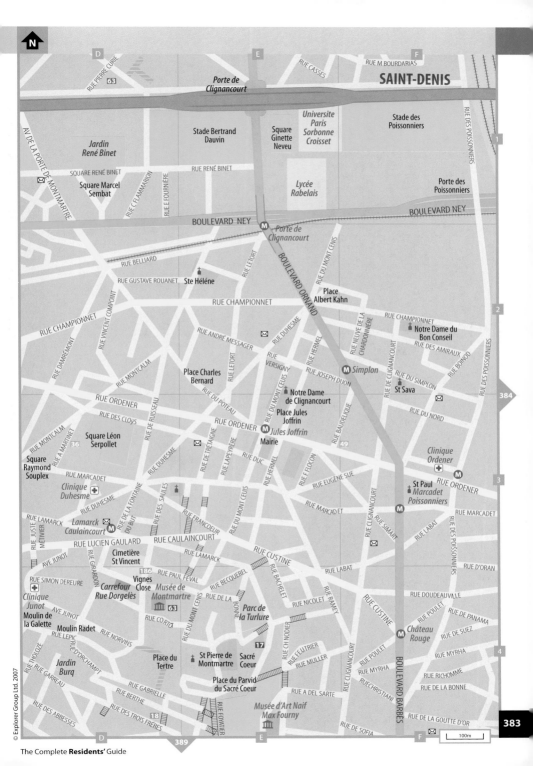

SAINT-DENIS

© Explorer Group Ltd. 2007

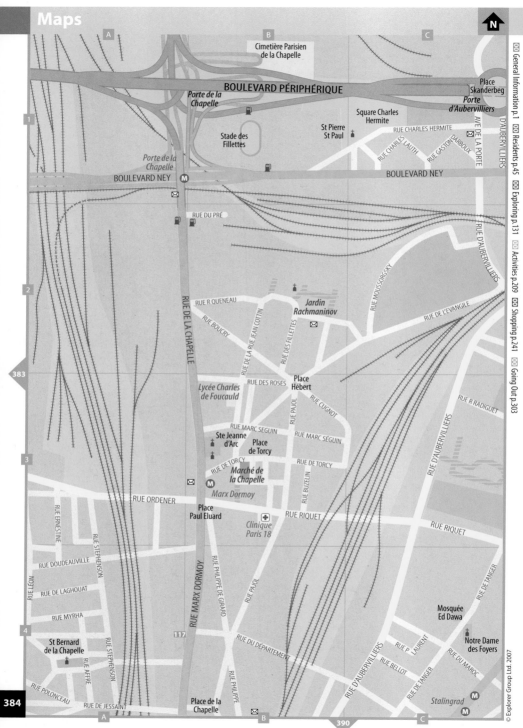

A   B   C

Cimetière Parisien
de la Chapelle

BOULEVARD PÉRIPHÉRIQUE

Porte de la
Chapelle

Place
Skanderbeg

*Porte
d'Aubervilliers*

Square Charles
Hermite

1

St Pierre
St Paul

RUE CHARLES HERMITE

RUE CHARLES LAUTH

RUE GASTON DARBOUX

AVE DE LA PORTE

D'AUBERVILLIERS

*Porte de la
Chapelle*

Stade des
Fillettes

BOULEVARD NEY

BOULEVARD NEY

M

RUE DU PRÉ

RUE D'AUBERVILLIERS

2

RUE R QUENEAU

RUE BOUCRY

RUE DE LA RUE JEAN COTTIN

RUE DES FILLETTES

*Jardin
Rachmaninov*

RUE MOUSSORGSKY

RUE DE L'EVANGILE

383

*Lycée Charles
de Foucauld*

RUE DES ROSES

Place
Hébert

RUE PAJOL

RUE CUGNOT

RUE R RADIGUET

RUE MARC SEGUIN

RUE MARC SÉGUIN

Ste Jeanne
d'Arc

Place
de Torcy

RUE DE TORCY

RUE DE TORCY

RUE D'AUBERVILLIERS

3

*Marché de
la Chapelle*

RUE BUZELIN

M

Marx Dormoy

RUE ORDENER

Place
Paul Eluard

RUE RIQUET

RUE RIQUET

RUE ERNESTINE

RUE STEPHENSON

*Clinique
Paris 18*

RUE DOUDEAUVILLE

RUE LÉON

RUE DE LAGHOUAT

RUE MYRHA

RUE MARX DORMOY

RUE PHILIPPE DE GIRARD

RUE PAJOL

Mosquée
Ed Dawa

RUE DE TANGER

4

St Bernard
de la Chapelle

RUE STEPHENSON

RUE AFFRE

117

RUE DU DÉPARTEMENT

RUE D'AUBERVILLIERS

RUE BELLOT

RUE P. LAURENT

RUE DE TANGER

Notre Dame
des Foyers

RUE DU MAROC

RUE POLONCEAU

RUE DE JESSAINT

Place de la
Chapelle

RUE PHILIPPE

Stalingrad

M

M

A   B   C

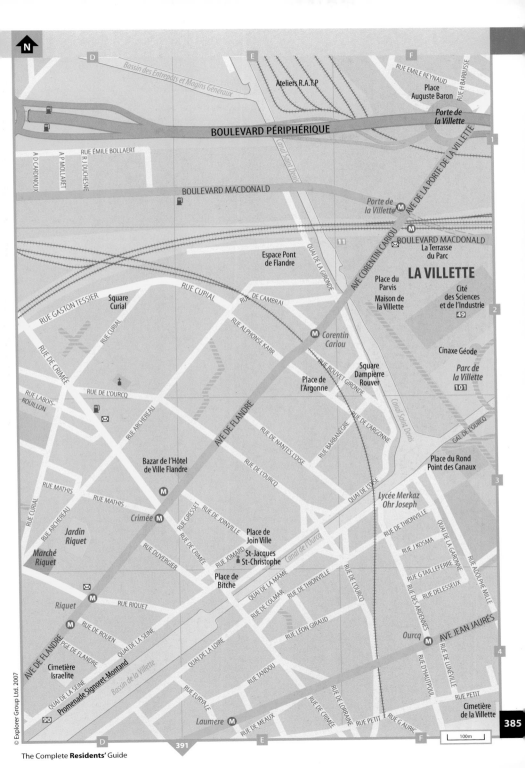

© Explorer Group Ltd. 2007

N

General Information p.1 Residents p.45 Exploring p.131 Activities p.209 Shopping p.241 Going Out p.303

A B C

RUE CINO DEL DUCA

RUE A CHARPENTIER

RUE GALVANI

RUE VERNIER

RUE LAUGIER

RUE GUILLAUME

RUE D'HÉLIOPOLIS

Péreire

Stade Paul Faber

BOULEVARD DE DIXMUDE

RUE DU DOBROPOL

BOULEVARD GOUVION ST CYR

RUE E ALLEZ

RUE ROGER BACON

RUE JB DUMAS

Porte de Villiers

RUE R U

Square Bayen

BOULEVARD PEREIRE NORD

BOULEVARD PEREIRE (SUD)

RUE FARADAY

AVE NIEL

RUE TH DE BANVILLE

RUE PIERRE DEMOURS

Square M Long Notre Dame de la Compassion

RUE GUERSANT

RUE DE ST SENOCH

RUE DES RENNEQUIN

Marche des Ternes

RUE LEBON

RUE TORRICELLI

RUE PIERRE DEMOURS

RUE FOURCROY

Porte des Ternes

RUE BAYEN

RUE LAUGIER

Bus Station

10

Palais des Congrès de Paris

BOULEVARD PEREIRE (SUD)

AVE DES TERNES

RUE NIEL

RUE SAUSSIER LEROY

RUE PONCELET

RUE LABIE

AVE MACMAHON

34

Porte Maillot

RUE SAINT FERDINAND

Hôpital Marmottan

AVE DE MONTENOTTE

St Germaine

Ternes

Place des Ternes

Place de la Porte Maillot

Neuilly Porte Maillot Palais des Congrès

RUE DU DÉBARCADÈRE

Place St Ferdinand

RUE DU COLONEL MOLL

RUE D'ARMAILLE

RUE DE L'ARC DE TRIOMPHE

RUE DE L'ETOILE

Porte Maillot

AVE DE LA GRANDE ARMÉE

Étoile

RUE DENIS POISSON

RUE BRUNEL

RUE DES ACACIAS

RUE DE TROYON

Hôtel Arc de Triomphe Etoite

RUE BREY

AVE DE WAGRAM

St Joseph

Square Alexandre et René Parodi

RUE WEBER

RUE PERGOLESE

AVE DE MALAKOFF

RUE PERGOLESE

RUE DURET

RUE ALP HAND

Clinique Alphand Pergolese

RUE LE SUEUR

Place Y et C Morandt

Argentine

AVE DE LA GRANDE ARMÉE

RUE ANATOLE DE LA FORGE

RUE DE SAIGON

RUE RUDE

Charles de Gaulle Etoile

RUE CARNOT

ÉTOILE

RUE DE TILSITT

Charles de Gaulle Etoile

RUE L PICHAT

RUE PICCINI

AVE FOCH

Arc de Triomphe

29

RUE A HOUSSAYE

AVE FOCH

AVE FOCH

AVE FOCH

Place Charles de Gaulle

AVE FOCH

V D'EYLAU

AVE VICTOR HUGO

RUE DE PRESBOURG

AVE D'IÉNA

RUE VERNET

Musée Arménien Musée d'Ennery

RUE DE VINCI

RUE LEROUX

Musée Dapper

Clinique Victor Hugo

Kleber

AVE DES PORTUGAIS

RUE MARCEAU

RUE GALILÉE

RUE PICOT

RUE DE SFAX

AVE RAYMOND POINCARE

RUE GEORGES VILLE

RUE PAUL VALERY

Centre de Conférences Internationales

RUE NEWTON

RUE EULER

RUE DE LA POMPE

AVE BUGEAUD

RUE DE SONTAY

Victor Hugo

Centre de Reservoirs de Passy

RUE LAURISTON

RUE LA PEROUSE

RUE DUMONT D'URVILLE

RUE A VACQUERIE

Place de l'Uruguay

St Georgès

RUE KEPLER

St Honoré d'Eylau

Place Victor Hugo

RUE COPERNIC

RUE DE BELLOY

RUE GALILÉE

RUE JEAN GIRAUDOUX

90

AVE VICTOR HUGO

RUE MESNIL

RUE BOISSIERE

Hôtel Victor Hugo

AVE KLEBER

RUE DE BELLOY

33

RUE DE BASSANO

RUE MESNIL

Ste Therése

RUE LAURISTON

RUE CIMAROSA

20

51

Square Thomas Jefferson

Clinique Bizet

St Pierre de Chaillot

Marché St Didier

Musée Baccarat

Place Amiral de Grasse

A B C

© Explorer Group Ltd 2007

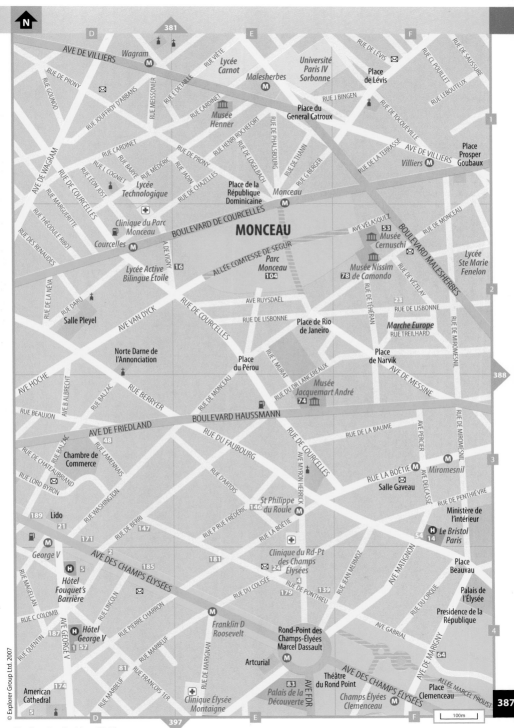

A   B   C

Lycée Jules Ferry   151
RUE DES BATIGNOLLES
RUE DE LA CONDAMINE
RUE DU LONG
RUE BOURSAULT
RUE BEUDANT
RUE DE ROME
Grande Loge
Institut Universitaire de Formation des Maîtres
RUE DARCET
RUE DE MI
DORE
RUE BIOT
RUE LÉCLUSE
L'Européen
Clinique Vintimille   Place Blanche   160
BOULEVARD DE CLICHY
Musée de l'Erotisme   58
Place de Clichy   Place Adolphe Max   Blanche
RUE DE BRUXELLES
RUE FONTAINE

BOULEVARD DES BATIGNOLLES   26
Rome
RUE DE FLORENCE
RUE DE ST PETERSBOURG
Place Lili Boulanger
RUE DE VINTIMILLE
RUE DE CALAIS
RUE BALLU
RUE MANSART
RUE DE DOUAI
RUE BLANCHE
Musée de la Vie Romantique   62
RUE CHAPTAL

1

RUE DU ROCHER
Lycée Chaptal
RUE ANDRIEUX
RUE BERNOULLI
RUE LARRIBE
RUE DE MOSCOU
RUE DE BERNE
St André de l'Europe
Place de Dublin
RUE DE PARME
Lycée St Louis
RUE HENNER
RUE DE NAPLES
RUE DE CONSTANTINOPLE
RUE D'EDIMBOURG
Clinique Turin
RUE DE TURIN
RUE DE MOSCOU
RUE DE BUCAREST
Fédération Protestante de France
RUE J LEFEBVRE
Liège
RUE DE LIÈGE
Deutsche Evangelische Christuskirche
RUE MONCEY
RUE JEAN BAPTISTE PIGALLE
RUE DE LA ROCHEFOUCAULD

Europe
Place de l'Europe
RUE DE MADRID
RUE D'AMSTERDAM
Clinique Milan
RUE DE MILAN
Musée Gustave Moreau   73

2

Mairie
RUE PORTALIS
RUE DE VIENNE
Place de Budapest
RUE D'ATHÈNES
RUE DE CLICHY
RUE DE LONDRES
Ste Trinité
Place d'Estienne d'Orves
Trinité d'Estienne d'Orves
RUE BLANCHE

RUE DE LA BIENFAISANCE
Gare St Lazare
ST LAZARE
RUE DE ROME
RUE DE BUDAPEST

387

St Augustin   18
PL H BERGSON
RUE DE LABORDE
St Lazare
Place G Péri
RUE ST LAZARE
Haussmann St Lazare
RUE DE MOGADOR
RUE DE LA CHAUSSÉE D'ANTIN

RUE DE RIGNY
Place St Augustin
RUE DE LA PÉPINIÈRE
St Augustin
RUE PASQUIER
Lycée Condorcet   41
RUE DE CAUMARTIN
RUE JOUBERT
RUE DE PROVENCE
RUE DE PROVENCE

17
RUE LA BOÉTIE
RUE D'ASTORG
BOULEVARD MALESHERBES
RUE LAVOISIER
31   24   BOULEVARD HAUSSMANN   32   Printemps
Galeries Lafayette
Chaussée d'Antin
Place Adrien Oudin

3

St Esprit
RUE ROQUÉPINE
RUE TRONSON DU COUDRAY
RUE D'ANJOU
Havre Caumartin
RUE DES MATHURINS
RUE AUBER
Auber   109
Place Jacques Rouché
RUE HALÉVY

RUE CAMBACÉRÈS
RUE DE LA VILLE L'EVÊQUE
RUE PASQUIER
RUE DE CASTELLANE
RUE TRONCHET
Office du Tourisme
Opéra Garnier   39
OPÉRA

St Michael's English Church
RUE DE DURAS
RUE D'AGUESSEAU
RUE DE SURÈNE
RUE VIGNON
RUE DE MAUROY
RUE GODOT DE MAUROY
RUE DE CAUMARTIN
Hôtel Scribe Paris   11
Opéra
Place de l'Opéra   51

4

RUE DU FAUBOURG ST HONORÉ
RUE DE SÉZE   12
Ste Marie Madeleine   7
Madeleine   15
BOULEVARD DE LA MADELEINE
Opéra   114
RUE DAUNAU
RUE VOLNEY
RUE DE LA PAIX
AVE DE L'OPÉRA
RUE LE PELETIER
RUE D'ANTIN   22
RUE DE LA MICHODIÈRE

AVE GABRIEL
RUE BOISSY D'ANGLAS
RUE ROYALE
RUE DUPHOT
RUE DU ST FLORENTIN
Hôtel Crillon   2
Musée des Lunettes et Lorgnettes
Galerie des Trois Quartiers
RUE CAMBON
Crédit Foncier de France   155
Ministère de la Justice   111
Place Vendôme
RUE DES CAPUCINES
Michelin   21
RUE DANIELLE CASANOVA   16
RUE GAILLON

A   B   C

398

388

© Explorer Group Ltd 2007

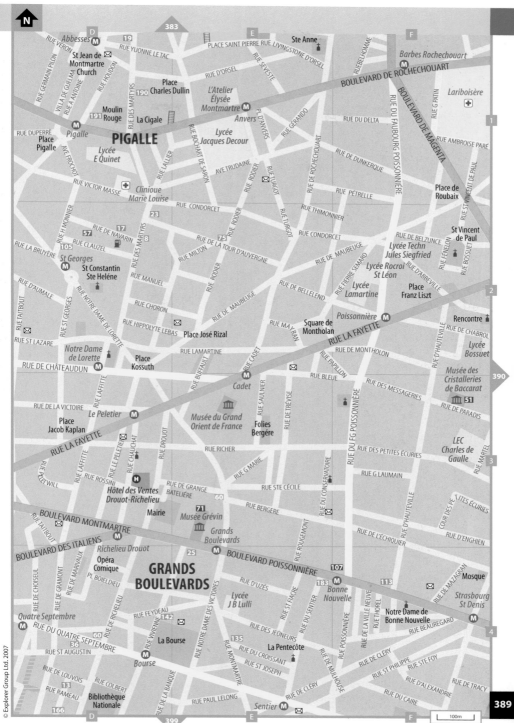

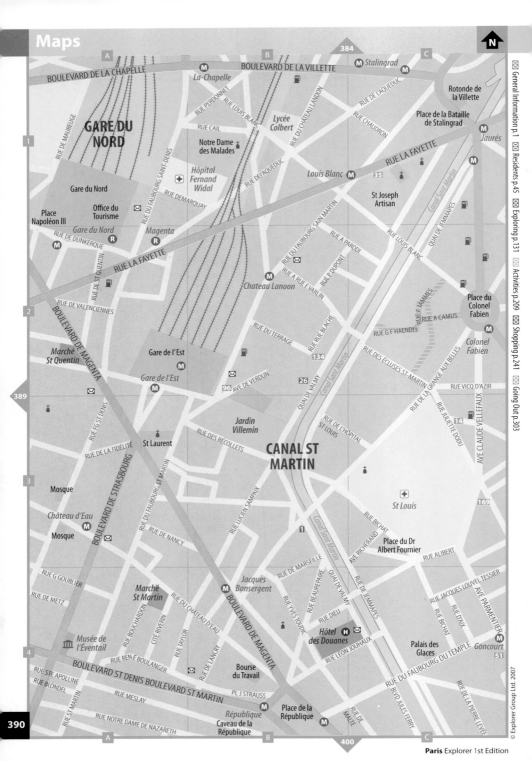

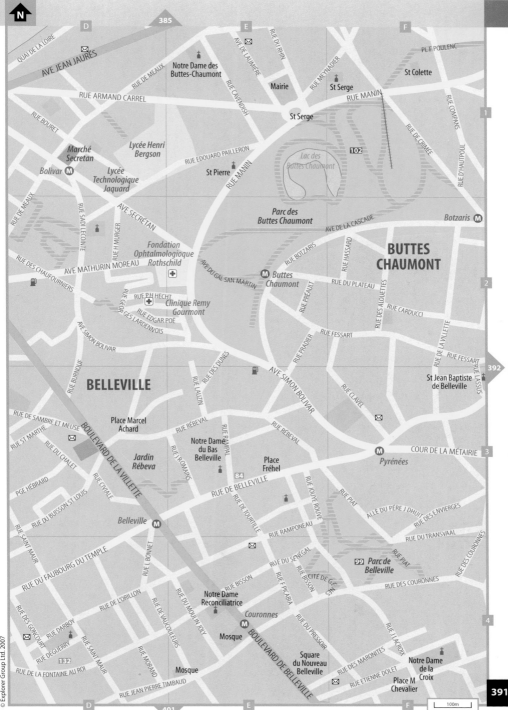

100m

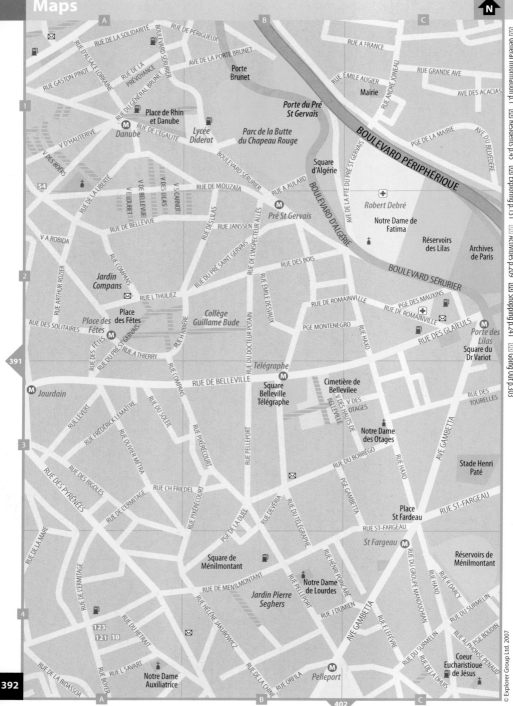

Porte Brunet

Porte du Pré St Gervais

Mairie

RUE A FRANCE

RUE ÉMILE AUGIER

RUE GRANDE AVE

AVE DES ACACIAS

AVE ANDRÉ JOINEAU

BOULEVARD PÉRIPHÉRIQUE

PGE DE LA MAIRIE

AVE DU BELVÉDÈRE

Place de Rhin et Danube

Danube

Lycée Diderot

RUE DE L'EGALITE

Parc de la Butte du Chapeau Rouge

Square d'Algérie

Robert Debré

Notre Dame de Fatima

Réservoirs des Lilas

Archives de Paris

RUE DE LA SOLIDARITE

RUE GASTON PINOT

RUE D'ALSACE LORRAINE

BOULEVARD SÉRURIER

RUE DE LA PRÉVOYANCE

AVE DE LA PORTE BRUNET

RUE DU GÉNÉRAL BRUNET

RUE DE PÉRIGUEUX

V D'HAUTERIVE

V DES BOERS

RUE DE LA LIBERTÉ

BOULEVARD SÉRURIER

RUE DE MOUZAÏA

RUE A AULARD

AVE DE LA PTE DU PRÉ ST GERVAIS

BOULEVARD D'ALGÉRIE

Pré St Gervais

RUE DES LILAS

RUE JANSSEN

RUE DE BELLEVUE

V DE BELLEVUE

V DES LILAS

V SCARNOT

V ELOUBET

V A ROBIDA

RUE ARTHUR ROZIER

RUE COMPANS

Jardin Compans

RUE L THULIEZ

Place des Fêtes

Place des Fêtes

RUE DES SOLITAIRES

Collège Guillame Bude

RUE DU PRÉ SAINT GERVAIS

RUE DE L'INSPECTEUR ALLES

RUE DES BOIS

RUE ÉMILE DESVAUX

RUE DU DOCTEUR POTAIN

RUE H RIBIÈRE

RUE DES FÊTES

RUE DU PRÉ ST GERVAIS

RUE A THIERRY

RUE DE ROMAINVILLE

RUE DE ROMAINVILLE

PGE DES MAUXINS

PGE MONTENEGRO

RUE HAXO

BOULEVARD SÉRURIER

Porte des Lilas

Square du Dr Variot

RUE DES GLAÏEULS

Jourdain

RUE COMPANS

RUE DE BELLEVILLE

Télégraphe

Square Belleville Télégraphe

Cimetière de Belleville

Notre Dame des Otages

V DES HAUTS DE BELLEVILLE

V DES OTAGES

Stade Henri Paté

RUE DES TOURELLES

AVE GAMBETTA

RUE LEVERT

RUE FRIÉDERICK LEMAITRE

RUE DU SOLEIL

RUE OLIVIER METRA

RUE PIXÉRÉCOURT

RUE PELLEPORT

RUE DU BORRÉGO

RUE HAXO

PGE GAMBETTA

PGE DU TÉLÉGRAPHE

Place St Fardeau

RUE ST-FARGEAU

RUE DES RIGOLES

RUE DES PYRÉNÉES

RUE CH FRIEDEL

RUE DE L'ERMITAGE

PGE DE LA DUÉE

RUE DEVÉRIA

RUE ST-FARGEAU

St Fargeau

Réservoirs de Ménilmontant

RUE DE LA MARE

Square de Ménilmontant

Jardin Pierre Seghers

Notre Dame de Lourdes

RUE HENRI POINCARÉ

AVE GAMBETTA

RUE J DUMIEN

RUE E LEFÈVRE

RUE DU GROUPE MANOUCHIAN

RUE HAXO

RUE R DARCY

PGE BOUDIN

RUE DU SURMELIN

RUE DE MÉNILMONTANT

RUE HÉLÈNE JAKUBOWICZ

RUE PELLEPORT

RUE DE L'ERMITAGE

RUE DU RETRAIT

RUE DE LA BIDASSOA

RUE BOYER

RUE L SAVART

Notre Dame Auxiliatrice

RUE DE LA CHINE

RUE ORFILA

Pelleport

RUE DU SURMELIN

RUE ALPHONSE PENAUD

Coeur Eucharistioue de Jésus

RUE DE LA DHUIS

123 121 10

402

© Explorer Group Ltd. 2007

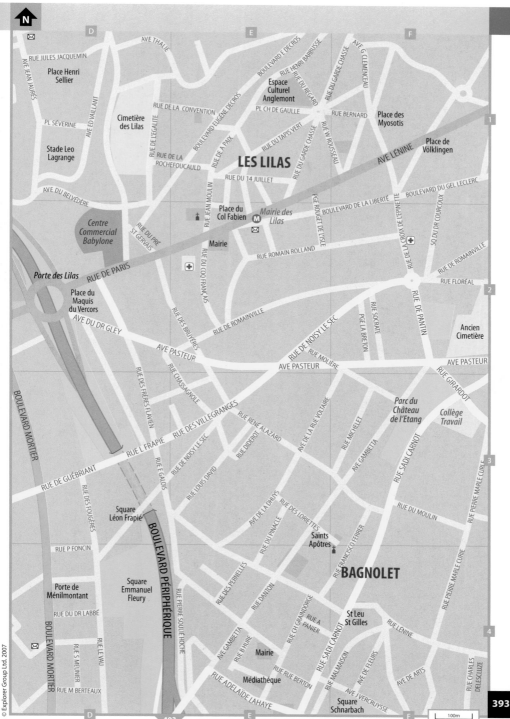

N

General Information p.1

Residents p.45

Exploring p.131

Activities p.209

Shopping p.241

Going Out p.303

ALLÉE DE LONGCHAMP

ROUTE DE SURESNES

ROUTE DE SURESNES

ROUTE DU PRÉ CATELAN

ALLÉE DE LA REINE MARGUERITE

ROUTE DE SURESNES

ROUTE DE SURESNES

Pré Catelan

Racing Club de France

Châlet des îles

CHEMIN DE CEINTURE DU LAC INFÉRIEUR

43

LE PRÉ CATELAN

Châlet du Pré Catelan

Lac Inférieur

CHEMIN DE CEINTURE DU LAC INFÉRIEUR

ROUTE DE LA GRANDE CASCADE

ALLÉE CAVALIÈRE SAINT DENIS

93

BOIS DE BOULOGNE

ALLÉE CAVALIÈRE SAINT DENIS

ROUTE DE LA VIERGE AUX BERCEAUX

Garde Républicaine à Cheval

Carrefour des Cascades

Porte de Passy

AVE DE L'HIPPODROME

ALLÉE SAINT-DENIS

Lac Supérieur

Pelouse de St Cloud

ROUTE D'AUTEUIL AUX LACS

Square Henry Bataille

Stade Suchet

Hippodrome d'Auteuil

AVE DE SAINT-CLOUD

Butte Mortemart

16

Practice de Golf

ALLÉE DES FORTIFICATIONS

AVE DE MONTMORENCY

AVE DES SYCOMORES

Paris Explorer 1st Edition

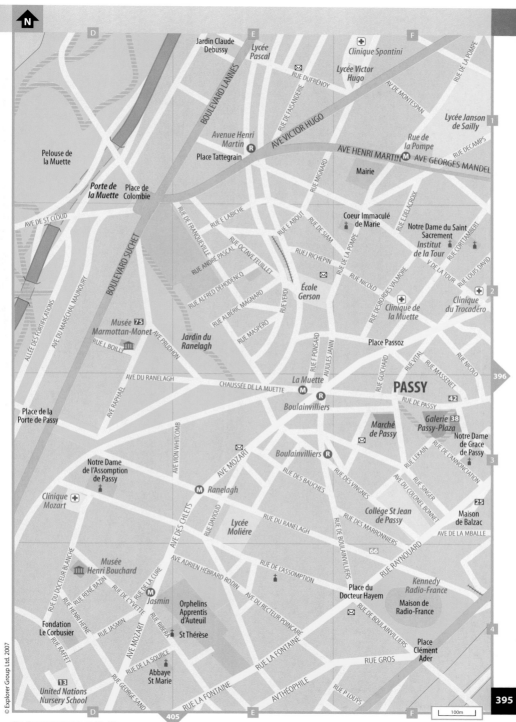

A

B

386

C

RUE DES BELLES FEUILLES

RUE SAINT DIDIER

RUE LAURISTON

RUE LÉO DELIBES

M Boissière

RUE BOISSIÈRE

RUE DE L'AMIRAL HAMELIN

Lycée Assomption

Place Rochambeau

RUE G. BIZET

St Étienne

AVE RAYMOND POINCARE

RUE KLEBER

RUE DE LUBECK

AVE PIERRE 1ER DE SERBIE

RUE FREYCINET

RUE PIERRE 1ER DE SERBIE

Place de Mexico

RUE DES SABLONS

AVE D'EYLAU

RUE GREUZE

RUE DE MAGDEBOURG

RUE DE LONGCHAMP

Musée Guimet

🏛 72

Iena

Palais Galliera

Place de Tokyo

M Place d'Iéna

RUE GASTON DE ST PAUL

Musée d'Art Moderne

57 🏛

Palais de Tokyo

AVE DU PRÉSIDENT WILSON

AVE GEORGES MANDEL

ALLÉE MARIA CALLAS

TROCADÉRO

M Trocadéro

Gonseil Économique et Social

173

AVE ALBERT DE MUN

118

RUE FRESNEL

Port Debilly

Cimetière de Passy

Place du Trocadéro et du 11 Novembre

M

Musée de l'Homme Chaillot

Jardin du Trocadéro

Port de la Bourdonnais

RUE SCHEFFER

Place José Marti

Palais de Chaillot

AVE G V DE SUEDE

AVE DE NEW YORK

RUE BENJAMIN FRANKLIN

🏛 60

Musée de la Marine

AVE ALBERT 1ER DE MONACO

Jardin Trocadéro

Place de Varsovie

27

QUAI BRANLY

56 🏛

69

Musée du Quai Branly

AVE PAUL DOUMER

Musée Clemenceau

RUE VINEUSE

RUE DE LA TOUR

65

École St Loui de Gonzague

RUE LE NÔTRE

RUE HARDIN

17

PONT D'IÉNA

3

RUE DE L'UNIVERSITÉ

AVE DE LA BOURDONNAIS

Place de Costa Rica

395

RUE DE PASSY

RUE RAYNOUARD

Musée du Vin M Passy

RUE CHERNOVIZ

Eiffel Tower

32

AVE GUSTAVE EIFFEL

AVE ELISÉE RECLUS

24

La Seine

Champ de Mars Tour Eiffel

R

Parc du Champ de Mars

3

AVE MARCEL PROUST

AVE RENÉ BOYLESVE

AVE DU PRÉSIDENT KENNEDY

PONT DE BIR HAKEIM

Stade Emile Anthoine

Place Jacques Rueff

RUE D'ANKARA

Place de Bolivie

Port Autonome de Paris

ALLÉE DES CYGNES

RUE JEAN REY

Place de Kyoto

AVE DE SUFFREN

AVE JOSEPH BOUVARD

AVE CHARLES FLOQUET

M Bir Hakeim

RUE NÉLATON

RUE SAINT SAËNS

Direction Journaux Officiels

RUE DE LA FEDERATION

AVE DE SUFFREN

RUE DE PRESLES

PORT DE GRENELLE

Square Bartók Bela

RUE DU DOCTEUR FINLAY

BLVD DE GRENELLE

RUE CLODION

RUE HUMBLÔT

Place Dupleix

QUAI DE GRENELLE

64

RUE DE FLERS

RUE EMERALD

RUE ST CHARLES

RUE VIALA

RUE B DUSSANE

RUE JUGE

Dupleix

M

RUE AUGUSTE BARTHOLDI

406

RUE ALASSEUR

A

B

C

© Explorer Group Ltd. 2007

Paris Explorer 1st Edition

General Information p.1   Residents p.45   Exploring p.131   Activities p.209   Shopping p.241   Going Out p.303

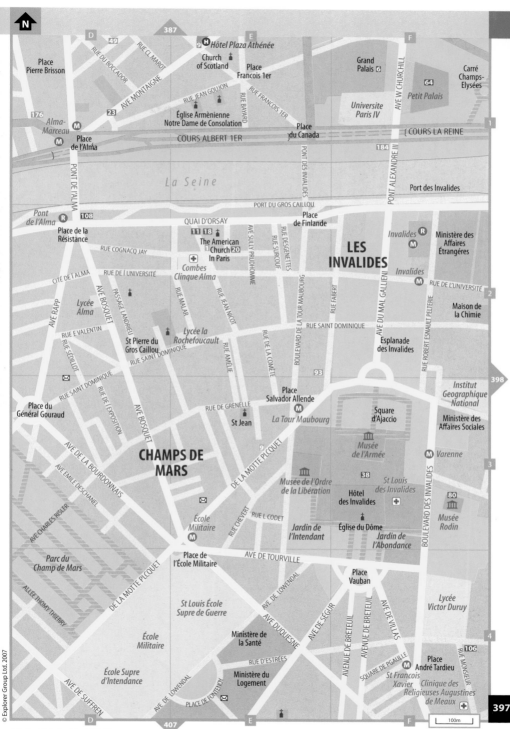

Place
Pierre Brisson

Church
of Scotland

H Hôtel Plaza Athénée

Place
Francois 1er

Grand
Palais G

Carré
Champs-
Elysées

RUE DU BOCCADOR

RUE CL MAROT

49

AVE MONTAIGNE

23

AVE W CHURCHILL

176

Alma-
Marceau

M

M
Place
de l'Alma

PONT DE L'ALMA

RUE JEAN GOUJON

RUE BAYARD

RUE FRANCOIS 1ER

Église Arménienne
Notre Dame de Consolation

Petit Palais

64

Universite
Paris IV

Place
du Canada

COURS ALBERT 1ER

PONT DES INVALIDES

COURS LA REINE

PONT ALEXANDRE III

184

La Seine

Port des Invalides

Pont
de l'Alma

R

108

QUAI D'ORSAY

PORT DU GROS CAILLOU

Place
de Finlande

Invalides

R

M

Ministère des
Affaires
Étrangéres

Place de la
Résistance

RUE COGNACQ JAY

11 18

The American
Church
In Paris

20

AVE SULLY PRUDHOMME

RUE DESGENETTES

RUE SURCOUF

**LES
INVALIDES**

Invalides

M

RUE DE L'UNIVERSITÉ

CITÉ DE L'ALMA

RUE DE l UNIVERSITÉ

Combes
Clinique Alma

BOULEVARD DE LA TOUR MAUBOURG

RUE FABERT

AVE DU MAL GALLIENI

RUE ROBERT ESNAULT PELTERIE

Maison de
la Chimie

Lycée
Alma

PASSAGE LANDRIEU

RUE MALAR

RUE JEAN NICOT

RUE SAINT DOMINIQUE

Esplanade
des Invalides

Institut
Geographique
National

398

AVE RAPP

AVE BOSQUET

RUE E VALENTIN

Lycée la
Rochefoucault

RUE AMELIE

RUE DE LA COMÈTE

St Pierre du
Gros Caillou

RUE SAINT DOMINIQUE

RUE SÉDILLOT

RUE SAINT DOMINIQUE

RUE DE l'EXPOSITION

Place
Salvador Allende

Square
d'Ajaccio

Ministère des
Affaires Sociales

Place du
Général Gouraud

AVE BOSQUET

RUE DE GRENELLE

St Jean

M

La Tour Maubourg

93

**CHAMPS DE
MARS**

AVE DE LA BOURDONNAIS

AVE EMILE DESCHANEL

DE LA MOTTE PICQUET

9

Musée
de l'Armée

Musée de l'Ordre
de la Libération

38

St Louis
des Invalides

M Varenne

BOULEVARD DES INVALIDES

80

Musée
Rodin

AVE CHARLES RISLER

École
Militaire

M

RUE CHEVERT

RUE L CODET

Hôtel
des Invalides

Église du Dôme

Jardin de
l'Intendant

Jardin de
l'Abondance

Parc du
Champ de Mars

Place de
l'École Militaire

AVE DE TOURVILLE

Place
Vauban

ALLEE THOMY THIERRY

DE LA MOTTE PICQUET

St Louis École
Supre de Guerre

AVE DE LOWENDAL

AVE DE SÉGUR

AVENUE DE BRETEUIL

AVENUE DE BRETEUIL

AVE DE VILLAS

Lycée
Victor Duruy

École
Militaire

Ministère de
la Santé

AVE DUQUESNE

SQUARE DE P GAULLE

RUE MONSIEUR

106

École Supre
d'Intendance

RUE D'ESTRÉES

AVE DE LOWENDAL

PLACE DE FONTENOY

Ministère du
Logement

Place
André Tardieu

M

St Francois
Xavier

Clinique des
Religieuses Augustines
de Meaux

AVE DE SUFFREN

100m

© Explorer Group Ltd. 2007

The Complete **Residents'** Guide

N

A   B   388   C

Espace
Pierre Cardin

Ⓜ Ⓗ Hôtel de
la Marine

Cour des
Comptes

Hôtel Ritz
39 Ⓗ 3 115
116 Ⓗ 52
10

PLACE DE
LA CONCORDE

Ⓜ Concorde

46

RUE DU MONTHABOR

Hôtel de
Vendôme

AVE DES CHAMPS ELYSEES

8

RUE ST HONORÉ

St HONORÉ
AVE DE L'OPÉRA
RUE ST ROCH
RUE DE LA SOURDIÈRE

Pyramides

Galerie Nationale
du Jeu de Paume

Hôtel
Meurice
8 91
2
Ⓗ

RUE DE RIVOLI

11

Ⓜ

RUE D'ALGER
RUE DES PYRAMIDES
RUE D'ARGENTEUIL

St Roch
♱
22

178

Place de la
Obélisque Concorde

Musée de
l'Orangerie

59

RUE DE RIVOLI

Ⓜ Tuileries

RUE DE L'ECHELLE

Port de la
Concorde

🏛

Jardin
des Tuileries

Musée de la
Mod du et Textile 🏛 55

Place
A Malraux

65

PONT DE LA CONCORDE

Musée des Arts Décoratifs
Musée de la Publicité

Assemblée
Nationale

Passerelle
Solférino

Port des
Tuileries

QUAI DES TUILERIES

Terrasse
des Tuileries

Palais
Bourbon

QUAI ANATOLE FRANCE

RUE A BRIAND

Assemblée
Nationale

La Seine

Jardin du
Carrousel

Place du
Carrousel

112

Ⓜ

Place du
Palais Bourbon

Palais de la
Légion d'Honneur

QUAI FRANÇOIS MITTERRAND

PONT ROYAL

Ministère de la Défense

RUE DE BOURGOGNE

RUE DE SOLFERINO

Musée d'Orsay 🏛

QUAI VOLTAIRE

Musée 56
d'Orsay

PONT DU CARROUSEL

QUAI MALAQUAIS

Institut des Langues et
Civilisations Orientales

École Nationale
Superière des
Beaux Arts

Place
Jacques Bainville

RUE DE BELLECHASSE

RUE DE LILLE

Solferino Ⓜ

397

Solférino

RUE DE MARTIGNAC
RUE CASIMIR PERIER

Solferino Ⓜ

RUE LAS CASES

RUE DE
VILLERSEXEL

RUE DE VERNEUIL

RUE DE BEAUNE

RUE DU BAC

L'Hôtel
Ⓗ
13

Basilique Ste
Clotilde

RUE DE L'UNIVERSITE

ST GERMAIN
DES PRÉS

Ⓜ

28

Lycée
Paul Claudel

BOULEVARD SAINT GERMAIN

Ministère de
L'Equipment
des Transports

RUE MONTALEMBERT

Don
Camilo

RUE JACOB

49

Ministère de
l'Agriculture ✉

RUE DE GRENELLE

♱

RUE P.L. COURIER

St Thomas
d'Aquin ♱

RUE DU PRE AUX CLERCS

✉

Université
Paris V

RUE ST BENOIT
RUE BONAPARTE
RUE DE L'ABBAYE

Ruf du Bac Ⓜ

✉

RUE DES SAINTS PÈRES

5

RUE SAINT GUILLAUME

94 103

RUE DE VARENNE

Hôtel
Lutetia
Ⓗ
7

Lycée
St Thomas
d'Aquin

22

31 Ⓜ

♱ 21

Musée
Maillol 🏛

RUE DE GRENELLE

Fondation
Nationale
des Sciences
Politique

St Germain des Prés

Clinique St
François
Xavier

RUE BARBET DE JOUY

CITE VANEAU

Hôtel
Matignon Ⓗ

RUE VANEAU

RUE DU BAC

Lycée
d'Hulst

BOULEVARD RASPAIL

RUE DE LA CHAISE

RUE RECAMIER

RUE DU DRAGON

✉

18

RUE DE L'ABBAYE
RUE DES CANETTES
RUE PRINCESSE

152
175

✚

St Dominique ♱

RUE DE VARENNE

Square
Récamier

136

7
♱

Clinique
St Jean de Dieu ✚

RUE VANEAU

Jardin
Catherine
Labouré

Notre Dame de
la Médaille
Miraculeuse

Bon
Marché
44

Sèvres
Babylone

Square
Boucicaut Ⓜ

✉ St Ignace

RUE DE SEVRES

RUE DE BABYLONE

Ⓜ St Sulpice

RUE DU CHERCHE MIDI

RUE DE RENNES

Ⓜ St Sulpice

Place
St Sulpice

St Sulpice
24

RUE BONAPARTE
RUE FEROU
RUE SERV
ANDONI

398

A   B   408   C

RUE COETLOGON

[01] General Information p.1 [02] Residents p.45 [03] Exploring p.131 [04] Activities p.209 [05] Shopping p.241 [06] Going Out p.303

© Explorer Group Ltd. 2007

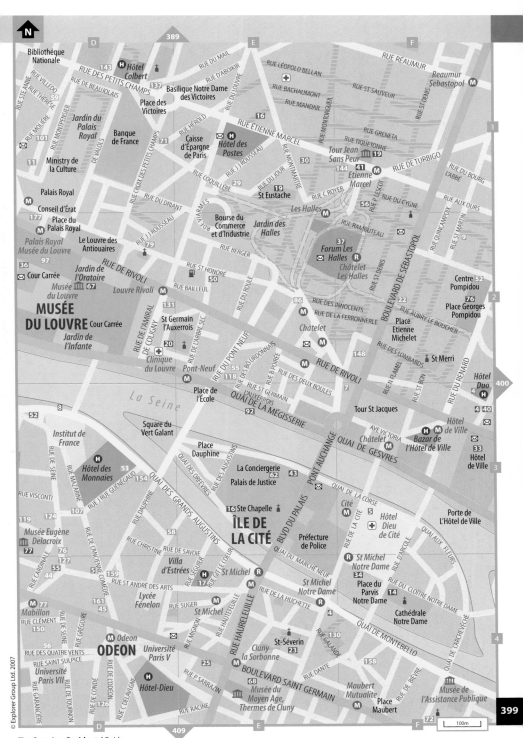

© Explorer Group Ltd. 2007

100m

N

A B C

390

66 Musée des Arts et Métiers
Musée National des Techniques
St Nicolas des Champs

Temple

45

AVE DE LA REPUBLIQUE

RUE VAUCANSON
RUE DU VERTBOIS
RUE VOLTA
RUE MONTGOLFIER
RUE DU TURBIGO
RUE RAMPON
RUE DE LA FOLIE MERICOURT
RUE DE LA FOLIE MERCOURT
RUE DU GRAND PRIEURE
BOULEVARD RICHARD LENOIR
BOULEVARD VOLTAIRE

Lycée Turgot

Arts et Métiers

73
108

RUE AU MAIRE
BEAUBOURG
RUE REAUMUR

RUE DES FONTAINES DU TEMPLE

145

RUE DE TEMPLE

Lycée Technique Ouperre

Square du Temple

61

BOULEVARD DU TEMPLE

Oberkampf

RUE JP TIMBAUD
62

Oberkampf

RUE AMELOT
133
RUE DE CRUSSOL
RUE DE MALTE

RUE BEAUBOURG
RUE DES GRAVILLIERS
RUE CHAPON

58

RUE SAINTONGE

RUE CHARLOT

RUE DE NORMANDIE

Cirque d'Hiver

RUE DE MONTMORENCY

RPORTEFON
RUE DE BRETAGNE

53

Filles du Calvaire
51

PGE ST PIERRE AMELOT

Musée de la Poupée
2
165
55

Musée d'Art et d'Histoire du Judaïsme

167

RUE MICHEL LE COMTE
RUE DU TEMPLE
RUE PASTOURELLE

Marché Enfants Rouges

RUE CHARLOT

RUE COMM INES

RUE FROISSART

RUE AMELOT
140

RUE SAINT SEBASTIEN

RUE RAMBUTEAU
20

Archives Nationales
Musée de l' Histoire de France

RUE DES ARCHIVES
RUE DES QUATRE FILS

Musée de la Chasse et de la Nature
27 4

Cathédrale Ste Croix

33

RUE DU PERCHE
RUE VIEILLE DU TEMPLE

5

RUE DEBELLEYME
RUE DEBELLEYME

RUE DU PONT AUX CHOUX

Lycée Simone Weil
3

BOULEVARD DES FILLES DU CALVAIRE

St Sebastien Froissart

BOULEVARD BEAUMARCHAIS

RUE SIMON LE FRANC
RUE DES FRANCS BOURGEOIS

Hôtel de Rohan
125

Musée Picasso
79

RUE DE THORIGNY

IMPST CLAUDE

St Denys du St-Sacrement

COUR DU COQ

RUE A BAUDIN

RUE DU PLATRE

Musée de la Serrure

RUE DES BLANCS MANTEAUX

19

RUE BARBETTE

RUE DE LA PERLE

RUE DU PARC ROYAL

RUE DE TURENNE

RUE ST SABIN

170

399

172

165

14

Billettes

138 104 99 120

RUE DE MOUSSY
RUE VIEILLE DU TEMPLE

Clinique du Sport du Marais

RUE ELZEVIR
54

Musée Cognacq-Jay

RUE PAVEE

Musée Carnavalet

RUE ST GILLES

RUE DES MINIMES

Chemin Vert

RUE DES ARQUEBUSIERS

Square Brégut Sabin

59

Bréguet Sabin

RUE DE RIVOLI

Hôtel de Ville
Mairie

RUE DU ROI DE SICILE

163 164

29
20

RUE DES ROSIERS

RUE DE SEVIGNE

52

RUE DU FOIN RUE R VERLOMME

34

Pavillon de la Reine
H 15 29

RUE DU PAS DE LA MULE

Foyer de l'Âme

102

70

RUE DUVAL
RUE MALHER

Centre Malher

THE MARAIS

RUE DE TURENNE

Place des Vosges

RUE DE BROSSE
RUE DU LOUIS PHILIPPE

RUE FR MIRON

RUE DE JOUY

RUE DE FOURCY

St Paul

RUE SAINT PAUL

RUE DE BIRAGUE

26 Maison de Victor Hugo

110

Maison de Victor Hugo

BOULEVARD RICHARD LENOIR
BOULEVARD RICHARD LENOIR
RUE DAVAL

QUAI DEL'HÔTEL DE VILLE

PONT LOUIS PHILIPPE

Lycée St German

Lycée Charlemagne

3

Bastille

Bastille

Place de la Bastille

Colonne de Juillet

Bastille

Opéra Bastille

Pont Marie

Hôtel de Sens

RUE DES NONMANS D'HYERES
QUAI DES CELESTINS

RUE DE L'AVE MARIA

68

ANTOINE RUE ST ANTOINE

École des Francs Bourgeois

RUE CASTEX

RUE JACQUES COEUR

RUE DE LA CERISAIE

RUE BISCORNET

DE BOURBON

ÎLE SAINT LOUIS

30

Porte des Célestins

QUAI D'ANJOU

35 St Louis

92

QUAI D'ORLEANS
QUAI DE BETHUNE
QUAI DES DEUX PONTS

Hôtel de Lauzun

Hôtel Lambert

Pavillon de l'Arsenal

École Massillon

Sully Morland

BLVD HENRI IV

Annexe Mairie de Paris

Bibliothèque de l'Arsenal

BOULEVARD BOURDON

RUE DE L'ARSENAL

4

A B C

410

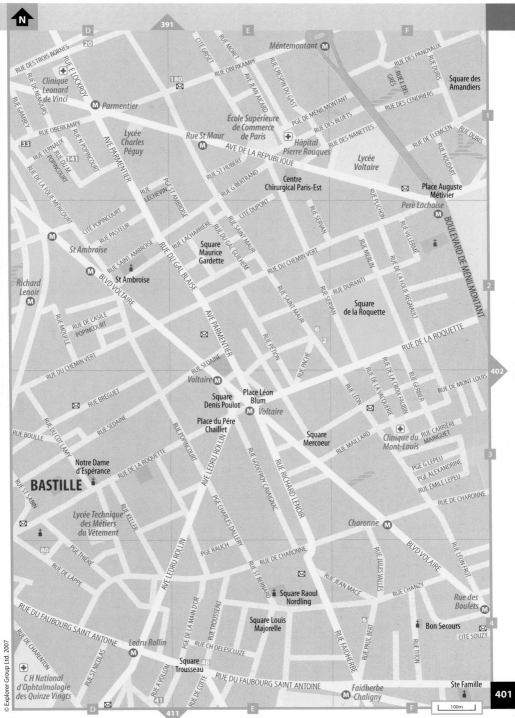

391

20

D

E

F

Square des
Amandiers

1

RUE DES TROIS BORNES
RUE E LOCKROY
Clinique
Leonard
de Vinci
RUE DE NEMOURS
RUE GAMBEY
RUE OBERKAMPF
33
141
RUE TERNAUX
RUE N POPINCOURT
RUE J M POPINCOURT
AVE PARMENTIER
RUE DE LA FOLIE MÉRICOURT
Parmentier
Lycée
Charles
Péguy
CITÉ GRISET
RUE MORET
RUE OBERKAMPF
RUE ST MAUR
180
Rue St Maur
AVE JEAN AICARD
AVE JEAN AICARD
École Supérieure
de Commerce
de Paris
Méntemontant
RUE CRESPIN DU GAST
PGE DE MÉNILMONTANT
RUE DES BLUETS
RUE DES NANETTES
Hôpital
Pierre Rouques
AVE DE LA RÉPUBLIQUE
RUE ST HUBERT
RUE G BERTRAND
Centre
Chirurgical Paris-Est
RUE DES PANOYAUX
RUE DES CENDRIERS
RUE DEL GRÈS
RUE DURIS
RUE DE TLEMCEN
RUE HOUDART
RUE DURIS
Lycée
Voltaire
Place Auguste
Métivier
Perè Lachaise

2

Richard
Lenoir
St Ambroise
RUE PASTEUR
CITÉ POPINCOURT
RUE SAINT AMBROISE
St Ambroise
BLVD VOLTAIRE
RUE MOUFLE
RUE DE L'ASILE
POPINCOURT
RUE CHEMIN VERT
RUE LÉCHEVIN
PGE ST AMBROISE
RUE DU GAL BLAISE
RUE LACHARRIÈRE
Square
Maurice
Gardette
CITÉ DUPONT
RUE SAINT MAUR
RUE DU GAL GUILHEM
RUE DU CHEMIN VERT
AVE PARMENTIER
RUE SAINT MAUR
RUE SERVIAN
RUE MERLIN
RUE SERVIAN
RUE DURANTI
Square
de la Roquette
RUE PUCHON
RUE DE LA FOLIE REGNAULT
RUE VILLERME
BOULEVARD DE MÉNILMONTANT
6
2

402

BASTILLE
RUE ST SABIN
RUE BOULLE
RUE DU CDT LAMY
RUE SEDAINE
RUE BRÉGUET
RUE DE LA ROQUETTE
RUE POPINCOURT
RUE SEDAINE
RUE PÉTION
RUE PACHE
Voltaire
Square
Denis Poulot
Place du Pére
Chaillet
Place Léon
Blum
Voltaire
AVE LEDRU ROLLIN
Square
Mercoeur
RUE MAILLARD
RUE LÉON
RUE DE LA VACQUERIE
RUE DE LA CROIX FAUBIN
RUE GERBIER
RUE DE MONT LOUIS
Clinique du
Mont-Louis
RUE CARRIÈRE
MAINGUET
PGE G LEPEU
PGE ALEXANDRINE
RUE ÉMILE LEPEU
RUE DE CHARONNE

3

Notre Dame
d'Espérance
Lycée Technique
des Métiers
du Vêtement
80
PGE THIÈRE
RUE DE LAPPE
RUE KELLER
AVE LEDRU ROLLIN
PGE CHARLES DALLERY
PGE RAUCH
RUE DE CHARONNE
RUE ST BERNARD
RUE GODEFROY CAVAIGNAC
RUE RICHARD LENOIR
RUE JEAN MACE
RUE JULES VALLÈS
BLVD VOLAIRE
Charonne
RUE CHANZY
RUE LÉON FROT
Rue des
Boulets

4

RUE DU FAUBOURG SAINT ANTOINE
RUE DE CHARENTON
Ledru Rollin
RUE ST NICOLAS
PGE DE LA MAIN D'OR
RUE A VOLLON
RUE DE COTTE
RUE CH DELESCLUZE
RUE TROUSSEAU
Square
Trousseau
48
Square Raoul
Nordling
Square Louis
Majorelle
RUE DU FAUBOURG SAINT ANTOINE
RUE FAIDHERBE
RUE PAUL BERT
6
RUE TITON
Bon Secours
CITÉ SOUZY
Faidherbe
Chaligny
Ste Famille

C H National
d'Ophtalmologie
des Quinze Vingts

41

411

D

E

F

100m

401

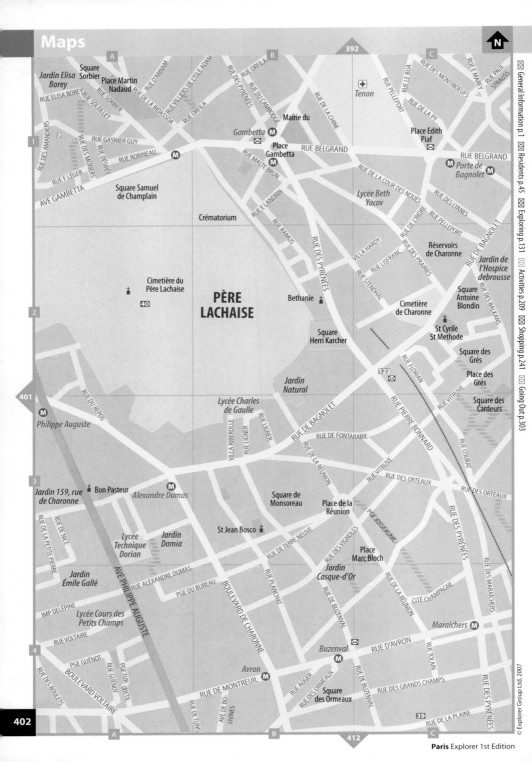

N

Jardin Elisa Borey
Square Sorbier
Place Martin Nadaud
RUE ELISA BOREY
RUE SOLEILLET
RUE D'ANNAM
RUE VILLIERS DE L'ISLE ADAM
RUE DES PYRÉNÉES
RUE ORFILA
RUE ORFILA
RUE DU CAMBODGE
RUE DE LA CHINE
Tenon
RUE PELLEPORT
RUE LE BUA
RUE DES MONTIBOEUFS
RUE DE LA PY
RUE MAREY
RUE PAUL STRAUSS

RUE DES AMANDIERS
RUE GASNIER GUY
RUE DES MURIERS
RUE DÉSIRÉE
RUE ROBINEAU
RUE DE LA BIDASSOA
Mairie du Gambetta
Place Gambetta
RUE BELGRAND
Place Edith Piaf
RUE BELGRAND

1

AVE GAMBETTA
RUE F LÉGER
Square Samuel de Champlain
RUE MALTE BRUN
RUE DE LA COUR DES NOUES
Porte de Bagnolet
Lycée Beth Yacov
RUE DES LYANES

Crématorium
RUE E LANDRIN
RUE RAMUS
RUE DES PYRÉNÉES
Lycée Beth Yacov
RUE DE L'INDRE
RUE PELLEPORT
Réservoirs de Charonne
RUE DE BAGNOLET
Jardin de l'Hospice debrousse

Cimetière du Père Lachaise
40
PÈRE LACHAISE
Bethanie
VILLA HARDY
RUE LISFRANC
RUE STENDHAL
RUE DES PRAIRIES
Cimetière de Charonne
Square Antoine Blondin
RUE DES BALKANS

2

Square Herri Karcher
St Cyrille St Methode
Square des Grés
Place des Grés

Jardin Natural
RUE FLORIAN
RUE VITRUVE
122
Square des Cardeurs

401
Philippe Auguste
RUE DU REPOS
Lycée Charles de Gaulle
RUE LIGNER
RUE DE BAGNOLET
RUE DE FONTARABIE
RUE PIERRE BONNARD
RUE VITRUVE
RUE COURAT

3

Jardin 159, rue de Charonne
Bon Pasteur
Alexandre Dumas
VILLA RIBEROLLE
RUE LIGNER
RUE DE LA RÉUNION
RUE DES ORTEAUX
RUE DES ORTEAUX

RUE DE NICE
Square de Monsoreau
Place de la Réunion
PGE JOSSEAUME
RUE DES PYRÉNÉES

RUE DE LA PETITE PIERRE
Lycée Technique Dorian
Jardin Damia
St Jean Bosco
RUE DE TERRE NEUVE
RUE DES VIGNOLES
Place Marc Bloch
RUE DE LA RÉUNION
RUE DES MARAICHERS

Jardin Émile Gallé
RUE ALEXANDRE DUMAS
PGE DU BUREAU
RUE PLANCHAT
Jardin Casque-d'Or
RUE DE BUZENVAL
CITÉ CHAMPAGNE

IMP DELÉPINE
Lycée Cours des Petits Champs
AVE PHILIPPE AUGUSTE
Maraichers

RUE VOLTAIRE
BOULEVARD DE CHARONNE
Buzenval
RUE D'AVRON
RUE TOLAIN

4

PGE GUENOT
RUE DES BOULETS
BOULEVARD VOLTAIRE
PGE TUR QUETIL
RUE GUENOT
Avron
RUE DE MONTREUIL
AVE DE BO-UVINES
RUE AUGER
RUE DES ORMEAUX
Square des Ormeaux
RUE DE BUZENVAL
RUE DES GRANDS CHAMPS
39
RUE DE LA PLAINE
RUE DES PYRÉNÉES

A General Information p.1
A Residents p.45
A Exploring p.131
A Activities p.209
A Shopping p.241
A Going Out p.303

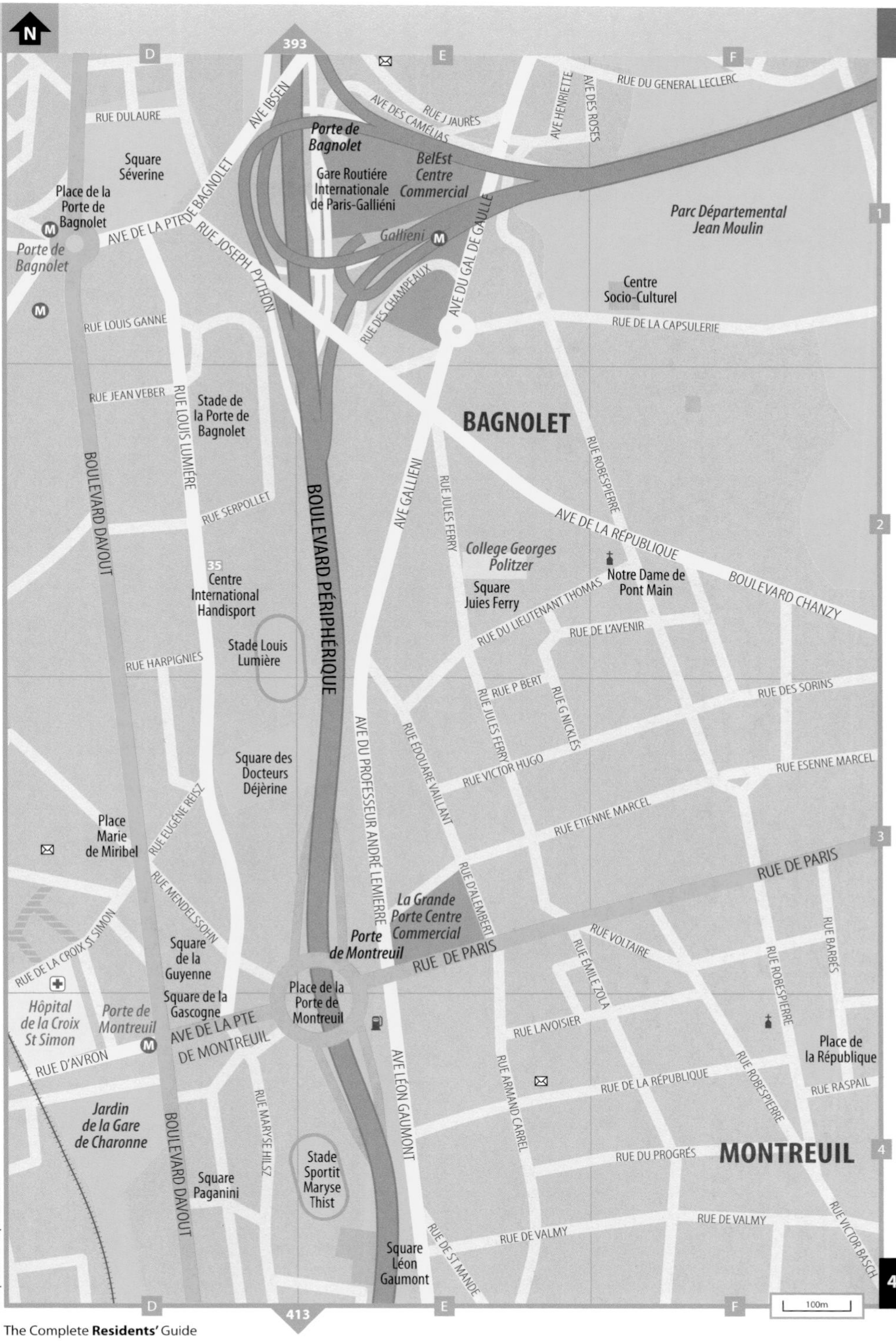
N
393
D
E
F
RUE DULAURE
AVE IBSEN
Square Séverine
Place de la Porte de Bagnolet
Porte de Bagnolet
AVE DE LA PTE DE BAGNOLET
RUE JOSEPH PYTHON
Porte de Bagnolet
Gare Routiére Internationale de Paris-Galliéni
BelEst Centre Commercial
AVE DES CAMÉLIAS
RUE J JAURÉS
AVE HENRIETTE
AVE DES ROSES
RUE DU GENERAL LECLERC
Parc Départemental Jean Moulin
Gallieni
RUE DES CHAMPEAUX
AVE DU GAL DE GAULLE
Centre Socio-Culturel
RUE DE LA CAPSULERIE
RUE LOUIS GANNE
RUE JEAN VEBER
RUE LOUIS LUMIÉRE
Stade de la Porte de Bagnolet
BAGNOLET
BOULEVARD DAVOUT
BOULEVARD PÉRIPHÉRIQUE
AVE GALLIENI
RUE JULES FERRY
RUE ROBESPIERRE
AVE DE LA RÉPUBLIQUE
RUE SERPOLLET
College Georges Politzer
Notre Dame de Pont Main
Square Jules Ferry
BOULEVARD CHANZY
35
Centre International Handisport
RUE DU LIEUTENANT THOMAS
RUE DE L'AVENIR
Stade Louis Lumière
RUE HARPIGNIES
RUE P BERT
RUE G NICKLÉS
RUE DES SORINS
RUE JULES FERRY
AVE DU PROFESSEUR ANDRÉ LEMIERRE
RUE ÉDOUARE VAILLANT
Square des Docteurs Déjèrine
RUE VICTOR HUGO
RUE ESENNE MARCEL
RUE ETIENNE MARCEL
Place Marie de Miribel
RUE EUGÉNE REISZ
1
2
3
4
RUE DE PARIS
RUE MENDELSSOHN
RUE D'ALEMBERT
La Grande Porte Centre Commercial
Porte de Montreuil
RUE DE LA CROIX ST SIMON
Square de la Guyenne
RUE DE PARIS
RUE VOLTAIRE
RUE ÉMILE ZOLA
RUE ROBESPIERRE
RUE BARBÉS
Place de la Porte de Montreuil
Square de la Gascogne
Hôpital de la Croix St Simon
Porte de Montreuil
AVE DE LA PTE DE MONTREUIL
RUE LAVOISIER
Place de la République
RUE D'AVRON
RUE DE LA RÉPUBLIQUE
RUE ROBESPIERRE
RUE RASPAIL
RUE ARMAND CARREL
AVE LÉON GAUMONT
Jardin de la Gare de Charonne
RUE MARYSE HILSZ
BOULEVARD DAVOUT
Stade Sportit Maryse Thist
RUE DU PROGRÉS
MONTREUIL
Square Paganini
RUE DE VALMY
RUE DE VALMY
RUE VICTOR BASCH
Square Léon Gaumont
RUE DE ST MANDE
413
100m

N

A

B

C

General Information p.1 Residents p.45 Exploring p.131 Activities p.209 Shopping p.241 Going Out p.303

Porte d'Auteuil

Espace d'Auteuil

AVE DES PEUPLIERS

RUE POUSSIN

Place de la Porte d'Auteuil

1

RUE D'AUTEUIL

M 78

Stade Roland Garros

AVE DE LA PORTE D'AUTEUIL

AVE GORDON BENNETT

Square des Poètes

Jardin des Serres d'Auteuil

47

Porte d'Auteuil

M

RUE CHANEZ

Lycée ENIO

Lycée des Oiseaux

RUE DES PINS

Stade Georges Hébert

StFrancois de Moutor

RUE MICHEL ANGE

Porte Molitor

AVE DE LA PORTE MOLITOR

Lycée la Fontaine

M

Michel Ange Molitor

RUE GUTENBERG

RUEMAX BLONDAT

Musée Paul Landowski

RUE DU CHÂTEAU

RUE NUNGESSER ET COLI

BOULEVARD PÉRIPHÉRIQUE

RUE MERYON

AVE DU GENERAL

BOULEVARD MURAT

RUE DE CIVRY

RUE BERANGER

Auteuil

Place Denfert Rochereau

RUE DARCEL

RUE S REINACH MARCEL LOYAU

AVE ROBERT SCHUMAN

RUE DE LA TOURELLE

Stade Jean Bouin

Apparition de la Ste Vierge

Exelmans

M

BOULEVARD EXELMANS

2

Bibliothèque-Musée Marmottan

RUE CLAUDE FARRÈRE

RUE LECOMTE DU NOÜY

Lycée Claude Bernard

RUE DU GENERAL DELESTRAINT

RUE MICHEL ANGE

EXELMANS

Ste Geneviéve

RUE CLAUDE LORRAIN

Parc des Princes

RUE DE JARIZE

Cimetière d'Auteuil

Tous les Saints de la Terre Russe

RUE BOILEAU

Rond Point André Malraux

RUE DU PAVILLON

RUE DU BELVEDERE

RUE DE LA TOURELLE

RUE DU COMMANDANT GUILBAUD

Place Juies Rimet

RUE DU SERGENT MAGNOY

AVE DU PARC DES PRINCES

BOULEVARD MURAT

RUE PARENT DE ROSEN

Place du General Stefanik

Place Paul Reynaud

RUE DES PRINCES

RUE DES PRINCES

RUE DE PARIS

Centre Sportif Géo André

Place du Docteur Paul Michaux

Ste Jeanne de Chantal

M

AVE DE VERSAILLES

RUE CLAUDE TERRASSE

RUE CH TEL

3

ROUTE DE LA REINE

AVE DE LA PORTE DE SAINT CLOUD

RUE E MAROIS

RUE E DETAILLES

RUE GALLIENI

RUE GALLIENI

RUE SAMARCO

RUE HENRI MARTIN

Porte de St Cloud

Place de la Porte

M

Saint Cloud

AVE MARCEL DORET

Porte du Point du Jour

RUE A FERRY

RUE THIERS

AVE EDOUARD VAILLANT

RUE FERDINAND BUISSON

Porte de St Cloud

AVE DODE DE LA BRUNERIE

RUE DU GENERAL MALLETERRE

RUE RIEULX

RUE MARCEL DASSAULT

Stade Pierre de Coubertin

Place de l'Abbé Franz Stock

RUE HENRY DE LA VAULX

4

Paris V René Descartes

RUE DE VANVES

Jardin L'arroseur Arrosé

Place R Clair

Port de la Petite Arche

BOULOGNE-BILLANCOURT

RUE DU DÔME

RUE DU POINT DU JOUR

St Pierre

Direction Générale de la Poste

A

B

C

Paris Explorer 1st Edition

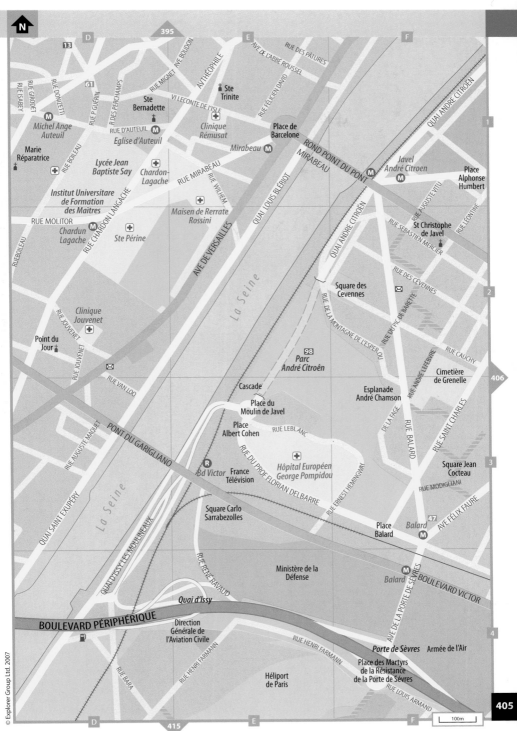

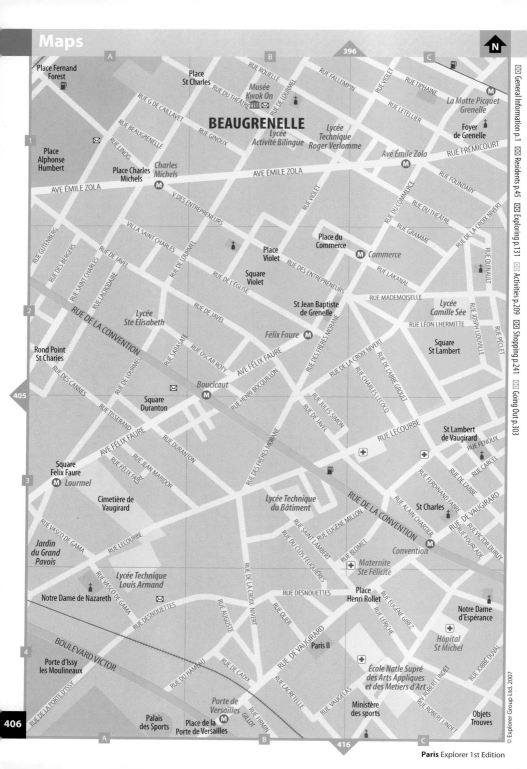

N

BEAUGRENELLE

© Explorer Group Ltd. 2007

Paris Explorer 1st Edition

General Information p.1 · Residents p.45 · Exploring p.131 · Activities p.209 · Shopping p.241 · Going Out p.303

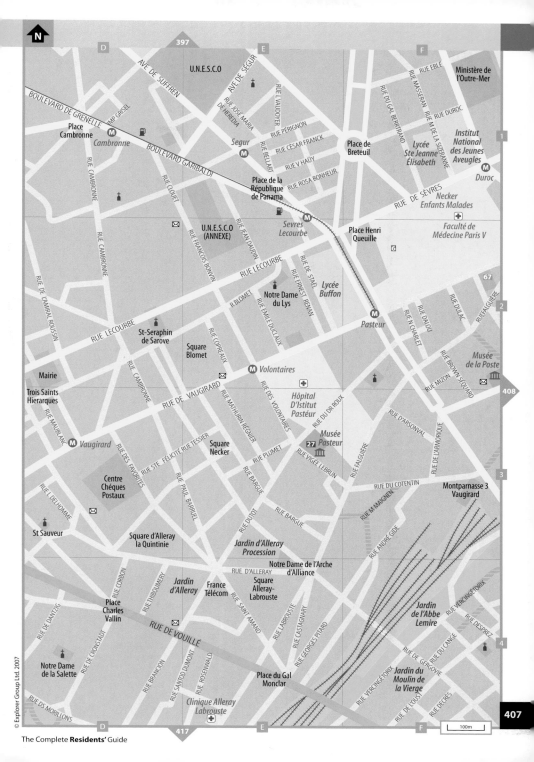

D E F

Ministère de
l'Outre-Mer

U.N.E.S.C.O

AVE DE SUFFREN

BOULEVARD DE GRENELLE

CHAMP GRISEL

Place
Cambronne

Cambronne

RUE CAMBRONNE

BOULEVARD GARIBALDI

RUE CLOUET

RUE DE L'AMIRAL ROUSSIN

RUE CAMBRONNE

AVE DE SÉGUR

RUE JOSÉ MARIA DE HEREDIA

RUE L'VAUDOYER

RUE PÉRIGNON

Segur

RUE BELLART

RUE CÉSAR FRANCK

RUE V HAÜY

Place de la
République
de Panama

RUE ROSA BONHEUR

U.N.E.S.C.O
(ANNEXE)

RUE FRANÇOIS BONVIN

RUE JEAN DAUDIN

Sèvres
Lecourbe

RUE LECOURBE

R BLOMET

Notre Dame
du Lys

RUE ÉMILE DUCLAUX

RUE ERNEST RENAN

RUE DE STAËL

Lycée
Buffon

RUE EBLÉ

RUE MASSÉRAN

RUE DU GAL BERTRAND

RUE DE LA SÉRRANNE

RUE DUROC

Place de
Breteuil

Lycée
Ste Jeanne
Élisabeth

Institut
National
des Jeunes
Aveugles

Duroc

RUE DE SÈVRES

Necker
Enfants Malades

Place Henri
Queuille

Faculté de
Médecine Paris V

RUE LECOURBE

St-Seraphin
de Sarove

RUE COPREAUX

Square
Blomet

RUE CAMBRONNE

RUE DE VAUGIRARD

RUE DES VOLONTAIRES

Volontaires

Hôpital
D'Istitut
Pastéur

RUE MATHURIN RÉGNIER

Pasteur

RUE N CHARLET

RUE DALOU

RUE DULAC

RUE FALGUIÈRE

RUE BROWN SÉQUARD

Musée
de la Poste

RUE MIZON

Mairie

Trois Saints
Hierarques

RUE MAUBLANC

Vaugirard

RUE DES FAVORITES

RUE STE FÉLICITÉ

RUE TESSIER

Square
Necker

Musée
Pasteur

27

RUE VIGÉE LEBRUN

RUE DU DR ROUX

RUE FALGUIÈRE

RUE D'ARSONVAL

RUE DE L'ARMORIQUE

Centre
Chéques
Postaux

RUE DELHOMME

RUE PAUL BARRUEL

RUE PLUMET

RUE BARGUE

RUE DUTOT

RUE BARGUE

RUE DU COTENTIN

RUE M MAIGNEN

RUE ANDRÉ GIDE

Montparnasse 3
Vaugirard

St Sauveur

Square d'Alleray
la Quintinie

RUE CORBON

RUE THIBOUMERY

Jardin
d'Alleray

France
Télécom

Jardin d'Alleray
Procession

RUE D'ALLERAY

Notre Dame de l'Arche
d'Alliance

Square
Alleray-
Labrouste

RUE SAINT AMAND

RUE LABROUSTE

RUE CASTAGNARY

RUE GEORGES PITARD

Jardin
de l'Abbé
Lemire

RUE VERCINGÉTORIX

RUE DESPREZ

Place
Charles
Vallin

RUE DE DANTZIG

RUE DE CRONSTADT

RUE DE VOUILLÉ

RUE SANTOS DUMONT

RUE ROSENWALD

Place du Gal
Monclar

RUE VERCINGÉTORIX

RUE DE GERGOVIE

RUE DU CANGE

Jardin du
Moulin de
la Vierge

RUE DE L'OUEST

RUE DÉCRÈS

Notre Dame
de la Salette

RUE BRANCION

RUE DS MORILLONS

Clinique Alleray
Labrouste

100m

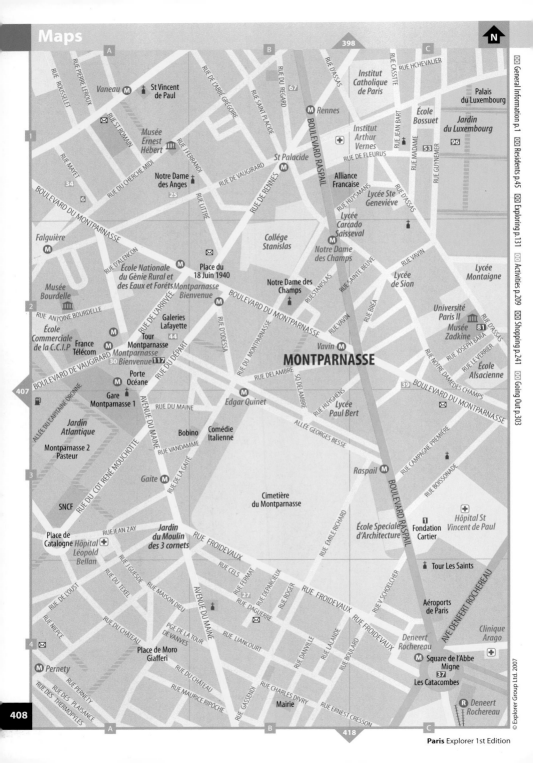

General Information p.1

Residents p.45

Exploring p.131

Activities p.209

Shopping p.241

Going Out p.303

398

A   B   C

RUE PIERRE LEROUX

RUE ROUSSELET

Vaneau Ⓜ ✠ St Vincent de Paul

Institut Catholique de Paris

RUE CASSETTE

RUE H.CHEVALIER

RUE DE L'ABBÉ GRÉGOIRE

RUE DU REGARD

RUE D'ASSAS

Palais du Luxembourg

École Bossuet

RUE JEAN BART

RUE SAINT PLACIDE

RUE DU CHERCHE MIDI

RUE ST ROMAIN

Musée Ernest Hébert

Rennes

BOULEVARD RASPAIL

Institut Arthur Vernes

Jardin du Luxembourg

1

RUE MAYET

RUE DE VAUGIRARD

St Palacide

RUE DE FLEURUS

53

RUE MADAME

RUE GUYNEMER

96

34

6

Notre Dame des Anges

25

RUE LITTRÉ

RUE DE RENNES

Alliance Française

RUE HUYSMANS

Lycée Ste Geneviève

RUE D'ASSAS

Falguière Ⓜ

BOULEVARD DU MONTPARNASSE

Lycée Carcado Saisseval

Notre Dame des Champs

RUE VAVIN

Lycée Montaigne

Musée Bourdelle

École Nationale du Gènie Rural et des Eaux et Forêts

Place du 18 Juin 1940

Collège Stanislas

Notre Dame des Champs

RUE STANISLAS

RUE SAINTE BEUVE

RUE BRÉA

Lycée de Sion

Université Paris II

Musée Zadkine 81

RUE D'ASSAS

2

RUE ANTOINE BOURDELLE

Montparnasse Bienvenue

RUE DE L'ARRIVÉE

BOULEVARD DU MONTPARNASSE

RUE VAVIN

RUE JOSEPH BARA

École Commerciale de la C.C.I.P

Galeries Lafayette

Tour Montparnasse

44

RUE D'ODESSA

RUE DU MONTPARNASSE

Vavin Ⓜ

RUE NOTRE DAME DES CHAMPS

RUE LE VERRIER

École Alsacienne

France Télécom Ⓜ

Montparnasse Bienvenue

30   117

RUE DU DÉPART

MONTPARNASSE

39

BOULEVARD DU MONTPARNASSE

BOULEVARD DE VAUGIRARD

Porte Océane

RUE DELAMBRE

407

Gare Montparnasse 1

AVENUE DU MAINE

RUE DU MAINE

Edgar Quinet Ⓜ

SQ DELAMBRE

RUE HUYGHENS

Lycée Paul Bert

BOULEVARD RASPAIL

Jardin Atlantique

Bobino

Comédie Italienne

RUE VANDAMME

ALLÉE GEORGES BESSE

RUE CAMPAGNE PREMIÈRE

RUE BOISSONADE

Montparnasse 2 Pasteur

RUE DU CDT RENÉ MOUCHOTTE

Gaité Ⓜ

RUE DE LA GAÎTE

Raspail Ⓜ

3

SNCF

Cimetière du Montparnasse

Hôpital St Vincent de Paul

Place de Catalogne Hôpital Léopold Bellan

RUE JEAN ZAY

Jardin du Moulin des 3 cornets

RUE FROIDEVAUX

RUE ÉMILE RICHARD

École Speciale d'Architecture

Fondation Cartier

RUE J.GUESDE

RUE DU TEXEL

RUE CELS

AVENUE DU MAINE

Tour Les Saints

RUE DE L'OUEST

RUE MAISON DIEU

RUE FERMAT

27

RUE DEPARCIEUX

RUE ROGER

RUE FROIDEVAUX

RUE SCHOELCHER

Aéroports de Paris

AVE DENFERT ROCHEREAU

Clinique Arago

RUE NIEPCE

RUE DU CHATEAU

PGE DE LA TOUR DE VANVES

RUE DAGUERRE

RUE LIANCOURT

RUE DANVILLE

RUE LALANDE

RUE BOULARD

Deneert Rochereau

4

Pernety Ⓜ

Place de Moro Giafferi

RUE DU CHATEAU

Ⓜ Square de l'Abbe Migne

37

RUE PERNETY

RUE DES PLAISANCE

RUE MAURICE RIPOCHE

RUE GASSENDI

RUE CHARLES DIVRY

Mairie

RUE ERNEST CRESSON

Les Catacombes

Ⓡ Deneert Rochereau

RUE DES THERMOPYLES

A   B   C

408

418

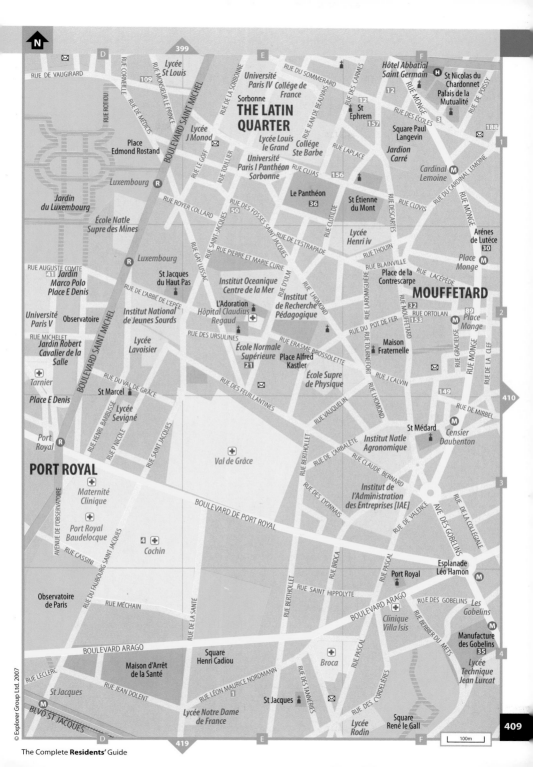

RUE DE VAUGIRARD

D

Lycée
St Louis

RUE CORNEILLE

RUE MONSIEUR LE PRINCE

109

RUE ROTROU

RUE DE MÉDICIS

RUE DE LA SORBONNE

Université
Paris IV Collège de
France

RUE DU SOMMERARD

E

Sorbonne

**THE LATIN
QUARTER**

RUE JEAN DE BEAUVAIS

RUE DES CARMES

12

St
Ephrem
157

Hôtel Abbatial
Saint Germain

F

12

St Nicolas du
Chardonnet
Palais de la
Mutualité

RUE DE POISSY

RUE MONGE

RUE DES ÉCOLES

3

188

1

Place
Edmond Rostand

BOULEVARD SAINT MICHEL

Lycée
J Monod

RUE LE GOFF

RUE TOULLIER

Lycée Louis
le Grand
Université
Paris I Panthéon
Sorbonne

Collège
Ste Barbe

RUE CUJAS

RUE LAPLACE

156

Square Paul
Langevin

Jardion
Carré

Cardinal
Lemoine M

RUE DU CARDINAL LEMOINE

RUE MONGE

Luxembourg R

Jardin
du Luxembourg

École Natle
Supre des Mines

RUE ROYER COLLARD

RUE DES FOSSES SAINT JACQUES

50

Le Panthéon
36

RUE CLOTILDE

St Étienne
du Mont

RUE DESCARTES

RUE CLOVIS

Lycée
Henri iv

RUE THOUIN

Arènes
de Lutèce
30

Place
Monge M

RUE AUGUSTE COMTE

41 Jardin
Marco Polo
Place E Denis

Luxembourg R

RUE DE L'ABBÉ DE L'EPÉE

RUE GAY LUSSAC

RUE SAINT JACQUES

RUE PIERRE ET MARIE CURIE

RUE DE L'ESTRAPADE

RUE D'ULM

RUE BLAINVILLE

Place de la
Contrescarpe

RUE LACÉPÈDE

MOUFFETARD

RUE DE L'ARBALÈTE

Université
Paris V

Observatoire

St Jacques
du Haut Pas

Institut National
de Jeunes Sourds

Institut Oceanique
Centre de la Mer

RUE LHOMOND

Institut
de Recherche
Pédagogique

RUE DU POT DE FER

32

RUE ORTOLAN

89

153

Place
Monge M

RUE MONGE

RUE GRACIEUSE

2

RUE MICHELET

Jardin Robert
Cavalier de la
Salle

Tarnier

Lycée
Lavoisier

RUE DES URSULINES

L'Adoration
Hôpital Claudius
Regaud

École Normale
Supérieure
21

Place Alfred
Kastler

École Supre
de Physique

RUE ERASME BROSSOLETTE

Maison
Fraternelle

RUE TOURNEFORT

RUE J CALVIN

RUE DE LA CLEF

410

Place E Denis

BOULEVARD SAINT MICHEL

RUE DU VAL DE GRÂCE

St Marcel

RUE DES FEUILLANTINES

RUE VAUQUELIN

149

RUE DE MIRBEL

Port
Royal R

RUE HENRI BARBUSSE

RUE P NICOLE

Lycée
Sévigné

RUE SAINT JACQUES

Val de Grâce

St Médard

RUE DE L'ARBALÈTE

Institut Natle
Agronomique

Censier
Daubenton M

PORT ROYAL

RUE BERTHOLLET

RUE CLAUDE BERNARD

3

AVENUE DE L'OBSERVATOIRE

Maternité
Clinique

Port Royal
Baudelocque

RUE CASSINI

4 Cochin

BOULEVARD DE PORT ROYAL

RUE DES LYONNAIS

Institut de
l'Administration
des Entreprises [IAE]

RUE DE VALENCE

AVE DES GOBELINS

RUE DE LA COLLÉGIALE

Esplanade
Léo Hamon M

Observatoire
de Paris

RUE DU FAUBOURG SAINT JACQUES

RUE MÉCHAIN

RUE DE LA SANTÉ

RUE BROCA

RUE SAINT HIPPOLYTE

BOULEVARD ARAGO

Port Royal

Clinique
Villa Isis

RUE DES GOBELINS

Les
Gobelins M

RUE BERBIER DU METS

Manufacture
des Gobelins
35

4

RUE LECLERC

St Jacques

BLVD ST JACQUES

BOULEVARD ARAGO

RUE JEAN DOLENT

Maison d'Arrêt
de la Santé

Square
Henri Cadiou

RUE LÉON MAURICE NORDMANN

1

RUE DES TANNERIES

RUE PASCAL

Broca

St Jacques

RUE DES CORDELIÈRES

Lycée
Technique
Jean Lurcat

Lycée Notre Dame
de France

Lycée
Rodin

Square
René le Gall

F

409

100m

© Explorer Group Ltd. 2007

The Complete **Residents'** Guide

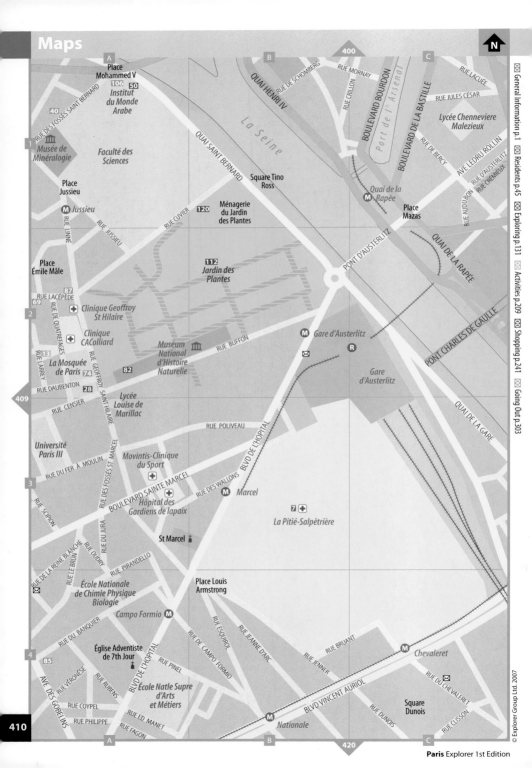

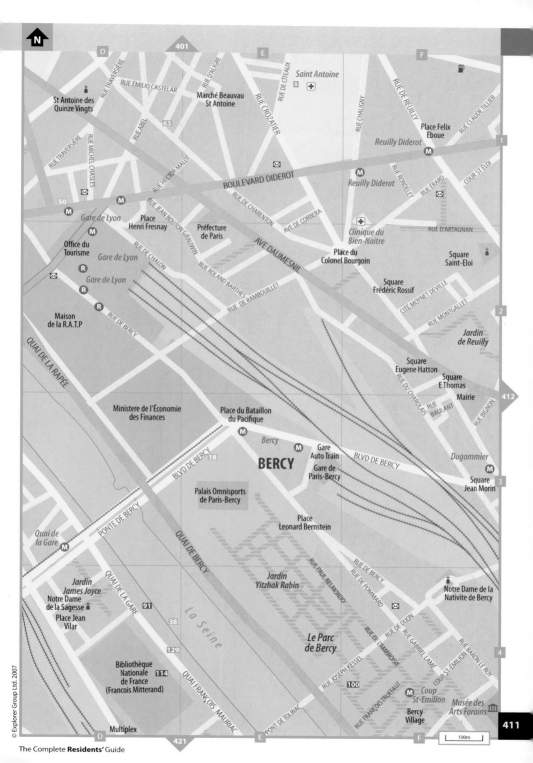

402

Square
Sarah Bernhardt

PGE DU GENE

RUE DU FAUBOURG SAINT ANTOINE

R

Place
de la
Nation

R

Place des
Antilles

Printemps
Nation

Square
Réjane

St Gabriel

Lycée
Hélène
Boucher

BOULEVARD DIDEROT

Lycée
Arago

M

Nation

M

COURS DE VINCENNES

RUE PIERRE BOURDAN

AVE DORIAN

RUE DORIAN

RUE MARIE-BENOIST

RUE TAILCOURT

RUE FABRE D'ÉGLANTINE

AVE DU BEL AIR

NATION

RUE DU RENDEZ-VOUS

BOULEVARD DE PICPUS

RUE MARSOULAN

Immaculée
Conception

IMP MOUSSET

RUE DU SERGENT BAUCHAT

Diacônesses

Montgallet

M

Office National
des Foréts

Institute
Supérieur du Bois

AVE DE SAINT MANDE

Picpus

Square
Courteline

AVE DE SAINT MANDE

Cimetière
de Picpus

RUE DE PICPUS

Rothschild

BOULEVARD DE PICPUS

BOULEVARD DE PICPUS

RUE SIBUET

AVE DU DOCTEUR ARNOLD NETTER

RUE MOUSSET ROBERT

RUE LASSON

RUE HÉNARD

RUE DE REUILLY

Lycée
St Michel
de Picpus

RUE SANTERRE

RUE DAGORNO

RUE VICTOR CHEVREUIL

Armand
Trousseau

ALLEE VIVALDI

RUE DE LA GARE DE REUILLY

Bel Air

M

RUE DE AMBERVILLERS

RUE DU SAHEL

411

RUE DUBRUNFAUT

RUE DUGOMMIER

M

RUE LAMBLARDIE

RUE DU DR GOUJON

PGE CHAUSSIN

RUE DE TOUL

AVE DU GENERAL MICHEL BIZOT

BOULEVARD DE BERCY

M

RUE TAINE

Daumesnil

Place
Félix Éboué

M

BOULEVARD DE REVILLY

RUE DE PICPUS

Square
Charles
Péguy

RUE DE CHARENTON

RUE TAINE

RUE DE LA
DURANCE

RUE DE LA BRECHE AUX LOUPS

Saint
Esprit

RUE SIDI BRAHIM

RUE GOSSEC

AVE DAUMESNIL

RUE ROTTEMBOURG

RUE DE LA VEGA

RUE PROUDHON

38

IMP TOURNEUX

Michel Bizot

M

VILLA JEAN GODARD

RUE CORIOLIS

RUE NICOLAI

RUE DES MEUNIERS

RUE DE WATTIGNIES

RUE DE GRAVELLE

RUE DE CAPRI

RUE CLAUDE DECAEN

RUE DE FÉCAMP

Jardin 54

RUE DE PICPUS

RUE E LACOSTE

Porte
Dorée

M

RUE M DUBOIS

Porte
Dorée

M

AVE DU GAL DODDS

RUE DE CHARENTON

RUE DES JARDINIERS

RUE DES MEUNIERS

RUE DE MADAGASCAR

AVE DU GÉNÉRAL MICHEL BIZOT

Porte
de Reuilly

RUE J CHALLEY

Cimetière
de Bercy

BOULEVARD PONIATOWSKI

Stade
Léo Lagrange

Square
Croix Rouge

General Information p.1 · Residents p.45 · Exploring p.131 · Activities p.209 · Shopping p.241 · Going Out p.303

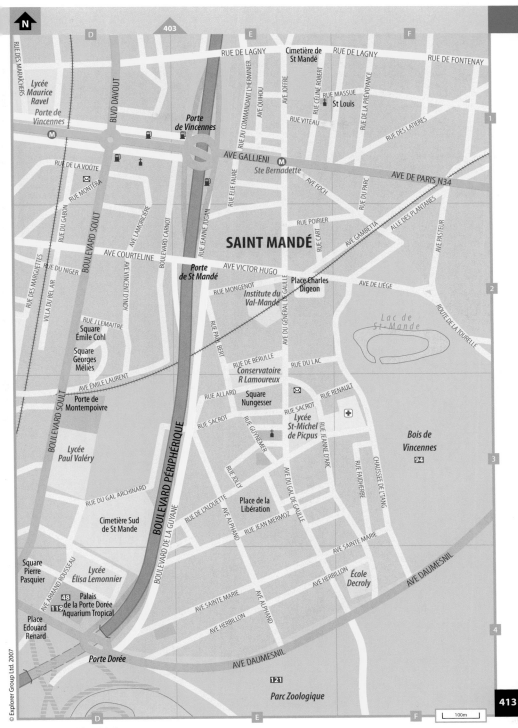

RUE DES MARAICHERS

Lycée
Maurice
Ravel

Porte de
Vincennes

BLVD DAVOUT

RUE DE LAGNY

Cimetière de
St Mandé

RUE DE LAGNY

RUE DE FONTENAY

AVE JOFFRE

AVE QUIHOU

RUE DU COMMANDANT L'HERMINIER

RUE CÉLINE ROBERT

RUE MASSUE

St Louis

RUE DE LA PRÉVOYANCE

RUE VITEAU

RUE DES LATIÈRES

Porte
de Vincennes

RUE DE LA VOÛTE

RUE MONTÉRA

RUE DU GABON

RUE DU NIGER

RUE DES MARGUETTES

VILLA DU BEL AIR

RUE ÉLIE FAURE

BOULEVARD SOULT

AVE LAMORICIÈRE

AVE COURTELINE

AVE VINCENT D'INDY

BOULEVARD CARNOT

RUE JEANNE JUGAN

AVE GALLIENI

Ste Bernadette

AVE FOCH

AVE DE PARIS N34

RUE DU PARC

RUE POIRIER

RUE CART

AVE GAMBETTA

ALLÉE DES PLATANES

AVE PASTEUR

SAINT MANDÉ

Porte
de St Mandé

AVE VICTOR HUGO

RUE MONGENOT

Institute du
Val-Mandé

Place Charles
Digeon

AVE DE LIÈGE

AVE DU GÉNÉRAL DE GAULLE

ROUTE DE LA TOURELLE

Lac de
St-Mande

RUE J LEMAITRE

Square
Émile Cohl

Square
Georges
Méliès

RUE PAUL BERT

RUE DE BÉRULLE

RUE DU LAC

AVE ÉMILE LAURENT

Conservatoire
R Lamoureux

Square
Nungesser

RUE RENAULT

BOULEVARD SOULT

Porte de
Montempoivre

RUE ALLARD

RUE SACROT

RUE SACROT

RUE GUYNEMER

Lycée
St-Michel
de Picpus

RUE JEANNE D'ARC

Bois de
Vincennes
94

Lycée
Paul Valéry

BOULEVARD PÉRIPHÉRIQUE

RUE FAIDHERBE

CHAUSSÉE DE L'ÉTANG

RUE DU GAL ARCHINARD

RUE JOLLY

RUE DE L'ALOUETTE

Place de la
Libération

AVE DU GAL DE GAULLE

Cimetière Sud
de St Mande

BOULEVARD DE LA GUYANE

AVE ALPHAND

RUE JEAN MERMOZ

AVE SAINTE MARIE

AVE DAUMESNIL

Square
Pierre
Pasquier

AVE ARMAND ROUSSEAU

Lycée
Élisa Lemonnier

AVE HERBILLON

École
Decroly

Place
Edouard
Renard

48
Palais
119
de la Porte Dorée
Aquarium Tropical

AVE SAINTE MARIE

AVE ALPHAND

AVE HERBILLON

Porte Dorée

AVE DAUMESNIL

121

Parc Zoologique

100m

The Complete **Residents'** Guide

404

General Information p.1

Residents p.45

Exploring p.131

Activities p.209

Shopping p.241

Going Out p.303

N

RUE DES LONGS PRÉS

RUE THIERS

RUE DU FER

BLVD DE LA REPUBLIQUE

AVE PIERRE GRENIER

⛪ Immaculée
Conception

Nouveau Cimetière
de Boulogne Billancourt

QUAI DU PONT DU JOUR

PONT D'ISSY

QUAI DU PRÉSIDENT ROOSEVELT

Issy Val Ⓡ
de Seine

RUE DU PONT DU JOUR

RUE DE SEINE

RUE ÉMILE DUCLAUX

La Seine

✉

BOULEVARD JEAN JAURÈS

Cours des
Longs Prés

RUE DE SEINE

La Tour
aux Figures

Place St Germain
des Longs Prés

AVE PIERRE GRENIER

Porte de
Boulogne-Studio

RUE YVES KERMEN

Place du Pont
de Billancourt

QUAI DU PONT DU JOUR

Parc
Départemental
de l'Île St
Germain

RUE TRAVERSIÈRE

⛽

QUAI DE STALINGRAD

**ÎLE
ST-GERMAIN**

QUAI DE STALINGRAD

PONT DE BILLANCOURT

Place
Jacques Madauie

ALLÉE D'ISSY

AVE DU BAS MEUDON

RUE PIERRE POLI

QUAI DE STALINGRAD

RUE JEAN JACQUES ROUSSEAU

BOULEVARD GARIBALDI

Billancourt

Place de
la Resistance

Square du
Colombier

RUE ARISTIDE BRIAND

Place
Léon Blum

QUAI DE STALINGRAD

RUE MARCEL MIQUEL

Centre Commercial
des 3 Moulins

✉

RUE JEAN-PIERRE TIMBAUD

COUR ST VINCENT

AVE DE VERDUN

Issy Valle Ⓡ

BLVD RODIN

RUE DE MEUDON

ALLÉE STE LUCIE

RUE D'EREVAN

RUE DE LA DÉFENSE

Parc de
la Résistance

RUE DU DOCTEUR LOMBARD

Parc de
la Ferme

Ste Lucie

Natter
Ste Lucie

Parc
Rodin

RUE D'EREVAN

SENTIER DES EPINETTES

AVE DE VERDUN

⛪

RUE DES MONTALETS

Jardin
Botanique

Mairie
Annexe

✉ Place du
Souvenir
Francais

RUE BENOIT MALOT

RUE DE L'EGALITÉ

BLVD RODIN

MEUDON

AVE HENRI BARBUSSE

RUE D'ARM
ENIE

Cimetière
d'Issy les Moulineaux

A   B   C

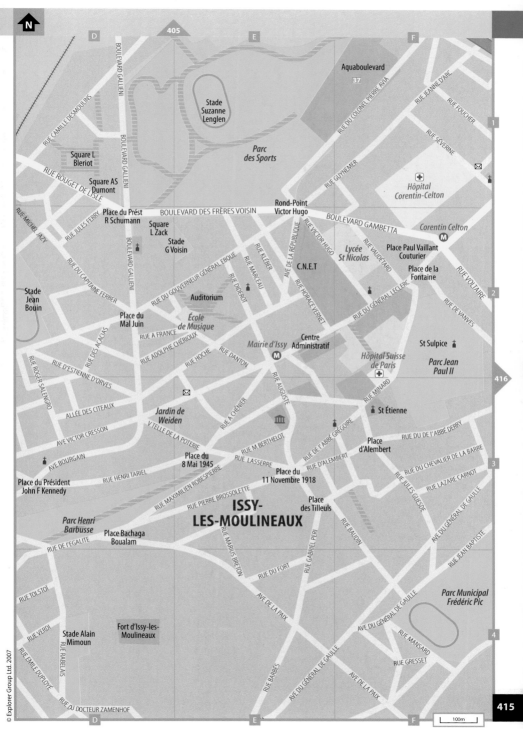

Aquaboulevard

37

RUE DU COLONEL PIERRE AVIA

RUE JEANNE D'ARC

RUE FOUCHER

RUE SÉVERINE

Hôpital
Corentin-Celton

BOULEVARD GALLIENI

Stade
Suzanne
Lenglen

Parc
des Sports

RUE CAMILLE DESMOULINS

Square L
Bleriot

RUE ROUGET DE L'ISLE

Square AS
Dumont

BOULEVARD GALLIENI

RUE GUYNEMER

Place du Prést
R Schumann

Rond-Point
Victor Hugo

BOULEVARD DES FRÈRES VOISIN

BOULEVARD GAMBETTA

Corentin Celton

RUE MICHEL JAZY

RUE JULES FERRY

Square
L Zack

Stade
G Voisin

BOULEVARD GALLIENI

RUE DU GOUVERNEUR GÉNÉRAL EBOUE

RUE KLEBER

RUE MARCEAU

RUE DIDEROT

AVE DE LA RÉPUBLIQUE

RUE VICTOR HUGO

C.N.E.T

Lycée
St Nicolas

RUE VAUDETARD

Place Paul Vaillant
Couturier

Place de la
Fontaine

RUE VOLTAIRE

RUE DE VANVES

RUE DU CAPITAINE FERBER

Auditorium

RUE HORACE VERNET

RUE DU GÉNÉRAL LECLERC

Stade
Jean
Bouin

Place du
Mal Juin

École
de Musique

RUE A FRANCE

RUE DES ACACIAS

RUE D'ESTIENNE D'ORVES

RUE ADOLPHE CHÉRIOUX

RUE HOCHE

RUE DANTON

Mairie d'Issy
M

Centre
Administratif

Hôpital Suisse
de Paris

St Sulpice

Parc Jean
Paul II

RUE MINARD

RUE ROGER SALENGRO

ALLÉE DES CITEAUX

RUE A CHÉNIER

RUE AUGUSTE

St Étienne

Jardin de
Weiden

V TELLE DE LA POTERIE

AVE VICTOR CRESSON

AVE BOURGAIN

Place du
8 Mai 1945

RUE M BERTHELOT

RUE LASSERRE

RUE DE L'ABBÉ GRÉGOIRE

RUE D'ALEMBERT

RUE DU DE L'ABBÉ DERRY

Place
d'Alembert

RUE DU CHEVALIER DE LA BARRE

Place du
11 Novembre 1918

RUE JULES GUESDE

RUE LAZARE CARNOT

Place du Président
John F Kennedy

RUE HENRI TARIEL

RUE MAXIMILIEN ROBESPIERRE

RUE PIERRE BROSSOLETTE

**ISSY-
LES-MOULINEAUX**

Place
des Tilleuls

RUE BAUDIN

AVE DU GÉNÉRAL DE GAULE

RUE JEAN BAPTISTE

Parc Henri
Barbusse

Place Bachaga
Boualam

RUE DE L'EGALITE

RUE MARIUS BRETON

RUE DU FORT

RUE GABRIEL PERI

Parc Municipal
Frédéric Pic

RUE TOLSTOÏ

RUE VERDI

RUE RABELAIS

Stade Alain
Mimoun

Fort d'Issy-les-
Moulineaux

AVE DE LA PAIX

RUE BARBES

AVE DU GÉNÉRAL DE GAULLE

AVE DE LA PAIX

RUE MANSARD

RUE GRESSET

RUE EMILE DUPLOYE

RUE DU DOCTEUR ZAMENHOF

N

General Information p.1

Residents p.45

Exploring p.131

Activities p.209

Shopping p.241

Going Out p.303

406

103

Paris Expo

AVE ERNEST RENAN

Porte de Versailles

BOULEVARD LEFEBVRE

RUE OLIVIER

RUE DE DANTZIG

BOULEVARD PÉRIPHÉRIQUE

Place Amédée
Gordini

RUETHUREAU DANGIN

AVE DE LA PORTE DE LA PLAINE

Porte de
Plaisance

Square des
Perichaux

RUE A THEURIET

Paris
Expo

St Antoine
de Padoue

RUE GASTON BOISSIER

Square du
Dr
Calmette

RUE JEAN SICARD

AVE ERNEST RENAN

RUE DU QUATRE SEPTEMBRE

AVE ALBERT BARTHOLOME

RUE MICHELET

RUE EUGÈNE BAUDOUIN

Paris
Expo

Place des Insurgés
de Varsovie
Porte de la Plaine

Stade de la
Porte de la
Plaine

Stade Charles
Rigoulot

RUE JULLIEN

RUE DE L'AGRICULTURE

RUE DU MOULIN

AVE PASTEUR

RUE LOUIS VICAT

1

2

415

3

4

Centre National
d'Enseignement

RUE JULLIEN

RUE MARCEL YOL

RUE JEAN JAURÈS

Square E
Jarrousse

RUE JEAN JAURÈS

Lycée
Michelet

RUE RAPHAEL

RUE PAUL LEFÈVRE

AVE PASTEUR

RUE SADI CARNOT

St Francois

RUE GAMBETTA

RUE JEAN BLEUZEN

RUE MURILLO

AVE VICTOR HUGO

RUE JULES MICHELET

Square du
General de Gaulle

Malakoff
Plateau
de Vanves

RUE MARY BESSEYRE

RUE LAMARTINE

Cimetière de
Vanves

AVE MARCEL MARTINE

RUE BARBÈS

RUE JEAN BLEUZEN

Place du Mal
de Lattre de Tassigny

RUE SADI CARNOT

RUE RENO SAHORS

Stade
Lénine

RUE GAMBURGLIN

RUE DE L'ÉGLISE

Centre
Administratif

Mairie

RUE ANTOINE FRATACCI

Square de
l'Insurrection

RUE KLÉBER

Place du
President
Kennedy

Square Jean
Monnet

BLVD GABRIEL PERI

AVE JULES FERRY

RUE FALRET

RUE DE LA RÉPUBLIQUE

VANVES

Place
Albert Culot

RUE RAYMOND DAVID

RUE PAUL BERT

AVE J J ROUSSEAU

Parc Municipal
Frédéric Pic

RUE RAYMOND MARCHERON

RUE RENE COCHE

Gare de
Vanves Malakoff

AVE MAURICE THOREZ

RUE G
CLEMENCEAU

RUE DIDEROT

RUE ETIENNE DOLET

RUE LARMEROUX

RUE DU G LAFOSSE

VILLA FRANCOD RUSSE

V DES MATRAIS

RUE PAUL VAILLANT

BOULEVARD CAMÉLINAT

COUTURIER

RUE JULES DALOU

RUE HOCHE

BOULEVARD DE STALINGARD

A

B

C

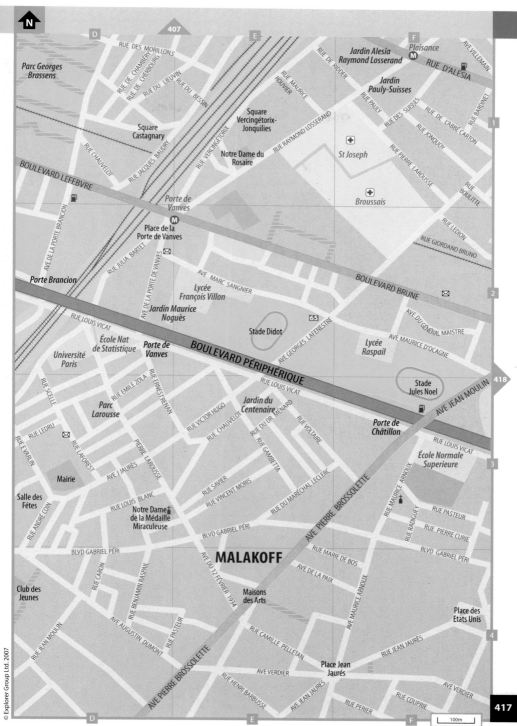

Parc Georges
Brassens

RUE DES MORILLONS

RUE DE CHAMBÉRY

RUE DE CHERBOURG

RUE DU LIEUVIN

RUE DU BESSIN

RUE MAURICE
ROUVIER

RUE DE RIDDER

Jardin Alesia
Raymond Losserand

Plaisance

AVE VILLEMAN

RUE D'ALESIA

Jardin
Pauly-Suisses

RUE PAULY

RUE DES SUISSES

RUE DE L'ABBÉ CARTON

RUE JONQUOY

RUE DE L'ABBÉ CARTON

RUE BARDINET

1

Square
Castagnary

RUE JACQUES BAUDRY

RUE CHAUVELOT

RUE VERCINGÉTORIX

Square
Vercingétorix-
Jonquilies

Notre Dame du
Rosaire

RUE RAYMOND LOSSERAND

St Joseph

RUE PIERRE LAROUSSE

RUE
BOULITTE

BOULEVARD LEFEBVRE

Porte de
Vanves

Place de la
Porte de Vanves

Broussais

RUE LEDION

RUE GIORDANO BRUNO

AVE DE LA PORTE BRANCION

RUE JULIA BARTET

AVE DE LA PORTE DE VANVES

Porte Brancion

AVE MARC SANGNIER

BOULEVARD BRUNE

2

RUE LOUIS VICAT

Lycée
François Villon

Jardin Maurice
Noguès

Stade Didot

RUE GEORGES LAFENESTRE

65

AVE DU GÉNÉRAL MAISTRE

Lycée
Raspail

AVE MAURICE D'OCAGNE

École Nat
de Statistique

Porte de
Vanves

BOULEVARD PÉRIPHÉRIQUE

Université
Paris

RUE SCELLE

RUE EMILE ZOLA

RUE ERNEST RENAN

RUE LOUIS VICAT

Stade
Jules Noel

AVE JEAN MOULIN

418

Parc
Larousse

RUE LEDRU

PIERRE LAROUSSE

RUE VICTOR HUGO

RUE CHAUVELOT

Jardin du
Centenaire

RUE DU DR MENARD

RUE VOLTAIRE

Porte de
Châtillon

RUE LOUIS VICAT

École Normale
Superieure

3

RUE EVARLIN

RUE LAFOREST

AVE J JAURÈS

RUE GAMBETTA

RUE DU MARÉCHAL LECLERC

AVE PIERRE BROSSOLETTE

RUE MAURICE ARNOUX

Mairie

RUE SAVIER

RUE VINCENT MORIS

RUE RADIGUEY

RUE PASTEUR

RUE PIERRE CURIE

Salle des
Fétes

RUE ANDRE COIN

RUE LOUIS BLANC

Notre Dame
de la Médaille
Miraculeuse

BLVD GABRIEL PÉRI

RUE MARIE DE BOS

BLVD GABRIEL PÉRI

RUE JEAN MOULIN

RUE CARON

RUE BENJAMIN RASPAIL

BLVD GABRIEL PÉRI

MALAKOFF

AVE DU 12 FÉVRIER 1934

AVE DE LA PAIX

AVE MAURICE ARNOUX

Place des
Etats Unis

4

Club des
Jeunes

AVE AUGUSTIN DUMONT

RUE PASTEUR

Maisons
des Arts

RUE CAMILLE PELLETAN

AVE PIERRE BROSSOLETTE

Place Jean
Jaurés

RUE HENRI BARBUSSE

AVE VERDIER

AVE JEAN JAURÈS

RUE JEAN JAURÈS

RUE PERIER

RUE COUPRIE

AVE VERDIER

100m

RUE DE GERGOVIE

Square du Viollet

RUE DE LA SABLIÈRE

RUE BÉNARD

RUE DES PLANTES

RUE MOUTON DUVERNET

RUE BREZIN

La Rochefoucauld

St Dominique

Place du Lieutenant Stephane Piobetta

RUE HIPPOLYTE MANDRON

RUE LÉONIDAS

RUE DU MOULIN VERT

AVE DU MAINE

Mouton Duvernet

RUE SOPHIE GERMAIN

AVE RENE COTY

RUE HALLÉ

RUE DIDOT

RUE JACQUIER

RUE DELBET

RUE D'ALESIA

RUE LECURIOT

RUE BAILLOU

VILLA D'ALÉSIA

GÉNÉRAL LECLERC

RUE DU COUËDIC

RUE REMY DUMONCEL

RUE HALLÉ

RUE DE L'ABBÉ CARTON

RUE LOUIS MORARD

St Pierre de Montrouge

N D'ORLÉANS

PGE MONTBRUN

RUE MONTBRUN

RUE DE LA SAÔNE

RUE DE BIGORRE

Alesia

RUE DE CHÂTILLON

Place Victor et Héléne Basch

RUE D'ALÉSIA

Notre Dame de Bon Secours

RUE DES PLANTES

RUE ANTOINE CHANTIN

RUE MARGUERIN

RUE DU LUNAIN

RUE SARRETTE

RUE DE L'AUDE

RUE DES ARTISTES

AVE JEAN MOULIN

RUE ALPHONSE DAUDET

RUE ADOLPHE FOCILLON

St Francois Clinique Sarrette

RUE SAINT

RUE AUGUSTE CAIN

RUE FRIANT

RUE SARRETTE

RUE DU PÈRE CORENTIN

RUE LACAZE

RUE DE LA TOMBE ISSOIRE

Réservoirs de Montsouris

Place de la Porte de Châtillon

AVE JEAN MOULIN

Clinique Ste Geneviève

RUE MORÈRE

RUE DE COULMIERS

RUE POIRIER DE NARCAY

RUE HENRI REGNAULT

RUE BEAUNIER

Place Jules Hénaffe

AVE REILLE

Square Jean Moulin

RUE NTXINAY

RUE CH LE GOFFIC

RUE ACHILLE

RUE GUSTAVE LE BON

St Paul

Porte de Montrouge

RUE PAUL FORT

Institut Mutualiste Montsouris

RUE ALBERT SOREL

Place du 25 Août 1944

Porte d'Orléans

RUE FLEURY BARBOUX

BOULEVARD BRUNE

Cimetière de Montrouge

AVE DE LA PORTE DE MONTROUGE

AVE DE LA PORTE D'ORLÉANS

Square du Serment de Koufra

AVE PAUL APPELL

RUE MONTICELLI

RUE MANSOUTY

Porte d'Arcueil

BOULEVARD PÉRIPHÉRIQUE

RUE DE LA LÉGION ETRANGÈRE

Porte d'Orléans

Stade Elisabeth

RUE DU PROF HYACINTHE VINCENT

Cité Internationale Universitaire de Paris

AVE ANDRE RIVOIRE

Institution Jeanne d'Arc

RUE GUTENBERG

RUE DELERUE

AVE E BOUTROUX

Place de la Libération

Mairie

Place Gabrielle de Guerchy

RUE GABRIEL PÉRI

RUE T GAUTIER

RUE LOUIS LEJEUNE

RUE FRANCOIS ORY

AVE DES CAVES

RUE SYLVINE CANDAS

St Jacques le Majeur

RUE SADI CARNOT

MONTROUGE

AVE ARISTIDE BRIAND

RUE BARBÈS

AVE PAUL VAILLANT COUTURIER

AVE DE LA RÉPUBLIQUE

PL DU MAL LECLERC

RUE LOUIS ROLLAND

RUE DE LA VANNE

RUELLE NINNE

RUE VICTOR HUGO

RUE D'ESTIENNED'ORVES

A B C

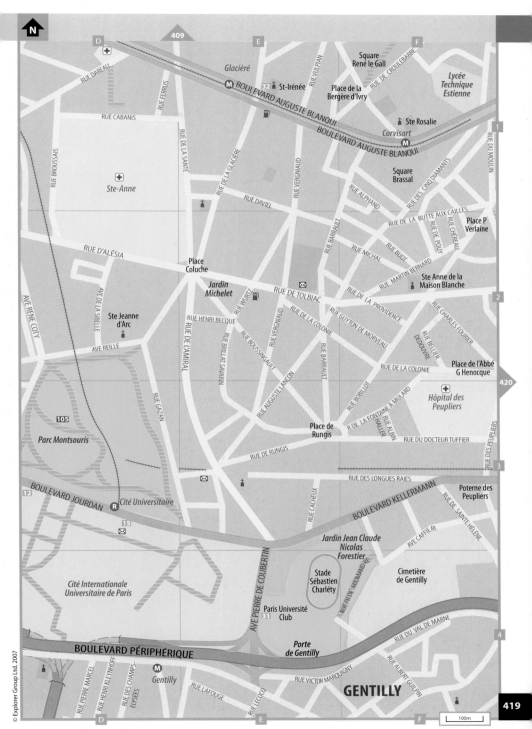

419

GENTILLY

100m

N

410

RUE GODEFROY †

Place
d'Italie

Place d'Italie

Jardin
Louis Say

St Jean des
Deux Mopulins

Centre de Rééducation
Sainte Marie

RUE DUNOIS

RUE DUCHEDELVILLE

Square
Héloise
et Abélard

Place
Jeanne d'Arc

RUE CHARCOT

RUE XAINTRAILLES

Notre Dame
de la Gare

Place
Soubam

RUE DE PATAY

Jardin des
Deux-Moulins

Centre
Commercial

PLACE
D'ITALIE

Lycée Technique
Henry Chasles

RUE NICOLAS FORTIN

RUE GEORGE EASTMAN

Centre de Soins
Dentaires
G Eastman

AVE EDISON

RUE RICAUT

RUE DU DR CHARLES RICHET

RUE JEANNE D'ARC

RUE NATIONALE

RUE JS BACH

RUE CLISSON

RUE LAHIRE

Place
Nationale

Place
André Masson

RUE VANDREZANNE

RUE DU MOULINET

RUE TOUSSAINT FÉRON

Parc de
Choisy

RUE CHARLES MOUREU

Stade
Charles Moureu

RUE BAUDRICOURT

Square
Blumenthal

RUE JEAN COLLY

RUE B RENARD

RUE DE TOLBIAC

Tolbiac

Lycée
Glaude Monet

Université Paris I

RUE DE TOLBIAC

LA BUTTES
AUX CAILLES

RUE PONCCARME

Clinique
Jeanne d'Arc

RUE DU CHÂTEAU DES RENTIERS

RUE ERNEST ET HENRI

RUE DU DR
LAURENT

RUE DAMÉSME

RUE DIEULAFOY

RUE HENRI PAPE

RUE DU DR LERAY

RUE AUGUSTE PERRET

AVE DE LA PORTE D'ITALIE

AVE DE CHOISY

AVE D'IVRY

Olympiades

RUE NATIONALE

RUE M DUCHAMP

PGE BOURGOIN

RUE DE L'INTERNE

RUE DU DOCTEUR

RUE DU TAGE

RUE BOURGON

Lycée
Gabriel Fauré

RUE DE LA VISTULE

RUE CAILLAUX

RUE PHILIBERT LUCOT

Jardin
Baudricourt

RUE DE LA POINTE D'IVRY

Square
Ulysse Trélat

RUE REGNAULT

Maison
Blanche

Jardin du
Moulin de
la Pointe

RUE DU MOULIN DE LA POINTE

RUE GANDON

St Hippolyte

Place de
Vénétie

Centre
Commercial

Porte d'Ivry

RUE E LEVASSOR

BOULEVARD MASSÉNA

Stade Poterne
des Peupliers

RUE MAX JACOB

Porte d'Italie

Jardin
Juan-Miro

Porte de Choisy

AVE DE LA PORTE DE CHOISY

RUE A FOUILLÉE

Place de
Port au Princes

Stade
Georges Carpentier

Parc
Kellermann

RUE JACQUES DESTRÉE

RUE DU DOCTEUR BOURNEVILLE

RUE EWIDAL

Lycée
Yabne

AVE LÉON BOLLÉE

Institut Mutualiste
Montsouris

BOULEVARD HIPPOLYTE MARQUÉS

Porte d'Italie

RUE ÉLISÉE RECLUS

BOULEVARD PÉRIPHÉRIQUE

RUE VOLTAIRE

RUE CHARLES LEROY

AVE DE VERDUN

RUE MAURIC BERTEAUX

RUE BARBÉS

Dépôt
R.A.T.P

© Explorer Group Ltd 2007

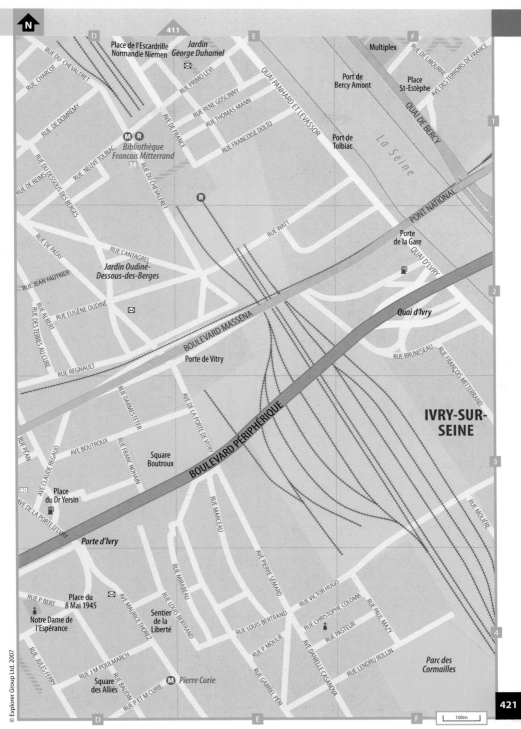

Place de l'Escardrille Normandie Niemen

Jardin George Duhamel

Multiplex

RUE DU CHEVALERET

RUE CHARCOT

RUE PRIMO LEVI

RUE DE LIBOURNE

RUE DES TERROIRS DE FRANCE

Port de Bercy Amont

Place St-Estèphe

RUE DE DOMRÉMY

RUE RENE GOSCINNY

RUE THOMAS MANN

QUAI PANHARD ET LEVASSOR

QUAI DE BERCY

RUE NEUVE TOLBIAC

M R *Bibliothèque Francois Mitterrand*

AVE DE FRANCE

RUE FRANCOISE DOLTO

Port de Tolbiac

La Seine

RUE DE REIMS DESSOUS DES BERGES

RUE DU CHEVALERET

38

R

PONT NATIONAL

RUE DE PATAY

RUE WATT

Porte de la Gare

QUAI D'IVRY

RUE CANTAGREL

Jardin Oudiné-Dessous-des-Berges

RUE JEAN FAUTRIER

RUE EUGÈNE OUDINÉ

Quai d'Ivry

RUE ALBERT

RUE DES TERRES AU CURE

BOULEVARD MASSENA

RUE REGNAULT

Porte de Vitry

RUE BRUNESEAU

RUE FRANÇOIS MITTERRAND

RUE DARMESTETER

AVE DE LA PORTE DE VITRY

BOULEVARD PÉRIPHÉRIQUE

IVRY-SUR-SEINE

RUE PÉAN

AVE CLAUDE REGAUD

AVE BOUTROUX

RUE FRANC NOHAIN

Square Boutroux

40

Place du Dr Yersin

RUE MOLIÈRE

AVE DE LA PORTE D'IVRY

Porte d'Ivry

RUE MARCEAU

RUE P BERT

Place du 8 Mai 1945

AVE MAURICE THOREZ

Sentier de la Liberté

RUE MIRABEAU

RUE LOUIS BERTRAND

RUE PIERRE SEMARD

RUE VICTOR HUGO

RUE CHRISTOPHE COLOMB

RUE PAUL MAZY

Notre Dame de l'Espérance

RUE LOUIS BERTRAND

RUE P MOULIE

AVE DANIELLE CASANOVA

RUE PASTEUR

RUE JULES FERRY

RUE J M POULMARCH

RUE BAUDIN

Square des Alliés

RUE P ET M CURIE

M *Pierre Curie*

RUE GABRIEL PÉRI

RUE LENDRU ROLLIN

Parc des Cormailles

100m

421

CROSS
BORDERS
WITHOUT
BARRIERS.

Whether you're connecting with family and friends or sending goods for business, you'll find all the help you need to cross borders without barriers at one of our many offices around the world.

www.dhl.com

Index

Index

Index

433

Notes

Residents' Guides

All you need to know about living, working and enjoying life in these exciting destinations

Mini Guides
The perfect pocket-sized
Visitors' Guides

Abu Dhabi — Amsterdam — Bahrain — Barcelona

Beijing * — Berlin — Dubai — Dublin — Hong Kong — Kuala Lumpur — London *

Los Angeles — New York — New Zealand — Oman — Paris — Qatar — Shanghai

Singapore — Sydney — Tokyo — Vancouver *

Mini Maps
Wherever you are,
never get lost again

Abu Dhabi — Amsterdam — Auckland — Bahrain

Beijing * — Barcelona — Berlin — Doha — Dubai — Dublin — Hong Kong

Kuala Lumpur * — Kuwait — London — Los Angeles — Muscat — New York — Paris

Shanghai — Sharjah — Singapore — Sydney — Tokyo * — Vancouver — UAE

Photography Books
Beautiful cities caught through the lens

Calendars
The time, the place, and the date

Maps
Wherever you are, never get lost again

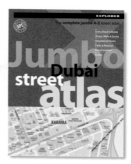

Activity and Lifestyle Guides
Drive, trek, dive and swim... life will never be boring again

Retail sales
Our books are available in most good bookshops around the world, and are also available online at Amazon.co.uk and Amazon.com. If you would like to enquire about any of our international distributors, please contact retail@explorerpublishing.com

Bulk sales and customisation
All our products are available for bulk sales with customisation options. For discount rates and further information, please contact corporatesales@explorerpublishing.com

Licensing and digital sales
All our content, maps and photography are available for print or digital use. For licensing enquiries please contact licensing@explorerpublishing.com

Ahmed Mainodin
AKA: Mystery Man

We can never recognise Ahmed because of his constantly changing facial hair. He waltzes in with big lambchop sideburns one day, a handlebar moustache the next, and a neatly trimmed goatee after that. So far we've had no objections to his hirsute chameleonisms, but we'll definitely draw the line at a monobrow.

Bahrudeen Abdul
AKA: The Stallion

Having tired of creating abstract sculptures out of papier maché and candy canes, Bahrudeen turned to the art of computer programming. After honing his skills in the southern Andes for three years he grew bored of Patagonian winters, and landed a job here, 'The Home of 01010101 Creative Freedom'.

Ajay Krishnan R
AKA: Web Wonder

Ajay's mum and dad knew he was going to be an IT genius when they found him reconfiguring his Commodore 64 at the tender age of 2. He went on to become the technology consultant on all three Matrix films, and counts Keanu as a close personal friend.

Ben Merrett
AKA: Big Ben

After a short (or tall as the case may have been) career as a human statue, Ben tired of the pigeons choosing him, rather than his namesake, as a public convenience and decided to fly the nest to seek his fortune in foreign lands. Not only is he big on personality but he brings in the big bucks with his bulk!

Alex Jeffries
AKA: Easy Rider

Alex is happiest when dressed in leather from head to toe with a humming machine between his thighs – just like any other motorbike enthusiast. Whenever he's not speeding along the Hatta Road at full throttle, he can be found at his beloved Mac, still dressed in leather.

Cherry Enriquez
AKA: Bean Counter

With the team's penchant for sweets and pastries, it's good to know we have Cherry on top of our accounting cake. The local confectioner is always paid on time, so we're guaranteed great gateaux for every special occasion.

Alistair MacKenzie
AKA: Media Mogul

If only Alistair could take the paperless office one step further and achieve the officeless office he would be the happiest publisher alive. Wireless access from a remote spot somewhere in the Hajar Mountains would suit this intrepid explorer – less traffic, lots of fresh air, and wearing sandals all day - the perfect work environment!

Claire England
AKA: Whip Cracker

No longer able to freeload off the fact that she once appeared in a Robbie Williams video, Claire now puts her creative skills to better use – looking up rude words in the dictionary! A child of English nobility, Claire is quite the lady – unless she's down at Jimmy Dix.

Andrea Fust
AKA: Mother Superior

By day Andrea is the most efficient manager in the world and by night she replaces the boardroom for her board and wows the pants off the dudes in Ski Dubai. Literally. Back in the office she definitely wears the trousers!

David Quinn
AKA: Sharp Shooter

After a short stint as a children's TV presenter was robbed from David because he developed an allergy to sticky back plastic, he made his way to sandier pastures. Now that he's thinking outside the box, nothing gets past the man with the sharpest pencil in town.

Derrick Pereira
AKA: The Returnimator
After leaving Explorer in 2003, Derrick's life took a dramatic downturn – his dog ran away, his prized bonsai tree died and he got kicked out of his thrash metal band. Since rejoining us, things are looking up and he just found out he's won $10 million in a Nigerian sweepstakes competition. And he's got the desk by the window!

Iain Young
AKA: 'The Cat'
Iain follows in the fine tradition of Scots with safe hands – Alan Rough, Andy Goram, Jim Leighton on a good day – but breaking into the Explorer XI has proved frustrating. There's no match on a Mac, but that Al Huzaifa ringer doesn't half make himself big.

Enrico Maullon
AKA: The Crooner
Frequently mistaken for his near-namesake Enrique Iglesias, Enrico decided to capitalise and is now a regular stand-in for the Latin heartthrob. If he's ever missing from the office, it usually means he's off performing for millions of adoring fans on another stadium tour of America.

Ieyad Charaf
AKA: Fashion Designer
When we hired Ieyad as a top designer, we didn't realise we'd be getting his designer tops too! By far the snappiest dresser in the office, you'd be hard-pressed to beat his impeccably ironed shirts.

Firos Khan
AKA: Big Smiler
Previously a body double in kung fu movies, including several appearances in close up scenes for Steven Seagal's moustache. He also once tore down a restaurant with his bare hands after they served him a mild curry by mistake.

Ingrid Cupido
AKA: The Karaoke Queen
Ingrid has a voice to match her starlet name. She'll put any Pop Idols to shame once behind the mike, and she's pretty nifty on a keyboard too. She certainly gets our vote if she decides to go pro; just remember you saw her here first.

Hashim MM
AKA: Speedy Gonzales
They don't come much faster than Hashim – he's so speedy with his mouse that scientists are struggling to create a computer that can keep up with him. His nimble fingers leave his keyboard smouldering (he gets through three a week), and his go-faster stripes make him almost invisible to the naked eye when he moves.

Ivan Rodrigues
AKA: The Aviator
After making a mint in the airline market, Ivan came to Explorer where he works for pleasure, not money. That's his story, anyway. We know that he is actually a corporate spy from a rival company and that his multi-level spreadsheets are really elaborate codes designed to confuse us.

Helen Spearman
AKA: Little Miss Sunshine
With her bubbly laugh and permanent smile, Helen is a much-needed ray of sunshine in the office when we're all grumpy and facing harrowing deadlines. It's almost impossible to think that she ever loses her temper or shows a dark side... although put her behind the wheel of a car, and you've got instant road rage.

Jake Marsico
AKA: Don Calzone
Jake spent the last 10 years on the tiny triangular Mediterranean island of Samoza, honing his traditional cooking techniques and perfecting his Italian. Now, whenever he returns to his native America, he impresses his buddies by effortlessly zapping a hot dog to perfection in any microwave, anywhere, anytime.

Henry Hilos
AKA: The Quiet Man
Henry can rarely be seen from behind his large obstructive screen but when you do catch a glimpse you'll be sure to get a smile. Lighthearted Henry keeps all those glossy pages filled with pretty pictures for something to look at when you can't be bothered to read.

Jane Roberts
AKA: The Oracle
After working in an undisclosed role in the government, Jane brought her super sleuth skills to Explorer. Whatever the question, she knows what, where, who, how and when, but her encyclopaedic knowledge is only impressive until you realise she just makes things up randomly.

Jayde Fernandes
AKA: Pop Idol
Jayde's idol is Britney Spears, and he recently shaved his head to show solidarity with the troubled star. When he's not checking his dome for stubble, or practising the dance moves to 'Baby One More Time' in front of the bathroom mirror, he actually manages to get some designing done.

Johny Mathew
AKA: The Hawker
Caring Johny used to nurse wounded eagles back to health and teach them how to fly again before trying his luck in merchandising. Fortunately his skills in the field have come in handy at Explorer, where his efforts to improve our book sales have been a soaring success.

Kate Fox
AKA: Contacts Collector
Kate swooped into the office like the UK equivalent of Wonderwoman, minus the tights of course (it's much too hot for that), but armed with a superhuman marketing brain. Even though she's just arrived, she is already a regular on the Dubai social scene – she is helping to blast Explorer into the stratosphere, one champagne-soaked networking party at a time.

Katie Drynan
AKA: The Irish Deputy
Katie is a Jumeira Jane in training, and has 35 sisters who take it in turns to work in the Explorer office while she enjoys testing all the beauty treatments available on the Beach Road. This Irish charmer met an oil tycoon in Paris, and they now spend the weekends digging very deep holes in their new garden.

Kiran Melwani
AKA: Bow Selector
Like a modern-day Robin Hood (right down to the green tights and band of merry men), Kiran's mission in life is to distribute Explorer's wealth of knowledge to the fact-hungry readers of the world. Just make sure you never do anything to upset her – rumour has it she's a pretty mean shot with that bow and arrow.

Lennie Mangalino
AKA: Shaker Maker
With a giant spring in her step and music in her heart it's hard to not to swing to the beat when Lennie passes by in the office. She loves her Lambada… and Samba… and Salsa and anything else she can get the sales team shaking their hips to.

Mannie Lugtu
AKA: Distribution Demon
When the travelling circus rode into town, their master juggler Mannie decided to leave the Big Top and explore Dubai instead. He may have swapped his balls for our books but his juggling skills still come in handy.

Maricar Ong
AKA: Pocket Docket
A pint-sized dynamo of ruthless efficiency, Maricar gets the job done before anyone else notices it needed doing. If this most able assistant is absent for a moment, it sends a surge of blind panic through the Explorer ranks.

Grace Carnay
AKA: Manila Ice
It's just as well the office is so close to a movie theatre, because Grace is always keen to catch the latest Hollywood offering from Brad Pitt, who she admires purely for his acting ability, of course. Her ice cool exterior conceals a tempestuous passion for jazz, which fuels her frenzied typing speed.

Matt Farquharson
AKA: Hack Hunter
A career of tuppence-a-word hackery ended when Matt arrived in Dubai to cover a maggot wranglers' convention. He misguidedly thinks he's clever because he once wrote for some grown-up English papers.

Matthew Samuel
AKA: Mr Modest
Matt's penchant for the entrepreneurial life began with a pair of red braces and a filofax when still a child. That yearning for the cut and thrust of commerce has brought him to Dubai, where he made a fortune in the sand-selling business before semi-retiring at Explorer.

Michael Samuel
AKA: Gordon Gekko
We have a feeling this mild mannered master of mathematics has a wild side. He hasn't witnessed an Explorer party yet but the office agrees that once the karaoke machine is out, Michael will be the maestro. Watch out Dubai!

Pamela Grist
AKA: Happy Snapper
If a picture can speak a thousand words then Pam's photos say a lot about her – through her lens she manages to find the beauty in everything – even this motley crew. And when the camera never lies, thankfully Photoshop can.

Mimi Stankova
AKA: Mind Controller
A master of mind control, Mimi's siren-like voice lulls people into doing whatever she asks. Her steely reserve and endless patience mean recalcitrant reporters and persistent PR people are putty in her hands, delivering whatever she wants, whenever she wants it.

Pete Maloney
AKA: Graphic Guru
Image conscious he may be, but when Pete has his designs on something you can bet he's gonna get it! He's the king of chat up lines, ladies – if he ever opens a conversation with 'D'you come here often?' then brace yourself for the Maloney magic.

Mohammed Sameer
AKA: Man in the Van
Known as MS, short for Microsoft, Sameer can pick apart a PC like a thief with a lock, which is why we keep him out of finance and pounding Dubai's roads in the unmissable Explorer van – so we can always spot him coming.

Rafi Jamal
AKA: Soap Star
After a walk on part in The Bold and the Beautiful, Rafi swapped the Hollywood Hills for the Hajar Mountains. Although he left the glitz behind, he still mingles with high society, moonlighting as a male gigolo and impressing Dubai's ladies with his fancy footwork.

Mohammed T
AKA: King of the Castle
T is Explorer's very own Bedouin warehouse dweller; under his caring charge all Explorer stock is kept in masterful order. Arrive uninvited and you'll find T, meditating on a pile of maps, amid an almost eerie sense of calm.

Rafi VP
AKA: Party Trickster
After developing a rare allergy to sunlight in his teens, Rafi started to lose a few centimeters of height every year. He now stands just 30cm tall, and does his best work in our dingy basement wearing a pair of infrared goggles. His favourite party trick is to fold himself into a briefcase, and he was once sick in his hat.

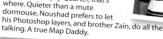

Noushad Madathil
AKA: Map Daddy
Where would Explorer be without the mercurial Madathil brothers? Lost in the Empty Quarter, that's where. Quieter than a mute dormouse, Noushad prefers to let his Photoshop layers, and brother Zain, do all the talking. A true Map Daddy.

Richard Greig
AKA: Sir Lancelot
Chivalrous to the last, Richard's dream of being a mediaeval knight suffered a setback after being born several centuries too late. His stellar parliamentary career remains intact, and he is in the process of creating a new party with the aim of abolishing all onions and onion-related produce.

Roshni Ahuja
AKA: Bright Spark
Never failing to brighten up the office with her colourful get-up, Roshni definitely puts the 'it' in the IT department. She's a perennially pleasant, profound programmer with peerless panache, and she does her job with plenty of pep and piles of pizzazz.

Sunita Lakhiani
AKA: Designlass
Initially suspicious of having a female in their midst, the boys in Designlab now treat Sunita like one of their own. A big shame for her, because they treat each other pretty damn bad!

Sean Kearns
AKA: The Tall Guy
Big Sean, as he's affectionately known, is so laid back he actually spends most of his time lying down (unless he's on a camping trip, when his ridiculously small tent forces him to sleep on his hands and knees). Despite the rest of us constantly tripping over his lanky frame, when the job requires someone who will work flat out, he always rises to the editorial occasion.

Steve Jones
AKA: Golden Boy
Our resident Kiwi lives in a nine-bedroom mansion and is already planning an extension. His winning smile has caused many a knee to weaken in Bur Dubai but sadly for the ladies, he's hopelessly devoted to his clients.

Shabsir M
AKA: Sticky Wicket
Shabsir is a valuable player on the Indian national cricket team, so instead of working you'll usually find him autographing cricket balls for crazed fans around the world. We don't mind though – if ever a retailer is stumped because they run out of stock, he knocks them for six with his speedy delivery.

Tim Binks
AKA: Class Clown
El Binksmeisterooney is such a sharp wit, he often has fellow Explorers gushing tea from their noses in convulsions of mirth. Years spent hiking across the Middle East have given him an encyclopaedic knowledge of rock formations and elaborate hair.

Shawn Jackson Zuzarte
AKA: Paper Plumber
If you thought rocket science was hard, try rearranging the chaotic babble that flows from the editorial team! If it weren't for Shawn, most of our books would require a kaleidoscope to read correctly so we're keeping him and his jazz hands under wraps.

Tom Jordan
AKA: The True Professional
Explorer's resident thesp, Tom delivers lines almost as well as he cuts them. His early promise on the pantomime circuit was rewarded with an all-action role in hit UK drama Heartbeat. He's still living off the royalties – and the fact he shared a sandwich with Kenneth Branagh.

Shefeeq M
AKA: Rapper in Disguise
So new he's still got the wrapper on, Shefeeq was dragged into the Explorer office, and put to work in the design department. The poor chap only stopped by to ask for directions to Wadi Bih, but since we realised how efficient he is, we keep him chained to his desk.

Tracy Fitzgerald
AKA: 'La Dona'
Tracy is a queenpin Catalan mafiosa and ringleader for the 'pescadora' clan, a nefarious group that runs a sushi smuggling operation between the Costa Brava and Ras Al Khaimah. She is not to be crossed. Rival clans will find themselves fed fish, and then fed to the fishes.

Shyrell Tamayo
AKA: Fashion Princess
We've never seen Shyrell wearing the same thing twice – her clothes collection is so large that her husband has to keep all his things in a shoebox. She runs Designlab like clockwork, because being late for deadlines is SO last season.

Zainudheen Madathil
AKA: Map Master
Often confused with retired footballer Zinedine Zidane because of his dexterous displays and a bad head-butting habit, Zain tackles design with the mouse skills of a star striker. Maps are his goal and despite getting red-penned a few times, when he shoots, he scores.

The *Paris Explorer* Team
Lead Editor David Quinn
Deputy Editor Helen Spearman
Editorial Assistants Ingrid Cupido, Mimi Stankova
Designer Shawn Jackson Zuzarte
Cartographers Sunita Lakhiani, Zainudheen Madathil,
Fariya Thaniyattil, Noufal Madathil, Sudheer Mekkatu
Photographers Victor Romero, David Quinn,
Pamela Grist, Anthony Maragou, Maria Howell,
Mark Ludbrook
Proofer Monica Degiovanni

Publisher
Alistair MacKenzie

Editorial
Managing Editor Claire England
Lead Editors David Quinn, Jane Roberts, Matt Farquharson,
Sean Kearns, Tim Binks, Tom Jordan
Deputy Editors Helen Spearman, Jakob Marsico,
Katie Drynan, Pamela Afram, Richard Greig, Tracy Fitzgerald
Editorial Assistants Grace Carnay, Ingrid Cupido, Mimi Stankova

Design
Creative Director Pete Maloney
Art Director Ieyad Charaf
Senior Designers Alex Jeffries, Iain Young
Layout Manager Jayde Fernandes
Layouters Hashim Moideen, Rafi Pullat,
Shefeeq Marakkatepurath
Junior Layouter Shawn Jackson Zuzarte
Cartography Manager Zainudheen Madathil
Cartographers Noushad Madathil, Sunita Lakhiani
Design Admin Manager Shyrell Tamayo
Production Coordinator Maricar Ong

Photography
Photography Manager Pamela Grist
Photographer Victor Romero
Image Editor Henry Hilos

Sales & Marketing
Area Sales Managers Laura Zuffa, Stephen Jones
Corporate Sales Executive Ben Merrett
Marketing Manager Kate Fox
Marketing Executive Annabel Clough
Retail Sales Manager Ivan Rodrigues
Retail Sales Coordinator Kiran Melwani
Retail Sales Supervisor Matthew Samuel
Merchandiser Johny Mathew
Sales & Marketing Coordinator Lennie Mangalino
Distribution Executives Ahmed Mainodin, Firos Khan, Mannie Lugtu
Warehouse Assistants Mohammed Kunjaymo, Najumudeen K.I.
Drivers Mohammed Sameer, Shabsir Madathil

Finance & Administration
Finance Manager Michael Samuel
HR & Administration Manager Andrea Fust
Accounts Assistant Cherry Enriquez
Administrators Enrico Maullon, Kelly Tesoro
Driver Rafi Jamal

IT
IT Administrator Ajay Krishnan R.
Software Engineers Bahrudeen Abdul, Roshni Ahuja
Digital Content Manager Derrick Pereira

Contact Us
Reader Response
If you have any comments and suggestions, fill out
our online reader response form and you could win prizes.
Log on to **www.explorerpublishing.com**

General Enquiries
We'd love to hear your thoughts and answer any questions
you have about this book or any other Explorer product.
Contact us at **info@explorerpublishing.com**

Careers
If you fancy yourself as an Explorer, send your CV
(stating the position you're interested in) to
jobs@explorerpublishing.com

Designlab & Contract Publishing
For enquiries about Explorer's Contract Publishing arm
and design services contact
designlab@explorerpublishing.com

PR & Marketing
For PR and marketing enquries contact
marketing@explorerpublishing.com
pr@explorerpublishing.com

Corporate Sales
For bulk sales and customisation options, for this book or
any Explorer product, contact
sales@explorerpublishing.com

Advertising & Sponsorship
For advertising and sponsorship, contact
media@explorerpublishing.com

Explorer Publishing & Distribution
PO Box 34275, Dubai
United Arab Emirates
Phone: +971 (0)4 340 88 05
Fax: +971 (0)4 340 88 06
www.explorerpublishing.com

Useful & Emergency Numbers

Police (emergency)	17
SAMU	15
Sapeurs-pompiers	18
Europe-Wide Emergency Number	112
24 Hour Pharmacy	01 45 62 02 41
Anti-Poison Centre	01 40 05 48 48
Dental Emergency	01 43 37 51 00
Domestic Violence Hotline	01 40 33 80 60
Gaz de France	08 10 80 08 01
Lost Property	08 21 00 25 25
Lost/Stolen Credit Cards	08 92 70 57 05
Paediatric Emergency	01 44 09 84 85
Rape Victim Hotline	08 00 05 95 95
SOS Help (English-language helpline)	01 46 21 46 46
Tourist Information	08 92 68 30 00
Veterinary Emergency	01 43 96 23 23

Airport Information

Paris – Orly

Information (06:00 to 23:45)	01 49 75 15 15
Medical centre (24 hour)	01 49 75 45 12
Terminal Sud – Lost and Found	01 49 75 34 10
Terminal Ouest – Lost and Found	01 49 75 42 34
Police (24 hour)	01 49 75 43 04
Customs (24 hour)	01 49 75 09 10

Paris – Roissy CDG

Information (24 hour)	01 48 62 22 80
Medical centre (24 hour)	01 48 62 28 00
Terminal 1 – Lost and Found	01 48 62 13 34
Terminal 2 – Lost and Found	01 48 16 63 83
Police (24 hour)	01 48 62 31 22
Customs (24 hour)	01 48 62 62 85

Hospitals

Ambroise-Pare	01 49 09 50 00
The American Hospital of Paris	01 46 41 25 25
Armand-Trousseau	01 44 73 74 75
Bichat – Claude-Bernard	01 40 25 80 80
Cochin	01 58 41 41 41
Hertford British Hospital	01 46 39 22 22
Hôtel Dieu	01 42 34 82 34
Necker – Enfants Malade	01 44 49 40 00
Pitie-Salpetriere	01 42 16 00 00
Saint-Antoine	01 49 28 20 00

Recovery Services & Towing

ABDR	08 00 10 43 05
ADA	01 46 55 22 36
Alfauto	01 58 46 10 00
Auto Guy's Depannage	06 98 81 41 92
CHL Depannage	08 00 10 43 05
Dan Dépann	08 00 25 10 00
Kablé	01 42 28 33 33

Main Hotels

Four Seasons Hôtel George V	01 49 52 70 00
Hôtel de Crillon-Concorde	01 44 71 15 00
Hôtel de Vendôme	01 55 04 55 00
Hôtel Fouquet's Barrière	01 40 69 60 00
Hôtel Lutetia	08 00 05 00 11
Hôtel Meurice	01 44 58 10 10
Hôtel Plaza Athénée	01 53 67 66 65
Hotel Ritz Paris	01 43 16 45 33
Hôtel Scribe Paris	01 44 71 24 24
L'Hôtel	01 44 41 99 00
Le Bristol Paris	01 53 43 43 00
Pavillon de la Reine	01 40 29 19 19
Terrass Hôtel	01 46 06 72 85
Villa d'Estrées	01 55 42 71 11

Embassies & Consulates

Australia	01 40 59 33 00
Belgium	01 43 80 61 00
Canada	01 44 43 29 00
Denmark	01 44 31 21 21
Finland	01 44 18 19 20
Germany	01 42 99 78 00
Greece	01 47 23 72 28
Ireland	01 45 00 20 87
Italy	01 45 44 38 90
The Netherlands	01 43 06 61 88
New Zealand	01 45 00 24 11
Norway	01 47 23 72 78
Portugal	01 47 27 35 29
South Africa	01 45 55 92 37
Spain	01 44 43 18 18
Sweden	01 44 18 88 00
Switzerland	01 49 55 67 00
United Kingdom	01 42 66 91 42
United States	01 43 12 22 22

Public Holidays

New Year's Day	January 1
Labour Day	May 1
1945 Armistice Day	May 8
'La Fête Nationale', or Bastille Day	July 14
Assumption	August 15
All Saints' Day	November 1
1918 Armistice Day	November 11
Christmas	December 25
Easter Monday	One day after Easter
Ascension Thursday	39 days after Easter
Pentecost Monday	50 days after Easter

Taxis

City of Paris (central number)	01 45 30 30 30
Les Taxis Bleus	08 91 70 10 10
Taxis G7	01 47 39 47 39